RECEPTION STUDY

RECEPTION STUDY

FROM LITERARY THEORY
TO CULTURAL STUDIES

Edited by
JAMES L. MACHOR AND PHILIP GOLDSTEIN

Routledge • *New York and London*

Published in 2001 by
Routledge
29 West 35th Street
New York, NY 10001

Published in Great Britain by
Routledge
11 New Fetter Lane
London EC4P 4EE

Copyright © 2001 by Routledge
Routledge is an imprint of the Taylor & Francis Group.

Printed in the United States of America on acid-free paper.

10 9 8 7 6 5 4 3 2 1

Library of Congress Cataloging-in-Publication Data

Reception study : from literary theory to cultural studies / edited by James L. Machor
and Philip Goldstein.
    p. cm.
  Includes bibliographical references and index.
  ISBN 0-415-92649-1 (acid-free paper) -- ISBN 0-415-92650-5 (pbk.: acid-free paper)
   1. Reader-response criticism. 2. Mass media--Audiences. I. Machor, James L. II.
Goldstein, Philip.

PN98.R38 R434 2000
801'.95--dc21

00-036593

CONTENTS

PREFACE

This book is the result of an extensive collaborative effort that both of us have appreciated. As joint editors, we have been equally responsible for the design, the introductory sections, and the bibliographical scholarship of this volume and, thus, take equal credit and blame for its merits and shortcomings. We would like to thank the University of Delaware and Kansas State University for their financial support toward the completion and publication of this volume. We would also like to thank Steven Mailloux for suggesting that we undertake this project in the first place, as well as Julien Devereux, Nick Syrett, and Damien Treffs at Routledge for their editorial assistance at various stages of the work.

James L. Machor
Kansas State University

Philip Goldstein
University of Delaware, Parallel Program

INTRODUCTION

In 1992 Robert Holub complained that reception theory, remarkably successful in Germany, was "still an optional and marginal theoretical tendency in the United States" (23). However truly such a claim may describe the American reception of German reception theory, it does not assess very accurately reception theory and practice as a whole. Since the mid-1980s collections and casebooks have reexamined the reception of *Hamlet, Huckleberry Finn, Pride and Prejudice,* and *Their Eyes Were Watching God,* to mention just a few titles, and major works, including Steven Mailloux's *Rhetorical Power* and *Reception Histories,* Gary Taylor's *Reinventing Shakespeare,* Jane Tompkins's *Sensational Designs,* and Peter Widdowson's *Hardy in History,* have contributed markedly to Anglo-American reception criticism. Add to this work the reception studies in cultural studies—from Janice Radway's *Reading the Romance* and Tony Bennett and Janet Wollacott's *Bond and Beyond* to Michael Bérubé's *Public Access*—as well as work in the history of the book, and it becomes apparent that reception study has been anything but marginal. Indeed, over the last ten years the number of British and American articles, book chapters, and full-length works in reception study has marked a virtual explosion in the field.[1]

These new reception studies divide into modern and postmodern types. Both types reconstruct the historical method that Anglo-American formal criticism, first established in the 1940s and 1950s, had so severely discredited; however, while the modern preserves traditional notions of textual autonomy, the postmodern challenges such aesthetic "foundations."

Initially, scholars treated reception only as an aspect of the author's development. Since an author's work often responds to commentary provided by friends, reviewers, or critics, scholars assumed that the study of these responses would help explain how and why the style, ideas, aims, or forms of a writer evolved. As Jerome McGann says in *The Beauty of Inflections,* a work's "critical history . . . dates from the first responses and reviews it receives. These reactions . . . modify the author's purposes and intentions, sometimes drastically, and they remain part of the processive life" of the work "as it passes on to future readers" (24).

McGann goes on to suggest that a work has "two interlocking histories, one that derives from the author's expressed decisions and purposes, and the other that derives from the critical reactions of the . . . various readers" (24). Traditional literary historians adopt the contrary view: to attribute meaning to a text is to engage in an impersonal act independent of the reader's expectations. For example, E. D.

Hirsch, Jr., argues that since "meaning" is a "constant, unchanging pole" of the "relationship" binding the text and the reader, the critic must establish a text's "objective" meaning before he or she assesses its subjective "significance" (8). Similarly, traditional Marxists believe that objective, public "understanding" precedes and transcends "interpretation"; however, while Hirsch considers the author's intention an autonomous, universally binding norm, the Marxists, who expect understanding to overcome the historical and institutional changes alienating the reader from the author, maintain that an objective account of the author's social conditions reveals the historical import of the author's meaning.

It is not surprising that these historians incisively explained the emergence of realism, naturalism, modernism, and other literary movements and genres; at the same time, these historians neglected the impact of the artist's and the reader's productive activities (see Macherey, 18–19). Because of such difficulties, the formal critics, who came to dominate Anglo-American literary study after World War II, discredited the historical method. Raymond Williams points out that during the 1940s and 1950s American New Critics and British Leavisites considered Historical Marxism the worst culprit because it reduced the work to an expression of the author's socioeconomic context, but they severely condemned all historical analyses because, instead of attending to the text itself, they described a work's causes or influences and an author's development (197). As McGann says, "[A] text-only approach has been so vigorously promoted during the last thirty years that most historical critics have been driven from the field" (17).

In response, some traditional literary historians simply dismissed the formal critiques, while others sought more subtle, complex accounts of a writer's style. McGann argues, for example, that, to overcome the "disciplinary crisis" resulting from the historians' defeat, critics should "integrate the entire range of sociohistorical and philological methods with an aesthetic and ideological criticism of individual works" (3). Similarly, in *Marxism and Literary Criticism*, Terry Eagleton claims that, to explain a poem like "The Waste Land" "as a poem which springs from a crisis of bourgeois ideology," one does not reduce the poem "to the state of contemporary capitalism"—rather, "Marxist criticism looks for the unique conjuncture" of such elements as "the author's class-position, ideological forms and their relation to literary forms, 'spirituality' and philosophy, techniques of literary production, aesthetic theory" (15–16; see also Jameson, 10).

The reception study of Hans Robert Jauss also reconstructs the historical method discredited by formalism; however, since he rejects what Hans-Georg Gadamer terms the Enlightenment's prejudice against prejudice, Jauss faults both the historians' neutral objectivity and the formal critics' figural indeterminacy. In the influential essay "Literary History as a Challenge to Literary Theory," he argues that traditional historians rightly emphasize art's social insight but ignore their own subjective involvement; as he says, they set themselves "outside of history and beyond the errors of . . . the historical reception" (9). Formalist critics, by contrast, ignore the author's original audience but emphasize their values and their methods. These critics evaluate texts and canons, overturn old traditions, and introduce new ones, but dismiss such factors as a genre's history and a writer's life and era (16–18).

Jauss maintains, in addition, that the reader's constructive activity, which brings together the author's historical context and the reader's models, paradigms, beliefs, and values, overcomes the destructive opposition between historical truth and formal methods. While the traditional defense of the historical method preserves the autonomy of the critic or the inherent identity of the text, Jauss's reception study emphasizes the reader's constructive activity, which grasps both the author's historical context or "other" and the reader's own models, paradigms, beliefs, and values. By examining readers' changing horizons and sociohistorical contexts, reception study reveals literature's historical influence, what Jauss terms the "coherence of literature as an event" (22).

Modern reception study, which accepts Jauss's assumption that as positive constructive influences the prejudices of the reader establish his or her subjective horizon and divide it from the historical other, examines the changing horizons of a text's many readers. Consider, for example, the reception of *Hamlet*. The many works that examine the reception of this play acknowledge that formal, authorial, Derridean, feminist, Marxist, New Historical, and other interpretations pursue very different ends and aims, but, far from examining their historical development or their diverse historical contexts, these studies demand that the critic transcend his or her school by accepting the common view or the rational truth.[2] These studies admit that divergent schools of interpretation produce equally divergent readings but still consider the quest for a rational consensus desirable and even obligatory; however, such studies fail to acknowledge the diverse institutional positions, literary methods, and social, sexual, and ideological beliefs that inform the play's formal, authorial, historical, psychoanalytic, and poststructuralist readings.

For instance, the traditional Marxist reading of *Hamlet* claims that, upset by Gertrude's "o'erhasty" marriage and the ghost's disturbing revelations, Hamlet discovers that a shocking corruption and brutal inhumanity pervade the Danish court. In Victor Kiernan's terms, "Sins of individuals open his eyes to deep faults in the society he has hitherto taken for granted" (68; see also Kettle, 238; Kernan, 1979, 93; Margolies, 66–67; and Siegel). As a consequence, Hamlet tries but fails to reform Claudius, Gertrude, the court, and even the theater. For example, he directs the play within the play to "catch the conscience of the king" (2.2.561–62), sets up a spiritual "glass" to show Gertrude her "inmost part" (3.4.19–20), and recommends a nunnery to Ophelia to save her from "calumny" (3.1.134). That is, in an idealist fashion he imagines that the glass, the play, and his other "deep plots" will reform the court and even the times; as he says, "The Time is out of joint. O curséd sprite that ever I was born to set it right" (1.5.187–88). In act 5, when he returns to Denmark, he admits that his "deep plots" did "pall," and he abandons his idealist tactics. Taking concrete action, he declares his love of Ophelia, reconciles the angry Laertes, avenges his poisoned father, and preserves his princely name and the royal succession.

Hence, for Marxists, the play depicts the dilemmas of the Renaissance and even the modern intellectual idealist. Besides offering its own reading, however, the conventional Marxist view takes to task interpretations in which a melancholy, repressed, or speculative Hamlet proves incapable of decisive action. For instance, an interpretation that is authorial because it appreciates Hamlet's analytical mind, Shakespeare's autonomous imagination, or tragedy's generic features claims that Hamlet believes the ghost and wants to take revenge, but, because of the world's evils, his speculative mind, his melancholy nature, or his mother's unseemly sexual appetite, he grows too depressed to do anything. This view began in the Romantic era when, to defend middle-class English literature against the aristocratic classical tradition, critics construed the play as the overflowing expression of Shakespeare's genius. In the Victorian and early modern era, when criticism entered the university and assimilated the classical tradition, scholars such as A. C. Bradley construed Hamlet as a tragic hero whose melancholy state of mind, not his inability to act, brings about his downfall.

The authorial account made the play accessible to the nineteenth century's new middle-class reading public and "disinterested" academic humanists. Similarly, the development of specialized fields and independent professional associations justify the formal or textual account, which denies that Hamlet takes meaningful action, occupies a world of his own, or experiences a disabling disgust with life, because it is the play's images of poison, disease, corruption, and death that unify the work. Other institutional grounds support the Derridean or poststructuralist account, which also denies that Hamlet takes meaningful action and experiences a disabling disgust, but which goes on to show that the play's figural language undermines the language's literal import, the text's unity, the play's generic conventions, and even the traditional critics' methodology. Still other grounds support historical criticism, which claims that the religious beliefs of the Elizabethans, the conventions of revenge tragedy, or the ideals of Senecan stoicism, not the evils of nascent Renaissance capitalism nor the indecision of the analytical intellectual, explain why Hamlet hesitates. While the Marxist seeks to refute these diverse views, reception study maintains that these divergent readings of the play, radically incommensurable, reveal the sociohistorical grounds and the divided state of modern literary study, not the confused views of elitist, withdrawn critics. Indeed, these differences indicate the play's rich import and criticism's evolving practices and changing contexts.

As the case of *Hamlet* suggests, modern reception study limits the governing powers of theory and undertakes the historical analysis of changing interpretive practices. Jane Tompkins rightly says that

> classic texts, while they may or may not have originally been written by geniuses, have certainly been written and rewritten by the generations of professors and critics who make their living by them. . . . Rather than being the repository of eternal truths, they embody the changing interests and beliefs of those people whose place in the cultural hierarchy empowers them to decide which works deserve the name of classic and which do not (37).

Because it recognizes that the traditional canon embodies the "changing interests and beliefs" of authoritative readers or critics, reception study examines the sociohistorical contexts of interpretive practice.

Reception study also has within it a postmodern turn. That is, in its postmodern form, reception study adopts the philosophical assumption that, to justify particular claims of knowledge, it must reject grand narratives or philosophical ideals in favor of local histories (see Bertens, 6–8; Fairlamb, 57; and Lyotard, 37–41). This reception study may be neopragmatic, in which case it assumes that the epistemological critique of foundational theory reveals the biases or local interests that have always governed criticism. As Richard Rorty points out in *Consequences of Pragmatism,* the epistemological norms of traditional philosophy seek but fail to escape the philosopher's determinate historical context or "vocabularies." Philosophers who recognize their epistemological limits would not seek an irrefutable argument or defend the scientific method; they would redescribe the vocabularies of others. This reception study may also be post-Marxist, in which case it presupposes that the reader's interpretive practices articulate the established methods of "hegemonic" literary discourse. As Ernesto Laclau and Chantal Mouffe argue, since hegemonic ideological practices fail to construct a full identity, the antagonisms and conflicts of diverse social contexts matter more than the systematic contradictions and predetermined stages of the Marxist "grand narrative" (97–105).

The Foucauldian or New Historical approach, which construes historical knowledge as anonymous, dispersed discourses organizing society as well as the body, also critiques the foundational norms of traditional theory; however, instead of explaining the historical contexts of readers' interpretive activities, this approach preserves the complexity of the literary text, which may assert both subversive and dominant discourses, and the autonomy of the critic, who may freely "affiliate" with established or with oppositional institutions (see Horwitz, 799–800). As Claire Colebrook says, the New Historicism considers "the cultural/aesthetic domain . . . an area of contestation where various forces (aesthetic, political, historical, economic, etc.) circulate" (24), yet the New Historicism also defends the traditional notion that historical texts are referential or that, as "self-fashioning," representation is fundamental to human experience (226–27). Thus, Stephen Greenblatt argues that Shakespeare's text constructs alien, subversive outlooks that anticipate but resist modern views, doctrines, and beliefs. As he says, "It was true that I could only hear my own voice, but my own voice was the voice of the dead" (1).

To reconstruct the historical method, both New Historicism and (post)modern reception study deny the transcendent status or transformative power of figural or theoretical ideals; however, instead of preserving the text's intrinsic complexity or the critic's autonomy, reception study undertakes the historical analysis of the changing conditions and reading practices through which texts are constructed in the process of being received. Both modern and postmodern reception study defend the historical against the purely formal approach, undertake the historical study of a text's diverse readings, and repudiate the autonomous norms and values of traditional theory; however, postmodern reception study also adopts the poststructuralist critique of "foundational" theory. Moreover, more fully than modern reception study, postmodern reception study examines women's, African-American, and multicultural literatures, popular culture, the ordinary reader, the history of the book, and so on. That is, modern reception study critiques the norms of theory but still assumes that canonical texts produce what Jauss terms the "emancipation of mankind from its natural, religious, and social bonds" (25), whereas, instead of defending canonical literature or preserving a utopian autonomy, postmodern reception study explores the rhetoric, politics, and/or interpretive communities of the traditional canon and the excluded literatures and culture.

Of course, cultural theorists of all sorts also repudiate the conventional distinction between high art and nontraditional literatures, popular culture, or ordinary readers' practices. Many cultural theorists have demonstrated that such literatures and practices do not always conform to established doctrines and views, nor does high art invariably subvert them (see, for example, Collins, 7–16; Easthope, 79; Polan; and Gendron); however, while these theorists reject the privileged status of canonical art, they do not question the universal values or objective truth of traditional aesthetics, even though this aesthetics justifies the privileged status of canonical art.[3] John Frow, who rejects not only that privileged status but also the absolute complexity of formal methods, claims, by contrast, that incompatible "regimes of value" govern the reception of high and popular texts. Instead of reflecting or representing an exterior social group or an institutional hierarchy, these regimes of value establish their own hierarchy of values and methods (146; see also Bennett and Woollacott). In other words, even though many traditional and postmodern critics reject the privileged status of high art, they preserve an illusory hierarchy of uniformity. Reception theorists like Frow maintain, however, that the differences between high and popular culture reveal their equally diverse regimes of value or, as other reception theorists say, "interpretive communities," "rhetorical practices," or "reading formations."

Although the final section of this collection discusses objections to and critiques of reception study, we would like to mention here the widespread concern that the study of such diverse regimes of value cannot establish a consensus, engage in rational debate, or reform the profession or society. Some traditional and radical scholars argue that abandoning the Arnoldian faith in rational, objective truth opens literary and historical study to transient fashions, sectarian politics, and ethical relativism.[4] Reception study maintains, however, that abandoning this Arnoldian faith changes nothing because our local gender, class, and racial biases have always influenced interpretive practices. As Rorty and others maintain, philosophical critiques of foundational truth do not alter the everyday business of philosophy, history, or criticism; these critiques simply prepare the way for an examination of what was always taking place. In the past decade, when poststructuralist theory has established itself in English departments and when unfriendly legislatures and increased public opposition and political scrutiny threaten the careers of worthy students and faculty and the survival of many university programs, reception study may be the wiser option—it moves beyond theoretical critique and acknowledges, explains, and justifies the very different interests, contexts, and interpretive communities that compose our pluralistic society.

Initially a way of explaining an author's development, reception study has become an important mode of historical inquiry because to rehabilitate the historical method discredited by formalist criticism, reception study limits or rejects the transformative force of theoretical ideals and examines the changing "reading formations" or "interpretive communities" governing readers' practices. To illustrate this new importance, the sections of this collection present the various forms that reception study has taken in major disciplinary and interdisciplinary fields. In the first section, the four readings set forth the main theoretical trajectories in reception study, which range from Jauss's traditional, modern form to Bennett's radical, poststructuralist approach. In section II, the readings demonstrate some of the ways reception study has been put into practice in literary-critical studies. Essays discussing methodology and exemplifying the shape of reception work in the field of the "history of the book" comprise section III. Since attention to reception has been a significant component of work in cultural studies as well as media and mass-communication studies, the essays in section IV exemplify and address important versions of that work. To provide a different perspective, the readings in the last section enunciate the major challenges and objections that have been raised against reception theory and its practice. Lastly, for reference and further reading, a bibliography lists works in the following categories of reception study: general theoretical works; studies treating particular authors, texts, and/or historical contexts; books and articles on reception and the history of the book; and books and articles on reception within mass communication and popular culture.

NOTES

1. The MLA *Bibliography* provides a telling index to this explosion, listing more than 3,900 items under "reception study" published during the last ten years.
2. For example, C. S. Lewis grants that the play has had many contrary readings, but they embarrass him because he fears that absurdities and weaknesses in the play must explain them. To avoid this damaging conclusion, he suggests that we examine "the poetry and the situation," not the main character (175). A. L. French also says that critics should not confuse the play and the main character, but he readily blames the many readings on the play's lapses, incoherence, and failures. In HAMLET *and the Philosophy of Criticism*, Morris Weitz admits that "there is no true, best, correct, or right explanation, reading, interpretation, or understanding of *Hamlet*, nor can there be" (258), but he still expects critics to overcome their differences and arrive at a consensus. Similarly, in *The Meanings of* HAMLET, Paul Gottshalk says that "no interpretation can explain *Hamlet* utterly" but then argues that many interpretations "may be coordinate. . . . [T]he possibilities of cooperation [among critical schools] are great and the impediments less than many seem to feel" (131). More recently in HAMLET's *Perfection* (1994), William Kerrigan grants that a "finite number" of conceptual frameworks explain the play's many readings (2) but denies that these frameworks justify our abandoning the pursuit of a "coherent understanding" (3). He even calls the play's poststructuralist critics "decadent" because their "new methods and concerns" give these critics "no way to solve the mysteries and unravel the cruxes" of the play(3).
3. For instance, Anthony Easthope complains that in the Frankfurt school's account, popular culture dupes ordinary readers into enjoying it (79), but he still says that his postmodern juxtaposition of high and popular art confirms the school's critique of modernity (1991, 100). In *Crusoe's Footprints*, Patrick Brantlinger admits that Adorno and Horkheimer's critique of Enlightenment science is too negative and despairing (185) and even that "art or high culture is no more radical or liberating in and of itself than is commodified mass culture" (196); at the same time, he dismisses the "status quo" functionalism of postmodern theory and defends the mimetic realism and the utopian potential with which humanist Marxism and the Frankfurt School endow canonical art.
4. For example, in "Authors as Rentiers," Alvin Kernan complains that in American literature departments "criticism's power grab" has expressed itself

> as a variety of aggressive social causes such as feminism, racial tolerance, moral relativism, ethnicity, and sexual freedom, all rejecting traditional forms of authority, intellectual and social, and demanding that literature be used to further their own social and political programs (1990, 83).

Paul Bové, opposes reception study on grounds that are radical but comparable: "Critical intelligence involves a demystification of intellectuals' sense of their independence, a constant genealogical self-criticism, and research into specific discourses and institutions as part of the struggle against oppressive power" (47; see also O'Hara, 7; Dasenbrock, 182; and Sprinker, 155).

WORKS CITED

Bennett, Tony, and Janet Woollacott. *Bond and Beyond: The Political Career of a Popular Hero.* New York: Methuen, 1987.
Bertens, Hans. *The Idea of the Postmodern: A History.* New York: Routledge, 1995.
Bérubé, Michael. *Public Access: Literary Theory and American Cultural Politics.* London: Verso, 1994.
Bové, Paul. *In the Wake of Theory.* Hanover, N.H.: Wesleyan University Press, 1992.
Bradley, A. C. *Shakespearean Tragedy: Lectures on* HAMLET, OTHELLO, KING LEAR, MACBETH. London: MacMillan, 1911.
Brantlinger, Patrick. *Crusoe's Footprints: Cultural Studies in Britain and America.* New York: Routledge, 1990.
Colebrook, Claire. *New Literary Histories: New Historicism and Contemporary Criticism.*

Manchester, England: Manchester University Press, 1997.

Collins, Jim. *Uncommon Cultures: Popular Culture and Post-modernism.* New York: Routledge, 1989.

Dasenbrock, Reed Way. "We've Done It to Ourselves: The Critique of Truth and the Attack on Theory." In *PC Wars: Politics and Theory in the Academy,* edited by Jeffrey Williams, 172–83. London: Routledge, 1995.

Eagleton, Terry. *Marxism and Literary Criticism.* Berkeley and Los Angeles: University of California Press, 1976.

Easthope, Anthony. *Literary into Cultural Studies.* London: Routledge, 1991.

Fairlamb, Horace L. *Critical Conditions: Postmodernity and the Question of Foundations.* Cambridge, England: Cambridge University Press, 1994.

French, A. L. *Shakespeare and the Critics.* London: Cambridge University Press, 1972.

Gendron, Bernard. "Theodor Adorno Meets the Cadillacs." In *Studies in Entertainment: Critical Approaches to Mass Culture,* edited by Tania Modleski, 18–38. Bloomington: Indiana University Press, 1986.

Gottschalk, Paul. *The Meanings of HAMLET: Modes of Literary Interpretation since Bradley.* Albuquerque: University of New Mexico Press, 1972.

Hirsch, E. D., Jr. *Validity in Interpretation.* New Haven: Yale University Press, l967.

Holub, Robert C. *Crossing Borders: Reception Theory, Poststructuralism, Deconstruction.* Madison: University of Wisconsin Press, 1992.

Horwitz, Howard. "'I Can't Remember': Skepticism, Synthetic Histories, Critical Action." *SAQ* 87 (1988): 787–820.

Jameson, Fredric. *The Political Unconscious: Narrative as a Socially Symbolic Act.* Ithaca, N.Y.: Cornell University Press, 1981.

Jauss, Hans Robert. *Toward an Aesthetic of Reception.* Translated by Timothy Bahti. Minneapolis: University of Minnesota Press, 1982.

Kernan, Alvin. *The Death of Literature.* New Haven: Yale University Press, 1990.

———. *The Playwright as Magician: Shakespeare's Image of the Poet in the English Public Theater.* New Haven: Yale University Press, 1979.

Kerrigan, William. *HAMLET's Perfection.* Baltimore: Johns Hopkins University Press, 1994.

Kettle, Arnold. "From *Hamlet* to *Lear.*" In *Shakespeare in a Changing World,* edited by Arnold Kettle, 146–71. New York: International Publishers, 1964.

Kiernan, Victor. *Eight Tragedies of Shakespeare: A Marxist Study.* London: Verso, 1996.

Laclau, Ernesto, and Chantal Mouffe. *Hegemony and Socialist Strategy.* Tranlated by Winston Moore and Paul Cammack. London: Verso, 1985.

Lewis, C. S. "Hamlet The Prince or the Poem?" Rpt. in Claire Sacks and Edgar Whan. *Hamlet: Enter Critic,* 170–87. New York: Appleton-Century-Crofts, 1960.

Lyotard, Jean-François. *The Postmodern Condition: A Report on Knowledge.* Translated by Geoff Bennington and Brian Massumi. Minneapolis: University of Minnesota Press, 1984.

Macherey, Pierre. *A Theory of Literary Production.* Translated by Geoffrey Wall. London: Routledge and Kegan Paul, 1978.

Mailloux, Steven. *Reception Histories: Rhetoric, Pragmatism, and American Cultural Politics.* Ithaca, N.Y.: Cornell University Press, 1998.

———. *Rhetorical Power.* Ithaca, N.Y.: Cornell University Press, 1989.

Margolies, David. *Monsters of the Deep: Social Dissolution in Shakespeare's Tragedies.* Manchester, England: Manchester University Press, 1992.

McGann, Jerome J. *The Beauty of Inflections: Literary Investigations in Historical Method and Theory.* Oxford: Clarendon Press of Oxford University Press, 1985.

O'Hara, Daniel. *Radical Parody: American Culture and Critical Agency After Foucault.* New York: Columbia University Press, 1992.

Polan, Dana. "Postmodernism and Cultural Analysis Today." In *Postmodernism and Its Discontents,* edited by E. Ann Kaplan, 45–58. London: Verso, 1988.

Radway, Janice. *Reading the Romance: Women, Patriarchy, and Popular Literature*. Chapel Hill: University of North Carolina Press, 1984.

Rorty, Richard. *Consequences of Pragmatism (Essays: 1972–1980)*. Minneapolis: University of Minnesota Press, 1982.

Shakespeare, William. *Hamlet*. Edited by Cyrus Hoy. 2nd ed. New York: Norton, 1992.

Siegel, Paul N. *Shakespeare In His Time and Ours*. Notre Dame, Ind.: University of Notre Dame Press, 1968.

Sprinker, Michael. "The War Against Theory." In *PC Wars: Politics and Theory in the Academy*, edited by Jeffrey Williams, 149–71. London: Routledge, 1995.

Taylor, Gary. *Reinventing Shakespeare: A Cultural History from the Restoration to the Present*. New York: Weidenfeld & Nicholson, 1989.

Tompkins, Jane. *Sensational Designs: The Cultural Work of American Fiction 1790–1860*. New York: Oxford University Press, 1985.

Widdowson, Peter. *Hardy in History: A Study in Literary Sociology*. London: Routledge, 1989.

Weitz, Morris. *HAMLET and the Philosophy of Criticism*. Chicago: University of Chicago Press, 1964.

Williams, Raymond. *Writing in Society*. London: Verso, 1985.

I

THEORETICAL ACCOUNTS
OF RECEPTION

For the most part, reception theorists, who include Tony Bennett, Stanley Fish, Hans Robert Jauss, and Steven Mailloux, claim that the interpretive activities of readers—formal, historical, authorial, Derridean, feminist, Marxist, and so on—explain a text's significance and aesthetic value. The most traditional, Jauss emphasizes the reader's "horizon of expectations" but takes the author's intention to ground the text's historical "other" and to preserve its capacity to critique social life and transform readers. More radical, Bennett, Fish, and Mailloux claim that the activity of diverse readers addresses equally diverse interpretive communities or "reading formations" whose norms and values determine the validity of the interpretation. In doing so, Fish preserves the disciplinary limits of literary study; Mailloux posits a broad, cultural notion of rhetoric; and Bennett argues that the institutional practices or reading formations establish the norms and ideals of the literary subject.

A. THE HERMENEUTICS OF HANS ROBERT JAUSS
In "The Identity of the Poetic Text in the Changing Horizon of Understanding," Jauss maintains that the evolution of the audience, not the historical period of the author, explains the history of a literary text. He grants that the author's original audience establishes the intended meaning, but he argues that this historical meaning and the modern meaning are radically incommensurate. To describe the author's life or era, critics must not assume that they have privileged access to a text or ignore their subjective involvement with it; rather, to preserve what Jauss terms the "hermeneutic difference of self and other," they open themselves to the historical or cultural other presented by a text. In a platonic fashion, literary hermeneutics fosters an unending dialogue of self and other.

Jauss acknowledges that the literary histories of Mikhail Bakhtin and Georg Lukács involve a dialogue of self and other: texts require an act of comprehension in which the reader/critic distinguishes his modern self from the author's historical self. Lukács argues that great literature transcends such unending historical dialogues, while Bakhtin maintains that the dialogue primarily reveals the author's conditions of production. Jauss, by contrast, accepts the Heideggerian belief that, because understanding is circular, hermeneutic experience requires openness or letting be. A text constructs a world but not a totality that cancels and preserves partial methods or distinct historical periods, as Hegelian and Marxist critics claim. The Heideggerians maintain, however, that, bringing "what is into the 'clearing,'" a text undermines traditional Western notions of truth or value and discloses the unique import of being, whereas Jauss adopts Hans-Georg Gadamer's belief that, just as a festival exists only in its celebration, so a text exists only as an event that reveals the reader's self, not being's unique import. As a consequence, Jauss argues that, to preserve the hermeneutics of self and other, criticism must examine what he terms the audience's "horizon of expectations." Derived from Heidegger and Gadamer, the "horizon of expectations" stipulates that, to interpret a text or a society, readers bring to bear the subjective models, paradigms, beliefs, and values of their necessarily limited background. Jauss says that the reader's prejudices do not distort or misconstrue the text's meaning or the author's intention; a positive constructive influence, these prejudices establish the subjective horizon of the reader.

At the same time, reading for Jauss is not an entirely subjective process because a text can resist its reception and transform readers and society. That is, Gadamer grants that the reader's horizon of expectations exercises a constructive import but still expects the traditional canon to embody objective truth; similarly, Jauss claims that great texts transcend their historical context and establish new beliefs and values. On the one hand, Jauss frees the reader to dismiss the traditional canon and to constitute a new one. He faults his earlier "modernist" belief that great texts demonstrate their aesthetic value by resisting the reader's assumptions. Rejecting the distinction between resistance and affirmation, he claims that even texts serving traditional religious or political ends can demonstrate aesthetic value. On the other hand, in *Toward an Aesthetic of Reception*, he argues that a great text can "result in a 'change of horizons' through negation of familiar experiences or through raising newly-articulated experiences to the level of consciousness" (25). Similarly, in "Identity," he claims that the aesthetic experience can make it "possible for new expectations of the seemingly unmovable horizon of a social order to open up."

B. THE NEOPRAGMATISM OF STANLEY FISH

In "Yet Once More," Fish also says that the reception of a text governs its meaning, but he repudiates a text's transformative force more consistently than Jauss does. Fish's account of reception derives from his belief that a text's effects on the reader explain a text's meaning. In early works, he argued that the irreducible effects of language move readers to produce interpretations, yet, like Jauss, he construed the author as a normative force teaching or fashioning the reader. In later work, Fish grants that this assumption does not explain why we read different texts differently nor why some readings are authoritative and others are not.

To explain these variations, Fish argues that the reader's views conform with her interpretive conventions, rather than the text's structure or the author's intention.

Just as Jauss denies that critics have unmediated access to texts, Fish denies that fact and rhetoric or concepts and conventions exclude each other; however, Fish draws on the speech act theory of J. L. Austin, particularly his distinction between "constative" assertions, which describe facts, and performative assertions, which must meet conventional requirements if they are to indicate action authoritatively (Austin 3–9). Although Fish provisionally accepts this distinction between constative and performative assertions, he also argues that it breaks down. He claims that Austin finally does not allow any assertion a purely factual, descriptive, or constative status because, as Austin admits, all assertions presuppose a conventional, social context in which they represent actions (1975, 67, 91). Like Derrida, who claims that Austin's distinction cannot effectively exclude misfires, failures, or literary figures (385-87), Fish shows that this breakdown effectively establishes the reader's conventions, not the language's conceptual rigor or denotative clarity, as the authoritative basis of a speech act's meaning (1980, 198; see also Petry, 22–41, 138, and 149).

To prevent the reader's lapse into an arbitrary subjectivity, Jauss claims that her hermeneutic practices enable her to distinguish the modern self or "horizon" from the historical or cultural "other." For similar reasons, Fish, who adopts the pragmatist's belief that the community of inquirers establishes the truth of a theory, claims that the modern "interpretive community" whose norms, ideals, and methods the reader accepts determines an interpretation's validity. As Fish's lengthy interpretation of Milton's *Lycidas* indicates, he construes the interpretive community of Milton's readers as specialized Milton or Renaissance scholars who already know the many, contrary generic features of pastoral poetry.

Moreover, Fish claims that composed of such professional communities, literary study precludes interdisciplinary or political activity. That is, Fish critiques the normative force of literary theory, but, unlike Jauss, he denies that literary study changes the reader's beliefs or transforms social life. In "Consequences," he argues that theory does not ensure a reader's self-consciousness, govern interpretive practice, or change political beliefs. He admits that theorists may examine the rhetorical figures of a text, the unifying intention of its author, its play of gender differences, or its critiques of ideology, but he considers these diverse interpretive practices a matter of local, Derridean, authorial, feminist, or Marxist beliefs, not of valid theory, which he restricts to general rules determining correct interpretations. Theory's project inevitably fails because practical interpretation never overcomes its local, particular contexts and achieves general or universal status. While Jauss still expects a text to transform the reader's norms, Fish insists that the reader's activity never escapes its disciplinary limits.

C. THE RHETORICAL PRAGMATISM OF STEVEN MAILLOUX

In "Interpretation and Rhetorical Hermeneutics," Steven Mailloux also assumes that the interpretive or "rhetorical" practices of the reader explain her interpretation of a text, but, unlike Fish's disciplinary and Jauss's traditional accounts, his "rhetorical hermeneutics" acknowledges political divisions and accommodates the new feminist, African-American, and cultural studies programs of modern literary study.

Mailloux grants the traditional belief that authors communicate meanings to readers and thereby teach readers how to read, but he defends a broad notion of rhetoric in which the conventions adopted by readers, not an author's intention or the foundational aesthetic norms of a text, account for established interpretive methods. Derived from Jonathan Culler's *Structuralist Poetics,* this broad notion of rhetoric explains the conventions and procedures whereby readers make sense of texts (1982, 56–57). Mailloux argues that objective truth does not transcend rhetorical conventions, as Plato says; rather, different readers produce different interpretations and even different texts because diverse conventions govern their interpretive practices.

Like Fish, Mailloux goes on to show that the rhetorical practices of a community or discipline, rather than the norms of "foundational" theory, justify or limit the reader's interpretive practice. Mailloux objects that Fish consigns too much to the reader's beliefs and too little to theory, which, he says, directs research, precludes unacceptable views, and exposes concealed interests (1989, 151–66), yet he too argues that rhetorical practices, not theoretical norms, govern interpretive practices. He does not dismiss universal theory in favor of local beliefs, as Fish does, or the Hegelian totality in favor of a partial horizon, as Jauss does; instead, Mailloux adopts Richard Rorty's neopragmatist belief that philosophy ought to abandon the metaphysical quest for ultimate grounds, irrefutable arguments, or foundational truths. Consequently, Mailloux urges critics to abandon (foundational) literary theory. As he says in *Rhetorical Power,* "The way to answer the realist/idealist question 'Is meaning created by the text or by the reader or by both?' is simply not to ask it, to stop doing Theory" (14).

More fully than Fish's or Jauss's critiques of theory, Mailloux's call for critics to "stop doing Theory" opens reception study to broad historical and cultural analyses; as he says in "Interpretation and Rhetorical Hermeneutics," "[R]hetorical hermeneutics uses rhetoric to practice theory by doing history." His rhetorical hermeneutics explains the changing history of a text's readings and creates a platform for "rhetorical" cultural studies, which includes a variety of untraditional genres and nonliterary texts. More importantly, he considers interpretation a "politically interested act" because it takes place "within the power relations of a historical community." At the same time, he grants Fish's belief that literary interpretation differs markedly from political activity, for he maintains that "it is better to keep the issue of foundationalism versus antifoundationalism logically separate from the issue of reactionary versus progressive politics" (1998, 40).

D. THE (POST-)MARXISM OF TONY BENNETT

Like Jauss, Fish, and Mailloux, Tony Bennett assumes that the reception of a text explains its importance, but, more consistently than Mailloux, he construes reception study as a political intervention in cultural affairs.

Fish, Jauss, and Mailloux say that the reader's "horizon," "interpretive community," or "rhetorical practices" govern her interpretive activity; similarly, Bennett says that what governs interpretive practices are "reading formations," which situate readers within institutional structures determining what counts as a text and a context or what distinguishes literary from nonliterary concerns. Bennett goes on to maintain, however, that authoritative institutions, with their justifying ideologies, foster certain interpretive methods and preclude others. Like Mailloux, who argues that good rhetoric establishes a community by restating the community's common sense (*doxa*), Bennett assumes that discourse creates a community, but he accepts the post-Marxist belief that hegemonic discourse constructs its own social relations and does not mirror or resist established socioeconomic structures. In *Outside Literature,* he complains that the post-Marxism of Ernesto Laclau and

Chantel Mouffe "can specify no postitive limits for the conduct of articulatory practices" (264); however, in "Texts in History," he accepts Laclau and Mouffe's belief that objects do not simply or literally mirror their sociohistorical contexts, as traditional Marxists say; rather, the distinction between object and context, discursive and nondiscursive practices, or "thought and reality" breaks down because, as Laclau and Mouffe say, "[s]ynonomy, metonomy, metaphor . . . are part of the primary terrain itself in which the social is constituted" (110).

As a consequence, Bennett also denies that an ideal text, true to itself, can justify interpretive practices or undermine contrary readings. He maintains, however, that to interpret a text is to contest its terrain, to vindicate one's methods and ideologies, and, by implication if not by explicit assertion, to debunk opposed methods and ideologies (1987, 59–60). While Fish and Mailloux hold that disciplinary or rhetorical norms govern interpretive practices, Bennett claims that a Marxist reception study reinterprets texts, disrupting the institutional reproduction of established ideologies in order to situate texts in "different reading formations." As he says in "Texts," the "business" of Marxist criticism is to "move" texts "about—to locate them within different reading formations, producing them as different texts for different readers—in accordance with shifting and variable calculations of political objectives." In his recent *Culture: A Reformer's Science,* he disavows such political interventions, but in "Texts," he identifies the different reading formations with working-class, feminist, and African-American struggles.

Jauss also considers reading a transformative practice, but he claims that texts change a reader's and, as a result, a society's norms; by contrast, Bennett denies texts such transformative power even though he takes Marxist reading practices to resituate texts. For example, he doubts that the scientific standpoint of the Althusserian critics transcends its enabling discourse and grants the critic a privileged perception; as he says, "there is no such thing as an Absolute science which escapes the constraints of its own discursivity." Bennett also complains that Marxist humanists like Georg Lukács explain canonical works in profound, sociohistorical terms but expect such works to escape the historical relativity of their subsequent interpretations or reception because these Marxists believe that when history ends and communism begins, "man" will be restored to himself, and the universality of a text's values will be self-evident. Closer to Fish and Mailloux than to Jauss, Bennett takes the reader's changing interpretive practices, not theoretical norms or textual figures, to explain a text's changing significance and repudiates these Marxist theories because they attribute universal validity to judgments of value but fail to overcome the opposition between universal values and criticism's political import.

As a post-Marxist reception theorist working in literary and cultural studies, Bennett, among the four theorists represented here, takes the most aggressively political position in articulating an oppositional relation between theory and practice. Nonetheless, the relation between theory and practice, in the broadest sense of the term, has been important to all four, as well as to others working in reception study. As the readings in the next section of this collection demonstrate, even when practice has been the primary concern of reception critics, some have made forays into theory an important component of their practical criticism. In a wider sense, however, such linkage represents an unavoidable condition. As postmodern reception theory reminds us, theory is always a form of practice, always embedded within a set of local conditions, epistemic frames, and interpretive protocols that mark it as a contextually constituted regime of value.

WORKS CITED

Austin, J. L. *How to Do Things with Words*. 2nd ed. Edited by J. O. Urmson and Marina Sbisà. Cambridge: Harvard University Press, 1975.

Bennett, Tony. *Culture: A Reformer's Science*. London: Sage, 1998.

———. "Marxism and Popular Fiction." *Literature and History* 7 (1981): 149–64.

———. *Outside Literature*. New York: Routledge, 1990.

Bennett, Tony, and Janet Woollacott. *Bond and Beyond: The Political Career of a Popular Hero*. New York: Methuen, 1987.

Derrida, Jacques. "Signature, Event, Context." *Glyph* 1 (1977): 172–97.

Fish, Stanley. "Consequences." *Critical Inquiry* 11 (1985): 433–58.

———. *Is There a Text in This Class? The Authority of Interpretive Communities*. Cambridge: Harvard University Press, 1980.

Laclau, Ernesto, and Chantal Mouffe. *Hegemony and Socialist Strategy*. Translated by Winston Moore and Paul Cammack. London: Verso, 1985.

Mailloux, Steven. *Interpretive Conventions: The Reader in the Study of American Fiction*. Ithaca, N.Y.: Cornell University Press, 1982.

———. *Reception Histories: Rhetoric, Pragmatism, and American Cultural Politics*. Ithaca, N.Y.: Cornell University Press, 1998.

———. *Rhetorical Power*. Ithaca, N.Y.: Cornell University Press, 1989.

Petry, Sandy. *Speech Acts and Literary Theory*. New York: Routledge, 1989.

HANS ROBERT JAUSS

THE IDENTITY OF THE POETIC TEXT IN THE CHANGING HORIZON OF UNDERSTANDING

INTRODUCTION

Since the 1960s, the renewal of literary hermeneutics has brought to the foreground of methodological reflection a notion which the historico-philological disciplines have always presupposed, but which has rarely ever been developed methodically in its own terms. The notion I am alluding to is that of horizon, which constitutes all creation of meaning in human behaviour and in our primary understanding of the world both as historical limitation and as the condition of possibility of any experience.

The level of understanding to be achieved in order to bridge the historical distance between the alien horizon of the text and the interpreter's own horizon did not become problematic as long as the notion of *Geist* from German idealism or the ideal of precision from positivism appeared to guarantee for interpretation an unmediated access. The historicist paradigm, however, recognized the limitations of the interpreter's point of view and thereby established the qualitative difference between past and present as a hermeneutical problem. It considered the problem of understanding the alien horizon as being resolved if only the interests or biases of the interpreter were excluded. Thus, the scope of historical understanding was radically diminished, being limited to the undifferentiated reconstruction of past life in the horizon of its historical distinctness. The renewed critique of historicism, led for the most part by Gadamer, has brought to light the objectivist illusion of this one-sided hermeneutic and has insisted that the past event cannot be understood without taking into account its consequences, that the work of art cannot be separated from its effects. The very history of effects and the interpretation of an event or work of the past enables us to understand it as a plurality of meanings that was not yet perceivable to its contemporaries. If the horizon of our present did not always already include the original horizon of the past, historical understanding would be impossible, since the past in its otherness may only be grasped in so far as the interpreter is able to separate the alien from his own horizon. It is the task of historical understanding to take both horizons into account through conscious effort. To believe that it is possible to gain access to the alien horizon of the past simply by leaving out one's own horizon of the present is to fail to recognize that subjective criteria, such as choice, perspective, and evaluation, have been introduced into a supposedly objective reconstruction of the past.

The recent trend towards historical knowledge, provoked by the success of the structural method, can be distinguished from classic historicism mainly through a methodological consideration of the historicity of understanding. Such an understanding requires that the horizons of the past and the present assert themselves as the central problem and achieve once more the complete hermeneutical triad of understanding, explanation, and application. Such a requirement has established the notion of horizon as a fundamental concept in both literary and historical hermeneutics. It poses the problem of understanding what is alien by insisting on the distinctness of the horizons not only of past and present experience, but also of familiar and culturally different worlds. One may state it as the problem of aesthetic experience when the horizon of expectation, evoked in the contemporary experience of the reading of the literary text, is reconstructed. It may also be conceived as a problem of intertextuality when one considers the function of other texts that constitute the horizon of a literary work and gain new meaning by this transposition. As well it encompasses the problem of the social function of literature mediating between the horizons of aesthetic and everyday experience. Historical knowledge may also be approached as the problem of the transformation of horizons, a perspective which arises when the teleological or evolutionist theory of tradition is invalidated and when, even in the arts, historical processes are drawn into the dialectic of appropriation and selection, conservation and rejuvenation. Finally we encounter the problem of ideological criticism when we have to elucidate the latent horizon of concealed interests and repressed needs that seems to challenge today the humanist trust in the transparency of communication in our dealings with art.

This sketch of the history of the problem might well be expanded to include other disciplines, the implications of which we will only briefly allude to here. Most disciplines have recently begun to question the hermeneutical presuppositions of their theoretical foundations and have raised explicitly or implicitly the notion of horizon: as a thematic field in the sociology of knowledge and its theory of relevancies (Schütz), as frame of reference that ultimately conveys meaning to actions and perceptions in the theory of science (Popper), as a presupposition of reasoning in the analysis of logical language (Frege), in generative semantics (Brekle) and in linguistic pragmatics (Wunderlich), as the isotopic level in structural semantics (Greimas), as the cultural code in semiotics (Lotman), as the situational context in the theory of speech-acts (Stierle), as the intertext in structural stylistics (Riffaterre), and finally as the language game in analytical language-philosophy, which, in Wittgenstein's later period, ultimately makes all understanding of meaning possible and thereby succeeds in replacing what was, until then, a precise world-portraying aspect of language.[1]

My own contribution to this change in the history of science was the attempt in *Literaturgeschichte als Provokation* (1967) to introduce the notion of horizon as an instrument in literary hermeneutics. By returning to it now I intend to re-examine the biases and lacunae of this enterprise, using my own work to test it. Rather than seeking to resolve problems raised by my critics, I shall attempt to summarize my argument by addressing myself to those examples in my critical work where the problem of bringing into play the notion of horizons focused on new aspects which as yet cannot claim to have been solved.

DIALOGICAL UNDERSTANDING IN LITERARY COMMUNICATION

Recent interest in aesthetic theory relating to the problem of the experience of art and its communicative function, to the experience of other historical periods and other cultures, and to the understanding which it brings of temporal remoteness and unfamiliarity has once again brought to the fore the problem of the circularity of literary communication and, at the same time, its dialogical nature.

Just as the producer of a text becomes also a recipient when he sets out to write, so the interpreter has to bring himself into play as reader when he wants to participate in the dialogue of literary tradition. A dialogue consists not only of two interlocutors, but also of the willingness of one to recognize and accept the other in his otherness. This is even more true when the other is represented by a text which does not speak to us immediately. Literary understanding becomes dialogical only when the otherness of the text is sought and recognized from the horizon of our own expectations, when no naïve fusion of horizons is considered, and when one's own expectations are corrected and extended by the experience of other.

The recognition and acceptance of the "dialogicity" of literary communication brings into play in more than one way the problem of otherness: between producer and recipient, between the past of the text and the present of the recipient, between different cultures. Today hermeneutical reflection and semiotic analysis compete as methods to grasp the otherness of a text that is unfamiliar to us. Neither the continuum of meaning of history nor the universality of semiotic systems can claim to have a better guarantee of understanding. In this respect one might appropriately recall Schleiermacher's axiom: that non-understanding is the rule rather than an exception when we come to deal with speech which is unfamiliar to us. The question to which literary hermeneutics must address itself, when faced with the otherness of a text, is how to bridge the gap between otherness and speechlessness.

Because of the aesthetic distance of the spectator, one cannot resolve the problem by asserting that the literary work will open up, as it were, by itself. For this reason precisely, Bakhtin's claim to base understanding on the "dialogicity of the word" went beyond contemplative hermeneutics. If, in a literary dialogue spanning different temporal moments, an embodiment of the experience of others becomes possible, the aesthetically mediated otherness has to include something identifiable which can also be discerned in the alien text. The topical interest in historical anthropology can be explained by this line of argument. Although it was taboo, until only recently, even to formulate the question of "anthropological constants," anthropology, which developed historically a theory of human needs or an archaeology of knowledge, and reconstructed the knowledge of elementary distinction and orientation of past worlds, has regained today an unchallengeable validity. Literary communication has the advantage that agreement about the work of art and the understanding of oneself in the alien object attains transparency. Literary hermeneutics can therefore take heart from the fact that its object—the experience of men in a productive and receptive relationship with art—makes available what is hidden by religious ritual from the uninitiated and repressed or concealed by a political or judicial document. It is characteristic of the aesthetic object that it conserves and, at the same time, reveals the historically other, since it not only allows the representation of subjective experience of the world but also makes it available within the framework of art as experience of itself in the experience of other. This brings us back to our question: to what extent is dialogical understanding an aid to us and what are its limitations when it has to make accessible art and literature in their temporal or spatial, historical or cultural otherness, thereby involving them in the progressive dialogue of aesthetic communication?

Theology may (as Magass explains with reference to Rosenzweig and Buber)[2] consider experience in conjunction with a theory of types of speech or speech-acts elucidating in turn the problem of dialogical understanding in otherwise exceptional cases. "Dialogicity" is characteristic of the Christian religion in a particular way, specifically as the speech situation of I and Thou between God and Man. This I-Thou relationship is constituted as early as God's address and call to man in Genesis 3:9: "Adam, where are you?" The dialogue between God and man initiated by this sentence is dominated throughout the rest of the Old Testament by the vocative, which awakens man from mute elements by the articulation of his name as an individual and makes of him a partner in the covenant. This dimension of question and answer distinguishes the Christian origin of dialogue from the "idealism of productive notions" that inhabits a monological world. The first monologue by God in the Bible (*And God said: Let there be light*) is drawn into the story of the creation, enabling us to deduce a theological triad of speech-acts. The *dialogue,* as a mode of revelation, occupies a middle position between the *tale* as the mode of creation and song or *hymn* as praise, leading to the *I* and *Thou* being transcended at a third stage by the liturgical paradigm of *we.* Thus dialogue in the end fades in the song and silence of the Sabbath. What remains an open question is how this theological triad is represented, functionally, in types of speech beyond the Bible, or whether every tale is an attempt to produce order akin to that ordering of elements which Genesis 1 seems to suggest, or whether dialogue, by definition, transgresses or breaks through established orders, or finally whether there exist ways to open and close a dialogue other than that of God and man with its beginning in the vocative and its end in a contented silence ("those that are separated still have to talk, the reunited can be silent—one keeps silent because all is said and done"— but one can also keep silent as a protest!).

Theological hermeneutics studies both the ideal form of the dialogue which achieves transcendence in contented communication and in forms of disintegrating "dialogicity." The Christian dialogue, which refers in the Last Supper to taking, giving and sharing, to the Revelation, may degenerate into an unchristian polemic about the mass—into a *Religionsgespräch* ("because the participants only wanted interpretations") or into apologetics, which in its crudest form degenerates into a catalogue of invectives, turned by the heretic opponent against himself, culminating in a refusal to engage in a dialogue. The progressive dogmatization of the *ecclesia militans* is revealed also in subtler ways of refusing a dialogue: in contempt for any searching on the part of both the *curiositas* and the *novitas,* confirmed by catechisms with fixed answers to the only questions which are allowed and crowned by the dialogically closed confession of faith that expresses "political intolerance of otherness and an incompatibility with dialectic." We might ask the theologian whether such a pattern is inevitable or whether it can only be explained historically in terms of the history of Christian apologetics and of the risk that the profession of faith (reinforced by the text which is spoken in unison in the first person) would become monological. At the same time, the speech-act of confession does not have to prevent dialogue in any way since it can sometimes open it up or initiate it again. We might question whether dialogically open forms of religious confession do, in fact, exist?

The "master dialogue," which is usually determined by the superiority of the one participant over the other, e.g., the teacher over the pupil, needs from a theological point of view a third perspective, the absent present in the person of the authoritative third, which can be represented as participant by Scripture or by the binding direction of Christ. In the formulation of the New Testament, the "master dialogue" is characterized by several stages: the *conversatio*, which seeks to relate the dialogue to the local circumstances; the *quaestio*, which reveals the deficiency or despair that a teacher may feign when he actualizes the past or delivers the questioner from an all-powerful past; the *interpretatio*, in which the rabbi becomes the giver of the gift or reaches agreement by a masterly maxim. Literary hermeneutics up until now has paid little attention to the "master dialogue." It can no longer be dismissed simply as repressive canonization, but must begin to be understood in its literary forms and interpreted as a medium for the creation of experience (e.g., by learning, in sequences of questions and answers).

Moreover, there is a considerable difference between the "master dialogue" in the New Testament and the Platonic dialogue. In the former the conversation is directed all the time by the teacher, the authoritatively pre-existing meaning is concretized by explanation in terms of the present situation, whereas the latter is a free conversation proceeding through digressions of question and answer, in which meaning is primarily constituted as a result of a joint quest through the mastery of the unknown. This typological opposition might certainly be modified by looking at it in new and interesting ways. Is it possible for the New Testament dialogue to regain openness by removing constraints from the pupil's questioning and by demanding that the master explain the Scripture from the point of view of the present situation and thereby reinterpret it differently? The effectiveness of the two rival forms of dialogue is beyond doubt, but their reception in the history of European literature seems to have almost completely escaped modification.

As long as the *philosophy of art* remained under the influence of the work-aesthetic, it has envisaged "dialogicity" as being primarily revealed in a dialogue of poets who soar above the chain of tradition of mediocrity into timelessness, thus opening eyes to the genesis of great works, viewed as a dialectic of imitation and creation, of constitution and revision of the aesthetic canon. To engage the recipient of literature in dialogue with its producer, to recognize the latter's part in the establishment of meaning and to ask how the work of art might be a whole, both closed in upon itself and open, and yet dependent on interpretation, would require a turning away from contemplative hermeneutics and its substantialist notion of the work. A long-unknown but extremely informative document relevant to the movement towards modern-day aesthetic theory has been introduced into the discussion by Bonyhai.[3] It deals with an important but little-known forerunner of the contemporary hermeneutics of art and literature, Leo Popper, and demonstrates his importance in the history of science by revealing his various insights, specifically his pioneering theory of "double misunderstanding." A more personal and historical reason for Leo Popper's obscurity is the success of his contemporary, friend and opponent Georg Lukács, whose *Heidelberger Philosophie der Kunst* (written in 1912–14 and published in 1974) was openly a reworking of the former's ideas, after which their paths quickly separated.

Popper and Lukács's common point of departure was an attempt to overcome divinatory hermeneutics, the aesthetics of expression and the theory of empathy. Aloys Riegel's notion of *Kunstwollen*, which would effortlessly become part of the work in accordance with the artist's intention and thus constitute the norm for adequate understanding by the recipient, indicates very clearly the opposing position they challenged. Popper opposed this brand of hermeneutics with a new hermeneutic which sought to recognize and justify the problem of inadequate understanding as the condition and characteristic of all understanding of art. His theory of "double misunderstanding" is in fact an aesthetic of nonidentity, founded on the notion that the work of art does not so much reveal, monologically, a transcendental meaning (in which both the will of the artist and the understanding of the observer disappear), but creates rather a double gap between the intention of the writer, the finished work, and its significance for the observer. In this way the constitution of meaning may be seen as a never-ending process between the production and reception of the work. An essentially analogous theory of the "open work" was argued at about the same time, but independently, by Paul Valéry. In Valéry's view the product of an author's aesthetic activity cannot be completely finished by him. The finished work is much more the illusion of the recipient, but also the beginning of his necessarily inadequate interpretation ("mes vers ont le sens qu'on leur prête"), reintroducing thereby the never-ending process of productive understanding. Thus Bonyhai rightly claims that Popper's theory indicates the beginning of a development which leads from the monological work-aesthetic to dialogical understanding, to the hermeneutical history of influence, and finally to the reception aesthetics of the present.

Lukács's evolution towards a "synthesis of sociology and aesthetics," even in its later materialistic drift towards the theory of mimesis, retains a platonizing tendency, and may already be identified by his adaptation of Popper's premises. Lukács explains the notion of double misunderstanding as the duplicity of the work of art that transcends life and man's yearningly familiar attitude to it, that separates the creative from the purely receptive attitude and at the same time ultimately sustains the distinction between the historicity and timelessness of the work of art. Popper's until now unpublished *Dialog über die Kunst* illustrates the basic difference between his position and that of Lukács, and casts an interesting light on the crossroads at which aesthetic theory found itself at the beginning of this century.

Their dialogue begins with the introduction of the opposition between closed and open works of art. Lukács interprets these as two fundamental possibilities of art, the moment of wish (Rodin's *Paolo et Francesca*) or that of fulfilment (Rodin's *Le Baiser*). Consequently, the theory of double misunderstanding, which Popper relates to two moments of non-identity in productive and receptive understanding, is separated into two different types of art and is qualified historically, since Lukács's distinction implies from the outset (with its dichotomy of the last or limited and the penultimate or unlimited) the historical and typological opposition between classical and romantic notions of art. To Popper's reply that the closed/open distinction must prove its validity in the wholeness of the form, Lukács refers (as he will do even in his later work) to the classical principle of the adequacy of form and content, thus attributing open works of art to the contemporary avant-garde and insisting that only the most recent art has used this medium, "this breaking off, this desertion." Popper counters this argument by revealing the romantic substratum (the unfulfilled as the only ending) of Lukács's presentation of modernism as fragmentary, and opposes it with the contention that the notion of completeness is no longer an ontological quality which lends the work expression, but is born out of man's desire for completeness (which he himself has to create) in the face of matter and ultimately of nature, where man finds himself confronted with "only transitions, never closure itself."

Thus the diametrically opposed positions of the debate concerning the work of art may be summed up in Lukács's formula: "in its finishedness unfinished" and in Popper's: "in its unfinishedness finished." Popper implicitly undermines the original distinction: the work of art is in its unfinishedness *finished*, because "art creates out of the penultimate, a last," meaning that "through art we take from nature what nature itself takes from us in our lives: unendedness." In Popper's view, art is a-cosmic, "the formula of people in things," i.e. the work of art is finished in its *unfinishedness*, because, whether it is open or closed, it attains its closedness only when the recipient is involved in it: "The ultimate end of the work of art is the recipient." Lukács on the other hand retains his own distinction by justifying it transcendentally: the work of art is in its finishedness *unfinished*, because "it relates the temporal to the eternal," which is another way of saying that the "question involves an absolute" and presupposes the "great answer," under which yoke man struggles without realizing it. In this way the recent theory of the open work offers the hermeneutics of art a choice. From Popper's viewpoint the work opens itself to the recipient and directs aesthetics towards the dialogicity of communication, while from that of Lukács it leads to the transcendental, regaining for aesthetics the Platonic feedback of a timeless absolute which, by its monological truth, grants the recipient little more than the role of contemplative understanding.

In the area of *philosophical hermeneutics*, Gadamer has defined dialogicity as the prerequisite of all understanding, both of foreign speech and of a temporally alien text. As a result of his work, the Platonic dialogue comes to be viewed as a hermeneutical model, where meaning is constituted not by a monological explanation but by a dialogical search for understanding, achieved by bringing experience into the open: "The dialectic of question and answer has always preceded the dialectic of explanation. It is the former which has made an event out of understanding."[4] To understand something means to conceive it as an answer, or, more precisely, to test one's own opinion against the opinion of the other through question and answer. This is true for the understanding of both an unfamiliar text and another's speech. One part of the hermeneutical project is to recuperate the text which has become alien through temporal distance and reinsert it "in the living presence of dialogue, constituted originally as question and answer." The expression "to enter into conversation with the text" remains metaphoric since the interpreter himself has to embody the role of the other before the text can speak, answer a question, or be understood ultimately as a "question to me." Just as a traditional text becomes a question only for a questioning person, the "dialogue with the past," if it is not to become a victim of the one-sidedness of traditionalism or "actualism," demands an appropriating understanding to become completed, i.e. one which takes into account both the alien horizon of the text and the interpreter's own horizon (a process which is often misunderstood in the ocular metaphor of "fusion of horizons").

The other concern of the hermeneutical project consists of elucidating the "dialogicity" of understanding involved in a conversation, where one's own speech enters into an unmediated relationship with speech which is alien. Gadamer defines such understanding, in an actual conversation, as "to understand-oneself-in-an-object" and thereby forges a relationship between the understanding of a text and understanding which occurs in a dialogue. But this obscures a second (equally original and interesting) aspect of dialogue: the understanding of the other in his otherness. It is clear that the understanding-of-oneself-in-an-object may also entail, in a dialogue, an understanding of the otherness of the interlocutor. However, such is not always the case and there undoubtedly exists, as well, an understanding of the other through dialogue, where agreement about the object is deemed irrelevant. In his criticism of the hermeneutics of empathy (which he sees foreshadowed in the psychological explanation of Schleiermacher) Gadamer has attributed interest in the understanding of alien speech to the fascination with the "dark thou."[5] Schleiermacher's shift from the problem of understanding texts to that of understanding speech as such requires a hermeneutics of dialogicity to replace the understanding-of-oneself-in-an-object with the understanding-of-one-self-in-the-other, as of equally important epistemological interest. Since literary hermeneutics has as its real point of departure the understanding of the aesthetic experience of a work of art (in the *how*, not the *what* of what is said) and does not therefore require agreement about an object, the aesthetic and literary writings of Mikhail Bakhtin offer, without doubt, an innovative approach to the question of how the otherness of other may be disclosed by literary speech.

Bakhtin's aesthetic theory can be viewed, in its hermeneutical premises and implications, as occupying a similar place in the theory of science to that of Popper and Lukács; specifically in relationship to the movement away from the aesthetics of expression and the theory of empathy which dominated the years after the turn of the century.[6] One of Bakhtin's points of departure is Wilhelm Worringer's *Abstraktion und Einfühlung* (1918), which views (in line with Theodor Lipps's theory of empathy) aesthetic activity as an act of self-expression, where the "I" loses itself in the outside world so as to produce the work of art in the objectification of what has been experienced: "Aesthetic enjoyment is objectified self-enjoyment. To enjoy aesthetically is to enjoy myself in a sensible object which is different from me and to feel myself in it."[7] From this model Bakhtin borrowed the act of self-expression, but saw it as a twofold counter-current movement. Empathy as a movement outside, in order to put oneself knowingly and consciously in the position of the other, has to be followed by a turning-back on oneself, which makes the experienced identification through distancing or "finding oneself outside" (*vnenachodi-most*) into a productive and once more receptive aesthetic experience.[8] Empathy constitutes a necessary transitory stage and does not represent the goal of aesthetic experience. A prior identification with the other is necessary in order to attain, by means of the withdrawal of oneself, a position of aesthetic eccentricity (Plessner's notion comes very close to Bakhtin's *vnenachodimost*), making it possible, in turn, to experience the other in his difference and oneself in one's otherness. The reciprocal nature of experience of the alien and experience of the self is the decisive innovative aspect of Bakhtin's reformulation of the theory of empathy. It not only asserts that human consciousness is inherently dialogical ("The consciousness of oneself is always experienced against the background of the consciousness that somebody else has of one"),[9] but also that aesthetic experience is characterized by its capacity to facilitate (if not render possible) the experience of oneself in the experience of the other:

I cannot imagine myself as contained in my own external form, as surrounded and expressed by it. . . . In this sense it is possible to say that man depends in an aesthetically absolute way upon the other and his seeing, remembering, gathering and synthesizing activity, because only this can give him an externally finished personality; this personality does not exist, when the other does not create it.[10]

This audacious theory of the dialogical nature of consciousness, which Bakhtin developed in an early essay (only recently published), has hermeneutical implications and is the basis of his later *Esthetika slovesnogo tvorchestva*. The basic theses developed in this essay are as follows: dialogue as initial form of human language; language as social event of linguistic interaction; a fundamental opposition between speaking (hearing) and writing (reading); the dialogical principles of the open truth and the monological principle of the closed truth; the three categories of the direct word, the represented word, and the word that is focused on alien speech; the historical genesis of the multivocal expression in Socratic dialogue, its subversive survival in the Menippean satire and the polyphonic novel (whereas official monologism reinforces constantly univocal aspects of discourse); prose as the place of the bivocal expression; poetry as the medium of the word (without witnesses) about oneself and the world. Bakhtin's *Esthetika slovesnogo tvorchestva* with its antithetical characterizations of the dialogical principle offers a framework of categories which makes possible a new definition of the communicative function of types of speech and literary genres. As well, Bakhtin ultimately broadened his notion of dialogue into a model with three stages.

Dialogue has to find its own truth in understanding a reply and is therefore, in principle, uncompletable. This notion is illustrated by the history of the conflict of interpretations in the unending dialogue maintained with the art of the past. Such dialogue presupposes the higher authority of the third or "super-addressee," "whose absolutely perfect understanding is postulated either in the metaphysical distance or in temporally distant historical times. . . . In different periods and in different world-views this super-addressee and his ideal answering and understanding are expressed in distinct ideological ways (God, the absolute truth, the judgment of the impartial human conscience, the people, the judgment of history, science etc.)."[11] We already know this third stage from theological hermeneutics. It is no longer an ultimate guiding authority, but an ultimate "absolutely perfect" understanding super–addressee who, as the postulated third, is always present (but also absent) in the dialogue between text and interpreter—between the alien voice and the interpreter's voice—and functions as the guarantee of any possibility of understanding. This rather beautiful but peculiar secularity betrays an embarrassment in *Esthetika slovesnogo tvorchestva*. Bakhtin designed his aesthetic theory of otherness initially from the point of view of aesthetic production alone, considering the counter-current movement of self-expression and the experience-of-oneself-in-the-other. Only in his later writings did he begin to develop them further, from the point of view of reception.[12]

Thus he did not address himself to the hermeneutical problem of what makes it possible for the reader to understand the text in its otherness or what the reader at a second stage has to invest in this dialogue from his own experience in order to allow his understanding to enter into a dialogue with the text and its earlier interpreters. Bakhtin's aesthetic of otherness, which has so effectively revalidated the dialogical principle of the poetic word, requires a hermeneutical basis to account for the historical continuity of dialogical understanding.

If one agrees with Bakhtin's idea (which I arrived at without any knowledge of his works by approaching it from the perspective of an aesthetics of reception), that the experience of art is an excellent way to experience the alien "you" in its otherness and, with that, one's own "I" enriched by it, one cannot expect that the understanding-of-oneself-in-the-other, through aesthetic communication, needs anything more than the counter-current movement of empathy and its withdrawal in self-reflection (*vnenachodimost*). When a work of art is excellent, it is capable of representing and disclosing the alien *"I"* as subject and when especially the polyphonic word of the novel, according to Bakhtin's brilliant interpretation of Dostoevsky, can represent and disclose alien speech in its own speech, the recipient is unable to bridge the hermeneutical difference from the otherness of the text and therefore from the "alien speech in speech" except by an aesthetically mediated self-reflection. If the understanding of literary texts is not to be allowed to degenerate into a free-floating production of differences (a danger posed by the fashionable theory of "intertextuality," which Julia Kristeva's abridgment of Bakhtin's dialogic is not able to avoid),[13] then the understanding-of-oneself in the otherness of the text and the everyday-understanding-of-oneself when one speaks and another replies have to be anchored in a prejudgment of what has already been said and understood together, and what is still operative. Although Bakhtin's dialogical principle illustrates the difference of polyphony between grammatical persons and "speech-distance," it still seems, so far as I can discern, to presuppose the transparency of the poetic word and fails to take into account, really, the hermeneutical difference between the intention of the author, the meaning of the text, and its significance for the reader. This hermeneutical difference of the text (which begins from the very outset when the hearer or reader of the discourse does not necessarily picture the same thing as the speaker or the writer) increases as a function of historical distance. It may also become more acute when it is used consciously in ideology or unconsciously in the poetic text, thereby developing into the problem of the deceptive use of indirect speech. Bakhtin's dialogical principle can only do justice to these aspects of the otherness of the text when it is supplemented by other modes of understanding and when access to the understanding-of-oneself in other is achieved through constructing hermeneutical bridges.

Another hermeneutical bridge is already implied in Bakhtin's thesis of the character of the word as answer, in so far as the word only becomes an answer when it responds dialogically to a question. This makes the dialectic of question and answer into a genuine hermeneutical instrument to transgress the dialectics of its own horizon, to question the alien horizon of the other, and to take up again the dialogue with the text which may only respond a second time when the text is once again engaged. However, not every literary text has the hermeneutical structure of the word as answer. This is especially true for poetry. Here the attitude towards the world which is revealed in the lyrical voice may become by itself a hermeneutical bridge of the understanding-of-oneself in other, since such openness of speech towards the subjective world-experience delineates, according to Ricoeur, the character of the text fixed in a written form. The literary word distinguishes itself from the purely informative or utilitarian one in so far as the significance of the text can be detached both from the intention of its producer and, simultaneously, from the pragmatic limitation of a speech situation, thereby gaining semantic autonomy which may also reveal itself to a later recipient in the fullness of meaning of a world that is seen differently. One may doubt whether the semantic autonomy of the poetic word, as it is defined here, does not still presuppose some sort of prejudgment about the "world" which is peculiar to Western culture and would therefore be unsuitable in bridging the gap to the otherness of different cultures. Here the understanding of alien speech may be helped by this sort of prejudgment, based in anthropology and having recourse to the forgotten stock of myths, and which in turn makes it possible to construct a bridge of understanding between various figures and configurations of the imaginary. Since, according to Blumenberg, the mythic world experience always brings about the supposed otherness of an "original condition" and, at the same time, actualizes itself in the "Albeit am Mythos,"[14] aesthetic understanding may begin where the imaginary envelops the forms and configurations of myths with the aura of completeness, thereby satisfying an aesthetic need. If it is true that completeness is the (or at least *one* strong) reason for fascination with the imaginary, then in the "anticipation of completeness" lies, according to Gadamer,[15] what amounts to a privileged possibility of understanding, determining in its turn the understanding -of-oneself-in-the-other; this understanding comes about when, in the gradual emancipation of the subject, the other is accepted precisely as completeness and contingency-as-individual, when the other becomes idealized in literature and is raised to the real problem of dialogical understanding.

MY OWN WORK: A RETROSPECTIVE AND PROSPECTIVE GLANCE

My initial incentive to examine the problem of the horizon of expectation of the reader for whom the literary text was originally written was the result of my study of a literature that is very distant and strange to us. The limits of traditional philology very quickly became apparent. This approach held that a work which had become foreign could be understood either literally or through interpretation by disregarding the distance in time and by studying the text alone, or by returning historically to its sources and compiling factual knowledge about its time. It was medieval literature in the vernacular, more precisely its characteristic animal epic, which blossomed in the twelfth century, that presented me with the foreign horizon of a closed past as the barrier against understanding. The literature of the Middle Ages, because of the break in continuity created by the Renaissance, has been endowed with a high degree of otherness. By comparing it with the literature of antiquity, which, until recently, remained canonical in the history of Western education, hermeneutic reflection encounters if not a less significant problem then a different one. The fact that medieval literature might serve as an example for contemporary research precisely because of this otherness was obscured by the philological research of the 1950s with its insistence on the practice of interpreting "from sources," a procedure which was unexpectedly and massively legitimized by E. R. Curtius's *Europäische Literatur und lateinische Mittelalter* (1948), considered at that time to be paradigmatic. This encouraged the positivists, who were as philologically exact as they were aesthetically blind, to reduce the humanistic motto *ad fontes* to an interest in sources for their own sake and to claim that even the least significant discovery made by their pursuit contributed to the proof of the unbroken, albeit latent, continuity of the "indispensable" heritage of antiquity, in which the Middle Ages served as a link in a "golden chain of literary tradition" and lost almost completely any historical independence. The famous interpretation of Villon which Leo Spitzer, in his provocatively titled *Etude ahistorique d'un texte,* had used as early as 1938 in fighting for an aesthetic approach in opposition to the objective search for sources was barely influential at all. The ideal of serious research was Italo Siciliano's *François Villon et les thèmes poétiques du moyen âge* (1934), which pushed reliance on sources so far that it found for almost every element of Villon's revolutionary poetry an antecedent in the universal repertoire of previous poetry.

The implicit presuppositions of this search for sources were promoted by Lansberg as a principle for the study of tradition,[16] developing thereby Curtius's program for a historical topology founded on a rhetoric that was equated with literature. The substantialist postulate was that every new literary work not only potentially presupposed the *summa* of the complete previous literary tradition but ultimately varied the archetypical substance of tradition to create only the appearance of historical innovation. Such a theory and metaphysic of tradition is based upon the allegedly humanist conviction that, "in a book, literature is timelessly present,"[17] thus making of the philologist the real reader for whom the text is written and who, as "super-reader," best understands the writer. Only the philologist, then, is capable of recognizing, through the later horizon of a more complete if not universal knowledge, the sources from which the author not only consciously but also unconsciously creates his work. Hermeneutically, the study of tradition, as it was understood at this stage, remained completely virginal: the philologist as super-reader naïvely presupposed that the later horizon of his knowledge existed in the earlier horizon of the creation of a work. Hence the distance in time (and also the limitedness of future historical horizons) disappeared in the timeless present of great literature, and even minor literature remained in the "unbreakable chain of the tradition of mediocrity."[18]

The hermeneutical innocence of this uncritical research in philology was simultaneously challenged about this time by Guiette and Nisin in France and by Bulst in Germany, in the paradoxically formulated statement: no text was ever written to be read and interpreted philologically by philologists or historically by historians. This stance raised the basic problem of a new literary hermeneutics by attempting to eradicate the fallacy that the text is as immediate to the philologist as—according to Rank—every epoch is to God, and to deny the necessity of recovering the meaning of the text for the reader as the actual addressee. This hermeneutical project entailed a twofold problem. On the one hand the reconstructed intention of the author could no longer constitute the final word on the understanding of the text, though the author still had to have some controlling function. On the other hand, the reading experience of a reader of the past could only be reached through the actual reading of the reader of the present. This meant that the difference between past and present horizons of the reading had to be brought into play in the interpretation itself.

The critics that I alluded to earlier did not yet have a methodological solution for this twofold problem. Bulst[19] leaned towards distinguishing between the subjective experience of reading and the objective investigation of the genesis of the text and doubted whether it was possible to reconstruct the experience of a past reader if it were not expressly stated. Guiette[20] tried to rehabilitate the unmediated enjoyment of medieval texts by interpreting the Artus-novel as a fascination with darkness, with the "not yet dissolved," and the poetry of the troubadours as a fascination for a "poésie formelle," a conscious pleasure in unending variation. In this way he discovered specific aesthetic attitudes that were implied by these and other literary types, but failed to recognize how far this discovery depended on a later point of view: the modern prejudgment of anti-romantic poetics which developed with Verlaine and Mallarmé. To Nisin, in his (undeservedly neglected) book *La Littérature et le lecteur* (1959),[21] we owe the disclosure of the latent Platonism of academic philology, its belief in the timeless essence of classic works and in the neutral point of the observer. Nisin's pioneering work towards a hermeneutics of reading insisted that the literary work had to be viewed like a musical score, and could only be realized through an act of reading. Genuine understanding of an aesthetic text requires also that the philologist integrate this explanation and his critically evaluative reflection with his primary experience as a reader. This requirement is not merely a way of sanctioning a purely subjectivist reading; the text continues to oppose an arbitrary attitude on the part of readers. The literary work as score becomes an instance of understanding in so far as the reader, in his returning for a second reading or in the second realization of what has been read in the experience of the whole, verifies in the wording of a text what seemed to him to be a possible sense in his first aesthetic observation. The deficiency of this theory is that Nisin makes of the spontaneity of the first reading (which seems to transfer the reader immediately into the unknown of another world of the imaginary) an absolute. To this extent his theory is limited; the *sens vécu* of a text of the past is not available any longer without the mediation or the translation by a philologist or without historical understanding. That there "is no virginity in aesthetic experience" (since one cannot understand any work of art without bringing to it a past and can only judge its aesthetic value by contrasting a literary work as an unknown with the horizon of already known works) had already been stressed by Picon in his aesthetics of literature.[22] But how was one to avoid the fallacy of a pure, spontaneously emotional reception of literature, without relegating interpretation to the primary experience of the reading? How was one to make clear the sense of prejudgment which already governs the spontaneous reading of a text, and what did one have to do to gain access to the sort of experience which the historically first addressee may have had in his reading?

These were the questions I attempted to come to grips with in my *Untersuchungen zur mittelalterlichen Tierdichtung* (1959). The medieval *Reineke Fuchs,* revived by Goethe, alienates the reader of our time specifically because of the so-called "anthropomorphisms" of its animal characters, in other words because of human attributes, chivalric gestures and courtly speech, fictitious behaviour in short, which can be understood neither mimetically (as observable life of animals in nature) nor allegorically (as spiritual meaning of their "natures"). In the history of the criticism of the *Roman de Renart* since Jacob Grimm, this peculiar mixture of human characteristics and animal form was resolved in various ways, though the romantic distinction between nature-poetry and art-poetry as latent paradigm remained operative even in the historico-positivist interpretation. As the shapes of the loosely connected tricks were seen as naïve, as the nature-poetry of an original agreement between man and animals, one could postulate behind the anthropomorphic traits (which were considered to be later aberrations) the pure form of original animal fairy tales. However, if one considered the animal characters as time-conditioned disguises of epic heroes, it was possible to see the feud between Renart and Ysengrim as the satirical art form of an animal epic, which, as parody of the chivalric epic and mirror of the feudal society, used the animal form as representative of eternal folly or as a form of decorum. By their contradictory one-sidedness, both paradigms of interpretation disregarded the obvious question,[23] namely, what the analogy of animal being and human nature played out in the *Roman de Renart* may have meant to the addressees for whom this work, begun in 1176, was written. Might the answer to this question not be linked to the pleasures which the medieval reader experienced in the novel's animal tricks and might this not also explain why this work, by Pierre de Saint-Cloud, had so many limitations? What could explain the inexhaustible interest in continuing the fable of the "real beginning of why the wolf and the fox are mortal enemies," in revising again and again the opening of the trial at the court-day of the lion, and in making the oldest animal epic in the French popular language into the unending adventures of the rake in the feudal kingdom of the animals, a story which along with *Tristan* and the *Roman de la Rose* alone survived the fall of medieval literature?

An answer to these questions was suggested by the fact that Pierre de Saint-Cloud, author of the oldest part (II-Va) of the *Roman de Renart,* made, in his prologue, the typical declaration: "I bring something that has never been said!" and then proceeded to name both single works and genres in previous literature which were to be overshadowed by his new work and which were well loved by his audience: *Troja* and *Tristan* and consequently the ancient and chivalric novel, the poetic farce (*fabliau*) and the chivalric epic (*chanson de geste*). From this canon, from further reference to already known facts and especially by viewing it as continuing the work of a predecessor (the Latin *Ysengrimus* by Magister Nivardus) unmentioned in the prologue, I was able to infer the horizon of expectation of the contemporary public, which the author evoked in order to contrast it with the novelty of his work. The textual analysis that was based on this insight indicated that the writer had, indeed, fulfilled his announcement in the prologue in the tale itself. He returns to the expectations that he evoked earlier, satisfies or disappoints them implicitly, and sometimes even explicitly and critically, when he wants to parody the chivalric epic or when he wants to make a travesty of the casuistic aspects of courtly love. This fact enables the later interpreter to reconstruct the prejudgments of the original addressee even when the distance in time is great and to trace out the difference between retrospective expectation and prospective experience which is progressively constituted in the reading. It is this transformation of horizon which the text must have brought into play for the public of the *chansons de geste* and courtly poetry, about 1176. The enjoyment of the new genre of fox's nasty tricks appears and reappears in so far as the reader interprets the "anthropomorphisms" as signals prompting him to recognize in the animal figures an element of human nature. Thus the "unheard-of war of two barons" may be read as an imitation of heroic poetry which for the first time questioned the elevated ethics of the chivalric world and the ideals of courtly love by clearly showing as playful satire the less than ideal, indeed purely human, nature of men in the projections of its perfection.

My attempt to interpret this medieval text from the horizon of expectation of its contemporary public opened new vistas to modern understanding. I do not at all deny that this reconstruction of the otherness of an aesthetic experience which has become alien to us presupposes the hermeneutical anticipation of an anthropological theory. It was Lipps's phenomenological analyses of the *Natur der Menschen* that made me see that the animal, with "its character written across its face" and marked by an "unbroken relationship with its nature," allows us to recognize in the character of man the natural substratum of his spiritual being.[24] Though this theoretical anticipation surely cannot engender the spontaneous experience of a first reader, it can disclose the attitude implied by the text, which initially makes it understandable as a condition of possible meaning. The spontaneous reading experience of a historically alien and distant reader has no hermeneutical value, and it is an illusion to try to reconstruct it as such, since spontaneity can never be completely covered by reflection. A misguided attempt of this sort also fails to see that aesthetic experience is, by nature, an observation which is mediated and therefore intensified; it cannot consequently be absorbed by emotional spontaneity. However, such a theoretical anticipation, especially when it brings into play (as is the case here) prospects of a vague, yet to be developed, generalization based on phenomenological anthropology, at least opens up these mediations, making aesthetic experience on the whole communicable, systematically as the attitude which the text implies and historically as a series of prejudgments which are evoked with the transformation of the horizon of expectation and experience and made accessible for interpretation.

The new significance brought to the *Roman de Renart* arises certainly from a modern perspective: an inquiry into the historical and literary genesis of individuation. It is therefore not just the projection of a modern interest, but succeeds also in disclosing an experience of the character and nature of people that was new in the everyday life of the twelfth century. It is accomplished by consciously removing the horizon which historically actualized the theoretical anticipation. The work of Pierre de Saint-Cloud reveals, as an anti-heroic parody of chivalric and courtly ideals, a complete world of characters removed from historical change, and establishes at the same time a negative hero, Renart, who, outwitting others by taking advantage of their less-than-ideal and all-too-human nature, with the wit of the rake becomes the first character with individuality. Although this innovation would not have been recognized or interpreted by the majority of the contemporary addressees, there exists extra-literary evidence which demonstrates that it might well have been understood. The threshold of individuation, which is apparent in the earlier parts of the *Roman de Renart* to later interpreters, is also historically mentioned for the first time by Otto von Freising, who by *persona* not only means the interchangeable mask, role, but also implies the uninterchangeable *individualitas* of worldly people.[25]

The threshold metaphor indicates for historical hermeneutics that the transition from the old to the new did not have to happen only once or, for all contemporaries, at the same time. In order to go beyond the field of experience of medieval life, which seemed hardly changeable, the Christian understanding of the world, hitherto limited to its closed horizon of the future, had to transgress the prohibition of *curiositas*. Licence to break the charm of the ideal norms of chivalric and courtly living and to portray human nature on the other side of good and evil in its imperfect ordinariness was obviously easier to achieve by means of the fiction of the animal kingdom. Thus, literary hermeneutics is able to participate in historical understanding in its own way and to show, through the transformation of the horizon of aesthetic experience, what for the contemporaries of a past world was still a latent need, wish, or presentiment of the future, and what may only be made conscious in its still-incalculable significance by the history of interpretation.

While the work of the medievalist introduced me to the hermeneutical problem of the lifting of horizon and led me to argue against the traditionalism of positivist philology, my initial attempt to turn these insights into a blueprint for a reception-aesthetic of literature (*Literaturgeschichte als Provokation*, 1967) grew out of a somewhat different situation. The concept of a new literary history, which would extend the short-circuited relationship of author and world in order to include the recipient and would raise the latter, as reader or public, to a mediating position between past and present, had to be asserted in the face of the discredited ideal of objectivity of the old literary history and of the claims of objectivity made by both sociological and structuralist opponents of historical understanding. The central feature of this position was the transformation of horizons, a paradigm which was introduced into modern literature. It was to be illustrated in certain ideal cases in works such as *Don Quixote* and *Jacques le fataliste* that "evoke the reader's horizon of expectations, formed by a convention of genre, style or form, only in order to destroy it step by step—which by no means serves a critical purpose only, but can also once again produce poetic effects."[26] In this transformation of horizon between preliminary expectations and the indicated new experience, I discerned the principle of aesthetic mediation in the literary historical process, leading by an actual transformation of the canon to a revision of our ideas about all past works. This idea of the transformation of horizons allowed me also to see the artistic character of a work as related to implicit aesthetic distance (i.e. the distance of expectation and experience, tradition and innovation) and to contrast its constitutive negativity with the affirmative character of the norm-sustaining trait of consumer literature.

My formulation of this paradigm was undoubtedly influenced (though to some degree unconsciously) by the opinion of the Russian formalists that aesthetic innovation is the agent of literature's evolution, and by Adorno's aesthetics of negativity, according to which the autonomous work can only acquire a social function by a certain negation of the existing norms. The flagrant modernist bias of this first paradigm of reception aesthetics reflects the position I took in my inaugural lecture at Constanz, which generated an unexpected and lively polemical debate.[27] My attempt to respond to my critics allowed me to develop this first project for a reception aesthetics step by step in a dialogue with them and to test it practically. The next stage was to introduce the notion of a horizon of expectation as a device for the analysis of the experience of the reader:

> The analysis of the literary experience of the reader avoids the threatening pitfalls of psychology if it describes the reception and the influence of a work within the objectifiable system of expectations that rises for each work in the historical moment of its appearance, from a preunderstanding of the genre, from the form and themes of already familiar works, and from the opposition between poetic and practical language.[28]

Directed against those who thought that an analysis of the reader's experience ended inevitably in the subjectivism of individual reaction ("so many readers, so many interpretations") or in the collectivism of a sociology of taste, this stance made it possible to conceive of literary experience in the objectifiable difference between normative expectation and norm-creating experience; it was therefore more internally literary. It had the advantage of leaving out of consideration what, in such a transformation of horizons, had to be ascribed to the influence of the text and what was appropriated by the initial and subsequent addressees. This posed the problem of distinguishing, in the process of literary history, between the two aspects of the relation between text and reader, i.e., *effect* as that element of the actualization of meaning which is determined by the text and *reception* as that which is determined by the addressee. In opposition to the notion that a literary tradition constitutes itself spontaneously as a passive synthesis of a "fusion of horizons," it became necessary to stress the event-character of a literary work as a moment of a process, in which two horizons are always at play in an active synthesis of understanding. In other words, the horizon of expectation evoked by the work confirms or transcends the horizon of experience introduced by the recipient.

The active participation of the reader in the historically progressive actualization of meaning (the possibility of its "productive reception"—Sartre) was also left unclear so as not to present literary history as autonomous of the historical process but rather to stress its *Partialität,* where its own relation to general history had to be seen in order to grasp its social function and history-making energy: "The social function of literature manifests itself in its genuine possibility only where the literary experience of the reader enters into the horizon of expectations of his lived praxis, preforms his understanding of the world, and thereby also has an effect on his social behaviour."[29] Directed towards the theory of mimesis, which Lukács had once again brought into favour but which had hardened into the closed circle of the aesthetics of production and representation, my final "Constanzer" thesis insisted on the precedence of the norm-constituting function of literature over the representational one. What was left open was the question of how the horizon of the experience of practical life might be included, if not by the mute determination of economic forces then by the primary attitudes of people concerned, by latent interests, needs, and wishes. What also remained to be considered was its relationship to the horizon of aesthetic experience. Such a relationship could only be elucidated with the provocative stance I took at the end of *Literaturgeschichte als Provokation.* Here I insisted on the expectation that literature today, as in the past, might renew the "consolidated observation" of things and destroy the taboos of prevailing morality. This necessitated transposing reception-aesthetics, constituted from an internally literary point of view, into the force field of a social praxis and inquiring if and how the historical actualization of a literary work, through the passive or the productive reception of its reader, reacts to a social situation, assesses its contradictions, and attempts to solve them projectively. This meant, above all, responding seriously to the ideological and critical suspicion that literary tradition does not have the privilege of developing in complete freedom but may be enforced so that one does not merely presuppose the transparency of literary communication between people and time-periods, but seeks to recover it in the face of the tendency of tradition to annex everything which is heterogeneous to the harmonic classical canon.

For the majority of my critics,[30] the theses which I developed in my inaugural lecture at Constanz were not sociological enough. There were others, however, who considered them too sociological, claiming that my attempt to found a new reception aesthetics failed to go beyond a hermeneutical and function-analytical sociology of reception, thereby missing what was aesthetic in the reader's experience. Petrovic has asserted that, by engaging in what he acknowledges as an absolutely necessary critique of the dominant ontology of art relating to the notion of the work in classic aesthetics and to that of mimesis in orthodox Marxist aesthetics, I have moved to the other extreme of a theory of literature, sacrificing along with the work its aesthetic value as object of reception and thereby reducing aesthetic experience to the transformation of the social norms of taste. But taste is only the condition of possibility of literary communication, not its content nor even its result. Literary communication really becomes aesthetic experience (and this renders comprehensible its difference from pragmatic experience) when its constitution is sought in the "materialization of the aesthetic object" both at the level of the pre-reflective reception of aesthetic meaning (*aistheton*) and at the reflective level of aesthetic judgment, when it is finally characterized as the specifically aesthetic activity of the producing and receiving subject.[31] I considered it a rare yet encouraging coincidence of scientific work that Petrovic had asserted *de facto* in his critique (read at a symposium in Belgrade in 1976) the continuation of the first paradigm of my reception-aesthetics and had outlined what was lacking in the theory of aesthetic experience. I myself had addressed these problems, meanwhile, in my second university lecture at Constanz (entitled *Apologie der ästhetischen Erfahrung*) and developed them further in the *Theorie und Geschichte der ästhetischen Erfahrung* (1972; published in 1977). I shall therefore only briefly summarize this book.

My purpose was to define the particular nature and everyday function of aesthetic experience (1) historically, as process of its liberation from the authority inherited from Platonic aesthetics, and (2) systematically, in its three basic forms of productive, receptive, and communicative aesthetic experience, otherwise known historically as the triad of *poiesis, aisthesis,* and *katharsis,* whose common fundamental attitude constitutes aesthetic pleasure. This point of departure made it possible to consider aesthetic experience at work not initially in the manifestations of autonomous modern art which rejects all enslavement, but already present in the practical (i.e. religious and social) functions of older art. Thus it was possible to bridge the gap, opened up by the reigning aesthetics of negativity, between pre-autonomous and autonomous, "affirmative" and "emancipatory" art. This revision of the modernist bias of my first project began therefore with a critique of the aesthetic theory of Adorno, and necessitated rehabilitating the notion of "pleasurable understanding" as the determining factor in aesthetic reflection and aesthetic judgment, demanding a consensus, as a specific social effect of aesthetic communication, despite the fact that the latter has been blocked in the age of the mass-media and the culture industry.

My contribution to research in literary hermeneutics is represented by several essays. *Racines und Goethes Iphigenie* (1973) was written to confront the Marxist theory of literature and illustrates the basic problem of literary hermeneutics: the limitedness of the historical horizon of understanding and the dialogical nature of production and reception in the processes of literary communication.

In order to reconstruct the original provocatory effect of Goethe's *devilishly human risk,* which was obscured by the transformation of horizon from historical to aesthetic classicism and by the incorporation of the neo-humanist ideals of education in specific instances, it was necessary to remove the first "concretization" (that of Hegel), of the near horizon of French classicism and of the alien horizon of Greek tragedy. It thus became possible to interpret the new *Iphigenie* as Goethe's answer to Racine and as a new version of the classical myth, in which Iphigenia's *outrageous deed* achieves man's liberation from his mythic entanglement with nature. But this victory over the mythic meteronomy is ultimately attained in Goethe's play at the expense of a new myth, that of all-redeeming pure woman-

hood, and turns the end with Thoas into a false solution in terms of modern understanding. It is here that one confronts the problem of the possibilities and limitations of an actualization of the classic work. After reconstructing the temporally
alien horizon and considering those normative interpretations ("actualization") in
the history of the reception available to the modern understanding, literary
hermeneutics faces the problem of application and is able to complete in its own
manner the triad of understanding, explanation, and application. I reconsidered
this problem in *Klassik-wieder modern?* (1977) and explored it in terms of contemporary theatre, where it revealed itself initially in avant-garde experiments and,
more recently, has had a broader effect both in literary production and in the practice of staging. The specific issue at stake is how a classic work may be decanon-
ized, how it may be introduced into the horizon of contemporary experience,
countering any pretence of timeless validity and being rejuvenated on the modern
stage in such a way that the link between past and present experience is not broken, as it undoubtedly is in a naïve actualization or rigorous historicization. A "reju-
venating" reception requires that the fusion of horizons not be silently
presupposed but be consciously achieved as a dialectic mediation of the past and
present horizons in a new actualization of meaning. The new *Mary Stuart* of
Hildesheimer and *Die neun Leiden des jungen W.* by Plenzdorf were signs of a
change in literary history, in that they transgressed the taboo of the untouchable
text and the unchangeable form of classic works; it is precisely because of this that
they succeeded in reviving classics which were already considered to be dead.
What they achieved was applied hermeneutics, i.e. the historical distance between
text and present is presented to the observer and the familiar horizon of the classic
is merely quoted, firstly to bring to the observer's attention the real otherness of a
past world, and then to disclose the other meaning of the past experience which
has again been brought to the observer's attention in the continuous confrontation
of self with other. In this way, by the renewed interplay with a separated past, a
horizon of new experience is revealed to contemporary understanding.

I have attempted to solve the hermeneutical problem of how the transformation
of the horizons of expectation and experience in the inner horizon of literature may
influence the outer horizon of everyday life. The process of transformation involves
three stages. In *La Douceur du foyer* (1974) I made use of the theory of the constitution of social reality from the sociology of knowledge to illustrate the communicative function of poetry in the transmission, internalization, legitimization, and
transformation of social norms. I used specifically the example of the Second
Empire bourgeois family's expectation of happiness at home. The sociology of
knowledge developed by Schütz and Luckmann contributed a perspective which
had not been explored by historical studies, even after their transformation into
social history. I am referring to a historically applicable theory of the perspectivist
organization of everyday reality, the pre-orientation of the experience of environment (i.e. the here-and-there of reality), the present situation (i.e. the reciprocally
generated present) and the flow of time, and the horizon of limited spheres of
meaning (*Subsinnwelten*) of human behaviour. The transcendental scheme of the
organization of the social world alone was not enough to comprehend the past
horizon of predominantly latent attitudes and norms but, by fulfilling an anticipa-
tory theoretical role, it made it possible to look for the latent horizon of expectation
of the historical view of life in 1857 within the pattern of contemporary poetry,
and to describe it as a system of literary communication which makes visible
what remained self-evident and therefore latent in the routine and the pressure of

everyday life. The sociology of knowledge did not inquire into the status of aesthetic experience in the social praxis. Aesthetic experience remained hidden as long as it was located as a *Subsinnwelt* among other sub-meaning-worlds and as long as one failed to realize that its specific social function begins at the point where aesthetic experience illuminates, in fiction, the unshakeable horizons and ideological legitimizations of other (e.g., religious, political, professional) sub-meaning-worlds, and where it makes possible communication with the world, within whose limits the other lives, thereby making it possible for new expectations of the seemingly immovable horizon of a social order to open up.

The limit-situation of aesthetic experience, as compared with the other functions of action as defined here, justifies the hermeneutical priority of the approach offered by reception aesthetics. When one seeks to reconstruct the social situation out of derivative knowledge drawn from historical and economic sources, one indeed easily succeeds in finding, in the mirror of "literary evidence," confirmation for what one already knows historically. The responsive character of literature may only be recognized when one uncovers its mediations which, principally, become transparent in the medium of literary experience and intelligible in lifting the horizon. Goethe answers Rousseau's *Julie* with his *Werther,* although he fails to mention anywhere the provocative model of his admired predecessor. The fact that the French and then the German *Catechism of Sentimentality* responds to the resulting social situation only becomes a problem again when one reconstructs the horizon of literary expectations transmitted in Germany by *Die Leiden des jungen Werthers* and by the enthusiastically received *La Nouvelle Héloïse.* My analysis of horizon led then to the thesis that the unexpected success enjoyed widely by both books created not only literary but also social norms. The *homme sensible* incarnated in the figure of Rousseau's couple and in Goethe's *Werther* as a "German Saint-Pierre" appeared to offer a solution for the self-alienation of bourgeois existence diagnosed by Rousseau in his first and second *Discours.* The dissatisfaction which Goethe may have felt about Rousseau's solution can be concretized in the way in which he picks up the contradictions of his predecessor, who effortlessly conceals the *ménage-à-trois* in the utopia of Clarens, and solves it by qualifying the proclaimed autonomy of consciousness, with the result of *sickness unto death.* This transformation of horizons makes it also possible to show how different the social substratum of the bourgeois institutions of status, family, religion, and work were and how they were experienced before and after the threshold which divides French enlightenment and German idealism.

My concluding essay, *Der poetische Text im Horizontwandel der Lektüre* (1980), sought to meet Gadamer's demand to develop fully again, for poetry, the triadic unity of the hermeneutic process. If the horizon-structure of aesthetic experience is the superior hermeneutic bridge enabling one to understand a text from the past in its otherness and to bring it into contact once again with the horizon of personal experience, it has to be possible to discover by hermeneutical reflection in reading itself what is really aesthetic about the aesthetic experience and thereby what makes historical understanding possible. My interpretation of Baudelaire's second *Spleen* poem is an attempt to separate the act of the aesthetic observation and that of explicatory understanding, which, in reading, are always mutually supportive. I approach this problem methodologically by withdrawing the still-open horizon of a first reading from the retrospective horizon of a second one. This allows the reader to follow, in the first stage of the analysis, the constitution of an aesthetic observation in the process of happening and to describe it as an effect of both the poetic structures and the still-open expectations of significance of the text. In the second stage of the analysis the aesthetic experience of the first reading, with the return of the end and the accomplished whole to the beginning of the poem, may become the horizon of an explicatory understanding, creating out of its conjectures and unanswered questions a context of meaning. Since this meaning fails to distinguish between what is implied by the text and what is brought to bear by the interpreter, a third stage of analysis has to reintroduce the distance in time initially omitted and reconstruct the author's intended meaning as a historical alternative, thereby elucidating the personal prejudgment from the point of view of the history of reception which determines the interpreter's horizon of interpretation. At this stage the validity of personal interpretation must be tested by inquiring whether it permits us to understand the text in a new and different way and whether it takes into account the work of predecessors. This last requirement alone can give literary hermeneutics its specific purpose which, according to Marquard, is to fight the battle of interpretations in such a way that it does not end in a political duel of life or death. In the horizon of the aesthetic experience, different meanings do not necessarily result in contradiction. Literary communication opens up a dialogue, in which the only criterion for truth or falsity depends on whether significance is capable of further developing the inexhaustible meaning of the work of art.

NOTES

1. References in the article "Horizont" in *Historisches Wörterbuch der Philosophie*, Basel and Stuttgart 1974, especially pp. 1204f., by M. Scherner; see also Karlheinz Stierle, "Sprechsituation, Kontext und Sprachhandlung," in *Handlungstheorien-interdisziplinär*, ed. H. Lenk, München 1980, I, 439–83 and Michael Riffaterre, "Interpretation and Undecidability," *New Literary History*, 12 (1981), 227–39.

2. In his essays "Der Religionsphilosophische Aspekt des Dialogischen," "Der grosse Sabbat—oder vom Ende des Dialogs," and "Episkopales und Pastorales zum Dialog/ zur Dialektik," in *Dialogizität in Prozessen literarischer Kommunikation*, Konstanzer Kolloquium 1980, ed. R. Lachmann (to be published shortly by W. Fink Verlag, München).

3. In his article "Leo Popper (1886–1911) und die moderne Hermeneutik," in *Dialogizität*, ed. Lachmann, which discusses the appendixes of the then unpublished *Dialog über die Kunst* (written by Popper, who represented with A and B the positions of himself and Lukács). I have used the names in the rest of this paper.

4. Hans-Georg Gadamer, *Wahrheit und Methode*, Tübingen 1960, p. 447. English translation: *Truth and Method*, translation ed. Garrett Barden and John Cumming, New York 1975, p. 429.

5. For the latest Schleiermacher research and for a critique of the primacy of the understanding-of-oneself in the object, in which "the being of the other as other disappears," we refer to M. Frank, *Das individuelle Allgemeine-Textstrukturierung und-interpretation nach Schleiermacher*, Frankfurt 1977, pp. 20–34, esp. p. 33.

6. I rely here on Mikhail Bakhtin, *Problems of Dostoevsky's Poetics*, trans. R.W. Rotsel, Ann Arbor 1973 and *Die Ästhetik des Wortes*, trans. Sabine Reese and Rainer Grübel, Frankfurt 1979; see also Tzvetan Todorov, "Bakhtine et l'altérité," *Poétique*, 40 (1979), 502–23 (included in his book, *M. Bakhtine et le principe dialogique*, Paris 1981, pp. 145ff.).

7. Wilhelm Worringer, *Abstraktion und Einfühlung*, München 1918, p. 4.

8. "The first movement of the aesthetic activity is one of empathy: I have to perceive his perceptions, learn them, even live them, I have to occupy his place, even identify with him. . . . But is this total merging the final aim of the aesthetic activity? Not at all! The really aesthetic activity has not even started. . . . And the aesthetic activity only begins when we return to ourselves and to the position outside the other and shape the contents of our

emphatic experience and raise it into a finished completeness." "Avtor i geroi v esteticeskoj dejatel'nosti," written around 1924, published in Mikhail Bakhtin, *Esthetika slovesnogo tvorchestva*, Moscow 1979, quoted from pp. 26–8 passim, from an as yet unpublished German translation by A. Sproede.

9. Bakhtin, *Problems*, p. 213.

10. From the already quoted German translation of "Avtor i geroj v esteticeskoj dejatel'nosti," pp. 39–41 passim.

11. Mikhail Bakhtin, "Problema teksta-Opyt filosofskogo analiza," *Voprosy literatury*, 10 (1976), 149f. (Quoted from R. Grübel's introduction to Bakhtin, *Die Ästhetik*, p. 48, revised from the Russian original.)

12. My definition of aesthetic enjoyment as "enjoyment of self in the enjoyment of the alien," or as "experience of oneself in the possibility of this being different" (Jauss, *Ästhetische Erfahrung und literarische Hermeneutik*, München 1977, p. 59), which I formulated in a critique of Geiger rather than of Worringer, almost coincides with Bakhtin's model of *vnenachodimost*, all the more because it implies the same criticism and development of the already quoted formula of Worringer.

13. The abridgment lies in the moment of the voice, which makes polygraphy take the place of polyphony, while at the same time the subject of the other disappears out of the "dialogue of the text with itself." See R. Lachmann in his essay "Bachtins Dialogizität und die akmeistische Mythopoetik als Paradigma dialogisierter Lyrik," in *Poetik und Hermeneutik XI* (unpublished).

14. H. Blumenberg, *Arbeit am Mythos*, Frankfurt 1979.

15. H.-G. Gadamer, "Vom Zirkel des Verstehens," in *M. Heidegger zum 70. Geburtstag*, Pfullingen 1959, pp. 24–35.

16. Henriquez Ivan Lansberg, *Handbuch der literarischen Rhetorik*, München 1960; see also the programmatic essay by his pupil W. Babilas, *Tradition und Interpretation*, München 1961.

17. E. R. Curtius, *Europäische Literatur und lateinisches Mittelalter*, Bern 1948, p. 22. English translation: *European Literature and the Latin Middle Ages*, trans. Willard R. Trask, Princeton 1973, p. 14.

18. Curtius, *Europäische Literatur*, p. 404. English translation, p. 400.

19. "Bedenken eines Philologen" (1954), in *Medium Aevum Vivum*, Festschrift for W. Bulst, ed. Jauss and D. Schaller, Heidelberg 1960, pp. 7–10.

20. *Questions de littérature* (1960/72); see also Jauss, *Alterität und Modernität der Mittelalterlichen Literatur: Gesammelte Aufsätze 1956–1976*, München 1977, pp. 411–27.

21. See also my review in *Archiv für das Studium der neueren Sprachen*, 197 (1960), 223ff.

22. See my review in *Philosophische Rundschau*, 4 (1956), 113ff.

23. With the exception of L. Olschki, K. Vossler, and L. Spitzer, whose controversy I tried to solve with my interpretation; see Jauss, *Alterität*, pp. 106ff.

24. Hans Lipps, *Die Menschliche Natur*, Frankfurt 1941, p. 19/25. See also Jauss, *Alterität*, p. 201.

25. According to A. Borst in *Poetik und Hermeneutik VIII*, p. 638.

26. Jauss, *Literaturgeschichte*, p. 176.

27. For this I refer to "Die Partialität der Rezeptions-ästhetischen Methode," special issue (*Rezeptions-ästhetik-Zwischenbilanz*) of *Poetica*, 7 (1975), to *Rezeptions-ästhetik–Theorie und Praxis*, ed. R. Warning, München 1975 (his critical introduction summarizes the theory up to 1975), and especially to Manfred Naumann's critique in Naumann et al., *Gesellschaft, Literatur, Lesen*, Berlin 1973. See also B. Pinkerneil in *Methodische Praxis der Literaturwissenschaft*, ed. D. Kimpel and B. Pinkerneil, Kronberg 1975, pp. 60–8, and S. Petrovic in *Teorijska Istrazivanja*, ed. Z. Konstantinovic, Beograd 1980, pp. 63–74.

28. Jauss, *Literaturgeschichte*, pp. 173ff.

29. Jauss, *Literaturgeschichte*, p. 199.

30. See Pinkerneil, *Methodische Praxis*, p. 67.

31. Petrovic, *Teorijska Istrazivanja*, pp. 63ff.

STANLEY FISH

YET ONCE MORE

To the ears of many in this audience, the lectures I am about to give will sound retrograde and reactionary because they go against the grain of much that has been said in recent years about literary and cultural studies. Specifically, I shall be questioning the possibility of transforming literary study so that it is more immediately engaged with the political issues that are today so urgent: issues of oppression, racism, terrorism, violence against women and homosexuals, cultural imperialism, and so on. It is not so much that literary critics have nothing to say about these issues, but that so long as they say it *as* literary critics no one but a few of their friends will be listening, and, conversely, if they say it in ways unrelated to the practices of literary criticism, and thereby manage to give it a political effectiveness, they will no longer be literary critics, although they will still be something and we may regard the something they will then be as more valuable.

The literary critic as I imagine him is anything but an organic intellectual in the Gramscian sense; instead he is a specialist, defined and limited by the traditions of his craft, and it is a condition of his labours, at least as they are exerted in the United States, that he remain distanced from any effort to work changes in the structure of society. It is not that society's structure is unalterable or that there could never come a day when the words of a literary critic will resound in the halls of congress; it is just that I do not see that day coming soon and I do not think that anything you or I could do will bring it closer. Samuel Goldwyn once said in response to someone who asked him why his movies were not more concerned with important social issues, "If I wanted to send a message, I'd use Western Union." I say, if you want to send a message that will be heard beyond the academy, get out of it. Or, if I may adapt a patriotic slogan, "the academy—love it or leave it."

I am aware of course that simply to utter such pronouncements is to invite a barrage of objections—who are you to say? isn't this a return to the discredited notion of the mandarin intellectual? aren't you presenting one more brief for the status quo?—and in the course of writing and revising these lectures I have tried to anticipate those objections and to reply to them. I have used as a heuristic device someone I thought of as The Cultural Critic, and at every point I have asked myself, "What would The Cultural Critic say?" Providence always provides, and in this case Providence provided a book by Alan Sinfield entitled *Faultlines: Cultural Materialism and the Politics of Dissident Reading* (Berkeley, Los Angeles, 1992). In that book Sinfield has some harsh things to say about me, although not so harsh as the things said recently by Christopher Norris, who at times seems to hold me (along with Richard Rorty, Baudrillard, and Lyotard) responsible for the Gulf War. Sinfield says that I "totalize"—a major crime in his lexicon, perhaps equivalent to serial murder; that I employ a "bullying tone"—well, he has a point there; that I desire to entrap "understanding within a closed system"; and that I am "complacent" in contrast to the new historicists who have the good grace to be "*anxious about* entrapment" (288–90). I would say instead that anxiety about entrapment is the new historicist's version of complacency; anxiety, of a particularly self-righteous kind, is what they do for a living. At any rate the difference between me and Sinfield is helpfully stark and it can be measured by one of his pronouncements: "Literary criticism tells its own stories. It is, in effect, a subculture, asserting its own distinctive criteria of plausibility" (51). I couldn't agree more; in fact the word "distinctive" will play a large part in my argument and the ways of plausibility—or, as I put it, of "immanent intelligibility"—are my subject. Sinfield, however, regards the plausibility of literary criticism as a sham and a lure; "coherence," he announces, "is a chimera"; it obscures the multiform nature of what it tries to domesticate and it is often in complicity with the most "regressive aspects of our cultural formation" (51). My view of coherence, plausibility, and distinctiveness is more benign; together they underwrite the culture in which I am privileged to work (and indeed any culture in which anyone could work), and in what follows I trace out the lineaments of that culture without apologizing for it.

I shall begin by offering an example of the kind of story the literary culture characteristically tells, and I have chosen as my vehicle the first three words of Milton's *Lycidas*. What follows is an analysis that would seem familiar and even ordinary to literary actors in general and Miltonists in particular. The analysis is thus a sample piece of work rather than the work I would do if I were writing an essay for submission to *Milton Studies*. In that essay, which I will now *not* write, I would focus on the image of a body weltering to the parching wind, and thereby becoming parchment, and I would observe that such a body/surface is available for inscription by forces indifferent to its previous history. I would then link this observation to the tropes of writing on water, walking on water, and drowning in water, all of which, I would say, are refractions of Milton's fear of strong women who will either overwhelm you, abandon you, or tear you to pieces and send your head down the stream toward the Lesbian shore.

However, you're not going to hear any of that; rather, you will hear a reading of the poem that assigns it meanings most workers in the field would find (relatively) uncontroversial. I will be committed to that reading only as an example of the present state of the art, an example that will allow me to pose some general questions about the art and about the conditions of its intelligibility. The difference between the two analyses, the one I shall withhold and the one I shall elaborate, is the difference between the answers to two (different) questions: (1) what reading of *Lycidas* do I believe to be true? and (2) what reading of *Lycidas* will best serve the purpose of the present study? The point may seem laboured or uninteresting, but I ask you to keep it in mind and promise you that in time it will connect up with some larger issues.

The first three words of Milton's *Lycidas* are "Yet once more," and any reading of the poem must begin with those words. But how does one begin? Is "yet" to be read as "despite" and therefore as referring to a previously noted reluctance to act that has now been overcome? "Forget what I've just been saying; we're going to do it again." "*Yet,* once more." Or is this the "yet" of exasperation, introducing a repetition whose occurrence is regretted even as it is announced? Is the "once-moreness" of the yet-to-be described action infused with a profound and disappointed weariness: "My God, must we do this *again*?" "Yet once *more*?" To choose between these readings (and they of course are not the only possible ones) is to choose between alternative imaginings of the situation from which the words issue, where "situation" is an inadequate shorthand for such matters as the identity of the speaker— what kind of person is he? where has he been? where is he going?; the nature of his project—what is he trying to do?; the occasion of its performance—what has moved him to do it?

It might seem that these and related questions are conveniently answered by the headnote that stands between the title and the first line:

> In this Monody the author bewails a learned Friend, unfortunately drown'd in his Passage from *Chester* on the *Irish* Seas, 1637. And by occasion foretels the ruine of our corrupted Clergy, then in their height.

But rather than narrowing interpretive options, the headnote proliferates them, if only because of its own publishing history. When the poem first appeared in 1638 there was no headnote, although a manuscript dated November 1637 includes the first sentence. The second sentence, "And by occasion foretels the ruine of our corrupted Clergy, then in their height," was added in 1645 when the author published a volume entitled *Poems of Mr. John Milton.* These few facts raise a distressing number of questions. If the first half of the headnote was written before the 1638 publication, why was it omitted?

One answer might be that since the poem was printed along with other tributes to the "unfortunately drown'd" learned friend in a memorial collection entitled *Justa Edovardo King,* there was no need for an identification of its occasion. If this common-sense explanation were taken seriously it would demand a reading of the poem in the context of its companion pieces. We would be obliged to consider it not as a free-standing artefact produced by a single consciousness, but as a component in an ensemble effort. This, however, would have the problematic effect of suggesting that the 1645 version, differently situated, was a different poem, for instead of offering itself as one of a number of responses to a distressing fact—the death of a mutual friend—the poem would offer itself as evidence of the talent of a newly emerged poet. It would then be read in the context of the other productions in the same volume, which would include poems that find Milton worrying obsessively about the late maturing of his talent ("How soon hath time the subtle thief of youth, / Stol'n on his wing my three and twentieth year") and wondering whether he is making the best possible use of his gifts. These same concerns are expressed often in the prose writings of this period where, typically, they take the form of a complaint by the poet that he has been interrupted in his studies and forced to take on a task he would rather have declined. He has been compelled, he says in *The Reason of Church Government,* to "write . . . out of mine own season, when I have neither yet compleated to my minde the full circle of my private studies" (*The Complete Prose Works of John Milton,* ed. Don Wolfe *et al.,* New Haven, 1953, i. 807). With passages like this in mind, *Lycidas,* with its elaborate metaphor of a "season due" that has not been allowed to mature, will seem but *one more* such interruption: "Yet once more." Yet once more I have been plucked from the "still time" of contemplation and thrust willy-nilly into the world of chance and mischance.

So far we have been proceeding (if that is the word, for after all we are still stuck on the poem's opening phrase) by looking backward to the possible antecedents of this moment of utterance; if we now go only slightly forward to the poem's next phrase, we find still further complications in the shape of additional interpretive alternatives: "Yet once more, O ye laurels." Note first the oddness of the address; one does not usually talk to trees. Of course, one does talk to trees and to all manner of other things in *poems*, and one is obligated to talk to trees in poems that belong to the category of *pastoral*. The generic identification is made in a note by Thomas Warton in 1791 when he observes that "by plucking the berries and the leaves of the laurel, myrtle and ivy, [Milton] might intend to point out the pastoral or rural turn of his poem" (*Poems upon Several Occasions, English, Italian, and Latin with Translations, by John Milton*, ed. Thomas Warton, 2nd edn., 1791, 2). But this can only be pointed out to a reader who already knows it, who already knows (among other things) that there is a genre called pastoral and that one of its conventions is an address to nature and natural processes. When I say "knows" I don't mean that the reader holds in reserve, and then applies, knowledge in order to give shape to a landscape that is as yet undifferentiated; rather it is within the requisite knowledge that the reader proceeds, and he quite literally sees the landscape into shape, filling in its details not after a first, uninterpretive reading but in the course of a first (not really the first since it is motored by all the previous readings that make it possible if not inevitable) reading. The direction of inference in Warton's observation (despite the footnote which suggests a process more inductive) is neither from a knowledge of the genre to a specification of the laurel's significance, nor from a noting of the laurel's significance to a specification of the genre; indeed it is not an inference he makes at all, but an (involuntary) act of recognition (*re*-cognition) in which the genre and the significance of particular details come into view immediately and simultaneously.

That act occurs as early as the taking in of the poem's title, for among the things that a reader like Warton knows is that "Lycidas" and like names are commonly found in poems that depict an idealized shepherd life that is used as a backdrop or frame within which a poet meditates on a range of issues including (the list is not exhaustive) agricultural policies, urban decay, civic responsibility, ecclesiastical corruption, military ambitions, economics, the pains of love, and the place of poetry in a world hostile to its existence. This last is particularly important because it marks the genre as a self-reflexive one. Moreover, it has been self-reflexive from the beginning, or rather, since its *non*-beginning. Theocritus, the "first" pastoral poet, was not situated in a rural scene from which his successors were progressively more removed; he was himself already removed; a participant in the "decadent" literary life of third-century Alexandria, his representation of an idyllic pastoral landscape is at best a remembered re-creation of a childhood in Sicily, a re-creation that breathes *loss* from its very first word. It is a paradox (and strength) of the genre that its preferred values are in a state of disintegration long before they are celebrated. The valorization of the "natural" and simple life of shepherds and shepherdesses is made in the context of a pervasive nostalgia, which means that the very notion of "the natural" is a construction of high artifice, a point emphasized by George Puttenham in 1589 when he declared that the intention of pastoral poetry is not to "represent the rusticall manner . . . but under the vaile of homely persons . . . to insinuate and glaunce at greater matters" (*The Arte of English Poesy,* London, 1589, 55).

What this means is that everyone who writes in the genre does so with a sense of belatedness, of having missed the beauty and equanimity of a form of life that can be invoked only after the fact of its passing. The poet who would add his voice to a long line of lamenting predecessors knows that he takes up a task (of sounding the "oaten" note) only in order to re-experience its failure, *yet once more.* In another tradition, however—a tradition also formative of a practised reader's consciousness—"yet once more" is strongly associated with a force that turns temporal failure into eternal success. The force is, quite simply, the force of God, whose apocalyptic promise (or is it a threat?) is reported by Paul in his Epistle to the Hebrews: "Yet once more I shake not the earth only but also heaven." Almost as if he were a literary critic, Paul immediately supplies the gloss: "this word, Yet once more, signifieth the removing of those things that are shaken, as of things that are made, that those things which cannot be shaken may remain. Wherefore, receiving a kingdom which cannot be moved, let us have grace, by which we may serve God acceptably with reverence and godly fear: For our God is a consuming fire" (Heb. 12: 26–9). That is, if I may gloss Paul's gloss (notice how we become ever more deeply embedded in the layered history of hermeneutics), the godly "Yet once more" announces the firm and everlasting foundation that underlies a world of *apparent* contingency announced by the secular "Yet once more." The "shaking" men and women experience from the vantage-point of their limited perspective is from God's perspective a "shaking down," at the end of which will remain only those things that abide. But since no one of us inhabits God's perspective, the permanence that underwrites and finally mitigates temporal instability is not something we can apprehend, and, as Paul explains elsewhere (notably in the eleventh chapter of Hebrews), we must therefore take it on faith, defined famously as "the substance of things hoped for, the evidence of things not seen."

It would seem, then, incumbent on us to hear two distinctive notes or voices in the opening words of Milton's poem: the weary voice of the beleaguered mortal who has just experienced what seems to him to be a cataclysmic shaking (the early and apparently senseless death of a good and talented man) and the confident voice of a deity who proclaims a truth that can be neither questioned nor verified (it is, by definition, its own evidence). Not coincidentally, these two voices correspond to the two strains of the pastoral in which Milton is necessarily (he has no choice) participating: the historically prior strain of the classical pastoral as established, in a kind of godly fiat, by Theocritus, and the biblical pastoral which takes its cue from Christ's declaration, "I am the good shepherd; the good shepherd giveth his life for the sheep" (John 10:11). The intersection of these two strains creates a double discourse in which landscapes and the values associated with them are systematically opposed. On one hand an idyllic landscape imagined as a safe (if precarious) retreat from the pressures of "modern" life, especially the life of the city; on the other a harsh and forbidding landscape whose central figure is not an immature, lovestruck shepherd, but an older and much burdened minister of the gospel who must give aid and comfort to a (human) flock beset with every trouble against which one might take arms.

The contrast is between the pastoral of ease or *otium* and the pastoral of care or moral responsibility, and it is a contrast that itself becomes a commonplace theme in medieval and Renaissance instances of the genre. Spenser's *February Eclogue*, for example, is structured as a dialogue between the two traditions as represented by the frivolous Cuddie and the oh-so-serious Thenot, who lectures his younger compatriot thus:

> Selfe have I worne out thrise threttie yeares,
> Some in much joy, many in many teares:
> Yet never complained of cold nor heate,
> of Sommers flame, nor of Winters threate,
> Ne ever was to fortune foeman,
> But gently tooke, that ungently came.
> And ever my flocke was my chief care,
> Winter or Sommer they mought well fare. (17–23)

In the *May Eclogue* the same opposition is continued by two other shepherds, Palinode and Piers (obviously intended to recall Langland's Piers the Ploughman), who looks beyond the present moment of pain and care to a day of final judgement:

> Thilke same bene shepeheards for the Devils stedde,
> That playen, while their flockes be unfedde . . .
> I muse what account both these will make . . .
> When great Pan account of shepeherdes shall aske.
> (43–4, 51, 54)

Thenot's forward-looking vision rebukes the *carpe diem* sentiments expressed by Palinode (shepherds should "Reapen the fruite . . . / The while they here liven, at ease and leasure") and points to a salient difference between the two pastoral strains, the one with its emphasis on the moment-to-moment passing of carnal time, the other with at least one eye (and that the clear-sighted eye) on the treasure that *already* awaits those who endure this life in the hope ("the substance of things hoped for") of another in eschatological time. It is a prime thesis of the biblical pastoral that carnal time is finally unreal, that, as Milton puts it in another poem, time's primary task is to cannibalize itself:

> Fly envious Time . . .
> And glut thyself with what thy womb devours,
> Which is no more than that what is false and vain,
> And merely mortal dross.
> (*On Time*, I, 4–6)

When this process is completed,

> Then all this earthly grossness quit,
> Attir'd with stars, we shall forever sit,
> Triumphing over death and chance and thee, O Time.
> (20–22)

This view of time is also a view of both the location and production of *meaning*. In the world of carnal or secular time meaning lies waiting at the end of a sequence; it emerges, quite literally, only in the "fulness of time." In the Christian vision, sequence is not productive of meaning, but rather marks out spaces (like the tick-tock of a metronome) in which an already full meaning, the meaning of Christ's redemptive act, is available to those who have the eyes to apprehend it; those, that is, for whom the evidence need *not* be seen. In this vision time is reversible, as it is for the God of *Paradise Lost,* who "from his prospect high / . . . past, present future . . . beholds" (III. 78–9). Moreover, since the spaces of time are filled always by the same meaning, individual agency is finally unimportant: in the eyes or ears of the faithful, God's message is manifest no matter who speaks. Intention is not a property of limited consciousnesses but of the spirit that makes of them an involuntary vehicle. For centuries Virgil's fourth eclogue, known as the messianic eclogue, was read as a prophecy of the birth of Christ, a reading that would be dismissed as anachronistic by a post-Enlightenment mind, but one that would seem quite appropriate and even inevitable to a mind schooled in the ways of interpretation by St Augustine's *On Christian Doctrine* and accustomed to thinking of Dante's *Divine Comedy,* graced by a Christianized Virgil, as a sacred text.

Augustine himself builds on an interpretive strategy already present in the epistles of Paul. It is called typology and it emerged first as a way of reading events chronicled in the Old Testament as prefigurations, or "shadows," of events in the life of Christ. In typological interpretations the actions of men and nations derive their significance not only from the conditions of their historical production, but from a master significance, Christ's work of incarnation and redemption, which is "before" history, in the sense of already having occurred in eternity, and yet is nevertheless the content of history in that every apparently discrete action at once reflects and anticipates it. In the course of the centuries strict typological interpretation is relaxed and the method is extended to the lives and deeds of contemporary agents, both individual and collective, and in the seventeenth century Puritans of Milton's temper routinely saw themselves as re-enacting the Old Testament "remnant," those few faithful who followed the call of God and, led by Moses (a type of Christ), struck out for the Promised Land, for Canaan, the type of Paradise and eternal life. It is not too much to say that from the typological perspective each moment is equivalent to all others, offering the same challenge, the challenge of affirming God's promise in the face of the contrary evidence often thrown up by "the world," and holding out the same reward, salvation and reunion with divinity, to those who hold fast; each moment in short is a repetition of the same, and therefore an instance of a meaning that is proclaimed *yet once more.*

It is not proclaimed by anyone in particular, although anyone at all can be its vehicle. That is why Milton is able to present himself in the headnote to *Lycidas* as a non-privileged reader of his own poem, or rather, of what has turned out to be *not* his own poem. When he says "And by occasion foretels the ruine of our corrupted Clergy, then in their height" he is not so much claiming the power of prophecy (although Virgilian precedent—and Milton self-consciously modelled his career on Virgil's—would have authorized him to do so) as he is finding (with the delight of the believer) meanings that he did not himself intend. In *The Reason of Church Government,* written in 1642, he had declared, "When God commands to take the trumpet, and blow a dolorous and jarring blast, it lies not in man's will what he shall say, or what he shall conceal" (*Complete Prose Works,* i. 803). Now, in 1645 he discovers just how jarring was the blast he unwittingly blew in 1637 when he thought he was simply lamenting the death of a friend and a loss to the Church but was in fact (God's fact, God's intention) foretelling, with an authority for which he was not responsible, the fall of Bishop Laud and of the entire institution of prelacy. Read this way, the headnote instructs us in how to read the poem's first three words, not as the anguished cry of a belated and ineffectual singer, as would be the case were the context limited to the classical strain inaugurated by Theocritus, but as the confident affirmation by a voice that will always make itself heard no matter how weak or transitory its vessel. In effect, by making this reading of his poem available—that is, by reporting in the headnote, with no hint of resentment, that this poem was commandeered "by occasion" by a power greater than his—Milton acknowledges and accepts his radical dependency, accepts and acknowledges his "yet-once-moreness."

I could go on for ever in this vein—I haven't been a Miltonist these thirty years for nothing—adding to the contexts I have already introduced the context of Italian verse forms, the context of the myth of Orpheus, even the context of Jungian archetypes; but enough has been done, I trust, to support my point, which is not that *Lycidas* is complex, but that *Lycidas* is a poem. I would not deny *Lycidas* the attribute of complexity; I merely assert that the compliment is tautological. Simply to *be* a poem, that is, to have been categorized in that way rather than as a political pamphlet or a sermon, is to have been credited with linguistic and semantic density, even in advance of its discovery. Moreover, that discovery, once the categorization has been granted, is *assured* not in its details (which can vary in all the ways we have already seen) but in a general shape that will be filled out by the interpretive activities generated by the knowledge (quite literally *working* knowledge) that it is a poem one is interpreting.

Linguistic and semantic density is not something poems announce, but something that readers actualize by paying to texts labelled poetic a kind of attention they would not pay to texts not so labelled. Were "yet once more" the first three words of a parliamentary speech or an address by a general to his troops, the addressees would not be hearing them as they hear them when they are the first three words of *Lycidas;* or, and this is to make the same point from the other direction, were the parliamentarians or the infantrymen to ring the interpretive changes I have rung in the preceding paragraphs, they would be understood (and understand themselves) to be acting in ways inappropriate to the community of which they were, at that moment, members. It is not that it couldn't be done (in fact it can *always* be done), but that doing it—treating a political speech or a hortatory appeal as a poem—would be recognized by everyone concerned, including the doers, as play of a kind that was not to the institutional point and, indeed, flouted it.

When I use words like "institution" or "community" I refer not to a collection of independent individuals who, in a moment of deliberation, *choose* to employ certain interpretive strategies, but rather to a set of practices that are defining of an enterprise and fill the consciousnesses of the enterprise's members. Those members include the authors and speakers as well as their interpreters. Indeed they are *all* interpreters: when Milton puts pen to paper he no less than those in his intended audience is a reader of his own action. That is, as he begins, he thinks of himself, or, to be more precise, he conceives of himself, as a worker in a long-established field; and as such a worker he knows what gestures are available to him and the extent to which he is obliged to perform them, and the meaning they will have for those who are situated as he is, in the same field. If one understands the relationship between writers and their readers in this way, not as a relationship between agents with differing tasks and objectives but as one between agents engaged in the mutual performance of a single task, my assertion a moment ago that complexity is something that readers actualize will seem less disturbing than it perhaps was when it could be heard as an assertion of an interpretive will to power. Readers who perform in the ways I have been describing—in ways I have been exemplifying—do not ride roughshod over an author's intention; rather they *match* it by going about their business at once constrained and enabled by the same history that burdens and energizes those whom they read. Like all interpreters they are engaged in the project of determining intention, of asking "What does he or she or they or it *mean?*," but that determination itself depends on the assumption (not self-consciously arrived at but deployed in some sense involuntarily) of an intention, the intention, imputed to the author and directive of the reader's activities, of making a *poem.*

Another way to put this is to say that both readers and interpreters begin (exactly the wrong word) *in medias res;* they go about their business not in order to discover its point, but already in possession of and possessed by its point. They ask questions and give answers—not, however, any old questions and answers, but questions and answers of the kind they know in advance to be relevant. In a sense they could not even ask the questions if they did not already know the answers to questions deeper than the ones they are explicitly asking. My own practice to this point can serve as an example. In the preceding pages I have been asking questions about the interpretation of literary texts, but I have been guided, unselfconsciously, by my pre-assumed understanding of what kind of thing literary interpretation *is,* an understanding which itself rests on a (tacit) understanding of what kind of thing literature is. The ease with which I multiplied interpretive alternatives in the supposed service of posing a question—what is literary interpretation?—is an answer to it. That is, I knew (not in a way that guided my practice, but in a way that constituted its intelligibility for me and for my peers) that literary texts are polysemous, that they are multivoiced, that they often assert A and not-A simultaneously and that they can be read from right to left as well as from left to right.

It was this knowledge that led me to put an interpretive *pressure* on the first three words of *Lycidas* that would have been inappropriate (and, presumably, unrewarding, although this is a matter less straightforward than it might seem) in relation to a text that was not identified as literary. It might have appeared that I was telling you what you have to know before you can read *Lycidas,* but in fact I was telling you what you have to know in order even to ask what you have to know before you can read *Lycidas.* Or, rather, I was not *telling* you what you have to know in order even to ask what you have to know before you can read *Lycidas;* I was *showing* you, offering myself as an example, much as a tennis coach does when he says to a pupil, "Do it like this." Indeed, I could not have told you, if I had tried, what you have to know in order even to ask what you have to know before you can read Lycidas, for the words that I would have used and the directions I might have given would have been intelligible only within the knowledge they purport to convey.

Where does that knowledge—which I wasn't offering discursively but exemplifying, which is, in some sense, too deep for words—come from? Surely not from the text, which acquires its generic shape and particular details only in the light of that knowledge. It comes, if it "comes" from anywhere, from the fact of my embeddedness (almost embodiment) in a field of practice that marks its members with signs that are immediately perspicuous to one another. These signs are not visible on the surface; rather they emerge when a member is offered a piece of behaviour by a non-member—by an outsider—and responds (the response may be nothing more than a discreet nod to another member) by saying ("saying," strictly speaking, isn't required; a change in expression caught and read by another member will suffice) "That's not the kind of thing we do around here." It would not be to the point to ask what exactly "the kind of thing we do here" is, because it is known precisely in the way suggested by the statement, not as a discrete item, but in contrast with the kind of thing done by members of other enterprises (history, sociology, statistics). As Bruce Robbins has put it, "professionalism in any one discipline is inseparable from, and indeed, defined by, the relations *among* disciplines" (*Secular Vocations: Intellectuals, Professionalism, Culture*, London, 1993, 115). The content of "kind of thing we do here" is differential; it comes into view against a background of the practices it is *not*; and it must "show" in that way—as something we, not others, do—because if it did not it could not sustain a challenge to its usefulness.

John Crowe Ransom made the point a long time ago when he found it "atrocious" for an English department "to abdicate its own self-respecting identity" by failing to establish and defend "the peculiar constitution and structure of its product." English, he thundered, "might almost as well announce that it does not regard itself as entirely autonomous, but as a branch of the department of history, with the option of declaring itself occasionally a branch of the department of ethics" ("Criticism, Inc.," in *The World's Body*, Port Washington, NY, 1964, 335). Ransom would seem here to be prophetic in foreseeing the eagerness of many literary academics to do just that in the name of the new historicism and of political criticism, and I shall have much to say about the unwisdom of these two projects. For the moment, however, I am content simply to register my agreement with Ransom's insistence that it is a requirement for the respectability of an enterprise that it be, or at least be able to present itself as, *distinctive*.

S T E V E N   M A I L L O U X

INTERPRETATION AND
RHETORICAL HERMENEUTICS

*I am, in the deepest sense, a translator. I go on translating, even if I must but trans-
late English into English.*

—Kenneth Burke, letter to Malcolm Cowley, 4 June 1932

*When I think back on all the crap I learned in high school,
It's a wonder I can think at all.
The lack of education hasn't hurt me none.
I can read the writing on the wall.*

—Paul Simon, "Kodachrome"

Reading words on walls. Explicating poems in classrooms. Making sense of dreams
from the gods. Reading, explicating, making sense: these are three names given to
the activity of interpretation. In English, "interpret" has most often meant "to
expound the meaning of (something abstruse or mysterious); to render (words,
writings, an author, etc.) clear or explicit; to elucidate; to explain" (*OED*). But an
earlier sense of the verb was "to translate," and so interpretation is also "the action
of translating; a translation or rendering of a book, word, etc." (*OED*). The word
"interpretation" itself derives from the Latin, *interpretatio,* meaning not only "the
action of expounding, explaining" but also "a translation, rendering." In Latin
rhetoric, *interpretatio* referred to "the explanation of one word by another, the use
of synonyms." *Interpretatio* was formed on *interpres:* "an intermediary, agent, go-
between" and "an interpreter of foreign languages, translator."[1] In its etymology,
then, "interpretation" conveys the sense of a translation pointed in two directions
simultaneously: *toward* a text to be interpreted and *for* an audience in need of the
interpretation. That is, the interpreter mediates, Hermes fashion, between the

translated text and its new rendering *and* between the translated text and the audience desiring the translation.

It is the heritage of these two etymological senses—translation *of* a text and translation *for* an audience—that we might try to capture in a heuristic definition: "interpretation" is "acceptable and approximating translation."[2] Each term here provokes additional questions: (1) Approximating *what*? (2) Translating *how*? and (3) Acceptable *to whom*? For the next few pages, we can use these questions to organize our discussion of interpretation and work toward a clearer understanding of its rhetorical aspects.

INTERPRETATION

Approximating *what*? Translation is always an approximation, which is to say that interpretation is always directed. It is always an approximation of something; it is always directed *toward* something: situations, actions, gestures, graffiti, poems, novels, dreams, etc. Such objects of interpretation we can call "texts." Ultimately anything can be viewed as a text, anything can be interpreted: walls, letters on walls, even poems about letters on walls, such as this one by Emily Dickinson:

> Belshazzar had a Letter—
> He never had but one—
> Belshazzar's Correspondent
> Concluded and begun
> In that immortal Copy
> The Conscience of us all
> Can read without its Glasses
> On Revelation's Wall—

If we think of interpreting as the translation of texts, then this is clearly a text requiring translation. In fact, here we have two texts in need of interpreting: Dickinson's poem and the "Letter . . . on Revelation's Wall" to which the poem refers. Just as the words of the "Letter" are missing, so too are some of the usual textual markers in the poem, like traditional punctuation. Dickinson's idiosyncratic dashes do give us some guidance but not much.

The poem itself translates a biblical story. In chapter 5 of the Book of Daniel, Belshazzar, king of the Chaldeans, holds a feast using sacred vessels taken from the Jewish temple at Jerusalem. During the feast, a hand appears and writes on the wall the words "Mene, Mene, Tekel, Upharsin." The king cannot interpret the writing, nor can any of his advisors. The problem of reading, making sense of texts, thus becomes foregrounded in the story. Daniel is summoned for help, and he ends up interpreting the "Letter" from the "Correspondent," God: "This is the interpretation of the thing: Mene, God hath numbered thy kingdom, and finished it. Tekel, Thou art weighed in the balances, and art found wanting. Peres, Thy kingdom is divided, and given to the Medes and Persians."

The three words written on the wall refer literally to three measures of weight: a mina, a shekel, and two half minas. Daniel interprets the message by punning off these words: the first resembles a Hebraic verb meaning "numbered," the second "weighed," and the third "to divide." He uses these verbal puns to interpret the message as an accusation and a prophecy. And in the chapter's final lines the prophecy of punishment is indeed fulfilled: "In that night was Belshazzar the king of the Chaldeans slain. And Darius the Median took the kingdom." Here we have an interpretation made in the context of political oppression and presented as a consequence of the oppressor's moral iniquity: Israel had been conquered, the Jews enslaved, and now their religious vessels desecrated. The reading of the wall-writing both advertises the king's crime and announces his punishment.[3]

It is possible that Dickinson meant her poem to serve as a similar announcement. Adding the inscription, "Suggested by our Neighbor," she sent it to her brother, probably after the 1879 Lothrop scandal in Amherst. This local affair involved newspaper reports of a father's physical cruelty to his daughter and resulted in a libel suit filed against the *Springfield Republican* by Reverend C. D. Lothrop, the accused father. The court found against Lothrop in April, and Dickinson may have been commemorating the occasion with this poem. From this biographical perspective, the poem refers to the judgment made by the court, which found Lothrop guilty of patriarchal oppression.[4]

More generally, Dickinson's poem takes the biblical tale and makes it into an allegory for the conscience "of us all," through which God points out and warns us about our sins, giving each of us our own private "Letter." This allegorizing of the poem translates the literary text, which itself translates a biblical story into a poem. Just as the poem approximates—is directed toward—the Biblical story, so too does my interpretation approximate the poem.

Now there are various ways to take the question—What does interpretation approximate?—and develop it into a hermeneutic theory, a general account of how readers make sense of texts. For example, we could say that the words of my reading approximately translate those of the poem and that Daniel's words approximately translate those on the wall. Such a formalist theory could go on to claim that what determines our interpretations is what they approximate, the words on the page. A different theoretical approach argues that what is approximately translated—for example, by Dickinson's reader and by Daniel—is, ultimately, the author's intention. Such an intentionalist theory could go on to claim that interpretations are constrained by the intention behind or in the words.[5] Dickinson in the poem and God in the letter intended a meaning that the interpreter must decipher to read the text correctly. Both formalist and intentionalist theories attempt to provide a foundation for constraining the interpretive relationship between reader and text. Often, such theories not only claim to *describe* how interpretation takes place but to *prescribe* how it should take place. These foundationalist theories present themselves as both general accounts of making sense and specific guides to correct interpretations. Antifoundationalism charges that such philosophical guarantees are theoretically incoherent or otherwise problematic and fail to make good on their claims in actual interpretive practice.[6]

Translating *how*? Our second question moves away from the *object* of interpretation—the text and its sense—to the *activity* of interpreting—the process of sense-making. In reading the Dickinson poem above, I provided two kinds of interpretive approaches, both grounded in a theory of author's intention: historicizing and allegorizing. In the former approach, I suggested that Dickinson intended to refer specifically to Rev. Lothrop getting a well-deserved public humiliation. In the latter, I suggested that Dickinson intended a more universal message about the conscience of us all. It is not necessary to choose between these two complementary meanings, but it is important to recognize the contrasting methods used to arrive at these different interpretations. In historicizing I used a strategy of placing the text in the historical context of its production. In allegorizing I followed a strategy that assumes poetry can refer to a second, more universal level of meaning beyond its particular historical reference. These reading strategies or interpretive conventions provide a way of describing the process of interpretation rather than its textual object. They are ways of characterizing how interpretive translation takes place. They emphasize what the reader contributes to interpretation rather than what the text gives the reader to interpret.[7]

We have now seen displayed several different strategies for interpreting texts. For example, Daniel uses puns or verbal resemblances to read the writing on the king's wall, and I earlier used etymologies to explore meanings for "interpretation" itself. Methods or strategies of making sense are associated with various theories of how interpretation does or should take place. Above I connected historicizing and allegorizing a text's meaning with intentionalist theories of interpretation. Punning and etymologizing are as often associated with formalist theories of interpretation as they are with intentionalist approaches. All these strategies—historicizing, allegorizing, punning, and using etymologies—can be restated as rules for correct interpretation. That is, certain interpretive conventions become in certain contexts the privileged way of making sense of texts. Identifying puns may be acceptable for interpreting ancient and contemporary graffiti but not for reading constitutions. Allegorizing may be appropriate for poetry and scripture but not for legislated statutes. For these supposedly more straightforward legal texts, theories of *neutral principles* are often proposed as ways to guarantee that interpreters resist more literary methods of making sense.[8]

Theories of neutral principles posit rules for guaranteeing correct interpretations, e.g., formalist rules for looking at "the words on the page" or intentionalist rules for respecting authorial purposes. These rules or interpretive principles are presented as neutral in the sense that they are viewed as capable of being applied in a disinterested manner safe from personal idiosyncrasy or political bias. Antifoundationalism rejects the possibility of such "neutral principles" and questions whether constitutions are in fact inherently more straightforward than literary texts and whether interpretive theories can actually constrain readings or avoid political entanglements. To approach these issues more closely, let us now turn to our third question: Acceptable *to whom*?

In *Adventures of Huckleberry Finn* the boy narrator and Jim, the runaway slave, are separated in the fog while traveling down the Mississippi River. Despairing after a night-long search, Jim gives Huck up for dead and, exhausted, falls into a troubled sleep. Meanwhile, Huck finds his way back to the raft, and, after Jim awakes, Huck plays a rather insensitive trick on his companion, convincing him that the pain and horrors of the night before never really happened. It was all just a dream. Jim then says "he must start in and ' 'terpret' it, because it was sent for a warning." After Jim presents a wild translation of the dream that wasn't a dream, Huck tries to clinch the joke by responding: "Oh, well, that's all interpreted well enough, as far as it goes, Jim . . . but what does *these* things stand for?" as he points to the leaves, rubbish, and smashed oar, all evidence of the previous night's catastrophe. Now one way to view Jim's dream interpretation is to see it as a rather laughable misreading. This is Huck's view and the view he wants his readers to share so that they get the joke on Jim.

But Huck's request for another interpretation, not of the dream but of the proof that there was no dream, produces a more serious response that makes Huck's joke backfire.

> Jim looked at the trash, and then looked at me, and back at the trash again . . . [H]e looked at me steady, without ever smiling, and says:
> "What do dey stan' for? I's gwyne to tell you. When I got all wore out wid work, en wid de callin' for you, en went to sleep, my heart wuz mos' broke bekase you wuz los', en I didn' k'yer no mo' what become er me en de raf'. En when I wake up en fine you back agin, all safe en soun', de tears come en I could a got down on my knees en kiss' yo' foot I's so thankful. En all you wuz thinkin 'bout wuz how you could make a fool uv ole Jim wid a lie. Dat truck dah is *trash*; en trash is what people is dat puts dirt on de head er dey fren's en makes 'em ashamed."

If we saw Jim's dream interpretation as a misreading, we certainly see nothing wrong with his allegorical reading of the trash. We get the point and so does Huck, as he writes that Jim then "got up slow, and walked to the wigwam, and went in there, without saying anything but that. But that was enough. It made me feel so mean I could almost kissed *his* foot to get him to take it back." Twain turns the incident into another episode in Huck's struggle with his racist upbringing when he has the boy write further: "It was fifteen minutes before I could work myself up to go and humble myself to a nigger—but I done it, and I warn't ever sorry for it afterwards, neither."[9] Interpreting this passage, readers recognize how Huck's apology undercuts his continuing racial prejudice, how his respect and affection for Jim work to undermine his society's ideology of white supremacy.

If you agree that Jim misread the "dream" but convincingly interpreted the "trash," if you agree with my reading of these readings and with my interpretation of the final passage, then we are agreeing on what to count as a correct interpretation for these various texts. Correct interpretations are those that are considered accurate, valid, acceptable. But acceptable to whom? One answer is suggested by another Dickinson poem:

> Much Madness is divinest Sense—
> To a discerning Eye—
> Much Sense—the starkest Madness—
> 'Tis the Majority
> In this, as All, prevail—
> Assent—and you are sane—
> Demur—you're straightway dangerous—
> And handled with a Chain—

This poem is about how correct interpretations are established, how sense-making is defined as right or wrong, sense or nonsense, sanity or madness. Read literally, it simply states that sense or meaning is in the eye of the beholder, rather than in the object beheld. The poem suggests further that the majority of interpreters determine what counts as sense. Of course, the point of the poem does not end there. Dickinson is not simply describing the conditions of "correct" interpreting—majority rules—but is sarcastically protesting against that fact. Thus the poem rewrites the question—To whom are correct interpretations acceptable?—as a problem

about the politics of interpretation, about a reading's status within the power relations of a historical community. These questions point us away from the exchange
between interpreter and text and toward that between interpreter and interpreter
—that is, from the hermeneutic problem of how text and reader interact to the
rhetorical problem of how interpreters interact with other interpreters in trying to
argue for or against different meanings. For rhetorical hermeneutics, these two
problems are ultimately inseparable.

When we move from foundationalist theories about reading texts to the rhetorical politics of interpretive disputes, we do not abandon the issues raised by my
original three heuristic questions. In one sense, we will simply be broadening our
area of concern. When we focus only on the text, an author's intention, or a
reader's interpretive conventions, as we have done, there is a strong tendency to
view interpretation as a private reading experience involving only an independent
text (and author) and an individual reader. Many foundationalist theories give in to
this temptation and compound the mistake by completely ignoring the socio-
political context in which interpretation takes place. . . . [I]nterpretation functions
repeatedly as a politically interested act of persuasion.

In the cases of reading discussed earlier, I hinted at this politics of interpretation
whenever I noted how an interpretive act took place within the context of power
relations in a historical community. For example, we saw how Daniel's reading of
the wall-writing functioned within a national situation of political oppression and
then how Dickinson's poem translated this biblical story into a new context involving the politics of family and gender. Similarly, Jim's dream interpretation and
Huck's reactions play a part in Mark Twain's commentary on the politics of race in
nineteenth-century U.S. culture. In each of these cases, interpretation takes place
in a political context and each interpretive act relates directly to the power relations
(whether of nation, family, gender, class, or race) involved in that context.

However, what is not quite as clear in these examples is how interpretation itself
can be politically interested, how claims for a reading are always direct attempts to
affect power relations through coercion or persuasion. These effects can be subtle
and microscopic as in cases where students ask a teacher to explain a line of poetry
and she convinces them to accept a particular reading. The effects become more
obvious when there are radical disagreements over interpretations, when the correct reading is in actual dispute. At such times, the least persuasive interpretation
loses out. Indeed, in some extreme cases of interpretive controversy, Dickinson
seems to be right:

> 'Tis the Majority
> In this, as All, prevail—
> Assent—and you are sane—
> Demur—you're straightway dangerous—
> And handled with a Chain—

Most situations involving interpretive disagreement do not result in such blatant
suppression of dissent. However, a poem protesting a majority's tyranny over an
individual dissenter does foreground what is always the case: any interpretive dispute involves political interests and consequences.

Old news in some intellectual quarters, such general claims remain empty without detailed illustrations of how they apply in specific historical contexts. In

[*Reception Histories*] . . . I provide an extended example of this rhetorical politics: pro- and antislavery interpretations of the Christian Bible in the 1840s. This interpretive dispute involved not only readings of Scripture but also theories for reading it. We can conclude our brief look at "interpretation" by quoting some of this hermeneutic theory from Reverend William Graham's *The Contrast; or, The Bible and Abolitionism: an Exegetical Argument:*

> Abolitionism assumes to demonstrate . . . that the relation of master and slave is a gross sin—a violation of the laws of our being. From this, it follows, by necessary consequence, that no book authorizing this relation can come from God. The Christian Abolitionist denies that this relation is authorized by the Bible and adopts a system of exegetical rules that make the Scriptures teach according to his theory.[10]

Instead of using "the strict laws of interpretation" (40), abolitionists adopt a hermeneutic theory to suit their political ideology, and in so doing they reject the obvious meanings of the Bible. For these biased readers, scriptural evidence supporting slavery is interpreted out of existence. For them,

> Abraham's "servants, bought with his money," are religious converts, and *eved* and *doulos,* instead of meaning slave, mean in fact only hired servant. The effect of such a mode of interpreting the Scriptures is obvious. Men learn to believe that the Bible is an unintelligible book. It ceases to speak to the heart and conscience with divine authority. The writing upon the wall may be from God, but the impression is according to their confidence in the interpreter. (40)

Having the wrong hermeneutic theory leads to relativism and interpretive distortion, according to Graham. But, from the perspective of rhetorical hermeneutics, what counts as the right theory, the legitimate "laws of interpretation," is not independent of one's ideological position in the political and religious debates. That is, the biblical interpretation and its hermeneutic justification are part of the same rhetorical configuration. Indeed, a hermeneutic theory provides no guarantees for correctly interpreting Scripture or any other text, though it does provide additional argumentative strategies for making one's case.[11] Doing rhetorical hermeneutics means writing rhetorical histories of such interpretive debates, focusing on the use of theory in rhetorical practice and on the practice of theory in doing history.

WHY RHETORICAL HERMENEUTICS?

Rhetorical hermeneutics *uses rhetoric to practice theory by doing history.* The rest of the chapter explains why and how this is so. The present section outlines the rhetorical context of critical theory and academic disciplines in the 1980s to account for why a rhetorical hermeneutics was proposed in the first place, and the final section describes its major theoretical claims by responding to specific objections to its arguments.

Rhetorical hermeneutics is the theoretical practice that results from the intersection between rhetorical pragmatism and the study of cultural rhetoric. Thus, one way of explaining rhetorical hermeneutics is to define the latter two modes of inquiry more fully and then describe how the overlap between them constitutes a rhetorical approach to specific historical acts of cultural interpretation.[12]

In the 1980s cultural studies became an influential outgrowth of several interdisciplinary projects in the human sciences. In his mid-decade essay "What Is Cultural Studies Anyway?" Richard Johnson began his answer, "Cultural studies is now a movement or a network. It has its own degrees in several colleges and universities and its own journals and meetings. It exercises a large influence on academic disciplines, especially on English studies, sociology, media and communication studies, linguistics and history." Johnson went on to address the problems of institutionalization and definition, offering his own view of the interdisciplinary field: "For me cultural studies is about the historical forms of consciousness or subjectivity, or the subjective forms we live by, or, in a rather perilous compression, perhaps a reduction, the subjective side of social relations."[13] Other quite different definitions of cultural studies also circulated in the eighties, but a certain consensus began to emerge. As Vincent Leitch commented near the end of the decade, "During the eighties, advocates of cultural studies influenced by poststructuralist thought advanced the argument that a pure pre-discursive, precultural reality or socioeconomic infrastructure did not exist: cultural discourse constituted the ground of social existence as well as personal identity. Given this 'poetic,' the task of cultural studies was to study the conventions and representations fostered by the whole set of cultural discourses."[14]

Cultural studies as an academic movement had varying effects on disciplines in the humanities and social sciences. In English departments, for example, cultural studies helped expand the discipline's subject matter to include nonliterary as well as literary texts and also cultural genres such as film and television and social practices more generally. In the new English and Textual Studies major at Syracuse University, a predominantly cultural studies approach replaced the usual coverage model of literary historical periods. Instead of focusing exclusively on literature organized into periods such as Medieval, Renaissance, Victorian, and so on, the ETS major takes as its subject matter a variety of cultural texts and organizes their study through different modes of inquiry—historical, theoretical, and political. Courses offered during the first full year of the ETS curriculum (1990–91) included in the history group Introduction to Reception Aesthetics (Cases in American Culture), Introduction to Literary History—1700 to Contemporary (English Romantic Writers), and Studies in Periodization and Chronology (The American 1890s); in the theory group, Introduction to Semiotic Theories of Representation (Film Theory), Studies in Hermeneutics (Interpreting Law and Literature), Studies in Psychological Theories of Representation (Feminism and Psychoanalysis), Studies in Semiotics (Hearing and Textuality), Studies in Theory of Genre (Epistolarity and the Novel), and Studies in Cultural Theories of Representation (Eurocentrism, Postcoloniality, Revolution); and in the politics group, Introduction to Feminisms (Politics, Culture, Theory), Studies in Feminisms (Gender and the Culture of Television), and Studies in Sexualities (Power, Gender, and Shakespeare).[15] Most of these sample courses indicate the influence of recent cultural studies on the new Syracuse major and suggest some of the ways that an interdisciplinary cultural studies movement can change the shape of a traditional discipline.

A specifically *rhetorical* form of cultural studies begins by rethinking this contemporary interdisciplinary approach in terms of a rhetorical framework with a vocabulary of terms such as "cultural conversation," "textual effects," "tropes," "arguments," etc. In such a reconceptualization, "culture" gets defined as "the network of rhetorical practices that are extensions and manipulations of other practices—social, political, and economic."[16] Rhetoric is not simply an expression or reflection of "deeper" historical forces, whether psychological, social, political, or economic. Rather, rhetorical practices are (at least partly) constitutive of these other historical categories. A rhetorically oriented cultural studies, then, describes and explains past and present configurations of rhetorical practices as they affect each other and as they extend and manipulate the social practices, political structures, and material circumstances in which they are embedded at particular historical moments.

A cultural rhetoric studies might, for example, interpret the function of a trope like "reading as eating" within a particular historical community during a specific historical period. How, for instance, was the trope tied to arguments about children reading fiction in the United States during the second half of the nineteenth century? How did the tropes and arguments about reading fiction relate to cultural narratives about "moral degeneracy" and "juvenile delinquency"? How did this cultural rhetoric of reading (its tropes, arguments, and narratives) circulate within different social institutions such as the family, the factory, the church, the primary school, the state reformatory, and the university and within different discourses such as popular novels, religious treatises, professional studies of child rearing, newspaper editorials and literary reviews, and political speeches about censorship? How did the figurative meaning of such tropes as "reading as eating" or "critical reading as mental discipline" get literalized in proposals to establish physical exercise classes alongside required courses in studying literature within state reformatories for juvenile delinquents in the 1880s? And how did this cultural rhetoric of reading get deployed differently according to gender in children's literature and in reformatories for male and female adolescents?[17] Questions of this kind focus most projects in cultural rhetoric studies and put into play such working definitions of rhetoric as "the political effectivity of trope and argument in culture."[18]

Rhetorical hermeneutics is a form of cultural rhetoric studies that takes as its topic specific historical acts of interpretation within their cultural contexts. But before expanding this description, I need to present rhetorical hermeneutics as a theoretical stance toward interpretation, a position related to . . . rhetorical pragmatism. . . . There are several ways of characterizing rhetorical pragmatism of the 1980s: a recent form of antifoundationalist historicism; a poststructuralist instance of sophistic rhetoric; a rhetoricized version of contemporary neopragmatism. The last of these descriptions is especially useful for my current purposes.

Arguably, Richard Rorty was the most influential neopragmatist during the eighties. His *Philosophy and the Mirror of Nature* set the stage for a significant revival of North American pragmatism in philosophy and other related disciplines.[19] Here I will use one of Rorty's essays as a synecdoche for the rhetorical aspects of his whole anti-Philosophical project.

To provide another rhetorical perspective on and from neopragmatism, we can start with a quotation from early in Rorty's article "Is Derrida a Transcendental Philosopher?":

> On my view, the only thing that can displace an intellectual world is another intellectual world—a new alternative, rather than an argument against an old alternative. The idea that there is some neutral ground on which to mount an argument against something as big as 'logocentrism' strikes me as one more logocentric hallucination. I do not think that demonstrations of 'internal incoherence' or of

'presuppositional relationships' ever do much to disabuse us of bad old ideas or institutions. Disabusing gets done, instead, by offering us sparkling new ideas, or utopian visions of glorious new institutions. The result of genuinely original thought, on my view, is not so much to refute or subvert our previous beliefs as to help us forget them by giving us a substitute for them.[20]

This passage strikes me as an especially rich example of rhetorical pragmatism. Among the rhetorical points made are two on argumentation that Rorty makes again and again throughout his writings in the eighties. First is the antifoundationalist point that there is no transcendental ground, no Archimedian standpoint beyond all argumentation, beyond all rhetoric, from which truth-claims can be adjudicated. And second is the nominalist, Wittgensteinian point that propositional argumentation does not bring about persuasion or conversion between two different paradigms or language games.

In developing the first, antifoundationalist claim, Rorty rejects the "specifically *transcendental* project—a project of answering some question of the form 'what are the conditions of the possibility of . . . ?'—of, for example, experience, self-consciousness, language or philosophy itself." Rorty admits "that asking and answering that question is, indeed, the mark of a distinct genre"—foundationalist philosophy—but argues that "it is a thoroughly self-deceptive question. The habit of posing it—asking for noncausal, nonempirical, nonhistorical conditions—is the distinctive feature" of the Kantian tradition. "The trouble with the question is that it looks like a 'scientific' one, as if we knew how to debate the relative merits of alternative answers, just as we know how to debate alternative answers to questions about the conditions for the *actuality* of various things (e.g., political changes, quasars, psychoses). But it is not" (210).

Instead of continuing the Kantian foundationalist tradition in philosophy, Rorty wants to redescribe the rhetorical strategies and purposes of this philosophical genre, abandon some of its projects, and move philosophy in a different direction with new self-definitions. As traditionally viewed within the genre, transcendental projects are treated as if one could argue over their alternative proposals in some common vocabulary:

If one thinks of writers like Hegel, Heidegger, and Derrida as digging down to successively deeper levels of noncausal conditions—as scientists dig down to ever deeper levels of causal conditions (molecules behind tables, atoms behind molecules, quarks behind atoms . . .)—then the hapless and tedious metaphilosophical question "How can we tell when we have hit bottom?" is bound to arise. More important, so will the question "Within what language are we to lay out arguments demonstrating (or even just making plausible) that we have *correctly* identified these conditions?" (212).

When and how can the philosophical conversation end and how could we recognize the conclusion? "The latter question causes no great embarrassment for physicists, since they can say in advance what they want to get out of their theorizing. But it *should* embarrass people concerned with the question of what *philosophical* vocabulary to use, rather than with the question of what vocabulary will help us accomplish some specific purpose (e.g., splitting the atom, curing cancer, persuading the populace)" (212). Rorty argues that there is no transcendental ground with a common vocabulary from which to carry out a comparison between theories of ontological conditions of possibility and that we should be thinking of vocabularies as tools to accomplish rhetorical purposes instead of searching for the ultimate vocabulary beyond all others.

The point of foundationalist philosophy is to end all conversation by proposing the final argument, the all-encompassing system, the ground of grounds. Some think Derrida has found this with notions like *différance,* but Rorty sees such notions as "merely abbreviations for the familiar Peircean-Wittgensteinian anti-Cartesian thesis that meaning is a function of context, and that there is no theoretical barrier to an endless sequence of recontextualizations" (212). That is, foundationalist theory (or any other kind) cannot guarantee an end to the sequence of counter-arguments. There is always the possibility of arguing against, of proposing new tropes, of offering a conflicting story, of putting forward a different context. Though, we might add, there is not always the probability that a particular rhetorical move of this kind will occur or will work within historically situated debates. Often a story becomes standard, an argument goes unchallenged, an ideology comes to dominate a historical community, and in those rhetorical contexts, the sequence of recontextualizations temporarily stops. Rorty's point is that no foundationalist theory can ever guarantee permanent closure to debate or ensure beforehand even a temporary consensus.

For Rorty, it would be better to redescribe transcendental philosophical projects not as making arguments that can be adjudicated in a common vocabulary but as proposing different worlds with different rhetorical structures. "For my purposes, the important place to draw a line is not between philosophy and non-philosophy but rather between topics which we know how to argue about and those we do not. It is the line between the attempt to be objective—to get a consensus on what we should believe—and a willingness to abandon consensus in the hope of transfiguration" (210). In distinguishing between "argumentative problem-solvers like Aristotle and Russell and oracular world-disclosers like Plato and Hegel" (211), Rorty seems to be making the rhetorical point that we should recognize a distinction between two uses of language: one (problem-solving) that argues among different positions with a common or overlapping vocabulary within the same (philosophical) world; and another (world-disclosing) that cannot argue across different worlds because there is not a common or significantly overlapping vocabulary and not enough shared argumentative criteria among the different (philosophical) positions, which themselves establish new vocabularies and criteria for problem solving.

This leads to the second point concerning the initial passage quoted above, which addresses the question of refuting versus forgetting previous beliefs in displacing an intellectual world. Rorty draws a distinction between the suitability of argumentation within paradigms and the unsuitability of argumentation between paradigms. We know how to argue within a paradigm, he says, but we do not know how to argue across different paradigms; and, further, argumentation is completely irrelevant to changing position from one paradigm to another. I think Rorty here overstates the rhetorical case. The conversion to a new paradigm is often dependent upon the weakening of the old, and the weakening of the old paradigm includes refutation through propositional argumentation. Indeed, the combination of refutation within an old vocabulary and the offering of an attractive new vocabulary is exactly what Rorty himself is so good at. His rhetorical strategies include both maneuvers.

Rorty at times seems to agree with this point when he writes: "Argumentation requires that the same vocabulary be used in premises and conclusions—that both be part of the same language-game. Hegelian *Aufhebung* is something quite different. It is what happens when we play elements of an old vocabulary off against each other in order to make us impatient for a new vocabulary. But that activity is quite different from playing old beliefs against other old beliefs in an attempt to see which survives. An existing language-game will provide 'standard rules' for the latter activity, but *nothing* could provide such rules for the former" (213). Rorty could be seen as describing here two kinds of propositional argumentation: One that argues for the self-contradiction, incoherence, or inadequacy of the old vocabulary (pushing us toward the new) and one that argues for one belief over the other within old vocabularies. It appears that Rorty wants to say that propositional argumentation applies only to the latter activity. But in both instances such argumentation is part of making a case: for a new world or an old belief. In each, argumentation is the means to a rhetorical end, not an end in itself.

Rorty could, I suppose, preserve his point by weakening his claim for a rigid distinction between the two rhetorical activities of problem solving within an old vocabulary and problem problematizing leading to a new vocabulary. That is, solving problems and disclosing a new world are two radically different rhetorical goals, but the means to achieve these goals can share rhetorical strategies, including propositional argumentation. But instead Rorty chooses to emphasize the rhetorical consequences of two very different kinds of philosophy: "We should . . . recognize that the writers usually identified as 'philosophers' include both argumentative problem-solvers like Aristotle and Russell and oracular world-disclosers like Plato and Hegel—both people good at rendering public accounts and people good at leaping in the dark" (211). And he goes on, "I object to the idea that one can be 'rigorous' if one's procedure [as world-discloser] consists in inventing new words for what one is pleased to call 'conditions of possibility' rather than playing sentences using old words off against each other. The latter activity is what I take to constitute argumentation. Poetic world-disclosers like Hegel, Heidegger and Derrida have to pay a price, and part of that price is the inappropriateness to their work of notions like 'argumentation' and 'rigor'" (211). Rorty agrees with Habermas in a "nominalist, Wittgensteinian rejection of the idea that one can be nonpropositional and still be argumentative" (212). Perhaps this is true, but one can be nonpropositional and still be persuasive or rhetorical.

We can end this gloss on Rorty's essay with another of his rhetorical pragmatist points: "The practice of playing sentences off against one another in order to decide what to believe—the practice of argumentation—no more requires a 'ground' than the practice of using one stone to chip pieces off another stone in order to make a spear-point" (217, n. 16). Similarly, we might say that interpretive arguments over texts need no general hermeneutic foundations, no theoretical description of interpretation in general that provides ahistorical prescriptions for achieving correct meanings. Interpretive arguments get their work done within the historical clash of opinion. Even from this brief sketch of Rorty's views and their implications, it is easy to see why rhetoricians in speech communication, literary studies, and other disciplines have cited his neopragmatism as further evidence of the (latest) return of rhetoric to the humanities.[21]

Rhetorical hermeneutics is the intersection of rhetorical pragmatism and cultural rhetoric studies. Just as rhetorical pragmatism rejects the notion of foundationalist philosophy, rhetorical hermeneutics attempts to move critical theory from general theories about the interpretive process to rhetorical histories of specific interpretive acts.[22] As hermeneutic theory becomes rhetorical history, the focus moves from pragmatist antifoundationalism to studies of cultural rhetoric. But in rhetorical hermeneutics the claim is that a rhetorical analysis of a particular historical act of interpretation *counts as* a specific piece of rhetorically pragmatic theorizing about interpretation. Thus, rhetorical hermeneutics uses rhetoric to practice theory by doing history.

Such a project takes an historical act of interpretation—for example, the Concord (Massachusetts) Library's banning of *Adventures of Huckleberry Finn* in March 1885—and attempts to do a rhetorical analysis of the cultural conversation in which that act participated. One might investigate why the issue of the "Negro Problem" played no role in the 1880s reception of Mark Twain's novel, a novel that twentieth-century readers have found deeply implicated in the cultural politics of race. How did Samuel Clemens's public persona as a humorist affect interpretations and evaluations of *Huckleberry Finn*; that is, in what way is any 1885 reading of the novel more significant as an event in the evolving cultural reception of Mark Twain than as a part of some purely literary reception of *Huckleberry Finn* (whatever that would mean)? How was the Concord Library committee's reading of the novel connected to debates over the "Bad Boy Boom" of the mid-1880s, anxieties over gang juvenile delinquency and the negative effects of reading crime stories and dime novels?[23] For rhetorical hermeneutics, this reception study provides an instance of interpretive theory as a form of rhetorical history. Unlike foundationalist theories, rhetorical hermeneutics focuses on the rhetorical histories of specific interpretive acts and makes no transcendental claims for its theoretical observations and the historical narratives it tells about interpretation.

OBJECTIONS TO RHETORICAL HERMENEUTICS

Every theory is defined quite specifically by the tropes and arguments it uses to state and defend its claims. Rhetorical hermeneutics is no exception. In this section I place the arguments of rhetorical hermeneutics in relation to those of its best critics as a way of further explaining its theoretical positions.

In "History and Epistemology: The Example of *The Turn of the Screw*," Paul Armstrong mounts a vigorous critique of rhetorical hermeneutics as part of his own proposed epistemology of interpretive conflict.[24] Armstrong begins by presenting a fair summary of the rhetorical turn in hermeneutics: "Some contemporary critics have suggested that history offers a way out of the impasses of epistemology. . . . [I]f the inability of epistemology to legislate correctness means that different communities can regard different kinds of argumentation as persuasive, then perhaps we should study concretely the various rhetorical practices in which interpreters have engaged instead of attempting to define absolutely what a right reading must look like. This maneuver would turn epistemology into a historical issue by asking how ways of seeing are institutionalized in discursive practices" (*Conflict* 89). So far so good. But then Armstrong adds that for such a theory "historical study seems to offer a means of avoiding irreconcilable epistemological disputes." Armstrong then (rightly) asserts his strong opposition to any "hope" that historical study represents a guaranteed solution to interpretive disagreement (*Conflict* 89–90).

The problem here is that Armstrong has confused foundationalist theories of knowledge (called collectively "epistemology") and historical claims about how knowledges are generated, contested, revised, etc. (generalizations we can call "epistemologies"). That is, rhetorical hermeneutics does call into question the usefulness of disputes within "epistemology" but then itself puts forward histories of conflicts among competing knowledge claims. Rhetorical hermeneutics avoids epistemological debates (e.g., between textual realism and readerly idealism) by setting their questions aside (e.g., refusing to ask "Does the text or the reader determine interpretation?"). But it does not try to avoid "irreconcilable epistemological disputes," as Armstrong asserts; rather, it attempts to take such historical disputes as a rhetorical focus of study. Again: rhetorical hermeneutics rejects foundationalist theories of epistemology which attempt to prescribe correct interpretations in general, but it does not avoid addressing historical debates over particular epistemic claims.

Armstrong similarly confuses foundationalist epistemology with historical epistemologies in his critique of Rorty's neopragmatism. Again he clearly summarizes his opponent's position: Rorty rejects philosophy as the "'most basic' discipline" whose responsibility it is to establish foundations for judging the knowledge-claims of other disciplines.[25] "In a multiple world of conflicting practices of thinking and speaking, it makes no sense to try to promulgate laws for how the mind should work, because to do so would be to propose only another manner of interpreting and talking about the world, not the way to end all ways. Consequently, Rorty advises, in order to come to grips with certain perpetually vexing philosophical problems, one should not try to develop an improved model of mind but should examine the historical record to see how they arose" (Conflict 92). Defining "epistemology" as the "project of learning more about what we could know and how we might know it better by studying how our mind worked,"[26] Rorty advocates the abandonment of epistemology as a philosophical project. Here Armstrong strongly disagrees, arguing that "Rorty's call for the demise of epistemology is self-contradictory because a theory of knowledge is implicit in his description of disciplines as diverse, changing conversations" (Conflict 92–93).

But again it is a question of what is meant by "epistemology" or "theories of knowledge." Rorty rejects foundationalist theory but not all reflection about knowledge claims. Indeed, as Armstrong points out, Rorty is constantly making rhetorical generalizations and telling conversational stories about how disciplines produce knowledge. Armstrong has simply missed Rorty's theoretical point. Another way of putting this: we can answer Armstrong's charge of self-contradiction against Rorty by using his own analysis of "theory," a term that has "a variety of meanings" (Conflict 91). Armstrong notes two current definitions: (1) "'theory' as the general activity of reflecting on the characteristics of literature and the implications of critical practice" and (2) "local 'theories' about the assumptions and aims that should guide interpretation" (Conflict 91). The first kind of theory gives us descriptions and the second prescriptions. What Armstrong does not mention is that foundationalist theory (including epistemology) combines these two forms: it attempts to move from general descriptions to specific prescriptions, for example, from how the interpretive process works in general to how it should work in particular to produce correct interpretations. Rorty does not reject theory as reflection on practice, but he does advocate abandoning foundationalist theory in philosophy (epistemology). Thus, Rorty's call for "the demise of [foundationalist] epistemology" does not contradict his continuing concern with questions of knowledge production, his continuing theoretical reflection on the rhetorical practices of disciplines.

I should note, however, that for Rorty "reflection" is a problematic term for characterizing the kind of philosophy he advocates. He writes that "in its unobjectionable sense, 'theory' just means 'philosophy.' One can still have philosophy even after one stops arguing deductively and ceases to ask where the first principles are coming from." That is, even when one rejects foundationalist theory— "the attempt to get outside practice and regulate it" from the ground of transcendental first principles—one can continue to do a form of theory. "I take 'literary theory,' as the term is currently used in America, to be a species of philosophy, an attempt to weave together some texts traditionally labeled 'philosophical' with other texts not so labeled," e.g., poems, novels, literary criticism.[27] Rorty resists characterizing this as a reflective practice, arguing that this philosophical activity "is not exactly what Mailloux calls 'metapractice (practice about practice),' for that term suggests a vertical relationship, in which some practices are at higher levels than others."[28]

Indeed, I would argue (and would seem to agree more with Armstrong than Rorty here) that in certain rhetorical situations, particular practices are on a "higher level" both in the sense that the topic of one practice can be another practice (interpretive disputes as the topic for theoretical practices such as rhetorical hermeneutics and epistemologies of interpretive conflict) *and* in the sense that at particular historical moments certain practices are privileged over others. Perhaps this is just to argue that the trope of spatial levels is still useful in characterizing the rhetorical activity of theoretical practice despite its traditional associations with foundationalist theory.

But in Armstrong's critique there are theoretical issues at stake more significant than whether he understands Rorty's view of epistemology or whether he agrees with my characterization of theory as practice about practice. These issues involve what Armstrong takes to be the major failing of Rorty's neopragmatism and my rhetorical hermeneutics. One issue concerns his questions: "Are there no 'enduring constraints on what can count as knowledge' (*Mirror* 9), as [Rorty] argues, or are there transhistorical tests for validity? Is it sufficient to regard interpretive standards as totally internal to the community, or should we preserve some notion of otherness as the object to which interpreters are responsible and at which their various conversations aim, even if this otherness can vary radically according to how it is construed?" (*Conflict* 93).

To answer these questions, Armstrong does a reception history of Henry James's *Turn of the Screw*. This move from theory to history is exactly what a rhetorical hermeneutics advocates, but Armstrong somehow believes his study refutes rhetorical hermeneutics and rhetorical pragmatism more generally. There are several reasons for this (I think) mistaken conclusion. Armstrong seems to reject Rorty's attack on epistemology at least partly because it entails a theoretical displacement of the confrontation model of subject and object with a conversation model of disputes among reading subjects. Armstrong agrees that "accurate representation" is not useful as a model for describing understanding and sees as more useful a notion of "variable conversations concerned with shifting, often incommensurable problems" for explaining the reception of James's story. However, he argues that the "history of this work shows as well that the process of validation has certain constant forms across different communities and that validation cannot be collapsed into social agreement because it entails a *responsibility to otherness*" (*Conflict* 93, my emphasis). He implies that Rorty overemphasizes conversation and social agreement to such an extent that he loses all "transhistorical tests for validity" such as "a responsibility to otherness."

But rhetorical pragmatism claims that interpretive disputes and social agreements (and disagreements) are *about* otherness—of texts, of disputants, of cultures. A rhetorical hermeneutics, for instance, argues that in most cases of literary reception, each of the disputants is holding the other responsible to the text; it is just that, as Armstrong himself admits, what counts as a relevant or significant part of the text is exactly what is under dispute. "Attempts to mediate or resolve such conflicts by pointing to what is really there in the text extend the debate instead of stopping it" (*Conflict* 94).

But this rhetorical point can also be applied to the question of a text's "otherness" or difference. That otherness cannot serve as a transhistorical test for interpretive validity when the makeup of the text, its identifiable otherness, and responsibility to that difference are all more or less at stake in particular historical debates over a text's interpretation. It is not that rhetorical pragmatism denies the relevance of a text's otherness to an interpretive debate; it is just that often otherness or difference is exactly what the debate is about and thus it cannot be a "transhistorical test" of a particular side's interpretive claims. This is not to say that charging your opponent with failing to respect the text's otherness might not be a very effective rhetorical strategy. It is to say that such a charge must be made to stick in a particular rhetorical context. Respecting difference is a historically specific activity quite relevant to interpretive disputes over texts today, and thus any rhetorical analysis of how contemporary textual interpretation functions must take such a factor into account.

Armstrong provides some insightful comments on the rhetoric of interpretive disputes in his reception analysis of *The Turn of the Screw*. He notes how "if, as Rorty claims, different partners in a discussion may not see eye to eye because they are concerned about different problems, such divergences occur because the interpreters have conflicting beliefs about what the object is and how best to engage it" (*Conflict* 95). In another place he observes, "An antagonist in hermeneutic conflict not only has the option of questioning the opposing community's assumptions and procedures but also may attempt to create embarrassing anomalies for it by pointing to textual details that its readings have not yet accounted for. On the other hand, however, these details are not simply empirical facts, for an interpreter may defend the validity of his or her reading by assimilating anomalous evidence through ingenious hypotheses that the opponent refuses to accept" (*Conflict* 99). Armstrong makes these and other useful theoretical/historical observations in the course of his reception study of *The Turn of the Screw* and thus provides a skillful example of using rhetoric to practice theory by doing history; that is, his study is a convincing instance of rhetorical hermeneutics.

Yet Armstrong takes his history and commentary to be a refutation, not a confirmation of rhetorical hermeneutics. Why? Again the problem is partly a matter of definition: Armstrong takes my agreement with Rorty to mean an abandonment of all historical, epistemological questions rather than a plea for setting aside the foundationalist questions of epistemology. But our differences (misunderstandings?) go deeper than assumed definitions. As Armstrong notes, a rhetorical hermeneutics proposes that "the way to answer the realist/idealist question 'Is meaning created by the text or by the reader or by both?' is simply not to ask it."[29] Against this view, Armstrong argues, "The dispute about *The Turn of the Screw* suggests that the 'realist/idealist question' cannot be bypassed in the history of reception but turns up there again when critics with incompatible beliefs give incommensurable readings to 'the facts of the text'" (*Conflict* 101).

However, again, Armstrong has missed my point if he thinks I disagree with him. I am certainly not saying that "realist" and "idealist" theories of interpretation never play a role in specific historical debates over texts (they do), nor am I saying that as an historian I won't be pointing to texts and assumptions as a way of telling a story about a text's reception and the debates that make it up. It is just that talking about a critic who appeals to foundationalist theories is not an instance of *doing* foundationalist theory. And to argue a specific history for a text's reception or to suggest tips on how to do such histories is not to put forward a realist or idealist epistemology. A rhetorician has no problem with arguing about facts and for heuristics, as long as "facts" are not taken to be noninterpretive givens and as long as "rules" are only seen as proposals to "try doing it this way." To bypass the "realist/idealist question" means simply to refrain from doing foundationalist epistemology.[30]

But in doing historical reception studies, does rhetorical hermeneutics claim to escape the historical problem of its own rhetorical situation? Is rhetorical hermeneutics guilty of ignoring its *own* history and rhetoric when it describes a particular example of interpretive conflict over a particular text? This seems to be what Armstrong suggests when he follows his description of rhetorical hermeneutics with objections that history "does not provide a neutral ground" and that history is itself a "hermeneutic construct" (*Conflict* 90). Is he implying that rhetorical hermeneutics denies these claims? But how could it? Rhetorical hermeneutics rejects foundationalist theory precisely because that theory attempts to place itself outside history and rhetoric in order to describe and prescribe interpretation in general. Any theoretical practice (including rhetorical hermeneutics) is within history as it reflects upon history, within rhetoric as it tropes and argues over interpretations and their histories. There is no ahistorical, nonrhetorical "neutral ground" from which historical arguments can be made. My history of *Huckleberry Finn*'s 1885 reception is an interpretive argument made within the rhetorical situation of the 1980s. It would be self-contradictory for a rhetorician to claim otherwise.

And this same rhetorical, historical embeddedness holds true for the therapeutic *theoretical* claims I am making as well. Another critic, Dieter Freundlieb, takes me to task when I propose that "textual realism" and "readerly idealism" have led to dead ends in epistemology and when I suggest a rhetorical turn to history be taken instead. He writes: "Mailloux thinks he can simply describe the institutional history of literary criticism and explain why realism and idealism seemed attractive to those who subscribed to them without himself engaging in any questions of epistemological validity. The philosophical naivety of Mailloux's move is astounding. He believes that normative questions of historical accuracy and interpretive validity can be dealt with adequately by adopting the position of the epistemologically disengaged historian who can discuss these issues as purely rhetorical moves in a sequence of factual events."[31] Astounding or not, the claim of rhetorical hermeneutics is that there are no standards for "epistemological validity" available if by "standards" one means the ahistorical criteria proposed by various realisms and idealisms throughout the history of epistemology. There are, of course, historically specific "standards" (traditions for argumentative appeal) accepted within particular communities, disciplines, discourses, and so on, but these are local, contingent, rhetorical constructs, which have all the force of such constructs, which is all the force needed for interpretive debate and knowledge production to take place.[32]

But, again, the claim here is not that rhetorical hermeneutics assumes an "epistemologically disengaged historian" even when the rhetorical historian is telling an institutional story about literary criticism and its relevant hermeneutic theories. Such stories are always told by an "engaged" historian—that is, an historian embedded, in this case, in the very history he is attempting to articulate. The only "disengagement" is with the foundationalist questions of epistemology, *not* with the history of interpretive disputes, conflicting theoretical arguments, and changing epistemological assumptions. Thus, rhetorical historians must take all of these into account even as they realize (and at certain moments foreground) their own rhetorical situations in writing the histories they write. Freundlieb is correct in his speculation that I assume my own institutional story of the old New Criticism is "nothing but further rhetoric" (838). But for a practitioner of rhetorical hermeneutics to accept this characterization (without the derogatory "nothing but") is not the fatal admission Freundlieb takes it to be. Rather it is the simple conclusion that follows from taking seriously that there is no escape from rhetoric and history into some transcendental realm from which the past can be heard speaking itself through a chronicler beyond all rhetoric.

Though I argue that it is desirable to use rhetoric to practice theory by doing history, I am not claiming that theory and history never form part of separate disciplinary language games. Contemporary theory, as metapractice about practice, continues philosophical arguments with long traditions. Giles Gunn, a fellow pragmatist, raises one such argument in challenging me to define more clearly the hermeneutic relation between past and present:

> The main issue for interpretation, it seems to me, has to do with the density and opacity of that dimension known as the historical, a density and opacity which involves at the very least, I would think, some sort of interpretive traffic—if not, in addition, some kinds of interpretive negotiations—between our by-whatever-means excavated and reconstructed sense of that prior historical moment and our by-whatever-means intuited and elaborated sense of our own contemporary moment.[33]

I am taken with Gunn's metaphors of interpretive traffic and negotiation between past and present. In one pragmatic sense, this traffic always goes on no matter what; it defines doing history as such and describes the dynamic but delimited process during which new truth is established about past, present, or future. As James puts it, "New truth is always a go-between, a smoother-over of transitions. It marries old opinion to new fact so as ever to show a minimum of jolt, a maximum of continuity."[34] Historical truth results from a requisite traffic between old opinion and new experiences: facts, desires, contradictions, reflections, and so forth. This formulation might not at first seem to coincide with what Gunn means by traffic between past and present, but I suggest returning to his carefully chosen phrases quoted above: he refers to traffic and negotiation "between our by-whatever-means excavated and reconstructed sense of that prior historical moment and our by-whatever-means intuited and elaborated sense of our own contemporary moment." True to our shared pragmatist premises, Gunn here makes no suggestion of some raw and unmediated past or some pure and immediate present that carry on an exchange. Thus, I think he might accept my theoretical restatement of his point. But if he does, then it seems that I cannot help but do history the way he recommends. That is, his prescription of what should be done turns into a description of what's always done.

However, there is another sense in which the past and present can be negotiated: when an interpreter explicitly compares past and present meanings, for example, the readings of *Huckleberry Finn* made in 1885 and 1995. Gunn raises the issue of relativism precisely in relation to this problem of evaluative comparison. Rhetorical hermeneutics, Gunn argues, associates "with a view of experience that, while acknowledging the historicity of all interpretive acts, including its own, in effect denies the possibility of critically comparing and evaluating them. We are thus left hermeneutically with the spectacle of history as a conflict (where there isn't a consensus) of interpretations among which it is impossible, from what I can tell, to adjudicate." I wish to disassociate rhetorical hermeneutics from at least certain versions of this relativism and claim instead that interpreters can make valid comparisons and evaluate which reading is a more persuasive interpretation of the text in question. Not only do I believe in the superiority of my reading of the rhetorical context of *Huckleberry Finn's* reception, I also think my own interpretation of *Huckleberry Finn* (in chapter 3 of *Rhetorical Power*) is a correct reading of the novel. I can thus say that, though I understand why certain 1885 readers could read the novel as being primarily or most significantly about bad boys (i.e., I am persuaded by my historical explanation), I believe *Huckleberry Finn* is more importantly about race relations in post-Reconstruction America (i.e, I am persuaded by my textual reading). A rhetorical hermeneutics simply acknowledges that such evaluations take place within present assumptions and practices; yet this recognition does not change one's belief in the truth of one's own historical and textual interpretations.

Now, such rhetorical pragmatist claims about our hermeneutic situation do not mean that we are somehow trapped once and for all within an unchanging web of present beliefs and practices. It's just that past events, including rhetorical acts, can only be encountered in our present. James articulates the implications of this pragmatist truth for doing explanations in general: Any new idea adopted as the true one "preserves the older stock of truths with a minimum of modification, stretching them just enough to make them admit the novelty, but conceiving that in ways as familiar as the case leaves possible. An *outrée* explanation, violating all our preconceptions, would never pass for a true account of a novelty" (*Pragmatism* 35). Again, this does not mean change is impossible, only that it is evolutionary, not revolutionary. Explaining the past, interpreting texts, talking with other people: all these rhetorical activities can have significant consequences for a particular person or group; but "the most violent revolutions in an individual's beliefs leave most of his [or her] old order standing" (*Pragmatism* 35). Rhetorical hermeneutics attempts to chart specific historical instances of how these changes take place through reading and to have these explanations and their implications count as instances of hermeneutic theorizing.

NOTES

1. *Oxford Latin Dictionary*, ed. P. G. W. Glare (Oxford, 1982), p. 947.
2. See my *Interpretive Conventions: The Reader in the Study of American Fiction* (Ithaca, 1982), p. 144.
3. For the biblical story and its exegesis, see "The Book of Daniel" in George A. Buttrick et al., eds., *The Interpreter's Bible* (New York, 1956), vol. 6, pp. 418–33.
4. For the texts of Dickinson's poems quoted in this chapter, see *The Poems of Emily Dickinson*, ed. Thomas H. Johnson, 3 vols. (Cambridge, Mass., 1958). On the Lothrop trial, see Jay Leyda, *The Years and Hours of Emily Dickinson* (New Haven, 1960), vol. 2, esp. pp. 245–50, 257–59, 310.
5. On formalist and intentionalist theories, see Section II of Sanford Levinson and Steven Mailloux, eds., *Interpreting Law and Literature* (Evanston, Ill., 1988), esp. pp. 37–42.
6. Tom Rockmore provides a working definition of "foundationalism" and usefully unpacks its constitutive tropes: "Foundationalism" refers to "the assumption that 'there are secure foundations, that is a firm, unshakable basis, on which to erect any edifice of knowledge.' Knowledge, from this angle of vision, is understood as like a building or structure that reposes directly on a conceptual underpinning. For both a building and the theory of knowledge, if the underpinnings of the edifice can be made secure, then nothing can shake the higher stories" (Rockmore, introduction to *Antifoundationalism Old and New*, ed. Rockmore and Beth J. Singer [Philadelphia, 1992], p. 6). For other recent accounts of foundationalism and antifoundationalism, see Evan Simpson, ed., *Anti-Foundationalism and Practical Reasoning: Conversations between Hermeneutics and Analysis* (Edmonton, Alta., 1987); my *Rhetorical Power* (Ithaca, 1989), chap. 1; and Hugh J. Silverman, ed., *Questioning Foundations: Truth/Subjectivity/Culture* (New York, 1993).
7. See Jonathan Culler, *Structuralist Poetics* (Ithaca, 1975); Mailloux, *Interpretive Conventions*; and Peter J. Rabinowitz, *Before Reading: Narrative Conventions and the Politics of Interpretation* (Ithaca, 1987).
8. Herbert Wechsler, "Toward Neutral Principles of Constitutional Law," *Harvard Law Review* 73 (1959): 1–35.
9. Mark Twain, *Adventures of Huckleberry Finn*, ed. Walter Blair and Victor Fischer (Berkeley, Calif., 1985), pp. 104–5. See my *Rhetorical Power*, chap. 3, for an extended rhetorical analysis of Twain's novel as an ideological performance within post-Reconstruction debates over "the Negro problem"; also see Peter Messent, "Racial Politics in *Huckleberry Finn*," chap. 5 of his *Mark Twain* (New York, 1997), pp. 86–109.
10. William Graham, *The Contrast; or, The Bible and Abolitionism: An Exegetical Argument* (Cincinnati, 1844), pp. 39–40.
11. See my *Rhetorical Power*, "Conclusion: The ABM Treaty Interpretation Dispute."
12. I return here to the definition of "interpretation" presented in Chap. 1 [of *Reception Histories*] —"the practice of establishing textual meaning"—and note again that I am using the term "hermeneutics" in its broad sense to refer to "theories of interpretation." A powerful influence on recent hermeneutics has been the German hermeneutical tradition, ably described in Richard E. Palmer, *Hermeneutics: Interpretation Theory in Schleiermacher, Dilthey, Heidegger, and Gadamer* (Evanston, Ill., 1969). Also, working within Heideggerian hermeneutics and very influential on my own rhetorical hermeneutics is Hubert L. Dreyfus, *What Computers Can't Do: The Limits of Artificial Intelligence*, rev. ed. (New York, 1979); also see Dreyfus and Paul Rabinow, *Michel Foucault: Beyond Structuralism and Hermeneutics*, 2d ed. (Chicago, 1983). For several more recent discussions of topics related to rhetorical hermeneutics, see George Pullman, ed., "Reconfiguring the Relation of Rhetoric/Hermeneutics," special issue of *Studies in the Literary Imagination* 28 (fall 1995); and Walter Jost and Michael J. Hyde, eds., *Rhetoric and Hermeneutics in Our Time* (New Haven, Conn., 1997).
13. Richard Johnson, "What Is Cultural Studies Anyway?" *Social Text*, no. 16 (winter 1986/87): 38, 43.
14. Vincent B. Leitch, *American Literary Criticism from the Thirties to the Eighties* (New York, 1988), p. 404. For other overviews of cultural studies in the 1980s, see Judith Newton and

Deborah Rosenfelt, eds., *Feminist Criticism and Social Change: Sex, Class, and Race in Literature and Culture* (New York, 1985); Tania Modleski, ed., *Studies in Entertainment: Critical Approaches to Mass Culture* (Bloomington, Ind., 1986); Cary Nelson and Lawrence Grossberg, eds., *Marxism and the Interpretation of Culture* (Urbana, Ill., 1988); Lynn Hunt, ed., *The New Cultural History* (Berkeley, Calif., 1989); H. Aram Veeser, ed., *The New Historicism* (New York, 1989); and Patrick Brantlinger, *Crusoe's Footprints: Cultural Studies in Britain and America* (New York, 1990).

15. For full descriptions of these courses and the ETS major, see *The English Newsletter: Undergraduate News from the English Department, Syracuse University* 1, no. 1 (March 1990) and no. 2 (November 1990). I discuss the production and reception of this major in Chap. 7 [*of Reception Histories*].

16. Mailloux, *Rhetorical Power*, p. 165.

17. See Chap. 6 [in *Reception Histories*] . . . on the cultural rhetoric of "eating books" and (mis) using fiction. There are many related examples of rhetorically oriented cultural studies in such disciplines as symbolic anthropology, speech communication, cultural history, and interpretive sociology, and one could cite a growing number of proposals and examples of related approaches from contemporary literary studies influenced by poststructuralist theory. The genealogies of Michel Foucault and Edward Said stand behind some of the most interesting studies of cultural rhetoric—see Foucault, *Discipline and Punish: The Birth of the Prison*, trans. Alan Sheridan (New York, 1977), and *Power/Knowledge: Selected Interviews and Other Writings, 1972–1977*, ed. Colin Gordon (New York, 1980); Said, *Orientalism* (New York, 1978), and *The World, the Text, and the Critic* (Cambridge, Mass., 1983); and my *Rhetorical Power*, chap. 5. And, of course, there's always Kenneth Burke; for a useful recent collection, see Burke, *On Symbols and Society*, ed. Joseph R. Gusfield (Chicago, 1989). For additional bibliography and discussion, see Thomas Rosteck, "Cultural Studies and Rhetorical Studies," *Quarterly Journal of Speech* 81 (August 1995): 386–421; and Rosteck, ed., *At the Intersection: Cultural Studies and Rhetorical Studies* (New York, 1998).

18. Mailloux, *Rhetorical Power*, p. xii.

19. See Richard Rorty, *Philosophy and the Mirror of Nature* (Princeton, 1979); and for recent commentary and detailed bibliographies, see Alan R. Malachowski, ed., *Reading Rorty: Critical Responses to "Philosophy and the Mirror of Nature" (and Beyond)* (Oxford, 1990), and Herman J. Saatkamp, Jr., ed., *Rorty and Pragmatism: The Philosopher Responds to His Critics* (Nashville, 1995).

20. Rorty, "Is Derrida a Transcendental Philosopher?" *Yale Journal of Criticism* 2 (spring 1989): 208–9; further references to this essay are given in the text.

21. See, for example, Janet Horne, "Rhetoric after Rorty," *Western Journal of Speech Communication* 53 (summer 1989): 247–59; Robert E. Smith III, "Reconsidering Richard Rorty," *Rhetoric Society Quarterly* 19 (fall 1989): 349–64; John Trimbur and Mara Holt, "Richard Rorty: Philosophy without Foundations," in *The Philosophy of Discourse: The Rhetorical Turn in Twentieth-Century Thought*, ed. Chip Sills and George H. Jensen (Portsmouth, N.H., 1992), vol. 1, pp. 70–94; and essays in Steven Mailloux, ed., *Rhetoric, Sophistry, Pragmatism* (Cambridge, 1995). My own rhetorical pragmatism has been significantly influenced by the work of Stanley Fish, Walter Michaels, and Steven Knapp. See my *Rhetorical Power*, chap. 6; Fish, *Doing What Comes Naturally: Change, Rhetoric, and the Practice of Theory in Literary and Legal Studies* (Durham, N.C., 1989); and W. J. T. Mitchell, ed., *Against Theory: Literary Studies and the New Pragmatism* (Chicago, 1985).

22. I will not here analyze in detail the historical connections between epistemology (theories of knowledge) and hermeneutics (theories of interpretation), but only say that the two enterprises have traditionally figured their projects in structurally similar ways and have developed analogous arguments within their theoretical debates; for example, both enterprises ask theoretical questions about a relation between subjects and objects (knower and world, reader and text), have proposed variations on realist and idealist answers to these questions, and have framed those answers in similar vocabularies of conditions or constraints (in terms, for example, of what counts as true knowledge about reality or what counts as a correct inter-

pretation of a text). For hermeneutic treatments of the relation between knowledge and interpretation, see Hans-Georg Gadamer, *Truth and Method*, 2d ed., rev. trans. Joel Weinsheimer and Donald G. Marshall (New York, 1989), pp. 220–24, 254–64, 505–6; and E. D. Hirsch, Jr., *The Aims of Interpretation* (Chicago, 1976), pp. 146–58. Also see debates in epistemic rhetoric: Robert L. Scott, "On Viewing Rhetoric as Epistemic: Ten Years Later," *Central States Speech Journal* 27 (winter 1976): 258–66; Richard A. Cherwitz and James W. Hikins, *Communication and Knowledge: An Investigation in Rhetorical Epistemology* (Columbia, S.C., 1986); and Robert L. Scott, "Rhetoric Is Epistemic: What Difference Does That Make?" in *Defining the New Rhetorics*, ed. Theresa Enos and Stuart C. Brown (Newbury Park, Calif., 1993), pp. 120–36. Recent obituaries for epistemic rhetoric strike me as a bit premature.

23. See my *Rhetorical Power*, chap. 4. For a rhetorical analysis of the novel's later reception history, see Jonathan Arac, *"Huckleberry Finn" as Idol and Target: The Functions of Criticism in Our Time* (Madison, Wis., 1997).

24. Paul B. Armstrong, "History and Epistemology: The Example of *The Turn of the Screw*," *New Literary History* 19 (winter 1988): 693–712; rpt. Armstrong, *Conflicting Readings: Variety and Validity in Interpretation* (Chapel Hill, N.C., 1990), pp. 89–108. Further references are to the book version, cited as *Conflict* in the main text.

25. Rorty, *Philosophy and the Mirror of Nature*, p. 132.

26. Rorty, *Philosophy and the Mirror of Nature*, p. 137, quoted in Armstrong, *Conflict*, p. 92.

27. Rorty, "Philosophy without Principles," in Mitchell, *Against Theory*, p. 136.

28. Rorty, "Philosophy without Principles," p. 136; quoting Mailloux, "Truth or Consequences: On Being Against Theory," in Mitchell, *Against Theory*, p. 71.

29. Mailloux, "Rhetorical Hermeneutics," *Critical Inquiry* 11 (1985): 628; rev. and rpt. in Mailloux, *Rhetorical Power*, p. 14; quoted by Armstrong, *Conflict*, p. 100.

30. See my "The Turns of Reader-Response Criticism," in *Conversations: Contemporary Critical Theory and the Teaching of Literature*, ed. Charles Moran and Elizabeth F. Penfield (Urbana, Ill., 1990), pp. 38–54.

31. Dieter Freundlieb, "Semiotic Idealism," *Poetics Today* 9, no. 4 (1988): 837; further references are in the text.

32. This is, of course, the rhetorical lesson many readers take from Thomas S. Kuhn, *The Structure of Scientific Revolutions*, 2d ed. (Chicago, 1970).

33. Giles Gunn, "Approaching the Historical" in *Reconceptualizing American Literary/Cultural Studies: Rhetoric, History, and Politics in the Humanities*, ed. William E. Cain (New York, 1996), p. 60.

34. William James, *Pragmatism: A New Name for Some Old Ways of Thinking* (1907; rpt. Cambridge, Mass., 1975), p. 35.

TONY BENNETT

TEXTS IN HISTORY: THE
DETERMINATIONS OF READINGS
AND THEIR TEXTS

I

While the issues I want to address fit into the general set of concerns of "poststructuralism and history," it is clear that one ought to be speaking about *poststructuralisms*, since more than one variety of the beast has been in evidence over the past few years. For the greater part, "poststructuralism" has been equated with the work of Derrida or, more generally, with the ever mobile and flexible strategy of deconstruction. While not entirely shifting this center of gravity, my concerns tend rather in the direction of a poststructuralist Marxism. I mean, by this, a Marxism that comes after structuralism, that is responsive to its criticisms—and, indeed, to those of other poststructuralisms—and that seeks to take account of them in reformulating its theoretical objectives and the means by which it should both represent and pursue them.

I also want slightly to tilt the balance of the discussion of "poststructuralism and history" in another respect. So far, poststructuralism has been posed largely as a set of tendencies both inimical to Marxism and problematic for it, in the sense of its calling into question a good many of its founding premises and theoretical procedures. That is obviously right insofar as the major currents of interaction between the two traditions are concerned. Still, it seems to me to be misleading in at least two respects. First, it tends to neglect the degree to which the antimetaphysical and de-essentializing orientation of poststructuralist deconstruction has been paralleled by—in turn fuelling and being fuelled by—related tendencies within Marxism. Admittedly, this has often resulted in forms of Marxism that have been so thoroughly revised theoretically that they bear scarcely any recognizable relationship to their classical antecedents. This need not in itself, however, occasion any embarrassment. It is only by being ongoingly revised that a body of theory retains any validity or purchase as a historical force. To construe the relations between the formulations of classical Marxism and those which have been developed in the wake of structuralism as if the latter could be assessed in terms of the degree of their fidelity to or compatibility with the former would be unduly restricting. That way, a body of theory could never be allowed to develop other than by means of the germination of the seeds of development sown during the crystallizing phase of its inception—a profoundly unhistorical conception of the ways in which theoretical ideologies are adapted to changing theoretical and political circumstances. Rather than testing the value of theoretical innnovations by means of such backward-looking glances, the acid test should always be: What do they enable one to do? What possibilities do they open up that were not there beforehand? What new fields and types of action do they generate?

It is in view of considerations of this kind that the construction of relations of *necessary opposition* between poststructuralism and Marxism is not only misleading but also counterproductive. This is not to suggest that Marxism could, or even should, want to ingest deconstruction wholesale. Yet it is to suggest that poststructuralism confronts Marxism not just with a series of negative problems (although it does that), but also with a field of positive possibilities. Secondly, therefore, I want to suggest that, through a critical sifting of the diverse elements of poststructuralism, Marxism may be able to reformulate its problems and objectives, not because it has to in order, so to speak, to keep its theoretical credentials in good condition, but because, by doing so, it may open itself into a differently constituted field of political possibilities. Such "revisionism," that is to say, may contribute to the urgent task of rethinking Marxism's conception of its relationship to the spheres of political action that it constitutes for itself and of the strategies by which it seeks to intervene within them.

I want, then, to consider the relations between poststructuralism, as a general tendency, and poststructuralist Marxism largely in their potentially positive aspects. First, however, some brief comments on those aspects of poststructuralism that widely have been regarded as posing a series of negative problems for Marxism. What are these problems? "The work of Derrida and others," Terry Eagleton has argued, has " . . . cast grave doubt upon the classical notions of truth, reality, meaning and knowledge, all of which could be exposed as resting on a naively representational theory of language."[1] Why is this a problem? (The question is rarely put, but it is well worth asking.) The reason that it has been *felt* to be a problem—indeed, has sometimes been conceived and, very often, has been perceived as an explicit challenge to Marxism—is that it calls into doubt all those mechanisms (theories of knowledge; metaphysical conceptions of meaning; eschatological or historicist versions of History) that purport to provide a warrant, a certainty of rightness (epistemological, ethical or historical), in the light of which our orientation to and practice within the present might be validated, secured in—and by means of—some set of criteria that transcends our local, limited, and irremediably muddied calculations.

Obviously, acceptance of such criticisms entails that Marxists should critically review all those economistic, scientistic, and historicist conceptions by means of which Marxism has traditionally sought to supply itself with such warrants. Yet need this be a problem? Again, the question is worth asking, if only because the major theoretical developments within Marxism over the past two decades have been pushing in precisely this direction. It is singularly odd to expect that Marxists should feel placed on the defensive by the "discovery" that there neither are, nor can be, any transcendental guarantees, any absolute certainties, or any essential truths since, in recent years, they have devoted some considerable effort to expunging from Marxist thought precisely such residues of nineteenth-century theologies, philosophies of history, or ideologies of science. Nor has this been a process of theoretical self-criticism undertaken purely for its own sake. Such essentializing tendencies have been opposed, above all, because of their political effects—the quietism produced by the scientism of the Second International, for example, or the class essentialism that informed the political strategies of the Third International.

To the degree that such tendencies within Marxism have proved politically unhelpful, the only fitting Marxist response to the discovery that there can be no transcendental guarantees is: who needs them, anyway? If it is further argued that Marxism cannot secure its own relation to reality as a knowledge relation, if it must accept its own discursivity and acknowledge that it is submitted to the effects of language and writing: so be it! How could it be otherwise? Still, such acceptance should be accompanied by a demand: that deconstruction prove its worth by showing that it can do more than to stand on the side-lines and undermine the terms in which every and any body of theory constructs itself. To argue that Marxism "is shot through with metaphors disguised as concepts," or that it is dependent on a whole battery of rhetorical and figurative devices, is all very well but, in itself, hardly matters a jot.[2] What would matter, what would count as helpful, would be to show that the existing stock of metaphorical, rhetorical, and figurative devices used in Marxism had disabling theoretical and political consequences that could be remedied by the use of another set of similar devices. If this is not the point at issue, then deconstruction seems likely to do no more than to lock itself into a historical *cul-de-sac* in which it keeps alive the demand for transcendence simply by never-endingly denying its possibility—a criticism of essentialism that can rapidly become a lament for its loss, a consolation for the limitations of the human condition that is simultaneously a recipe for political quietism.

To put this another way, it has been argued that one of the major critical effects of deconstruction consists in the claim: "There is no metalanguage."[3] That is not true of course. If by "metalanguage" is meant a language that constitutes other languages or discourses as objects of analysis within itself, then the world is full of them. What, then, does this claim amount to? Simply that there is no metametalanguage, no language which can claim an absolute or transcendental validity for its ways of "fixing" other languages, discourses, or texts as objects within itself, or which can efface the traces of writing or language within itself. Fine. God is dead, and there is no such thing as an Absolute Science that escapes the constraints of its own discursivity. Meanwhile, the struggle between metalanguages—the struggle as to which discursive framing of other discourses is to predominate—continues. What matters for Marxism, as a party to such struggles, is not that it should be able to secure *absolutely* its discursive construction of the "real" and its framing of other texts and discourses within that "real"; rather, it is a matter of securing such constructions and framings *politically* in the sense of making them count above contending ones in terms of their ability to organize the consciousness and practice of historical agents.

If it is objected—"But what can the justification for such a practice be?"—the answer must be, "None," if it is a case of looking for absolute justifications, be they epistemological, ethical, or historical. In *Language, Semantics and Ideology*, Michel Pêcheux tells the story of Baron von Munchausen, who rode into a bog only to extricate himself from this predicament by dragging himself—and his horse—out "by pulling with all the strength of one arm on a lock of my own hair."[4] Pêcheux

likens this to the way in which an individual, in being hitched into a subject position within ideology, is also subjected to a "phantasy effect" whereby, once in place,
such a subject represents himself to himself as "cause of himself."[5] While I intend
the argument only analogically, it seems to me that socialism can extricate itself
from the mire of an epistemological and ethical relativism only by yanking itself
out by means of a political desire that functions as cause and justification of itself
(although, of course, produced by and within the complex play of social forces and
relationships) and that supplies the criteria—always contested—for the determination of the ends to which political and theoretical practice are directed. If that is
not felt to be enough, I would ask: what other foundation could there be that is not
a demand for transcendence and that—in order to preserve things as they are—
simultaneously denies the possibility that such a demand might ever be realized?

II

The issues I want now to consider, in the context of these more general problems,
concern the ways in which, if at all, texts either can or should be constituted as
objects of analysis within a Marxist framework. I shall do so by considering the
work of Ernesto Laclau who, perhaps more probingly than anyone else, has sought
to reformulate the concerns of Marxism in requiring it to acknowledge and accept
the consequences of its own discursivity. The spirit in which he has done so, however, has been consistently positive and political. Whereas Christopher Norris, for
example, sees in deconstruction merely a negative challenge to Marxism, particularly to the attempt to constitute the literary text as the object of its scientific
knowledge, Laclau translates this challenge into a positive means of expanding
Marxism's field of political possibilities.

I should say straightaway, in case the "if at all" above seems gratuitously polemical, that it is clear that Marxism is and cannot but be concerned with the analysis
of textual phenomena. The issues I want to explore concern the means by which
Marxism should represent to itself its relationship to the texts with which it
engages and the political issues which hinge on such considerations. Laclau enormously expands the significance of these problems in arguing, in fact, that
Marxism is concerned with little else other than textual phenomena in the sense
that even its primary object—the prevailing system of economic and social relationships—is constituted entirely within discourses whose conditions of existence
are largely textual.[6]

At the same time, however, Laclau disputes the more usual way in which
Marxism has represented its relationship to the textual phenomena it analyzes. In
its more scientistic formulations, Marxism typically has represented its own relation to reality as one of pure transparency, thereby denying its own discursivity and
textuality. Furthermore, in doing so, it has represented its relationship to the texts
it has analyzed as a knowledge relation. In construing them as forms of the appearance of the real which it knows (the economy, society, history), Marxism has represented itself as having produced a valid knowledge—or, more accurately, a
knowledge that is *tendentially* valid—of such texts "in themselves." In opposition
to this view, Laclau argues that Marxism, rather than seeking to efface its own discursivity, should conceive of itself as a set of discursive interventions, interventions
which must prove their validity through their effects rather than by claiming any
kind of prior ontological privilege. Such interventions, he argues, must seek to
interrupt, to uncouple, and to disrupt the prevailing array of discourses through

which subject identities are formed—and, thereby, through which forms of political alliance and cleavage are constructed—so as to produce new discursive articulations that will produce new subjects and new forms of political alliance, and, above all, discursively construct relations of contradiction through which moments of possible historical rupture might be constituted.[7] Since the conditions of existence of discursive practices are, in good part, textual, this is tantamount to saying that Marxism should regard itself as, again in good part, if not entirely, a set of textual practices that seeks to rearticulate the relations among other textual practices so as to produce those systems of ideological interpellation and patterns of political alliance that are calculated, in a particular conjuncture, to be the best bet for socialism.

While I am not sure that I should like to go as far as Laclau in, in fact, collapsing the social into the discursive, I go along with his view sufficiently to think that the way in which Marxism represents its relationship to the textual phenomena it engages is not merely a recondite theoretical question but one with far-reaching political implications. I want, therefore, to dispute the view that Marxism should represent texts as possible objects of knowledge (as opposed to defending such a view against the criticisms of deconstruction), to review a range of the devices through which Marxism has sought to do this, and to comment on their, in my view, largely negative consequences.

So regarded, texts cannot figure within Marxism, I shall argue, in the sense that there is no space other than a transcendent, ahistorical one within which they can be constituted as possible objects of knowledge. They should not so figure in the sense that such a representation of textual phenomena, and of Marxism's relationship to them, is both theoretically and politically disabling. It is theoretically disabling in the respect that it inhibits the adequate formulation and development of what I regard as the proper concerns of Marxist literary theory: namely, the development of a historical and materialist theory of the interactions among texts classified as literary, other ideological phenomena, and broader social and political processes and relationships, recognizing that the systems of classification within which the "literary" is produced are always culturally specific and that, therefore, their functioning and effects are a part of what needs to be studied. While that is, perhaps, a fairly uncontentious view, I want to add a rider that calls into question an essentializing orientation that has lain behind much of the work that has been developed within the Marxist tradition: that is, that such a theory cannot be adequately developed if predicated on the assumption—an assumption which usually has obtained implicitly—that the relations among literary texts, other ideological phenomena, and broader social and political processes can be determined or specified for all time by referring such texts to the conditions of production obtaining at the moment of their origin. To the contrary, the actual and variable functioning of texts in history can only be understood if account is taken of the ways in which such originary relations may be modified through the operation of subsequent determinations—institutional and discursive—that retrospectively may cancel out, modify, or overdetermine those which marked the originating conditions of the production of a text.

This is to take issue with the "metaphysics of origin" that characterizes scientistic representations of the relationship between Marxism and the literary texts with which it engages, according to which such texts are construed as forms of the appearance of the real which Marxism "knows." The characteristic discursive move of such approaches has consisted in the claim that Marxism, through "the appliance of science," rescues literary texts from the history of their misunderstanding in revealing, for the first time and by means of the application of the principles of historical materialism, their objective historical meaning. Such claims are not to be taken at their face-value. Their primary effect has been to disguise the active and interventionist nature of Marxist criticism, to shield from itself, and from others, a recognition of its own inescapably ideological nature. The stress placed within Marxism on returning the text to the originating conditions of its production, while *represented* as a scientific move producing a knowledge of the text, *in fact* has functioned as the distinguishing hermeneutic device whereby Marxist criticism, in rewriting the relations of a text to past history, has sought to reorganize its significance and functioning, its meaning in and for the present. In this, Marxist criticism has always functioned in the way Laclau suggests it should: namely, as a discourse of intervention. Interrupting and contesting the ideological production of literary texts effected by bourgeois criticism, it has consistently sought to reorganize the systems of intertextual, ideological, and cultural reference through which reading practices are organized and animated. It has, *practically,* functioned as a bid to reorder the discursive determinations of reading and as an attempt to produce both readings and the appropriate texts for such readings, while, *theoretically,* it has represented itself as producing a valid knowledge of texts "in themselves."

This theoretical misrepresentation of the nature of its own activity to itself has had two consequences. First, at the theoretical level, it has entailed that analysis of the functioning of texts within history has been conceived as a once and once only affair. For once a text is coupled to the conditions of its origin by means of "the appliance of science," the analysis of its subsequent functioning in history, prior to the point at which Marxism reveals its objective historical meaning, is thereby rendered unimportant or is representable only as a history of errors. There are, accordingly, scarcely any—if any—such analyses within the Marxist tradition. Yet it is clear that the determinations and accretions that bear in upon, remold and reconfigure texts may have a more consequential bearing on the nature of their functioning within the present—and, thereby, on the ways in which this may need to be modified—than do those specified by their relations to the originating conditions of their production. Perhaps more damagingly, and as the second consequence of scientistic representations of the relationship between Marxism and the texts with which it engages, the scope for the political maneuverability of texts is thereby severely limited. In effect, one move and one move only is possible: that ordained by the knowledge of the text produced by referring it to the originating conditions of its production.

In view of these considerations, then, I want to suggest that the proper object for Marxist literary theory consists not in the study of texts but in the study of reading formations. By a reading formation, I mean a set of discursive and intertextual determinations that organize and animate the practice of reading, connecting texts and readers in specific relations to one another by constituting readers as reading subjects of particular types and texts as objects-to-be read in particular ways. This entails arguing that texts have, and can have, no existence independently of such reading formations, that there is no place independent of, anterior to, or above the varying reading formations, through which their historical life variantly is modulated, within which texts can be constituted as objects of knowledge. Texts exist only as always-already organized, or as activated to be read in certain ways, just as readers exist as always-already activated to read in certain ways: neither can be granted a virtual identity that is separable from the determinate ways in which they are gridded onto one another within different reading formations. The consequence of this so far as Marxist *criticism* is concerned—and the distinction between theory and criticism I have in mind here is that, whereas the concern of theory is to analyze the determinations that are operative in the processes whereby meanings are produced in relation to textual phenomena, the concern of criticism is to intervene within such processes, to make texts mean differently by modifying the determinations which bear in upon them—is that it should seek to detach texts from socially dominant reading formations and to install them in new ones. The accent here should be placed on the use of the plural mood. Its business is not to subject textual phenomena to a singular move by means of a scientistically represented reevaluation of their objective historical meaning, but to move them about in different ways, to locate them within different reading formations and to produce them as different texts for different readers, in accordance with shifting and variable calculations of political objectives, rather than in accordance with the fixed calculation of such objectives which scientistic formulations produce.

III

I can think of two major forms of objection that might be advanced in relation to this line of reasoning. The first is that it is merely another version of neo-Kantianism, according to which the text is conceived as an unknowable *ding an sich*. I do not think this is the case. If it were, I would certainly be unhappy with it, as that is not the sort of company I should like to keep. As I shall try to show, the approach I am advocating is one that aims to suspend the neo-Kantian problematic, to displace its essentialism by following Laclau toward an absolute historicalization of textual phenomena that is, at the same time, uncompromisingly materialist and that thereby affords no space in which "the text itself" might be constituted as an object, knowable or otherwise. I shall come back to this point later. The second line of objection would be that I merely am reducing texts to contexts, and I must admit that there is much truth in this. However, I am also proposing a way of rethinking context such that, ultimately, neither text nor context are conceivable as entities separable from one another. According to most formulations, context is conceived as social; that is, as a set of extradiscursive and extratextual determinations to which the text is related as an external backdrop or set of reading conditions. The concept of reading formation, by contrast, is an attempt to think of context as a set of discursive and intertextual determinations, operating on material and institutional supports, that bear in upon a text, not just externally, from the outside in, but internally, shaping it, in the historically concrete form in which it is available as a text-to-be-read, from the inside out.

I can perhaps best expand on this concept and its implications by contrasting these with the ways in which the relations between texts and readers are construed in other approaches to the question of reading. Such approaches fall within two broad categories. First, there are those approaches that are concerned to analyze the formal mechanisms by which a text produces a position or positions for reading, organizing its own consumption in the implied, model, or preferred reader (the terms vary, but the approach is essentially the same) that it constructs as a condition of its own intelligibility. Clearly, work of this type is of considerable importance, and I do not mean to belittle the significance of the considerations with which it is concerned. Nonetheless, the supposition on which it is predicated, namely, that the intratextual processes through which reading is organized can be specified independently of the extratextual determinations that mold and configure the reading practices of empirically diverse groups of readers, is problematic. "No text," Umberto Eco has argued, "is read independently of the reader's experience of other texts."[8] If that is so, its implication, although Eco does not draw it, is that reading cannot be accounted for first by analyzing the fixed properties of the text and only then by considering the intertextual determinations that may explain how those fixed properties come to be received and interpreted differently. Rather, analysis should deal with the ways in which such intertextual determinations organize the text internally through the specific constitution of the text as a text-to-be-read. It is clear, for example, that reading practices are, in part, organized by the systems of genre expectations brought to bear on specific texts. It is equally clear that such expectations are largely culturally determined and, hence, variable. Given that such genre expectations may predispose the readers to relate themselves to a text in a specific way, it is not clear how or where intratextual mechanisms of reader positioning might be constituted independently of a set of assumptions concerning the operation of particular genres and, therefore, independently of culturally engendered reader predispositions.

Or, to take another example, John Frow has argued that that literary space is marked off by the operation of a "frame" that establishes "the particular historical distribution of the 'real' and the 'symbolic' within which the text operates."[9] Such frames, he argues, organize the "inside" and the "outside" of a text and the relations between them. In the case of texts operating within the constructed space of "the literary," they produce such texts "both as an enclosure of the internal fictional space and as an exclusion of the space of reality against which the work is set."[10] Since the functioning of such frames is culturally dependent, Frow argues, "changes in the context of reception of a work alter the kinds of expectation governed by the frame and are thus translated into structural changes in the work."[11] In short, there is no fixed boundary between the extratextual and the intratextual that prevents the former from pressing in upon the latter and reorganizing it. The intratextual, in fact, is always the product of a definite set of intertextual relations.

The second approach to reading has concentrated largely on considerations of social positionality; that is, on the role of class and gender relations, for example, in organizing reading practices. The chief difficulty with this approach consists in the tendency to theorize such relations as comprising an extratextual context of reception since, in this case, no mechanisms are provided that could connect such extratextual determinations to the process of reading. Recent approaches have tried to overcome this difficulty in suggesting that considerations of social positionality bear upon reading only mediately and indirectly, as a consequence of the structure of access they produce in relation to the discourses that comprise the ideological level of a social formation. If social position determines the ways in which individuals are exposed to and inserted within ideological discourses, it is the properties of those discourses that actually mold and organize the activities of those individuals as reading subjects. Except for some suggestive comments by Stephen Heath, however, such discursive determinations have been conceived as operating only at a level of highly abstract generality.[12] The concept of reading formation is not meant to displace these considerations but, rather, to refine them by requiring that the effectivity of such general discursive determinations be regarded as conditioned by the way they are processed through the operation of those inter-discursive and intertextual relations that bear most specifically and most closely on the process of reading.

The concept of reading formation, then, is an attempt to weave a way between these two approaches to the study of reading by conceiving the intratextual determinations of reading as being overdetermined by the operation of determinations which, while they cannot be derived from the text concerned, are not reducible to an extratextual social context either. It is an attempt to identify the determinations that, in operating on both texts and readers, mediate the relations between text and context, connecting the two and providing the mechanisms through which they productively interact in representing context, not as a set of extradiscursive relations, but as a set of intertextual and discursive relations that produce readers for texts and texts for readers. This is to question conventional conceptions of texts, readers, and contexts as separable elements, fixed in their relations to one another, by suggesting that they are variable functions within a discursively ordered set of relations. Different reading formations, that is to say, produce their own texts, their own readers, and their own contexts.

In an interview he gave, Pierre Macherey asked what the study of literature would look like once the supposition that it consisted of fixed works—of texts, given and completed—was abandoned.[13] Well, I think it would look very different. The implication of the perspectives I have been developing is that it would consist, not in the study of texts as self-contained givens, but in the study of texts as constituted objects-to-be-read within the different reading formations that have modulated their existence as historically active, culturally received texts. This, it is important to add, would mean not studying texts first and then their readings, as if the history both of the diverse patterns of readings that have been produced within different reading formations and of the different social and ideological relations of reading of which they form a part need not be allowed to complicate the analytical exchange between analyst and text. To the contrary, it would be a question of studying texts in the light of their readings, readings in their texts. The relations between textual phenomena and social and political processes can be theorized adequately only by placing in suspension the text as it appears to be given to us in our own reading formation so as to be able to analyze the differential constitution and functioning of that apparently same but different text within different reading formations. The aim of such an analysis would not be to reveal the meaning or effects of textual phenomena but, rather, to make them hum and reverberate with (ideally) the full range of meanings and effects for which they have furnished a site.

None of this in any way queries the objective, material existence of textual phenomena. To the contrary, it stresses it. It is precisely because texts are material phenomena that their social and ideological articulations may be reordered discursively, and reordered by social and material means since, of course, discursive processes are social and material processes produced within specifiable institutional conditions. By reverse, the only way of fixing a text as the source of a specifiable range of meanings or effects is by means of idealist constructions, according to which there is conjured up the notion that there is somehow and somewhere, at the back of the materiality of textual phenomena, an ideal text—the "text itself"—that it is the purpose of analysis to reach and to reveal, always (if the rhetoric is to be believed) for the first time, or, in an eschatology of meaning, to anticipate. It is for this reason that I do not think my arguments lead in the direction of neo-Kantianism, according to which the text is posited as an unknowable *ding an sich*. My argument is not that the text is somewhere "there" (wherever that might be) but unknowable, but that there is no "there" in which its existence might be posited, other than in the varying reading formations through which the actual history of its functioning is modulated and that, therefore, to seek to produce a knowledge of it is to engage in a Sisyphean labor.

IV

In short, and contrary to appearances, it is the concept of the "text itself," rather than criticisms of it, that rests on idealist principles and procedures. It is a construction and, furthermore, a variable construction, since the means by which such a concept of the text is produced vary from one school of criticism to another. Indeed, what is constructed as the "text itself" is the product of a particular bid for the terms of intertextual, ideological, and cultural reference that are to prevail in organizing reading practices; therefore, it cannot supply the means of arbitrating between readings. It follows that to seek to determine the limits of what can and cannot be said on the basis of the "text itself" is to engage in a pursuit that is necessarily metaphysical, since it rests on the supposition that the discursive wrappings that have been placed around a text within different reading formations can somehow be peeled away to yield an unfettered access to its irreducible kernel, thereby establishing analysis in a relationship of pure and unmediated transparency to its object. Either that, or it is merely myopic, overlooking the history that, in determining the form in which a text is currently available as an object-to-be-read—the whole ensemble of material, social and ideological relations that condition the apparent givenness of "the text on one's desk"—simultaneously occludes itself.

However, this is not to suggest that all the readings that either have or might be produced in relation to textual phenomena should be regarded as of equal value. It is merely to argue that the differences between them cannot be resolved epistemologically by claiming for a particular reading the warrant of a relationship to the "text itself" such that all other readings are thereby automatically disqualified in its favor. Rather, readings can only be assessed politically in terms of a calculation of their consequences in and for the present. Texts, according to such a view, cannot be conceived as extradiscursive points of reference which may be appealed to as a means of adjudicating between readings. Rather, they exist only as variable pieces of play within the processes through which the struggle for their meaning is socially enacted: kept alive within the series of bids and counterbids that different critical tendencies advance in their attempts to organize reading practices, to make texts mean differently by rewriting their relations to history. Texts are thus kept alive only at the price of being always other than "just themselves."

Paradoxically, it is precisely at this level, the level of the social struggle for the meaning of textual phenomena, that the concept of the "text itself" is produced and has effects as an essentially rhetorical device used to enhance the claims of a particular ideology of reading. It provides the means by which a new reading seeks to clear a space for itself and to displace the cultural power of prevailing readings by producing, in its construction of the "text itself," the criteria of validity in relation to which other readings can be found wanting. It is for this reason that the functioning of the concept of the "text itself" is always paradoxical. While forming a part of activist and interventionist critical projects that implicitly recognize the "mobility" of texts in the very process of their attempts to shift them or to make them mean differently, that movement is represented always as a final movement, as, at last, a pinning down of texts so that their intrinsic nature can be recognized. There are, of course, a variety of means by which such a concept of the "text itself" may be produced discursively. Barthes argues that the category of the author typically functions in this way. "To give a text an Author," he writes, "is to impose a limit on that text, to furnish it with a final signified, to close the writing."[14] Whatever the details of the devices used, however, a necessary condition for, and complement to, the discursive production of the "text itself" consists in the discursive production of a unified subject by whom that text can, even if only tendentially, be recognized.[15]

This is as true of Marxist criticism as it is of any other. I argued earlier that the distinguishing hermeneutic gambit of Marxist criticism has consisted in the contention that the objective historical meaning of a text can only be understood by placing it in the context of the originating conditions of its production. The precise way in which this move operates, as well as its consequences, however, are considerably more complicated than this bald description suggests. In fact, detailed analyses of texts in the light of the originating conditions of their production are somewhat rare in the Marxist tradition, and they rarely stop at that. Indeed, there is a sense in which such considerations are the last things to be taken into account. To take Lukács—and I would argue that, on these matters, Lukács is the paradigm case—the way in which he construes the relations between a text and the social and ideological conditions of its period is always informed by a prior conception of the relations of that text to earlier and subsequent texts, and to the social and ideological conditions of their respective periods, as specified by the degree to which it does or does not continue the realist tendencies of earlier texts, or anticipates and paves the way for those of subsequent texts. In short, the objective historical meaning of texts is determined, not so much by relating texts to the conditions of their production, as by locating them within the metatext of a History which Marxism claims to know but yet whose final judgments—which can only be delivered once the process of History has been completed—it can only anticipate. Hence Lukács's constant insistence that the meaning of a period and its texts will become clear to us the more distant we are from it, not just because, with time, perspectives settle, but because, with the unfolding of each stage of historical development, we move a little closer to the post-historical unified subject, "Man," to whom the meaning of the text of History and, therefore, of each text within it, will finally be rendered luminously transparent. In Lukács's work, the means by which the text itself is fixed and its objective historical meaning is deciphered is thus accomplished by means of the determination which the future is allowed to exert on that text and its history.

The idealism of such an approach is apparent. The "text itself," which such a criticism posits, turns out to be that text which achieves a full and adequate relationship to itself only when the text of History has been completed. It is an ideal text which assumes a social and material form that is fully adequate to itself only at the end of History and that, pending this consummation, exists only as a shadowy presence, an ideal form lodged behind the diverse social, material, and ideological relations that regulate the real history of its reading, until it is given in such a form that its "in-itselfness," in being completed, is made transparent. Not only idealist but ideological: the critical project that is produced and supported by such a view ends up constituting literary texts as a privileged region for the reproduction of an ideological view of history. Althusser has argued that an ideological conception of history, "far from functioning as (provisional) truth for the production of new knowledges," presents itself "as the *truth* of History, as exhaustive, definitive and absolute knowledge of it, in short as a system closed in on itself, without any development because without any object in the scientific sense of the term, and only ever finding in the real its own mirror reflection."[16] This perfectly describes Lukács's criticism and, indeed, the entire tradition of Marxist criticism which constitutes texts as the pretexts for the elaboration of a historicized humanist aesthetics. For, such an aesthetic can only ever find in the real historical lives of texts the mirror reflection of its conditioning premise: namely, that texts are a reflection of the historical process through which "Man" makes himself, as will eventually be made clear once they are slotted into the foreordained hermeneutic sprocket-holes that await them at the end of that process.

It is not that I object to the fact that there can be no surprises within such an approach, nor even to its manifestly ideological nature, since it seems to me that any critical practice that hopes to be a historical force must be deeply ideological, in the sense that its concern will be to engage in the struggle for the terms in which individuals are to be produced and mobilized as subjects in history. Rather, I take issue with the form of this ideology and, therefore, with the subject it produces. I argued earlier, following Laclau, that Marxism should be conceived as a set of discursive interventions that seeks to interrupt, to uncouple, and to disrupt the subject identities and forms of political alliance constructed by dominant ideological discourses in order to forge new ones. The implications of this for Marxist criticism are that it should contribute to such struggles by seeking both to disarticulate those texts that are classified as literary from the system of ideological connections in which they are inscribed through the functioning of bourgeois reading formations and to order their ideological articulations differently—to make them mean differently—by reorganizing the systems of intertextual, ideological, and cultural reference—the reading formations—within which they are constituted as objects-to-be-read. I also argued that, in practice, this is how Marxist criticism mostly has functioned, albeit that it has misrepresented the nature of its activity to itself through the application of scientistic formulations, with the result that it has permitted itself one move and one move only in relation to literary texts: that of bringing them into line with the knowledge of their objective historical meaning as produced by Marxism.

I here shall take the case of Lukács again, since it is clear, first, that his criticism was motivated by a definite political project (the attempt to produce an alliance between the progressive wings of the bourgeoisie and the proletariat) and, second, that this project depended on the idealist principles I have just outlined whereby Lukács sought to fix texts into history. The system of articulations that Lukács sought to weave through his studies of literary texts can be roughly summarized as follows: literary texts are reflections of the process, yet to be completed, of Man's historical self-creation; the texts which most adequately reflect this process are those which embody the maximum form available in a particular epoch of Man's historical self-consciousness; the supports for such forms of historical self-consciousness are provided by the worldviews of progressive social classes, the bourgeoisie yesterday, the proletariat today; therefore, the progressive sections of the bourgeoisie should support the working class in order to support those humanist values they once had championed. In this way, Lukács's criticism forms an attempt to construct a system of political alliances—particularly in the context of the struggle against fascism—that would operate, not along class, but along cultural lines. It seeks to reformulate an essentialist conception of class struggle as being articulated around a single contradiction, the proletariat versus the bourgeoisie, as a cultural struggle conceived in equally essentialist terms. The struggle between the proletariat and the bourgeoisie thus is conceived as merely a contingent stand-in for the struggle between a system of opposing cultural values: reason versus unreason; socialism versus barbarism; the human versus the inhuman. In short, the way in which Lukács related texts to history, fixing them within it by referring them forward to the imminent *telos* of their soon-to-be revealed objective historical meaning, served as a means of articulating bourgeois humanist values to those of socialism, but only at the price of representing the struggle between the proletariat and the bourgeoisie as merely the given, contingent form of the more essential struggle between the humanizing and dehumanizing forces in history. Clearly, once texts have been shifted by being moved into such an interpretive system, there is no other way that they can be moved which is not, at the same time, a breach with that system and with the fixing of texts that it proposes. All criticism can do, so long as it remains within the confines of such a system, is to perfect its anticipations of the judgments of the posthistorical unified subject that it posits as a condition of its own practice.

What can be done with such a criticism today? Not very much, it seems to me. Apart from the fact that the way of fixing texts in history which it proposes rests on a secularized eschatology of meaning, the political calculations of which it formed a part surely have been called into question. It is clearly not the case that all of the struggles that need to be coordinated in the struggle for socialism can be grouped around an essential contradiction that is expressed in terms of the bourgeoisie versus the proletariat. To the contrary, the successful articulation of such struggles into a provisional unity depends on a recognition of their relative autonomy, of the separate interests of women and blacks, for example, which cannot be subordinated to an essential class contradiction. This being so, the political value of producing an objective meaning within history for literary texts is called into question. If such texts are to be—and I think they should be—regarded as strategic sites for the contestation of dominant ideological subject identities, it needs to be recognized that, as such, they are implicated in different struggles (and not just one) and that, therefore, they may need to be moved around differently—and then only provisionally—within different social and ideological relations or reading, rather than being moved just once by an attempted scientist fixing of their meaning. As to whether the "text itself" might encounter, at the end of history, the unified subject of judgment that can sustain and recognize it, it seems to me that such an issue, together with a good many others of the same nature, is one that we safely can leave to the future, precisely because there are more pressing problems with which to deal.

NOTES

1. Terry Eagleton, *Literary Theory: An Introduction* (Oxford: Basil Blackwell Publisher Ltd., 1983), 143.
2. See Christopher Norris, *Deconstruction: Theory and Practice* (London: Methuen & Co., Ltd., 1982), 74–75.

3. Ibid., 84.
4. Michel Pêcheux, *Language, Semantics and Ideology* (London: Macmillan Press Ltd., 1982), 17.
5. Ibid., 108–109.
6. See Ernesto Laclau, "Politics as the Construction of the Unthinkable" (unpublished paper).
7. Laclau deals with the problem of the discursive construction of relations of contradiction in "Populist Rupture and Discourse," *Screen Education* 34 (Spring 1980).
8. Umberto Eco, *The Role of the Reader: Explorations in the Semiotics of Texts* (London: Alan Hutchinson Publishing Co., Ltd., 1981), 21.
9. John Frow, "The Literary Frame," *Journal of Aesthetic Education* 16, 2 (1982): 25.
10. Ibid., 27.
11. Ibid., 28.
12. See Stephen Heath, "Difference," *Screen* 19, 3 (Autumn 1978).
13. See the interview with Pierre Macherey in *Red Letters* 5 (Summer 1977).
14. Roland Barthes, "The Death of the Author," *Image-Music-Text* (London: Fontana Paperbacks, 1977), 147.
15. In this respect I believe that the discursive conditions for the production of the "text itself" are similar to those required by theories of value. I have discussed the latter in "Marxism and Popular Fiction," *Literature and History* 7, 2 (Autumn 1981).
16. Louis Althusser, "The Conditions of Marx's Scientific Discovery," *Theoretical Practice*, nos. 7–8, (1973): 7.

II

LITERARY CRITICAL

STUDIES OF RECEPTION

The last section explained the varieties and the philosophical grounds of reception theory. This section turns to "practical" reception criticism: the application of theory to the study of literary texts' reception histories. Theory and practice repeatedly have intersected in reception study since the earliest work in the field at Germany's University of Konstanz in the 1970s. As empirical surveys of the way contemporary readers responded to literature, these early studies drew on the theories of Hans Robert Jauss and, to a lesser extent, Wolfgang Iser.[1] The work of Jauss himself included "practical" essays, which were first translated into English in the late sixties and early seventies. In 1982, two important translated collections, *Toward an Aesthetic of Reception* and *Aesthetic Experience and Literary Hermeneutics,* devoted chapters to such works as the Faust texts of Goethe and Valéry, and Baudelaire's "Spleen II." In these and other studies, Jauss, focusing on his aesthetics of reception, examined the way canonical literature has been received and reformulated by other writers and the way literary works reconfigure horizons of expectation created "intraliterarily" by previous aesthetic texts.

Like his theories, Jauss's practical criticism became influential in Anglo-American critical circles, in part because of its affinities with traditional formalist methods and historical criticism, especially studies of source and influence and the history of ideas. But Jauss's significance also emanated from the way his analyses of the reception of texts coincided with the newly developing attention to audience in Anglo-American criticism, from the psychological approaches of Norman Holland and David Bleich to the early work of Stanley Fish, Judith Fetterley, Jane Tompkins, and Steven Mailloux.[2] All shared an assumption that the meaning and significance of literary texts depended on the models, codes, and values of readers. Also significant has been an affinity between reception study and the humanities' new cultural programs. As we have explained, Jauss defends the transformative force of canonical texts, but he argues that reception study challenges the traditional notion of the historically transcendent literary masterpiece. Because this challenge parallels those mounted by feminist, African-American, postcolonial, and gay and lesbian criticism, reception study has become increasingly important to criticism concerned with interrogating the literary canon and exploring the politics of race and gender. Critical practice within Anglo-American reception study, in other words, has emerged from an interlarded variety of theory and praxis manifested in a diversity of forms.

The four essays comprising this division reflect a cross section of that diversity. It begins with Gary Taylor's essay "1790," which was published in 1989. Though chronologically the second most recent of the readings in this section, it could be said to be the most traditional of the four. Part of his full-length study of the reception and "reinvention" of Shakespeare from the Restoration to the twentieth century, Taylor's essay is perhaps the most Jaussian in that it indicates how literary artists and members of the English "literary classes" from the mid-eighteenth century through the early romantic era reinterpreted or "received" the earlier Shakespeare. Taylor, however, departs from a purely modern approach to Shakespeare's reception and in the process goes beyond an interest in the aesthetics of reception in several ways.

While attending to the manner writers such as Wordsworth, Keats, and Hazlitt interpreted *Hamlet* and other plays, Taylor explores how the significance and growing reputation of Shakespeare at this time depended on the way institutions of literary culture, from the English theater to the work of publishers who issued new editions of his plays, re-presented his texts within a matrix of cultural conditions. More importantly, Taylor does not essentialize Shakespeare's plays by ascribing to them intrinsic merit as "high art" or claiming that they possess inherent features that transcend the contexts in which they were received. Instead, he demonstrates that Shakespeare's ascendancy during an age of political revolutions hinged on both a reactionary political strain among romantic writers and a broad "growth of cultural conservatism" and an "expansive imperialism" in British society. This cross-examination of literary and political culture, along with its antiessentialism, gives Taylor's essay a postmodern turn, which acknowledges Shakespeare's canonical status but reveals that status as a product of the specific conditions of the plays' reception history.

The other essays in this section also devote substantial attention to canonical writers, but, more markedly than Taylor's, they evince postmodern turns, especially in the way they address the politics of excluded literatures and cultures. Henry Louis Gates, whose work is heavily inflected by poststructuralist and postmodern theory, is not usually identified with reception study, but his "Literary Theory and the Black Tradition" provides a significant example of how reception study and African-American and poststructuralist criticism intersect.

This intersection appears not only in the essay's attention to non-canonical texts but also in its examination of the racial politics informing the late-eighteenth- and early-nineteenth-century white reception of African and African-American writing. This connection with a broader version of reception study obtains as well in the inflection Gates gives to the leading term of his title. By "literary theory" he means not just the crafted principles guiding the practice of literary critics but the entire panoply of beliefs, values, and interpretive codes that constitute the reception of texts (Gates, introduction). In the late eighteenth century that panoply was, Gates says, heavily marked by a racial and racist conception of both "black texts" and African identity. Gates devotes his sharpest attention not to the obvious racism of responses by apologists for slavery but to the racial politics of reception by those who configured early black texts—from slave narratives to the poetry of Phyllis Wheatley—as vehicles demonstrating "the African potential to deserve inclusion in the human community." Employing the Eurocentric logic of the Enlightenment to define membership in civilized society, these responses valued such texts for displaying the capacity of Africans, and especially African Americans, to move beyond their indigenous "bestial" origins. By constituting for such literature a "documentary status," such readings depended on a "confusion of . . . art with propaganda" that colored the reception and production of African American writing into the next century and that, Gates implies, diminished the status of black literature as art. One interesting result of this last implication is the way it moves Gates's essay away from its otherwise strong postmodernism. In asserting that studies of black texts must "respect the integrity, the traditions, of the black work of art" by attending to "the text itself," Gates's writing aligns itself with modern reception theory, which attributes to texts intrinsic properties and status that exist independently of historical acts of reception.

Claudia Johnson's "The Divine Miss Jane" and Jane Tompkins's "Masterpiece Theater" keep their focus largely on canonical literature, but both emphasize the role that gender politics plays in reception histories. In a postmodern approach informed by gay and lesbian criticism, Johnson's essay examines the reception of Jane Austen by exploring the vexed "heteronormative" status surrounding Austen's novels. Contrary to the obstreperous objections of conservatives such as Roger Kimball and Roger Rosenblatt, Johnson reveals that the "queering" of Austen has not been the product of a misguided political criticism of the late twentieth century; rather, as early as the 1850s, the view of Austen and her characters as not "properly underwritten by the institutions of heterosexuality" and female love for virile men marked the reception of her novels. As Johnson demonstrates, efforts to erase this version of Austen occurred only after World War II, when the disciplinary study of the novel was taking shape within the academy. At that time, academic critics took custody of Austen's reception by wresting it away from upper-class "Janite" devotees. The process of "straightening Austen out" thus transpired within an institutional framework determined to discredit the authority of Janite reception by repositioning her novels within heteronormative cultural codes. In exploring both the Janite response to Austen and the academic reception of Janite reception, Johnson's postmodern approach discloses the reception of Austen as a *mis en abyme* linked to larger cultural processes involving a crisis in masculine identity and in English and American nationalism that surfaced in the wake of the century's two world wars.

The earliest of the four essays, Tompkins's "Masterpiece Theater" is arguably the most immersed in the principles of postmodern reception study. Influenced by the feminist critique of the canon and by the neopragmatist theory of Stanley Fish, Tompkins examines the link between Nathaniel Hawthorne's canonical status and the reception history of his fiction. Far from inhering in their intrinsic merit as masterpieces, the canonicity of Hawthorn's novels and tales has developed out of a political and social process of reception that included the work of literary artists, editors, the publishing industry, and other institutions of a literary culture shaped and dominated by men. As a point of contrast, Tompkins interrogates the status of Hawthorne's contemporary, Susan Warner, whose novels were praised alongside his in the mid-nineteenth century but who fell into virtual oblivion after 1900. Tompkins' purpose is not to reveal how *The Scarlet Letter* "stood the test of time" while Warner's *The Wide, Wide World* did not. Instead, her juxtaposition of the receptions of Hawthorne and Warner unfolds in a persuasive argument that the relative positions of these two writers in and outside of the canon—and by extension, the canonical status of any writer—depends on a politics of reception that repeatedly has been coded by the gender norms of patriarchal culture.

In making a case not against the political nature of canon formation—which Tompkins rightly points out can never avoid being political—but against the particular shape that politics has taken, Tompkins adopts a strong postmodern position even as her union of feminist criticism and reception study reinforces traditional feminist arguments for recovering and revaluing women's writing. Among the four essays, Tompkins's is, moreover, the one that unites practice to an overt discussion of reception theory while looping that theory back to practice. For in her last section, Tompkins directly articulates a postmodern position against any claim for intrinsic textual properties that transcend contexts of reception and argues for the value of reception study for critical inquiry into the nature and history of neglected texts.

Besides demonstrating the close connections between theory and practice within critical studies of literary reception, these essays also tellingly address an early and oft-repeated objection to reception study: the critique that it is too one-sided in its emphasis on consumption at the expense of literary production. The essays by Gates, Taylor, and Tompkins, in particular, demonstrate in different ways the interrelations between the activities of production and reception. For Gates, that relation emerges in his argument that the documentary emphasis in the reception of African-American texts influenced the subsequent production of black literature, especially the way writers designed their works' purposes. Taylor examines a phase of reception that was itself a form of production: the staging of Shakespeare's plays in the eighteenth-century theater. By contrast, Tompkins's arguments implicitly suggest that the very critique of reception study as one-sided is based on a false dichotomy, since reception is a form of production more "durable" than any other. As Tompkins puts it, "Rather than being the repository of eternal truths," significances, and forms produced by gifted writers, "literary texts, like everything else, are humanly created, historically produced objects, whose value has been created and re-created" by a "succession of interpretations . . . wholly adequate to the text that each interpretive framework makes possible." Although this strong postmodern argument has itself been cited as one more manifestation of one-sidedness, the point is that literary-critical practice in reception study, as exemplified in these essays, addresses this and other theoretical issues while demonstrating the importance and contributing to the growth of reception's role in literary studies.

NOTES

1. While the Konstanz school, as it has come to be called, can rightly be identified as a major source for literary-critical reception study today, various precursors have been cited, from the rhetorical criticism of Wayne Booth and Kenneth Burke to Russian formalism and the phe-

nomenology of Roman Ingarden. For a useful discussion of these and other precursors and their influence on the development of reception study in Germany in the early 1970s, see Holub, 13–52. For the empirical work growing out of the Konstanz school, see Holub 134–46, where he points out that the connection has also been, paradoxically, a gap, in that empirical studies developed out of what was seen as a "deficiency" in the theories of the Konstanz school. Hence, a divide between the empiricists and what Holub calls the "hermeneutical reception theorists" marked reception study in Germany in the 1970s and '80s.

2. Although this early work in Anglo-American audience-oriented criticism was characterized less by an emphasis on reception than by a shared orientation to reader response, the differences between the two were far from clear, and the overlap has become even greater since the late 1980s. For useful discussions of the distinctions and affinities between reader response and reception criticism, as a well as the problematics of differentiating between the two, see Kuenzli; Holub, xi–xiv; Freund, 134–36; and Machor, vii–xi. It is worth adding that the interest of Anglo-American literary critics in Jaussian reception study was facilitated by the concurrent impact of French reader-oriented work, from the phenomenology of Georges Poulet to the poststructuralist studies of Roland Barthes.

WORKS CITED

Freund, Elizabeth. *The Return of the Reader: Reader-Response Criticism.* London: Methuen, 1987.
Gates, Henry Louis, Jr. introduction to *Figures in Black: Words, Signs, and the "Racial" Self.* New York: Oxford University Press, 1987.
Holub, Robert C. *Reception Theory: A Critical Introduction.* London: Methuen, 1984.
Kuenzli, Rudolf E. "The Intersubjective Structure of the Reading Process: A Communication-Oriented Theory of Literature." *Diacritics* 10 (1980): 47–56.
Machor, James L. "Introduction: Readers/Texts/Contexts." In *Readers in History: Nineteenth-Century American Literature and the Contexts of Response,* edited by James L. Machor, vii–xxix. Baltimore: Johns Hopkins University Press, 1993.

1790

. . . By his own account "Hamlet was the play, or rather Hamlet himself was the Character, in the intuition and exposition of which" Coleridge in 1798 first demonstrated his gift for "Philosophical criticism."[1] Three decades later he confessed, "I have a smack of Hamlet myself, if I may say so."[2] The Hamlet of which Coleridge had a smack was a character typified by "aversion to action," who

> is all meditation, all resolution as far as words are concerned, but all hesitation &
> irresolution when called upon to act; so that resolving to do everything he in fact
> does nothing. He is full of purpose, but void of that quality of mind wch wo^d lead
> him at the proper time to carry his purpose into effect . . . the great purpose of life
> defeated by continually resolving to do, yet doing nothing but resolve.[3]

You would hardly gather from this description that Hamlet actively isolates himself from the court by conspicuously continuing to wear mourning, or that he faces the Ghost alone, murders Polonius, forges an order for the execution of Rosencrantz and Guildenstern, leaps from his own ship in order to fight the pirates hand to hand on their own, leaps into Ophelia's grave, outduels Laertes, and kills Claudius. Whether or not Coleridge had a smack of Hamlet, the Hamlet he described had more than a smack of Coleridge, Wordsworth, and Southey, literary intellectuals who flirted with revolution but who could not "at the proper time" commit themselves.

Coleridge's interpretation of Hamlet distanced and idealized the political irresolution of his own generation. Coleridge projected that collective indecision onto Hamlet and then made an artistic fetish of his own weakness; even as he criticized it, he made "doing nothing" seem Shakespearian, heroic, and tragic. And, as if to ensure that we do not overlook such meanings, Coleridge himself intruded contemporary political parallels into his discussion of the play. In some notes for a lecture on Hamlet, written in 1813, he praised Shakespeare for his "tenderness with regard to all innocent Superstitions"; Shakespeare spares us "Tom Paine declarations and pompous philosophy." Coleridge proposed to end the lecture by speaking "of the honest pride of our Englishmen—Milton, Shakespear, Bacon, Newton—& now Wellington."[4] Elsewhere, Coleridge applauded "the wonderfully philosophic impartiality of Shakespeare's politics"; the phrase has since been echoed by innumerable Coleridgettes, who do not usually notice that in the next sentence he claims that Shakespeare was "devoted to patriotism."[5] For Coleridge "impartiality in politics" meant rejecting Thomas Paine's egalitarian *Rights of Man* in favor of the Duke of Wellington's monarchist victories.

In the same notes, describing Hamlet's "aversion to real action," Coleridge quoted the first line of the most memorable speech in Wordsworth's verse tragedy *The Borderers:*

> Action is transitory, a step, a blow—
> The motion of a muscle—this way or that—
> 'Tis done—and in the after vacancy
> We wonder at ourselves like men betray'd.[6]

The hero of that play is a noble, young, procrastinating, disgusted idealist; the text repeatedly, consciously or involuntarily, echoes *Hamlet* (and Shakespeare's other tragedies). Wordsworth was working on *The Borderers* from 1796 to 1799, and by his own account the play grew out of his "long residence in France, while the Revolution was rapidly advancing to its extreme of wickedness";[7] the famous speech is spoken by a character named after and based upon an English Jacobin who was in revolutionary Paris at the same time as Wordsworth.

Like his elders Coleridge and Wordsworth, John Keats quoted *Hamlet* more often than any other play. In quoting it he too interpreted it. First, the title character could be identified with Shakespeare himself:

> a miserable and mighty Poet of the human Heart. The middle age of Shakspeare was all c[l]ouded over; his days were not more happy than Hamlet's who is perhaps more like Shakspeare himself in his common every day Life than any other of his Characters—.[8]

Second, the title character could be identified with Keats himself:

> Hamlet's heart was full of such Misery as mine is when he said to Ophelia "Go to a Nunnery, go, go!" Indeed I should like to give up the matter at once—I should like to die. I am sickened at the brute world which you are smiling with. I hate men and women more.[9]

Keats=Hamlet=Shakespeare; by eliminating the middle term, Keats=Shakespeare. But eliminating it obscures the character of the two poets' proposed identity. They are identical because they are miserable and in love. Hamlet's political mission and social status have, in Keats, simply disappeared; Shakespeare has become the poet of love and melancholy. Coleridge and his Hamlet agonized inconclusively over a decisive political act; Keats and his Hamlet abdicated into a deliberately depoliticized private world.

Charles Lamb retreats even further, into the security of an elected insignificance:

> You might pit me
> For height
> Against Kean.

> But in a grand tragic scene
> I'm nothing.
> It would create a kind of loathing
> To see me act Hamlet.
> There'd be many a damn let
> Fly
>
> At my presumption
> If I should try
> Being a fellow of no gumption—.[10]

Lamb has, he insists, the diminutive stature, but none of the talent of the actor Edmund Kean; Lamb cannot act either in the theatre or in the political world; he cannot even act Hamlet, let alone be Hamlet; he lacks "the gumption" even to play the part of a character who, in the prevailing Romantic interpretation, spent his life averting action. The flippancy of his rhymes advertises Lamb's pose of triviality.

Lamb's Hamlet could be acted by Kean, or someone else perhaps, but not Lamb; William Hazlitt's Hamlet could not be acted at all:

> We do not like to see our author's plays acted, and least of all, HAMLET. There is no play that suffers so much in being transferred to the stage. Hamlet himself seems hardly capable of being acted. . . . Mr. Kemble plays it like a man in armour, with a determined inveteracy of purpose, in one undeviating straight line, which is as remote from the natural grace and refined susceptibility of the character, as the sharp angles and abrupt starts which Mr. Kean introduces into the part. Mr. Kean's Hamlet is as much too splenetic and rash as Mr. Kemble's is too deliberate and formal.

No representation can be adequate to Hazlitt's idea of the character; and if he cannot have a perfect performance, Hazlitt wants none. In this attitude the critic resembles his Hamlet, "the prince of philosophical speculators," who, "because he cannot have his revenge perfect, according to the most refined idea his wish can form, he declines it altogether." Hamlet cannot be acted because Hamlet, at heart, does not belong on stage at all but in the audience. "It is we who are Hamlet" (Hazlitt's sociable "we" in place of Coleridge's egotistical "I"); whoever "goes to a play as his best resource to shove off, to a second remove, the evils of life by a mock representation of them—this is the true Hamlet." Hamlet is anyone who watches a play (like *Hamlet*) instead of confronting and opposing "the evils of life," particularly the evils of corrupt and illegitimate political power. "It is we," Hazlitt tells readers in 1817, "It is we" who, when we are "most bound to act," remain "puzzled, undecided, and sceptical" and dally with our purposes "till the occasion is lost."[11] Hazlitt defines himself and his contemporaries as the spectators to a performance, always inadequate, of a play about a character who would rather watch than act, because acting is always inadequate, and because watching the play is an alternative to changing the world. In Shakespeare's text the inset "Mousetrap" play contributes to the plot; in Hazlitt's text the inset *Hamlet* play is an alternative to plotting.

"We love Hamlet even as we love ourselves"; in Byron's mouth the Romantic glorification of Hamlet is phrased in terms that satirize its self-satisfaction. Byron himself, by contrast, declares, "O I am sick of this most lame and impotent hero"—

and then falls asleep.[12] Physically lame himself, he is sick of lameness; politically impotent, he is sick of inaction. He might as well have said, "I hate Hamlet even as I hate myself." He makes these remarks in Pisa early in 1822. By then he is deeply involved in revolutionary Italian politics; a year later he will leave Italy to contribute physically and financially (and fatally) to the battle for Greek independence.

These interpretations of Hamlet, however varied and even contradictory, all belong to the Romantic obsession with works unfinished, closure postponed: Wordsworth's epic by titular definition a mere *Prelude,* itself deferred by endless revisions; Byron's unfinished and unfinishable *Don Juan,* formally promiscuous, knowing that no episode or orgasm can be any more definitive than the one before; Coleridge's volumes of fragments, notes, talk, plans—including plans for an edition of Shakespeare; Keats' abandoned *Hyperion,* his *Fall of Hyperion* suspended in midsentence; Edmond Malone's biography of Shakespeare, the goal and focus of a lifelong scholarly enterprise, published posthumously, a ragged fragment. (This experience—even glorification—of artistic incompleteness leads naturally, in the next generation, to the suggestion that one of Shakespeare's own plays, *Timon of Athens,* was left unfinished.)[13] Completedness, the rondure of achievement, is an aesthetic and spiritual injunction—Wordsworth describes his muse in a phrase quoted from Shakespeare, who had used it of the ghost of Hamlet's father[14]—but artistic and social wholeness seems unattainable.

In its place they have only fragments. They create fragments, like Coleridge's *Kubla Khan,* and they transform Shakespeare into a treasure-house of stray puzzle-pieces. In 1814 Edmund Kean bursts upon the London theatre with successive impersonations of Shylock, Richard III, Hamlet, Othello, and Iago; everyone faults his style as "fitful, flashy" and "spasmodic,"[15] but that unevenness cannot be separated from new and irresistible bits of business that "had an electrical effect" upon audiences. When Kean reaches the end of one of Shylock's famous set pieces ("You call'd me dog; and for these courtesies / I'll lend you thus much moneys"), his "struggle of outward humility and inner rage ends at the last word, the word 'moneys,' with an eerily prolonged laugh which suddenly breaks off, while the face, convulsively distorted into submission, remains for some time mask-like, unmoving, while the evil eye stares out of it, threatening and deadly"—that eye which observers described as "a magic lightning-flash, a fiery flame."[16] Kean's Richard III stands at Bosworth Field oblivious of those around him, "for some moments fixed in reverie, drawing figures on the sand" with the point of his sword.[17] To see Kean act was "like reading Shakspeare by flashes of lightning."[18]

As an actor Kean could make one moment—a line, a gesture—leap out of its context to demand attention (and applause). Audiences appreciated these revelations because they already knew the plays, and knew too how they had been performed by others; whenever Kean did something new his audience recognized the novelty and could grasp its relevance to the whole character. In the same way, writers could expect readers to recognize quotations from Shakespeare and relish the aptness of an allusion or the novelty of an interpretation. Shakespeare was quotable precisely because he was already familiar. William Blake could entitle an image "Jocund Day" or "Fiery Pegasus" and expect the two-word quotation to recall its context in *Romeo and Juliet* or *Henry IV.*[19] The Reverend Thomas Ford could publish in *The Gentleman's Magazine* one hundred and fifty parodies of speeches from Shakespeare, including twenty-two from *Hamlet* alone, and expect his readers to note and appreciate how he was transforming each original.[20] As John Poole explained in the preface to *Hamlet Travestie,* a popular burlesque of 1810, "to derive entertainment from the perusal of a travesty . . . a familiar acquaintance with the original is indispensable.[21] No English writer was more familiar than Shakespeare, no play more familiar than *Hamlet.*

Quoting *Hamlet,* and all the other plays and poems, the Romantics paste bits and pieces of Shakespeare into their lives and letters and essays and poems. The main character in John O'Keefe's *Wild Oats,* a theatrical hit of 1791–93, is a "Strolling Gentleman" named Rover, who can apply and mix quotations from Shakespeare on any occasion. Hazlitt quotes Shakespeare more than 2,400 times (and over a fifth of those quotations come from *Hamlet*).[22] Keats declares that in reading Shakespeare and Milton he looks "upon fine Phrases like a Lover,"[23] presumably contrasting "Lover" with an implied "pedant"; unlike editors of Shakespeare from Theobald to Malone, Keats does not break down the poetic text into specimens for philological inquiry. But although Keats sees the lover and the pedant as antithetical, both disintegrate the text into minute verbal constituents. The editor sections off obscure phrases; Keats sections off fine phrases, both highlighting fragments at the expense of continuity. This process can be seen not only in the quotiness of Hazlitt's essays and Keats' letters but also in Keats' underlining of words and phrases in the editions of Shakespeare he read.

The Tatler, at the beginning of the eighteenth century, had quoted whole speeches; the Romantics quote phrases. In his edition of Shakespeare, Pope had visually emphasized "the most shining passages" and had appended an index to *sententiae*; but those passages were later wholly extracted from the text of the plays and printed in enormously popular and influential collections like William Dodd's *The Beauties of Shakespeare* (first published in 1752), William Enfield's *The Speaker; or, Miscellaneous Pieces, Selected from the Best English Writers* (1774), Elizabeth Griffith's *The Morality of Shakespeare's Drama Illustrated* (1775), and Vicesimus Knox's *Elegant Extracts: or, Useful & Entertaining Passages in Poetry* (1789). Lord Kames' *Elements of Criticism* (1762) owed much of its popularity to the "numerous illustrations and quotations from Shakespeare" with which its arguments were substantiated, making it another handy anthology of purple passages.[24] All these books went through numerous reprintings.

Shakespeare's plays had been, throughout the seventeenth century, actions. They happened; they enacted a story temporally; they were acted out by particular persons from beginning to end; they acted upon an audience assembled in a certain place at a certain time. In the eighteenth century they became things; they became, primarily, books. Books are spatial, not temporal; any reader can skip backward or forward, dip in, pull out, pause, repeat. Books can be cut up and rearranged, as time cannot. The transformation of Shakespeare's actions into books thus permitted and encouraged their disintegration into assemblages of quotable fragments. Unlike a moment of time, the physical space of a book can also be systematically enlarged; and as the eighteenth century progresses Shakespeare editions surround the text with an expanding border of annotation, an undertext of commentary that repeatedly interrupts a reading of the uppertext. The commentary beneath the text whispers to us visually, like a conversation at the next table, audible but not comprehensible until we stop to listen, turning our eyes away from Shakespeare to focus upon someone else. The experience of reading *Hamlet* in a late eighteenth-century edition was an experience of directed action repeatedly interrupted, postponed by eddies of subsidiary meditation. Books abstract, impersonalize, idealize; what had been an interaction between a cast and an audience became instead a kind of message left by an unreachable author for any and all possible readers. The text became a thing, a perfect timeless thing, and any attempt to transform it back into an action came to be regarded as a transgression; any actualization diminishes the ideal by confining it to a particular time and place and person. "*Action, Action, Action,*" Garrick had demanded of drama.[25] The Romantics replied, "Action is transitory"; "We do not like to see our author's plays acted."

The French Revolution enacted the philosophy of the Enlightenment: it turned books back into actions, ideals back into tangible particulars. It performed thought, and the performance was, predictably, inadequate. Edmund Burke, politician and aesthetician, sitting in a Channel-side seat, had an excellent view of the action and was seized at first by "astonishment at the wonderful Spectacle . . . what Spectators, and what actors!"[26] But within a year he had condemned the whole "monstrous tragi-comic scene."[27] It was monstrous to Burke in part because it was "tragi-comic"; in an ironic reversal of perspectives the English critic berated the French actors for abandoning neoclassical decorum and mixing dramatic genres.

Burke too quoted *Hamlet,* although the play hardly recommends itself to a critic contemptuous of tragicomedy. In his correspondence, as in that of Keats, it is quoted more often than any other Shakespeare play. Writing in 1790 of events in France, he declares, in Hamlet's words, "It is not nor It can not come to good."[28] In what would become the most famous sequence in *Reflections on the Revolution in France,* Burke condemned the French revolutionaries for their lack of "chivalry" toward Marie Antoinette. Burke's longtime friend and political associate Philip Francis, who saw the book in proof, particularly objected that this defense of Marie Antoinette was "pure foppery." Burke responded:

> What, are not high Rank, great splendour of descent, great personal Elegance and outward accomplishments ingredients of moment in forming the interest we take in the Misfortunes of Men? The minds of those who do not feel thus are not even Dramatically right. "What's Hecuba to him or he to Hecuba that he should weep for her?" Why because she was Hecuba, the Queen of Troy, the wife of Priam, and suffered in the close of Life a thousand calamities. I felt too for Hecuba when I read the fine Tragedy of Euripides upon her Story. . . .[29]

The quoted lines from *Hamlet* in the middle of this diatribe were (and are) so familiar that Burke did not even need to attribute them. They belong to the soliloquy in which Hamlet upbraids himself for his own cold inaction, contrasting it with the "passion" that an actor wastes upon a fiction. The quotation rose into Burke's mind because he was, like so many of his contemporaries, obsessed with English inaction. Hamlet is trying to rouse himself to kill a king; Burke was trying to rouse the English people to defend a king.

But Burke's quotation itself illustrates the extent to which Shakespeare's lines had already floated free of their context; for in context Hamlet finds it "monstrous" —the word Burke would use of the Revolution—that the actor's passion is "all for nothing! For Hecuba! . . . What would he do, / Had he the motive and the cue for passion, / That I have?"[30] As Burke uses the quotation, the "he" in question has been transformed into a spectator, a reader not an actor; those who are not moved by Euripides' play or Burke's book are not responding as an audience should. Hamlet's incredulity at an exaggerated overemoting response has become Burke's condemnation of a response (Philip Francis' or the English people's), which is not extravagant or emotional enough. Burke argues that we should indeed weep for the distant Hecuba and that consequently we should, even more, both weep for and defend Marie Antoinette, regardless of her guilt or innocence.

Burke's allusion to *Hamlet* here jostles with one to Euripides; in his work as a whole, Shakespeare belongs with Milton, Virgil, Cicero, and the Bible among the venerable relics of a culture threatened by the irrational energy of change. In 1790 Edmond Malone gave his fellow Irishman Edmund Burke a complimentary copy of his edition of the *Plays and Poems of William Shakspeare*; Burke in turn gave Malone a copy of "a pamphlet which I have lately published," *Reflections on the Revolution in France*.[31] In the preface to his edition Malone described The Right Honourable Edmund Burke as "a great orator, philosopher, and statesman" who would rival Dr. Johnson as "the brightest ornament of the eighteenth century."[32] Some readers of Burke's *Reflections* explicitly compared its author to the author of *Hamlet* ("Shakespeare himself is come again!").[33] In 1796 Burke, congratulating Malone on his scholarship, congratulated him on his politics as well: "Your admiration of Shakespeare would be ill sorted indeed, if your Taste (to talk of nothing else) did not lead you to a perfect abhorrence of the French Revolution, and all its Works."[34] Shakespeare's *Works*, for Burke and Malone, are natural enemies to the "Works" of the French revolutionaries.

The quoting of *Hamlet* by English critics and poets in the decades after 1789 not only expresses their obsession with political inaction and artistic failure; it also constitutes, in itself, a form of cultural inertia. As Jane Austen observed, Shakespeare's "thoughts and beauties are so spread abroad that one touches them every where, one is intimate with him by instinct.— . . . His celebrated passages are quoted by every body; they are in half the books we open, and we all talk Shakespeare, use his similies, and describe with his descriptions"; consequently, "Shakespeare one gets acquainted with without knowing how. It is a part of an Englishman's constitution."[35] "Constitution" was, of course, a word electrified with political meaning. An Englishman's political constitution was not, like the new American or French alternatives, an identifiable piece of paper, a rational construct, any more than an Englishman's physical constitution could be located in a specific organ of the body. Instead, that mystical entity existed somehow, one had to believe, organically, as an effusion of the whole. "Organic" was the adjective Coleridge used to define and defend both the English class system and Shakespeare's poetry. Shakespeare's plays were broken down into fragments and then disseminated through the bloodstream of English society, droplets of poetry suspended in a stable cultural solution. By the end of the eighteenth century, Shakespeare had become part of the English constitution.

As all their quoting from *Hamlet* demonstrates, the English managed to avoid a revolution in their literary institutions just as surely as they avoided one in their political institutions. In the forty years after the storming of the Bastille, Blake, Wordsworth, Coleridge, Byron, Keats, and Shelley wrote their Romantic masterpieces, one by one, and died or decayed, romantically, one by one. But Shakespeare and Milton, the twin crowned monarchs of the literature of Great Britain— English poetry's royal family—still reigned at the end of those forty years—if anything, even more secure in their preeminence, no longer simply enthroned but also fixed atop "the two glory-smitten summits of the poetic mountain."[36] Postrevolutionary Romanticism in France toppled, temporarily at least, Racine and Corneille; in Germany, Russia, and eastern Europe, Romanticism tore down neoclassicism and erected a new vernacular pantheon; in Italy it canonized Dante, after long neglect. But in England literary loyalties held. Shakespeare and Milton still commanded the apex of the cone, on top and central.

It ought to surprise us that the English literary classes remained so loyal to Shakespeare's reputation. After all, Hazlitt, describing in 1818 the writers of his own generation, recognized that the new English poetry:

> had its origin in the French revolution, or rather in those sentiments and opinions which produced that revolution. . . . The change in the belles lettres was as complete, and to many persons as startling, as the change in politics, with which it went hand in hand. . . . [A]ll was to be natural and new. Nothing that was established was to be tolerated.

Shakespeare, of course, was one of those unnew "established" things, which should have been intolerable, and Hazlitt repeatedly quotes him in cataloguing all that the new poets rejected:

> It could not be said of these sweeping reformers and dictators in the republic of letters, that "in their train walked crowns and crownets; that realms and islands, like plates, dropt from their pockets" [quoted from *Antony and Cleopatra*]. . . . They scorned "degrees, priority, and place, insisture, course, proportion, season, form, office, and custom in all line of order" [quoted from *Troilus and Cressida*]. . . . Their poetry . . . has "no figures nor no fantasies" [quoted from *Julius Caesar*] . . . "no trivial fond records" [quoted from *Hamlet*] . . . "the marshal's truncheon, nor the judge's robe" [quoted from *Measure for Measure*]; neither tradition, reverence, nor ceremony, "that to great ones 'longs" [quoted from *Measure for Measure*].

Condemning such newfangled "metre ballad-mongering" (quoted from *Henry IV, Part I*), Hazlitt concludes that the typical Romantic poet "hates prose; he hates all poetry but his own; he hates the dialogues in Shakespeare."[37]

Hazlitt moves from prose to poetry to Shakespeare's mixture of poetry and prose. Politically, as Burke suggests, the long, costly, bloody war against France was undertaken to restore decorum; yet Shakespeare, jumbling prose and poetry, kings and clowns, was the most notorious of all disrespecters of aesthetic decorum. Shakespeare was a playwright; the English Romantics achieved their greatness in epics and essays, lyrics and lectures and letters, not drama. Shakespeare did not die young, did not leave fragments, did not despair, did not devote his poetry to prophecy or spiritual autobiography; proportionally, few of his lines stooped or rose to descriptions of nature; he could hardly be celebrated as an exemplar of the egotistical or geographical sublime. The Romantics valued originality far more than their predecessors had; Shakespeare had stolen much of his material from others. He could not be considered an exponent of the stylistic simplicity advocated by Coleridge's and Wordsworth's Preface to *Lyrical Ballads;* he had been condemned by every generation of critics since his own for his deviations from simplicity, for verbal obesity and farfetched mutations of phraseology. When Hazlitt says that in the new poetry "kings and queens were dethroned from their rank and station in legitimate tragedy or epic poetry, as they were decapitated elsewhere,"[38] he was almost certainly defining "legitimate tragedy" in terms of Shakespeare.

As Hazlitt's reference makes clear, aesthetic and political objections to Shakespeare went hand in hand. John Philip Kemble's sympathetic portrayal of Coriolanus was one of the most successful theatrical performances of the period, and according to Hazlitt, "The whole dramatic moral of CORIOLANUS is that those who have little shall have less, and that those who have much shall take all that others have left." He concluded that "Shakespear himself seems to have had a leaning to the arbitrary side of the question, perhaps from some feeling of contempt for his own origin."[39] Even more fundamentally, Hazlitt argued that tragedy itself was an absolutist genre and that poetry and the theatre almost inevitably idealized and romanticized tyrants like Coriolanus and Henry V. Likewise, Tom Paine, the champion of democratic common sense in America and France, condemned Burke's *Reflections on the Revolution* as "a dramatic performance" full of "theatrical exaggerations"; for Paine the theatre was a realm of aristocratic falsehood, and "Mr. Burke should recollect that he is writing History, and not *Plays*."[40] When Paine alluded to Shakespeare at all, he associated him with the ancien régime; Burke's pamphlet and the system of government it defended would soon disappear into "the family vault of all the Capulets"; in England's corrupt Parliament "the Comedy of Errors concludes with the Pantomime of HUSH."[41] William Cobbett, the most influential English agitator of the period, objected to Shakespeare's "bombast and puns and smut" and characterized his plays as a concoction of "wild and improbable fiction, bad principles of morality and politicks, obscurity in meaning, bombastical language"; he complained that "hundreds of thousands of pounds had been expended upon embellishing his works; [and] numerous commentators and engravers and painters and booksellers had got fat upon the trade." Cobbett's explanation for Shakespeare's reputation is equally damning. He asks, "What can make an audience in London sit and hear, and even applaud, under the name of Shakespear, what they would hoot off the stage in a moment, if it came forth under any other name?"—and he answers, "It is *fashion*. These books are in fashion. Every one is ashamed not to be in the fashion." *Hamlet* and *King Lear* are like fad foods; it is "the *fashion* to extol the virtues of potatoes, as it has been to admire the writings of Milton and Shakespear."[42]

Shakespeare could have been dethroned, just as George III could have been, but for some reason neither was. Why did Shakespeare's cultural supremacy survive and, indeed, expand during a revolutionary period when idols were being replaced all over Europe? It is as though Hamlet had failed to kill Claudius.

But before we can explain why the English Romantics failed to topple Shakespeare, we first have to explain when and how Shakespeare had made it to the top. The "when" is easy to define. Everyone agrees that, after a slow but steady upward climb, Shakespeare's coronation as the King of English Poets finally occurred in the middle of the eighteenth century, at some time between the death of Alexander Pope (1744) and the birth of William Wordsworth (1770); or, to put it another way, between the second Jacobite rebellion (1745) and the first year of Lord North's ministry (1770), which would precipitate and then lose the war in America. In 1751–56 William Hawkins, Professor of Poetry at Oxford, gave (in Latin) the first academic lectures on "Shakesperio" in a British university;[43] on the Sunday before Christmas, 1772, Mrs. Hester Thrale "heard for the first Time

Shakespear's Plays quoted in the Pulpit the Passage was from Hamlet."[44] Between 1751 and 1772 Shakespeare had conquered both academia and ecclesia.

If you insist on naming a particular year, 1760 will do as well as any. In 1760 a professor of Greek at Cambridge University publicly declared that the excellencies of Æschylus, Sophocles, and Euripides were "all united and surpass'd in the immortal and inimitable Shakespear"; in 1760 *The British Magazine,* comparing "the two great dramatic genius's of France and England," found Corneille "greatly inferior to Shakespear"; in 1760 *The Critical Review* remarked that "our immortal Shakespear" possessed "vast powers as a tragic writer [which] remain unrivalled"; in 1760 the first major exhibition of contemporary English art included five paintings of scenes or characters from Shakespeare; in 1760 a peer of the realm, in a little book so popular that it ran through three editions in that year alone, declared that "If Human Nature were quite destroyed, and no Monument left of it except [Shakespear's] Works, other Beings might know *what Man was* from those Writings."[45] It would not be entirely perverse to suggest that in 1760 William Shakespeare and George III together simultaneously ascended the English throne.

• • •

By every measure of material prosperity—wealth, military power, political stability, population growth, upward mobility, industrial innovation—the eighteenth century was good to England. The theatres prospered. From 1747 to 1776 David Garrick ran Drury Lane, combining the functions of leading actor and what we would call artistic director, to the considerable profit both of himself and the theatre. During that time he made repeated improvements and alterations to the building; its capacity gradually swelled from about 1,200 at midcentury to almost 2,300 by the 1780s. During Garrick's tenure the rival theatre at Covent Garden could accommodate almost 2,200 spectators; in 1782 it was expanded again, to hold another 300. During the early years of the French Revolution the two theatres ballooned once more: Covent Garden by September 1792 could hold 3,013 customers; while Drury Lane, having leapfrogged it in size, could open its doors to over 3,600 by the spring of 1794. This expansion of theatrical auditoriums in London was accompanied by the erection of new theatres in the provinces. Bath built a new theatre in 1705, York was supporting its own regular repertory company by 1730, by the 1740s Norwich had one; Birmingham, Bristol, Liverpool, Portsmouth—every English town of any size or self-importance had its own theatre. Outside London, England was better equipped with theatres in the late eighteenth century than in the late twentieth. Both the demand that justified such expansions and the capital that financed them demonstrate the commercial vitality of the entertainment industry.

Artistic vitality was another matter altogether. The expanding theatrical market created an increased demand for plays: twice as many new plays were written between 1750 and 1800 as in the preceding fifty years.[46] But in the century after John Gay's *The Beggar's Opera* (1728), English theatres produced only three and a half new plays that have been canonized by later generations: Goldsmith's *She Stoops to Conquer* (1773), Sheridan's *The Rivals* (1775) and *The School for Scandal* (1777), and his short comic afterpiece *The Critic* (1779). Noticeably, all were comedies; even more than at the beginning of the century Shakespeare dominated the serious repertoire by default. In the three decades of Garrick's tenure at

Drury Lane, for instance, six of Shakespeare's seven most popular plays were tragedies; all six featured among the twenty most frequently performed plays of the period.[47] In the last quarter of the eighteenth century all but four of the most popular dramatic entertainments were comedies, many of them musical comedies; the four exceptional serious plays were all by Shakespeare.[48]

Many critics throughout this period remarked upon the garish shoddiness of new plays. Burke, for instance, complained that the stage had "sunk . . . into the lowest degree; I mean with regard to the trash that is exhibited on it"; but he did not blame this decline upon "the taste of the audience" because when Shakespeare was performed "the boxes, pit, and gallery, are crowded."[49] An enthusiasm for Shakespeare was proof, by definition, of good taste, even if in every other respect the taste of such audiences seemed execrable.

As contemporary drama sank, theatre managers clung to the wreckage of past success; and Shakespeare was the safest dramatist in the repertoire. They exercised their ingenuity by attempting to make greater use of a brand name that had attracted customers in the past, scouring the canon for revivable or adaptable plays that had been relatively neglected in previous decades. Thus, Garrick made his own reputation in (Cibber's adaptation of) *Richard III;* in his performances, it became the third most popular play of the period. Earlier that year (1741) Charles Macklin, playing Shylock, had transformed *The Merchant of Venice* into a thrilling tragicomedy, which he went on playing for almost half a century.

· ·

Garrick belongs beside Josiah Wedgwood and William Hogarth among the most astute eighteenth-century entrepreneurs of culture. Like most marketing claims before and since, his were misleading, if not deliberately dishonest. Shakespeare did not need Garrick to rescue him from any looming oblivion. As for restoring Shakespeare's words to the stage, in the case of *Macbeth* that meant cutting one-eighth of the 1623 text, retaining some of Davenant's scenic and musical elaborations in the witches' scenes, and writing a new death speech for Macbeth (played by Garrick). Garrick's *Macbeth* was undoubtedly much closer to Shakespeare's than Davenant's adaptation had been; but it was still a considerable distance from the play "as written by Shakespeare." Likewise, Garrick proclaimed his "Plan/To lose no *Drop* of that immortal Man" in the prologue to an adaptation of *The Winter's Tale* that omitted three of its five acts. Amid all the odes and ovations at the Shakespeare jubilee, not a word of Shakespeare was spoken. Garrick did not adapt all of Shakespeare's plays—but then, no one ever had. Like his predecessors, he adapted some but not others, and adapted some more heavily than others.

In his advertised aspirations to authenticity Garrick simply reverted to the appeal of the original patent companies at the Restoration. Like Davenant, he combined this authenticity with novelty: the novelty of new adaptations, of reviving plays that had not been seen before, of reverting to the original texts in place of adaptations, and throughout it all the novelty of Garrick's own interpretation of his roles. The advertisements for *Macbeth* juxtaposed the claim "As written by Shakespeare" with the promise "The Characters new Dress'd."

Such novelties should not obscure the essential conservatism of Garrick's appeal. Although he made a number of changes to the body of the theatre—gradually removing spectators from the stage itself, improving stage lighting and the artistry of set design—they all merely reformed and refined the spirit of the early eighteenth century without radically redirecting it. Garrick gave—and his audience welcomed—not much new but, rather, more and better of the old. The rise of Shakespeare coincided with the growth of cultural conservatism.

It also coincided with upsurgent nationalism and expansive imperialism. While Garrick managed Drury Lane, Britain fought and decisively defeated France in the Seven Years War; the Tories, after decades in the wilderness, were readmitted to some measure of influence at court; Samuel Johnson, the nation's most visible literary Tory, was granted a pension; and a series of ministries tried to impose Britain's will on its American colonies. In 1753 an impassioned reply to Voltaire's criticisms of Shakespeare observed that in Britain, "SHAKESPEAR is a kind of establish'd Religion in Poetry."[50] In 1756 Joseph Warton berated the "nauseous cant" of French and Frenchified critics who found Shakespeare "INCORRECT."[51] In 1760 an anonymous "Ode to the Muses," celebrating Shakespeare, recalled that in *Henry the Fifth* he had shown:

> . . . how great Henry's vengeful lance
> Humbled the crested pride of France,
> With arms triumphant shook the haughty state,
> And rear'd his banners in their vanquish'd land;[52]

During the 1760s writers fell over one another in proclaiming Shakespeare the world's greatest dramatist and poet. Such praises were almost always nationalistic in tone and often specifically anti-French. In 1768 Capell's edition described Shakespeare's works as "a part of the kingdom's riches" that were "talk'd of wherever the name of *Britain* is talk'd of, that is, (thanks to some late counsels) wherever there are men."[53] The next year at the jubilee—sitting smack in the middle between the end of the French war and the beginning of the American one— Garrick proclaimed that "*England* may justly boast the honour of producing the greatest dramatic poet in the world."[54] (This speech was probably written for Garrick by Burke.)

Like the critics, the theatres were openly chauvinistic. The French-supported, pro-Catholic Jacobite rebellion of 1745 prompted successful revivals of Cibber's anti-Catholic satire *The Non-juror* and Shakespeare's *Henry V*, "With the glorious Victory of the English against the French in the Battle of Agincourt"; when Covent Garden produced *Papal Tyranny in the Reign of King John* (Cibber's adaptation of *King John*), Drury Lane responded with a revival of Shakespeare's play. In the same year the theatres began the practice, which would continue for two centuries, of commencing every performance with a rendition of "God Save the King." *Henry V* was revived annually during the Seven Years War; in 1761, incorporating a theatrical replica of George III's coronation procession, it achieved a phenomenal run of twenty-four performances in six weeks. During the reign of George III the king and queen regularly attended the theatres. In the 1790s Sadler's Wells produced a string of successful musicals glorifying English victories against the French, culminating in 1804 with the construction of a large tank filled with water for miniature reenactments of naval battles; the patent theatres responded with a spectacular new production of *Henry V; or, The Conquest of France* and with periodic revivals of *King John*. Henry V was one of John Philip Kemble's most acclaimed roles; his sister Mrs. Siddons was even more celebrated for her portrayal of Constance in *King John*, driven to madness and death by French perfidy.

England's victory in the Seven Years War was a decisive event in the growing international resistance to French political and cultural hegemony, and Shakespeare was the chief artistic beneficiary of that resistance. First in Germany, then successively in other parts of southern and eastern Europe, emergent literary nationalism and romanticism defined themselves, almost inevitably, in opposition to the dominant classical models. Politically, the only visible alternative to French absolutism was English liberty, as guaranteed by the English mixed constitution; aesthetically, the only visible alternative to the rules of the French Academy was the practice of English genius, a freedom from arbitrary critical decrees exemplified by the mixture of tones, genres, and social classes found in the plays of "Sachespir."[55] The English acclaimed Shakespeare as their greatest and most characteristic genius, as the paradigm of artistic freedom, in the very decade when England seemed to itself and others the modern world's most assured and successful experiment in political and social liberty. In that same decade Lessing's *Hamburgische Dramaturgie* praised the ghost in *Hamlet* and mocked the ghost in Voltaire's *Semiramis*, adopting as standards the dramatization of love in *Romeo and Juliet* and of jealousy in *Othello*, rebuking Voltaire's treatment of similar material in his most famous play, *Zaire*.

Most of the political revolutions of the later eighteenth century were attempts by disenfranchised peoples—American colonists, native Irishmen, colonized Italians, Haitian slaves, the French third estate—to claim for themselves liberties like those which native Englishmen already enjoyed. One of those enviable English liberties was a right, and a determination, to celebrate their native literature, in defiance of the fact that it did not conform to the prevailing international aesthetic system. Any European critic who wanted to raise the banner of Dante or Cervantes or medieval romance could take comfort from English cultural independence. The opposition between Shakespeare's practice and French aesthetic theory, the focus of critical argument for a century, became the foundation of Shakespeare's expanding international reputation. Shakespeare became the exemplar of literary liberty, the titular champion of anyone who wanted to overthrow an exhausted critical system.

This interpenetration of aesthetic and political values can be seen clearly enough in Pierre Le Tourneur's preface to the first complete French translation of Shakespeare's plays. The translation was undoubtedly stimulated in part by Garrick's visits to Paris in 1763–65 and by the international publicity generated by the jubilee in 1769; the first volume was published, coincidentally, in 1776. Le Tourneur professedly does no more in his preface than string together extracts from the prefaces to existing English editions from Rowe to Johnson. But when he comes to Pope's statement that "To judge . . . of *Shakespear* by *Aristotle*'s rules, is like trying a man by the Laws of one Country, who acted under those of another," he transforms it into "condamner Shakespeare d'après ces règles, c'est juger un Républicain sur les loix d'une Monarchie étrangère."[56] Pope's neutral opposition between one country and another has been translated into Le Tourneur's image of an English republican condemned by the laws of a (French) monarchy—a monarchy defined, by the ambiguity of *étrangère*, not only as "foreign" (from Shakespeare's perspective) but also as "strange, unnatural" (from any perspective).

England's prosperity in the eighteenth century was built in part on its success as a trading nation, and Shakespeare was one of its most successful cultural exports. The English economy is still banking a handsome profit from the international market for Shakespeare opened up by eighteenth-century entrepreneurs. And once that market had become truly international, foreign demand could act as a periodic stimulus to domestic production. The *Hamlet* of English Romantic criticism was, for instance, deeply in debt to Goethe's novel *Wilhelm Meisters Lehrjahre* (1795–96) and August Wilhelm von Schlegel's *Vorlesungen über dramatische Kunst und Litteratur* (1809–11); it was Goethe who, more memorably than any English writer, described the play as a story of "the effects of a great action laid upon a soul unfit for the performance of it," a story in which "There is an oak tree planted in a costly jar, which should have borne only pleasant flowers in its bosom; the roots expand, the jar is shivered."[57] Coleridge's appropriations from Schlegel and other German critics could be justified as nationalistic expropriations of foreign technologies, like the American theft of the design for the spinning jenny, expropriations designed to secure domestic markets for domestic producers. To the German "unser Shakespeare" Coleridge replied with "our Shakespear"; he appropriated and then further developed German critical innovations in order to ensure that England retained its threatened supremacy in the Shakespeare market.

England in the late eighteenth century exported Shakespeare; it also exported prints. English engravings, particularly caricatures, were the most popular art form of the 1790s and early 1800s. England's most successful exporter of prints was Alderman John Boydell. Like Garrick, Boydell set out to alloy Shakespeare, patriotism, and the profit motive. This must have seemed a natural combination, because Shakespeare was already the most popular source of allusions and captions in the work of English engravers.[58] In the late 1780s Boydell organized an exhibition of specially commissioned paintings of scenes from Shakespeare's plays, which were made the basis of a folio edition of large engravings. This ambitious project—and Boydell himself—was ruined commercially by England's war with France, which cut Boydell off from his vital Continental markets. Though in most respects the increasing association of Shakespeare with English nationalism fostered his European reputation, in France it created understandable hostility, lasting well into the next century: as late as 1822 a French audience, recognizing in Shakespeare "*un lieutenant de Wellington*," prevented *Othello* from being performed.[59]

But the commercial failure of Boydell's "Shakespeare Gallery" does not detract from its cultural importance. It was designed, among other things, to provide commercial encouragement for the development of "an *English School of Historical Painting*";[60] Shakespeare was chosen as the "one great National subject concerning which there could be no second opinion."[61] Boydell's new Pall Mall Gallery opened on May 4, 1789, displaying what one reviewer acclaimed as "a treasure of graphic excellence in the highest degree creditable to British genius."[62]

Shakespeare had, along with Milton, already been instrumental in the development of a consciously English art during the eighteenth century. Hogarth, the first native visual artist to acquire an international reputation, in a self-portrait emblematically rests his palette on the works of Shakespeare, Milton, and Swift. Shakespeare provided matter, and a manner, that was perceived as quintessentially English; his artistic identity was defined for Georgian England in opposition to Continental traditions. Shakespeare, moreover, was the repository of a specifically English mythology, which artists could expect any educated viewer to recognize; in George III's England the satirical prints of Samuel Rowlandson and James Gilray quoted Shakespeare as automatically, and as confidently, as did Thomas Sheridan's parliamentary speeches and Horace Walpole's letters.

Shakespeare was also a dominant figure in two cultural forms that provided models for the native school of painting: books and theatres. Engravings could be used to illustrate books or could be sold separately as prints; often the same engraving served both purposes, and both incarnations could be bought in the same shop. At the same time, the theatre provided a new model, specifically native and contemporary, for the organization of visual space. Hogarth defined his own art in explicitly theatrical terms: "my Picture was my Stage and men and women my actors who were by Mean of certain Actions and express[ions] to Exhibit a dumb shew."[63] Popular actors and scenes from popular plays were among the most popular subjects for popular prints. And in an age when English art drew so much of its inspiration from the theatre, the theatre itself drew much of its inspiration from Shakespeare.

English artists were felt, and felt themselves, to be particularly adept at portraiture; since the Restoration, Shakespeare too had been especially praised for his portrayal of individuals, and his characters accordingly became natural subjects for Georgian artists. Portrait painting, and its ugly younger brother political caricature, expressed a more general Georgian fascination with individuality, a fascination bound up with the triumphal energies of expanding entrepreneurial capitalism, with the increasing upward pressure for political liberation of many kinds, with the rise of the Methodist movement and lesser spiritualist sects. Garrick gave his last Shakespearian performance in the year which defined every individual's right to "life, liberty, and property" (the draft text) or "life, liberty, and the pursuit of happiness" (the revised text). This period also gave birth to the English eccentric, and Shakespeare's apotheosis took place during the eight years of serial publication of the greatest literary glorification of eccentricity, that unpredictable celebrity of the century, *Tristram Shandy*. (One of the eccentrics celebrated in that novel, Parson Yorick, is descended,—in fact,—fictitiously,—from *"Hamlet's Yorick,* in our *Shakespear."*)[64]

As the birth of political caricature demonstrates, this fascination with individuality does not entail untroubled endorsement of it. *Richard III,* that exorcism of grasping egocentric villainy, became after a century of neglect one of Shakespeare's most popular tragedies, its title role played by the vulnerable little parvenu David Garrick; *The Merchant of Venice,* that exorcism of ruthless financial villainy, became for the first time one of Shakespeare's most popular comedies, its leading role played with sullen intensity by Macklin. But whether Shakespeare's enactments of egotism left Georgian spectators appalled or applauding—or, often, both —those enactments satisfied a newly intensified curiosity about the nature of individuality. The ambition of portrait painters who visualized Shakespeare's plays drew upon and contributed to an increasingly exclusive interest in defining characters. Commentators on and illustrators of Shakespeare's plays might be weak on overall composition and structure, but they were keen on individual faces.

Such preoccupations shaped the very texts that eighteenth-century readers read. Rowe's 1709 edition had not only, for the first time, provided lists of dramatis personae and a consistent designation of each character in speech prefixes; it had also sometimes substituted personal names for the generic labels found in the original texts. Rowe's successors carried this nominative process further, gradually mopping up any pockets of generic identification he had missed. "Bastard" in *King Lear* became Edmund, "Bastard" in *King John* became Falconbridge, "Bastard" in *Much Ado about Nothing* became Don John; "Clowne" in *As You Like It* became

Touchstone, in *Measure for Measure* Pompey, in *Love's Labour's Lost* Costard; "King" throughout the English history plays and in half a dozen comedies and tragedies was broken down into individuated subsets. So long as a character was named at least once in the text, editors could impose that name throughout. Theatrical managers could go further, and invent individualities for characters Shakespeare had neglected ever to denominate. In *Henry IV, Part I*, John Philip Kemble baptized with the good Scots nickname "Raby" a succession of speeches given to Hotspur's servant in scene 7 (2.4), to a messenger who reports to Hotspur in scene 12 (4.1), and to a messenger who reports to Hotspur in scene 17 (5.2), thereby creating an entirely plausible minor identity. In *All's Well That Ends Well* Kemble sorted the confusion of minor French lords into Lewis, Biron, Jaquez, and Tourville. *Et cetera.*

Speech prefixes were systematically relabeled in order to emphasize the individuality of all Shakespeare's characters; particular prefixes were also singled out for emendation in order to make the text more appropriate to received notions of character. One example out of many: in all editions of Shakespeare's plays from 1623 to 1732 Miranda had addressed Caliban as an "Abhorred Slave" and then violently rebuked him for another eleven lines;[65] in 1733 Theobald's edition, following the Dryden/Davenant adaptation, transferred the speech to Prospero, who kept it for two centuries. The coarse energy of the lines did not accord with editorial notions of feminine decorum.

The editorial rage for individuation was not limited to speech prefixes. Pope alphabetically indexed Shakespeare's characters (historical and fictional) by name, subdividing some of them into elaborated analytical outlines of their more important attitudes and actions. Johnson's commentary differed most obviously and memorably from that of his predecessors in its attention to critical assessment of character. In *Henry the Fifth*, for instance, the offstage death of Falstaff provokes a four-paragraph note on his character, the offstage execution of Bardolph another note, the final exit of Pistol yet another; an analysis of King Henry's character is appended to one of his speeches wooing Catherine; Johnson's endnote on the play devotes two of its five sentences to summary critiques of the characters of King Henry and Pistol.

The fascination with character was not limited to editors of Shakespeare. In 1774 William Richardson, Professor of Humanity at Glasgow University, published *A Philosophical Analysis and Illustration of some of Shakespeare's remarkable Characters*, which was soon followed by other influential works like *An Essay on the Dramatic Character of Sir John Falstaff* by the civil servant Maurice Morgann (1777) and *Remarks on Some of the Characters of Shakespeare* by Member of Parliament Thomas Whateley (written 1768–69; published 1785). Excerpts from these and similar works soon found their way into editorial commentaries. To Johnson's edition Edmund Burke contributed a note on *Timon of Athens*, admiring Shakespeare's careful differentiation of Apemantus' misanthropy from Timon's;[66] to the later editions of Edmond Malone and George Steevens, Sir Joshua Reynolds contributed observations on the portrayal of Macbeth, Lear, and others.[67] Although we usually label those editions with the names of Johnson or Steevens or Malone or Boswell, their commentaries were in fact compilations that mixed the editor's own observations, those of previous editors, and those contributed by a widening circle of educated readers. In Steevens' case they also included notes written by the editor but facetiously or maliciously attributed to others. Those commentaries and texts were certainly shaped to a degree by the personalities of their titular editors, but they were also shaped by the social character of an entire period.

One spinoff of Boydell's Shak[e]speare Gallery was a new edition of Shakespeare, illustrated by small prints and edited by that ubiquitous Shakespearian, George Steevens. That edition, though of no importance to the history of editing, contributed to the incoming tide of Shakespeare texts, rising throughout the eighteenth century. Publishing of all kinds—of books, magazines, newspapers, prints—was one of the most successful industries of the period; in the bookshops as in the theatres, Shakespeare was a safe investment. Just as the audience capacity of theatres grew, so the number of editions of Shakespeare's complete works grew.[68] In the hundred years up to 1708 there had been four; in the hundred years after 1708 there were sixty-five, with each successive twenty-year period producing more such editions than its predecessor.

Theatres searched for new Shakespeare plays to perform and new ways to perform them; publishers searched for new ways to package the same old product. In 1709 Tonson shifted from single–volume folio to multivolume octavo. In 1711–12 Thomas Johnson began issuing *A Collection of the Best English Plays*, copying Shakespeare's texts from Tonson's 1709 edition but printing them "in small Volumes fit for the pocket"; they could be purchased separately but could also be bound together as a set of "10 handsom Volumes."* Pocket books and serial publication became two of the most profitable innovations in the eighteenth-century book trade. Tonson responded with a pocket Shakespeare of his own; the 1714 reprint of Rowe's edition was published in a small duodecimo format. In 1725 Tonson published the six volumes of Pope's edition in large elegant quartos, followed three years later by a second edition in a more manageable duodecimo. In 1744 Sir Thomas Hanmer published at Oxford an edition in quarto volumes even more sumptuous than Pope's. In 1773 readers could buy *Bell's Edition of Shakespeare's Plays, As they are now performed at the Theatres Royal in London; Regulated from the Prompt Books of each House, by Permission;* in 1784 they could purchase the first new single-volume edition published in a century. In 1795–96 American readers could buy an edition printed on their side of the Atlantic.

But this proliferation of editions should not obscure the continuity and conservatism of the reading tradition. The editorial succession passed from Rowe to Pope to Theobald to Hanmer to Warburton to Johnson to Steevens to Reed and Malone. Other editions contributed to the marketing of Shakespeare throughout and beyond the English-speaking world; but only that continuous central tradition determined the text that others would disseminate. Moreover, that tradition was more homogenous in the second half of the century than it had been in the first. Unlike his predecessors, Johnson chose his own successor, Steevens, who in turn adopted Reed and Malone; Steevens and Malone eventually quarreled, but both continued to pay homage to Johnson, correcting him politely or silently. Johnson was thus granted a retrospective centrality that the quality of his editorial work hardly merited. Steevens, Reed, and Malone—unlike their predecessors—each worked on more than one major edition, so that between them they wholly dominated Shakespeare editing from 1773 to 1821. And each of the editions in that

---

* Johnson, though an English bookseller catering to the English market, operated out of the Netherlands in order to evade the 1709 copyright act; his piracies of Tonson's text were therefore legal.

legitimate succession was based, literally, upon its immediate predecessor; each editor created his own new edition by marking up a copy of the previous edition, deleting some of his predecessors' observations, adding his own, adding or subtracting emendations, and then dispatching this palimpsest to the printer. Johnson institutionalized the practice, already initiated to a lesser degree by Theobald and Warburton, of incorporating the remarks of previous editors even when he disagreed with them, and thereafter the main editions were relentlessly assimilative; as a result they grew in size from the eight volumes of Johnson in 1765 to the twenty-one volumes of Boswell in 1821.

Editions of Shakespeare grew organically, like the English constitution, like English law, by corporate incorporation, a prolonged and collaborative process of accumulation and inclusion. Moreover, old editions continued to be reprinted alongside the editions that superseded them. Thomas Hanmer's 1744 text, for instance, rose again in 1745, 1747, 1748, 1751, 1760, 1761, and 1771; that first American edition, of 1795–96, was simply a reincarnation of Johnson's edition, first published three decades earlier; the title pages of reprints continued to parade the names of Steevens and Malone until 1864. Like vestigial organs, outdated editions became part of the constitution of Shakespeare.

The form in which these editions reproduced themselves was conservative; the burden of material carried over from the past increasingly tended to dwarf the commentary original to each new edition. Editors wished to conserve as much as possible of the past. The material and intellectual relics of Elizabethan England had, for them, an intrinsic interest, beyond any question of their utility to the present. This privileging of the past soon liberated itself from any immediate pertinence to the text. Malone's prolix investigations of Shakespeare's biography and the history of the English stage did not limit themselves to questions that might affect the determination or explication of the text. Malone belonged to a society increasingly conscious of the difference between its habits and those of earlier epochs, increasingly curious about the texture of past cultures. After all, Edward Gibbon's *History of the Decline and Fall of the Roman Empire* was published in installments between 1776 and 1788; its author was a member of Dr. Johnson's literary club, to which Malone also belonged, as did the finest practitioner and theorist of the English school of historical painting, Sir Joshua Reynolds.

In this intellectual climate it is not surprising that Shakespeare's history plays became more popular than ever, both in and out of England. In 1768 Lessing wrote that Shakespeare's histories "stand to the tragedies of French taste much as a large fresco stands to a miniature painting intended to adorn a ring." Friedrich Schiller, whose achievement in dramatizing German history was inspired and guided by Shakespeare's example, earned his living as a professor of history from 1789 to 1791. A. W. von Schlegel described Shakespeare's cycle of English chronicle plays as "a historical heroic poem in the dramatic form";[69] of the seventeen plays he translated between 1797 and 1810, nine were English histories. And the nineteenth-century Briton most often compared to Shakespeare was not Keats or any of the Romantic poets but Sir Walter Scott, who redirected the energies of the English novel by creating an immensely popular model of historical romance.

As Scott's novels demonstrate, the eighteenth century's new historicism produced a new aesthetic appreciation of antiques. The works of antiquity had, of course, long been admired; but previous critics had extolled them for a universality that transcended the passage of time. Now, by contrast, evidence of the passage of time itself became part of their charm. *A Discourse on Ancient and Modern Learning* recognized that modern readers lose much of the meaning of an ancient work but suggested that in compensation such works "appear to us in the Splendor and Formality of Strangers," embellished with "several Graces that arise merely from the Antiquity of an Author."[70] Oldness became a relished attribute. The age that produced the run of great Shakespeare editions from Johnson to Malone was also the age that celebrated and even constructed ruins; that purchased innumerable curios carved from the wood of a mulberry tree Shakespeare had planted in Stratford; that avidly read *The Castle of Otranto,* the first Gothic novel, said to be printed from an ancient manuscript; that thrilled to the wrinkles of the ancient Gaelic bard Ossian; that discovered and acclaimed the poetry of the fifteenth-century Bristol monk Thomas Rowley.

This age of antiques was also, inevitably, an age of fakes. Rowley's poems, Ossian's epic, and *The Castle of Otranto* were all written by eighteenth-century writers, consciously creating the appropriately discolored documents of an imagined past, satisfying the appetite for antiques better than the antiques themselves. This impulse to create a literary past, to invent the manuscripts that should have been written, spread throughout Europe, from Britain to Bohemia, Russia to Rumania. To this period also belong the most famous of all Shakespeare impostures, a series of documents, poems, and plays forged by William Henry Ireland, admired at the time by many readers until they were discredited by Malone.

It is no coincidence that the rise of historicism coincided with a boom in literary frauds. In the historicist dispensation the value of an object no longer depended upon a judgment of its aesthetic merit but upon a determination of its origin. By putting a price tag on antiquity, this system of evaluation created a market for faked obsolescence and therefore needed to develop the critical machinery for distinguishing genuine from spurious. Malone began his career as a Shakespeare editor with an edition of the seven apocryphal plays added to the canon in 1664 and peremptorily ejected by Pope in 1725. Malone concluded, essentially, that Pope had been right about six of the seven (all but *Pericles*); but his method radically differed from Pope's. Pope had justified the expulsion of all seven plays on the basis of his own judgment of "all the distinguishing marks of [*Shakespear's*] style, and his manner of thinking and writing";[71] Malone documented those stylistic impressions and at the same time investigated the reliability of the documents that had assigned the plays to Shakespeare.

This pursuit of documentary authenticity contributed to the increasing critical dissatisfaction with performances of Shakespeare's plays. Even when eighteenth-century admirers praised Garrick as "the best commentator" on Shakespeare, they were unconsciously proclaiming the primacy of the book; actors were judged as commentators, marginal servants of the printed text. What reviewers called the "new readings" of performers were evaluated just as critically as the new emendations of editors. And for the most part, when the theatre was judged "by the book," it was found wanting. On the one hand the theatre continued to make use of adapted texts, performing passages that were "spurious" (because written by someone other than Shakespeare) and omitting passages that were "genuine" (because written by Shakespeare). On the other hand performances were not historically accurate in their treatment of costume and setting. Accordingly, Boydell's "first instruction" to the artists contributing to his Shakspeare Gallery was to "forget, if possible, they had ever seen the plays of Shakespeare, as they are absurdly decorated in modern theatres." Why? Among other reasons, because "In a playhouse, anachronisms are so little guarded against, that discordant devices, and modern arms, are frequently associated with ancient ensigns and weapons peculiar to distinct nations, and ages remote from each other."[72] The theatre was not authentic; the authentic Shakespeare could be found only in books or in paintings, in fixed historical idealizations.

We still rely upon documents first discovered by Malone and Steevens and their contemporaries; their conclusions about many matters of historical interpretation have been vindicated by subsequent scholarship. But the cast of mind that produced those discoveries also produced the political philosophy of Edmund Burke. Burke judged events in France against the native canonical standard established by the Glorious Revolution of 1688, a paradigm characterized by a limited program based on gentlemanly consensus and the unwritten common law. The French Revolution did not follow that pattern; instead, as always, the chaotic variety of the present contrasted painfully with the apparently perfect order and closure of the past. Burke and Malone judged the French Revolution as though it were a new work of literature or a new emendation, seeking admittance to the canon. They rejected it because, like French drama, it insisted that cultural practice should be governed by a logical, rigorous, unforgiving, formally articulated set of intellectual ideals. As the Glorious Revolution was to politics, Shakespeare was to literature: an ad hoc native model, scornful of a priori principles, adopting and adapting accepted national practice, endorsed by subsequent generations. In Malone's treatment of Shakespeare, as in Burke's treatment of the French Revolution, what is altogether new is by definition spurious; the past validates; past authority authenticates present actions. The most influential editors and interpreters of Shakespeare shared with Burke that compound allegiance to the past which Tom Paine questioned in Rights of Man:

> The circumstances of the world are continually changing, and the opinions of men change also; and as government is for the living, and not for the dead, it is the living only that has any right to it. That which may be thought right and found convenient in one age, may be thought wrong and found inconvenient in another. In such cases, Who is to decide, the living, or the dead?[73]

Malone and Burke would have answered in unison, "the dead." Shakespeare was part of that past which they wanted to protect from a radical future, part of the past with which they protected England from a revolution.

. . . .

"Why did a revolution not happen in England?" The question is as important and as obvious as, "Why did one happen in France?" But most literary critics do not ask themselves why Shakespeare stayed on top during the Romantic period, because they assume that he belongs on top, and they assume too that continuity is normal. Inertial motion is, indeed, a large part of the explanation for his continued predominance; his reputation had developed so much momentum that it could have been stopped only by an obstacle or countermovement of enormous force. No such obstacle presented itself; instead, Shakespeare's momentum was accelerated.

In 1850 an aging Leigh Hunt recalled that at the end of the eighteenth century "people of all times of life were much greater play-goers than they are now." That addiction to theatre was actually intensified by events of the 1790s, for "the French Revolution only tended at first to endear the nation to its own habits."[74] "As the history of the preceding decades so clearly demonstrates, Shakespeare, like playgoing, was one of those habits. An initially enthusiastic, or at least cautious, welcome for the French Revolution turned within a few years into a panicking chauvinistic rejection of it. Shakespeare's reputation had been fed by nationalism, and the intensified nationalism dominant during the twenty years of Napoleonic wars only fattened it further.

For England the balance did not tilt in 1789, the year of the fall of the Bastille, but in 1790, the year of Burke's *Reflections on the Revolution in France*. In 1790 Malone published his edition of *The Plays and Poems of William Shakspeare,* and Boydell became Lord Mayor. In the same year Isaac Reed, whose first edition of Shakespeare had been published in 1785, recorded in his diary that on April 23 "(Shakespeare's Birthday)," he had dined at Boydell's house, where the company included Sir Joshua Reynolds, Benjamin West, and Paul Sandby, who all contributed paintings to Boydell's Shakspeare Gallery. The next night Reed went to see *Twelfth Night;* on June 9 to *Hamlet;* on June 22 to *The Merchant of Venice;* on July 18, he "Dined at Mr Malone's with Boswell & Johnson. Afterw^{ds} Sr Joshua Reynolds came"; on October 21 he saw *Richard III* in the company of Dr. Richard Farmer, the Cambridge classicist who had written an influential *Essay on the Learning of Shakespeare.*[75] While France gave bloody birth to the future, the guardians of Shakespeare's England dined and theatred.

In the contest between French neoclassicism and English drama Shakespeare had been and would continue to be praised for his freedom from the rules, and that freedom had always had a political significance. But that political significance was altered and intensified by the French Revolution. There could no longer be a contrast between French absolutism and English liberty; the French had gotten rid of their king, the English still had one. Instead, the French (and American) belief that a society could be rationally planned, that a blueprint could be intellectually conceived and then imposed upon recalcitrant human materials, was contrasted with the English belief that a society naturally evolved, organically, by gradations and consolidations, like a tree, like Burke's British royal oak in particular. This political contrast has, obviously, its aesthetic corollary: French plays were constructed by rule, English drama grew organically.

The connection between these two ideas is expressed most directly in Coleridge's *Biographia Literaria*. Shakespearian critics tend to read the parts devoted to Shakespeare as brilliant exercises in critical theory or practice, because —along with published and unpublished passages from many other sources—they have been conveniently collected, organized, and decontextualized in various editions of *Coleridge's Shakespearean Criticism*. But as originally published they belong to a sustained argument for political and social reaction, written in the turbulent aftermath of Napoleon's defeat, when national self-defense could no longer be used as an excuse for repressing or postponing reform.

Shakespeare was not deposed *because* George III was not deposed; or, George III was not deposed *because* Shakespeare was not deposed. From 1790 on, the defense of political and social privilege was justified as a defense of the culture of the English people, and any such defense would inevitably entail the preservation of Shakespeare, already widely regarded as England's greatest artist. Indeed, Shakespeare was certain to be further glorified by such a movement. Milton, after all, had been an accomplice to the execution of an English king—a rather uncomfortable precedent in the years between 1790 and 1820. Shakespeare caused no such embarrassment. His mixing of genres, his representation of all ranks of society, clowns rubbing shoulders with kings, social diversity aesthetically united—the very aspects of his art that neoclassicism had found objectionable—became admirable, because culturally useful. The openness of Shakespeare's art embodied —indeed, proved—the openness of English society.

Like the Romantics themselves, in some moods, romantic readers believe in abrupt change, enjoy the excitement of cataclysms (avalanches in the Alps, and all that). Romanticism, on its own account, provides just such a cataclysm. The threat and promise of the revolution next door exhilarated English poets; the disparate elements of an evolving late-Enlightenment taste suddenly crystallized into a strong new aesthetic compound. Acolytes of Romanticism are interested in Milton or in Shakespeare only secondarily, because of their professed importance to the Romantics themselves; and they tend to believe the story the Romantics tell them. The Romantics tell them that the Romantics discovered Shakespeare—just as, in the middle of the eighteenth century, Garrick's admirers said that Garrick had discovered Shakespeare.

The historical record makes it perfectly clear that the playwright's works were in no danger of impending oblivion, in either case. But this is probably clearer to us than it was to them. Among authors quoted in literary anthologies from 1771 to 1801, Shakespeare ranks fourth (after Pope, Thomson, and Cowper).[76] Much of the most innovative criticism of Shakespeare in the second half of the eighteenth century was scattered in ephemeral periodicals and in books on other topics; it was not collected into a single widely accessible compendium until the 1970s. For the Romantics, what was accessible, what was inescapable, was the eighteenth-century editorial tradition, which brought Shakespeare's text into the nineteenth century encumbered with all the outmoded baggage of prefaces and critical notes from Rowe to Steevens. The Romantics took arms against the big books, against the anthologies, against the variorum editions, against the strictures in popular collected editions of *The Tatler* and *The Spectator*, against David Hume's *History of England*, its midcentury disparagements of Shakespeare monumentalized by reprintings, translations, and Hume's own prestige. In doing so they fought a battle won long before on the bloody fields of polemical journalism. Having mistaken him for David, the Romantics rushed to defend Goliath—and prided themselves on their part in his victory.

The Romantic attack on Shakespeare's eighteenth-century editors and critics belonged, socially, to a much more general attack on the intelligentsia. It was wrongly but widely believed that the French Revolution had been the work of a cabal of Enlightenment intellectuals and that a similar cabal of radicals, epitomized by Tom Paine and Mary Wollstonecraft, was at work in England. A conspiracy of pedants had overturned the French state and was busy planting its little lever under the foundations of the English one. The Romantic poets and critics were themselves, of course, intellectuals; they could not simply join the popular clamor against the class to which they belonged. But some of them did respond to the same emotions and, at the same time, usefully distanced themselves from such criticism, by attacking Shakespeare's eighteenth-century editors and critics, thus deflecting the outrage onto another set of intellectuals.

The English Romantics displaced their revolutionary fervor away from politics onto literature. Such displacements are also characteristic of their attitude toward Shakespeare. They did not challenge, but appropriated, Shakespeare or Milton; the energies of their rebellion against the literature of the past were channeled into attacks on lesser poets in the vernacular pantheon. Rather than confront Shakespeare, they directed their hostility onto his editors, critics, and adapters. Dryden, Pope, and Johnson conveniently belonged to both categories of target. Anyone familiar with political history will recognize such tactics: in the face of growing popular protest, the president/prime minister/general secretary/emperor sacrifices members of his staff. By toppling underlings a society presumes and ensures the inviolability of the high center of power. The Romantic manifesto did not call for the overthrow of the reigning literary dynasty; it called, instead, only for a change of ministry. Schlegel contended that English critics had never properly appreciated their greatest poet; they had abdicated, and Germany could therefore claim Shakespeare for herself. Coleridge and his contemporaries could endorse Schlegel's condemnation of eighteenth-century critical practice, but they wanted to retain English control of this strategic literary territory. The greatness of the "sovereign" Shakespeare would be better served and sustained by Prime Minister Coleridge than it had been by the corrupt pensioners of the old regime.

Shakespeare, simultaneously supreme and central, commanded the apex of the cone of English literature. Although given the opportunity and the injunction to overthrow the literary past, to make everything natural and new, the Romantics could not often, or for long, take arms against a sea of Shakespeare. Although he intended otherwise, the man whom Hamlet stabbed behind the arras was Polonius, not Claudius: the minister, not the king.

· ·

NOTES

[Notes have been renumbered to adjust for omitted material]

1. *Lectures 1808–1819 on Literature*, ed. R. A. Foakes, 2 vols. (1987), in *The Collected Works of Samuel Taylor Coleridge*, gen. ed. Kathleen Coburn: II, 293 (manuscript note dated January 7, 1819).
2. *Specimens of the Table Talk of the late Samuel Taylor Coleridge*, ed. H. N. Coleridge, 2 vols. (1835), I, 69 (June 24, 1827).
3. Coleridge, *Lectures 1808–1819*, I, 386, 390.
4. Ibid., 540, 542.
5. *The Literary Remains of Samuel Taylor Coleridge*, ed. H. N. Coleridge, 4 vols. (1836), II, 135.
6. William Wordsworth, *The Borderers*, ed. Robert Osborn, Cornell Wordsworth (1982), III v.60–65 (1797 manuscript).
7. *The Borderers*, 812 (1842 note).
8. *The Letters of John Keats 1814–21*, ed. Hyder Edward Rollins, 2 vols. (1958), II, 115–16 (June 9, 1819).
9. *Letters of John Keats*, II, 312 (August [?] 1820).
10. *The Letters of Charles and Mary Anne Lamb*, ed. Edwin W. Marrs, Jr., 3 vols. (1975–78), III, 243–44 (May 12, 1817).
11. "Hamlet," from *Characters of Shakespear's Plays* (1817), in *The Complete Works of William Hazlitt*, ed. P. P. Howe, 21 vols. (1930), IV, 232–37.
12. "Byron and Shelley on the Character of Hamlet," *New Monthly Magazine* 29 (1830), 328, 329, 336. The authenticity of the account is defended by Earl Wasserman, "Shelley's Last Poetics: A Reconsideration," in *From Sensibility to Romanticism*, ed. Frederick W. Hilles and Harold Bloom (1965), 505–11; evidence for Mary Shelley's authorship of the unsigned arti-

cle is given by Charles E. Robinson, *Shelley and Byron: The Snake and Eagle Wreathed in Fight* (1976), 270. The 1830 article does not date the conversation, but the independent testimony of Samuel Rogers places it in Pisa in April 1822.

13. Hermann Ulrici, *Shakspeare's dramatische Kunst* (1839), trans. as *Shakspeare's Dramatic Art* (1846), 238–39.

14. Wordsworth's Muse, in the 1812 manuscript of *The Waggoner*, "scents the morning air" (MS 3, line 680; *Benjamin the Waggoner*, ed. Paul Betz, Cornell Wordsworth [1981], 305); at *Hamlet* 1.5.58/675, the Ghost "scent[s] the morning air." The parallel is discussed by Jonathan Bate, *Shakespeare and the English Romantic Imagination* (1986), 103–5.

15. George Vandenhoff, *Leaves from an actor's note-book* (1860), 22; George Henry Lewes, *On Actors and the Art of Acting* (1875), 5.

16. Siegbert Prawer, *Heine's Shakespeare: An Inaugural Lecture* (1970), 37, translating an account written by Heine in 1938; quoting *Merchant of Venice* 1.3.126–27/443–44.

17. Leigh Hunt, "Theatrical Examiner. No. 163," *The Examiner* (February 26, 1815), 138–39.

18. Coleridge, *Table Talk*, I, 24 (April 27, 1823).

19. Alluding to *Romeo and Juliet* 3.5.9/1943 and *I Henry IV* 4.1.100/2234.

20. Jonathan Bate, "Parodies of Shakespeare," *Journal of Popular Culture* 19 (1985-86), 75–89.

21. John Poole, *Hamlet Travestie*, 2nd ed. (1811), 10.

22. A. Jonathan Bate, "Hazlitt's Shakespearean Quotations," *Prose Studies* 7 (1984), 26.

23. *Letters of John Keats*, II, 139 (August 14, 1819).

24. James Beattie, Letter XXI (January 1, 1768), in Sir William Forbes, *An Account of the Life and Writings of James Beattie, LL.D.*, 2 vols. (1806), I, 110–11.

25. *The Letters of David Garrick*, ed. David M. Little and George M. Kahrl, 3 vols. (1963), II, 542 (September 12, 1766).

26. *The Correspondence of Edmund Burke*, ed. Alfred Cobban and Robert A. Smith, 10 vols. (1958–70), VI, 10 (letter of August 9, 1789).

27. Burke, *Reflections on the Revolution in France* (1790), 11.

28. Burke, *Correspondence*, VI, 126 (July 29, 1790), quoting *Hamlet* 1.2.158/314.

29. Ibid., 86 (February 19, 1790, from Philip Francis), 90 (February 20, 1790).

30. *Hamlet* 2.2.558–63/1488–93; quoted from Malone's edition, 9.280–81.

31. Burke, *Correspondence*, VI, 182 (ca. November 29, 1790).

32. Edmond Malone, ed., *The Plays and Poems of William Shakspeare*, 10 vols. (1790), vol. I, pt. 1, lxviii.

33. Burke, *Correspondence*, VI, 206 (note).

34. Ibid., VIII, 456.

35. Jane Austen, *Mansfield Park*, 3 vols. (1814), III, 60 (Chapter 34 in modern editions).

36. Coleridge, *Biographia Literaria* (1817), ed. James Engell and W. Jackson Bate, 2 vols. (1983), in *Collected Works*: II, 27.

37. Hazlitt, *Lectures on the English Poets* (1818), in *Works*, 5.161–64.

38. Ibid., 162.

39. Hazlitt, *Characters of Shakespear's Plays*, in *Works*, IV, 216, 214.

40. Thomas Paine, *Rights of Man* (1791), 16, 15, 9.

41. Ibid., 39, 28.

42. William Cobbett, *A Year's Residence, in the United States of America* (1818), pars. 270–71 (pp. 278–85).

43. William Hawkins, *Praelectiones poeticae in schola naturalis philosophiae Oxon. habitae* (1758); see J. W. Binns, "Some Lectures on Shakespeare in Eighteenth-Century Oxford: *The Praelectiones poeticae* of William Hawkins," in *Shakespeare: Text, Language, Criticism: Essays in Honour of Marvin Spevack*, ed. Bernhard Fabian and Kurt Tetzeli von Rosador (1987), 19–33.

44. *Thraliana: The Diary of Mrs. Hester Lynch Thrale (Later Mrs. Piozzi)*, 1776–1809, ed. Katherine C. Balderston, 2 vols. (1942; rev. 1951), I, 97 (June 1777).

45. Thomas Francklin, *A Dissertation on Antient Tragedy* (1760), 59; "An Essay on the Merits of Shakespear and Corneille," *The British Magazine* 1 (June 1760), 362-65; *The Critical Review* 10 (September 1760), 247; George Lyttleton, *Dialogues of the Dead* (1760), 118.

46. J. H. Plumb, "The Commercialization of Leisure," in Neil McKendrick, John Brewer, and J. H. Plumb, *The Birth of a Consumer Society: The Commercialization of Eighteenth-Century England* (1982), 276.
47. Stone, "The Making of the Repertoire," 201.
48. C. B. Hogan, *The London Stage, 1660–1800. Part 5: 1776–1800*, 3 vols. (1968), I, clxxi–clxxiii.
49. Burke, *Correspondence*, I, 360–61 (letter of uncertain date; apparently 1750s or 1760s).
50. Arthur Murphy, *The Gray's Inn Journal*, No. 12 (December 15, 1753).
51. Joseph Warton, *An Essay on the Writings and Genius of Pope* (1756), 202.
52. *The Critical Review*, 10 (September 1760), 248.
53. Edward Capell, ed., *MR. WILLIAM SHAKESPEARE his Comedies, Histories, and Tragedies*, 10 vols. (1768), I, sig. a3^v-a4.
54. David Garrick, *An Ode Upon Dedicating A Building, And Erecting A Statue, To Shakespeare, At Stratford Upon Avon* (1769), "Advertisement."
55. Carlo Goldoni, *Malcontenti* (1754), quoted in Lacy Collison-Morley, *Shakespeare in Italy* (1916), 35–38.
56. Pope, "The Preface of the Editor to The Works of William Shakespear," *Prose Works*, II, 16; *Shakespeare, traduit de L'Anglois*, trans. Pierre Le Tourneur, 20 vols. (1776–83), I, xciii.
57. Johann Wolfgang von Goethe, *Wilhelm Meister's Apprenticeship*, trans. Thomas Carlyle (1824), Book IV, chap. 13.
58. Jonathan Bate, "Shakespearean Allusion in English Caricature in the Age of Gillray," *Journal of the Warburg and Courtauld Institutes* 49 (1986), 196–210.
59. Joseph-Léopold Borgerhoff, *Le Théâtre Anglais à Paris sous la Restauration* (1912), 14.
60. John Boydell, "A Catalogue of the Pictures in the Shakespeare Gallery" (May 1789), in *Collection of Prints, from pictures painted for the purpose of illustrating the dramatic works of Shakspeare, by the artists of Great-Britain* (1803); reprinted as *The Boydell Shakespeare Prints* (1968).
61. Winifred H. Friedman, *Boydell's Shakespeare Gallery* (1976), 5.
62. "Historical Chronicle," *Universal Magazine* 84 (May 1789), 274.
63. William Hogarth, "Autobiographical Notes" (British Library Add. MS. 27,991), fol. 10; printed in *The Analysis of Beauty*, ed. Joseph Burke (1955), 209.
64. Laurence Sterne, *The Life and Opinions of Tristram Shandy, Gentleman* (1759–67), ed. Melvyn New and Joan New, 3 vols. (1978–84), I, 26 (chapter XI).
65. *The Tempest* 1. 2.354–65/420–31.
66. *Johnson on Shakespeare*, ed. Arthur Sherbo, 2 vols. (1968), in *The Yale Edition of the Works of Samuel Johnson*: II, 737 (added in 1773).
67. Edmond Malone *et al.*, *Supplement to the edition of Shakspeare's Plays Published In 1778*, 2 vols. (1780), I, 152; Isaac Reed, ed., *The Plays of William Shakspeare*, 10 vols. (1785), IX, 607–8.
68. George Walton Williams, "The Publishing and Editing of Shakespeare's Plays," in *William Shakespeare: His World, His Work, His Influence*, ed. John F. Andrews, 3 vols. (1985), III, 595–98.
69. G. E. Lessing, *Hamburg Dramaturgy*, trans. Helen Zimmern (1962), 173 (No. 73: January 12, 1768); A. W. von Schlegel, *Vorlesungen über dramatische Kunst und Litteratur* (1809–11), II, ii, 181–82, trans. by John Black as *A Course of Lectures on Dramatic Art and Literature*, 2 vols. (1815), II, 217.
70. Joseph Addison (?), *A Discourse on Ancient and Modern Learning* (1739), 23, 2.
71. Pope, "Preface," *Prose Works*, II, 23.
72. *The Gentleman's Magazine and Historical Chronicle* 58 (1788), 778: unsigned letter dated September 11, 1788.
73. Paine, 5.
74. Leigh Hunt, *Autobiography*, 2 vols. (1850), I, 162.
75. Folger MS. M. a. 129.
76. Ian Michael, *The Teaching of English: From the Sixteenth Century to 1870* (1987), 196–98.

HENRY LOUIS GATES, JR.

LITERARY THEORY AND THE

BLACK TRADITION

We have dreamed a dream, and there is no interpreter of it.

GENESIS 40:8

Criticism is the habitus *of the contemplative intellect, whereby we try to recognize with probability the genuine quality of a literary work by using appropriate aids and rules.*

. . . The interpreter must know the writer's idiom well, aim at truth without partiality and inquire into the true and false reading.

Note. A painter is known by his painting, a writer by his writing.

The art of interpretation or hermeneutics is the habitus *of the contemplative intellect of probing into the sense of a somewhat special text by using logical rules and suitable means.*

Note. Hermeneutics differs from criticism as the species does from the genus and the part does from the whole.

. . . In every interpretation there occur the author, the literary work, and the interpreter.

ANTONIUS GUILLELMUS AMO, an African from Guinea.
"On Criticism, Hermeneutics, Method," *Treatise on the Art
of Philosophising Soberly and Accurately* (1738)

The idea of a determining formal relationship between literature and social institutions does not in itself explain the sense of urgency that has, at least since the publication in 1760 of *A Narrative of the Uncommon Sufferings and Surprising Deliverance of Briton Hammon, a Negro Man*, characterized nearly the whole of Afro-American writing. This idea has often encouraged a posture that belabors the social and documentary status of black art. Indeed, the earliest discrete examples of written discourse by the slave and ex-slave came under a scrutiny not primarily literary. Black formal writing, beginning with the five autobiographical slave narratives published in English between 1760 and 1789, was taken to be collective as well as functional. Because these narratives documented the black's potential for "culture"—that is, for manners and morals—the command of written English virtually separated the African from the Afro-American, the slave from the ex-slave, titled property from fledgling human being. Well-meaning abolitionists cited these texts as proof of the common humanity of bondsman and lord, yet these same texts also demonstrated the contrary for slavery's proponents: the African imagination was merely derivative.

The command of a written language, then, could be no mean thing in the life of the slave. Learning to read, the slave narratives repeat again and again, was a decisive political act; learning to write, as measured against an eighteenth-century scale of culture and society, was an irreversible step away from the cotton field toward a freedom larger even than physical manumission. What the use of language entiled for personal social mobility and what it implied about the public Negro mind made for the onerous burden of literacy, a burden having very little to do with the use of language as such, a burden so pervasive that the nineteenth-century quest for literacy and the twentieth-century quest for form became the central, indeed controlling, metaphors (if not mythical matrices) in Afro-American narrative. Once the private dream fused with a public and therefore political imperative, the Negro arts were committed; the pervasive sense of urgency and fundamental unity of the black arts became a millennial, if not precisely apocalyptic, force.

I do not mean to suggest that these ideas were peculiar to eighteenth-century criticism of black texts. For example, William K. Wimsatt argues that we learn from Herder's Prize Essay of 1773 on the *Causes of the Decline of Taste in Different Nations* that in Germany "the appreciation of various folk and Gothic literatures and the comparative study of ancient, eastern, and modern foreign literatures (the criticism of literature by age and race) were strongly established, and these interests profoundly affected theories about the nature of literature as the expression of, or the power that shaped, human cultures or human nature in general." Wimsatt also reminds us that Friedrick Schlegel "only accented an already pervasive view when he called poetry the most specifically human energy, the central document of any culture."[1] It should not surprise us, then, that *Poems on Various Subjects, Religious and Moral, by Phillis Wheatley, Negro Servant to Mr. Wheatley of Boston,* the first book of poems published by an African in English, became almost immediately after its publication in London in 1773 the international antislavery movement's most salient argument for the African's innate mental equality. That the book went to five printings before 1800 testified far more to its acceptance as a "legitimate" product of "the African muse," as Henri Grégoire wrote in 1808, than to the merit of its sometimes vapid elegiac verse.[2] The eighteen signatures, or "certificates of authenticity," that preface the book, including one by John Hancock and another by the governor of Massachusetts, Thomas Hutchinson, meant to "leave no doubt, that [Phillis Wheatley] is its author."[3] Literally scores of public figures—from Voltaire to George Washington, from Benjamin Rush to Benjamin Franklin—reviewed Wheatley's book, yet virtually no one discussed the book as poetry. It was an unequal contest: the documentary status of black art assumed priority over mere literary judgment; criticism rehearsed content to justify one notion of origins or another. Of these discussions, Thomas Jefferson's proved most central to the shaping of the Afro-American critical activity.

Asserted primarily to debunk the exaggerated claims of the abolitionists, Thomas Jefferson's remarks on Phillis Wheatley's poetry, as well as on Ignatius

Sancho's posthumously published *Letters* (1782), exerted a prescriptive influence over the criticism of the writing of blacks for the next 150 years. "Never yet," Jefferson prefaces his discussion of Wheatley, "could I find a Black that had uttered a thought above the level of plain narration; never seen even an elementary trait of painting or sculpture." As a specimen of the human mind, Jefferson continues, Wheatley's poems, as poetry, did not merit discussion. "Religion," he writes, "indeed has produced a Phillis Whately [sic] but it could not produce a poet." "The compositions published under her name," Jefferson concludes, "are below the dignity of criticism. The heroes of the *Dunciad* are to her, as Hercules to the author of the poem." As for Sancho's *Letters,* Jefferson says:

> His imagination is wild and extravagant, escapes incessantly from every restraint of reason and taste, and, in the course of its vagaries, leave a tract of thought as incoherent and eccentric, as is the course of a meteor through the sky. His subjects should have led him to a process of sober reasoning: yet we find him always substituting sentiment for demonstration.[4]

The substitution of sentiment for demonstration is the key opposition in this passage, pitting unreflective emotion against reason. Writing, as I shall argue, was a principle sign of reason, especially since the *spoken* language of black people had become an object of parody at least since 1769 when *The Padlock* appeared on the American stage, including among its cast of characters a West Indian slave called Mungo. We know Mungo's essence by his language, a language represented by a caricature that signifies the difference that separated white from black:

> Me supper ready, and now me go to the
>   cellar—But I
> say, Massa, ax de old man now,
>   what good him watching do, him
> bolts, and him bars, him walls,
>   and him padlocks.[5]

No, blacks could not achieve any true presence by speaking, since their "African"-informed English seems to have only underscored their status as *sui generis,* as distinct in spoken language use as in their peculiarly "black" color. If blacks were to signify as full members of the Western human community, they would have to do so in their writings.

Even before Jefferson allowed himself the outrageous remark that "the improvement of the blacks in body and mind, in the first instance of their mixture with the whites, has been observed by every one, and proves that their inferiority is not the effect merely of their condition of life," advocates of the unity of the human species had forged a union of literary tradition, individual talent, and innate racial capacity. Phillis Wheatley's "authenticators," for instance, announced:

> We whose Names are under-written, do assure the world, that the POEMS specified in the following Page, were (as we verily believe) written by *Phillis,* a young Negro Girl, who was but a few years since, brought an uncultured Barbarian from Africa, and has ever since been and now is, under the Disadvantage of serving as a

Slave of a Family in this Town. She has been examined by some of the best judges, and is thought qualified to write them.[6]

Further, Wheatley herself asks indulgence of the critic, considering the occasion of her verse. "As her Attempts in Poetry are now sent into the World, it is hoped the critic will not severely censure their Defects; and we presume they have too much Merit to be cast aside with contempt, as worthless and trifling effusions." Wheatley clearly could not imagine a critic as harsh as Jefferson. "With all their Imperfections," she concludes, "the poems are now humbly submitted to the Perusal of the Public." Other than the tone of the author's preface, there was little here that was "humbly submitted" to Wheatley's public. Her volume generated much speculation about the nature of the "African imagination." So compelling did evidence of the African's artistic abilities prove to be to Enlightenment speculation on the idea of progress and the precise shape of the *scala naturae* that just nine years after Wheatley's *Poems* appeared, more than one thousand British lords and ladies subscribed to have Ignatius Sancho's collected letters published. Even more pertinent in our context, Joseph Jekyll, M.P., prefaced the volume with a full biographical account of the colorful Sancho's life, structured curiously around the received relation between "genius" and "species."

British readers were fascinated by the "African mind" presented in the collected letters to Ignatius Sancho. Sancho was named "from a fancied resemblance to the Squire of Don Quixote" and had his portrait painted by Gainsborough and engraved by Bartolozzi. He was a correspondent with Garrick and Sterne and, apparently, something of a poet as well. "A commerce with the Muses was supported amid the trivial and momentary interruptions of a shop," Jekyll writes. Indeed, not only were "the Poets studied, and even imitated with some success," but "two pieces were constructed for the stage." Moreover, Sancho composed and published musical compositions. In addition to his creative endeavors, Sancho was a critic—perhaps the first African critic of the arts to write in English. His "theory of Music was discussed, published and dedicated to the Princess Royal, and Painting was so much within the circle of Ignatius Sancho's judgment and criticism," Jekyll observes, "that several artists paid great *deference* to his opinion."[7]

Jekyll's rather involved biography is a pretext to display the artifacts of the "sable mind," as was the very publication of the *Letters* themselves. "*Her* motives for laying them before the publick," the publisher admits, "were the desire of showing that an untutored African may possess abilities equal to an European." Sancho was an "extraordinary Negro," his biographer relates, although he was a bit better for being a bit bad. "Freedom, riches, and leisure, naturally led to a disposition of African tendencies into indulgences; and that which dissipated the mind of Ignatius completely drained the purse," Jekyll puns. "In his attachment to women, he displayed a profuseness which not unusually characterizes the excess of the passion." "Cards had formerly seduced him," we are told, "but an unsuccessful contest at cribbage with a jew, who won his cloaths, had determined to abjure the propensity which appears to be innate among his countrymen." Here again we see drawn the thread between phylogeny and ontogeny. "A French writer relates," Jekyll explains, "that in the kingdoms of Ardrah, Whydah, and Benin, a Negro will stake at play his fortune, his children, and his liberty." Thus driven to distraction, Sancho was "induced to consider the stage" since "his complexion suggested an offer to the manager of attempting Othello and Oroonoko; but a defective and incorrigible *articulation* rendered it abortive" (emphasis added).

Colorful though Jekyll's anecdotes are, they are a mere pretext for the crux of his argument: a disquisition on cranial capacity, regional variation, skin color, and intelligence. The example of Sancho, made particularly human by the citation of his foibles, is meant to put to rest any suspicion about the native abilities of the Negro:

> Such was the man whose species philosophers and anatomists have endeavored to degrade as a deterioration of the human; and such was the man whom [Thomas] Fuller, with a benevolence and quaintness of phrase peculiarly his own, accounted "God's Image, though cut in Ebony." To the harsh definition of the naturalist, oppressions political and legislative have added; and such are hourly aggravated towards this unhappy race of men by vulgar prejudice and popular insult. To combat these on commercial principles, has been the labour of [others]—such an effort here [he concludes ironically] would be an impertinent digression.[8]

That Sancho's attainments are not merely isolated exceptions to the general morass is indicated by the state of civilization on the African "slave-coast." Jekyll continues:

> Of those who have speculatively visited and described the slave-coast, there are not wanting some who extol the mental abilities of the natives. [Some] speak highly of their mechanical powers and indefatigable industry. [Another] does not scruple to affirm, that their ingenuity rivals the Chinese.

What is more, these marks of culture and capacity signify an even more telling body of data, since the logical extensions of mechanical powers and industry are sublime arts and stable polity:

> He who could penetrate the interior of Africa, might not improbably discover negro arts and polity, which could bear little analogy to the ignorance and grossness of slaves in the sugar-islands, expatriated in infamy; and brutalized under the whip and the task-master.

"And he," Jekyll summarizes, "who surveys the extent of intellect to which Ignatius Sancho had attained self-education, will perhaps conclude, that the perfection of the reasoning faculties does not depend on the colour of a common integument."

Jekyll's preface became a touchstone for the literary anthropologists who saw in black art a categorical repository for the African's potential to *deserve* inclusion in the human community. Echoes of Jekyll's language resound throughout the prefaces to slave testimony. Gustavus Vassa's own claim in 1789 that the African's contacts with "liberal sentiments" and "the Christian religion" have "exalted human nature" is vouched for by more than one hundred Irish subscribers. Charles Ball's editor asserts in 1836 that Ball is "embued by nature with a tolerable portion of intellectual capacity."[9] Both Garrison's and Phillips's prefaces to *The Narrative of the Life of Frederick Douglas* (1845) and James McCune Smith's introduction to Douglass's *My Bondage and My Freedom* (1855) attest to Douglass's African heritage, former bestial status, and intellectual abilities. McCune Smith, a black physician, proffers the additional claims for literary excellence demanded by the intensity of doubt toward the black African's mental abilities:

> The Negro, for the first time in the world's history brought in full contact with high civilization, must prove his title first to all that is demanded for him; in the teeth of unequal chances, he must prove himself equal to the mass of those who oppress him—therefore, absolutely superior to his apparent fate, and to their relative ability. And it is most cheering to the friends of freedom, to-day, that evidence of this equal-ity is rapidly accumulating, not from the ranks of the half-breed colored people of the free states, but from the very depths of slavery itself; the indestructible equality of man to man is demonstrated by the ease with which black men, scarce one remove from barbarism—if slavery can be honored with such a distinction—vault into the high places of the most advanced and painfully acquired civilization.[10]

An 1845 review of Douglass's *Narrative* emphasizes the relevance of each "prod-uct" of the African mind almost as another primary argument in the abolitionist's brief against slavery:

> Considered merely as a narrative, we have never read one more simple, true, coherent, and warm with genuine feeling. It is an excellent piece of writing, and on that score to be prized as a specimen of the powers of the black race, which preju-dice persists in disputing. We prize highly all evidence of this kind, and it is becom-ing more abundant.[11]

If an abolitionist reviewer in 1845 would admit that "we prize highly all evidence of this kind," he was only summarizing an antislavery emphasis that was at least a century and a half old. Wheatley and Sancho, and much later even the articulate ex-slave Frederick Douglass, commenced their public careers as the result of experiments to ascertain just how much "natural capacity" lay dormant in the "sable mind." Several enlightened aristocrats in the first half of the eighteenth cen-tury abstracted individual black children from the daily routine of slavery and edu-cated them with their own children in experiments to ascertain if the "perfectibility of man" applied equally to blacks and to whites. What was at stake in these exper-iments was nothing less than the determination of the place of the African on the Great Chain of Being, a place that hovered rather precariously well beneath the European (and every other) "race of man," yet just above—or parallel to—that place reserved for the "orang-outang." As Edward Long put the matter in *The History of Jamaica* (1774), there was a *natural* relation between the ape and the African, and

> If such has been the intention of the Almighty, we are then perhaps to regard the orang-outang as,
> —the lag of human kind,
> Nearest to brutes, by God design'd.

For Long, the ape and the African were missing links, sharing "the most intimate connexion and consanguinity," including even "amorous intercourse." While it might sound hyperbolic to state this today, enlightened antislavery advocates turned to writing to determine and to demonstrate in the most public way just how far removed from the ape the African was in fact. Let us examine briefly four instances of blacks whose literacy would serve as an argument against the bestial status of all black people.

Literacy—the literacy of formal writing—was both a technology and a commodity. It was a commodity with which the African's right to be considered a human being could be traded. The slave narratives repeat figures of the complex relationship between freedom and literacy. But well before the first slave narrative was published, the freedom of literacy became inscribed in the curious education of Wilhelm Amo. In 1707, Amo, at the age of four an African slave, was given to the reigning Duke of Brunswick-Wolfenbuttel as a gift. The duke, in turn, gave the slave as a present to his son, Augustus Wilhelm. Augustus Wilhelm ascended the throne in 1714 and became the influential protector and benefactor of the young slave. Amo was christened Anton Wilhelm in 1708 and was educated in the same manner as were the other children of the royal family. Amo matriculated at the Prussian University of Halle on June 9, 1727. In 1732, he defended his thesis, entitled "De jure Maurorum in Europa," and was promoted to the academic degree of a Candidate of the Laws. In 1730, he received the degree of Magister of Philosophy and Liberal Arts at the University of Wittenberg, a degree to be renamed Doctor of Philosophy within a few years. In 1734, Amo published a dissertation entitled *Inaugural philosophical dissertation on the APATHY of the human mind, or the absence of feeling and the faculty of feeling in the human mind and the presence of them in our organic living body,* a thesis on a subject that borders upon psychology and the medical sciences. In 1738, Amo published his treatise on logic, from which the second epigraph here is taken, while a university lecturer at Halle. In 1739, Amo assumed a position in the Faculty of Philosophy of Jena. Not much else is known of Amo's life. Fredrick Blumenbach in 1787 wrote that he had been appointed Councillor at the court of the Prussian king some time between 1740 and 1750. We do know, however, that in 1753 Amo was living back in Africa, near his birthplace on the Gold Coast, known today as Ghana, where he lived as a hermit and was widely known as a magician and a doctor. We also know that Amo returned to Africa willingly.[12]

What is remarkable about Amo's life and writings is that during his lifetime and throughout the Enlightenment they were seized upon by philosophers and critics as proof that the African was innately equal to the European, because this one African had demonstrated mastery of the arts and sciences. His thesis supervisor, for example, wrote that just as Terence, Tertullian, St. Cyprian, and St. Augustine had done for North Africa, Amo proved that those parts of sub-Saharan Africa, populated by beings whose humanity was in doubt, could produce superior intellects. Amo, moreover, demonstrated that from among other "uncivilized" nations outstanding individuals could emerge with the proper formal training.

Let us examine another instance of this curious phenomenon, one that occurred well beyond the confines and luxuries of the palace and the academy. One early eighteenth-century slave's experiences represent the relationship between freedom and literacy dramatically and more directly, indeed, than would seem possible. Job, the son of Solomon (Suleiman), a priest of the Fulani, apparently was a person of some distinction in West Africa, until he was captured by the Mandingos and sold into slavery in 1731. From a plantation in Maryland, Job wrote a letter in Arabic to his father. Mail services between early eighteenth-century Maryland and Senegal, of course, were not quite as direct as they are today. Job, now a slave, had absolutely no chance of seeing a letter written in Arabic reach his African father. This letter, nevertheless, by a remarkable set of accidents eventually came into the possession of James Oglethorpe, one of the founders of the colony of Georgia and then the deputy governor of the Royal African Company. Oglethorpe sent the Arabic text up to Oxford, where the Huguenot John Gagnier held the Laudian Chair of Arabic. Gagnier's translation so moved Oglethorpe—about whom Pope wrote, "One, driv'n by strong Benevolence of Soul/Shall fly, like Oglethorpe, from Pole to Pole"—and so impressed him with the strength of Job's character that in June 1732 he gave his bond for the payment of this slave at the price of forty-five pounds. Job, I should add, came to London, was the toast of the Duke of Montague (who would soon thereafter repeat the Duke of Brunswick's experiment with Wilhelm Amo and become patron to Francis Williams and Ignatius Sancho) and of the British royal family, and fourteen months later in 1734 returned, as did Amo, to his father's land. Job Ben Solomon literally wrote his way out of slavery; his literacy, translated into forty-five pounds, was the commodity with which he earned his escape price.[13]

Lest we think that Job's was an isolated incident, there were dozens of instances of this use of literacy as a commodity. As late as 1829, in this country, George Moses Horton's master at North Carolina collected his slave's poems, published them as a book, and then falsely advertised widely in Northern black and antislavery newspapers that all proceeds from the book's sales would be used to purchase Horton's freedom! However, royalties of the 1879 edition of Francisco Calcagno's *Poetas de Color,* published at Habana, were used to purchase the freedom of the slave poet, José de Carme Díaz.

There were many other such experiments: "el negro" Juan Latino, who published three books of poems in Latin at Granada between 1573 and 1576; Jacobus Capitein, who graduated from the University of Leyden in 1742 and whose thesis was published in Latin and in Dutch that same year; and Phillis Wheatley, who in 1773 became the first African to publish a book of poems in English. All three, among several others, were the subject of experiments in literature mastery, whose lives and works came to serve as black figures for the idea of progress and the perfectibility of man, as well as human synecdoches for the capacity of the African to assume a parallel rank with the European on the Great Chain of Being.

Amo and his fellow writers, Othello's countrymen, suffered under the sheer burden of literacy: to demonstrate that the person of African descent was indeed a human being. Amo was not competing, as it were, with Newton; he was distinguishing himself from the apes. How curious, how arbitrary that the written word, as early as 1700, signified the presence of a common humanity with the European. Any serious theory of the nature and function of writing in the Western tradition must, to put it bluntly, take the critical reception to this unique genre into full account. What more meaningful example of the eighteenth century's theories of writing can possibly exist? What a profoundly burdensome task to impose upon the philosopher such as Amo—indeed, to impose upon the human being. What an ironic origin of a literary tradition! If Europeans read the individual achievements of blacks in literature and scholarship as discrete commentaries of Africans themselves upon the Western fiction of the "text of blackness," then the figure of blackness as an absence came to occupy an ironic place in the texts of even the most sober European philosophers. In the next section of this chapter, I wish to outline the repetition of the relationship between blackness and writing, so that I may begin to demonstrate how the strategies of negation, so central to Black Aesthetic criticism, were locked in a relation of thesis to antithesis to a racist discourse embedded in Western philosophy.

. . . .

I would hope that it is obvious that the creation of formal literature could be no mean matter in the life of the slave, since the sheer literacy of writing was the very commodity that separated animal from human being, slave from citizen, object from subject. Reading, and especially writing, in the life of the slave represented a process larger than even "mere" physical manumission, since mastery of the arts and letters was Enlightenment Europe's sign of that solid line of division between human being and thing.

The letters of attestation of authorship that preface Phillis Wheatley's *Poems* of 1773 are an aspect of the commodity function of black writing, just as surely as we can describe the curious attempts of George Moses Horton's master in 1829 to raise his slave's manumission price by publishing and selling his slave's poetry through subscriptions advertised in Northern black and reform antebellum newspapers. Any theory of the origins of American literature, for example, must account for this process of the reification of the activity of writing into a commodity, . . . from Samuel Purchas in the seventeenth century to Fontenelle, Hume, Kant, Jefferson, and Hegel in 1813, down to William Dean Howells at the turn of the century, and beyond. Race and reason, ethnocentrism and logocentrism, together were used by the enlightened to deprive the black of his or her humanity.

Unlike almost every other literary tradition, the Afro-American literary tradition was generated as a response to eighteenth- and nineteenth-century allegations that persons of African descent did not, and could not, create literature. Philosophers and literary critics, such as Hume, Kant, Jefferson, and Hegel, seemed to decide that the absence or presence of a written literature was the signal measure of the potential, innate humanity of a race. The African living in Europe or in the New World seems to have felt compelled to create a literature both to demonstrate implicitly that blacks did indeed possess the intellectual ability to create a written art and to indict the several social and economic institutions that delimited the humanity of all black people in Western cultures.

So insistent did these racist allegations prove to be, at least from the eighteenth to the early twentieth centuries, that it is fair to describe the subtext of the history of black letters as this urge to refute the claim that because blacks had no written traditions they were bearers of an inferior culture. The relationship between European and American critical theory, then, and the development of African and Afro-American literary traditions, can readily be seen to have been ironic indeed. Even as late as 1911, when J. E. Casely-Hayford published *Ethiopia Unbound* (called the first African novel), that pioneering author felt compelled to address this matter in the first two paragraphs of his text. "At the dawn of the twentieth century," the novel opens, "men of light and leading both in Europe and in America had not yet made up their minds as to what place to assign to the spiritual aspirations of the black man. . . . Before this time, it had been discovered that the black man was not necessarily the missing link between man and ape. It has even been granted that for intellectual endowments he had nothing to be ashamed of in an *open* competition with the Aryan or any other type." *Ethiopia Unbound,* it seems obvious, was concerned to settle the matter of black mental equality, which had remained something of an open question for two hundred years. Concluding this curiously polemical exposition of three paragraphs, which precedes the introduction of the novel's protagonist, Casely-Hayford points to "the names of men like [W. E. B.] Du Bois, Booker T. Washington, [Edward Wilmot] Blyden, [Paul Laurence] Dunbar, [Samuel] Coleridge-Taylor, and others" as prima facie evidence of the sheer saliency of what Carter G. Woodson once termed "the public Negro mind." These were men, the narrative concludes, "who had distinguished themselves in the fields of activity and intellectuality," men who had demonstrated conclusively that the African's first cousin was indeed the European rather than the ape.

That the presence of a written literature could assume such large proportions in several Western cultures from the Enlightenment to this century is only as curious as the fact that blacks themselves, as late as 1911, felt the need to speak the matter silent, to end the argument by producing literature. Few literary traditions have begun or been sustained by such a complex and ironic relation to their criticism: allegations of an absence led directly to a presence, a literature often inextricably bound in a dialogue with its potentially harshest critics.

In Spanish and English, in Latin and French, in German and Dutch, the writings of blacks in the Enlightenment came under scrutiny not primarily literary, giving rise to an implicit theory of writing itself, at least of black writing, and its relation to what we have come to think of as the innate rights of a people to political freedom. Indeed, we can only begin to understand the resistance to theory in the Afro-American tradition if we qualify these terms somewhat and call this tendency the resistance to *Western* theory. Black writers and critics, since Amo, have been forced to react against an impressive received tradition of Western critical theory which not only posited the firm relation among writing, "civilization," and political authority, but which also was called upon by various Western men of letters to justify various forms of enslavement and servitude of black people. It is no surprise that black people have been theory-resistant. Because the history of this relationship between blacks and theory involves many Western philosophers, because its threads of influence have not been defined before, and because it has had such a determining effect upon black critics and writers since the eighteenth century, I have sketched its contours to begin to suggest its implications. Let us next consider how black writers and critics reacted to the racism of Western writings about the relationship between the written arts and the status of the black human being.

Hume, Kant, Jefferson, and Hegel's stature demanded response: from black writers, refutations of white doubts about their very capacity to imagine great art and hence to take a few giant steps up the Great Chain of Being; from would-be critics, encyclopedic and often hyperbolic replies to these disparaging generalizations. The critical responses include Thomas Clarkson's Prize Essay, written in Latin at Cambridge in 1785 and published as *An Essay on the Slavery and Commerce of the Human Species, Particularly the African* (1788), and the following rather remarkable volumes: Gilbert Imlay's *A Topographical Description of the Western Territory of North America* (1793); the Marquis de Bois-Robert's two-volume *The Negro Equalled by Few Europeans* (1791); Thomas Branagan's *Preliminary Essay on the Oppression of the Exiled Sons of Africa* (1804); the Abbé Grégoire's *An Enquiry Concerning the Intellectual and Moral Faculties, and*

Literature of Negroes . . . (1808); Samuel Stanhope Smith's *An Essay on the Causes of the Variety of the Human Complexion and Figure in the Human Species* (1810); Lydia Maria Child's *An Appeal in Favor of That Class of Americans Called Africans* (1833); B. B. Thatcher's *Memoir of Phillis Wheatley, a Native American and a Slave* (1834); Abigail Mott's *Biographical Sketches and Interesting Anecdotes of Persons of Color* (1838); R. B. Lewis's *Light and Truth* (1844); Theodore Hally's *A Vindication of the Capacity of the Negro Race* (1851); R. T. Greener's urbane long essay in *The National Quarterly Review* (1880); Joseph Wilson's rather ambitious *Emancipation: Its Course and Progress from 1481 B.C. to A.D. 1875* (1882); William Simmon's *Men of Mark* (1887); Benjamin Brawley's *The Negro in Literature and Art* (1918); and Joel A. Rodgers's two-volume *The World's Great Men of Color* (1946). There are well over 150 encyclopedias of black intellection, published to disprove racist aspersions cast upon the mind of "the race."

Even more telling for our purposes here is that the almost quaint authenticating signatures and statements that prefaced Wheatley's book became, certainly through the period of Dunbar and Chesnutt and even until the middle of the Harlem Renaissance, fixed attestations of the "specimen" author's physical blackness. This sort of authenticating color description was so common to these prefaces that many late nineteenth- and early twentieth-century black reviewers, particularly in the *African Methodist Episcopal Church Review, the Southern Workman,* the *Voice of the Negro, Alexander's Magazine,* and *The Colored American,* adopted it as a political as well as rhetorical strategy to counter the intense and bitter allegations of African inferiority popularized by journalistic accounts and "colorations" of social Darwinism. Through an examination of a few of these prefaces, I have tried to sketch an ironic circular thread of interpretation that commences in the eighteenth century but does not reach its fullest philosophical form until the decade between 1965 and 1975: the movement from blackness as a physical concept to blackness as a metaphysical concept. Indeed, this movement became the very text and pretext of the "Blackness" of the recent Black Arts movement, a solidly traced hermeneutical circle into which we all found ourselves drawn.

The confusion of realms, of art with propaganda, plagued the Harlem Renaissance in the twenties. A critical determination—a mutation of principles set in motion by Matthew Arnold's *Culture and Anarchy,* simplified thirty years later into Booker T. Washington's "toothbrush and bar of soap" and derived from Victorian notions of "uplifting" spiritual and moral ideals that separated the savage (noble or not) from the realm of culture and the civilized mind—meant that only certain literary treatments of black people could escape community censure. The race against social Darwinism and the psychological remnants of slavery meant that each piece of creative writing became a political statement. Each particular manifestation served as a polemic: "another bombshell fired into the heart of bourgeois culture," as *The World Tomorrow* editorialized in 1921. "The black writer," said Richard Wright, "approached the critical community dressed in knee pants of servility, curtseying to show that the Negro was not inferior, that he was human, and that he had a gift comparable to other men." As early as 1921, W. E. B. Du Bois wrote of this in the *Crisis:*

> Negro art is today plowing a difficult row. We want everything that is said about us
> to tell of the best and highest and noblest in us. We insist that our Art and

Propaganda be one. We fear that evil in us will be called racial, while in others it is viewed as individual. We fear that our shortcomings are not merely human.[14]

And as late as 1925, even as sedate an observer as Heywood Broun argued that only through art would the Negro gain freedom: "A supremely great negro artist," he told the New York Urban League, "who could catch the imagination of the world, would do more than any other agency to remove the disabilities against which the negro now labors." Further, Broun remarked that this artist-redeemer could come at any time, and he asked his audience to remain silent for ten seconds to imagine that coming![15] Ambiguity in language, then, and "feelings that are general" (argued for as early as 1861 by Frances E. W. Harper) garnered hostility and suspicion from the critical minority; ambiguity was a threat to "knowing the lines." The results for a growing black literature were disastrous, these perorations themselves dubious. Black literature came to be seen as a cultural artifact (the product of unique historical forces) or as a document that bore witness to the political and emotional tendencies of the Negro victim of white racism. Literary theory became the application of a social attitude.

By the apex of the Harlem Renaissance, then, certain latent assumptions about the relationships between art and life had become prescriptive canon. In 1925, Du Bois outlined what he called "the social compulsion" of black literature, built as it was, he contended, on "the sorrow and strain inherent in American slavery, on the difficulties that sprang from emancipation, on the feelings of revenge, despair, aspiration, and hatred which arose as the Negro struggled and fought his way upward."[16] Further, he made formal the mechanistic distinction between "method" and "content," the same distinction that allowed James Weldon Johnson to declare with glee that, sixty years after slavery, all that separated the black poet from the white was "mere technique"! Structure, by now, was atomized. Form was merely a surface for a reflection of the world, the world here being an attitude toward race; form was a repository for the disposal of ideas; message was not only meaning but value; poetic discourse was taken to be literal, or once removed; language lost its capacity to be metaphorical in the eyes of the critic; the poem approached the essay, with referents immediately perceivable; literalness precluded the view of life as allegorical; and black critics forgot that writers approached things through words, not the other way around. The functional and didactic aspects of formal discourse assumed primacy in normative analysis. The confusion of realms was complete: the critic became social reformer, and literature became an instrument for the social and ethical betterment of the black person.

. . . .

NOTES

[Notes have been renumbered to adjust for omitted material]
1. William K. Wimsatt and Cleanth Brooks, *Literary Criticism: A Short History* (New York: Knopf, 1969), p. 360.
2. *De la littérature des nègres, ou recherches sur leurs facultés intellectuelles, leurs qualités morales, et leur littérature* (Paris: Maradan, 1808), p. 140.
3. Eugene Parker Chase, *Our Revolutionary Forefathers, The Letters of Francois Marquis de Barbé-Marbois during His Residence in the United States as Secretary of the French Legation, 1779–1884* (New York: Duffield, 1929), pp. 84–85.
4. *Notes on the State of Virginia* (London: Stockdale, 1787), book II, p. 196.

5. These lines, along with an engraving of Ira Aldridge by T. Hollis, were combined to form a popular nineteenth-century broadside. The lines are from Act 2, Scene 1.
6. Phillis Wheatley, *Poems* (Philadelphia: A. Bell, 1773), p. vii.
7. *Letters of the Late Ignatius Sancho, an African* (London: J. Nichols and C. Dilly, 1783), p. vii.
8. Sancho, pp. xiv–xvi.
9. Charles Ball, *Fifty Years in Chains; Or, The Life of an American Slave* (New York: H. Dayton, 1858), p. 3.
10. Introduction, *My Bondage and My Freedom* (New York: Miller, Orton, and Mulligan, 1855), pp. xvii–xxxi.
11. *New York Tribune,* June 10, 1845, p. 1. Rpt. in *Liberator,* May 30, 1845, p. 97.
12. On Amo, see Wolfram Suchier, "A. W. Amo, Ein Mohr als Student und Privatdozent der Philosophie in Halle, Wittenburg and Iena, 1727–1740," *Akademische Rundschau,* Leipzig (1916) and "Weiteres über den Mohren Amo," *Altsachen Zeitschrift des Altsachenbundes für Heimatschutz und Heimatkunde,* Holminden, Nos. 1–2 (1981); Norbert Lochner, "Anton-Wilhelm Amo," *Transactions of the Historical Society of Ghana,* vol. III (1958); William Abraham, "The Life and Times of Anton-Wilhelm Amo," *Transactions of the Historical Society of Ghana,* vol. VII (1964); and Paulin J. Hountondji, "An African Philosopher in Germany in the Eighteenth Century," in *African Philosophy: Myth and Reality* (Bloomington: Indiana University Press, 1983), chapter V. Amo's work was translated into English in 1968 under the title *Antonius Gulielmus Amo Afer of Axim in Ghana, Translation of His Works* (Martin Luther University: Halle).
13. On Job-Ben Solomon, see Charles T. Davis and Henry Louis Gates, Jr., *The Slave's Narrative* (New York: Oxford University Press, 1985), pp. 2–3.
14. W. E. B. DuBois, "Negro Art," *Crisis* 22 (June 1921): 55–56.
15. *New York Times,* January 26, 1925, p. 3.
16. W. E. B. DuBois, "The Social Origins of American Negro Art," *Modern Quarterly* 3 (Autumn 1925): p. 53.

C L A U D I A   L .   J O H N S O N

THE DIVINE MISS JANE:

JANE AUSTEN, JANEITES, AND THE

DISCIPLINE OF NOVEL STUDIES

On the level of common sense it is not hard to wish Mr. Kimball well in his war [against "tenured radicals"]. Even when his examples of academic idiocy are funny, they are also hair-raising. . . . A proponent of feminist studies argues that "gynophobia is structured like a language." Sessions of the annual meeting of the Modern Language Association are devoted to "Jane Austen and the Masturbating Girl" and to "Desublimating the Male Sublime: Autoerotics, Anal Erotics and Corporeal Violence in Melville and William Burroughs."

—ROGER ROSENBLATT, "The Universities: A Bitter Attack"
(Review of Roger Kimball, *Tenured Radicals*),
New York Times Book Review, 22 April 1990

If we now turn to the significance of the macho-style for gay men, it would, I think, be accurate to say that this style gives rise to two reactions, both of which indicate a profound respect for machismo itself. One is the classic put-down: the butch number swaggering into a bar in a leather get-up opens his mouth and sounds like a pansy, takes you home, where the first thing you notice is the complete works of Jane Austen, gets you into bed, and—well, you know the rest. In short, the mockery of gay machismo is almost exclusively an internal affair, and it is based on the dark suspicion that you may not be getting the real article. The other reaction is, quite simply, sexual excitement.

—LEO BERSANI, "Is the Rectum a Grave?" in *AIDS: Cultural
Analysis, Cultural Activism*

Jane Austen always seems to inspire radically contradictory appeals to self-evidence. For Roger Rosenblatt, as for Roger Kimball, "common sense" dictates that Austen is obviously straitlaced and straight, and would have seemed off-limits to the nonsense of sex and gender analysis if tenured radicals had not turned the world, the obviously prim Miss Austen included, upside down. Pressing fantasies about the serenity of Regency England into the service of heterosexual presumption, Kimball and Rosenblatt place Austen *before* the advent of such ills as industrialization, dubiety, feminism, homosexuality, masturbation, the unconscious. In her novels, men are gentlemen, women are ladies, and the desires of gentlemen and ladies for each other are intelligible, complementary, mutually fulfilling, and, above all, *inevitable*. Not that such assumptions are articulated. The whole point is *not* that they do not have to be but that they must never be; as David Halperin has suggested, heterosexuality is the love that dares not speak its name, and argument would denaturalize and *out* it.[1] Recoiling from this possibility as from apocalypse itself, Rosenblatt describes Eve Kosofsky Sedgwick's paper on *Sense and Sensibility* as one of many "horror stories" that make Kimball seem like a bearded prophet of old: the world may indeed be coming to an end; even Jane Austen is not safe.[2]

For Leo Bersani, the case is different, testifying inadvertently as he does to Austen's status among gay men. His anecdote comes to us as an old and disappointing story. Like Rosenblatt, he relies on "common" knowledge and on an audience that similarly will recognize his anecdote as a *classic*, a story *you*—which is to say, "we gay boys"—all know and that for this reason will require no elaboration. Calling attention to ambivalences about effeminacy and macho within the gay community itself, Bersani's anecdote shows that homosexuality and the *Oxford Illustrated Jane Austen* are not strange bedfellows. Even as we speak, some leather-clad "butch number" may be "swaggering" up to a not-so-unsuspecting boy in a bar, his mind full of the ball at Netherfield and hot sex. Sure, he is, as Bersani puts it, a "pansy": "you" may pretend "you" had no inkling of this until later, but "you" knew it as soon as he "open[ed] his mouth" and obviously liked it well enough to go home with him in the first place. But his passion for Austen, recognized later, makes him doubly so, guaranteeing that he will be a bottom: "well, you know the rest." Bersani's complex and rather Austenian mockery aside, Austen's novels appear often to have facilitated rather than dampened conversation between men. In 1899, when he was a student at Cambridge, E. M. Forster was whisked to a fellow's room expressly to examine a new deluxe edition of Austen's novels;[3] and Montague Summers remembers "hotly championing the cause of Jane Austen" to the "charming" poet Robert Nichols, a man "distractingly violent . . . but most attractive in his flaming zeal and pale vehemence."[4] The precise nature of these Austenian encounters we do not know. This much is clear, however: the real joke in Bersani's story is not the "complete works of Jane Austen" but the "leather get-up," and their simultaneously denied and desired conjunction.

A comparable clash of assumptions over what Austen is like and what kind of converse her novels promote reerupted last fall in the *London Review of Books*, when Terry Castle discussed Austen's intense attachment to her sister Cassandra and claimed that sister-sister relations are just as important as marriage in the novels, if not more so. The editors of the *LRB* sought controversy: why else entitle the review "Was Jane Austen Gay?" without Castle's say-so? But no one expected the vehemence that followed, as scores of people rushed to rescue Austen from the charge of "sister-love": one reader, assuming "Terry" was a man, damned the "drip-drip" smuttiness of "his" discussions of women's familiarity; some swore up and down that marriages in Austen's novels were perfectly felicitous without requiring the supplemental pleasures of sororal love; others insisted testily, if inanely, that since sisters commonly shared beds in those days, it is anachronistic to imply that their intimacy meant anything "more." Austen scholar B. C. Southam entered the fray: does Austen describe women's bodies with "homophilic fascination," as Castle suggested? Not to worry: Austen was an amateur seamstress and thus had a perfectly innocent reason for attending to how gowns hugged the persons of her female acquaintance. The outcry, extensively covered in the British media, even reached *Newsweek* and *Time,* where one reader grumbled, "So Jane Austen may have been a lesbian. . . . Who cares?" only to continue by complaining about the "questionable practices" of psychoanalyzing historical subjects unable to speak for themselves and of reading too much into the "love language of women." Vainly did Castle plead that she never said that Austen had an incestuously lesbian relationship with her sister: the words *homophilic* and *homoerotic* provoked readers to announce that the limits of tolerance had been reached. Castle "polluted the shrine," and this would not be suffered.[5]

The heteronormativity of Austen seems as obvious to Rosenblatt, Kimball, and outraged readers of the *LRB* as her queerness does to Castle, Bersani, and the men in his anecdote. How can we account for this anomaly, and why should we bother? In attempting to answer this, I make no claims to neutrality. I cast my lot with the queer Austen and believe that the question of Austen's reception and readerships merits substantial consideration. Such is the enormity of Austen's status as a cultural institution, however, and such is her centrality to the canon of British literature in general, that the issues surrounding these controversies are really much larger. What if Austen *were* "gay" (as the *LRB* put it)? I hope to show that modern Austen criticism labored to occlude this possibility when a middle-class professoriate wrested Austen from upper-class Janeites and when the disciplined study of the novel was being founded. Central to this undertaking, then, is a consideration of different traditions, motives, and modes of valuation regarding Austen.[6] While I will begin by tracing the sexual politics of Austenian valuations and how these get appropriated by constituencies of different class and sexual positions, I will go on to uncover the terms on which Austen's place in the founding of the disciplined study of the novel was established. Although my principal aim will be to illuminate the history of Austenian reception as it sheds light on the institution of novel studies,[7] at the same time, by considering the phenomenon of "Janeitism," I also hope to genealogize the perceived queerness of many of her readers, as this queerness has been played out euphemistically in (sometimes overlapping) oppositions between macho and "effeminate" standards of masculinity, and between academic and belletristic models of novel criticism.

• • •

To listen to the readers who attacked Sedgwick and Castle, we might imagine that no one had *ever* doubted Austen's normativity before. This is so far from the case that the wonder is rather that Austen's normality itself now appears beyond question to so many. "Is she queer?—Is she prudish?"[8] So asks the rakish Henry Crawford of *Mansfield Park* as he wonders about Austen's nerdiest heroine, Fanny Price. For some reason, the erotic charm that makes married and unmarried women in that novel yield to Henry's desire fails to make a dent on this mousy, inhibited, and intense girl. Stymied by Fanny's resistance to his allure, Henry tries to determine Fanny's "character."[9] Is something *wrong* with her (is she odd, out of sorts, cold, and thus peculiarly resistant to normal heterosexual seduction)? Or is something "wrong" with him (do his multiple and serial flirtations deserve the censure this unusually, but not abnormally, moral young lady levels against them?)? Fanny decides in favor of the severity of rectitude, but the novel refuses to settle between propriety and pathology, and insists on their confusion.

Henry's reading of Fanny as either queer or prudish describes two traditions of Austenian reception.[10] Ever since Archbishop Whately claimed in 1821 that Austen was "evidently a Christian writer,"[11] many readers have been either pleased or infuriated to find that her novels are given over to orthodox morality, conservative politics, and strenuous propriety. This view is hardly the handiwork of the academic right wing, much less of heterosexist readers. Such are the asymmetries of the sex-gender system brilliantly elucidated by Judith Butler, among others, that it is not hard to find critics working within the camps of feminism, deconstruction, and queer studies who view Austen as Rosenblatt and Kimball might wish. D. A. Miller, for example, who has done so much for the study of "gay fabulation," reads Austen much as Allan Bloom does: what Bloom admired as wholesomely instructive and disciplinary in Austen's style and narrative structures, Miller can describe as violently hygienic and correctional. Different valuation; same Austen.[12]

Even though Kimball and Rosenblatt cast themselves as righteous amateurs opposing the lunacy rampant in the academy, the Jane Austen prevailing in the British and American academies today actually belongs to this normative tradition. It is only recently, however, that this Austen was the only widely visible one. Starting in the mid-nineteenth century, an anti-normative tradition developed. Ever since Mrs. Oliphant praised the "feminine cynicism" and "quiet jeering" of her fiction,[13] another set of readers has been either pleased or infuriated to find that Austen is not committed to the values of her neighborhood or to any values qua values at all, that she is disengaged from dominant moral and political norms, particularly as these are underwritten by the institutions of heterosexuality and marriage.

Because Austen's heterosexuality was not guaranteed by marriage, doubts about her sexuality have been played out in different historical moments as asexuality, as frigidity, and as lesbianism. This "queerness," as we might now term it, has been used to account for her fiction since the get-go. Charlotte Brontë linked the formal perfection of Austen's novels—her attention to "the surface of the lives of genteel English people"—to her indifference to "what throbs fast and full, though hidden, what the blood rushes through."[14] Lionel Trilling attributed the "feral" hostility of many readers to Austen to "man's panic fear at a fictional world in which the masculine principle, although represented as admirable and necessary, is prescribed and controlled by a female mind."[15] His explanation, however, misrepresents such animosity as a conflict between the sexes, when it is a conflict about sexuality. It is not because she is a woman that D. H. Lawrence and Brontë deplore her but because she is a woman whose fiction does not reverence the love of virile men. Thus, Lawrence decried "this old maid" for typifying "the sharp knowing in apartness" rather than the "blood connection" between the sexes; and George Sampson complained, "In her world there is neither marrying nor giving in marriage, but just the make-believe mating of dolls. . . . Jane Austen is abnormal . . . because [her characters] have no sex at all."[16]

The history of Austen criticism has often been darkened by the scorn Austen-haters express for novels in which men and women are more absorbed in village tittle-tattle than in each other. For this reason, male admirers of Austen have had much to endure at the hands of a world that frowns upon their love. H. W. Garrod's famous "Jane Austen: A Depreciation," an address delivered to the Royal Society for Literature in 1928, attacks the whole notion of Austen's greatness on sexual grounds. Austen is an "irredeemably humdrum" writer precisely because she holds herself aloof from sexual passion for men, and so "was as incapable of having a story as of writing one—by a story I mean a sequence of happenings, either romantic or uncommon." Garrod's misogynist "Depreciation" is aimed just as much at male Janeites in the audience as at Austen herself: "There is a time to be born and a time to die, and a time to be middle-aged and read Miss Austen." A man content to read novels by "a mere slip of a girl," as Garrod describes her, must be a mere slip of a girl himself. Having unmanned themselves not simply by admiring a woman writer— which is bad enough—but, even worse, by idolizing a sharp-tongued woman unimpressed with men (Garrod takes offense at Austen's quip, "Admiral Stanhope is a gentlemanlike man, but then his legs are too short and his tail too long"), men who *like* Austen are like the "pansy" in Bersani's story, doubly feminized.[17]

The Janeites Garrod ridicules are not the philistine consumers of "their 'dear,' our dear, everybody's dear, Jane" whom Henry James castigated decades earlier, readers who valued Austen as an instance of high culture in its least challenging form and whose Janeitism was a badge of gentility.[18] On the contrary, in its most influential forms, the Janeitism of the early twentieth century was, with the prominent exception of Shakespeare scholar Caroline Spurgeon, principally a male enthusiasm shared among an elite corps of publishers, professors, and literati, such as Montague Summers, A. C. Bradley, Lord David Cecil, Sir Walter Raleigh, R. W. Chapman, and E. M. Forster. At the Royal Society of Literature, in particular, Austen's genius was celebrated with a militantly dotty enthusiasm. Far from regarding their interest in Austen as "work," Janeites flaunt it as the ecstasy of the elect: she was not merely their *dear* Jane, but their *divine* Jane, their *matchless* Jane, and they were her *cult*, her *sect*, her *little company* (*fit though few*), her *tribe* of adorers who celebrate the *miracle* of her work in flamboyantly hyperbolic terms. Although their zeal is genuine, the self-parody implicit in these encomia tells us that we are in an insider's society of scholar-gentlemen at play.[19]

In a manner similar to how, as Henry Jenkins has shown, the trekkies, fans, and mass culture media enthusiasts of today are marginalized by dominant cultural institutions,[20] Janeites constitute a reading community whose practices violate a range of protocols later instituted by professional academics when novel studies emerged—dogmas holding, for example, that you cannot talk about characters as if they were real people; that reading novels requires specialist skills and knowledges developed at universities; that hermeneutic mastery—as exemplified in a comprehensive "reading"—is the objective of legitimate novel criticism; that the courtship plot celebrating marriage and maturity is the determinative event in Austen's fiction; and that the business of reading novels is solitary rather than sociable. To exemplify what Janeite reading looked like before novel criticism and readings per se existed, I will turn to Rudyard Kipling's "The Janeites."

• • •

A story within a frame-story and further enframed by poems, "The Janeites" is set at a London Masonic Lodge in 1920, where shell-shocked veteran Humberstall talks about a secret society into which he was inducted years earlier while serving under the supervision of Sergeant Macklin as an officers' mess waiter with his

World War I artillery battery in France.[21] One day, as the officers discuss whether "Jane" (*DC*, 124) died without leaving "direct an' lawful prog'ny" (*DC*, 124), Macklin (who is very drunk) loudly interrupts the officers' conversation with the claim, "She *did* leave lawful issue in the shape o' one son; an''is name was 'Enery James" (*DC*, 124). Puzzled that the superior officers, far from punishing this insubordinate intrusion, have the sergeant taken off to bed and cared for, Humberstall finds out more about the secret club whose membership brings such privileges. After selling him the password ("*Tilniz an' trap-doors*," from *Northanger Abbey*), Macklin imparts to him the mysteries of Jane, which make the war front companionable: "It *was* a 'appy little Group" (*DC*, 132), he later murmurs nostalgically. When half the battery is blown up in a German artillery attack, Humberstall is the only Janeite to survive. As he struggles to board a hospital train, only to be pushed back by a woman insisting the train is too crowded, Humberstall implores a nurse to "make Miss Bates, there, stop talkin' or I'll die" (*DC*, 136), and she—evidently an initiate herself—recognizes a fellow's allusion and obliges, even filching a spare blanket for his comfort.

Unlike most academic readings of Austen's fiction, this story backgrounds the courtship plot. The love story is less than inevitable for Janeites. In their civilian lives, they are chilly toward women (Jane "was the only woman I ever 'eard 'em say a good word for" [*DC*, 123], Humberstall remembers), and chary of domesticity (the senior Janeites are a divorce court lawyer and a private detective specializing in adultery cases). The Janeites recognize that novels are "all about young girls o' seventeen . . . not certain 'oom they'd like to marry" (*DC*, 126). But for them (unlike non-Janeites in the story), this detail is leveled with other details that are also part of what the novels are "all about"—including "their dances an' card parties an' picnics, and their young blokes goin' off to London on 'orseback for 'aircuts an' shaves" (*DC*, 126), a fact that, like the wearing of wigs, intrigues Humberstall, who is a hairdresser in civilian life. As for Austenian plots, "there was nothin' *to* 'em nor *in* 'em. Nothin' at all" (*DC*, 128).

Defended by school lads, equipped with superannuated cannons, and mobilized by a dilapidated train rather than modern transport caterpillars, the Janeites' battery is pitifully doomed. Indeed, they cathect onto Austen's novels precisely because "there was nothin' to 'em." Unlike current scholars of narrative, for whom plot bears the lion's share of narrative significance, Janeite readers ignore plot with its forward-moving momentums, its inevitabilities, its "maturity," and its closure, and dwell instead on atemporal aspects of narration, descriptive details, catchy phrases, and, especially, characterization (as the appreciations of real-life Janeites such as A. C. Bradley and Spurgeon attest). In this story, identifying people and things in their own experience and renaming them according to Austen's characters, the soon-to-be-slaughtered Janeites piece together a shattering world.

Because "real-life" Janeites would soon be decried as escapists retreating to the placidity of Austen's world, it is worth stressing that Kipling's Janeites do not do this. Their Jane Austen—as distinct from the Austen celebrated in the prefatory poem as "England's Jane" (*DC*, 120)—is never described by them as a repository of ethical wisdom; nor is she linked with a feminine elegiac ideal of England whose very vulnerability is what knightly menfolk must fight to protect. After the war, Humberstall reads Austen's novels not because they help him recover the prior world unshaken by war but precisely because they remind him of the trenches: "It brings it all back—down to the smell of the glue-paint on the screens. You take it from me, Brethren, there's no one to touch Jane when you're in a tight place" (*DC*, 137).

As for that tight place. We have already seen that many in the academy and outside it assume that Austenian admirers are properly and aggressively heteronormative. For this reason, it is also worth emphasizing that Janeite confederacies had little truck with domesticity. Kipling's story mentions two secret homosocial societies—the Masons and the Janeites—but several details suggest that Austen's fiction promoted a secret brotherhood of specifically homoerotic fellowship, too. When Humberstall chalks the names of Austenian characters onto the guns, he infuriates the battery sergeant major (BSM), who reads his Cockney spelling "De Bugg"—for De Burgh—as a reference to sodomy. Determined to punish him for "writin' obese words on His Majesty's property" (*DC*, 131), the BSM takes the case to the officers on the grounds that "'e couldn't hope to preserve discipline unless examples was made" (*DC*, 131). What the BSM does not know, of course, is that the Janeites exist and that the officers will not discipline one of their own: the officers dismiss the charges, send the BSM away, and entertain themselves by quizzing Humberstall on Jane. Janeite discourse—which would later be trivialized as "gossip" by presumptively masculine professional critics—has the cultural value of promoting fellowship among a group of people living under the aegis of the closet, and their coded and otherwise specialized speech indicates their membership in a "club" that exists covertly within a hostile world.

The narrator of the story, not a Janeite, closes by observing that Austen was "a match-maker" and her novels "full of match-making" (*DC*, 138), and by hinting at a secondary character's marriage to Humberstall's sister. Kipling also attaches a sequel-poem, entitled "Jane's Marriage," in which Austen enters the gates of heaven and is rewarded in matrimony by Captain Wentworth. These multiple efforts to reinstate the marriage plot are risible in themselves (Wentworth is not only fictional but already married) and at odds with the Janeitism elsewhere in the story: the frame-story is thus a sop thrown to "a pious post-war world" (*DC*, 129), which requires what the narrator calls "revision" of the truth. One of these truths is that Janeites are committed to club rather than domestic society. They are as barren of "direct an' lawful prog'ny" as Austen herself, leaving no issue, the surviving Humberstall being a stranger to women. The reproduction they are interested in pertains to the dissemination of Janeite culture itself. Just as Austen brought forth James, Janeites bring forth other Janeites—by recruitment. Macklin is pleased when Humberstall renames the guns after Austenian characters: "He reached up an' patted me on the shoulder. 'You done nobly,' he says. 'You're bringin' forth abundant fruit, like a good Janeite'" (*DC*, 130).

Early-twentieth-century Janeitism emerges from specific historical needs. Before World War I, Frederic Harrison described Austen as a "rather heartless little cynic . . . penning satires against her neighbors whilst the Dynasts were tearing the world to pieces and consigning millions to their graves."[22] Harrison deplored Austen's isolation, but once the dynasts of our century went at it, many readers loved her presumed ahistoricity, indulging in elegiac yearnings through Austen that Kipling's story both conjures and undermines. To Janeites outside Kipling's story, her novels evoked a world *before* history blew up, before manners were archaic. As Christopher Kent has shown, Austen's novels were recommended to British veterans suffering post-traumatic shock syndrome after the war.[23] For soldiers whose minds were shattered by dynastic history, the famously limited dimensions of

Austen's fictional world could feel rehabilitative; her parlors could feel manageable; her very triviality could feel redemptive. Assumptions about *feminine* propriety embedded within this fantasy—about transparency, restraint, poise—shore up masculine lucidity and self-definition when these, along with English national identity itself, were under duress.

D. A. Miller's compelling, latter-day conviction that when he was ill, Jane Austen's novels "did more than accompany [his] return to health; they accomplished it"[24] owes much to this postwar Janeite construction of Austen as a restorative to sensitive men. But as the more ambiguous core of Kipling's story attests, whatever "normality" Austen's novels might foster is attenuated given the indifference to heterosexual passion, domesticity, and heroic masculinity expressed there. In any case, when W. J. Blyton wrote in 1947, "Men as masculine as Scott and Kipling have been Janeites and have been enthralled by her sly humour and fidelity to reality,"[25] his defense of a manful readership demonstrated what he sought to deny: that Janeites were already suspected of being not masculine enough.

This suspicion motivates the emergence of what we now recognize as modern Austenian criticism, which begins with D. W. Harding's "Regulated Hatred: An Aspect of the Work of Jane Austen" (1940). The principle of this pathbreaking essay is that Austen's "books are . . . read and enjoyed by precisely the sort of people whom she disliked."[26] The "people" Harding refers to are clearly Janeites, described by Harding with withering contempt as the "exponents of urbanity," the "sensitive," and the "cultured," the "Gentlemen of an older generation than mine" who disseminate Austeniana "through histories of literature, university courses, literary journalism, and polite allusions" (RH, 166).[27] Although the Janeiteism of this period was actually more productive than he acknowledges—giving us, for one thing, Chapman's 1923 edition of Austen's novels, the first scholarly edition of any British novelist—Harding dismisses Janeites as weakling escapists who recur to the idyllic figure of Jane as a "refuge" when "the contemporary world grew too much for them" (RH, 166).[28]

Absolutely foundational to the practice of Austenian criticism in the academy was the discrediting of Janeites such as existed in Kipling's story and in the Royal Society of Literature. Deploying an invidious distinction between the "attentive" and "urbane," Harding calls Janeites her worst readers: "She is a literary classic of the society which attitudes like hers, held widely enough, would undermine" (RH, 167). Harding's qualifications as a good reader, it is implied, derive from his alienation from upper-class mores, an alienation Austen is said to have shared. Claiming Austen would never "have helped to make her society what it was, or ours what it is," Harding trumps the Janeite "posterity of urbane gentlemen" by disaffiliating Austen from them (RH, 179, 170).

Harding's depiction of Austen as subversive was valuable to the next generation of academics, especially feminists. But his motives were hardly emancipatory. In order to champion middle-class values, Harding and others after him reshuffle the relations between gender norms and sexual practices and/or identities. Defining Janeites as upper-class gentlemen of doubtful virility, Harding hinted that Austen was more of a real man—tough-minded, astringent, unblinking—than they were. F. R. Leavis carries this project of reshuffling forward in *The Great Tradition,* which is, among other things, a running diatribe against Janeite extraordinaire, Lord David Cecil. Leavis dignifies Austen and the great tradition of fiction she originated by insisting on her moral seriousness; accordingly, the leisured enjoyment of Janeites—

with their fondness for entertainment, character, and comedy—is hateful to him. Lord David's influence—detected in books, lectures, exam questions and answers at Cambridge—is so deep that Leavis treats him not as a scholar-dandy but as a downright pervert. The homophobic gender component of Leavis's class-based critique tars Lord David as a homosexual despite his evident heterosexuality. Leavis does this by playing up Lord David's Bloomsbury connections, taunting him for regarding Jane Austen as "an ideal contemporary of Lytton Strachey" rather than as a dour moralist and as a formative influence on George Eliot. Assailing Lord David's perceived preference for Austen's stylized comedy over Eliot's "puritan" morality, Leavis champions bourgeois virtue at the expense of Bloomsbury aestheticism: Eliot (like Austen, it is implied)

> admired truthfulness and chastity and industry and self-restraint, she disapproved of loose living and recklessness and deceit and self-indulgence. . . . I had better confess that I differ (apparently) from Lord David Cecil in sharing these beliefs, admirations and disapprovals. . . . [T]hey seem to me favourable to the production of great literature. I will add . . . that the enlightenment or aestheticism or sophistication that feels an amused superiority to them leads, in my view, to triviality and boredom, and that out of that triviality comes evil.[29]

Janeites might be so debilitated or so depraved or so despairing as to enjoy triviality as a reprieve from the business of productive signification, but the brisk and booming Leavis is here to assure us that triviality and its advocates alike are heinous.

What makes Harding's and Leavis's attacks on Janeites different from Garrod's, of course, is that they *like* Austen. They clear themselves from the charge of effeminacy by making Austen safe for real men engaged in real study, driving a wedge between the good (masculine) queerness of Austen and the bad (feminine) queerness of etiolated Janeites. Post–World War II Austenian reception thus participates in that demand to consolidate and reinvigorate masculinity elsewhere visible in the larger context of British and American culture. While such criticism conduced to the rise of Austen studies, it took some time before it generated a countermethod of reading that value-coded the marriage plot as the preeminent significance-bearing structural or thematic element of her novels, and devalued Janeite discussions as gossip that promoted the silly sociability of the brethren rather than the production of moral earnestness.[30] Edmund Wilson, for example, chides G. B. Stern and Sheila Kaye-Smith's Janeite book, *Speaking of Jane Austen* (1944), for treating characters "as actual people . . . and speculating on their lives beyond the story."[31] But when Wilson argues that Emma's offstage lesbianism is "something outside the picture which is never made explicit in the story but which has to be recognized by the reader before it is possible for him to appreciate the book," he carries on the Janeite practice of reading beyond what is printed.[32] And when he trails off into a fantasy about how Emma will bewilder Knightley by continuing to invite lovely new female protégées into the household after they are married, he shows that the marriage plot is no bar against the imagination or enactment of futures different from, or even inimical to, it.[33]

It is was not until the sixties that the marriage plot gained the prestige it now enjoys in academic readings of classic British fiction. Marvin Mudrick's profoundly influential *Jane Austen: Irony as Defense and Discovery* moved in this direction, but this, too, was by omission. Expecting Austen's novels to narrativize the maturing processes of heterosexual love, Mudrick is scandalized to find that her heart just isn't in this project. Whereas Harding and Leavis attacked the deviance of Janeites, Mudrick dwells on the deviance of Austen; he sees the bachelor-toughness they admired in her as a spinster's sick resentment. For him, irony—Austen's most celebrated stylistic achievement—is diagnosed as a defense mechanism against that "great, unknown, adult commitment," that is, "sexual love."[34] Mudrick's book elaborates earlier suspicions about Austen's sexual peculiarity by alluding to same-sex love directly in his chapter on Emma—that heroine deemed most like Austen in her fear of commitment, her coldness, her irony, her penchant for authorship, and her need to dominate, to "play God" by playing *man:* "The fact is that Emma," he writes, "prefers the company of women. . . . Emma is in love with [Harriet]: a love unphysical and inadmissible, even perhaps undefinable in such a society; and therefore safe" (*DD*, 193, 203).[35] Appearing in 1952, when a discourse of psychosexual pathology was readily at hand, Mudrick's book assumes that Austen's queerness is homosexuality tout court. All future attempts on behalf of Austen's normativity would succeed or fail to the extent that they could answer him.

Austen's massively definitive normalization came with Wayne Booth's widely reprinted "Control of Distance in Jane Austen's *Emma*" (1961), which not only passionately defends Emma Woodhouse's heterosexuality but also links the proper reading of Austenian narrative with a proper respect for the self-evidence of marital felicity in novels and outside them: "Marriage to an intelligent, amiable, good, and attractive man is the best thing that can happen to this heroine, and the readers who do not experience it as such are, I am convinced, far from knowing what Jane Austen is about—whatever they may say about the 'bitter spinster's' attitude towards marriage." According to Booth's formalism, marriage is not a matter of pairing character *x* to character *y*, as it is in Stern and Kaye-Smith's book *Speaking of Jane Austen.* If it were, novel studies would be a species of gossip (of the sort in which Janeites revel), novel critics would be lightweights, and novels themselves would not deserve the respect accorded to poetry and drama. Equating the ending of the novel with its telos, Booth elevates the structural and moral import of marriage as the novel's inevitable, its only possible, meaning: plot brings about "the reform of [Emma's] character," and heterosexual love is what Emma must "learn" for the novel to end. Evidence is unnecessary to sustain this standard of value. Countless readers have claimed that the infamous absence of "love scenes" in Austen's novels must mean *something.* Not so for Booth: norms about gender and sexuality are encoded onto plot so that representation in the form of kisses, palpitations, and embraces is superfluous.[36] If you don't see this, you don't know how to read novels.

Rescuing Austen from Mudrick,[37] Booth succeeded in celebrating Austen's mastery over voice and plot as a positive thing, advancing novel study as an analytic discipline. In the process, he equated the perversity of women who indulge same-sex "infatuations" with the perversity of readers who refuse to credit a happy ending when they see one. Sedgwick has remarked that Austenian criticism belongs to the bottom-spanking "Girl Being Taught a Lesson" mode of criticism.[38] As a description of criticism since the late fifties, this seems quite right. Critics as diverse as Tony Tanner, Ian Watt, and Mary Poovey all concur in maintaining that character development, formal control, voice, and ideological resistance/compliance are mediated through marriage, as an institution and plot device.

Indeed, so entrenched is this respect and so short our institutional memory that we have forgotten that there are other ways to read courtship plots. E. M. Forster, whose *Aspects of the Novel* was still taught in fiction courses when Booth's *Rhetoric of Fiction* was cresting, accorded the courtship plot less power: "A man and woman . . . want to be united and perhaps succeed." The compulsory nature of the love story as described here is acknowledged, and that compulsion has ideological import that we know weighed very heavily on Forster's own career. Still, it seems important to observe that Forster describes these events *not* under the headings "Plot" or "Story" but under the heading "People," classifying it not as an overarching structure but as one among many "facts of human life"—alongside birth, food, sleep, death, and other people—that interest people and novelists who write about them.[39] Many similar Janeite reading practices discussed earlier with respect to Kipling's story flourish today in the Jane Austen Societies, where fans convene to stage teas, balls, games, readings, and dramatic representations; to take quizzes (bringing together minutiae with no hierarchy or agenda-driven priority); and to imagine together how a character in one novel might behave toward a character from another, all of which practices render Austen's novels one loose, baggy middle.

The discipline of novel studies that evolved in England and America during the fifties and sixties was bent first on devaluing Janeites as effete—excessive, aberrant, frivolous, undomesticated, contemptibly weak yet morally pernicious at one and the same time—and next on eradicating everything in Austen and her fiction that might legitimize their way of reading. I began by asking what would happen if Austen *were* "gay," as the *LRB* put it. Now I will venture to answer with a hunch: If the "case" of Rock Hudson showed that our icon of masculinity was gay, the "case" of Jane Austen presented the unnerving possibility that *manners* are gay, that civility (of which Austen has been deemed the preeminent exemplar) may rest on a basis different from what is commonly imagined, and that (the terror of prophet Kimball about the end of the world notwithstanding) gay manners are indeed profoundly productive. This, indeed, seems to be Leavis's fear, and unless we recognize this, his attacks on Lord David will seem bizarrely out of place. Furiously resisting Lord David's seemingly innocuous statement that Austen's novels are "entertainment," Leavis attacks Lord David for holding that Austen creates "delightful characters" and "lets us forget our cares and moral tensions in the comedy of pre-eminently civilized life." Lord David's opinion might well seem so tepid as not to deserve attacking, but as Leavis sees it, the "idea of 'civilization' invoked [here] appears to be closely related to that expounded by Mr. Clive Bell," which is to say, conducing to "the cult of the stylized, the conventionalized, the artificial, just for their own sakes." In saying this, Leavis is damning the homosexual's Jane Austen, the decadent's Jane Austen, damning all persons for whom manners bear no relation to nature—which, here, is shorthand for bourgeois morality and heterosexual desire. Leavis's target is all readers who take for granted that manners and morality are different things, who regard manners as publicly recognized fictions that make it possible for people with other things on their mind to behave well.[40] Similarly, when Mudrick complained that Austen "was interested in a person, an object, an event, only as she might observe and recreate them free from consequences, as performance, as tableau" (*DD*, 3), he shows that Austen's novels yield up the amoral readings Leavis deplores as Bloomsburian, though Mudrick, of course, shares Leavis's anxiety about them. For Mudrick, Austen queers the courtship narrative so that the love story is presented "not sentimentally, not morally, indeed not [connected] to any train of consequences, but with detached discrimination among its incongruities" (*DD*, 3).

Fearful of the campy space Austen opens up between manners and desire, critics such as Booth and Trilling, as Susan Winnett has suggested, collapse manners into morals, making it possible to bring Austen (along with James) safely into a middle-class canon.[41] C. S. Lewis's essay, "A Note on Jane Austen," continues this process for Austen studies by regenealogizing her: "[Austen] is described by someone in Kipling's worst story as the mother of Henry James," he taunts, referring to "The Janeites," "[but] I feel much more sure that she is the daughter of Dr. Johnson." Assailing proponents of the comic, mannered Jane Austen—those who turn her into a Regency James, or, worse, a Regency Wilde—Lewis manfully insists that Austen's comedy is inspired by "hard core morality" and "religion."[42] The process of straightening Austen out, then, occurs in conjunction with the development of a view of narrative that presumes its province to be desire (hegemonic, heteronormative) rather than manners (which may be practiced self-consciously, skeptically, and strategically).

The success of this enterprise is proven by the present invisibility of what was so glaring in the forties and fifties. Even Sedgwick and Castle—in their initial papers, and in their responses to the furor they caused—appear unaware that their positions have ample and rather recent precedent. Likewise, when Southam accounts for Garrod's claim that Janeites liked women too much by insinuating that Garrod did not like women enough ("He spent much of his life at Oxford, unmarried, where he had rooms in Merton College for over fifty years"[43]), he, among other things, shows that Austen is presumptively a straight man's writer, putting admirers —from Wilde, to Swinburne, to Housman, to Forster, whose "I am a Jane Austenite" sounds like a coming-out statement—beyond consideration.[44] *because it was popular*

This review of Austen's recent revaluations suggests several opportunities for further study. First, it is now a given that the novel "rose" to ideological prominence by the 1740s; but this essay shows that the work of "raising" the novel was still undone as late as 1940, when the curriculum at Oxbridge was being revised, and that the elevation of novel studies has a distinct relation to Austen. Second, in attempting to resist what are, to my mind, rather inflexible desire-driven models of "realistic" narrative that prevail today, this project also suggests that it may be worth our while to distinguish between the theory of the novel and the theory of narrative, and to historicize both. While it is widely assumed that novels are a branch of the police, this discussion suggests that it is not novels but rather the professionalization of novel studies that deployed methods of reading that guaranteed certain outcomes and devalued others. And third, for Austen study more specifically, this review shows how much we have to gain by bringing non-normalizing Austenian readings back into view. For the denial and outrage of Kimball, Southam, and others notwithstanding, it has been not only Austen's detractors but her admirers, too, who have suspected that the "Passions" were (as Brontë put it) "entirely unknown" to her not because Austen was such a good girl but because in some secret, perhaps not fully definable way, she was so bad.

NOTES

1. David M. Halperin, *Saint Foucault: Towards a Gay Hagiography* (New York: Oxford University Press, 1995), 48. See also Paul Morrison's *Sexual Subjects,* forthcoming from Oxford University Press.

2. *New York Times,* 22 April 1990, 36. Sedgwick discusses neoconservative attacks on her MLA paper in "Jane Austen and the Masturbating Girl," in *Tendencies* (Durham: Duke University Press, 1993). I have found Sedgwick's remarks on self-evidence particularly suggestive.

3. See B. C. Southam, ed., *Jane Austen: The Critical Heritage,* vol. 2 (London: Routledge and Kegan Paul, 1987), 60.

4. Montague Summers, *The Galantry Show* (London: Cecil Woolf, 1980), 225.

5. Terry Castle's "Was Jane Austen Gay?" appeared as a review article of Deirdre Le Faye's new edition of Austen's letters in the *London Review of Books,* 3 August 1995. Her response, along with that of several other readers, appeared in the next issue, 24 August 1995. B. C. Southam's letter was published in the 7 September 1995 *LRB. Time* magazine reported on this "kerfuffle" in its 14 August 1995 issue; responses appeared in the 4 September 1995 issue.

6. My sense of Austen's cultural value owes much to John Guillory's *Cultural Capital* (Chicago: University of Chicago Press, 1993) in general, and more to Eric O. Clarke in particular, whose work on Shelley is profoundly suggestive. See "Shelley's Heart: Sexual Politics and Cultural Value," *Yale Journal of Criticism* 8 (spring 1995): 187–208. I am moreover grateful to Clarke for providing me with so many challenging suggestions for this essay.

7. The conflict rehearsed here about Austen not surprisingly recalls debates about the novel, too, whose narrative structures and agendas have been seen as repressive and "policing," or as resistant and theatrical. See, for example, D. A. Miller, *Novel and the Police* (Berkeley: University of California Press, 1988), and Joseph Litvak, *Caught in the Act: Theatricality in the Nineteenth-Century Novel* (Berkeley: University of California Press, 1992).

8. Jane Austen, *Mansfield Park,* ed. R. W. Chapman (Oxford: Oxford University Press, 1934), 230.

9. Austen, *Mansfield Park,* 230.

10. For a fuller discussion of the development of Austenian reception, see my "Jane Austen: Cults and Cultures," in *A Cambridge Companion to Jane Austen,* ed. Juliet McMaster and Ed Copeland (forthcoming from Cambridge University Press).

11. B. C. Southam, ed., *Jane Austen: The Critical Heritage,* vol. 1 (London: Routledge and Kegan Paul, 1968), 95.

12. Allan Bloom, *Love and Friendship* (New York: Simon and Schuster, 1993), 191–208. Bloom, interestingly enough, attributes Austen's disciplinary lucidity precisely to her sexual detachment: "Perhaps her position as a novelist outside of the marriage game that is her subject matter permits her relative clarity and freedom from self-deception" (205). D. A. Miller, "The Late Jane Austen," *Raritan* 10 (1990): 55–79.

13. From "Miss Austen and Miss Mitford," *Blackwood's Edinburgh Magazine* (Mar. 1870), reprinted in Southam, *Critical Heritage,* 1: 217.

14. Also: "Jane Austen was a complete and most sensible lady, but a very incomplete, and rather insensible (*not senseless*) woman" (Charlotte Brontë, letter to W. S. Williams, 12 April 1850, in Southam, *Critical Heritage,* 1: 128.

15. Lionel Trilling, *The Opposing Self* (New York: Viking Press, 1955), 209.

16. See D. H. Lawrence, *A Propos of Lady Chatterley's Lover,* in Southam, *Critical Heritage,* 2: 107; George Sampson, "Jane Austen," *The Bookman* 65, no. 388 (Jan. 1924): 193.

17. H. W. Garrod's "Jane Austen: A Depreciation" was originally delivered at the Royal Society for Literature in May 1928, and was published in *Essays by Divers Hands: Transactions of the Royal Society of Literature* 8 (1928): 21–40; it has been reprinted in numerous other places. The version I have quoted is from William W. Heath, ed., *Discussions of Jane Austen* (Boston: Heath and Company, 1961), 32–40.

18. James's remarks, originally appearing in "The Lesson of Balzac" (1905) and reprinted in *The House of Fiction,* are included in Southam, *Critical Heritage,* 2: 230. Jonathan Freedman's *Professions of Taste: Henry James, British Aestheticism, and Commodity Culture* (Stanford: Stanford University Press, 1990) traces James's at first satirical response to aestheticism, especially as exemplified by Wilde, which then modulates into an attempt to create a purified, creative, and moral (because productive) aestheticism in his major fiction. Although Freedman is hesitant about engaging the erotic transgressiveness and especially the homoeroticism associated with aestheticism, his discussion of professionalism is quite relevant to my study. In attempting to wrest criticism from the hoi polloi and assign it to professionals, James is anticipating strategies that would later marginalize him, and James's own place in the genealogy of the novel is curiously unstable.

19. See Montague Summers, "Jane Austen: An Appreciation," *Transactions of the Royal Society of Literature* 36 (1918): 1–33. Summers's language of divine election is typical of all Janeites.

20. Henry Jenkins, *Textual Poachers: Television Fans and Participatory Culture* (New York: Routledge, 1992). Jenkins draws from Michel de Certeau's *Practice of Everyday Life* (Berkeley: University of California Press, 1984) and from Pierre Bourdieu's *Distinction* (Cambridge: Harvard University Press, 1979) to show how high culturalists feel tainted by the adoption of their protocols for use with respect to low-culture objects and to suggest that fans transgress bourgeois structures of cultural valuation, which are bent on legitimizing their own objects and protocols of expertise.

21. Rudyard Kipling's "The Janeites" is included in *Debits and Credits* (1926). It was begun in 1922, finished in 1923, and first published in 1924, in a slightly different version from what appeared in the 1926 volume. All quotations are from *Debits and Credits*, ed. Sandra Kemp (Harmondsworth: Penguin, 1987), 119–40. Hereafter, this work is cited parenthetically as DC.

22. Frederic Harrison, letter to Thomas Hardy, 10 November 1913, cited in Southam, *Critical Heritage*, 2: 87–88.

23. According to Kent, H. F. Brett Smith, an Oxford tutor, served in World War I as an adviser in British hospitals. His special responsibility was the prescription of salubrious reading for the wounded, and he recommended Austen's novels to "severely shell-shocked" soldiers. I am much indebted to Kent's fine essay, "Learning History with, and from, Jane Austen," in *Jane Austen's Beginnings: The Juvenilia and Lady Susan*, ed. J. David Grey (Ann Arbor: UMI Research Press, 1989), 59.

24. Miller, "The Late Jane Austen," 55.

25. W. J. Blyton's quotation is cited in the supplement to the *Oxford English Dictionary* (3: 434), illustrating the word *Janeite*. The editors of the *OED* cite *English Language and Literature* 7 (1947) as their source, but I have been unable to locate this publication.

26. D. W. Harding, "Regulated Hatred: An Aspect of the Work of Jane Austen," in *Jane Austen: A Collection of Critical Essays*, ed. Ian Watt (Englewood Cliffs, N.J.: Prentice Hall, 1963), 166. Hereafter, this work is cited parenthetically as RH. Harding's essay was originally delivered before the Literary Society of Manchester University on 3 March 1939, and was originally printed in *Scrutiny* 8 (1940): 346–62.

27. In some respects, Harding's characterization recollects Woolf's review of the Chapman edition, which also codes Janeites as dotty and superannuated men, "elderly gentlemen living in the neighbourhood of London, who resent any slight upon her genius as if it were an insult offered to the chastity of their aunts"; in "Jane Austen at Sixty," *Nation* (15 Dec. 1923), 433, and reprinted without these opening swipes at the Chapman edition in *The Common Reader*.

28. Harding singles out Eric Linklater's Janeite prime minister in *The Impregnable Women* (1938) and Beatrice Kean Seymour's *Jane Austen: Study for a Portrait* (London: M. Joseph, 1937), where she wrote, "In a society which has enthroned the machine-gun and carried it aloft even into the quiet heavens, there will always be men and women—Escapist or not, as you please—who will turn to her novels with an unending sense of relief and thankfulness."

29. F. R. Leavis, *The Great Tradition* (Garden City, N.Y.: Doubleday and Co., 1954), 19. Although the Austenian criticism of Queenie and F. R. Leavis surely differs profoundly from earlier, more belletristic Janeites, Leavis's animus sometimes prompts him to misrepresent Lord David's positions. In his *Jane Austen* (London: Cambridge University Press, 1935), which originated as a lecture at Cambridge, Lord David flatly states, "Jane Austen was profoundly moral" (32), and though Leavis would probably scorn the conception of morality that Lord David attributes to her, it is stretching things, indeed, to suggest that Lord David describes Austen's morality as aesthetic or sophisticated.

30. The brilliance of Mary Lascelles's *Jane Austen and Her Art* (London: Oxford University Press, 1939) I regard as exceptional to the argument I am making here in its formal emphasis, which is in keeping with American models of fictional analysis. Although Lascelles's study is indeed blissfully free from nastier gender- and class-based attacks of Harding, Leavis, Mudrick, she does have a professional ax to grind, opening her book by noting that Austen's

"professed" admirers indulge in biographical minutiae rather than engage in the work of sustained criticism.

31. Austen seemed to have authorized this practice when she entertained her nieces and nephews by consenting, when asked, to tell them particulars about the careers of her characters subsequent to her novels' conclusions.

32. Edmund Wilson, "A Long Talk about Jane Austen," in *Classics and Commercials: A Literary Chronicle of the Forties* (New York: Farrar and Strauss, 1950), 196–203.

33. It is worth noting that Wilson's essay also argues that the homoerotic bond between Elinor and Marianne Dashwood in *Sense and Sensibility* is stronger than the heterosexual bond that yokes the sisters to their male lovers.

34. Marvin Mudrick, *Jane Austen: Irony as Defense and Discovery* (Princeton: Princeton University Press, 1952), 19. See also 194: "She convert[ed] her own personal limitations into the very form of the novel." Hereafter, this work is cited parenthetically as *DD*.

35. As Mudrick himself acknowledges, this take on Emma's lesbianism is indebted to Edmund Wilson's "A Long Talk about Jane Austen."

36. Wayne Booth's essay first appeared in *Rhetoric of Fiction* (Chicago: University of Chicago Press, 1961), 243–66; it was reprinted in David Lodge, *Jane Austen: Emma, A Casebook* (London: Macmillan, 1991), 137–69. A generation of "new critics" continued along the path Booth forged, claiming to discuss Emma's "growth" and "development" formally, but actually discussing narratives of gender and sexuality normatively.

37. According to Mudrick, Austen "converted her own personal limitations into the very form of the novel" (*DD*, 194).

38. Sedgwick, "Jane Austen and the Masturbating Girl," 125.

39. E. M. Forster, *Aspects of the Novel* (New York: Harcourt Brace Jovanovich, 1927), 67–82. In an excellent discussion of Forster's *Aspects*, Paul Morrison argues that Forster's remarks on narrative are much less emancipatory than what I suggest here. See "End Pleasure," *GLQ* 1 (1993): 53–78.

40. Leavis, *The Great Tradition*, 14–15, n. 6.

41. Susan Winnett pays particular attention to Trilling's 1950 essay, "Manners, Morals, and the Novel," in her *Terrible Sociability: The Text of Manners in Laclos, Goethe, and James* (Stanford: Stanford University Press, 1993), 27–32. While I admire Winnett's study, I think she may well inherit a view of Austen that Trilling and others handed down.

42. C. S. Lewis, "A Note on Jane Austen," originally published in *Essays in Criticism* (1954), 4: 359–71, reprinted in Watt, *Jane Austen*, 34, 33.

43. Southam writes that "a clue" to Garrod's dislike of Austen lies in the fact that he was "a distinguished classical scholar who moved to English studies in the 1920s" (in *Critical Heritage*, 2: 154). Of course, many passionate Janeites answer to this description, so this "clue" explains nothing.

44. Forster, cited in Southam, *Critical Heritage*, 2: 154. Wilde writes from Reading Gaol in a letter of 6 April 1897, "Later on, there being hardly any novel in the prison library for the poor imprisoned fellows I live with, I think of presenting the library with about a dozen good novels. Stevenson's, some of Thackeray. . . . Jane Austen (none here)." Wilde writes on 1 September 1890, "My dear Robbie, thank you for the cheque. Your letter is very maddening: nothing about yourself, and yet you know I love middle-class tragedies, and the little squabbles that build up family life in England. I have had delightful letters from you in the style of Jane Austen." According to biographer Richard Perceval Graves, A. E. Housman "enjoyed some of Hardy's novels, though he preferred Jane Austen." Evidently Housman's friend Arthur Platt, who held the chair in Greek at University College, London, "knew the novels of Jane Austen practically by heart." See *A. E. Housman: The Scholar-Poet* (New York: Charles Scribner's Sons, 1980), 84 and passim. Swinburne appears to have liked Austen as well, or at least he wrote Chatto (on 26 Dec. 1882), asking him to send the "Steventon [*sic*] edition of Miss Austen."

JANE TOMPKINS

MASTERPIECE THEATER: THE POLITICS OF HAWTHORNE'S LITERARY REPUTATION

The classic definition of a classic, as a work that has withstood the test of time, was formulated by Samuel Johnson in his *Preface to Shakespeare*. Where productions of genius are concerned, wrote Johnson, "of which the excellence is not absolute and definite but gradual and comparative, . . [.] no other test can be applied than length of duration and continuance of esteem." Once a great author has outlived his century, he continues:

> whatever advantages he might once derive from personal allusions, local customs, or temporary opinions, have for many years been lost. . . . The effects of favor and competition are at an end; the tradition of his friendships and enmities has perished. . . . His works . . . thus unassisted by interest or passion, have past [sic] through variations of taste and changes of manners, and, as they devolved from one generation to another, have received new honors at every transmission.[1]

The notion that literary greatness consists in the power of a work to transcend historical circumstances repeats itself in the nineteenth century, particularly in the work of Arnold and Shelley, and has been a commonplace of twentieth-century criticism.[2] T. S. Eliot and Frank Kermode, for instance, take it for granted that a classic does not depend for its appeal on any particular historical context and devote themselves to defining the criteria we should use to determine which works are classic, or to describing the characteristics of works already designated as such.[3] I propose here to question the accepted view that a classic work does not depend for its status upon the circumstances in which it is read and will argue exactly the reverse: that a literary classic is a product of all those circumstances of which it has traditionally been supposed to be independent. My purpose is not to depreciate classic works but to reveal their mutability. In essence what I will be asserting is that the status of literary masterpieces depends on arguments just like the one I am making here and that therefore the canon not only can but will change along with the circumstances within which critics argue.

I have chosen as a case in point the literary reputation of Nathaniel Hawthorne, a reputation so luminous and enduring that it would seem to defy the suggestion that it was based on anything other than the essential greatness of his novels and stories. Indeed, that assumption is so powerful that what follows may at times sound like a conspiracy theory of the way literary classics are made. As Hawthorne's success comes to seem, in my account, more and more dependent upon the influence of his friends and associates, and then upon the influence of their successors, it may appear that this description of the politics of Hawthorne's rise to prominence is being opposed, implicitly, to an ideal scenario in which the emergence of a classic author has nothing to do with power relations. Yet to see an account of the political and social processes by which a classic author is put in place as the account of a conspiracy is only possible if one assumes that classic status could be achieved independent of political and social processes. The argument that follows is not critical of the way literary reputations come into being, or of Hawthorne's reputation in particular. Its object, rather, is to suggest that a literary reputation could never be anything but a political matter. My assumption is not that "interest and passion" should be eliminated from literary evaluation—this is neither possible nor desirable—but that works that have attained the status of classic, and are therefore believed to embody universal values, are in fact embodying only the interests of whatever parties or factions are responsible for maintaining them in their preeminent position. Identifying the partisan processes that lead to the establishment of a classic author is not to revoke his or her claim to greatness, but simply to point out that that claim is open to challenge from other quarters, by other groups, representing equally partisan interests. It is to point out that the literary works that now make up the canon do so because the groups that have an investment in them are culturally the most influential. Finally, it is to suggest in particular that the casualties of Hawthorne's literary reputation—the writers who, by virtue of the same processes that lead to his ascendancy, are now forgotten—need not remain forever obliterated by his success.

To question the standard definition of the classic, and thus the canon as it is presently constituted, is also to question the way of thinking about literature on which the canon is based. For the idea of the classic is virtually inseparable from the idea of literature itself. The following attempt to describe the historically produced nature of a single author's reputation, therefore, is likely to arouse a host of objections because it challenges an entire range of assumptions on which literary criticism has traditionally operated. The strength of these assumptions does not stem from their being grounded in the truth about literature, however, but from the pervasiveness of one particular mode of constructing literature—namely, the one that assigns to literary greatness an ahistorical, transcendental ground. The overwhelming force of this conception lies in its seeming to have arisen not from any particular school of criticism or collection of interests, but naturally and inevitably, as a way of accounting for the ability of certain literary works to command the attention of educated readers generation after generation. That this theory is neither natural nor inevitable it will be the purpose of this essay to show. "The effects of favor and competition, . . . the tradition of friendships," the "advantages" of "local customs" and "temporary opinions," far from being the ephemeral factors Johnson considered them, are what originally created and subsequently sustained Hawthorne's reputation as a classic author. Hawthorne's work, from the very beginning, emerged into visibility, and was ignored or acclaimed, as a function of the circumstances in which it was read.

• • •

Between 1828 and 1836 Hawthorne published some of what are now regarded as his best short stories: "The Gentle Boy," "The Gray Champion," "Young Goodman Brown," "Roger Malvin's Burial," "The Minister's Black Veil," and "The Maypole of Merrymount." Yet although these are among the most frequently anthologized American short stories, to Hawthorne's contemporaries they were indistinguishable from the surrounding mass of magazine fiction. Until the *Token* of 1836 appeared, says Bertha Faust, author of the best study of Hawthorne's early reception, "no one singled out one of Hawthorne's pieces by a single word."[4] This indifference to what we now regard as Hawthorne's finest tales requires an explanation. If an author's reputation really does depend upon the power of his art to draw attention to itself regardless of circumstances, why then did Hawthorne's first readers fail utterly to recognize his genius as we understand it, or as his contemporaries would later understand it? The reason, Faust says, is that Hawthorne's tales would not have stood out on the basis of their subject matter, since tales involving American colonial history or depicting a person dominated by a single obsession had many parallels in contemporary fiction. Moreover, since Hawthorne's stories, like most of what appeared in the gift-book annuals, were published anonymously, there was no way of telling that they were the products of a single hand. Finally, since the annuals were rather lightly regarded at the time, critics had no expectation of finding anything of merit in them.[5]

This account of why Hawthorne's greatness went unrecognized initially argues that Hawthorne's readers could not have judged his tales accurately because of the misleading circumstances in which they were embedded. In this account, the context acts as a kind of camouflage, making Hawthorne's tales look exactly like those of lesser writers, and it implicitly assumes that under other circumstances, the tales would have been seen for what they "really" are. Yet what sorts of circumstances could these have been? If Hawthorne's tales had not appeared in the *Token*, they would have appeared in *Graham's Magazine* or *Godey's Lady's Book* or the *Southern Literary Messenger*; in each case the context supplied by the periodical would have altered readers' perceptions of the tales themselves.[6] If the tales had not appeared anonymously, but under Hawthorne's name, then whatever associations readers attached to that name would have influenced their responses. Of course, it could be argued that while some circumstances get in the way of accurate perception, others merely reinforce qualities already present in the work, and so do not distort readers' perceptions of the work itself. Yet the difficulty with this argument is that since there is no way of knowing what a work is like exempted from all circumstances whatsoever, we can never know which circumstances distort and which reinforce the work "as it really is." Since pure perception is a practical impossibility, given that a text must always be perceived under some circumstances or other, one cannot use the notion of "misleading" vs. "reinforcing" circumstances to explain why Hawthorne's first readers did not see his tales the way we do.

Another way to explain the indifference to Hawthorne's work in the 1830s is to consider the possibility that the circumstances in which a text is read, far from *preventing* readers from seeing it "as it really is," are what make the text available to them in the first place. That is, circumstances define the work "as it really is"— under those circumstances. They do this by giving readers the means of classifying a text in relation to what they already know. Thus, Hawthorne's first critics did not single out his tales for special commendation for the simple reason that they did not know anything about them beforehand. That is why the stories they did single out—stories by John Neal, N. P. Willis, and Catharine Sedgwick—were written by well-published, widely praised authors of whom they had already heard a great deal.[7] In praising *their* work, Hawthorne's contemporaries stood in exactly the same relation to it as modern critics stand in relation to Hawthorne's; that is, they were able to identify its merits because they already knew that it was good and were looking at it with certain expectations in mind. Thus, when Samuel Goodrich, the editor of the *Token,* began telling other editors about Hawthorne's work, they began to pay attention to it for the first time;[8] once the editors had a reason for seeing Hawthorne's work as exceptional, they began to see it that way. I am not suggesting that Goodrich had an especially keen eye for literary genius and so was able to point out to others what they had not been able to see for themselves, but that, as editor of the most prominent of the annuals, he was in a position to create a favorable climate for the reception of Hawthorne's work. Until 1836 Hawthorne's tales not only seemed but *were* completely ordinary because the conditions necessary to their being perceived in any other way had not yet come into being.

I have been suggesting that "external circumstances," far from being irrelevant to the way a literary work is perceived, are what make it visible to its readers in the first place. Yet, one might ask, once "circumstances" had alerted readers to the existence of Hawthorne's fiction, from that point on wouldn't it stand or fall on its own merits? This would seem to be a plausible suggestion, but the particulars of Hawthorne's early reception point in a different direction. What they show is that circumstances not only brought Hawthorne's tales to the attention of critics; they also shaped critics' reactions to the tales themselves.

The first notice of any length to appear following the publication of *Twice-told Tales* in 1837 was an extremely laudatory piece by the editor of the *Salem Gazette.* This man, according to Faust, "was indebted to Hawthorne for a number of early contributions, all presumably unpaid, and . . . was about to increase his debt by reprinting . . . pieces from the volume in question."[9] Any one of a number of factors—local pride, a sense of financial obligation, personal gratitude, or an eye to future self-interest—positioned the editor of the *Salem Gazette* in relation to what he read. Circumstances, one might say, weighed heavily on this editor, and he found the *Twice-told Tales* quite spectacular as a result. What is important to note here is not that the laudatory review was the product of circumstances favorable to Hawthorne but that this editor—like any reader—was *in a situation* when he read Hawthorne's work, and that that situation mediated his reading of it.

The other most laudatory review of the *Twice-told Tales,* the one that played the most decisive role in establishing Hawthorne's literary reputation, was a piece by Henry Wadsworth Longfellow published in the *North American Review.* Longfellow was no more neutral or disinterested a reader of *Twice-told Tales* than the editor of the *Salem Gazette.* He had been a classmate of Hawthorne's at Bowdoin College; they shared a common background and a common vocation. In the months preceding the publication of *Twice-told Tales* (which Hawthorne sent to Longfellow as soon as it appeared), Hawthorne had written Longfellow a series of letters suggesting that they collaborate on a volume of children's stories; shortly before the review in question came out, he had written to Longfellow speaking of his reclusive existence, nocturnal habits, and unavailing efforts to "get back" into "the main current of life."[10] While none of these circumstances could guarantee that Longfellow would admire Hawthorne's collection of stories, they constituted a situation in which a negative response would have been embarrassing and difficult.

It is possible, of course, that Longfellow and the editor of the *Gazette* may have felt pressured into admiring Hawthorne's work for what we could call, broadly speaking, "political" reasons, and that their true opinion of Hawthorne may have been quite different from what they publically expressed. Longfellow, for instance, might have harbored a secret dislike for Hawthorne because of some prank he had played in college, or he might have thought the tale an inferior literary genre, or been bored by stories that used a historical setting, and therefore might have found Hawthorne's tales dull and trivial. Yet even if that had been the case, *that* set of circumstances would have been no more neutral or disinterested than any other. If it seems that I have chosen to discuss only "special cases" in the reception of Hawthorne's early work—in other words, cases where special interests were involved—and have omitted examples in which the reviewer had no prior interests at stake, that is because readers are always situated, or circumstanced, in relation to a work—if not by their prior knowledge of it, then, as we have seen, by their ignorance. There is never a case in which circumstances do not affect the way people read and hence *what* they read—the text itself.

In the case of Longfellow's review, the circumstances in question had an extremely positive effect on Hawthorne's literary career. Longfellow was someone whose opinion carried weight in critical circles; he had just been appointed Smith Professor of Modern Languages at Harvard and was at the beginning of a long and distinguished career of his own. He wrote for a weighty and influential journal whose editors, contributors, and subscribers constituted New England's cultural elite in the 1830s, 1840s, and 1850s. When Longfellow announced in the pages of the *North American* that Hawthorne was a "man of genius" and that a new "star" had arisen in the heavens, a new set of circumstances was called into being within which Hawthorne's fiction would, from then on, be read.[11] He began to receive more, and more favorable, critical attention; and his works began to assume a shape and to occupy a place in the literary scene that made him eligible, in time, for the role of American literary hero.

It is not my intention here to describe how that process took place step by step, but rather to show, in a series of instances, how the "circumstances" surrounding the emergence of Hawthorne's texts onto the literary scene defined those texts and positioned them, so that they became central and, so to speak, inescapable features of the cultural landscape.

• • •

Once Hawthorne's tales had been called to their attention, nineteenth-century critics did not single out what we now consider his great short stories—"The Minister's Black Veil," "Young Goodman Brown," and "The Maypole of Merrymount"—but sketches now considered peripheral and thin. Their favorites, with virtually no exceptions, were "A Rill from the Town Pump," "Sunday at Home," "Sights from a Steeple," and "Little Annie's Ramble." Not only did these critics devote their attention almost exclusively to sketches that moralize on domestic topics and fail to appreciate what we now consider classic examples of the American short story, they "overlooked" completely those qualities in Hawthorne's writing that twentieth-century critics have consistently admired: his symbolic complexity, psychological depth, moral subtlety, and density of composition. Instead, what almost every critic who wrote on Hawthorne's tales in the 1830s found particularly impressive were his combination of "sunshine" and "shadow," the transparency of his style, and his ability to invest the common elements of life with spiritual significance.[12] It is these qualities that made Hawthorne a critical success among literary men in the 1830s and 1840s and it is on this foundation that his reputation as a classic author was built. Even the laudatory reviews by Poe and Melville, which critics take as proof of their "discernment" because in certain passages they seem to anticipate modern views, arise out of tastes and sympathies that are in many respects foreign to present-day critical concerns.[13] Thus, the texts on which Hawthorne's claim to classic status rested were not the same texts we read today in two senses. In the first and relatively trivial sense, they were not the same because the stories that made Hawthorne great in the eyes of his contemporaries were literally not the ones we read today: they preferred "Little Annie's Ramble" to "Young Goodman Brown." In the second and more important sense, they were not the same because even texts bearing the same title became intelligible within a different framework of assumptions. It is not that critics in the 1830s admired different *aspects* of Hawthorne's work from the ones we admire now, but that the work itself was different. Whatever claims one may or may not wish to make for the ontological sameness of these texts, all of the historical evidence suggests that what Hawthorne's contemporaries saw when they read his work is not what we see now. What I mean can be illustrated by juxtaposing a piece of Hawthorne criticism written in 1837 with one written 120 years later.

In praising Hawthorne's brilliance as a stylist, Andrew Peabody made the following comment on a phrase from "The Gentle Boy":

> These Tales abound with beautiful imagery, sparkling metaphors, novel and brilliant comparisons. . . . Thus, for instance, an adopted child is spoken of as "a domesticated sunbeam" in the family. . . . How full of meaning is that simple phrase! How much does it imply, and conjure up of beauty, sweetness, gentleness and love! How comprehensive, yet how definite! Who, after reading it, can help recurring to it, whenever he sees the sunny, happy little face of a father's pride or a mother's joy?[14]

No wonder, then, Hawthorne's contempories missed the point of his great short stories: they could not possibly have understood him, given the attitudes that must inform effusions such as these. Yet before dismissing Peabody completely, it is worthwhile asking if there isn't a point of view from which his commentary made good critical sense.

For Peabody, whose critical assumptions privileged the spiritualization of the ordinary and especially of domestic life, the phrase "a domesticated sunbeam" leaped immediately into view. "The Gentle Boy" became visible for him from within a structure of norms that nineteenth-century social historians refer to as "the cult of domesticity" and fulfilled a definition of poeticity that values fanciful descriptions of commonplace things (Peabody admired Hawthorne's tales because they were "flower-garlands of poetic feeling wreathed around some everyday scene or object").[15] The forms of apprehension that concretized the tale for him flag the phrase as a brilliant embodiment of his critical principles and moral presuppositions.

In the same way, one can readily see how a changed set of cultural beliefs and critical presuppositions have given rise to a modern commentary on the story. For example, Richard Adams has written in *The New England Quarterly* (1957) that Ilbrahim, the title character to whom the phrase "domesticated sunbeam" applies, "does not succeed" because he "is too young and weak."[16] He fails to "surmount the crisis of adolescence" and illustrates the "common theme" of all the *Provincial Tales* which is "not basically a question of good versus evil but rather of boyish dependence and carelessness versus manly freedom and responsibility. . . . It is very much a question of the protagonist's passing from the one state to the other or of failing to do so—a question of time, change, and development."[17]

The modern critic typically does not pause to exclaim over the beauties of a single phrase but sees the tale as a whole as the illustration of a "theme." He understands the character of Ilbrahim in the light of a psychological paradigm of human development in which childhood represents a stage that must be overcome. The ideal of human life implicit in Adams's descriptions of the story privileges individual self-realization, intellectual control, and a take-charge attitude toward experience. His beliefs about the nature of good fiction and the ideal shape of human life have interpreted "The Gentle Boy" for him as a story about "the protagonist's passing from one state to the other or failing to do so." He has not *imposed* this interpretation on the story; that is to say, he has not applied his convictions to "The Gentle Boy" in order to make its details conform to some predetermined outline. Rather, his convictions are what made the story intelligible to him in the first place.[18] This way of rendering stories intelligible means, among other things, that Adams would not have noticed the phrase "a domesticated sunbeam" at all, because there was nothing in his interpretive assumptions that would have made it noticeable. If someone were to call it to his attention, he would have had to read the phrase ironically—as Hawthorne's sneering comment on nineteenth-century prettifications of childhood—or as an unfortunate lapse, on Hawthorne's part, into the sentimental idiom of his age. In any case, the phrase is not the same phrase for him as it is for Peabody, except in a purely orthographic sense, because it becomes visible—if it is noticed at all—from within a completely different framework of assumptions from those that produced Peabody's reading of the tale.

The critical vocabulary, moreover, which each critic uses to formulate his comments, extends and elaborates his assumptions even as the text itself does. When Adams says that the protagonist's success or failure is a "question of time, change, and development," his vocabulary implicitly affirms the value of controlling experience through abstract categorization, an assumption not merely appropriate to but required by the institutional and professional situation within which he writes. In the same way, Peabody's rhetoric, full of exclamations and given to naming the tender emotions ("How full of meaning is that simple phrase! How much does it imply and conjure up of beauty, sweetness, gentleness, and love!"), embodies just the kind of excited representation of emotional experience that his critical stance privileges, and affirms the value of precisely those feelings which—to his mind—Hawthorne so splendidly evokes. The critic's rhetoric is not a secondary or detachable attribute of his enterprise but simultaneously its enabling assumption and final justification. When Peabody rhapsodizes over the domesticated sunbeam, when Longfellow exclaims "live ever, sweet, sweet book," when Charles Fenno Hoffman describes Hawthorne as "a rose, bathed and baptized in dew," their rhetorical performance embodies the same critical strategies that make Hawthorne's tales intelligible to them, and all three—rhetoric, critical strategies, and the tales themselves—are inseparable from a whole way of looking at life.[19]

The reading of fiction and the writing of criticism in the 1830s were activities rooted in beliefs about the sanctity of the home, the spirituality of children, the purifying effects of nature, the moral influence of art, and relation of material to spiritual essences that determined what shape the *Twice-told Tales* would have for its readers at the level of the individual phrase, and at the level of the volume as a whole. Longfellow and his peers did not admire "A Rill from the Town Pump" out of bad taste; their judgment was an affirmation of their ideals no less than Adams's belief that Hawthorne "chronicles the crisis of adolescence" is an affirmation of his. We may think that the beliefs of Peabody and Longfellow are silly or outmoded but we cannot accuse them of having *overlooked* in Hawthorne's work what they couldn't possibly have seen. One might just as well criticize F. O. Matthiessen, who holds that Hawthorne's greatness lies in his "wholeness of imaginative composition," for failing to notice that Hawthorne's prose is "as clear as running waters are" and that "his words are like stepping-stones."[20] In short, it is useless to insist that critics of the 1830s couldn't see the true nature of Hawthorne's work because of their naïve literary and cultural assumptions, but that that true nature was there all along, waiting to be discovered by more discerning eyes. Rather, the "true nature" of a literary work is a function of the critical perspective that is brought to bear upon it.

What remains to be explained is why—if it is true that literary texts only become visible from within a particular framework of beliefs—it is always *Hawthorne's* texts that are the subject of these discussions rather than the texts of other writers. If there was nothing "in" the *Twice-told Tales* that commanded critical attention, why has Hawthorne's collection of stories and sketches come down to us, rather than Harriet Beecher Stowe's *The Mayflower*? Wasn't there, right from the beginning, something unique about Hawthorne's prose that marked it as different from and better than the prose of other writers?

One can answer these questions by turning to the contemporary reviews. What the reviews show is that the novels of sentimental writers like Susan Warner and Harriet Beecher Stowe were praised as extravagantly as Hawthorne's and in exactly the same terms. Critics who admired Hawthorne's fondness for "lowly . . . scenes and characters," which they took as a sign of his "sympathy with everything human," also admired Warner's "simple transcript of country life" and "homely circumstances," which portrayed "the ordinary joys and sorrows of our common humanity."[21] They found that Hawthorne's "tales are national while they are universal," and that Warner's novels "paint human nature in its American type" and "appeal to universal human sympathy."[22] Warner is commended for her remarkable grasp of religious truth, and Hawthorne for his depiction of "spiritual laws" and "the eternal facts of morality."[23] Both writers display an extraordinary understanding of the "heart."[24]

Thus it is not the case that Hawthorne's work from the very first set itself apart from the fiction of his contemporaries; on the contrary, his fiction did not distinguish itself at all clearly from that of the sentimental novelists—whose work we now see as occupying an entirely separate category. This is not because nineteenth-century critics couldn't tell the difference between serious and sentimental fiction but because their principles of sameness and difference had a different shape. In the 1850s the aesthetic and the didactic, the serious and the sentimental were not opposed but overlapping designations. Thus, the terms "sentimental author" and "genius" were not mutually exclusive but wholly compatible ways of describing literary excellence. Differences in the way literature is defined necessarily produce differences in the way literary works are classified and evaluated. Thus, if Evert Duyckinck, who was arguably the most powerful literary man in New York, regarded "Little Annie's Ramble" as the high-water mark of Hawthorne's achievement in 1841, it is no wonder that other critics should subsequently have admired Susan Warner's novel about the tribulations of an orphan girl, and seen both works —moralized pictures of innocent girlhood in a characteristically New England setting—as exemplifying the same virtues.[25] Nor is it strange that when Phoebe Pynchon appeared to brighten the old family mansion in Salem, critics praised *The House of the Seven Gables* because it was full of "tenderness and delicacy of sentiment" "with a moral constantly in view."[26] *The House of the Seven Gables* succeeded in 1851 because it was a sentimental novel; that is, it succeeded not because it escaped or transcended the standards of judgment that made critics admire Susan Warner's work but because it fulfilled them. To critics who took for granted the moral purity of children, the holiness of the heart's affections, the divinity of nature, and the sanctity of the home, and who conceived of the poet as a prophet who could elevate the soul by "revealing the hidden harmonies of common things," sketches like "Sunday at Home," "Sights from a Steeple," "A Rill from the Town Pump," and novels like *The House of the Seven Gables* and *The Wide, Wide, World* formed a perfect continuum; it is not that these critics couldn't see the difference between Warner's work and Hawthorne's, but that, given their way of seeing, there *was* no difference.

This does not mean that antebellum critics made no distinction between various kinds of work, but that their principles of classification produced different groupings from the ones we are used to. *The House of the Seven Gables* and *The Wide, Wide World*, for example, were published in the same year as *Moby-Dick*, but whereas today Hawthorne and Melville are constantly seen in terms of one another, contemporary reviews of Hawthorne never even mention Melville's name. While in the 1850s there was no monolithic view of either Hawthorne or Melville, one can easily construct characterizations of their works, based on comments from contemporary reviews, that would place them at opposite ends of the critical spectrum. According to contemporary critics, Hawthorne, like the sentimental novelists, wrote a clear, intelligible prose accessible to everyone (a style suitable for artists in a self-consciously democratic nation); he told stories about recognizable people in humble settings and thus, like the writers of domestic fiction, illuminated the spiritual dimensions of ordinary life; his works, like theirs, firmly rooted in Christian precept, served as reliable guides to the truths of the human heart.[27] Melville, on the other hand, whose work was described as being full of stylistic extravagances, bizarre neologisms, and recondite allusions, emerges as a mad obscurantist; his characters inhabited exotic locales and ranted incomprehensibly about esoteric philosophical issues; and their ravings verged dangerously and irresponsibly on blasphemy.[28] Although many critics admired Melville's daring and considered his work powerful and brilliant, they nevertheless did not describe it in the terms they used to characterize Hawthorne. In their own day, Hawthorne and Melville were admired, when they were admired, for opposite reasons: Hawthorne for his insight into the domestic situation, Melville for his love of the wild and the remote.[29]

It is easy enough to see that Hawthorne's relation to Melville in the nineteenth-century wasn't the same as it is now; and it is easy enough to see that it wasn't the same because the criteria according to which their works were described and evaluated were different and that therefore the works themselves took on a different shape. Not only is Hawthorne in the 1850s not easily distinguishable from the sentimental novelists, and in most respects quite distinguishable from Melville; not only did antebellum critics have different notions about the nature and function of good literature, prize the domestic affections, and think children were spiritually endowed; more important, once one has accepted the notion that a literary text exists only within a framework of assumptions that are historically produced, it then becomes clear that the "complex" Hawthorne that we study, the Melville we know as Hawthorne's co-conspirator against the pieties of the age, the sentimental novelists we regard as having pandered to a debased popular taste, are not the novelists nineteenth-century readers read and that nineteenth-century critics wrote about. Even when nineteenth- and twentieth-century critics use the same or similar words to describe some element in Hawthorne's work, one can see that what they mean by what they say is not the same thing.

When a Unitarian clergyman writes that "the character of Chillingworth" illustrates "the danger of cherishing a merely intellectual interest in the human soul," he seems to be describing the same phenomenon that Donald Ringe describes when he writes that Chillingworth is a "cold, speculative, intellectual man who commits a sin of isolation which must ultimately destroy him."[30] Both writers clearly agree that Hawthorne, through the character of Chillingworth, is suggesting that the intellect alone is a dangerous guide. Yet what the modern critic means by Chillingworth's sin is isolation from the community, the separation of the head from the heart, and something he calls "dehumanization"; for him, Chillingworth sins by cutting himself off from "human sympathy and love."[31] The minister writing for the *Universalist Quarterly*, on the other hand, admires Hawthorne's treatment of character because it demonstrates "spiritual laws" and is "sternly true to the eternal facts of morality."[32] Those facts are not the same for him as they are for Ringe. Chillingworth is damned in the minister's eyes not because he is cut off from human sympathy and love, but from "God . . . the all-good and the all-beautiful."[33] These critics may use the same words to describe Hawthorne's character, but the Chillingworth of *PMLA* transgresses the social and psychological norms of a secular humanism, while the Chillingworth of Hawthorne's era dramatizes liberal Protestant convictions about the soul's relation to God. These accounts of what Hawthorne meant to convey are not interchangeable and do not testify to the existence of some central truth in Hawthorne's text that both critics have grasped. What they show is that the critic, the context within which the critic reads, and the text that is interpreted are simultaneously features of a single historical moment. As the concept of sin changes from theological fact to metaphor for a psychological state, as the critic changes from Unitarian clergyman to Professor of English, as the *Universalist Quarterly* gives way to *PMLA*, the text of *The Scarlet Letter* changes accordingly.

Because modern commentators have tended to ignore the context within which nineteenth-century authors and critics worked, their view of the criticism that was written on *The Scarlet Letter* in the nineteenth century has failed to take account of the cultural circumstances that shaped Hawthorne's novel for his contemporaries. They evaluate this criticism as if it had been written about the same text that they read, and so produce accounts of it that are unrelated to the issues with which that criticism was actually engaged.

This is not simply because each critic looks at the text from a different point of view or with different purposes in mind, but because *looking* is not an activity that is performed outside of political struggles and institutional structure but arises *from* them.

• • •

One such structure is the machinery of publishing and reviewing by means of which an author is brought to the attention of his audience. The social and economic processes that govern the dissemination of a literary work are no more accidental to its reputation, and indeed to its very nature (as that will be perceived by an audience), than are the cultural conceptions (of the nature of poetry, of morality, of the human soul) within which the work is read. The conditions of dissemination interpret the work for its readers in exactly the same way as definitions of poetry, in that they flow from and support widely held—if unspoken—assumptions about the methods of distribution proper to a serious (or nonserious) work. The fact that an author makes his or her appearance in the context of a particular publishing practice rather than some other is a fact about the kind of claim he or she is making on an audience's attention and is *crucial* to the success of the claim. Hawthorne's debut as a novelist illustrates this proposition rather strikingly.

In 1970, C. E. Frazer Clark, Jr., published an article that revealed some little-known facts surrounding the publication of *The Scarlet Letter*.[34] Clark observed that despite Hawthorne's habit of referring to himself as "the most unpopular author in America," he was much better known than he himself was aware. His satires and sketches had been pirated liberally by newspapers up and down the eastern seaboard; notices, advertisements, and reviews of his work had regularly appeared in the periodical press. So when Hawthorne lost his job as Surveyor of Customs at Salem, it caused a furor in the local papers.[35] The press took up the case of political axing not because such events were so extraordinary—nothing could have been more common with a change of administration—but because Hawthorne was already newsworthy. This publicity attracted the attention of James T. Fields, shortly to become New England's most influential publisher, who until then had not printed a word of Hawthorne's, but whose business instincts now prompted him to visit Salem on the off-chance that Hawthorne might have something ready for the press. Hawthorne, as it happened, did have something on hand which, very reluctantly, he gave to Fields. It was a story that Fields encouraged him to turn into a novel—novels being more marketable than short fiction—which Hawthorne did, and prefaced it with an introductory essay on his stint in the Custom-House to help achieve the desired length. As Fields suspected, Hawthorne's first book to appear after the Custom-House fiasco sold remarkably well: the advance publicity had guaranteed that *The Scarlet Letter* would be a success.

Encouraged by the attention paid to his novel, and prodded by the ever-vigilant Fields, who saw an opportunity to capitalize on the reputation so recently enlarged, Hawthorne, who until then had not been a prolific writer, turned out two more novels in rapid succession. These received a great deal of favorable attention from well-placed reviewers, with the result that, two years after the publication of *The Scarlet Letter*, Hawthorne was being referred to as a classic American writer—and so has been identified ever since. Yet the success of *The Scarlet Letter* and of the subsequent novels becomes fully explicable only within a larger frame of reference than the one Clark's essay supplies.

By the 1840s Washington Irving's reputation had sagged and James Fenimore Cooper had alienated large portions of the reading public and the critical establishment with his attacks on American manners and unpopular political stands. America needed a living novelist whom it could regard as this country's answer to Dickens and Thackeray, a novelist who represented both what was essentially American and what was "best" by some universal criteria of literary value. Hawthorne seemed well suited for the role, since, as almost every critic emphasized, his work made use of characteristically American materials. Hawthorne's feel for the humbler aspects of the American scene made him attractive both as an interpreter of "spiritual laws" that knew no nationality and as a spokesman for the democratic way of life. These qualities, however, as I have suggested, were shared equally by novelists like Warner and Stowe who, if anything, outdid him in this respect. What finally distinguished Hawthorne from his popular rivals was his relation to the social and institutional structures that shaped literary opinion; these associations ultimately determined the longevity of his reputation. The parallel but finally divergent careers of Hawthorne and Susan Warner illustrate dramatically how important belonging to the right network was as a precondition for long-standing critical success.

The circle of well-educated, well-connected men and women who controlled New England's cultural life at midcentury thought of themselves as spiritually and culturally suited to raise the level of popular taste and to civilize and refine the impulses of the multitude. Any writer whom they chose as a model of moral and aesthetic excellence, therefore, had to be someone whose work had not already been embraced by the nation at large, but had been initially admired only by the discerning few. Longfellow formulated the prevailing view of Hawthorne as a writer for a cultivated minority in his review of the second edition of *Twice-told Tales*:

> Mr. Hawthorne's . . . writings have now become so well known, and are so justly appreciated, by all discerning minds, that they do not need our commendation. He is not an author to create a sensation, or have a tumultuous popularity. His works are not stimulating or impassioned, and they minister nothing to a feverish love of excitement. Their tranquil beauty and softened tints, which do not win the notice of the restless many, only endear him to the thoughtful few.[36]

The "thoughtful few" to whom Longfellow refers are the people who controlled New England's cultural life before the Civil War. Once Hawthorne's work had been published by Ticknor and Fields, New England's most prominent publisher; once it had been reviewed by E. P. Whipple, a member of Fields's coterie and one of the most influential contemporary reviewers; and once it had become the subject of long discussions in the *Christian Examiner* and the *North American Review,* periodicals whose editors, in Sidney Ahlstrom's words, "alone constitute . . . a hall of fame of the New England flowering," he had gained a place in a socio-cultural network that assured his prominence because its own prominence was already an established and self-perpetuating fact.[37]

Lewis Simpson has characterized this group of literary and intellectual men who took the nation's spiritual welfare as their special charge as the "New England clerisy."[38] Simpson traces its beginnings in the passage from a theological to a literary clergy in the early years of the nineteenth century, using the career of Joseph Stevens Buckminster, a precocious young theology professor at Harvard, to exemplify the broadening of ecclesiastical authority to include general cultural matters and especially literature. Buckminster and his associates, who founded the *Monthly Anthology,* America's most serious literary journal at the time, spoke of literature as a "commonwealth" with its own "government," that along with Church and State fought for civilization against barbarism.[39] As a result of their activity, Simpson has written, "the image in the New England mind of the old theocratic polity begins to become the image of a literary polity. . . . The *Respublica Christiana* . . . becomes the *Respublica Litterarum.*"[40] The metaphor of the state as a means of conceptualizing literary activity is important because it suggests the need for centralized leadership and control in cultural affairs: the choice of proper reading matter was not something that could be left to the "restless many," but rightly belonged to the "thoughtful few" whose training and authority qualified them as arbiters of public taste. The formation of a literary canon in the nineteenth century was not a haphazard affair but depended on the judgment of a small group of prominent men, the members of the Anthology Society—clergymen, professors, businessmen, judges, and statesmen—who conceived of their task as a civic and moral duty. The power they had to determine who would be read and who would not is dramatically illustrated by the career of Richard Henry Dana, Sr., whose ardent admiration for the English Romantic poets drew scathing criticism from the Boston literati. He failed to be elected to the editorship of the *North American* (the direct descendant of the *Monthly Anthology*), and thereafter refused to contribute to it. When his essays and tales, his long poem, and the collected edition of his poems and prose elicited only a cool response from reviewers, he simply withdrew from the world, devastated by its failure to recognize his genius.[41]

This fate did not befall Nathaniel Hawthorne because he had been taken up by the second generation of the New England clerisy, whose power to shape literary opinion had been inherited from the first through an interlocking network of social, familial, political, and professional connections. William Tudor, an active member of the Anthology Society, the *Monthly Anthology's* editorial board, became the founding editor of the *North American Review.* John Kirkland, another of the Society's original members, became president of Harvard. Alexander Everett, another member, later a minister to Spain, also went on to edit the *North American,* as did Edward Everett, who had studied German at Göttingen with George Ticknor, both of them original members of the Anthology Society. Ticknor, who preceded Longfellow as Professor of Modern Languages at Harvard, was the cousin of William Ticknor, of Ticknor and Fields, who became one of Hawthorne's lifelong friends. William Emerson, pastor of the First Church of Boston, who edited the *Monthly Anthology* for two years before the Society took over, was Ralph Waldo Emerson's father.[42]

Joseph Buckminster's father had strenuously opposed the liberal theological tendencies of his son, just as the Unitarians of Buckminster's era and beyond would oppose the radical theorizing of Emerson and his circle, but the authority to speak on spiritual and cultural issues passed smoothly down from father to son undiminished by doctrinal differences. The men who thus assumed the role of cultural spokesmen at midcentury—Longfellow, Holmes, Lowell, Whittier, and Emerson—were particularly powerful since by then Boston had become the literary center of the nation.[43] These were the men whom Caroline Ticknor recorded as gathering to socialize at the Old Corner Bookstore, as Ticknor and Fields was familiarly known.[44] These were the men who in 1857 "all agreed to write for the *Atlantic,* and . . . made it immediately . . . the most important magazine in America."[45] These were the men who, as Sophia Hawthorne left the cemetery after her husband's funeral, stood with bared heads as the carriage passed.[46]

It is hard to overestimate the importance of Hawthorne's connections with these men who outlived him by a score of years and who launched the periodical that would dominate literary activity in the United States for the rest of the nineteenth century. When William Dean Howells returned to Boston in 1866, he became assistant editor of the *Atlantic Monthly* under James T. Fields (Hawthorne's publisher), who had taken over the editorship from Lowell (Hawthorne's good friend). Howells, whom Hawthorne had helped get his start by introducing him to Emerson, took over the editorship from Fields in 1871 and George Parsons Lathrop, Hawthorne's son-in-law, became an assistant editor.[47] Lathrop would publish the first full-length study of Hawthorne, which Howell's close friend, Henry James, would challenge three years later in *his* full-length study. This touched off a critical controversy—notably in an essay by Howells—over whether Hawthorne was an idealist or a realist, so that it was Hawthorne whose texts critics used to argue the merits of literary realism in the 1880s and 1890s.[48] Meanwhile, several friends published poems commemorating Hawthorne's death; relatives, friends, and associates printed their reminiscences; Sophia published excerpts from Hawthorne's journals; and other admirers wrote pieces with titles like "The Homes and Haunts of Hawthorne." Yet most important in assuring Hawthorne's continuing presence in the cultural foreground was James T. Fields. Fields, wanting to make good on his investment, followed his former practice of putting out anything he thought would pique the public's interest in his author and managed to produce eleven posthumous editions of Hawthorne's work between 1864 and 1883. This meant, twenty years after he was dead, that Hawthorne was still being reviewed as a live author. Osgood, the successor to Fields, pushed this strategy further by adding Hawthorne to his "Little Classics" series, and in 1884, Houghton Mifflin, the successor to Osgood, capped it off by publishing *The Complete Works of Nathaniel Hawthorne* in twelve volumes, edited by his son-in-law. Finally, Houghton Mifflin reinforced the image by including Hawthorne in two more series: "Modern Classics" and "American Classics for the Schools." In 1883 the academic establishment put its *imprimatur* on what the publishers had done. In that year, Yale allowed English literature students for the first time to write their junior essays on "Hawthorne's Imagination"—the only topic on the list that concerned an American author. Consequently, Hawthorne's texts were "there" to be drawn upon for ammunition in the debates over the question of realism that raged during the 1880s. By the end of the century, as Edwin Cady observes in his survey of Hawthorne criticism, "a minor critic might well have doubted his respectability if he failed to cite Hawthorne whether in praise of or attack against any writing in question."[49]

The prominence of Hawthorne's texts in the post-Civil War era is a natural consequence of his relation to the mechanisms that produced literary and cultural opinion. Hawthorne's initial connections with the Boston literati—his acquaintance with Longfellow at college, his residence next door to Alcott and a half mile from Emerson (his son and Emerson's nephew roomed together at Harvard), his marrying a Peabody, becoming fast friends with Ticknor and Lowell, being published by the indefatigable Fields, and socializing with Duyckinck and Whipple—these circumstances positioned Hawthorne's literary production so that it became the property of a dynastic cultural elite that came to identify itself with him.[50] The members of this elite could not fail to keep Hawthorne's reputation alive since it stood for everything they themselves stood for. America's literary establishment, no less than James T. Fields (who was part of it), had an investment in Hawthorne. In short, the friends and associates who outlived Hawthorne kept his fiction up-to-date by writing about it, and then *their* friends took over. Consequently, when the next generation of critics, Howells, James, and their contemporaries, came of age, they redefined his work according to the critical tastes of the new era. When the century turned, it seemed appropriate that a volume of Hawthorne criticism should appear in 1904 celebrating the hundredth anniversary of his birth. "By then," writes Edwin Cady, "figures like George Woodberry, William Peterfield Trent, and Paul Elmer More had come to maturity," who, with their "Arnoldian . . . neo-humanism" would "project Hawthorne toward the present century's Age of Criticism."[51]

During the same period, Susan Warner's critical reputation dwindled to nothing. Whereas critics writing before the Civil War had discussed her work alongside that of Hawthorne, Brockden Brown, Cooper, Irving, Longfellow, and Stowe, by the 1870s they had ceased to take her novels seriously as literature and finally stopped reviewing them altogether. Under the pressure of new conditions, Warner's work, like Hawthorne's, came to be redefined. The circumstances that create an author's literary reputation were of the same *kind* in either case—that is, they consisted of the writer's relation to centers of cultural domination, social and professional connections, blood relations, friendships, publishing history, and so on—but in Warner's case the circumstances were negative rather than positive.

Warner's connections—such as they were—sprang from New York rather than Boston, which at this particular period put her at a geographical disadvantage. Not having lived in Concord, she did not know Emerson and his circle, was not published by Fields, had not known Longfellow at college, had not roomed with a former president of the United States whose campaign biography she would write and who would get her a consulship when she needed money. Rather, she had been forced by her father's financial failure in the 1830s to retire to an island in the Hudson River where the family owned property, and where, along with her maiden sister, she wrote novels to earn a living. The Warners' poverty and their resulting social isolation affected both what they wrote and the way their work was perceived by contemporary audiences. As a consequence of their social isolation the Warners threw themselves into church-centered activities and became extremely devout followers of the Reverend Thomas Skinner—a New Light Presbyterian who preached the importance of faith over doctrine in religious conversion. They considered the novels and stories they wrote their best means of doing the Lord's work and—since they had to—of supporting themselves. These conditions (at one point their house was in receivership and creditors took their furniture away) determined not only what they wrote, but how much, how fast, for what kind of audience, and for which publishers.[52] Though they had started out with G. P. Putnam, a large commercial publisher in New York who had been a friend of their father's, in the 1860s they gave most of what they wrote to Robert Carter, a highly respected religious publisher who could guarantee a certain number of sales. The audience for religious books was large, stable, and provided an outlet for the Warners that answered their need both to win souls and to have bread on the table. Thus, at a time when changes in the economic and social environment created the context within which literary realism flourished, the Warner sisters guaranteed that their novels would be read as religious rather than literary discourse, labelling them with Carter's imprint and with titles—"Stories on the Lord's Prayer," "A Story of Small Beginnings," "The Word"—more reminiscent of tract society pamphlets than of high art.

Given a different cultural milieu, these conditions of production might have guaranteed the Warner sisters lasting fame. If the religious views that characterized the attacks on *The Scarlet Letter* in the 1850s had dominated literary criticism after the war, Hawthorne would have done well to experience a religious conversion and switch to Carter, too. However, the moral impulse behind American criticism, which had been evangelical and religious in the antebellum years, evolved during the 1870s and 1880s into a concern for the material conditions of social life. Novels that had previously appeared to contain superb renditions of American character and homely scenes imbued with universal human truths, now seemed to be full of idealized characters, authorial didacticism, and an overt religiosity that marked them as morally false and artistically naïve. Warner's work had become identified with an outmoded piety and a discredited Romanticism that assured its swift disappearance from the critical scene. It is not that critics suddenly discovered limitations they had previously failed to notice, but that the context within which the work appeared had changed the nature of the work itself. If Warner had had the kinds of connections that kept Hawthorne's works in the public eye, had commanded the attention of influential publishers, editors, and reviewers, her early novels might have remained critically viable as they came to be recast according to the prevailing standards. In that case *The Wide, Wide World* might have been passed down to us as one of the benchmarks of American literary realism.[53] Yet when she died in 1885 there were no famous men at her funeral who would write poems in her memory for the *Atlantic Monthly* to print or for Harvard Phi Beta Kappas to hear. She had no publisher whose commercial interests lay in bringing out posthumous editions of her work, whose friends would write retrospective evaluations of her career. There were no surviving relatives whose connections would allow them to publish excerpts from her journals in prestigious places, no son to write three volumes of reminiscences, no son-in-law to write a full-length critical study and then go on to edit her complete works in twelve volumes.

What these facts demonstrate is that an author's relation to the mechanisms by which his or her work is brought before the public determines the status of that work in the world's eyes. Hawthorne's canonization was the result of a network of common interests—familial, social, professional, commercial, and national—that, combined, made Hawthorne a literary and cultural artifact, a national possession; the same combination of circumstances in reverse reconstituted Warner's best-selling novels as ephemera that catered to the taste of a bygone age. Nor was there a conspiracy involved in keeping Hawthorne's reputation green while Warner's withered. By attributing the canonical status of Hawthorne's work to factors other than its "intrinsic" merit, I do not mean to suggest that the merits that critics and editors discerned in that work were not real, that they promoted work they believed was worthless or mediocre, or that they deliberately ignored work they believed was good. On the contrary, although a mixture of motives was bound to be present in any individual decision to publish or write about Hawthorne's work—friendship, family feeling, commercial gain, professional advancement—these motives are not distinguishable from a belief in Hawthorne's genius and the conviction that his novels were great works of art. For that conviction is itself a contextual matter; that is, it does not spring from a pure, unmediated perception of an author's work on the part of his admirers and supporters, but is determined by the situation in which they encounter it. To put it another way, the fact that an author's reputation depends upon the context within which it is read does not empty the work of value; it is the context—which eventually includes the work itself—that creates the value its readers "discover" there. Their reading is an activity arising within a particular cultural setting (of which the author's reputation is a part) that reflects and elaborates the features of that setting simultaneously.

* * *

The idea that great literary works are those that stand the test of time might seem at first to have a persuasive force that no amount of argument can dispel. Yet the moment one starts to investigate the critical history of even a single work, the notion that a classic is a book that outlasts its age becomes extremely problematic. What does it mean to say that *The Scarlet Letter* stood the test of time and *The Wide, Wide World* did not? Which test? Or rather, whose? It was the Custom-House essay and not Hester's story that drew the most unstinting praise from contemporary reviewers of *The Scarlet Letter*; and it was *The Marble Faun*, that, on the whole, Hawthorne's contemporaries deemed his finest work.[54] The reason for this, as I have shown, is that the criteria by which those critics judged Hawthorne were different from ours. Whose criteria then shall constitute the test? Certainly not Longfellow's: his standards belong to the "prose-like-running-waters" school. Henry James's admiration of Hawthorne was highly qualified: he believed *The Scarlet Letter* inferior to John Lockhart's *Adam Blair*.[55] The transcendental defense of Hawthorne is not, as I have indicated, one that twentieth-century critics could make. Yet if we use only modern critical criteria—assuming they could be agreed upon—then *The Scarlet Letter* would have passed *a* test but not the "test of time," since that presumably would have to include the critical judgments of more than one generation. The trouble with the notion that a classic work transcends the limitations of its age and appeals to critics and readers across the centuries is that one discovers, upon investigation, that the grounds of critical approval are always shifting. *The Scarlet Letter* is a great novel in 1850, in 1876, in 1904, in 1942, and in 1966, but each time it is great for different reasons. In the light of this evidence, it begins to appear that what we have been accustomed to think of as the most enduring work of American literature is not a stable object possessing features of enduring value, but an object that—because of its place within institutional and cultural history—has come to embody successive concepts of literary excellence. This is not to say that *The Scarlet Letter* is simply an "empty space" or that there is "nothing there"; to put it another way, it is not to assert that no matter what Hawthorne had written, his work would have succeeded because he had the right connections. The novel Hawthorne produced in 1850 had a specificity and a force within its own context that a different work would not have had. Yet as the context changed, so did the work embedded in it.

Yet that very description of *The Scarlet Letter* as a text that invited constant redefinition might be put forward, finally, as the one true basis on which to found its claim to immortality. For the hallmark of the classic work is precisely that it rewards the scrutiny of successive generations of readers, speaking with equal power to people of various persuasions. It is on just this basis, in fact, that one of Hawthorne's critics has explained his critical prominence in recent years. Reviewing Hawthorne criticism for *American Literary Scholarship* in 1970, Roy Male comments "on the way Hawthorne's work has responded to shifting expectations during the last two decades."

> In the fifties it rewarded the explicatory and mythic analyses of the New Critics; in the mid-sixties it survived, at the cost of some diminution, the rigorous inquest of the new historicists and the neo-Freudians; and now his fiction seems more vital than ever for readers aware of new developments in psychology and related fields.[56]

In a sense, what Roy Male describes here is a capsule version of what I have been describing throughout this essay; namely, the various ways in which Hawthorne's texts have been reinterpreted by critics of various persuasions. What is at issue is how to account for this phenomenon. In Male's view, these successive reinterpretations show that Hawthorne's work is "more vital than ever" because they testify to its capacity to reward a variety of critical approaches, each of which produces only a partial reading of it; the text itself must be deeper and broader than any of its individual concretizations, for there is no other way to explain how the same text could give rise to them all. The notion that the classic text escapes or outlasts history *must* hold that various attempts to capture it from within history (i.e., from within a particular perspective) are incomplete, for if one of them did succeed completely, not only would interpretation have to stop, it would mean that the classic was not universal but limited, could not speak to people in all times and places, was not, in short, a classic.

Yet as I have been suggesting, there is no need to account for the succession of interpretations by positing an ahistorical, transcendental text that calls them forth. History—the succession of cultural formations, social networks, institutional priorities, and critical perspectives—does that, and the readings thus produced are not partial approximations of an ungraspable, transhistorical entity, but a series of completions, wholly adequate to the text that each interpretive framework makes available. In each case, the reading can be accounted for by a series of quite specific documentable circumstances having to do with publishing practices, pedagogical and critical traditions, economic structures, social networks, and national needs which constitutes the text within the framework of a particular disciplinary hermeneutic. The "durability" of the text is not a function of its unique resistance to intellectual obsolescence; for the text, in any describable, documentable sense, is not durable at all. What endures is the literary and cultural tradition that believes in the idea of the classic, and which perpetuates that belief from day to day and from year to year by reading and rereading, publishing and republishing, teaching and recommending for teaching, and writing books and articles about a small group of works whose "durability" is thereby assured.

The fact is that literary classics do not *withstand* change; rather, they are always registering, or promoting, or retarding alterations in historical conditions as these affect their readers and, especially, the members of the literary establishment. For classic texts, while they may or may not have originally been written by geniuses, have certainly been written and rewritten by the generations of professors and critics who make their living by them. They are the mirrors of culture as culture is interpreted by those who control the literary establishment. Rather than being the repository of eternal truths, they embody the changing interests and beliefs of those people whose place in the cultural hierarchy empowers them to decide which works deserve the name of classic and which do not. For the idea of "the classic" itself is no more universal or interest-free than the situation of those whose business it is to interpret literary works for the general public. It underwrites their claim to be the servants—and not the arbiters—of truth, and disguises the historically conditioned, contingent, and partisan nature of the texts which their modes of construction make visible. The recognition that literary texts, like everything else, are humanly created, historically produced objects, whose value has been created and re-created by men and women out of their particular needs, suggests a need to study the interests, institutional practices, and social arrangements that sustain the canon of classic works. It also opens the way for a retrieval of the values and interests embodied in other, noncanonical texts, which the literary establishment responsible for the canon in its present form has—for a variety of reasons—suppressed.

NOTES

1. Samuel Johnson, *Preface to Shakespeare*, rpt. in *The Great Critics*, ed. James Harry Smith and Edd Winfield Parks, 3d ed. (New York: W.W. Norton, 1951), 444–45.

2. Matthew Arnold, "The Study of Poetry," *Essays in Criticism, Second Series* (London: MacMillan, 1958), 2–3: Matthew Arnold, "Sweetness and Light," ch. 1 of *Culture and Anarchy*, rpt. in *Lectures and Essays in Criticism*, ed. R. H. Super (Ann Arbor: Univ. of Michigan Press, 1962). 13; Percy Bysshe Shelley, *A Defense of Poetry*, rpt. in Smith and Parks, eds., *The Great Critics*, ed. Smith, pp. 563–64, 575.

3. T. S. Eliot, "What Is Minor Poetry?" "What Is a Classic?" *On Poets and Poetry* (New York: Farrar, Strauss and Cudahy[,] 1957), 34–51, 52–74. Frank Kermode devotes an entire chapter to Hawthorne's work without ever raising the question of why Hawthorne should be considered a classic author.

4. Bertha Faust, *Hawthorne's Contemporaneous Reputation: A Study of Literary Opinion in America and England, 1828–1864* (New York: Octagon, 1968). A reprint of the 1939 Univ. of Pennsylvania dissertation, 16.

5. Ibid., 16–17.

6. For characterizations of these periodicals, see Frank Luther Mott, *A History of American Magazines, 1741–1850* (New York: D. Appleton, 1930); *Graham's*, 544–55; *Godey's Lady's*, 580–94; *Southern Literary Messenger*, 629–57.

7. Faust, *Hawthorne's Contemporaneous Reputation*, 12, 15, 17.

8. Ibid., 16, 24, 25.

9. Ibid., 27.

10. J. Donald Crowley, ed., *Hawthorne: The Critical Heritage* (New York: Barnes and Noble, 1970), 55.
11. Henry Wadsworth Longfellow, from a review in the *North American Review*, 45 (1837), 59–73; rpt. in Crowley, *Hawthorne*, 55, 56.
12. See, for example, Charles Fenno Hoffman, in the *American Monthly Magazine*, 5, March 1838, 281–83, rpt. in ibid., 61: Longfellow, rpt. in ibid., 58–59; and Peabody, rpt. in ibid., 64–65.
13. In a headnote to Poe's second review of *Twice-Told Tales*, Richard Wilbur comments: "Poe proves his discernment by recognizing the merits of his contemporary." (See *Major Writers of America*, General Editor, Perry Miller [New York: Harcourt, Brace and World, 1962], I, 465.) Yet while Poe's reviews seem to confirm modern assessments of Hawthorne by pointing to his "invention, creation, imagination, originality," the chief merit Poe recognized in Hawthorne's tales was one that few modern commentators have seen: their repose. "A painter," Poe writes, "would at once note their leading or predominant feature, and style it *repose*. . . . We are soothed as we read." (See *Graham's Magazine*, May 1842, reprinted in *The Complete Works of Edgar Allan Poe*, ed. James A. Harrison [New York: Thomas Y. Crowell, 1902], XI, 105.) Hawthorne's current status as a major writer rests on exactly the opposite claim, namely that his vision is dark and troubled, the very reverse of that "hearty, genial, but still Indian-summer sunshine of his Wakefields and Little Annie's Rambles" which Poe admires so much and contrasts favorably to the "mysticism" of "Young Goodman Brown," of which he wishes Hawthorne would rid himself. "He has done *well* as a mystic. But . . . let him mend his pen, get a bottle of visible ink, come out from the Old Manse, cut Mr. Alcott, hang (if possible) the editor of the *Dial*, and throw out of the window to the pigs all his odd numbers of the "North American Review." (See *Godey's Lady's Book*, Nov. 1847, reprinted in Harrison, ed., *Complete Works*, XIII, 154–55.)
    Melville's wonderful encomium of Hawthorne in the *Literary World*, which sees Hawthorne's works as "deeper than the plummet of the mere critic," characterized above all by their "blackness," and possessed of a vision of truth as "terrific" and "madness to utter," comes much closer to modern criticism of Hawthorne (which quotes from it tirelessly) than Poe's reviews do. (See "Hawthorne and His Mosses," *The Works of Herman Melville*, ed. Raymond Weaver [London: Constable, 1922], XIII, 123–43.) Yet Melville's response to Hawthorne's "blackness" is not proof that he saw Hawthorne's tales as they really are, but rather of Melville's own preoccupation with the problem of innate depravity and original sin. He himself calls attention to the idiosyncracy of his views (for example, "the world is mistaken in this Nathaniel Hawthorne" and has an "absurd misconception of him"). Yet while Melville's reading of Hawthorne resembles modern interpretations in some respects, many of his critical observations—his pronouncements on "genius," his constant comparison of Hawthorne to natural phenomena (for example, "the smell of young beeches and hemlocks is upon him; your own broad prairies are in his soul"), his emphasis on the "repose" of Hawthorne's intellect, on his "Indian summer . . . softness," on the "spell" of "this wizard," testify to Melville's participation in the same romantic theories of art that dominate the mainstream reviews.
14. Peabody, in Crowley, *Hawthorne*, 66.
15. For an excellent discussion of the cult of domesticity, see Kathryn Kish Sklar, *Catherine Beecher: A Study in American Domesticity* (New Haven: Yale Univ. Press, 1973), 151–67; Peabody, in Crowley, *Hawthorne*, 64.
16. Richard P. Adams, "Hawthorne's *Provincial Tales*." *New England Quarterly*, 30 (1957), 50.
17. Ibid.
18. Of course, Adams's reading of "The Gentle Boy" may seem to *us* a willful imposition of his own ideas, and just as far off the mark, in its way, as Peabody's response. Yet what I am attempting to show is not that either critic is right or wrong, but that their readings of the tale flow naturally from their critical presuppositions.
19. Crowley, *Hawthorne*, 66, 60, 56.
20. F. O. Matthiessen, *American Renaissance: Art and Expression in the Age of Emerson and*

Whitman (New York: Oxford Univ. Press, 1941), 274–75; Crowley, *Hawthorne*, 58.

21. Samuel W. S. Dutton. "Nathaniel Hawthorne," *New Englander*, 5 Jan. 1847, 56–69, rpt. in Crowley, *Hawthorne*, 138; Carolyn Kirkland, "Novels and Novelists," *North American Review*, 76 (1853), 114. See also two reviews of *Queechy*, one from *Tait's Magazine*, the other from the *New York Evening Post*, rpt. in *Littel's Living Age*, 34 (July–Sept. 1852), 57–58.

22. Henry F. Chorley, in a review of *The Blithedale Romance*, in the *Athenaeum*, 10 (July 1852), 741–43, rpt. in Crowley, *Hawthorne*, 247. Chorley's remark is typical. Kirkland, "Novels and Novelists," 121.

23. Kirkland, "Novels and Novelists," 121; *The Literary World*, 7 (1850), 525; Amory Dwight Mayo, "The Works of Nathaniel Hawthorne," *Universalist Quarterly*, 8 (1851), 272–93, rpt. in Crowley, *Hawthorne*, 219, 221, 223.

24. Kirkland, "Novels and Novelists," 221. Most of Hawthorne's reviewers make this point in one way or another.

25. E. A. Duyckinck, *Arcturus*, 1 Jan. 1841, 125–26; as quoted in Faust, *Hawthorne's Contemporaneous Reputation*, 37–38.

26. E. A. Duyckinck, *The Literary World*, 8 (1851) 334–35, rpt. in Crowley, *Hawthorne*, 194; an unsigned review in the *Christian Examiner*, 50 (1851), 508–09, rpt. in Crowley, *Hawthorne*, 194.

27. These characterizations of Hawthorne are drawn from reviews by Edgar Allan Poe, Anne Abbot, Rufus Griswold, Henry Tuckerman, E. P. Whipple, R. H. Stoddard, Samuel S. W. Dutton, Evert Duyckinck, Charles William Webber, Amory Dwight Mayo, and George Loring. All are reprinted in Crowley, *Hawthorne*.

28. These characterizations of Melville come from reviews in *The Spectator*, the Boston *Post*, the *Literary World*, the *Democratic Review*, the London *New Monthly Magazine*, the *Southern Quarterly*, the *Albion*, the *Atlas*, the *Athenaeum*, *Today*, and *Peterson's Magazine*, as cited by Hugh Hetherington, "Early Reviews of *Moby-Dick*," *Moby-Dick Centennial Essays*, ed. with an introduction by Tyrus Hillway and Luther S. Mansfield (Dallas: Southern Methodist Univ. Press, 1953).

29. Though critics used the terms "original" and "deep" to praise both writers, Hawthorne's reviewers liked to characterize him as "gentle," "tasteful," "quiet," "delicate," "subtle," "graceful," and "exquisite," while Melville's admirers constantly used words like "racy," "wild," "extravagant," "brilliant," "eccentric," "outrageous," and "thrilling."

30. Amory Dwight Mayo, "The Works of Nathaniel Hawthorne." *Universalist Quarterly*, 8 (1851), 272–93; rpt. in Crowley, *Hawthorne*, 223; Donald A. Ringe, "Hawthorne's Psychology of the Head and Heart," *PMLA*, 65 (1950), 120.

31. Ringe, "Hawthorne's Psychology," 112, 122, 125.

32. Mayo, as reprinted in Crowley, *Hawthorne*, 223.

33. Ibid., 221.

34. Clark, "Posthumous Papers of a Decapitated Surveyor: *The Scarlet Letter* in the Salem Press," *Studies in the Novel*, 2 (1970), 395–419.

35. What happened was that Hawthorne, who had gotten the job through the influence of his old college friends and not through local connections or service to the party, lost his post when the Whigs took office. Because he was accused, in the process, of using his office for partisan ends, he became angry enough to stir up his friends on his behalf—hence the heated exchanges in the Salem and Boston papers. George Woodberry, *Nathaniel Hawthorne* (Boston: Houghton Mifflin, 1902), 163–77; Arlin Turner. *Nathaniel Hawthorne: A Biography* (New York: Oxford Univ. Press, 1980), 177–87.

36. Longfellow, in the *North American Review*, 56 (1842), 496–99, as reprinted in Crowley, *Hawthorne*, 83.

37. Sidney E. Ahlstrom, *A Religious History of the American People* (New Haven: Yale Univ. Press, 1972), 398. Ahlstrom's account of the emergence of Unitarianism is instructive for understanding the literary history of the period.

38. Lewis P. Simpson, *The Man of Letters in New England and the South* (Baton Rouge: Louisiana State Univ. Press, 1973).

39. Ibid., 22.
40. Ibid.
41. Robert E. Spiller, ed., *Literary History of the United States: History,* 3d ed. rev. (New York: Macmillan, 1963), 286–87.
42. Frank Luther Mott, *A History of American Magazines* (Cambridge: Harvard Univ. Press, 1957), I, 253–55.
43. Ibid., II, 32.
44. Caroline Ticknor, *Hawthorne and His Publisher* (Boston: Houghton Mifflin, 1913), 7.
45. Mott, *History of American Magazines,* II, 33, 494, 496.
46. Turner, *Nathaniel Hawthorne* 392–93.
47. *Literary History of the United States,* 888; Mott, *History of American Magazines,* II, 493ff.
48. Edwin Cady, "'The Wizard Hand': Hawthorne, 1864–1900," in *Hawthorne Centenary Essays,* ed. Roy Harvey Pearce (Ohio State Univ. Press, 1964), 324ff.
49. Ibid., 331.
50. Much of this interesting social information is contained in *The Memoirs of Julian Hawthorne,* ed. Edith Garrigue Hawthorne (New York: Macmillan, 1938).
51. Cady, "'The Wizard Hand,'" 334.
52. Anna Warner, *Susan Warner* (New York: G.P. Putnam's Sons, 1909).
53. Henry James, writing in the *Nation* in 1865, says that in its depiction of rural scenes *The Wide, Wide World* is superior to the realism of Flaubert. Yet later in the review he expresses exactly that critical doctrine that would eventually disqualify Warner's fiction from serious consideration as art. "They [novels written for both parents and children] frequently contain, as in the present case [James is reviewing *The Schönberg-Cotta Family*], an infusion of religious and historical information, and they in all cases embody a moral lesson. This latter fact is held to render them incompetent as novels; and doubtless, after all, it does, for of a genuine novel the meaning and the lesson are infinite; and here they are carefully narrowed down to a special precept" (See the *Nation,* 14 Sept. 1865, 344–45). It is interesting to compare James's comment with Brownson's review of *The Scarlet Letter* attacking the novel for failing to be Christian and moral enough.
54. Crowley, *Hawthorne,* 21; Faust, *Hawthorne's Contemporaneous Reputation,* 72, 141.
55. Henry James, *Hawthorne* (Ithaca: Cornell Univ. Press, 1956), 90–92.
56. Roy R. Male, in *American Literary Scholarship: An Annual, 1969* (Durham, N.C.: Duke Univ. Press, 1970), 19–20.

III

RECEPTION STUDY AND THE
HISTORY OF THE BOOK

Bringing together theory and practice, "practical" reception study has taken diverse forms but remains a well-defined literary field, whereas the history of the book is a territory still being charted. For example, several of its practitioners have maintained that "history of the book" examines the production, distribution, and reception of a variety of printed matter, from books, periodicals, and newspapers to pamphlets, broadsides, manuals, tracts, and even maps and posters. In that light, it is not surprising that Robert Darnton, one of the field's leading voices, has defined the history of the book as a set of practices concerned with "the social and cultural history of communication by print" during the five hundred years since Gutenberg invented movable type (65). Others, however, have claimed that this definition, despite its breadth, is too narrow because it ignores books that existed before print, whether in the form of the codex, the illuminated manuscript book, or the libellus (Davidson, 4). This argument has led to the claim that the history of the book is nothing less than "the history of texts and their transmittal" (Hall, 30).

The very generosity of these definitions raises questions about specific features of the field's history and contemporary profile. A central claim of its practitioners is that book history is a new field marked by significant departures from previous work. Most frequently, the origins of the field are identified with Lucien Febvre and Henri-Jean Martin's groundbreaking *L'Apparition du livre* (1958). That study and the work that followed in France applied the methods of the Annales school of socioeconomic history to the areas of print production and consumption, often via quantitative analyses of private libraries, sales figures, paper production, literacy rates, distribution channels, and print production technology. But in noting the relationship of this work to Anglo-American and German historiography of print, and in claiming for it an impact on German reception study (e.g., Darnton), those working in the field have simultaneously raised two problems that disrupt this neat narrative of origins. First, the claim of newness is troubled by the fact that studies of print, in forms similar to the "new" book history, were already being done in the 1940s and 1950s. Indeed, at least two of the leading figures in book history in the U. S. have admitted that historical study of books and print goes back at least to the nineteenth century and even to the Renaissance.[1] In the face of such a recognition, several book historians have subsequently argued—via a strategy that is especially germane to reception study—that what separates old studies of print from the new book history is the way the latter takes as its "core or center" a "concern with readers and the act of reading" (Hall, 30).[2] Yet such an assertion raises a second problem—or more accurately a series of related problems—about the composition of the field.

For instance, there has been over the last three decades important work in book history that has little or no concern with reading and reception, yet this assertion cashiers that work. The assertion also fails to solve the problem of demarcating the new book history from its antecedents, since studies by Richard Altick, H. S. Bennett, Robert Webb, and others in the early and mid-1950s made the relation between books and readers central to their investigations.[3] Even more problematic, the assertion has led book historians to claim as part of the field an inordinately wide range of work in contemporary literary criticism, cultural studies, and social history. Consequently, one can find pronouncements that book history includes the work of Hans Robert Jauss and German *rezeptionsästhetik* as a whole; the reader-response theory and practice of Wayne Booth, Wolfgang Iser, and Stanley Fish; and the poststructuralist criticism of Jonathan Culler and Barbara Herrnstein-Smith.[4] Although this colonization of fields would no doubt surprise Fish, Culler, Herrnstein-Smith, and perhaps even Iser and Jauss, the point is that such broad claims raise a central issue about how reception study and the history of the book relate to each other: Is reception study a subdivision of book history or are the two somehow coextensive?

Given that German and Anglo-American reception study, on the one hand, and French and American work in history of the book, on the other, have followed very different trajectories of development, it seems more appropriate to speak of these two as marking out complementary fields that partially overlap. That is, part of the work in the history of the book is concerned with examining the conditions under which and the manner in which written and printed texts have been available and consumed by their historical audiences. In this sense, history-of-the-book work complements literary-critical study by showing that reception involves such factors as the availability of different types of printed matter, the economics of book buying, literacy rates and practices, the treatment of books as physical objects, and the mechanisms (including institutional structures) through which printed matter has been censored, banned and canonized. The last of these factors points, moreover, to one of the ways book history shares analytical concerns and assumptions with reception theory and practice. That is, book historians recognize that the way a text is received varies in a markedly diachronic fashion: its significance is a product of the historical context in which it is being read as well as the composition of historically specific audiences. Book historians working in reception studies also share with their counterparts in literary and cultural studies a concern with what Roger Chartier calls "the great difference between the norms and conventions of reading that define, for each community of readers, legitimate uses of the book, ways to read, and the instruments and methods of interpretation" (1994, 4).

Such a concern has led book historians to draw from a number of disciplines, including literary criticism, social history, library science, and economics, to investigate reception. It also has led to discussion about analytical methods and resources for undertaking such study. To address these issues, Robert Darnton points out in the first essay of this section that book historians have done substantial work in identifying the who, what, where, and when of reception, which he calls the "external history" of reading. Yet it is the question of methods for probing the why and how of reading, particularly the practices through which readers relate to and process printed matter, that concerns Darnton. To get at the "how," he identifies five analytical foci related to different types of archival materials. Two of these are fairly traditional in literary study and reader-oriented criticism: work in textual bibliography that attends to the physical shape of books as an index to how they were read, and work in criticism that examines the way writers conceived of their audiences and inscribed their reading roles in texts. Beyond these, Darnton argues for the value of studying the "ideals and assumptions underlying reading" at various periods by examining advertisements, promotional materials, censors' reports, anti-novel tracts, and representations of reading in paintings and prints. Invoking the study of literacy (often central to the new book history), Darnton highlights a fourth area of historical research: the manner in which people learned to read and the social ways they practiced reading. Darnton's fifth area consists of examining autobiographies, letters, diaries, and commentary in book margins to describe the ways readers have made sense of texts. Central to Darnton's concern is the way histories of print and the book can disclose the specific shapes that have marked out reception as a historically constituted activity.

First published in 1986, Darnton's typology of historical inquiry at once reflected the reception study being done in book history at the time and projected the shapes such work would take in the following thirteen years. Particularly significant have been studies that attempt to get at the "how" of reception by examining "real readers," whether they be the monks and lay scribes who recorded their responses in the margins of medieval books, or middle-class readers in antebellum Boston and in turn-of-the-century Indiana, whose diaries and letters have provided an archival record of particular patterns of print reception.[5] Curiously, however, this concern with common readers has led to an argument opposing reception criticism to book history on the grounds that the latter is a superior form of reception study. Invoking a distinction between "reception history" and the "history of audiences," Jonathan Rose, for example, has claimed that "where reception histories have generally traced responses of professional intellectuals (literary and social critics, academics, clergymen), audience histories . . . focus on the common reader —defined as any reader who did not read books for a living" (51). Although substantial truth inheres in Rose's claim about the limited readership studied in literary-critical accounts of reception, his distinction is too stark and fails to account for the range of history-of-the-book reception study concerned with the "how" of reading, for some of the best work in the field has integrated both kinds of readerships.

Exemplifying this integrated approach to readership, James Smith Allen's "Reading the Novel," the second essay in this section, examines the nineteenth-century French reception of four novels by Eugene Sue, Emile Zola, Gustave

Flaubert, and Anatole France. Drawing on published reviews and "fan-mail" letters that these writers received from their general readership, Allen explores the common interpretive codes both communities of readers brought to bear in making sense of these texts. In a distinctive yet representative fashion, Allen's essay integrates elements from reception study within book history and from reader-response criticism to decipher these responses within the schema of "rules" that, Peter Rabinowitz has argued, govern textual decoding during the act of reading.

Yet if Allen's study exemplifies some of the insights that the history of the book has contributed to reception study, it also points to a limitation within book history. There is little doubt that this field has contributed materially to our understanding of who read and what they read in past eras, as well as the relation between readers and books as commodities and artifacts. It has even revealed some of the general ways readers have made sense of texts as vehicles of instruction and entertainment and as narrative analogues to their own lives. However, despite the assertions of some of its leading practitioners, it has been able to disclose little about the process of response and about historical variations in audience engagement with texts during the act of reading.[6] What book history has said little about, in other words, is the area of reception involving hermeneutics and the dynamics of interpretation.

Such a gap, however, hardly constitutes a fatal flaw or undermines the importance of reception study within book history. After all, inquiries into the dynamics of reading, which have been a characteristic concern of reader-response criticism, have also largely been missing from literary-critical work in reception. If the history of the books shares this gap, it only serves to demarcate an area of potentially productive inquiry for reception study in the future.

NOTES

1. On the history of the book in previous centuries see Darnton, 65–66; and Davidson, 4.
2. Roger Chartier makes a similar but more nuanced claim in asserting that the history of the book in the '60s and '70s came to be seen as excessively narrow for failing to address the full range of the production-reception circuit. Consequently, in the 1980s in its international (in contrast to its early French) form, book history became strongly marked by a concern with reading and reception (1988, 304–8, 322).
3. See Altick, *The English Common Reader,* 1957; Bennett, *English Books and Readers 1475 to 1557,* 1952; and Webb, *The British Working Class Reader,* 1955.
4. This colonizing tendency in book history extends to claims that the boundary of the field includes such studies as Frederic Jameson's *The Political Unconscious,* Robert Escarpit's *Sociology of Literature,* Pierre Bourdieu's *Distinction: A Social Critique of the Judgment of Taste,* and even Raymond Williams's *The Long Revolution* and *The Sociology of Culture* (see, for example, Davidson, 5; and Darnton. By such logic, just slightly extended, history of the book as history of reading would have to include a good part of the field of cultural studies and media studies, particularly if "reading" and "texts" are taken in their broad, poststructuralist sense.
5. For studies of marginal responses in medieval manuscript books, see Huot and Johnson. Textual reception by nineteenth-century American readers has been the subject of studies by Sicherman and by Zboray and Zboray.
6. Examples of such claims by book historians appear in Chartier, 1988, 325; Hall, 30; and Rose, 47.

WORKS CITED

Altick, Richard. *The English Common Reader: A Social History of the Mass Reading Public 1800–1900*. Chicago: University of Chicago Press, 1957.

Bennett, H. S. *English Books and Readers 1475 to 1557*. Cambridge: Cambridge University Press, 1952.

Chartier, Roger. "Frenchness in the History of the Book: From the History of Publishing to the History of Reading." *Proceedings of the American Antiquarian Society* 97 (1988): 299–329.

———. *The Order of Books: Readers, Authors, and Libraries in Europe between the Fourteenth and Eighteenth Centuries*. Translated by Lydia G. Cochrane. Cambridge, England: Polity, 1994.

Darnton, Robert. "What Is the History of Books?" *Daedalus 111*, no. 3 (summer 1982): 65–83.

Davidson, Cathy N. Introduction to *Reading in America: Literature and Social History*, edited by Cathy N. Davidson, 1–26. Baltimore: Johns Hopkins University Press, 1989.

Hall, David. "The History of the Book: New Questions? New Answers?" *Journal of Library History* 21 (1986): 27–36.

Huot, Sylvia. The Romance of the Rose *and Its Medieval Readers: Interpretation, Reception, Manuscript Transmmission*. Cambridge: Cambridge University Press, 1993.

Johnson, Barbara. *Reading* Piers Plowman *and* The Pilgrim's Progress. Carbondale: Southern Illinois University Press, 1992.

Rose, Jonathan. "Rereading the English Common Reader: A Preface to the History of Audiences." *Journal of the History of Ideas* 53 (1992): 47–70.

Sicherman, Barbara. "Sense and Sensibility: A Case Study of Women's Reading in Late-Victorian America." In *Reading in America: Literature & Social History*, edited by Cathy N. Davidson, 210–25. Baltimore: Johns Hopkins University Press, 1989.

Webb, Robert W. *The British Working Class Reader, 1790–1848: Literacy and Social Tension*. London: Allen & Unwin, 1955.

Zboray, Ronald J., and Mary Zboray. "'Have You Read . . . ?': Real Readers and Their Responses in Antebellum Boston and Its Region." *Nineteenth-Century Literature* 52 (1997): 139–70.

ROBERT DARNTON

FIRST STEPS TOWARD
A HISTORY OF READING

Ovid offers advice on how to read a love letter: "If your lover should make overtures by means of some words inscribed on tablets delivered to you by a clever servant, meditate on them carefully, weigh his phrases, and try to divine whether his love is only feigned or whether his prayers really come from a heart sincerely in love." It is extraordinary. The Roman poet might be one of us. He speaks to a problem that could arise in any age, that appears to exist outside of time. In reading about reading in *The Art of Love*, we seem to hear a voice that speaks directly to us across a distance of two thousand years.

But as we listen further, the voice sounds stranger. Ovid goes on to prescribe techniques for communicating with a lover behind a husband's back:

> It is consonant with morality and the law that an upright woman should fear her husband and be surrounded by a strict guard. . . . But should you have as many guardians as Argus has eyes, you can dupe them all if your will is firm enough. For example, can anyone stop your servant and accomplice from carrying your notes in her bodice or between her foot and the sole of her sandal? Let us suppose that your guardian can see through all these ruses. Then have your confidante offer her back in place of the tablets and let her body become a living letter.[1]

The lover is expected to strip the servant girl and read her body—not exactly the kind of communication that we associate with letter writing today. Despite its air of beguiling contemporaneity, *The Art of Love* catapults us into a world we can barely imagine. To get the message, we must know something about Roman mythology, writing techniques, and domestic life. We must be able to picture ourselves as the wife of a Roman patrician and to appreciate the contrast between formal morality and the ways of a world given over to sophistication and cynicism at a time when the Sermon on the Mount was being preached in a barbarian tongue far beyond the Romans' range of hearing.

To read Ovid is to confront the mystery of reading itself. Both familiar and foreign, it is an activity that we share with our ancestors yet that never can be the same as what they experienced. We may enjoy the illusion of stepping outside of

160

time in order to make contact with authors who lived centuries ago. But even if their texts have come down to us unchanged—a virtual impossibility, considering the evolution of layout and of books as physical objects—our relation to those texts cannot be the same as that of readers in the past. Reading has a history. But how can we recover it?

We could begin by searching the record for readers. Carlo Ginzburg found one, a humble miller from sixteenth-century Friulia, in the papers of the Inquisition. Probing for heresy, the inquisitor asked his victim about his reading. Menocchio replied with a string of titles and elaborate comments on each of them. By comparing the texts and the commentary, Ginzburg discovered that Menocchio had read a great deal of Biblical stories, chronicles, and travel books of the kind that existed in many patrician libraries. Menocchio did not simply receive messages transmitted down through the social order. He read aggressively, transforming the contents of the material at his disposition into a radically non-Christian view of the world. Whether that view can be traced to an ancient popular tradition, as Ginzburg claims, is a matter of debate; but Ginzburg certainly demonstrated the possibility of studying reading as an activity among the common people four centuries ago.[2]

I ran across a solidly middle-class reader in my own research on eighteenth-century France. He was a merchant from La Rochelle named Jean Ranson and an impassioned Rousseauist. Ranson did not merely read Rousseau and weep: he incorporated Rousseau's ideas in the fabric of his life as he set up business, fell in love, married, and raised his children. Reading and living run parallel as leitmotifs in a rich series of letters that Ranson wrote between 1774 and 1785 and that show how Rousseauism became absorbed in the way of life of the provincial bourgeoisie under the Old Regime. Rousseau had received a flood of letters from readers like Ranson after the publication of La Nouvelle Héloïse. It was, I believe, the first tidal wave of fan mail in the history of literature, although Richardson had already produced some impressive ripples in England. The mail reveals that readers responded as Ranson did everywhere in France and, furthermore, that their responses conformed to those Rousseau had called for in the two prefaces to his novel. He had instructed his readers how to read him. He had assigned them roles and provided them with a strategy for taking in his novel. The new way of reading worked so well that La Nouvelle Héloïse became the greatest best-seller of the century, the most important single source of romantic sensibility. That sensibility is now extinct. No modern reader can weep his way through the six volumes of La Nouvelle Héloïse as his predecessors did two centuries ago. But in his day, Rousseau captivated an entire generation of readers by revolutionizing reading itself.[3]

The examples of Menocchio and Ranson suggest that reading and living, construing texts and making sense of life, were much more closely related in the early modern period than they are today. But before jumping to conclusions, we need to work through more archives, comparing readers' accounts of their experience with the protocols of reading in their books and, when possible, with their behaviour. It was believed that The Sorrows of Young Werther touched off a wave of suicides in Germany. Is not the Wertherfieber ripe for fresh examination? The pre-Raphaelites in England provide similar instances of life imitating art, a theme that can be traced from Don Quixote to Madame Bovary and Miss Lonely Hearts. In each case the fiction could be fleshed out and compared with documents—actual suicide notes, diaries, and letters to the editor. The correspondence of authors and the papers of publishers are ideal sources of information about real readers. There are dozens of letters from readers in the published correspondence of Voltaire and Rousseau, and hundreds in the unpublished papers of Balzac and Zola.[4]

In short, it should be possible to develop a history as well as a theory of reader response. Possible, but not easy; for the documents rarely show readers at work, fashioning meaning from texts, and the documents are texts themselves, which also require interpretation. Few of them are rich enough to provide even indirect access to the cognitive and affective elements of reading, and a few exceptional cases may not be enough for one to reconstruct the inner dimensions of that experience. But historians of the book have already turned up a great deal of information about the external history of reading. Having studied it as a social phenomenon, they can answer many of the "who," the "what," the "where," and the "when" questions, which can be of great help in attacking the more difficult "whys" and "hows."

• • •

Studies of who read what at different times fall into two main types, the macro- and the microanalytical. Macroanalysis has flourished above all in France, where it feeds on a powerful tradition of quantitative social history. Henri-Jean Martin, François Furet, Robert Estivals, and Frédéric Barbier have traced the evolution of reading habits from the sixteenth century to the present, using long-term series constructed from the *dépôt légal,* registers of book privileges, and the annual *Bibliographie de la France.* One can see many intriguing phenomena in the undu- lations of their graphs: the decline of Latin, the rise of the novel, the general fasci- nation with the immediate world of nature and the remote worlds of exotic countries that spread throughout the educated public between the time of Descartes and Bougainville. The Germans have constructed a still longer series of statistics, thanks to a peculiarly rich source: the catalogues of the Frankfurt and Leipzig book fairs, which extend from the mid-sixteenth to the mid-nineteenth century. (The Frankfurt catalogue was published without interruption from 1564 to 1749, and the Leipzig catalogue, which dates from 1594, can be replaced for the period after 1797 by the *Hinrichssche Verzeichnisse.*) Although the catalogues have their drawbacks, they provide a rough index to German reading since the Renaissance; and they have been mined by a succession of German book historians since Johann Goldfriedrich published his monumental *Geschichte des deutschen Buchhandels* in 1908–1909. The English-reading world has no comparable source; but for the period after 1557, when London began to dominate the printing indus- try, the papers of the London Stationers' Company have provided H. S. Bennett, W. W. Greg, and others with plenty of material to trace the evolution of the English book trade. Although the British tradition of bibliography has not favoured the compilation of statistics, there is a great deal of quantitative information in the short-title catalogues that run from 1475. Giles Barber has drawn some French- like graphs from customs records. And Robert Winans and G. Thomas Tanselle have taken the measure of early American reading by reworking Charles Evans's enormous *American Bibliography* (18,000 entries for the period 1638–1783 including unfortunately an undetermined population of "ghosts").[5]

All this compiling and computing has provided some guidelines to reading habits, but the generalizations sometimes seem too general to be satisfying. The novel, like the bourgeoisie, always seems to be rising; and the graphs drop at the expected points—most notably during the Seven Years' War at the Leipzig fair, and during World War I in France. Most of the quantifiers sort their statistics into vague categories like "arts and sciences" and "belles-lettres," which are inadequate for identifying particular phenomena like the Succession Controversy, Jansenism, the Enlightenment, or the Gothic Revival—the very subjects that have attracted the most attention among literary scholars and cultural historians. The quantitative history of books will have to refine its categories and sharpen its focus before it can have a major impact on traditional strains of scholarship.

Yet the quantifiers have uncovered some significant statistical patterns, and their achievements would look even more impressive if there were more of an effort to make comparisons from one country to another. For example, the statistics suggest that the cultural revival of Germany in the late eighteenth century was connected with an epidemic-like fever for reading, the so-called *Lesewut* or *Lesesucht*. The Leipzig catalogue did not reach the level it had attained before the Thirty Years' War until 1764, when it included 1200 titles of newly published books. With the onset of *Sturm und Drang*, it rose to 1600 titles in 1770; then 2600 in 1780 and 5000 in 1800. The French followed a different pattern. Book production grew steadily for a century after the Peace of Westphalia (1648)—a century of great literature, from Corneille to the *Encyclopédie,* which coincided with the decline in Germany. But in the next fifty years, when the German figures soared, the French increase looks relatively modest. According to Robert Estivals, requests for authorizations to publish new books (*privilèges* and *permissions tacites*) came to 729 in 1764, 896 in 1770, and only 527 in 1780; and the new titles submitted to the *dépôt légal* in 1800 totalled 700. To be sure, different kinds of documents and standards of measurement could produce different results, and the official sources exclude the enormous production of illegal French books. But whatever their deficiencies, the figures indicate a great leap forward in German literary life after a century of French domination. Germany also had more writers, although the population of the French and German speaking areas was roughly the same. A German literary almanach, *Das gelehrte Teutschland* listed 3000 living authors in 1772 and 4300 in 1776. A comparable French publication, *La France littéraire,* included 1187 authors in 1757 and 2367 in 1769. While Voltaire and Rousseau were sinking into old age, Goethe and Schiller were riding a wave of literary creativity that was far more powerful than one might think if one considered only the conventional histories of literature.[6]

Cross-statistical comparisons also provide help in charting cultural currents. After tabulating book privileges throughout the eighteenth century, François Furet found a marked decline in the older branches of learning, especially the Humanist and classical Latin literature that had flourished a century earlier according to the statistics of Henri–Jean Martin. Newer genres such as the books classified under the rubric "sciences et arts" prevailed after 1750. Daniel Roche and Michel Marion noticed a similar tendency in surveying Parisian notarial archives. Novels, travel books, and works on natural history tended to crowd out the classics in the libraries of noblemen and wealthy bourgeois. All the studies point to a significant drop in religious literature during the eighteenth century. They confirm the quantitative research in other areas of social history—Michel Vovelle's on funeral rituals, for example, and Dominique Julia's investigation of clerical ordinations and teaching practices.[7]

The thematic surveys of German reading complement those of the French. Rudolf Jentzsch and Albert Ward found a strong drop in Latin books and a corresponding increase in novels in the fair catalogues of Leipzig and Frankfurt. By the late nineteenth century, according to Eduard Reyer and Rudolf Schenda, borrowing patterns in German, English, and American libraries had fallen into a strikingly similar pattern: seventy to eighty per cent of the books came from the category of light fiction (mostly novels); ten per cent came from history, biography, and travel; and less than one per cent came from religion. In little more than two hundred years, the world of reading had been transformed. The rise of the novel had balanced a decline in religious literature, and in almost every case the turning point could be located in the second half of the eighteenth century, especially the 1770s, the years of the *Wertherfieber*. *Die Leiden des jungen Werthers* produced an even more spectacular response in Germany than *La Nouvelle Héloïse* had done in France or *Pamela* in England. All three novels marked the triumph of a new literary sensitivity, and the last sentences of *Werther* seemed to announce the advent of a new reading public along with the death of a traditional Christian culture: "Handwerker trugen ihn. Kein Geistlicher hat ihn begleitet."[8]

Thus for all their variety and occasional contradictions, the macroanalytical studies suggest some general conclusions, something akin to Max Weber's "demystification of the world." That may seem too cosmic for comfort. Those who prefer precision may turn to microanalysis, although it usually goes to the opposite extreme—excessive detail. We have hundreds of lists of books in libraries from the Middle Ages to the present, more than anyone can bear to read. Yet most of us would agree that a catalogue of a private library can serve as a profile of a reader, even though we don't read all the books we own and we do read many books that we never purchase. To scan the catalogue of the library in Monticello is to inspect the furnishings of Jefferson's mind.[9] And the study of private libraries has the advantage of linking the "what" with the "who" of reading.

The French have taken the lead in this area, too. Daniel Mornet's essay of 1910, "Les enseignements des bibliothèques privées," demonstrated that the study of library catalogues could produce conclusions that challenged some of the commonplaces of literary history. After tabulating titles from five hundred eighteenth-century catalogues, he found only one copy of the book that was to be the Bible of the French Revolution, Rousseau's *Social Contract*. The libraries bulged with the works of authors who had been completely forgotten, and they provided no basis for connecting certain kinds of literature (the work of the philosophes, for example) with certain classes of readers (the bourgeoisie). Seventy years later, Mornet's work still looks impressive. But a vast literature has grown up around it. We now have statistics on the libraries of noblemen, magistrates, priests, academicians, burghers, artisans, and even some domestic servants. The French scholars have studied reading across the social strata of certain cities—the Caen of Jean-Claude Perrot, the Paris of Michel Marion—and throughout entire regions—the Normandy of Jean Quéniart, the Languedoc of Madeleine Ventre. For the most part, they rely on *inventaires après décès*, notarial records of books in the estates of the deceased. So they suffer from the bias built into the documents, which generally neglect books of little commercial value or limit themselves to vague statements like "a pile of books." But the notarial eye took in a great deal in France, far more than in Germany, where Rudolf Schenda considers inventories woefully inadequate as a guide to the reading habits of the common people. The most thorough German study is probably Walter Wittmann's survey of inventories from the late eighteenth century in Frankfurt am Main. It indicated that books were owned by

100 percent of the higher officials, 51 percent of the tradesmen, 35 percent of the master artisans, and 26 percent of the journeymen. Daniel Roche found a similar pattern among the common people of Paris: only 35 per cent of the salaried workers and domestic servants who appear in the notarial archives around 1780 owned books. But Roche also discovered many indications of familiarity with the written word. By 1789 almost all the domestic servants could sign their names on the inventories. A great many owned desks, fully equipped with writing implements and packed with family papers. Most artisans and shopkeepers spent several years of their childhood in school. Before 1789 Paris had 500 primary schools, one for every 1,000 inhabitants, all more or less free. Parisians were readers, Roche concludes, but reading did not take the form of the books that show up in inventories. It involved chapbooks, broadsides, posters, personal letters, and even the signs on the streets. Parisians read their way through the city and through their lives, but their ways of reading did not leave enough evidence in the archives for the historian to follow closely on their heels.[10]

He must therefore search for other sources. Subscription lists have been a favourite, though they normally cover only rather wealthy readers. From the late seventeenth to the early nineteenth century, many books were published by subscription in Britain and contained lists of the subscribers. Researchers at the Project for Historical Biobibliography at Newcastle upon Tyne have used these lists to work toward a historical sociology of readership. Similar efforts are under way in Germany, especially among scholars of Klopstock and Wieland. Perhaps a sixth of new German books were published by subscription between 1770 and 1810, when the practice reached its peak. But even during their *Blütezeit,* the subscription lists do not provide an accurate view of readership. They left off the names of many subscribers, included others who functioned as patrons instead of as readers, and generally represented the salesmanship of a few entrepreneurs rather than the reading habits of the educated public, according to some devastating criticism that Reinhard Wittmann has directed against subscription-list research. The work of Wallace Kirsop suggests that such research may succeed better in France, where publishing by subscription also flourished in the late eighteenth century. But the French lists, like the others, generally favour the wealthiest readers and the fanciest books.[11]

The records of lending libraries offer a better opportunity to make connections between literary genres and social classes, but few of them survive. The most remarkable are the registers of borrowings from the ducal library of Wolfenbüttel, which extend from 1666 to 1928. According to Wolfgang Milde, Paul Raabe, and John McCarthy, they show a significant "democratization" of reading in the 1760s: the number of books borrowed doubled; the borrowers came from lower social strata (they included a few porters, lackeys, and lower officers in the army); and the reading matter became lighter, shifting from learned tomes to sentimental novels (imitations of *Robinson Crusoe* went over especially well). Curiously, the registers of the Bibliothèque du Roi in Paris show that it had the same number of users at this time—about fifty a year, including one Denis Diderot. The Parisians could not take the books home, but they enjoyed the hospitality of a more leisurely age. Although the librarian opened his doors to them only two mornings a week, he gave them a meal before he turned them out. Conditions are different in the Bibliothèque Nationale today. Librarians have had to accept a basic law of economics: there is no such thing as a free lunch.[12]

The microanalysts have come up with many other discoveries—so many, in fact, that they face the same problem as the macroquantifiers: how to put it all together? The disparity of the documentation—auction catalogues, notarial records, subscription lists, library registers—does not make the task easier. Differences in conclusions can be attributed to the peculiarities of the sources rather than to the behaviour of the readers. And the monographs often cancel each other out: artisans look literate here and unlettered there; travel literature seems to be popular among some groups in some places and unpopular in others. A systematic comparison of genres, milieux, times, and places would look like a conspiracy of exceptions trying to disprove rules.

So far only one book historian has been hardy enough to propose a general model. Rolf Engelsing has argued that a "reading revolution" (*Leserevolution*) took place at the end of the eighteenth century. From the Middle Ages until sometime after 1750, according to Engelsing, men read "intensively." They had only a few books—the Bible, an almanach, a devotional work or two—and they read them over and over again, usually aloud and in groups, so that a narrow range of traditional literature became deeply impressed on their consciousness. By 1800 men were reading "extensively." They read all kinds of material, especially periodicals and newspapers, and read it only once, then raced on to the next item. Engelsing does not produce much evidence for his hypothesis. Indeed, most of his research concerns only a small sampling of burghers in Bremen. But it has an attractive before-and-after simplicity, and it provides a handy formula for contrasting modes of reading very early and very late in European history. Its main drawback, as I see it, is its unilinear character. Reading did not evolve in one direction, extensiveness. It assumed many different forms among different social groups in different eras. Men and women have read in order to save their souls, to improve their manners, to repair their machinery, to seduce their sweethearts, to learn about current events, and simply to have fun. In many cases, especially among the publics of Richardson, Rousseau, and Goethe, the reading became more intensive, not less. But the late eighteenth century does seem to represent a turning point, a time when more reading matter became available to a wider public, when one can see the emergence of a mass readership that would grow to giant proportions in the nineteenth century with the development of machine-made paper, steam-powered presses, linotype, and nearly universal literacy. All these changes opened up new possibilities, not by decreasing intensity but by increasing variety.[13]

I must therefore confess to some scepticism about the "reading revolution." Yet an American historian of the book, David Hall, has described a transformation in the reading habits of New Englanders between 1600 and 1850 in almost exactly the same terms as those used by Engelsing. Before 1800, New Englanders read a small corpus of venerable "steady sellers"—the Bible, almanachs, the *New England Primer*, Philip Doddridge's *Rise and Progress of Religion*, Richard Baxter's *Call to the Unconverted*—and read them over and over again, aloud, in groups, and with exceptional intensity. After 1800 they were swamped with new kinds of books —novels, newspapers, fresh and sunny varieties of children's literature—and they read through them ravenously, discarding one thing as soon as they could find another. Although Hall and Engelsing had never heard of one another, they discovered a similar pattern in two quite different areas of the Western world. Perhaps a fundamental shift in the nature of reading took place at the end of the eighteenth century. It may not have been a revolution, but it marked the end of an Old Regime —the reign of Thomas à Kempis, Johann Arndt, and John Bunyan.[14]

The "where" of reading is more important than one might think, because by placing the reader in his setting it can provide hints about the nature of his experience. In the University of Leyden there hangs a print of the university library, dated 1610. It shows the books, heavy folio volumes, chained on high shelves jutting out from the walls in a sequence determined by the rubrics of classical bibliography: *Jurisconsulti, Medici, Historici,* and so on. Students are scattered about the room, reading the books on counters built at shoulder level below the shelves. They read standing up, protected against the cold by thick cloaks and hats, one foot perched on a rail to ease the pressure on their bodies. Reading can not have been comfortable in the age of classical humanism. In pictures done a century and a half later, "La Lecture" and "La Liseuse" by Fragonard, for example, readers recline in chaises longues or well padded armchairs with their legs propped on footstools. They are often women, wearing loose-fitting gowns known at the time as *liseuses.* They usually hold a dainty duodecimo volume in their fingers and have a far-away look in their eye. From Fragonard to Monet, who also painted a "Liseuse," reading moves from the boudoir to the outdoors. The reader backpacks books to fields and mountain tops, where like Rousseau and Heine he can commune with nature. Nature must have seemed out of joint a few generations later in the trenches of World War I, where the young lieutenants from Göttingen and Oxford somehow found room for a few slim volumes of poetry. One of the most precious books in my own small collection is an edition of Hölderlin's *Hymnen an die Ideale der Menschheit,* inscribed "Adolf Noelle, Januar 1916, nord-Frankreich"—a gift from a German friend who was trying to explain Germany. I'm still not sure I understand, but I think the general understanding of reading would be advanced if we thought harder about its iconography and accoutrements, including furniture and dress.[15]

The human element in the setting must have affected the understanding of the texts. No doubt Greuze sentimentalized the collective character of reading in his painting of "Un père de famille qui lit la Bible à ses enfants." Restif de la Bretonne probably did the same in the family Bible readings described in *La vie de mon père:* "Je ne saurais me rappeler, sans attendrissement, avec quelle attention cette lecture était écoutée; comme elle communiquait à toute la nombreuse famille un ton de bonhomie et de fraternité (dans la famille je comprends les domestiques). Mon père commençait toujours par ces mots: 'Recueillons-nous, mes enfants; c'est l'Esprit Saint qui va parler.'" But for all their sentimentality, such descriptions proceed from a common assumption: for the common people in early modern Europe, reading was a social activity. It took place in workshops, barns, and taverns. It was almost always oral but not necessarily edifying. Thus the peasant in the country inn described, with some rose tinting around the edges, by Christian Schubart in 1786:

> Und bricht die Abendzeit herein,
> So trink ich halt mein Schöpple Wein;
> Da liest der Herr Schulmeister mir
> Was Neues aus der Zeitung für.[16]

The most important institution of popular reading under the Old Regime was a fireside gathering known as the *veillée* in France and the *Spinnstube* in Germany.

While children played, women sewed, and men repaired tools, one of the company who could decipher a text would regale them with the adventures of *Les quatre fils Aymon, Till Eulenspiegel,* or some other favourite from the standard repertory of the cheap, popular chapbooks. Some of these primitive paperbacks indicated that they were meant to be taken in through the ears by beginning with phrases such as, "What you are about to hear. . . ." In the nineteenth century groups of artisans, especially cigar makers and tailors, took turns reading or hired a reader to keep themselves entertained while they worked. Even today many people get their news by being read to by a telecaster. Television may be less of a break with the past than is generally assumed. In any case, for most people throughout most of history, books had audiences rather than readers. They were better heard than seen.[17]

Reading was a more private experience for the minority of educated persons who could afford to buy books. But many of them joined reading clubs, *cabinets littéraires,* or *Lesegesellschaften,* where they could read almost anything they wanted, in a sociable atmosphere, for a small monthly payment. Françoise Parent-Lardeur has traced the proliferation of these clubs in Paris under the Restoration,[18] but they went back well into the eighteenth century. Provincial booksellers often turned their stock into a library and charged dues for the right to frequent it. Good light, some comfortable chairs, a few pictures on the wall, and subscriptions to a half-dozen newspapers were enough to make a club out of almost any bookshop. Thus the *cabinet littéraire* advertised by P. J. Bernard, a minor bookseller in Lunéville: "Une maison commode, grande, bien éclairée et chauffée, qui serait ouverte tous les jours, depuis neuf heures du matin jusqu'à midi et depuis une heure jusqu'à dix, offrirait dès cet instant aux amateurs deux mille volumes qui seraient augmentés de quatre cents par année." By November 1779, the club had 200 members, mostly officers from the local *gendarmerie.* For the modest sum of three livres a year, they had access to 5,000 books, thirteen journals, and special rooms set aside for conversation and writing.

German reading clubs provided the social foundation for a distinct variety of bourgeois culture in the eighteenth century, according to Otto Dann. They sprang up at an astounding rate, especially in the northern cities. Martin Welke estimates that perhaps one of every 500 adult Germans belonged to a *Lesegesellschaft* by 1800. Marlies Prüsener has been able to identify well over 400 of the clubs and to form some idea of their reading matter. All of them had a basic supply of periodicals supplemented by uneven runs of books, usually on fairly weighty subjects like history and politics. They seem to have been a more serious version of the coffee house, itself an important institution for reading, which spread through Germany from the late seventeenth century. By 1760, Vienna had at least sixty coffee houses. They provided newspapers, journals, and endless occasions for political discussions, just as they had done in London and Amsterdam for more than a century.[19]

• • •

Thus we already know a good deal about the institutional bases of reading. We have some answers to the "who," "what," "where," and "when" questions. But the "whys" and "hows" elude us. We have not yet devised a strategy for understanding the inner process by which readers made sense of words. We do not even understand the way we read ourselves, despite the efforts of psychologists and neurologists to trace eye movements and to map the hemispheres of the brain. Is the cognitive process different for Chinese who read pictographs and for Westerners who scan lines? For Israelis who read words without vowels moving from right to left and for blind people who transmit stimuli through their fingers? For Southeast Asians whose languages lack tenses and order reality spatially and for American Indians whose languages have been reduced to writing only recently by alien scholars? For the holy man in the presence of the Word and for the consumer studying labels in a supermarket? The differences seem endless, for reading is not simply a skill but a way of making meaning, which must vary from culture to culture. It would be extravagant to expect to find a formula that could account for all those variations. But it should be possible to develop a way to study the changes in reading within our own culture. I would like to suggest five approaches to the problem.

First, I think it should be possible to learn more about the ideals and assumptions underlying reading in the past. We could study contemporary depictions of reading in fiction, autobiographies, polemical writings, letters, paintings, and prints in order to uncover some basic notions of what people thought took place when they read. Consider, for example, the great debate about the craze for reading in late eighteenth-century Germany. Those who deplored the *Lesewut* did not simply condemn its effects on morals and politics. They feared it would damage public health. In a tract of 1795, J. G. Heinzmann listed the physical consequences of excessive reading: "susceptibility to colds, headaches, weakening of the eyes, heat rashes, gout, arthritis, hemorrhoids, asthma, apoplexy, pulmonary disease, indigestion, blocking of the bowels, nervous disorder, migraines, epilepsy, hypochondria, and melancholy." On the positive side of the debate, Johann Adam Bergk accepted the premises of his opponents but disagreed with their conclusions. He took it as established that one should never read immediately after eating or while standing up. But by correct disposition of the body, one could make reading a force for good. The "art of reading" involved washing the face with cold water and taking walks in fresh air as well as concentration and meditation. No one challenged the notion that there was a physical element in reading, because no one drew a clear distinction between the physical and the moral world. Eighteenth-century readers attempted to "digest" books, to absorb them in their whole being, body and soul. The physicality of the process sometimes shows on the pages. The books in Samuel Johnson's library, now owned by Mrs Donald F. Hyde, are bent and battered, as if Johnson had wrestled his way through them.[20]

Throughout most of Western history, and especially in the sixteenth and seventeenth centuries, reading was seen above all as a spiritual exercise. But how was it performed? One could look for guidance in the manuals of Jesuits and the hermeneutical treatises of Protestants. Family Bible readings took place on both sides of the great religious divide. And as the example of Restif de la Bretonne indicates, the Bible was approached with awe, even among some Catholic peasants. Of course, Boccaccio, Castiglione, Cervantes, and Rabelais had developed other uses of literacy for the elite. But for most people, reading remained a sacred activity. It put you in the presence of the Word and unlocked holy mysteries. As a working hypothesis, it seems valid to assert that the farther back in time you go the farther away you move from instrumental reading. Not only does the "how-to" book become rarer and the religious book more common, reading itself is different. In the age of Luther and Loyola, it provided access to absolute truth.

On a more mundane level, assumptions about reading could be traced through advertisements and prospectuses for books. Thus some typical remarks from an eighteenth-century prospectus taken at random from the rich collection in the

Newberry Library: a bookseller is offering a quarto edition of the *Commentaires sur la coutume d'Angoumois,* an excellent work, he insists, for its typography as much as its content: "The text of the *Coutume* is printed *in gros-romain* type; the summaries that precede the commentaries are printed in *cicéro;* and the commentaries are printed in *Saint-Augustin.* The whole work is made from very beautiful paper manufactured in Angoulême."[21] No publisher would dream of mentioning paper and type in advertising a law book today. In the eighteenth century advertisers assumed that their clients cared about the physical quality of books. Buyers and sellers alike shared a typographical consciousness that is now nearly extinct.

The reports of censors also can be revealing, at least in the case of books from early modern France, where censorship was highly developed if not enormously effective. A typical travel book, *Nouveau voyage aux isles de l'Amérique* (Paris, 1722) by J.-B. Labat, contains four "approbations" printed out in full next to the privilege. One censor explains that the manuscript piqued his curiosity: "It is difficult to begin reading it without feeling that mild but avid curiosity that impels us to read further." Another recommends it for its "simple and concise style" and also for its utility: "Nothing in my opinion is so useful to travellers, to the inhabitants of that country, to tradesmen, and to those who study natural history." And a third simply found it a good read: "I had great pleasure in reading it. It contains a multitude of curious things." Censors did not simply hound out heretics and revolutionaries, as we tend to assume in looking back through time across the Inquisition and the Enlightenment. They gave the royal stamp of approval to a work, and in doing so they provided clues as to how it might be read. Their values constituted an official standard against which ordinary readings might be measured.

But how did ordinary readers read? My second suggestion for attacking that problem concerns the ways reading was learned. In studying literacy in seventeenth-century England, Margaret Spufford discovered that a great deal of learning took place outside the schoolroom, in workshops and fields where labourers taught themselves and one another. Inside the school, English children learned to read before they learned to write instead of acquiring the two skills together at the beginning of their education as they do today. They often joined the work force before the age of seven, when instruction in writing began. So literacy estimates based on the ability to write may be much too low, and the reading public may have included a great many people who could not sign their names.[22]

But "reading" for such people probably meant something quite different from what it means today. In early modern France the three *rs* were learned in sequence —first reading, then writing, then arithmetic—just as in England and, it seems, all other countries in the West. The most common primers from the Old Regime— A.B.C.s like the *Croix de Jésus* and the *Croix de par Dieu*—begin as modern manuals do, with the alphabet. But the letters had different sounds. The pupil pronounced a flat vowel before each consonant, so that *p* came out as "eh-p" rather than "pé," as it is today. When said aloud, the letters did not link together phonetically in combinations that could be recognized by the ear as syllables of a word. Thus *p-a-t* in *pater* sounded like "elhp-ah-eht." But the phonetic fuzziness did not really matter, because the letters were meant as a visual stimulus to trigger the memory of a text that had already been learned by heart—and the text was always in Latin. The whole system was built on the premise that French children should not begin to read in French. They passed directly from the alphabet to simple syllables and then to the *Pater Noster, Ave Maria, Credo,* and *Benedicite.* Having learned to recognize these common prayers, they worked through liturgical responses printed in standard chapbooks. At this point many of them left school. They had acquired enough mastery of the printed word to fulfil the functions expected of them by the Church—that is, to participate in its rituals. But they had never read a text in a language they could understand.

Some children—we don't know how many, perhaps a minority in the seventeenth century and a majority in the eighteenth—remained in school long enough to learn to read in French. Even then, however, reading was often a matter of recognizing something already known rather than a process of acquiring new knowledge. Nearly all of the schools were run by the Church, and nearly all of the schoolbooks were religious, usually catechisms and pious textbooks like the *Escole paroissiale* by Jacques de Batencour. In the early eighteenth century the Frères des Ecoles Chrétiennes began to provide the same text to several pupils and to teach them as a group—a first step toward standardized instruction, which was to become the rule a hundred years later. At the same time, a few tutors in aristocratic households began to teach reading directly in French. They developed phonetic techniques and audio-visual aids like the pictorial flash cards of the abbé Berthaud and the *bureau typographique* of Louis Dumas. By 1789 their example had spread to some progressive primary schools. But most children still learned to read by standing before the master and reciting passages from whatever text they could get their hands on while their classmates struggled with a motley collection of booklets on the back benches. Some of these "schoolbooks" would reappear in the evening at the *veillée,* because they were popular best-sellers from the *bibliothèque bleue.* So reading around the fireside had something in common with reading in the classroom: it was a recital of a text that everyone already knew. Instead of opening up limitless vistas of new ideas, it probably remained within a closed circuit, exactly where the post-Tridentine Church wanted to keep it. "Probably," however, is the governing word in that proposition. We can only guess at the nature of early modern pedagogy by reading the few primers and the still fewer memoirs that have survived from that era. We don't know what really happened in the classroom. And whatever happened, the peasant reader-listeners may have construed their catechism as well as their adventure stories in ways that completely escape us.[23]

If the experience of the great mass of readers lies beyond the range of historical research, historians should be able to capture something of what reading meant for the few persons who left a record of it. A third approach could begin with the best known autobiographical accounts—those of Saint Augustine, Saint Theresa of Avila, Montaigne, Rousseau, and Stendhal, for example—and move on to less familiar sources. J.-M. Goulemot has used the autobiography of Jamerey-Duval to show how a peasant could read and write his way up through the ranks of the Old Regime, and Daniel Roche discovered an eighteenth-century glazier, Jacques-Louis Ménétra, who read his way around a typical tour de France. Although he did not carry many books in the sack slung over his back, Ménétra constantly exchanged letters with fellow travellers and sweethearts. He squandered a few sous on broadsides at public executions and even composed doggerel verse for the ceremonies and farces that he staged with the other workers. When he told the story of his life, he organized his narrative in picaresque fashion, combining oral tradition (folk tales and the stylized braggadocio of male bull sessions) with genres of popular literature (the novelettes of the *bibliothèque bleue*). Unlike other plebeian authors—Restif, Mercier, Rousseau, Diderot, and Marmontel—Ménétra never won a place in the Republic of Letters. He showed that letters had a place in the culture of the common man.[24]

That place may have been marginal, but margins themselves provide clues to the experience of ordinary readers. In the sixteenth century marginal notes appeared in print in the form of glosses, which steered the reader through Humanist texts. In the eighteenth century the gloss gave way to the footnote. How did the reader follow the play between text and para-text at the bottom or side of the page? Gibbon created ironic distance by masterful deployment of footnotes. A careful study of annotated eighteenth-century copies of *The Decline and Fall of the Roman Empire* might reveal the way that distance was perceived by Gibbon's contemporaries. John Adams covered his books with scribbling. By following him through his copy of Rousseau's *Discourse on the Origin of Inequality*, one can see how radical Enlightenment philosophy looked to a retired revolutionary in the sober climate of Quincy, Massachussetts. Thus Rousseau, in the first English edition:

> There was no kind of moral relation between men in this state [the state of nature]; they could not be either good or bad, and had neither vices nor virtues. It is proper, therefore, to suspend judgment about their situation . . . until we have examined whether there are more virtues or vices among civilized men. . . .
>
> And Adams, in the margin:
>
> Wonders upon wonders. Paradox upon paradox. What astonishing sagacity had Mr. Rousseau! Yet this eloquent coxcomb has with his affectation of singularity made men discontented with superstition and tyranny.

Christiane Berkvens-Stevelinck has found an excellent site for mapping the Republic of Letters in the marginalia of Prosper Marchand, the bibliophile of eighteenth-century Leyden. Other scholars have charted the currents of literary history by trying to reread great books as great writers have read them, using the annotations in collectors' items such as Diderot's copy of the *Encyclopédie* and Melville's copy of Emerson's essays. But the inquiry needn't be limited to great books or to books at all. Peter Burke is currently studying the graffiti of Renaissance Italy. When scribbled on the door of an enemy, they often functioned as ritual insults, which defined the lines of social conflict dividing neighbourhoods and clans. When attached to the famous statue of Pasquino in Rome, this public scribbling set the tone of a rich and intensely political street culture. A history of reading might be able to advance by great leaps from the Pasquinade and the Commedia dell'Arte to Molière, from Molière to Rousseau, and from Rousseau to Robespierre.[25]

My fourth suggestion concerns literary theory. It can, I agree, look daunting, especially to the outsider. It comes wrapped in imposing labels—structuralism, deconstruction, hermeneutics, semiotics, phenomenology—and it goes as rapidly as it comes, for the trends displace one another with bewildering speed. Through them all, however, runs a concern that could lead to some collaboration between literary critics and historians of the book—the concern for reading. Whether they unearth deep structures or tear down systems of signs, critics have increasingly treated literature as an activity rather than an established body of texts. They insist that a book's meaning is not fixed on its pages; it is construed by its readers. So reader response has become the key point around which literary analysis turns.

In Germany, this approach has led to a revival of literary history as *Rezeptionsästhetik* under the leadership of Hans Robert Jauss and Wolfgang Iser. In France, it has taken a philosophical turn in the work of Roland Barthes, Paul Ricœur, Tzvetan Todorov, and Georges Poulet. In the United States, it is still in the melting-pot stage. Wayne Booth, Paul de Man, Jonathan Culler, Geoffrey Hartman, J. Hillis Miller, and Stanley Fish have supplied ingredients for a general theory, but no consensus has emerged from their debates. Nonetheless, all this critical activity points toward a new textology, and all the critics share a way of working when they interpret specific texts.[26]

Consider, for example, Walter Ong's analysis of the first sentences in *A Farewell to Arms*:

> In the late summer of that year we lived in a house in a village that looked across the river and the plain to the mountains. In the bed of the river there were pebbles and boulders, dry and white in the sun, and the water was clear and swiftly moving and blue in the channels.

What year? What river? Ong asks. Hemingway does not say. By unorthodox use of the definite article—"the river" instead of "a river"—and sparse deployment of adjectives, he implies that the reader does not need a detailed description of the scene. A reminder will be enough, because the reader is deemed to have been there already. He is addressed as if he were a confidant and fellow traveller, who merely needs to be reminded in order to recollect the hard glint of the sun, the coarse taste of the wine, and the stench of the dead in World War I Italy. Should the reader object—and one can imagine many responses such as, "I am a sixty-year-old grandmother and I don't know anything about rivers in Italy"—he won't be able to "get" the book. But if he accepts the role imposed on him by the rhetoric, his fictionalized self can swell to the dimensions of the Hemingway hero; and he can go through the narrative as the author's companion in arms.[27]

Earlier rhetoric usually operated in the opposite manner. It assumed that the reader knew nothing about the story and needed to be oriented by rich descriptive passages or introductory observations. Thus the opening of *Pride and Prejudice*:

> It is a truth universally acknowledged, that a single man in possession of a good fortune must be in want of a wife.
>
> However little known the feelings or views of such a man may be on his first entering a neighbourhood, this truth is so well fixed in the minds of the surrounding families that he is considered as the rightful property of some one or other of their daughters.
>
> "My dear Mr Bennet," said his lady to him one day, "have you heard that Netherfield Park is let at last?"

This kind of narrative moves from the general to the particular. It places the indefinite article first, and helps the reader get his bearing by degrees. But it always keeps him at a distance, because he is presumed to enter the story as an outsider and to be reading for instruction, amusement, or some high moral purpose. As in the case of the Hemingway novel, he must play his role for the rhetoric to work; but the role is completely different.

Writers have devised many other ways to initiate readers into stories. A vast distance separates Melville's "Call me Ishmael" from Milton's prayer for help to "justify the ways of God to men." But every narrative presupposes a reader, and every reading begins from a protocol inscribed within the text. The text may undercut itself, and the reader may work against the grain or wring new meaning from familiar words: hence the endless possibilities of interpretation proposed by the deconstructionists and the original readings that have shaped cultural history—Rousseau's reading of *Le Misanthrope*, for example, or Kierkegaard's reading of Genesis 22. But whatever one makes of it, reading has re-emerged as the central fact of literature.

If so, the time is ripe for making a juncture between literary theory and the history of books. The theory can reveal the range in potential responses to a text—that is, to the rhetorical constraints that direct reading without determining it. The history can show what readings actually took place—that is, within the limits of an imperfect body of evidence. By paying heed to history, the literary critics may avoid the danger of anachronism; for they sometimes seem to assume that seventeenth-century Englishmen read Milton and Bunyan as if they were twentieth-century college professors. By taking account of rhetoric, the historians may find clues to behaviour that would otherwise be baffling, such as the passions aroused from *Clarissa* to *La Nouvelle Héloïse* and from *Werther* to *René*. I would therefore argue for a dual strategy, which would combine textual analysis with empirical research. In this way it should be possible to compare the implicit readers of the texts with the actual readers of the past and, by building on such comparisons, to develop a history as well as a theory of reader response.

Such a history could be reinforced by a fifth mode of analysis, one based on analytical bibliography. By studying books as physical objects, bibliographers have demonstrated that the typographical disposition of a text can to a considerable extent determine its meaning and the way it was read. In a remarkable study of Congreve, D. F. McKenzie has shown that the bawdy, neo-Elizabethan playwright known to us from the quarto editions of the late seventeenth century underwent a typographical rebirth in his old age and emerged as the stately, neo-classical author of the three-volume octavo *Works* published in 1710. Individual words rarely changed from one edition to another, but a transformation in the design of the books gave the plays an entirely new flavour. By adding scene divisions, grouping characters, relocating lines, and bringing out *liaisons des scènes,* Congreve fit his old texts into the new classical model derived from the French stage. To go from the quarto to the octavo volumes is to move from Elizabethan to Georgian England.[28]

Roger Chartier has found similar but more sociological implications in the metamorphoses of a Spanish classic, *Historia de la vida del Buscón* by Francisco de Quevedo. The novel was originally intended for a sophisticated public, both in Spain where it was first published in 1626 and in France where it came out in an elegant translation in 1633. But in the mid-seventeenth century the Oudot and Garnier houses of Troyes began to publish a series of cheap paperback editions, which made it a staple of the popular literature known as the *bibliothèque bleue* for two hundred years. The popular publishers did not hesitate to tinker with the text, but they concentrated primarily on book design, what Chartier calls the "mise en livre." They broke the story into simple units, shortening sentences, subdividing

paragraphs, and multiplying the number of chapters. The new typographical structure implied a new kind of reading and a new public: humble people, who lacked
the facility and the time to take in lengthy stretches of narrative. The short
episodes were autonomous. They did not need to be linked by complex sub-themes
and character development, because they provided just enough material to fill a
veillée. So the book itself became a collection of fragments rather than a continuous story, and it could be put together by each reader-listener in his own way. Just
how this "appropriation" took place remains a mystery, because Chartier limits his
analysis to the book as a physical object. But he shows how typography opens onto
sociology, how the implicit reader of the author became the implicit reader of the
publisher, moving down the social ladder of the Old Regime and into the world
that would be recognized in the nineteenth century as "le grand public."[29]

A few adventuresome bibliographers and book historians have begun to specu-
late about long-term trends in the evolution of the book. They argue that readers
respond more directly to the physical organization of texts than to their surrounding social environment. So it may be possible to learn something about the
remote history of reading by practising a kind of textual archeology. If we cannot
know precisely how the Romans read Ovid, we can assume that like most Roman
inscriptions, the verse contained no punctuation, paragraphing, or spaces
between words. The units of sound and meaning probably were closer to the
rhythms of speech than to the typographical units—the ens, words, and lines—of
the printed page. The page itself as a unit of the book dates only from the third or
fourth century A.D. Before then, one had to unroll a book to read it. Once gath-
ered pages (the *codex*) replaced the scroll (*volumen*), readers could easily move
backwards and forwards through books, and texts became divided into segments
that could be marked off and indexed. Yet long after books acquired their modern
form, reading continued to be an oral experience, performed in public. At an
indeterminate point, perhaps in some monasteries in the seventh century and
certainly in the universities of the thirteenth century, men began to read silently
and alone. The shift to silent reading might have involved a greater mental
adjustment than the shift to the printed text, for it made reading an individual,
interior experience.[30]

Printing made a difference, of course, but it probably was less revolutionary
than is commonly believed. Some books had title pages, tables of contents,
indexes, pagination, and publishers who produced multiple copies from scriptoria
for a large reading public before the invention of movable type. For the first half
century of its existence, the printed book continued to be an imitation of the manuscript book. No doubt it was read by the same public in the same way. But after
1500 the printed book, pamphlet, broadside, map, and poster reached new kinds of
readers and stimulated new kinds of reading. Increasingly standardized in its
design, cheaper in its price, and widespread in its distribution, the new book transformed the world. It did not simply supply more information. It provided a mode of
understanding, a basic metaphor of making sense of life.

So it was that during the sixteenth century men took possession of the Word.
During the seventeenth century they began to decode the "book of nature." And in
the eighteenth century they learned to read themselves. With the help of books,
Locke and Condillac studied the mind as a tabula rasa, and Franklin formulated an
epitaph for himself:[31]

> The Body of
> B. Franklin, Printer,
> Like the cover of an old Book,
> Its Contents torn out,
> And stript of its Lettering & Gilding
> Lies here, Food for Worms.
> But the Work shall not be lost;
> For it will, as he believ'd,
> Appear once more
> In a new and more elegant Edition
> Corrected and improved
> By the Author.

* * *

I don't want to make too much of the metaphor, since Franklin has already flogged it to death, but rather to return to a point so simple that it may escape our notice. Reading has a history. It was not always and everywhere the same. We may think of it as a straightforward process of lifting information from a page; but if we considered it further, we would agree that information must be sifted, sorted, and interpreted. Interpretive schemes belong to cultural configurations, which have varied enormously over time. As our ancestors lived in different mental worlds, they must have read differently, and the history of reading could be as complex as the history of thinking. It could be so complex, in fact, that the five steps suggested here may lead in disparate directions or set us circling around the problem indefinitely without penetrating to its core. There are no direct routes or short cuts, because reading is not a distinct thing, like a constitution or a social order, that can be tracked through time. It is an actively involving a peculiar relation—on the one hand the reader, on the other the text. Although readers and texts have varied according to social and technological circumstances, the history of reading should not be reduced to a chronology of those variations. It should go beyond them to confront the relational element at the heart of the matter: how did changing readerships construe shifting texts?

The question sounds abstruse, but a great deal hangs on it. Think how often reading has changed the course of history—Luther's reading of Paul, Marx's reading of Hegel, Mao's reading of Marx. Those points stand out in a deeper, vaster process—man's unending effort to find meaning in the world around him and within himself. If we could understand how he has read, we could come closer to understanding how he made sense of life; and in that way, the historical way, we might even satisfy some of our own craving for meaning.

NOTES

1. Ovid, *Ars Amatoria,* Book III, lines 469–472 and 613–626. I have followed the translation by J. H. Mozley in *The Art of Love and Other Poems* (London, 1929), modifying it in places with the more modern version by Héguin de Guerle, *L'Art d'aimer* (Paris, 1963). All other translations in this essay are by me.
2. Carlo Ginzburg, *The Cheese and the Worms: The Cosmos of a Sixteenth-Century Miller,* tr. by Anne and John Tedeschi, Baltimore, 1980.
3. Robert Darnton, "Readers Respond to Rousseau: The Fabrication of Romantic Sensitivity" in Darnton, *The Great Cat Massacre and Other Episodes of French Cultural History,* New York,

1984, pp. 215–256.

4. As instances of these themes, see Kurt Rothmann, *Erläuterungen und Dokumente. Johann Wolfgang Goethe: Die Leiden des jungen Werthers*, Stuttgart, 1974, and James Smith Allen, "History and the Novel: *Mentalité* in Modern Popular Fiction," *History and Theory*, 22, 1983, pp. 233–252.

5. As examples of this literature, which is too vast to be cited in detail here, see Henri-Jean Martin, *Livre, pouvoirs et société à Paris au XVII siècle (1598–1701)*, Geneva, 1969, 2 vols; Robert Estivals, *La Statistique bibliographique de la France sous la monarchie au XVIIIe siècle*, Paris and The Hague, 1965; Frédéric Barbier, "The Publishing Industry and Printed Output in Nineteenth-Century France," in Kenneth E. Carpenter, ed., *Books and Society in History. Papers of the Association of College and Research Libraries Rare Books and Manuscripts Preconference, 24–28 June, 1980 Boston, Massachusetts*, New York and London, 1983, pp. 199–230; Johann Goldfriedrich, *Geschichte des deutschen Buchhandels*, Leipzig, 1886–1913, 4 vols; Rudolf Jentzsch, *Der deutsch-lateinische Büchermarkt nach den Leipziger Ostermesskatalogen von 1740, 1770 und 1800 in seiner Gliederung und Wandlung*, Leipzig, 1912; H. S. Bennett, *English Books & Readers 1475 to 1557*, Cambridge, 1952; Bennett, *English Books & Readers 1558 to 1603*, Cambridge, 1965; Bennett, *English Books & Readers 1603 to 1640*, Cambridge, 1970; Giles Barber, "Books from the Old World and for the New: the British International Trade in Books in the Eighteenth Century," *Studies on Voltaire and the Eighteenth Century*, 151, 1976, pp. 185–224; Robert B. Winans, "Bibliography and the Cultural Historian: Notes on the Eighteenth-Century Novel," in William L. Joyce, David D. Hall, Richard D. Brown, and John B. Hench, eds, *Printing and Society in Early America*, Worcester, 1983, pp. 174–185; and G. Thomas Tanselle, "Some Statistics on American Printing, 1764–1783," in Bernard Bailyn and John B. Hench, eds, *The Press & the American Revolution*, Boston, 1981, pp. 315–364.

6. Estivals, *La Statistique bibliographique*, p. 309; Paul Raabe, "Buchproduktion und Lesepublikum in Deutschland 1770–1780," *Philobiblon. Eine Vierteljahrsschrift für Buch- und Graphiksammler*, 21, 1977, pp. 2–16. The comparative statistics on writers are based on my own calculations.

7. François Furet, "La 'librairie' du royaume de France au 18e siècle" in Furet et al, *Livre et société dans la France du XVIIIe siècle*, Paris, 1965, pp. 3–32; Daniel Roche, "Noblesses et culture dans la France du XVIIIe: les lectures de la noblesse," in *Buch und Sammler. Private und öffentliche Bibliotheken im 18. Jahrhundert. Colloquium der Arbeitsstelle 18. Jahrhundert Gesamthochschule Wuppertal Universität Münster vom 26.–28. September 1977*, Heidelberg, 1979, pp. 9–27; Michel Marion, *Recherches sur les bibliothèques privées à Paris au milieu du XVIIIe siècle (1750–1759)*, Paris, 1978; Michel Vovelle, *Piété baroque et déchristianisation en Provence au XVIIIe siècle. Les attitudes devant la mort d'après les clauses des testaments*, Paris, 1973.

8. Jentzsch, *Der deutsch-lateinische Büchermarkt*; Albert Ward, *Book Production, Fiction, and the German Reading Public 1740–1800*, Oxford, 1974; Rudolf Schenda, *Volk ohne Buch. Studien zur Sozialgeschichte der populären Lesestoffe 1700–1910*, Frankfurt am Main, 1970, p. 467.

9. For Jefferson's model of a minimal library for an educated but not especially scholarly gentleman, see Arthur Pierce Middleton, *A Virginia Gentleman's Library*, Williamsburg, 1952.

10. Daniel Mornet, "Les Enseignements des bibliothèques privées (1750–1780)," *Revue d'histoire littéraire de la France*, 17, 1910, pp. 449–96. For an overview of the French literature with bibliographical references, see Henri-Jean Martin and Roger Chartier, eds, *Histoire de l'édition française* (Paris, 1982–), of which the first two volumes covering the period up to 1830 have appeared. Walter Wittmann's study and related works are discussed in Schenda, *Volk ohne Buch*, pp. 461–7. On the Parisian common reader, see Daniel Roche, *Le Peuple de Paris. Essai sur la culture populaire au XVIIIe siècle*, Paris, 1981, pp. 204–41.

11. Reinhard Wittmann, *Buchmarkt und Lektüre im 18. und 19. Jahrhundert. Beiträge zum literarischen Leben 1750–1880*, Tübingen, 1982, pp. 46–68: Wallace Kirsop, "Les mécanismes éditoriaux," in *Histoire de l'édition française*, Paris, 1984, vol. II, pp. 31–2.

12. John A. McCarthy, "Lektüre und Lesertypologie im 18. Jahrhundert (1730–1770). Ein Beitrag zur Lesergeschichte am Beispiel Wolfenbüttels," *Internationales Archiv für Sozialgeschichte der deutschen Literatur*, 8, 1983, pp. 35–82.
13. Rolf Engelsing, "Die Perioden der Lesergeschichte in der Neuzeit. Das statistische Ausmass und die soziokulturelle Bedeutung der Lektüre," *Archiv für Geschichte des Buchwesens*, 10, 1969, cols 944–1002 and Engelsing, *Der Bürger als Leser. Leserge–schichte in Deutschland 1500–1800*, Stuttgart, 1974.
14. David Hall, "The Uses of Literacy in New England, 1600–1850" in *Printing and Society in Early America*, pp. 1–47.
15. For similar observations on the setting of reading, see Roger Chartier and Daniel Roche, "Les pratiques urbaines de l'imprimé," in *Histoire de l'édition française*, vol. II, pp. 403–29.
16. Restif de la Bretonne, *La vie de mon père*, Ottawa, 1949, pp. 216–7. Schubart's poem is quoted in Schenda, *Volk ohne Buch*, p. 465, and can be translated: "When the evening time comes round, / I always drink my glass of wine. / Then the schoolmaster reads to me / Something new out of the newspaper."
17. On chapbooks and their public in France, see Charles Nisard, *Histoire des livres populaires ou de la littérature du colportage*, Paris, 1854, 2 vols; Robert Mandrou, *De la culture populaire aux 17e et 18e siècles: la bibliothèque bleue de Troyes*, Paris, 1964; and for examples of more recent scholarship the series "Bibliothèque bleue" edited by Daniel Roche and published by Editions Montalba. The best account of popular literature in Germany is still Schenda, *Volk ohne Buch*, although its interpretation has been challenged by some more recent work, notably Reinhart Siegert, *Aufklärung und Volkslektüre exemplarisch dargestellt an Rudolph Zacharias Becker und seinem "Nothund Hülfsbüchlein,"* Frankfurt am Main, 1978. As an example of workers reading to each other, see Samuel Gompers, *Seventy Years of Life and Labor. An Autobiography*, New York, 1925, pp. 80–1.
18. Françoise Parent-Lardeur, *Les cabinets de lecture. La lecture publique à Paris sous la Restauration*, Paris, 1982.
19. The studies by Dann, Welke, and Prüsener, along with other interesting research, are collected in Otto Dann, ed., *Lesegesellschaften und bürgerliche Emanzipation: ein europäischer Vergleich*, Munich, 1981.
20. Heinzmann's remarks are quoted in Helmut Kreuzer, "Gefährliche Lesesucht? Bemerkungen zu politischer Lektürekritik im ausgehenden 18. Jahrhundert," in Rainer Gruenter, ed., *Leser und Lesen im 18. Jahrhundert. Colloquium der Arbeitsstelle Achtzehntes Jahrhundert Gesamthochschule Wuppertal, 24.–26. Oktober 1975*, Heidelberg 1977. Bergk's observations are scattered throughout his treatise, *Die Kunst Bücher zu Lesen* (Jena, 1799), which also contains some typical remarks about the importance of "digesting" books: see its title page and p. 302.
21. Newberry Library, Case Wing Z 45.18 ser. la, n° 31.
22. Margaret Spufford, "First Steps in Literacy: The Reading and Writing Experiences of the [H]umblest [S]eventeenth-century Autobiographers," *Social History*, 4, 1979, pp. 407–35 and Spufford, *Small Books and Pleasant Histories. Popular Fiction and its Readership in Seventeenth-century England*, Athens, Georgia, 1981. On popular reading in nineteenth-and twentieth-century England, see R. K. Webb, *The British Working Class Reader*, London, 1955, and Richard D. Altick, *The English Common Reader: A Social History of the Mass Reading Public 1800–1900*, Chicago, 1957.
23. This discussion is based on the research of Dominique Julia, notably his "Livres de classe et usages pédagogiques" in *Histoire de l'édition française*, vol. 2, pp. 468–97. See also Jean Hébrard, "Didactique de la lettre et soumission au sens. Note sur l'histoire des pédagogies de la lecture," in *Les textes du Centre Alfred Binet: L'enfant et l'écrit*, 3, 1983, pp. 15–30.
24. Jean-Marie Goulemot, ed., Valentin Jamerey-Duval, *Mémoires. Enfance et éducation d'un paysan au XVIIIe siècle*, Paris, 1981; Daniel Roche, ed., *Journal de ma vie. Jacques-Louis Ménétra compagnon vitrier au 18e siècle*, Paris, 1982.
25. Adams' margin notes are quoted in Zoltán Haraszti, *John Adams & the Prophets of Progress*, Cambridge, Mass., 1952, p. 85. On glosses and footnotes, see Lawrence Lipking, "The

Marginal Gloss," *Critical Inquiry*, 3, 1977, pp. 620–31 and G. W. Bowersock, "The Art of the Footnote," *The American Scholar*, 53, 1983–84, pp. 54–62. On the Prosper Marchand manuscripts, see the two articles by Christiane Berkvens-Stevelinck, "L'Apport de Prosper Marchand au 'système des libraires de Paris'" and "Prosper Marchand, 'trait d'union' entre auteur et éditeur" in *De Gulden Passer*, 56, 1978, pp. 21–63 and 65–99.

26. For surveys and bibliographies of reader-response criticism, see Susan R, Suleiman and Inge Crosman, eds, *The Reader in the Text: Essays on Audience and Interpretation*, Princeton, 1980, and Jane P. Tompkins, ed., *Reader-Response Criticism: From Formalism to Post-Structuralism*, Baltimore, 1980. One of the most influential works from this strain of criticism is Wolfgang Iser, *The Implied Reader: Patterns of Communication in Prose Fiction from Bunyan to Beckett*, Baltimore, 1974.

27. Walter J. Ong, "The Writer's Audience Is Always a Fiction," *PMLA*, 90, 1975, pp. 9–21.

28. D. F. McKenzie, "Typography and Meaning: The Case of William Congreve," in Giles Barber and Bernhard Fabian, eds, *Buch und Buchhandel in Europa im achtzehnten Jahrhundert*, Hamburg, 1981, pp. 81–126.

29. Roger Chartier, *Figures de la gueuserie*, Paris, 1982. See also the general reflections of Chartier in his essay, "Une histoire de la lecture est-elle possible? Du livre au lire: quelques hypothèses," to which appear in the transactions of the Colloque de Saint-Maximin, October 1982.

30. Paul Saenger, "Manières de life médiévales," *Histoire de l'édition française*, vol. 1, pp. 131–41 and Saenger, "From Oral Reading to Silent Reading," Viator, 13, 1982, pp. 367–414. Of course one can find exceptional cases of individuals who read silently long before the seventh century, the most famous being Saint Ambrose as described in the *Confessions* of Saint Augustine. For further discussion of reading and the early history of the book, see Henri-Jean Martin, "Pour une histoire de la lecture," *Revue française d'histoire du livre*, new series, n° 16, 1977, pp. 583–610.

31. On the long-term history of the notion of the world as a book to be read, see Hans Blumenberg *Die Lesbarkeit der Welt*, Frankfurt am Main, 1981. Franklin's epitaph does not actually appear on his gravestone. He probably wrote it in 1728, when he was a young printer and a wit in the Junto club: see *The Papers of Benjamin Franklin*, Leonard W. Labaree, ed., New Haven, 1959-, vol. 1, pp. 109–11. The phrasing differs slightly in each of the three autograph texts.

JAMES   SMITH   ALLEN

READING THE NOVEL

In response to a proliferation of popular literature during the July Monarchy, Alfred Nettement wrote a series of critical essays on the serial novel.[1] A publicist with strong Catholic and legitimist sympathies, Nettement was especially outraged by the phenomenal success of Eugène Sue's *Les Mystères de Paris* (1842–43); he devoted all four of his "lettres à une femme du monde," first published in *La Gazette de France*, to deploring the threat that this work posed to the social order.[2] But in doing so, Nettement also felt the responsibility that all serious literary critics have to outline their analysis clearly, logically, and succinctly. "My observations bear on the conception, on the plan, on the outline of the book," he wrote. This analytical framework required Nettement to include commentary "on the types [that the novel] contains, on the author's literary procedures, on his style, on the morality of his work, [and] on the motives to which one must attribute its success."[3] Although some of these concerns, morality especially, no longer matter to most readers today, Nettement expressed a specific interpretive style, one as appropriate to prose fiction in general as it was to Sue's novel in particular. His other interests aside, this conservative writer responded self-consciously to the distinct nature of literary narrative. In effect, what Nettement did in his essays was to define the rules for reading the modern novel.

Nettement's attention to narrative conventions was far from complete; the work of recent reader-response critics is more extensive. Peter Rabinowitz, for example, has devoted the major portion of a book to the implicit rules that people follow in reading prose fiction.[4] What Nettement termed his "observations," Rabinowitz called the "rules of notice," the way in which a reader sorts out the relevant details from the plethora of stimuli in any narrative. The title, opening and closing scenes, and the like are important interpretive clues in every literary text, but especially in the novel because of all its extraneous material. Moreover, what Nettement called "conception," Rabinowitz termed the "rules of signification," that is, the work's larger meaning expressed in both form and content. Here narrative voice takes a leading role in defining the reader's understanding of the work. Another set of Rabinowitz's rules appeared in Nettement's "plan" or map of the work's unfolding. As Rabinowitz argues, the narrative's "configuring conventions" guide reader response as it develops over time from the first to the last chapters. And finally, Nettement's "outline" prefigures Rabinowitz's "rules of coherence," or how a narrative suggests to readers its unity as a literary work. On this issue, the reviewer is clearly distinguished from the ordinary reader, since until recently the critic's main task has been to characterize the narrative as an artistic whole; few other people are so concerned with a novel's coherence.[5] Nevertheless, all readers, critics or not, are subject to the same rules in their encounters with prose fiction.

In this fashion, a nineteenth-century writer anticipated the ideas of a twentieth-century literary specialist. Like Rabinowitz, though with far less deliberation, Nettement outlined the conventions of reading a genre for every interpretive community. Both book reviewers and fan-mail writers responded appropriately not only to Sue's *Les Mystères de Paris*, but also to Gustave Flaubert's *Madame Bovary* (1857), Émile Zola's *L'Assommoir* (1877), and Anatole France's *Le Lys rouge* (1894). Over a fifty-year period, from late romanticism to early symbolism, actual readers followed the narrative's rules of notice, signification, configuration, and coherence, all fundamental features of the French novel as it developed in the nineteenth century. Each work made certain demands of its readers, who responded appropriately, depending upon their skills and the narrative's clues. Different audiences thus interacted with specific works in yet one more element important to the history of interpretive practice: the text itself.[6] The contexts of publishing, education, ideology, and culture all shaped the literate experience, as did the tradition of response within reading publics and the nature of various genres. This much is clear. But the text also played a major role; it guided the act of reading in ways that can be well documented historically.

NOTICE

As any literature teacher knows, long fictional narratives pose special problems to young readers: What are the most significant details? How are they distinguished from the irrelevant? Of course, significance depends much upon the reader's ultimate interpretation, but the text does provide some obvious clues.[7] A reasonable narrative will help its audience to establish a hierarchy of detail, to privilege some information, in short, to suggest a framework of understanding. As literature, the novel naturally directs the reader's attention, even though the actual focus may shift somewhat from reader to reader. In most cases, people will attend to the title, to opening and closing scenes, and to dramatic changes in the course of the narrative. These are all common features of the modern novel. It is no accident, then, that French readers noticed and made good use of them in their responses. This is certainly true of Sue's audience for *Les Mystères de Paris;* this novel provoked considerable commentary from both the author's correspondents and his critics, who followed the rules of notice in the long narrative itself (especially its title, its first and last installments, and its shifts in theme, characterization, and setting). Each of these features guided the reader of Sue's text as it was published serially in the *Journal des débats* from June 1842 to October 1843.[8] Despite ambiguities, *Les Mystères de Paris* provided its readership the help it needed to make sense of an otherwise enormous and poorly conceived work.

In irregular biweekly installments, Sue spun out the diverse fates of a long list of characters. The novel had little unity of plot, structure, characterization, tone, or mood in its nearly 900 pages of narrative.[9] Rather, the work was organized episodically; its most consistent focus rested on the activities of Prince Rodolphe of Gerolstein in his quest for social justice in nineteenth-century Paris. A high-minded reformer, often disguised as a fan-painter in order to seek out honest but impoverished workers deserving of his charity, Rodolphe discovers his natural-born daughter, Fleur-de-Marie, whom he rescues from prostitution (despite the machinations of her hard-hearted mother, Lady MacGrégor). Before the resolution of this conflict, however, Rodolphe encounters the cutthroat Chourineur, the lapidary Morel, and the seamstress Rigolette—each of them possessing a heart of gold that an evil urban environment has endangered. Rodolphe rescues them, as well. But other characters are not so deserving: the brutal thief le Maître d'école and his ruthless accomplices, la Chouette and Tortillard; the grasping notary Jacques Ferrand; the homicidal Squelette; Calabash; and the widow Martial, among others. Like Lady MacGrégor, all of these evil figures seek to frustrate Rodolphe's generous designs, unsuccessfully, of course, in this deliberately melo-dramatic narrative. In the end, each villain dies. Otherwise, only the reiterated theme of bleeding-heart social reform—by individual charity and not by political action—provides a modicum of aesthetic unity to the innumerable details competing for the reader's attention.[10]

But one important convention did help Sue's audience: the work's title. By its very nature, *Les Mystères de Paris* suggested a world unfamiliar to the literate bourgeoisie, whether or not they lived in the French capital. The novel's particular mysteries—the poverty, crime, vice, and violence so common among the laboring classes—were its most obvious subject matter, as many readers testified.[11] Wrote Désiré Laverdant in the Fourierist newspaper *La Phalange,* "M. Eugène Sue wanted to investigate the mysteries of a civilized capital."[12] And he was echoed by more than two-thirds of the novel's reviewers. Socialist, liberal, and conservative commentators alike noted the work's call to reform "the mysteries of injustice, . . . these mysteries in society and Parisian civilization," as Nettement put it.[13] Occasionally, hostile critics like the reviewer in the Catholic *L'Univers* mocked the author's depiction of immorality, "a secret that he ought to explain."[14] C.-A. Sainte-Beuve appropriately quoted the abbé Combalot of Saint Sulpice: "The mysteries of Paris ooze with crime."[15] Such confusion of title and subject was deliberate. But Sue's correspondents were more generous in their responses. An overwhelming majority of them singled out the work's truths. Charity workers like Caroline Angebert and an anonymous letter writer sent serious proposals for social reform thanks to the narrative's heavy-handed commentary.[16] Clearly, the title alerted these readers to this particular feature in Sue's bewildering text.

Another textual clue guiding readers was the novel's dramatic first installment set in Paris's criminal underworld, the dark streets and wineshops of la Cité. Within a week of its appearance, Laverdant noted this bold scene: "Monsieur Eugène Sue, in effect, has opened to the public those obscure and frightful cesspools that accumulate criminal scum, the precise types in jailbird hangouts where men from the prison hulks are given refuge, where crime is contemplated, where trips to the gallows are prepared."[17] This graphic setting earned the attention of other readers, as well. One woman unwilling to sign her name admonished the author for having frightened her by his work's opening action. It was much too threatening for sensitive people like her.[18] Similarly, two years later Jules Michelet complained, without mentioning the author or his text by name, that Sue's first pages had defamed the working people: "A great and terribly phantasmagorical talent [has] given, in lieu of our urban communities, the life of a place where the police keep an eye on former offenders and released convicts."[19] Consequently, one of the novel's more notable features, the beginning, not only provoked its readers, but informed their views of the entire work as it unfolded for the next seventeen months. In actual interpretive practice, first impressions lingered.

Because of its privileged position in the text, the last word impresses at least as much as the first. And so as *Les Mystères* continued, installment after installment, book reviewers and correspondents often wondered when and sometimes how the novel would end. A hostile critic and a disgruntled letter writer both thought Sue's work "interminable."[20] In *La Revue des deux mondes,* Paulin Limayrac wrote angrily, "M. Sue accumulates volume upon volume, and his pen once launched never stops."[21] There seemed no obvious way for the work to conclude after hundreds of loosely linked episodes that, according to Nettement, made it "a nomad and vagabond narrative."[22] Less hostile readers sometimes spoke of the sense of closure they experienced with each installment, despite the deliberate suspense invariably created by the last line, "To be continued in the next issue." Noted Laverdant, "M. Eugène Sue's fecundity is marvellous. Each chapter of his book contains the elements of an entire play or novel."[23] But for the most part, the text provided few clues about its end until September 1843, when correspondents wrote of their impending disappointment. "Rumor has it that there will be several volumes. Is this true?" asked Ernestine Dumont, who hoped that the news she heard would delay the return of Prince Rodolphe and Fleur-de-Marie to the principality of Gerolstein, the logical end to their adventures in Paris.[24] In a serial novel like Sue's, however, the reader's need for conclusion was continuously frustrated.

Another novelistic feature that focuses the reader's attention is a shift in the narrative. Whenever a text adds new material or changes direction in the development of character or plot, the audience is sure to notice. As *Les Mystères* progressed, the narrative took up new themes, and Sue's readers responded. Most of them, like one anonymous correspondent, remarked the richness of the author's interests that invited suggestions of other worthy themes for him to develop. In this case, the reader proposed that Sue consider writing about a virtuous wife driven to prostitution by the incarceration of her husband for unpaid debts.[25] But most of the time, readers were surprised by the narrative's sudden shifts from one subject to another. Nettement complained of "continuous surprises." George Sand was hardly more indulgent: "This is a jumble of scenes that criss-cross, follow one another and seem to progress haphazardly, so vague and poorly indicated is its point."[26] Coming to the author's defense, Laverdant saw some merit in the text's many twists and turns: "M. Sue approaches the most incisive criticism of Society with a profundity, a wisdom, and an energy worthy of every glory; and if it is proclaimed only in the contrasts, it is solely because there are certain people who must be taught somehow by surprise."[27] However they reacted to shifts in Sue's work, readers noted them as the text grew longer and harder to understand as a unified narrative.

Besides material intrusions in the narrative—and occasionally long interruptions from installment to installment—readers noticed the work's change in setting.[28] As a German prince, Rodolphe also appears in elegant social circles, the *beau monde* of the French aristocracy, whose vices the narrative contrasts with those specific to the urban poor. "M. Eugène Sue has a manner," Laverdant wrote, "of comparing the fate of civilized people with the fate of beasts whose effect is striking and terrible."[29] The narrative's deliberate juxtaposition of these two worlds captured the attention of other readers, though rarely with Laverdant's evident enthusiasm. Louis Reybaud remarked, "The regions where the convict's language is spoken hold no more secrets for [Sue]; he has taken on the task of diminishing the distance that separates the criminal from the elegant world."[30] For another critic in *La Gazette de France,* the novel was nothing less than "a systematic attack" on the entire social order.[31] But the correspondents actually welcomed Sue's decision to bring Parisian high life and its problems into the work. When Clémence d'Harville first made her appearance in a March 1843 installment, two women wrote Sue to praise her fortitude in a tragically unhappy marriage. For Ernestine Dumont, this aristocrat was as much an example to the middle classes as Rigolette was to the laboring poor.[32] Meanwhile, Virginie Prignot could not praise Clémence's character enough, the same figure whom Nettement had called "la Goualeuse with 100,000 francs in dividends."[33] The narrative's sudden shift in focus, from the misery of the poor to the vices of the rich, was noted by contemporary readers.

Another major change remarked in the narrative was in the character of Fleur-de-Marie, whose motives intrigued Sue's audience. On the one hand, she was a prostitute, a fact that irremediably condemned her in the eyes of hostile respondents. Limayrac could not believe that the author had created this moral abomination: "Such is how the author imagines a prostitute in la Cité, innocent and completely candid, who in the novel's first chapter exercises her abominable trade and who at the end of the book becomes the princess of a royal court in Germany!"[34] Sand was similarly bemused: "What then does Fleur-de-Marie lack to be the most charming creature in modern poetry? The truth."[35] On the other hand, this character was a victim of circumstances beyond her control. More sympathetic readers seized on her relationship to Prince Rodolphe, surprisingly revealed in the twelfth installment of the novel, as evidence of her purity. "The prostitute breathes this frail and delicate grace that only privileged races breathe," stated Reybaud.[36] Given her parentage, she could do nothing truly wrong. The correspondents were particularly adamant in this conviction. Noted Castellane de Contades, "Marie . . . is a pretty person of whom you must be very proud."[37] Towards the end of the novel, readers worried about her fate. At least two people pleaded, in vain of course, that she not die.[38] Even though Fleur-de-Marie was not the central character in the novel, the narrative's unexpected revelations made her a much more prominent figure.

Fleur-de-Marie was only emblematic, however, of a much more pervasive feature that readers noticed in Sue's work: its thematic contradictions. The novel's title and dramatic changes in character, plot, and setting all indicated matters of import, but so did flagrant violations of narrative logic, the most obvious of which was the moral condition of the Parisian poor. While the text exonerated some characters like Fleur-de-Marie of personal responsibility for their acts, it condemned others like Lady MacGrégor and le Maître d'école, both of whom suffer painful deaths. There seemed no consistent rationale for the narrative's tone towards its characters. As Nettement put it, "M. Sue . . . has an astoundingly fecund imagination in finding excuses for the most blameworthy acts; and he pleads extenuating circumstances with a superiority that has assured him a fine place before the bar in a criminal court." Why should the reader, Nettement asked, respect le Chourineur, for example, who kills but never steals? He is an odious type, all the same.[39] Other readers could not accept the narrative's apparent "social fatality," or what Karl Marx called "false consciousness," at work in the narrative.[40] For those people better disposed to the author's theme, however, this illogic was more easily reiterated

than explained. Wrote one anonymous correspondent, *"Les Mystères de Paris . . .*
exposes the particular turpitudes and virtues that demonstrate the irresistible
influence of legal and social institutions on the deterioration or amelioration of
individuals."[41] This reader also noted the text's obvious contradictions, but chose to
ignore their implications.

Obviously, then, Eugène Sue's documented audience did follow some important
rules of notice. Both book reviewers and correspondents established a hierarchy of
detail within an analytical framework of their own making, one most certainly
guided by the text. These interpretive communities noted the work's title, *Les
Mystères de Paris,* and explained what it seemed to mean; they remarked the first
and last installments; and they responded to all disruptions in the narrative created
by the introduction of new material, by unexpected changes in plot, character, and
setting, and by various contradictions and inconsistencies in the work. Each of
these features of Sue's text was noted by his audience, even though the significance of these features varied from one person to the next. Ideology undoubtedly
intruded at this point, as many social and cultural commentators have observed
recently, but Sue's readers first had to respond to the text.[42] What they saw there
was in large part determined by the narrative itself, whose conventions directed
attention to specific elements. Not surprisingly, the debate over *Les Mystères de
Paris* concerned the details less than what those details meant. The details themselves were never in question; they were all too evident to readers in 1843.

SIGNIFICATION

Another set of rules implicit in the novelistic text facilitates the reader's sense of its
significance.[43] Beneath the literal surface, the narrative requires the attentive
reader to answer a series of questions that suggest a limited range of interpretations: Who is speaking—the author, a character, a narrator, or someone else? What
is one to make of that voice's judgment of character and action? Who is that voice
addressing? What does the text expect the reader to assume, and why?[44] In making
sense of fictional narratives, every reader needs to consider these conventions.
This is especially true of Flaubert's *Madame Bovary,* whose interest arises directly
from the different answers readers give to the questions it poses. Flaubert's free,
indirect style removes the author almost completely from the narrative and frustrates all pat conclusions drawn from the most apparent voice in the text. Similarly,
the narrative seems not to judge so much as to ridicule the characters, good and
bad alike, leaving its audience unsure whom it is addressing. In short, the text's
assumptions are ambiguous. Readers are therefore left without the assurances that
one expects from works like Sue's *Les Mystères de Paris.* An examination of the
actual responses *to Madame Bovary* highlights the narrative conventions of signification, largely because of their ambiguity throughout Flaubert's creative work.

The story itself is not difficult to summarize: Emma Bovary's adulterous infatuations with a local squire and a law clerk in a small provincial town lead in the end
to her suicide and her disillusioned husband's premature death. But the narrative
is much more complex. The critical problems it poses have been the object of considerable attention since the work's publication in *La Revue de Paris* in 1856.[45]
Despite Flaubert's apparent intention to portray an incurable romantic—a victim
of her extravagant novel-reading at odds with her more prosaic world—*Madame
Bovary* undermines the very ground on which this simple moral lesson stands. The
reader is distanced from every character, including the heroine, by long detailed

descriptions of surface detail provided by an utterly impersonal narrative voice. The result is confusion over what moves the characters. For the most part, their motives are inscrutable. Readers learn more explicitly about Charles Bovary's hat, for instance, than they do about the man's relationship with his wife; the audience is left alone to relate externals without guidance from the narrator. For this reason, the rules of signification in Flaubert's text are never very clear, and his contemporary reading public responded accordingly.[46]

From the very first page, *Madame Bovary* challenged its readers to identify the narrator.[47] The style was so impersonal that few of Flaubert's contemporaries could easily characterize its voice. Like most critics, Edmond Duranty disliked the narrative that was "always material description and never personal impression."[48] There was a sterile, antiseptic quality to what Léon Aubineau called "a medicinal style," because the narrative seemed so tightly controlled, crafted, or more precisely, tooled like a jewel.[49] Its language, Granier de Cassagnac remarked, was "full of ease, clarity, and force. It is supple without softness, correct without pedantry, concise without harshness. It is a firm and noble instrument."[50] That tool, however, was not a pen but a scalpel—both Paulin Limayrac and Marie-Sophie Leroyer de Chantepie borrowed Sainte-Beuve's famous surgical analogy—probing the hearts of the novel's characters "without tenderness, without idealism, without poetry, and . . . without soul."[51] Although Flaubert's correspondents were more comfortable with this cold narrative voice, they recognized its impersonality as well as the critics had. As a result, Edmond About wrote Flaubert, "From the first pages of your novel, one recognized the true life of the provinces studied up close," its stylistic objectivity a matter otherwise unexceptionable to the author's friends and family.[52]

Who, then, was speaking in the narrative? Few people claimed to know for sure. While readers answered the question variously, most of them turned to science for their terms. "M. Flaubert is not only a painter who has mistaken his vocation," wrote Gustave Merlet, "but a surgeon who applies to character analysis the cruel cold-bloodedness of an anatomist."[53] Only physicians would write such prose that contained "neither emotion, nor sentiment, nor life."[54] Sainte-Beuve used the same medical terminology in his assessment of the novel: "Son and brother of distinguished physicians, M. Gustave Flaubert holds the pen as others hold the scalpel. Anatomists and physiologists I still find you everywhere!"[55] Others agreed; they called the narrator a sawbones [carabin], an entomologist, and a mathematician.[56] Almost all critics, both friendly and hostile, recognized the detached scholarly features of Flaubert's apparent narrative persona. The more poetic voice at work in the text was hardly ever mentioned, except among the author's correspondents, who, like René de Marcourt, made the narrative into a sacred script: "I read and reread you as a true believer reads the *Imitation* [*of Christ*]," he wrote.[57] Otherwise, the voice speaking in the text could be none other than Flaubert himself, a logical resolution of the puzzle posed by the narrative's implacable, impassive surface that few readers liked, much less understood, whatever the terms they used to describe it.

In fact, the most common response to the narrative voice in *Madame Bovary* was to call it Flaubert's. Confusing narrator and author was, of course, habitual in the nineteenth century; readers often claimed to hear novelists in their texts throughout the period. But Flaubert's audience persisted despite the impersonality of the author's prose. Jean Rousseau, a critic for *Le Figaro,* spoke for many readers when he wrote, "There is in M. Gustave Flaubert's novel a forgotten character and that it does not name: it is the author."[58] As a rule, Flaubert's correspondents addressed both author and narrator; Charles Toirac, Ulric Guttinguer, and Champfleury, for instance, all considered Flaubert the narrator in this "fine study of the period, mores, [and] feelings."[59] "An author ordinarily puts his heart and soul into his work," Leroyer de Chantepie stated emphatically, "for this work is himself."[60] Consequently, even critics who decried the narrative's free, indirect style still tended to see the author in the text. Wrote M. Dumesnil in *La Chronique artistique et littéraire,* "*Madame Bovary* remains no less than one of the most curious and most personal works of our time."[61] Neither the prosecuting nor the defense attorney during Flaubert's obscenity trial ever made the critical distinction between the author and his narrative, for an obvious reason: the law held writers responsible for their language. "The principal accused," declaimed Ernest Pinard, "is the author, M. Flaubert."[62]

Some readers did make a distinction between the author and the narrative voice, and thereby understood better the significance of Flaubert's accomplishment. As Sainte-Beuve put it, "*Madame Bovary* is above all a book, a well-considered and composed book, where everything is in its place, where the pen leaves nothing to chance, and in which the author, the artist rather, has done precisely what he wanted from one end to the other."[63] By distinguishing the artist from the author, Sainte-Beuve implicitly distinguished the narrative from Flaubert. Similarly, Rousseau noted "the style of artist and poet where the picturesque word and image abound." These words and images, Rousseau thought, were prominent features of the text, not the author.[64] In this way the work took on a different meaning, one that A. A. Cuvillier-Fleury remarked in his careful review of the book:

> The scenes of a singular boldness and revolting crudeness abound in M. Flaubert's work. Has the author put them there complacently? In fairness, no, and I believe as well that once given the heroine's character, the situations force her author willy-nilly into these perilous analyses.[65]

The result was a new truth, a new realism in the novel that had never existed before. Readers were left to draw their own conclusions from the narrative, written in what Jules Habans called "the language of the daguerreotype."[66] The author was simply the photographer, his novel the reproduction of the world in which everyone existed.[67]

Because there was indeed a voice distinct from the author's addressing a different audience in the text, readers sought its judgment of the characters and their behavior. Some critics, like Charles de Mazade had difficulty assessing it: "This novel evidently contains an idea, a social thought, in such a way that it is not easy to disentangle."[68] But most people had no trouble discerning the implicit narrator's often bitter mockery. Despite the impersonality of the text written by "a stone pen," reviewers like Nestor Roqueplan found "an excellent store of irony, taste, and feeling."[69] "Irony is always just beneath the surface," wrote Sainte-Beuve, so much so that it tended to outright ridicule. "The raillery of a systematic hostility" was aimed at nearly every figure in the text.[70] "At heart M. Gustave Flaubert is a satirist," noted Cuvillier-Fleury.[71] Flaubert's correspondents remarked this feature of the narrative as well, one perhaps too harsh toward life in the provinces and the people who live there.[72] One correspondent simply stated, "I have also known this large and fine egoist of a farmer; this ridiculous bourgeois who discusses, judges, and settles without knowing anything . . . ; this avid and clever merchant who dupes you while he obliges you; and these young men ready to profit by a woman's weaknesses."[73] Consequently, Leroyer de Chantepie told Flaubert that the book's moral lesson was clear to all who had eyes to read: come what may, wives must be faithful to their husbands.[74]

But matters were hardly so clear to people less kindly disposed to the narrative's ironic stance. Those readers who confused author and narrator were particularly harsh in their response to the book's apparent (im)moral tone. Jules Barbey d'Aurevilly, a recent Catholic convert, wrote, "M. Flaubert is too intelligent not to have in himself firm notions of right and wrong, but he invokes them so rarely that one is tempted to believe that he does not have them."[75] Other reviewers threw up their hands in frustration and declared the book obscene. "Art ceases the very moment it is invaded by filth," opined Aubineau.[76] Both Pontmartin and Granier de Cassagnac considered the novel nothing less than a poison, like democratic politics, sure to destroy French society.[77] Other critics condemned the work's cruel, often lascivious irony. Nettement called the novel "a long calumny against human nature"; Émile Chevalet deplored its cynicism, "the crudeness with which M. Flaubert presents us licentious scenes."[78] To the extent that the narrative voice seemed to judge, its treatment of Emma seemed too severe, too superfluous in fact for prose realism; she was too trivial an individual to die in the end.[79] Only a handful of friendly critics and correspondents, like Frédéric Baudry, accepted the narrative voice's moral judgment.[80] Otherwise, whether or not readers recognized the integrity of the narrative, *Madame Bovary*'s apparent significance was sharply criticized. Its voice, its audience, and thus its meaning were not so easily discerned.

Given the text's ambiguous rules of signification concerning its narrative voice, readers sought what understanding they could. In his shrewd review of *Madame Bovary*, Charles Baudelaire identified the most common interpretive difficulty that Flaubert's audience encountered: "It is for the reader to draw conclusions by inference."[81] The text provided insufficient interpretive clues and thus forced readers to assess the novel's meaning all by themselves. Rousseau touched on this problem when he wrote, "A suspicion has come to me several times in running through this book: it is that I have not read a novel but a memorandum. . . . That would explain the faceless characters and banal situations—and at the same time it would also explain the minute care with which the author details these trivialities."[82] For Rousseau there were no causal links between the items on this aimless list of details. Rational explanation of the story also defeated Gustave Vapereau: "The entire unity of the book is in the heroine's character," he wrote, "and there is nothing sadder than such a unity; it is fatality, always fatality in its many different guises."[83] But this inevitability did not shed much light on either Emma's behavior or the lesson the reader was to draw from it. "From the heroine's first false step, you know that she was born and that she will die a *courtisane*. That is the sole formula that explains it."[84] The audience found no other source of meaning in a literary world without explicit suggestions from the narrative.

Second Empire readers, then, were troubled because the rules of signification in *Madame Bovary* were unclear. Few members of Flaubert's documented audience could make sense of the narrative voice; after the first chapter, in which the author seemed to be simply another figure in the novel, the narrator disappeared altogether. What voice there was, however, created an uncomfortable distance from the characters and their activities; the implicit narrator was detached, ironic, often satiric. This distant voice refused to assess or to judge any aspect of the story, except perhaps to ridicule good intentions and provincial life. Consequently, there was no causal or moral explanation that Flaubert's readers could identify with confidence in the plethora of textual detail. In an underdetermined text such as *Madame Bovary*, the normal conventions assisting, directing, guiding readers to some understanding of the author's achievement were obscure; and the response was confusion, frustration, bemusement, and for many readers, anger. Indeed, much of the moral outrage over the novel when it first appeared stems, in part at least, from these ambiguous features of the text. The ordinary narrative rules clearly defining its meaning simply did not apply in this case. Flaubert's audience made what it could from a text that permitted the Second Empire's moralism to determine its meaning.

CONFIGURATION

A third set of rules important to reading prose fiction made possible answers to a single question: How will this narrative, in all probability, work out?[85] As a novel unfolds, it typically creates expectations about its course and outcome. All characters generate speculation about the rewards the story holds in store for them; in most narratives, crime is punished and virtue rewarded. An audience naturally assumes a moralistic universe unless the text drops hints along the way that its world is structured differently. When a story fools the reader and belies these preliminary predictions, the response is either surprise or discomfiture, usually both. A reader's tolerance for reversals, for betrayals of expectations derived from the text, is often very limited. This is true for the novel's most prominent features—its characters, plot, and setting—on which a literate audience focuses its greatest attention from the very beginning. Most expectations concern who does what and where in the novel. One can see these rules at work in the responses to Zola's *L'Assommoir* when it was published both serially and in book form in 1876-77.[86] Here readers recognized the author's programmatic preface at work; they reacted sharply to how it seemed to achieve his stated intentions; and finally, they drew their conclusions from what they learned of Gervaise, Lantier, Coupeau, and their life in Paris. In this way Zola's audience responded to the conventions appropriate to the author's evolving narrative.

L'Assommoir provided its audience ample indication of the characters' implacable fate.[87] Once reaching Paris, Gervaise and her lover Lantier are destined to a difficult working-class existence. An incurable idler, Lantier leaves Gervaise to support their two children by herself. The struggling woman then marries Coupeau, a zinc worker, and together they manage a brief prosperity after Gervaise opens her own laundry business on borrowed money. But their life is troubled by heredity and circumstances beyond their control. Coupeau is badly injured in a roofing accident and turns to drink, squandering all of Gervaise's savings from the shop. Soon she, too, takes up drinking and loses customers. At Coupeau's suggestion, Lantier returns; he moves in with the unfortunate couple until they can no longer support him. Gervaise's laundry fails, Coupeau dies of delirium tremens, and Gervaise's rotting body is found soon afterward in a staircase closet. From the start, these characters have all too little chance to defy either the alcoholism they inherit or the environment they inhabit. The narrative presents an unrelieved portrait of Parisian brutality and degradation from which there is no escape. As the story develops, it draws the reader inexorably into the lives of its characters and their point of view; the narrative thereby creates a pessimism as unavoidable as the sympathy the reader feels for these apparent victims.

As one would expect, Zola's readers responded to the plot's inevitable course. Those people who felt that everyone is a responsible moral agent naturally condemned this feature of the narrative. "Beginning with this book *L'Assommoir*," wrote Barbey d'Aurevilly, "M. Émile Zola—and for me this is hardly praise—must be taken for the most accentuated, the most resolute, the most systematically exaggerated realist in a literature that has a heart for nothing and a heart sick from nothing."[88] By 1877 realism had become a more neutral term for Zola's deliberately provocative naturalism, a literary project first outlined in his "Le Roman expérimental." Because of naturalism's focus on the working class, however, Armand de Pontmartin objected as a matter of political principle: "M. Zola's work is the Republic."[89] And *L'Assommoir* was no exception; from the first page onward, it fit the mold perfectly. Consequently, when Anatole France reviewed the novel, he began with an overview of the author's previous work; for him *L'Assommoir* appeared in what was by then a predictable pattern.[90] Zola's naturalistic colleagues took up the same theme in their response to the novel. Observed Louis Jacquet, "*L'Assommoir* is thus not a novel for little girls, nor for prudes . . . but it pleases us, this novel where we find a living reality."[91] For readers like Jacquet and Zola's correspondents, literary expectations extraneous to the text itself complemented well the certain progress of the story and its characters.

So predictable did *L'Assommoir* seem to its original audience, critical reviews of it appeared long before the last serial installment in *La République des lettres*. Only one critic, Albert Wolff, admonished his colleagues for judging a work still in progress.[92] But this tendency to anticipate Zola's work continued unabated. Henry Houssaye expressed his disappointment in terms as unoriginal as he felt the author's work: "And it took M. Zola," he wrote sarcastically, "six hundred pages of close text to recount such an epic and to come to this new conclusion, that evil conduct engenders misery!"[93] Zola's severest critics expected and were not disappointed by his new work's ignoble material, which rendered all literary art impossible, according to Barbey d'Aurevilly.[94] The vast majority of reviews, however, noted the narrative's clear and unimpeded course. "From the perspective of the work's unity, of continuous plot development," remarked Jacquet, "this book is one of the best made that we have ever read."[95] Jacquet was particularly put out by the interruption of the novel's serialization in midstream when *Le Bien public* turned it over to *Le République des lettres*. Even more than the critics, Zola's correspondents, especially those thanking him for copies he had sent, spoke of the narrative in the future tense. Ferdinand Fabres intended to pass several "good hours" reading *L'Assommoir*, while Gabriel Guillemot looked forward to "ineffable enjoyments."[96] Writing from Warsaw, Jules Guillemain told Zola that he was not surprised by the critical debate over such "conscientious and unstinting work of exploration into reality."[97]

Consequently, Zola's audience expressed little satisfaction with those aspects of the novel which betrayed their expectations of it. A narrative on working-class life, one radical republican wrote, ought to be more sympathetic to the poor: "On first reading *L'Assommoir*, I asked myself if this work, with its ever brutal, often disgusting realism from which arises no philosophy, moral, or conclusion, was not a bad deed and more, a reactionary work?"[98] What Zola should have written and what

Secondigné promised to write himself was a novel depicting the true source of working-class degradation: the Second Empire's politics of debauchery. Other readers expressed their surprise at Zola's achievement. While most critics, like Wolff, resented the work's unrelenting attention to social ills, the correspondents had their own reservations about the narrative's unexpected turns. Paul Bourget thought that for so unified a work, *L'Assommoir* lacked a center; in light of the narrative's obvious sympathy for Gervaise, its tragic end was insufficiently intimate.[99] Anatole France was similarly bemused by the novel's artless quality:

> [Zola] believes that disorder is natural. He does not understand that all our conceptions of order come from nature alone and that ideas of the world and of order are identical. . . . I do not wish to impose on contemporaries the forms of the past; but art has its laws that will endure as long as humankind, because they conform to the nature of humankind.[100]

In short, France implied, Zola was not naturalistic enough.

Ordinarily, readers focused on the novel's most apparent message. But the nature of that theme varied from one person to another. These different assessments of *L'Assommoir*'s central idea resulted, of course, in a variety of expectations and predictions about the text as it unfolded. It is therefore no accident that the novel's most critical audience identified themes drawn from the text's most objectionable subject matter. Pontmartin in particular was struck by how "the municipal pawn shop, the hospital, the criminal court, the prison all preach the same antithetical homily."[101] These features of working-class life had no place in art. Readers more favorably inclined to Zola's text also varied remarkably in their assessments of *L'Assommoir*'s theme, but none of these differences was enough to disturb the author's fans; accordingly, none of their expectations was disappointed. Jacquet identified Zola's interest in the destructive aspects of poverty; Wolff remarked the determining roles of heredity and environment; Élizé de Montagnac understood the ambivalent consequences of work that leads as much to misery as it does to wealth; and Jan ten Brink analyzed the naturalistic principles in literary art.[102] As Frédéric Erbs put it, "Zola gives us a good idea of the mores appropriate to a certain class of people from eccentric localities—especially of those people who desert the home for the tavern, tools and books for gambling and drinking."[103] And his judgment of Zola's work followed logically: *L'Assommoir* was a perfect example of naturalism in prose.

What was true for perceptions of theme also held for views of characterization. Zola's readers responded to Gervaise, Coupeau, and Lantier in ways that affected their expectations of these figures in the narrative itself. Houssaye called them hideous exceptions.[104] Given such assumptions, the narrative's sympathetic tone could only provoke this critic's anger. On the other hand, those readers, like Jules Lermina, who considered Zola's characters superb types were less unpleasantly surprised by the text.[105] "The author wanted," wrote Philippe Gille, "by introducing everyone to the mores of Paris's lowest class of workers, to preach against the drunkenness that decimates them every day and to show us the real types who resemble none of Eugène Sue' s conventional workers. From this point of view, he has completely succeeded."[106] For Gille, the narrative's characterizations both promised and delivered. Théodore Bainville also thought the characters consistent; he told Zola, "Like you I think that pure heroes must resemble peasants and savages more, and that is why I like them so much. Moreover, one has always known these perfect primitives, how they drink as well as eat, where they sleep as well as why they act as they do."[107] The author understood all his characters so well, J.-K. Huysmans felt, that he was past master at portraying minor figures, even faceless crowds.[108] Consequently, so captured was he by the narrative's account of Gervaise, Ferdinand Fabres cried when he learned of her death in the last install-ment, even though he knew it was coming.[109]

Commentary on *L'Assommoir*'s plot varied much less, but the responses were still keyed to the continuities or ruptures that readers perceived in the text. Some correspondents were particularly struck by scenes that interrupted the flow of action. In his letter to Zola, Huysmans pointed out Gervaise in the street soliciting passersby in her desperation, and again Gervaise and Coupeau in the snow passing each other without saying a word.[110] These poignant moments, Huysmans believed, were the best of the novel, and more, the best of all Zola's work. But the dramatist William Busnach found that these scenes, strung together, did not make for a unified whole. As drama *L'Assommoir* promised "sketches and not a play."[111] The inevitable progress of Gervaise's demise, however, created other expectations of the text. Houssaye disliked the intrusion of chance events; they did not belong in a tightly structured plot; the characters did not need any help to die: "The progress of their fall is not well rendered. Their slow decline is entirely fortuitous."[112] Jacquet, on the other hand, saw the entire plot as of a piece: "*L'Assommoir*'s subject does not, in effect, take much conceptual effort. . . . It is the story of a worker's household that declines bit by bit to the lowest degrees of shame and misery."[113] Whatever happened to the characters came as no surprise, their fate was perfectly predictable.

Perhaps *L'Assommoir*'s most controversial feature was its setting, one that encouraged a wide variety of predispositions towards the rest of the novel. Few readers could restrain from judging the working-class world in which Gervaise struggled so unsuccessfully. In the minds of conservatives, Zola's deliberate choice of setting condemned his entire narrative *a priori*. Critics more favorably disposed to the author's naturalistic project were also uncomfortable with the novel's depic-tion of Paris. Deeply ambivalent himself about the narrative, Édouard Rod asked, "How can you wish to see with a tranquil eye the vice that approaches everywhere? And how can you wish it painted and branded without showing it in all its ugliness? That it be on display and make us shudder, such is what M. Zola wants."[114] But the author's apparent moral intention did not stand up to scrutiny. As Secondigné pointed out, Zola pretended to know more about this world than he actually did; his use of working-class argot, for instance, was merely a cover for this igno-rance.[115] In fact, the novel's crude language represented an extremely risky artistic strategy, noted Huysmans: "[It is] to have the people speak just as they speak, to recount in their language their miseries and their joys, and at the same time to cre-ate a work of art."[116] While Huysmans was convinced that the author had suc-ceeded, most other critics and some of Zola's correspondents were sure that he had not. *L'Assommoir*'s setting seems to have spoiled the literary experience for much of its readership.

Thus Zola's audience responded to the implicit rules of configuration in the novel. The unfolding narrative created specific expectations of the course that it would take. Undoubtedly, readers brought extratextual concerns to the text, espe-cially their interest in or loathing of naturalism. But these matters actually complemented rather than conflicted with predilections arising directly from the work itself. On the basis of a few installments in *Le Bien public,* readers anticipated the rest of the novel. Some predictions of the narrative's course were readily made within the first few pages. Consequently, Zola's audience developed a limited tolerance for sudden changes in ideological content or literary form; his reading public often felt betrayed whenever their predispositions ultimately proved wrong or inappropriate. Moreover, readers expressed a variety of perspectives on the work's theme, characters, plot, and setting that led to a variety of anticipations of where the narrative was headed. And not all people, not even Zola's friends, were necessarily pleased by the narrative's outcome. In this way the text played a part in shaping reader response, as much by what it promised as by what it ultimately did. The narrative's configuring conventions pervaded interpretive practice; actual readers' projections in fact depended upon them.

COHERENCE

Readers also respond to a novel's unity.[117] The rules of coherence inherent in the prose narrative enable people to answer the question, "How does one make sense of all this?" Most works provide ample evidence of their totality, and few readers have trouble comprehending them. But many novels are problematic because in one way or another they are incomplete, contradictory, or open-ended—sometimes all three.[118] Usually the reader is left to fill in gaps, to sort out irrelevancies, and to piece together the text's various elements, even though the narrative guides the process more or less adequately. A murder mystery, for example, rewards in particular the active reader who can make sense of the text's many clues. Achieving closure, that is, coming to a logical conclusion, is ultimately the reader's responsibility. To that extent, at least, a text cannot read itself. A good historical example of a literate audience's completing, resolving, and concluding a complex narrative arose in response to Anatole France's *Le Lys rouge.* The peculiar qualities of this *fin-de-siècle* novel required readers to seek its totality in the author's carefully crafted style. How the textual conventions suggesting the work's coherence actually worked appears in the responses that this text elicited from its original audience when symbolism was just becoming a force in French literature.[119] Again, the text explicitly shared in literate experience.

Le Lys rouge openly invites the reader to complete its narrative.[120] Thérèse Martin-Bellême, the central figure, grows disenchanted first with her husband, a prominent politician, and then with her lover, Robert Le Ménil, before she falls rapturously in love with the artist Jacques Dechartre. For the first time in her life Thérèse experiences passion to its fullest measure. And Jacques, too, seems enthralled by his new lover's awakening sensuality. But this passion is not meant to last. Jacques is fiercely jealous; he must possess Thérèse entirely. So when he inadvertently catches her in a lie about Robert and suspects that she still loves the man despite her protestations, Jacques leaves Thérèse. The narrative ends ambiguously, for it is unclear what will become of her. Readers must decide this matter for themselves as they attempt answers to other questions implied in the work: Is sensual love ever fulfilled? Does the Parisian *beau monde* preclude personal passion? How conducive to love is life in another culture, such as Italy, where most of the novel's action occurs? The author's ironic language throughout the novel drops few hints to help its audience. There are frequent omissions, digressions, and ambiguities that readers must address on their own. The lovers' passion is suggested indirectly;

curious secondary characters divert attention from the principal couple; and the
end is deliberately held in suspense. How readers actually resolved France's text
underscores the rules of coherence at work in his narrative—and in their response.

With few exceptions, readers of *Le Lys rouge* sought its unity in the author's stylistic persona.[121] Reviewers in particular noted Anatole France's special voice that,
for them, gave the novel its clearest form, in language itself. In his account of the
play derived from the narrative, drama critic Robert de Flers noted "the 'gentle
nihilism,' 'the inalterable skepticism,' and the serene indifference" of the original
text whose author was to be found in every word.[122] Gaston Deschamps was also
impressed by France's apparent "wide-ranging erudition, his active philosophy, his
irony moistened by tears."[123] It is hard to determine whether these qualities per-
tained to the novelist or to the novel he wrote. But few critics made much of a distinction; as if to make sense of the text, they identified the man with the work and
its particular style. Asked Paul d'Armon in *Le Voltaire,*

> Perhaps he wanted only to modulate ironic couplets on love and the political
> milieu of our time? Perhaps he sought only to express a literary refinement for his
> pleasure and even more for ours as well? Let us accept this latter suggestion in
> order to enjoy fully the exquisite grace of *Lys rouge,* however a bit deliquescent its
> style.[124]

Such impressionist attributions of the author in a text were most clearly expressed
in Jules Lemaître's assessment of the novel's language as "the latest flowering of
the Latin genius."[125] From this perspective, coherence lay in the author's voice as
evidenced most profoundly in the language of his work.

This personal stylistic approach to *Le Lys rouge* was even more obvious in the
correspondence the author received. It is interesting to note that in a sample of
270 letters sent to Anatole France over his long lifetime, only one letter—from the
Danish critic Georges Brandes—made direct reference to this novel.[126] In fact, relatively few letters concerned any one text in particular; most people spoke of his
work in general, citing oftentimes the charm of his characters and the wisdom of
his prose in a number of different novels. But for France's correspondents, the
heart of the literary experience was the author's voice. Like the critics, the letter
writers praised the novelist profusely for his style, his language, and the persona
they suggested. Jules Lecornu, for example, remarked "this skepticism . . . this secularity . . . this free thought" in *Le Puits de Sainte Claire.*[127] These stylistic features
were France himself. Similarly, Raymond Poincaré wrote the author of the charm
of his prose, what Madame Jean Peyret in her letter called his grace and finesse.[128]
His language was enchanting in itself, but it also represented the novelist's most
significant achievement. As Jules Puch put it in 1916, "It is your wisdom and your
taste that keep me in the present enchantment."[129] For France's audience, the narrative voice, the author's own, seemed to provide the underlying coherence to all
his work, and not just to *Le Lys rouge.*

Critics stressed the extent to which style actually unified an otherwise uncom-
posed novel. "We are much less interested in the course of the narrative so often
interrupted," wrote Georges Pellissier, "than in the diversions from which it wan-
ders on its way. However remarkable the novelistic part of *Le Lys rouge,* it is only
truly superior in its episodes," each one of which was exquisitely written.[130]
Charles Arnaud agreed: "Anatole France's *Le Lys rouge* is a news item garlanded by

treatises"—the better the individual discourses, the better the work.[131] Teodor de Wyzewa corrected the common sentiment that the novelist structured his works poorly; "on the contrary, I believe that he composes his work marvellously, but it has nothing to do with the novel form."[132] France's splendid language created a genre all its own. "There are in our literature no more polished models of free, abundant, ornate conversation that is enlivened by fantasy and fertile in its wingèd grace."[133] While René Doumic identified the form France had chosen, few other reviewers were so courageous. Asked Deschamps, "What is this? Is it a photographic album? A collection of rough sketches? A pack of epigrams? A fagot of thorns disguised beneath the flowers of incomparable rhetoric? . . . What does it matter? It is so well written!"[134] For most critics, the central feature of Le Lys rouge, like much else France wrote, was its beautiful style. What form it took or what it expressed seems not to have mattered. Language was all, the whole, the source of the work's unity.

This stylistic preference reinforced another important tendency: the coherence of the reader's response. Reviewers not only praised the author's language, they also reveled in how it affected them. From their deliberately subjectivist perspective, critics found a certain order in the extreme pleasure they took in France's text. Noted the Belgian poet and critic Émile Verhaeren, "It is very pleasant reading; as artistic flavoring, it is delicate; one sucks on it like a candy at once fragrant and pungent. But these last features dissolve in the mind's saliva; there is no other sensation (not without cost) than that of some charmingly spent hours."[135] Most such readers were willing to locate the unity of the work in their response. Philippe Gille, for example, was especially charmed by the details, the ingenious observations, the particular and personal way of seeing things in France's novel.[136] So was Wyzewa: "The reverie and conversation remain there strong enough to divert our minds and to charm our senses for the entire narrative."[137] Neither the plot, nor the characters, nor the setting sustained as much interest as the author's suggestive tone and mood. The reader's delight was justification and coherence enough for the critics. Consequently, the ambiguous ending did not disturb Albert Le Roy: "For a novelist, here is such supreme competence that it leaves the last chapter to mislead the female reader's imagination!"[138]

Even more than the critics, France's correspondents made their response the novel's focus. Jacques Bereilh-Liegaux's warm appreciation was typical. "Thank you," he wrote, "for having contributed to instilling in me so healthy a taste for beautiful, pure, clear, and concise French prose."[139] Younger readers expressed a similar enthusiasm for the author's influence on them. Wrote Renée Chevalier, "It seemed that after the student's arid, suffocating work, a fresh hand was placed on my forehead; my thoughts became harmonious and sweet."[140] For this student, notwithstanding France's impressionistic language, the text imposed a refreshing order on her own intellectual and emotional world. The author's classical style in particular seemed to have made this coherence possible, not only for Chevalier, but also for Lecornu. "What draws me to you especially," this reader wrote, "is the admirable and pure style. . . . It is this Attic form that characterizes you."[141] And so when Georges Brandes spoke of the remarkable passion in Le Lys rouge, he meant more than Thérèse's newfound sensuality; he experienced it as well in his own response.[142] France's correspondents frequently confused the text with its effects on them, as M. Harmigny noted in the verses that he sent the author about his work: "How he makes us smile or provokes a tear. / Whatever the subject he takes, he charms, / And his work forms a harmonious whole," as much in the reader as in the text.[143]

Although *Le Lys rouge* left readers room to create their own conceptions of its achievement, they still did so within the usual conventions of coherence. France's audience filled in gaps in the text, the uncertain conclusion for instance, to complete the narrative. His readership also sorted out extraneous details such as the long digressions on various topics of interest to the characters. And the author's reading public gave order to the chaotic narrative, whose elements did not in themselves constitute a unified whole. For critics and correspondents alike, these challenging tasks were facilitated by France's commanding persona in the text. His voice made closure, for example, much easier, because it offered a focus of attention, a foundation on which the work could be reconceived. Similarly, the very language identified this persona; its style constituted another source of unity in an otherwise disparate text. But ultimately France's readers found the surest resolution of his problematic work in their responses to it. *Le Lys rouge* was a delight, an enchantment, a sustained pleasure. Even if the novel had no structure whatsoever, its audience found order in an enjoyment derived from few other texts. Perhaps the reason why Anatole France is no longer read much now is that his narrative voice no longer speaks so immediately; his readers today are no longer willing to impose the same kind of order in their response to his works. In short, the rules of coherence in the text are perceived differently, and the result is another subjective, but less favorable, perspective on France's fiction.

The particular conventions at work in France's *Le Lys rouge* shaped its audience's sense of the whole. And they did so in much the same way that the rules of notice in Sue's *Les Mystères de Paris* had affected its readership fifty years earlier. In fact, what was true for the specific roles played by these texts in their readers' responses also held for those played by Flaubert's *Madame Bovary* and Zola's *L'Assommoir;* the rules of signification and of configuration helped audiences make sense of the latter novels, either as an authorial voice or as an unfolding narrative, even though the texts themselves were often deliberately ambiguous. In each case, the work and its clues gave rise to certain interpretive practices appropriate to the text as well as to the audience. The act of reading therefore appears historically as a dialogue between the work and the reader, between the text and the context, both functioning in the literate experience. Despite the vagaries of individual readers, the narratives did provide some boundaries within which people responded.

It should be noted that the conventions were not exclusive to the works themselves: the rules of notice guided readers in other texts besides *Les Mystères de Paris,* just as the rules of signification, configuration, and coherence promoted the interpretation of other novels besides *Madame Bovary, L'Assommoir,* and *Le Lys rouge,* respectively. People responded to titles, voices, expectations, and gaps in all the novels they read. Only rarely, as in serial novels, did some conventions seem to preclude the others. As a matter of course, readers require and use as many interpretive clues as they can find in every narrative they encounter.

But from 1800 onward, there was a discernible development in the textual conventions most appropriate to historical changes in literature and interpretive practice. For instance, at the height of romanticism in France before 1850, new kinds of texts privileged the rules of notice, at least among reviewers and fan-mail writers. The romantic reaction to the emotional and aesthetic sterility of neoclassicism meant that critics were reluctant to embrace any new literary enthusiasms; they focused on a work's subject matter, refusing to appreciate so much as to judge a text, like Stendhal's *Le Rouge et le noir* or Balzac's *La Peau de chagrin*, that seemed alarmingly new or potentially dangerous to its audience. Similarly, the rise of romantic literature contributed to serious contradictions in the correspondents' apparent nobility of sentiment. Despite the pervasive challenge to older literary forms, letter writers continued to express their allegiance to aristocratic ideals of neoclassicism and poetic truth; at the same time, they also projected their feelings onto texts, drew analogies to the plastic arts, and indulged in a deeply personal reverie, one frequently detached as much from empirical reality as from the literary work. In each interpretive community, romanticism and its explosive creativity fostered responses for which titles, openings, closings, and narrative shifts were especially important. These particular conventions focused attention on the dramatically new features of romantic literature, and above all on the contradictory elements of the texts themselves. In short, the rules of notice shared in the complexities already inherent in romantic works and their reception.

In time, with the appearance of realist works from 1850 to 1880, another set of rules guided interpretive practices. Realism's mirror held up to the everyday world, succeeded by naturalism's quasiscientific endeavor to explain that reality, encouraged critics and correspondents alike in concerns appropriate to signification and configuration. Reviewers now focused on the author and the impact this creative individual had on an impressionable audience. Like Sainte-Beuve, these critics considered novels by Flaubert and the Goncourts as enormously influential monuments to literature's special place in an increasingly literate society. Moreover, the letter writers reinforced this development with their heightened interest in morality. Critics also discussed this issue, but correspondents expressed perhaps more clearly the new social basis for this response, namely, the bourgeois ideals of proper subject matter and language in literature. The moral outrage provoked by realist and naturalist publications like Zola's *La Terre,* for example, stemmed from these new interpretive practices—and more, from the new importance of clues to meaning and chronology in the texts themselves. Flaubert's use of free, indirect style confused authorial and narrative voices, made the identification and judgment of those voices more difficult, and undermined the readers' understanding of causation. Likewise, Zola's inexorable plots created expectations about the unfolding narrative and limited the readers' tolerance for surprises in theme, characterization, setting, and action. Thus the textual conventions concerning narrative voice and continuity were called into play by the texts and audiences of both realism and naturalism.

Symbolism from the *fin-de-siècle* to the interwar period meant still more new works, new rules, and new responses. In a neoromantic reaction to realism, creating a new literary context for a limited audience of aesthetes, the symbolists' medley of metaphors challenged the more ordinary reader to make sense of some very difficult texts. Critics at the time naturally had relatively little trouble, since they shared with symbolism an abiding interest in self-discovery, especially their own. Consequently, book reviewers were far from hostile to the particular innovations they saw, for example, in Proust's *À la recherche du temps perdu*. Even Sartre's existentialist project in *La Nausée* seemed a bit dated. Anatole France's correspondents, on the other hand, adapted symbolism's creative concerns to a new personal sensibility. Their ideals were neither overtly aristocratic nor crudely bourgeois, but apparently were more literary; their quest for the self disavowed morality per se and embraced instead a more flexible aestheticism. Besides their tolerance for classicism and acceptance of prosaic truths in literature, these readers expressed a more detached sympathy for the characters, more eclectic analogies to all the arts, and a broader literary imagination. It is certainly no accident, then, that the conventions of coherence became increasingly central to both symbolist texts and audience responses. In works like France's *Le Lys rouge*, but also in even more ambiguous works, readers had to fill in gaps, to sort out details, to resolve contradictions—in effect, to unify their conception of the author's often opaque achievement. Symbolism actually required its audience to participate more actively in making sense of literary texts; from this new demand, neither critics nor correspondents were exempt.

So there was indeed a complex relationship between developments in literary expression and reader response throughout the modern period. At least two different communities of readers responded to different genres like the letter, the essay, the theater, and the novel, in ways that obviously required a text. To be sure, their interaction with literature changed over time not only as the reading public changed, but also as the works and their rules developed. From period to period, however, the immediate situation of that interaction changed as well. Notwithstanding the complexities that remain for further study, such as how reception delayed and distorted literary trends from romanticism onward, it is now clear that from a historical perspective, texts do not read themselves, readers do, and that audiences do so at a specific intellectual moment. Every reader functions within at least one interpretive community's tradition of response, as well as within the context of new literary movements, new genres, and their specific conventions. Clearly, a work has no meaning until readers make of it what they can, given certain changing historical circumstances and interpretive practices appropriate to them, even though all literate experience begins first and foremost with the printed text and the particular rules essential to its reception.

NOTES

1. See Edmond Biré, *Alfred Nettement* (1901).
2. Alfred Nettement, *Études critiques sur le feuilleton roman* (1847), 1: 231–330.
3. Ibid., 1: 236.
4. See Peter Rabinowitz, *Before Reading: Narrative Conventions and the Politics of Interpretation* (Ithaca, 1987), 15–169. Cf. Wayne Booth, *The Rhetoric of Fiction* (Chicago, 1961), 23–148.
5. See Frank Lentricchia, *After the New Criticism* (Chicago, 1980), 102–55; and Geoffrey H. Hartman, *Criticism in the Wilderness: The Study of Literature Today* (New Haven, 1980), 284–301.
6. See Jane Tompkins, ed., *Reader-Response Criticism from Formalism to Post-Structuralism* (Baltimore, 1980); Susan Suleiman and Inge Crosman, eds., *The Reader in the Text: Essays on Audience and Interpretation* (Princeton, 1980); and Elizabeth Flynn and Patrocinio Schweickart, eds., *Gender and Reading: Essays on Readers, Texts, and Contexts* (Baltimore, 1986).
7. See Rabinowitz, *Before Reading*, 47–75.
8. See Eugène Sue, *Les Mystères de Paris*, ed. Jean-Louis Bory (1963), based on the text in the *Journal des débats*.
9. See Jean-Louis Bory, *Eugène Sue. Le Roi du roman populaire* (1962), 243–97; Pierre Chaunu, *Eugène Sue et la Seconde République* (1948); Peter Brooks, "The Mask of the Beast: Prostitution, Melodrama, and Narrative," *New York Literary Forum* 7 (1980): 125–

40; Georges Jarbinet, *Les Mystères de Paris d'Eugène Sue* (1932); and *Europe: Revue littéraire mensuelle. Eugène Sue* 60 (1982): nos. 643–44.

10. See Edward Tannenbaum, "The Beginnings of Bleeding-Heart Liberalism: Eugène Sue, *Les Mystères de Paris,*" *Comparative Studies in History and Society* 16 (1981): 491–507; John Moody, *Les Idées sociales d'Eugène Sue* (1938); Marc Angenot, *Le Roman populaire. Recherches en paralittérature* (Quebec, 1975), 71–87; and Umberto Eco, *The Role of the Reader: Explorations in the Semiotic[s] of Texts* (Bloomington, 1984), 125–43.

11. See Louis Chevalier, *Labouring Classes and Dangerous Classes in Paris during the First Half of the Nineteenth Century,* trans. Frank Jellinek (London, 1973), 359–417.

12. D. L. [Désiré Laverdant], "Feuilleton de la Phalange. Revue critique," *Phalange* (13 Nov. 1842), col. 961.

13. Nettement, *Études critiques,* 1: 239.

14. Cited in D. L., "Feuilleton de la Phalange. Revue critique," *Phalange* (19 Feb. 1843), col. 1639.

15. C.-A. Sainte-Beuve, *Chroniques littéraires (1843–1845)* (1876), 132. Cf. Alexandre Privat d'Anglemont to Sue, 30 May 1843, in BHVP Fonds Sue fol. 180.

16. Caroline Angebert to Sue, 28 Feb. 1843, and Lecteur des Mystères de Paris to Sue, 28 Mar. 1843, in BHVP Fonds Sue fols. 96, 124.

17. D. L., "Feuilleton de la Phalange. Revue critique," *Phalange* (26 June 1842), col. 1235.

18. Une Inconnue to Sue, 20 June 1842, in BHVP Fonds Sue fol. 19.

19. Jules Michelet, *Le Peuple* (Lausanne, 1945), 28.

20. See review in *Le Constitutionnel,* quoted in D. L., "Feuilleton de la Phalange. Revue critique," *Phalange* (19 Feb. 1843), col. 1639; and H. D. to Sue, 25 April 1843, in BHVP Fonds Sue fol. 151.

21. Paulin Limayrac, "Simples essais d'histoire littéraire. IV. Le Roman philanthrope et moraliste. Les Mystères de Paris," *RdDM,* n.s. 2 (1844): 94.

22. Nettement, *Études critiques,* 1: 249.

23. D. L., "Feuilleton de la Phalange. Revue critique," *Phalange* (29 Mar. 1843), col. 1903.

24. Ernestine Dumont to Sue, 24 Sept. 1843, in BHVP Fonds Sue fol. 416.

25. Anon. to Sue, 26 April 1843, in ibid., fol. 153.

26. Nettement, *Études critiques,* 1: 327; Eugène Faure [George Sand], "Les Mystères de Paris, par M. Eugène Sue," *Revue indépendante* 8 (1843), in Helga Grubitzsche, ed., *Material zur Kritik des Feuilletons-Romans. "Die Geheimnisse von Paris" von Eugène Sue* (Weisbaden, 1977), 43.

27. D. L., "Feuilleton de la Phalange. Revue critique," *Phalange* (26 June 1842), cols. 1235–36.

28. See Sophie Dorloclot to Sue, 30 April 1843, and Dr. Frédéric Maîtrejean to Sue, 7 July 1843, in BHVP Fonds Sue fols. 157, 261.

29. D. L., "Feuilleton de la Phalange. Revue critique," *Phalange* (9 Dec. 1842), col. 1138.

30. Louis Reybaud, "La Société et le socialisme. La Statistique, la philosophie, le roman," *RdDM,* n.s. 1 (1843): 806.

31. Anon., no title, *Gazette de France* (15 Feb. 1843).

32. Ernestine Dumont to Sue, 13 July 1843, in BHVP Fonds Sue fol. 268.

33. Nettement, *Études critiques,* 1: 279; Virginie Prignot to Sue, 17 May 1843, in ibid., fol. 186.

34. Limayrac, "Simples essais d'histoire littéraire," 87.

35. Faure [Sand], "Les Mystères de Paris," 46.

36. Reybaud, "La Société et le socialisme," 806.

37. Castellane de Contades to Sue, 6 Sept. 1843, in BHVP Fonds Sue fol. 386.

38. E.g., Dumont to Sue, 24 Sept. 1843, and Louis Jacquet to Sue, 15 Feb 1843, ibid., fols. 416, 83.

39. Nettement, *Études critiques,* 1: 267, 295.

40. See Karl Marx and Friedrich Engels, *The Holy Family; or The Critique of Critical Criticism,* trans. Richard Dixon and Clemens Dutton (Moscow, 1975), 218–21.

41. Anon. to Sue, 18 Aug. 1843, in BHVP Fonds Sue fol. 338.

42. Cf. titles in note 10 above.
43. See Rabinowitz, *Before Reading*, 76–109.
44. See Booth, *The Rhetoric of Fiction*, 169–398.
45. See Bernard Weinberg, *French Realism: The Critical Reaction 1830–1870* (New York, 1937), 159–76; Raymond Giraud, ed., *Flaubert: A Collection of Essays* (Englewood Cliffs, N.J., 1964), 88–140; Benjamin Bart, ed., *"Madame Bovary" and the Critics: A Collection of Essays* (New York, 1966); and R. Debray-Genette, ed., *Flaubert: Miroir de la critique* (1970).
46. Cf. Dominick LaCapra, *"Madame Bovary" on Trial* (Ithaca, 1982), 126–49.
47. Cf. Francis Steegmuller, *Flaubert and Madame Bovary: A Double Portrait* (New York, 1950); Jonathan Culler, *Flaubert: The Uses of Uncertainty* (Ithaca, 1974); and Michael Riffaterre, "Flaubert's Presuppositions," *Diacritics* 11 (1981): 2–11.
48. Edmond Duranty, "Nouvelles diverses," *Réalisme* (15 Mar. 1857): 79.
49. Léon Aubineau, "Variétés. G. Flaubert et Paul Destuf," *Univers* (26 June 1857), in René Dumesnil, "*Madame Bovary* et son temps," *MdF* (1 Dec. 1911): 473.
50. Adolphe Granier de Cassagnac, "La Bohème dans le roman. *Madame Bovary,*" *Réveil* (16 Jan. 1858), in Dumesnil, "*Madame Bovary* et son temps," 479.
51. Paulin Limayrac, "Des causes et des effets dans notre situation littéraire," *Constitutionnel* (10 May 1857), in Dumesnil, "*Madame Bovary* et son temps," 468; Marie-Sophie Leroyer de Chantepie to Flaubert, 18 Dec. 1857, BSL H. 1364 (B.IV) fols. 229–30; C.-A. Sainte-Beuve, "*Madame Bovary,*" *Moniteur universel* (4 May 1857), in *Causeries du lundi* (1869), 13: 349, 350; and Jules Barbey d'Aurevilly, "M. Gustave Flaubert," *Pays* (6 Oct. 1857), in René Dumesnil, *La Publication de "Madame Bovary"* (1927), 116–17.
52. Edmond About to Flaubert, [1857], in Flaubert, *Oeuvres complètes: Madame Bovary* (1930), 525.
53. Gustave Merlet, "Le Roman physiologique. *Madame Bovary* par M. Gustave Flaubert," *Revue européenne* (15 June 1860), in idem, *Le Réalisme et la fantaisie dans la littérature* (1861), 114.
54. Duranty, "Nouvelles diverses," 79.
55. Sainte-Beuve, "*Madame Bovary,*" 13: 363.
56. Edmond Texier, "Chronique littéraire," *Illustration* (9 May 1857), in Flaubert, *Oeuvres complètes: Madame Bovary,* 536; Barbey d'Aurevilly, "M. Gustave Flaubert," 119; and Duranty, "Nouvelles diverses," 79, respectively.
57. René de Marcourt to Flaubert, 30 Dec. 1866, BSL H. 1364 (B.IV) fols. 286–91.
58. Jean Rousseau, "Les Hommes de demain. II. M. Gustave Flaubert," *Figaro* (27 June 1858).
59. Ulric Guttinguer to Flaubert, [1857], in Dumesnil, "*Madame Bovary* et son temps," *MdF* (16 Nov. 1911), 312. Cf. Charles Toirac to Flaubert, 30 April 1857, BSL H. 1364 (B.IV) fols. 60–61; and Champfleury to Flaubert, [30 Jan. 1857], BSL H. 1361 (B.I) fol. 302.
60. Leroyer de Chantepie to Flaubert, 15 Mar. 1857, in Flaubert, *Corr.,* ed. Jean Bruneau (1980), 2: 680.
61. Dumesnil, note, *Chronique artistique et littéraire,* in Flaubert, *Oeuvres complètes: Madame Bovary,* 534.
62. Ernest Pinard, "Réquisitoire," in Flaubert, *Madame Bovary,* ed. Édouard Maynial (Garnier frères edition, n.d.), 344.
63. Sainte-Beuve, "*Madame Bovary,*" 13: 347.
64. Rousseau, "Les Hommes de demain."
65. A. A. Cuvillier-Fleury, "*Madame Bovary,*" *Journal des débats* (26 May 1857).
66. Jules Habans, "*Madame Bovary.* Roman par M. Gustave Flaubert," *Figaro* (28 June 1857) in Dumesnil, "*Madame Bovary* et son temps," *MdF* (1 Dec. 1911): 475.
67. Jacques? to Flaubert, 28 April 1857, BSL H. 1364 (B.IV) fol. 349.
68. Charles de Mazade, "Chronique de la quinzaine," *RdDM* (1 May 1857): 218.
69. "Une Plume de pierre," according to Barbey d'Aurevilly, "M. Gustave Flaubert," 118. Cf. Nestor Roqueplan, "Courrier de Paris," *Presse* (16 May 1857), in Flaubert, *Oeuvres complètes: Madame Bovary,* 534.

70. Sainte-Beuve, *"Madame Bovary,"* 13: 358; Merlet, "Le Roman physiologique," 118.
71. Cuvillier-Fleury, *"Madame Bovary,"* in Flaubert, *Oeuvres complètes: Madame Bovary,* 531.
72. Anon. to Flaubert, n.d., BSL H. 1366 (B.VI) fols. 347–48.
73. Jacques? to Flaubert, 28 April 1857, BSL H. 1364 (B.IV) fol. 349.
74. Leroyer de Chantepie to Flaubert, 18 Dec. 1857, BSL H. 1364 (B.IV) fols. 229–30.
75. Barbey d'Aurevilly, "M. Gustave Flaubert," 117–18.
76. Aubineau, "Variétés. G. Flaubert et Paul Destuf," 473.
77. Armand de Pontmartin, "Le Roman bourgeois et le roman démocratique. MM. Edmond About et Gustave Flaubert," *Correspondant* (25 June 1857), in Flaubert, *Oeuvres complètes: Madame Bovary,* 533; and Granier de Cassagnac, "La Bohème dans le roman," 479.
78. Alfred Nettement, "Gustave Flaubert," in *Le Roman contemporain* (1864), 123; and Émile Chevalet, *"Madame Bovary,"* Les 365. *Annuaire de la littérature et des auteurs contemporains, par le dernier d' entre eux* (1858), 193.
79. Rousseau, "Les Hommes de demain."
80. Frédéric Baudry to Flaubert, 30 Dec. 1856, in BSL H. 1361 (B.I) fols. 122–23.
81. Charles Baudelaire, *"Madame Bovary par Gustave Flaubert,"* in Baudelaire, *Oeuvres,* ed. Y.-G. LeDantec (1954), 1008.
82. Rousseau, "Les Hommes de demain."
83. Gustave Vapereau, *L'Année littéraire et dramatique.* Première année 1858 (1859), 53.
84. Merlet, "Le Roman physiologique," 131 (emphasis in the original).
85. See Rabinowitz, *Before Reading,* 110–40.
86. See Léon Deffoux, *La Publication de "L'Assommoir"* (1931); Jacques Dubois, *"L'Assommoir" de Zola. Société discours, idéologie* (1973); Jacques Allard, *Le Chiffre du texte. Lecture de "L'Assommoir"* (Montreal, 1978); and Henri Mitterand, *Le Renard et le signe. Poétique du roman réaliste et naturaliste* (1987), 209–29.
87. Cf. David Baguley, "Event and Structure: The Plot of *L'Assommoir,"* PMLA 90 (1975): 823–33; and Auguste Dezalay, *Lectures de Zola* (1973).
88. Jules Barbey d'Aurevilly, "Zola. *L'Assommoir,"* Le XIXe siècle. *Des oeuvres et des hommes,* ed. Jacques Petit (1966), 2: 278.
89. Armand de Pontmartin, "M. Émile Zola," *Nouveaux samedis* (1877): 326.
90. Anatole France, "Variétés. Les Romanciers contemporains. M. Émile Zola," *Temps* (27 June 1877).
91. Louis Jacquet, "Chronique. *L'Assommoir,"* Bien public (7 Feb. 1877).
92. Albert Wolff, "Gazette de Paris," *Figaro* (5 Feb. 1877).
93. Henry Houssaye, "Variétés. Le Vin bleu littéraire. *L'Assommoir, par M. Émile Zola," Journal des débats* (14 Mar. 1877).
94. Barbey d'Aurevilly, "Zola. *L'Assommoir,"* 278.
95. Jacquet, "Chronique. *L'Assommoir."*
96. Gabriel Guillemot to Émile Zola, 17 May [1877], in BN NAFr 24519 fol. 428.
97. Jules Guillemain to Zola, 1 Feb. 1877, in EZRP Coll. Dr. F. Émile-Zola.
98. A. Secondigné, *Les Kerney-Séverol. Histoire d'une famille française au XIXe siècle. L'Assommé* (1877), iii.
99. Paul Bourget to Zola, [2 Feb. 1877], in BN NAFr 24511 fols. 184–85.
100. France, "Variétés. Les Romanciers contemporains."
101. Pontmartin, "M. Émile Zola," 331.
102. Jacquet, "Chronique. *L'Assommoir";* Wolff, "Gazette de Paris"; Élizé de Montagnac, *À propos de "l'Assommoir." Monseigneur Mermillod et Monsieur Zola. Étude contemporaine publiée en avril 1877 dans Le Courrier des Ardennes et le journal La Défense* (Chareville, 1877), 26; and Jan ten Brink to Zola, 31 Dec. 1876, in BN NAFr 24512 fol. 5.
103. Frédéric Erbs, *M. E. Zola et son Assommoir. Étude critique* (1879), 75.
104. Houssaye, "Variétés. Le Vin bleu littéraire"; and Montagnac, *À propos de "l'Assommoir,"* 15.
105. Jules Lermina to Zola, 27 Jan. 1877, in BN NAFr 24521 fol. 259.
106. Philippe Gille, "Revue bibliographique," *Figaro* (12 Oct. 1876), supplement.
107. Théodore Bainville to Zola, 27 Nov. 1876, in BN NAFr 24511 fol. 1.

108. J.-K. Huysmans, "Émile Zola et l'*Assommoir*," in Huysmans, *Oeuvres complètes* (n.d.), 2: 187–88.

109. Ferdinand Fabres to Zola, 31 Dec. 1876, in BN NAFr 24518 fol. 425.

110. Huysmans to Zola, 7 Jan. 1877, in BN NAFr 24520 fol. 410.

111. William Busnach to Zola, 21 Aug. 1877, in BN NAFr 24513 fols. 16–19.

112. Houssaye, "Variétés. Le Vin bleu littéraire."

113. Jacquet, "Chronique. *L'Assommoir.*"

114. Édouard Rod, *À propos de "l'Assommoir"* (1879), 33.

115. Secondigné, *Les Kerney-Séverol,* ix.

116. Huysmans, "Émile Zola et l'*Assommoir*," 2: 182.

117. See Rabinowitz, *Before Reading,* 141–69.

118. Cf. Wolfgang Iser, *The Implied Reader: Patterns of Communication in Prose Fiction from Bunyan to Beckett* (Baltimore, 1974), 274–94.

119. See Jean Pierrot, *The Decadent Imagination 1880–1900,* trans. Derek Coltman (Chicago, 1981), 147–237; Michel Raimond, *La Crise du roman. Des lendemains du naturalisme aux années vingt* (1985), 194-212; and Pierre-Olivier Walzer, *Littérature française. Le XXe siècle. I: 1896-1920* (1975), 209–32.

120. See Jean Levaillant, *Les Aventures du scepticisme. Essai sur l'évolution intellectuelle d'Anatole France* (1965); Drehan Bresky, *The Art of Anatole France* (The Hague, 1969); Julien Cain. "Le Drame amoureux du *Lys rouge,*" *Figaro littéraire* (20 Sept. 1955); and Edwin Preston Dargan, *Anatole France, 1844-1896* (New York, 1937).

121. See Paul Giselle, "Sur la popularité d'Anatole France," *Revue mondiale* (1 Nov. 1924).

122. Robert de Flers, "*Le Lys rouge,* de M. Anatole France," *Le Théâtre et la ville. Essais de critique—Notes et impressions* ([1895]), 18.

123. Gaston Deschamps, "M. Anatole France," *La Vie et les livres* (1899): 231.

124. Paul d'Armon, "*Le Lys rouge,*" *Voltaire* (11 Aug. 1894).

125. Jules Lemaître, "Anatole France. *Le Lys rouge,*" *Les Contemporains. Études et portraits littéraires,* 6th ser. (n.d.), 395.

126. Georges Brandes to France, 12 April 1899, in BN NAFr 15431 fols. 9–10.

127. J. Lecornu to France, 5 Feb. 1913, in BN NAFr 15435 fols. 427–28.

128. Raymond Poincaré to France, 11 Mar. [1901]; and Mme. Jean Peyret to France, 26 Nov. 1921, in BN NAFr 15437 fols. 320, 122.

129. Jules Puch to France, 10 Nov. 1916, in ibid., fol. 518.

130. Georges Pellissier, "*Le Lys rouge;* par A. France," *Revue encyclopédique* (15 Oct. 1894): 451.

131. Charles Arnaud, "*Le Lys rouge,* de M. Anatole France," *Polybiblion* (Feb. 1895): 112.

132. Teodor de Wyzewa, "Les Livres nouveaux. *Le Lys rouge,* de M. Anatole France," *Revue politique et littéraire. Revue bleue* (1 Sept. 1894): 284.

133. René Doumic, "Revue littéraire. M. Anatole France," *RdDM* (15 Dec. 1896): 933.

134. Deschamps, "M. Anatole France," 243, 244.

135. Émile Verhaeren, "Anatole France. *Le Lys rouge,*" *Art moderne* (30 Sept. 1894): 307.

136. Philippe Gille, "Anatole France. *Le Lys rouge,*" *Les Mercredis d'un critique* (1895): 172–73.

137. Wyzewa, "Les Livres nouveaux," 284.

138. Albert Le Roy, "Profiles littéraires. *Le Lys rouge,*" *Événement* (30 Aug. 1894).

139. Jacques Bereilh-Liegaux to France, 23 Aug. 1916, in BN NAFr 15430 fols. 284–85.

140. Renée Chevalier to France, 21 Dec. 1919, in BN NAFr 15432 fols. 180–81.

141. Lecornu to France, 5 Feb. 1913, in BN NAFr 15435 fols. 427–28.

142. Brandes to France, 12 April 1899, in BN NAFr 15431 fols. 9–10.

143. L. Harmigny to France, 3 Nov. 1917, in BN NAFr 15434 fol. 407.

IV

RECEPTION STUDY, CULTURAL STUDIES, AND MASS COMMUNICATION

The difficulty of defining the history of the book and its relation to reception study applies to an equal, if not greater, degree for cultural studies. In part, this problem arises because cultural studies, from its very beginnings, developed in deliberate resistance to any overarching paradigm and singular identity. The difficulty also stems from the fact that cultural studies has been marked by theoretical shifts, contending discourses, and cross-disciplinary practices that have made it "a set of unstable formations" with "a number of different histories" (Hall, 1992, 277). Those instabilities are evident in the many attempts to explain the field, not only in the way they highlight its shifts and multiple trajectories but also in the diverse shapes these explanations have taken.[1] Despite these differences, however, virtually every account of cultural studies and its development has recognized, as Janice Radway has pointed out, that audience study has comprised an important element of the field (236).

Several factors have contributed to the interest in audience and reception in cultural studies. One has been the claim that semiotic practices, social forms, and ideological frames operating within specific cultural contexts and historical moments configure human subjectivity. This conceptualization has led to analyses of the way the media have constructed the subjectivities of readers, viewers, and listeners. Equally important has been the impact of mass communication research, both as a shaping influence and as a set of practices and methods that cultural studies has called into question. Indeed, the work in audience and reception study in mass communication has overlapped with such work in cultural studies to the point that "a great deal of cultural studies," according to Stuart Hall, "is really very closely related to communication studies" (1994, 271).

Comprehending the shape and orientations of reception analysis in cultural studies thus requires some understanding of the changing contours of the work in mass communication that preceded and has become intertwined with the study of audiences in cultural studies. Since the 1930s and 1940s, when mass communication study began, the relation between media and the audience has been a subject of investigation. Mostly behaviorist and often market driven, this early work sought to measure the effects of the media on their audience by matching output with input following the communication model of sender→message→medium→receiver.[2] Although this effects model became the dominant paradigm of audience studies, its assumption that audiences are passive receivers was challenged by what came to be know as the "uses and gratifications" approach. This approach applied psychological models to show that individual audience members responded to the media to fulfill personal needs in a way that often differed from the producers' purposes.[3] But even as uses-and-gratifications study became a competing paradigm by the 1960s, it was challenged by a new turn in effects study, a turn influenced by the work of Theodore Adorno, Max Horkheimer, and the Frankfurt school. Critiquing uses and gratifications for its naive assumption of individualistic agency and the older effects model for failing to account for political economies, proponents of the Frankfurt School theorized media communication as the politically inflected work of the "culture industry," which imposed upon and reinforced in its (largely working-class) audience the ideology of the dominant culture. Emphasizing the power exerted over the audience by the culture industry, from films and television to advertising and music, this interrogation of mass media as conduits of commodification and ideological dominance reinforced the centrality of the effects model in mass communication. This critical version of the effects model also served as the initial paradigm for audience analysis within the newly developing field of cultural studies in Britain.[4]

Like the earlier effects model, however, this critical version quickly came under criticism. In *Television: Technology and Cultural Form* (1974), Raymond Williams faulted the technological and media determinism of the effects models for ignoring the way viewers might use a medium such as television for social change. By the late 1970s and early 1980s, that critique was extended within cultural studies in a series of theoretical essays by Stuart Hall and in several watershed research studies, particularly David Morley's and Charlotte Brundson's analyses of British responses to television news programming. In both mass communication and cultural studies, several new theories extended this critique and the accompanying reorientation in audience and reception studies. One was the revisionist Marxism of Louis Althusser and Antonio Gramsci, which argued that ideology was never total or imposed but was instead the result of the subject's negotiating position within the production-reception nexus. Semiotics, with its claim that the polysemy of signification prevented any text from conveying to an audience any single dominant meaning, also played a role, as did deconstruction, feminist theory, and reader-response criticism.[5]

Such influences helped produce a trenchant interrogation of both the effects and the uses-and-gratifications models. The former was called into question for following a simplistic "hypodermic injection" or "syringe" model of communication and for conceiving the audience as passive "dupes" of the culture industry. In addition, both the effects and the uses-and-gratifications paradigms came under criticism for leaving out any consideration of economic, political, and cultural influences at the receiving end. Feminist critiques took two forms. First, feminists pointed out that, since many mass media were aimed at a female audience, effects models were underwritten by a patriarchal logic that viewed women as vessels powerless to resist the thrusts of the culture industry. Just as importantly, feminist intervention, in conjunction with race studies, pointed out that the audience's position is imbricated within such cultural factors as gender, race, ethnicity, and age, not just economics and class, as the Frankfurt school maintained. Finally, practitioners in both mass media and cultural studies objected that little, if any, work had been done to test effects models by investigating the responses of actual audiences.

Because of these critiques and new theories, mass communication and cultural studies scholars retheorized reception, beginning with Hall's seminal essay "Decoding/Encoding" and continuing in the work of John Fiske, Tony Bennett, Janice Radway, Ien Ang, Martin Allor, and others. In place of the passive audience model, these scholars emphasized active audiences and the work they do. In the active audience model, signifying practices and their reception occur in a site marked by ideological and semiotic negotiation and contestation shot through with varying and at times contradictory meanings and significances generated by different audiences. Consequently, this new audience study focuses on reception as diverse arrays of particular experiences constituted by the social positions, interpretive practices, and culturally constructed subjectivities of viewers and readers. But whether it takes the form of dominant, negotiated, or oppositional responses (Hall, 1980) or a combination of all three, the reception experience still depends on the particular interpretive formations that viewers/readers inhabit. For the new audience studies, reception occurs as an active process of "production in use" that is always culturally activated within specific contexts and local histories.

Paralleling the premises of reception study in literary criticism and the history of the book, this emphasis on reception as an active, contextual process has led mass communication and cultural studies to investigate specific subgroups or "subcultures" of viewers and readers of mass media. One direction for such work has been the examination of fandom, which counters the notion of popular consumption as deluded or ideologically manipulated and discloses what Fiske calls the "semiotic productivity" of fan reception (1992, 37). More significant has been the turn to conducting ethnographies of reception (also called "qualitative" studies) within specific sociocultural audiences. Using questionnaires, interviews, examinations of letters and journals, and on-site observations and group discussions, such qualitative research has sought to provide "thick descriptions" of both the viewing and reading experience and the social and cultural conditions and practices that constitute particular contexts of reception.

Although audience and reception study within mass communication and cultural studies has undergone a number of important shifts, the history of this work is not as neatly linear or "progressive" as the preceding overview might suggest. Despite the advent of active audience models in the 1980s, uses-and-gratifications studies have continued through the 1990s.[6] Effects studies also have remained dominant in some sectors of mass media and cultural studies, particularly those concerned with the way the mass media construct audiences and promote the hegemonic formation of dominant cultural values.[7] It has also been suggested that the active audience model and qualitative analyses represent not so much a "new" audience study as a revision of earlier effects and uses-and-gratifications approaches (Curran). Nor has the new audience study gone uncontested. The active audience model has been upbraided for attributing too much power and freedom to viewers and readers or for being a form of "mindless populism" that reinforces the hegemony of the culture industry (Angus, Seaman). Although much of the work in active audience study belies such charges by displaying a keen awareness of the forces within cultural production, contributors to the qualitative study of reception have themselves raised questions about the "radical contextualism" underlying ethnographic analyses of audiences (see, e.g., Ang, Radway). Especially problematic has been the issue of how to determine the boundaries of any reception context in light of the poststructuralist recognition of the "boundlessness of context" (Culler, 128).

The relation between audience study and reception study poses a different question about boundaries. For one thing, not all audience study is reception study. Since most effects studies have defined reception merely as a function of production at the terminus of communication, such work leaves out the way textual signification and impact depend on the codes, practices, and conceptions of viewers, readers, and listeners. More specifically, target-audience research and studies of audience-directed programming, of technologies and their impact on audience access, or of the social use and proxemics of the material forms of media technology either fall outside of reception study or can be called such only by extending that label to include virtually any social practice of consumption. At the same time, some of this work underscores the difficulty of specifying the category of reception study. Indeed, within both mass communication and cultural studies, reception has tended to take a broad meaning that includes the significances and uses audiences make of the technologies of communication and the socially constituted contexts in which such activity takes place—what Fiske has called the "ethnosemiotics" of "places of reception" (1990).[8] By conceiving reception analysis with a breadth paralleling work in the history of the book, inquiries into the significances and selections audiences make of popular media and the way they employ them in relation to other cultural practices have productively blurred distinctions between audience study and reception study.

Audience and reception analysis has lead to equally problematic distinctions between mass communication and cultural studies. Although the preceding discussion has treated these areas as a consortium of shared interests, theories, and practices, other overviews of the fields have provided quite different typologies, in some cases collapsing everything under the umbrella of mass communication research, in others placing reception study, cultural studies, communication studies, and audience ethnography in different categories.[9] Certainly some distinctions are warranted. Since reception work in cultural studies has been characterized by its close attention to the social constitution of audience subjectivities and the role of ideological formations and vectors of power in marking reception as a process of cultural negotiation, some forms of mass communication reception study (e.g., uses-and-gratifications research or quantitative surveys of programming preferences) clearly occupy a different category of analysis. But distinctions between mass communication and cultural studies research into reception have become increasingly hard to make. Under the impact of revisionist Marxism, feminism, active audience theory, and ethnographic analysis, the social and cultural dynamics of reception have become central concerns of mass communication studies at the same time that cultural studies has extensively drawn on and grappled with the theories and approaches of mass media audience analysis. Hence, any attempt at clear-cut distinctions between the two fields, particularly over the last ten years, would oversimplify and distort the complex interrelations, articulations, and productive tensions that unite mass communication and cultural studies as overlapping fields of inquiry into the dynamics and contexts of reception.

The essays in this section exemplify these overlappings, beginning with Janice Radway's "Readers and Their Romances," which is a chapter from her *Reading the Romance*. In this pathbreaking study in the development of qualitative audience research, Radway employs an ethnographic method to examine how a locally defined, contextually specific audience—a group of approximately forty women readers of romances from the pseudonymous town of Smithton—has received a popular genre of mass-produced fiction. In the chapter reprinted here, Radway focuses on the shape and social characteristics of these women's reading choices and responses, including the way they are mediated by a local bookstore clerk, Dorothy Evans, who advises the Smithton women on their selection of romance novels. Radway points out that these women conceive the romance and differentiate among its types in particular ways that do not necessarily match the way publishers define that genre. Instead, these women's genre conceptions, preferences, and reading habits are "tied to their daily routines, which themselves are a function of education, social role, and [middle-] class position." For these women, the desire for a combination of leisurely pleasure and pleasurable reflection affects both why and how they read romances. Possessing considerable interpretive knowledge of the codes of the genre, the Smithton women read these novels within and against those codes while projecting themselves into the narratives in a way that treats plots and characters as a "'display' of contemporary cultural habits," particularly traditional and feminist conceptions of gender and the social reality of male power. Far from being mere escape or mindless entertainment, romance reading for these women functions as a site for exploring, explaining, and reflecting on the relation between such habits and their own lives.

The power of audiences to remake texts within specific social contexts also underscores John Fiske's essay on popular music, rock-and-roll videos, and fandom. Examining the lyrics and image of Madonna and their reception by her fans, Fiske readily grants that Madonna's persona is a product of the culture industry of late-twentieth-century patriarchal capitalism and that the culture's dominant ideology structures both the Madonna "text" and her fans' subjectivities. Unlike Frankfurt school theorists, however, Fiske does not treat Madonna's reception as a form of mindless consumption by "cultural dupes." Instead, he construes fans as active viewers and listeners for whom Madonna's persona and music become a "site of semiotic struggle between the forces of patriarchy and feminine resistance, of capitalism and the subordinate." Combining ethnographic and semiotic analysis, the essay reads the comments and behaviors of Madonna's (mostly female) fans as negotiated and oppositional acts of reception that struggle against both the patriarchal assumptions inscribed in Madonna's sexuality and the patriarchy within the fans' own subjectivities. These fans seize upon and take pleasure from Madonna's parodic excesses and stylistic bricolage, interpreting them as expressions of their own quest for independent female identity. Thus, while the media text of Madonna serves the dominant cultural construction of subjectivity, it also becomes a vehicle through which her fans achieve an empowerment with the potential, asserts Fiske, for social change.

In "Women Like Us," Andrea Press and Elizabeth Cole turn to a different dimension of socially constructed reception: the way class position affects responses to texts from the mass medium of television. In particular, the essay shows that television representations of abortion and their reception by female viewers are inscribed within class positions. Press and Cole point out that television has predominately represented women seeking abortions as working-class and has tended to code abortion as acceptable only for women in dire economic circumstances. To examine women's responses to such representations, the authors conducted a controlled, focus-audience ethnographic study with several groups of working-class and middle-class women who were shown two representative examples of such TV depictions: an episode of *Cagney and Lacey* and the made-for-TV movie *Roe vs. Wade*. While working-class pro-life women tended to resist such representations "in a very general way," working-class women who identified themselves as pro-choice were alienated from these images in a more "complicated" manner. The latter group objected especially to the depiction of working-class women seeking abortions as powerless victims, even as these viewers sympathized and identified with such women's struggle for social mobility. However, when such aspiration to middle-class status was lacking—as it was for the protagonist in *Roe vs. Wade*—one group of pro-choice working-class women disapproved of the character's lifestyle and values, interpreting her as irresponsible and lacking self-reliance. Such responses, that is, depended on the degree to which working-class women viewers identified with middle-class values. In light of these patterns, Press and Cole argue that working-class women respond to such shows by using them to resist middle-class perceptions of working-class women, but do so in two different ways. While some construct alternate working-class identities, others, especially those who identify with middle-class values, deny that social class plays any role in abortion decisions or in women's identity in contemporary society.

These first three essays, which exemplify work at the crossroads of mass communication and cultural studies, analyze the reception of mass-market fiction, rock music, and prime-time television, whereas Janet Staiger's "Taboos and Totems" concentrates on popular film through a "historical reception study" informed by gay studies. Staiger defines her project as one that "combines contemporary critical and cultural studies" to "illuminate the cultural meanings of texts in specific times" and within historically specific social formations. Analyzing the reception of the 1991 film *The Silence of the Lambs,* Staiger finds especially telling its relation to and embeddedness in contemporary cultural debates about gender and sexual orientation. In essays and in letters to newspapers and magazines, responses by viewers and reviewers "solidified" in divergent gender and sexual terms shortly after the release of Jonathan Demme's film. Some viewers characterized the movie as homophobic and charged it with irresponsibly abetting audience paranoia about AIDS, while others praised the film as offering a positive image of a professional working woman that empowered female viewers. To understand the formation of these responses by two nondominant groups (some gay men and some feminists), Staiger unpacks the interpretive strategies and accompanying cultural values that structure these divergent receptions. Like other qualitative reception studies, her essay does not claim that the patterns and dynamics she examines are representative of the culture as a whole. On the contrary, reflecting the principle that reception is always locally embedded within particular reading formations and social conditions, Staiger maps out a historically specific event of reception marked by varying interpretive patterns and carrying important ideological resonances.

To conclude, this section returns to theory with John Frow's "Economies of Value," which comes from his book *Cultural Studies and Cultural Value*. Earlier in that study, Frow maintains that in the wake of postmodernism and poststructuralism, cultural production no longer can be understood within a "general economy of value" under which divergent value judgments can be reconciled. In this essay, he argues that the reconceptualization of valuation as localized practices performed by culturally specific valuing communities raises the vexing issue of whether critical movement across incommensurate realms of interpretive evaluation is possible. This is no idle question but one central to cultural-studies inquiry into reception, which seeks not only to describe such localized practices but also to critically interrogate their operation and constitution within specific ideological and social formations. Several problems underscore this issue. On the one hand, in refusing to privilege any position external to the codes of the group being examined, cultural studies denies itself a metadiscourse ordinarily needed for the analytical critique of everyday practices. On the other, the very concept of a valuing community is problematic because it fails to account for the fact that communal boundaries are always porous and that interpretive position often entails membership in multiple communities. It is precisely at such borders, however, that Frow proposes a solution via the concept of "regimes of value." Frow argues that the mediating practices of regimes of value operate as mechanisms of inter-communal and cross-cultural value construction. Having "no directly expressive relation to social groups," such mediating regimes can be theorized and examined as interpretive formations operating as "semantic institution[s] generating evaluative regularity under certain conditions of use" that are always socially and historically specific. Besides opening a space for examining the overlappings and disjunctions marking evaluative practices and for disclosing the way interpretive evaluations become locally valid, the concept of regimes of value could, asserts Frow, help intellectuals engage more productively with the popular by providing an avenue for interrogating the way their own inquiries operate within and across cultural regimes.

Open to question is whether Frow's theoretical intervention solves the problem of how to analyze reception critically without in some way invoking a metacode of value that validates such critiques. However, such a question is part of the ongoing developments and debates that have marked reception study, not only in mass communication and cultural studies, but as a field as a whole. It is fitting, therefore, that in this collection's last section, the essays address several of the major questions about, and criticisms of, reception study as both theory and practice.

NOTES

1. See, for example, the descriptions of the field and the narratives of its development in Easthope; Storey; Turner; Hall, 1990; During; and Nelson et al. All of these, it should be noted, address the problematics of delineating cultural studies as a developing field.

2. Useful overviews and histories of the effects model in mass communication studies appear in Meehan and in McLeod, Kosicki, and Pan.

3. For more on the development and orientation of uses-and-gratifications audience studies, see McLeod and Becker.
4. On the Frankfurt school and its influence on audience study, especially in cultural studies, and for a critique of its assumptions, see Hall, 1977, 1982; and Turner, 197–210. It should be noted that the earlier effects model also had its critical dimension, but it came from conservative warnings that mass media were contaminating traditional values and beliefs—a position, of course, reiterated still today.
5. For a firsthand discussion of the impact of semiotics, Derridean deconstruction, the theories of Althusser and Gramsci, and the work of Stanley Fish and reader-response critics on cultural studies, see Hall, 1994. Oddly enough, one area that seems to have had little impact on audience analysis in mass communication and cultural studies is German reception theory and the work of Jauss in particular. For example, in the three most recent collections on audience and reception study in the two fields (Cruz and Lewis's *Viewing, Reading, and Listening* [1994]; Hay, Grossberg, and Wartella's *The Audience and Its Landscape* [1996]; and Dickinson, Harindranath, and Linn's *Approaches to Audience* [1998]) Jauss's work fails to appear in any of the bibliographies. Although others have occasionally mentioned the Konstanz school, it has been by reference to Iser rather than to Jauss (e.g., Allen) or by identifying the two as significant to literary-critical work in reception but not to reception and audience study in mass communication and cultural studies (Jensen and Rosengren).
6. For an overview of uses-and-gratifications research through 1998, see McQuail.
7. See, for example, Ettema and Whitney, Kellner, Jhally and Lewis, and Joyrich. Under the impact of Althusser and Gramsci, the work of Michel Foucault and Pierre Bourdieu, poststructuralism, feminist theory, and even the active audience model, such effects studies have become increasingly sophisticated to the point where the pejorative labels "syringe" or "hypodermic injection" have become misnomers.
8. Besides its extended use in the Fiske essay, the designation "reception study" has been claimed by or applied to such broad-ranging work as Silverstone and Morley, "Domestic Communication"; Silverstone, "From Audience to Consumers": Tulloch, "Approaching the Audience"; Lull, "Social Uses"; and Stacey, *Star Gazing*.
9. For such inclusions and divisions, see the overviews and typologies in Höijer, Jensen and Rosengren, Lorimer, Rosengren, and Schroder.

WORKS CITED

Allen, Robert C. "Reader-Oriented Criticism and Television." In *Channels of Discourse: Television and Contemporary Criticism,* edited by Robert C. Allen, 74–112. Chapel Hill: University of North Carolina Press, 1987.
Ang, Ien. "Ethnography and Radical Contextualization in Audience Studies." In *The Audience and Its Landscape,* edited by James Hay, Lawrence Grossberg, and Ellen Wartella, 247–62. Boulder, Colo.: Westview, 1996.
Angus, Ian. "Democracy and the Constitution of Audiences: A Comparative Media Theory Perspective." In *Viewing, Reading, Listening: Audiences and Cultural Reception,* edited by Jon Cruz and Justin Lewis, 233–52. Boulder, Colo.: Westview, 1994.
Cruz, Jon, and Justin Lewis, eds. *Viewing, Reading, Listening: Audiences and Cultural Reception.* Boulder, Colo.: Westview, 1994.
Culler, Jonathan. *On Deconstruction.* London: Routledge, 1983.
Curran, James. "The New Revisionism in Mass Communication Research: A Reappraisal." *European Journal of Communication* 5 (1990): 135–64.
Dickinson, Roger, Ramaswami Harindranath, and Olga Linn,, eds. *Approaches to Audience.* London: Arnold, 1998.
During, Simon. Introduction to *The Cultural Studies Reader,* edited by Simon During, 1–25. London: Routledge, 1993.
Easthope, Anthony. *Literary into Cultural Studies.* London: Routledge, 1991.
Ettema, James S., and D. Charles Whitney, eds. *Audience Making: How the Media Create the*

Audience. Thousand Oaks, Calif,: Sage, 1994.

Fiske, John. "The Cultural Economy of Fandom." In *The Adoring Audience: Fan Culture and Popular Media,* edited by Lisa Lewis, 30–49. London: Routledge, 1992.

———. "Ethnosemiotics: Some Personal and Theoretical Reflections." *Cultural Studies* 4 (1990): 85–99.

Hall, Stuart. "Culture, the Media, and the 'Ideological Effect.'" In *Mass Communication and Society,* edited by James Curran, Michael Gurevitch, and Janet Woollacott, 315–48. London: Arnold, 1977.

———. "Cultural Studies and Its Theoretical Legacies." In *Cultural Studies,* edited by Lawrence Grossberg, Cary Nelson, and Paula A. Treichler, 277–86. New York: Routledge, 1992.

———. "The Emergence of Cultural Studies and the Crisis of the Humanities." *October* 53 (1990): 11–90.

———. "Encoding/Decoding." In *Culture, Media, Language,* edited by Stuart Hall, Dorothy Hobson, Andrew Lowe, and Paul Willis, 128–38. London: Hutchinson, 1980.

———. "The Rediscovery of 'Ideology': The Return of the Repressed in Media Studies." In *Culture, Society and the Media,* edited by Michael Gurevitch, Tony Bennett, Colin Mercer, and Janet Woollacott, 56–90. London: Methuen, 1982.

———. "Reflections upon the Encoding/Decoding Model: An Interview with Stuart Hall." In *Viewing, Reading, Listening: Audiences and Cultural Reception,* edited by Jon Cruz and Justin Lewis, 253–74. Boulder, Colo.: Westview, 1994.

Hay, James, Lawrence Grossberg, and Ellen Wartella, eds. *The Audience and Its Landscape.* Boulder, Colo.: Westview, 1996.

Höijer, Birgitta. "Social Psychological Perspectives in Reception Analysis." In *Approaches to Audiences,* edited by Roger Dickinson, Ramaswami Harindranath, and Olga Linné, 166–83. Boulder, Colo.: Westview, 1998.

Jhally, Sut, and Justin Lewis. *Enlightened Racism:* The Cosby Show, *Audiences, and the Myth of the American Dream.* Boulder, Colo.: Westview, 1994.

Jensen, Klaus Bruhn, and Karl Erik Rosengren. "Five Traditions in Search of an Audience." *European Journal of Communication* 5 (1990): 207–38.

Joyrich, Lynne. *Re-Viewing Reception: Television, Gender, and Postmodern Culture.* Bloomington: Indiana University Press, 1996.

Kellner, Douglass. *Television and the Crisis of Democracy.* Boulder, Colo.: Westview, 1990.

Lorimer, Rowland. *Mass Communication: A Comparative Introduction.* Manchester: Manchester University Press, 1994.

Lull, James. "The Social Uses of Television." *Human Communications Research* 6 (1980): 198–209.

McLeod, Jack M., and Lee B. Becker. "The Uses and Gratifications Approach." In *Handbook of Political Communication,* edited by Dan D. Nimmo and Keith R. Saunders, 67–100. Beverly Hills, Calif.: Sage, 1981.

McLeod, Jack, Gerald M. Kosicki, and Zhongdang Pan. "On Understanding and Misunderstanding Media Effects." In *Mass Media and Society,* edited by James Curran and Michael Gurevitch, 235–66. London: Arnold, 1991.

McQuail, Denis. "With the Benefit of Hindsight: Reflections on Uses and Gratifications Research." In *Approaches to Audiences,* edited by Roger Dickinson, Ramaswami Harindranath, and Olga Linné, 151–65. Boulder, Colo.: Westview, 1998.

Meehan, Eileen R. "Why We Don't Count: The Commodity Audience." In *Logics of Television,* edited by Patricia Mellencamp, 117–37. Bloomington: Indiana University Press, 1990.

Nelson, Cary, Paul A. Treichler, and Lawrence Grossberg. "Cultural Studies: An Introduction." In *Cultural Studies,* edited by Lawrence Grossberg, Cary Nelson, and Paul A. Treichler, 1–16. New York: Routledge, 1992.

Radway, Janice. "The Hegemony of 'Specificity' and the Impasse of Audience Research: Cultural Studies and the Problem of Ethnography." In *The Audience and Its Landscape,* edited by James Hay, Lawrence Grossberg, and Ellen Wartella, 235–45. Boulder, Colo.: Westview, 1996.

Rosengren, Karl Erik. "Combinations, Comparisons, and Confrontations: Toward a Comprehensive Theory of Audience Research." In *The Audience and Its Landscape,* edited by James Hay, Lawrence Grossberg, and Ellen Wartella, 23–51. Boulder, Colo.: Westview, 1996.

Schroder, Kim Christian. "Convergence or Antagonist Traditions? The Case of Audience Research." *European Journal of Communication* 2 (1987): 7–31.

Seaman, William R. "Active Audience Theory: Pointless Populism." *Media, Culture and Society* 14 (1992): 301–11.

Silverstone, Roger. "From Audience to Consumers." In *The Audience and Its Landscape,* edited by James Hay, Lawrence Grossberg, and Ellen Wartella, 281–96. Boulder, Colo.: Westview, 1996.

Silverstone, Roger, and David Morley. "Domestic Communication: Technologies and Meaning." *Media, Culture and Society* 12 (1990): 31–55.

Stacey, Jackie. *Star Gazing: Hollywood and Female Spectatorship.* London: Routledge, 1994.

Storey, John. *Cultural Studies and the Study of Popular Culture: Theories and Methods.* Athens: University of Georgia Press, 1996.

Tulloch, John. "Approaching the Audience: The Elderly." In *Remote Control: Television, Audiences, and Cultural Power,* edited by Barbara Seiter, Hans Borcher, Gabriele Kreutzner, and Eva-Maria Warth, 180–203. London: Routledge, 1989.

Turner, Graeme. *British Cultural Studies: An Introduction.* Boston: Unwin Hymen, 1990.

Williams, Raymond. *Television: Technology and Cultural Form.* London: Fontana/Collins, 1974.

J A N I C E   R A D W A Y

READERS AND THEIR ROMANCES

Surrounded by corn and hay fields, the midwestern community of Smithton, with its meticulously tended subdivisions of single-family homes, is nearly two thousand miles from the glass-and-steel office towers of New York City where most of the American publishing industry is housed. Despite the distance separating the two communities, many of the books readied for publication in New York by young women with master's degrees in literature are eagerly read in Smithton family rooms by women who find quiet moments to read in days devoted almost wholly to the care of others. Although Smithton's women are not pleased by every romance prepared for them by New York editors, with Dorothy Evans's help they have learned to circumvent the industry's still inexact understanding of what women want from romance fiction. They have managed to do so by learning to decode the iconography of romantic cover art and the jargon of back-cover blurbs and by repeatedly selecting works by authors who have pleased them in the past.

In fact, it is precisely because a fundamental lack of trust initially characterized the relationship between Smithton's romance readers and the New York publishers that Dorothy Evans was able to amass this loyal following of customers. Her willingness to give advice so endeared her to women bewildered by the increasing romance output of the New York houses in the 1970s that they returned again and again to her checkout counter to consult her about the "best buys" of the month. When she began writing her review newsletter for bookstores and editors, she did so because she felt other readers might find her "expert" advice useful in trying to select romance fiction. She was so successful at developing a national reputation that New York editors began to send her galley proofs of their latest titles to guarantee their books a review in her newsletter. She now also obligingly reads manuscripts for several well-known authors who have begun to seek her advice and support. Although her status in the industry does not necessarily guarantee the representivity of her opinions or those of her customers, it does suggest that some writers and editors believe that she is not only closely attuned to the romance audience's desires and needs but is especially able to articulate them. It should not be surprising to note, therefore, that she proved a willing, careful, and consistently perceptive informant.

I first wrote to Dot in December 1979 to ask whether she would be willing to talk about romances and her evaluative criteria. I asked further if she thought some of her customers might discuss their reading with someone who was interested in what they liked and why. In an open and enthusiastic reply, she said she would be glad to host a series of interviews and meetings in her home during her summer vacation. At first taken aback by such generosity, I soon learned that Dot's unconscious magnanimity is a product of a genuine interest in people. When I could not secure a hotel room for the first night of my planned visit to Smithton, she insisted that I stay with her. I would be able to recognize her at the airport, she assured me, because she would be wearing a lavender pants suit.

The trepidation I felt upon embarking for Smithton slowly dissipated on the drive from the airport as Dot talked freely and fluently about the romances that were clearly an important part of her life. When she explained the schedule of discussions and interviews she had established for the next week, it seemed clear that my time in Smithton would prove enjoyable and busy as well as productive. My concern about whether I could persuade Dot's customers to elaborate honestly about their motives for reading was unwarranted, for after an initial period of mutually felt awkwardness, we conversed frankly and with enthusiasm. Dot helped immensely, for when she introduced me to her customers, she announced, "Jan is just people!" Although it became clear that the women were not accustomed to examining their activity in any detail, they conscientiously tried to put their perceptions and judgments into words to help me understand why they find romance fiction enjoyable and useful.

During the first week I conducted two four-hour discussion sessions with a total of sixteen of Dot's most regular customers. After she informed them of my interest, they had all volunteered to participate. About six more wanted to attend but were away on family vacations. These first discussions were open-ended sessions characterized by general questions posed to the group at large. In the beginning, timidity seemed to hamper the responses as each reader took turns answering each question. When everyone relaxed, however, the conversation flowed more naturally as the participants disagreed among themselves, contradicted one another, and delightedly discovered that they still agreed about many things. Both sessions were tape-recorded. I also conducted individual taped interviews with five of Dot's most articulate and enthusiastic romance readers. In addition, I talked informally to Dot alone for hours at odd times during the day and interviewed her more formally on five separate occasions. Along with twenty-five others approached by Dot herself at the bookstore, these sixteen all filled out a pilot questionnaire designed before I had departed from Philadelphia.

Upon returning from my visit to Smithton, I read as many of the specific titles mentioned during the discussions and interviews that I could acquire, transcribed the tapes, and expanded a field-work journal I had kept while away. In reviewing all of the information and evaluations I had been given, it became clear that I had neither anticipated all of the potentially meaningful questions that might be asked nor had I always included the best potential answers for the directed-response questions. Accordingly, I redesigned the entire questionnaire and mailed fifty copies to Dot in mid-autumn of 1980. I asked her to give the questionnaire to her "regular" customers (those who she recognized and had advised more than once about romance purchases) and to give no additional directions other than those on the questionnaire and in an attached explanatory letter. She returned forty-two completed questionnaires to me in early February 1981, during my second sojourn in Smithton.

At that time, I stayed with Dot and her family for a week, watched her daily routine, and talked with her constantly. I also spent three full days at the bookstore observing her interactions with her customers and conversing informally with them myself. I reinterviewed the same five readers during this period, checked points about which I was uneasy, and tested the hypotheses I had formulated already. I also talked at length with Maureen, one of Dot's most forthright readers who had recently begun writing her own romances.

It is clear that the Smithton group cannot be thought of as a scientifically designed random sample. The conclusions drawn from the study, therefore, should be extrapolated only with great caution to apply to other romance readers. In fact, this study's propositions ought to be considered hypotheses that now must be tested systematically by looking at a much broader and unrelated group of romance readers. Despite the obvious limitations of the group, however, I decided initially to conduct the study for two reasons.

The first had to do with Dot's indisputable success and developing reputation on the national romance scene. The second was that the group was already self-selected and stably constituted. Dot's regular customers had continued to return to her for advice *because* they believed her perceptions accorded reasonably well with theirs. They had all learned to trust her judgment and to rely on her for assistance in choosing a varied array of romance reading material. They found this congenial because it freed all of them from the need to rely solely on a single "line" of books like the Harlequins that had recently begun to offend and irritate them. It also enabled them to take back some measure of control from the publishers by selectively choosing only those books they had reason to suspect would satisfy their desires and needs. Although there are important variations in taste and habit within the Smithton group, all of the women agree that their preferences are adequately codified by Dorothy Evans.

The nature of the group's operation suggests that it is unsatisfactory for an analyst to select a sample of romances currently issued by American publishers, draw conclusions about the meaning of the form by analyzing the plots of the books in the sample, and then make general statements about the cultural significance of the "romance." Despite the industry's growing reliance on the techniques of semi-programmed issue to reduce the disjunction between readers' desires and publishers' commodities, the production system is still characterized by a fundamental distance between the originators, producers, and consumers of the fantasies embodied in those romances. Consequently, it must be kept in mind that the people who read romance novels are *not* attending to stories they themselves have created to interpret their own experiences. Because the shift to professional production has reduced self-storytelling substantially, there is no sure way to know whether the narratives consumed by an anonymous public are in any way congruent with those they would have created for themselves and their peers had they not been able to buy them.

Although repeated purchase and consumption of a professionally produced and mass-marketed commodity hints that some kind of audience satisfaction has been achieved, this is not a guarantee that each individual text's interpretation of experience is endorsed by all buyers. In fact, what the Smithton group makes clear is that its members continue to possess very particular tastes in romance fiction that are not adequately addressed by publishers. However, because these corporations have designed their products to appeal to a huge audience by meeting the few preferences that all individuals within the group have in common, they have successfully managed to create texts that are minimally acceptable to Dot and her readers. Moreover, because the Smithton women feel an admittedly intense need to indulge in the romantic fantasy and, for the most part, cannot fulfill that need with their own imaginative activity, they often buy and read books they do not really like or fully endorse. As one reader explained, "Sometimes even a bad book is better than nothing." The act of purchase, then, does not always signify approval of the product selected; with a mass-production system it can just as easily testify to the existence of an ongoing, still only partially met, need.

Precisely because romance publishers have not engineered a perfect fit between the product they offer and all of their readers' desires, the Smithton women have discovered that their tastes are better served when the exchange process is mediated by a trusted selector who assembles a more suitable body of texts from which they can safely make their choices. This particular reliance on a mediator to guide the process of selection suggests that to understand what the romance means, it is first essential to characterize the different groups that find it meaningful and then to determine what each group identifies as its "romance" before attempting any assessment of the significance of the form. Despite the overtly formulaic appearance of the category, there are important differences among novels *for those who read them* that prompt individual decisions to reject or to read. We must begin to recognize this fact of selection within the mass-production process, make some effort to comprehend the principles governing such selection, and describe the content that gives rise to those principles.[1] The Smithton women comprise only one small, relatively homogeneous group that happens to read romances in a determinate way. While their preferences may be representative of those held by women similar to them in demographic characteristics and daily routine, it is not fair to assume that they use romance fiction in the same way as do women of different background, education, and social circumstance. Conclusions about the romance's meaning for highly educated women who work in male-dominated professions, for instance, must await further study.

The reading habits and preferences of the Smithton women are complexly tied to their daily routines, which are themselves a function of education, social role, and class position. Most Smithton readers are married mothers of children, living in single-family homes in a sprawling suburb of a central midwestern state's second largest city (population 850,000 in 1970).[2] Its surrounding cornfields notwithstanding, Smithton itself is an urbanized area. Its 1970 population, which was close to 112,000 inhabitants, represented a 70 percent increase over that recorded by the 1960 census. The community is essentially a "bedroom" community in that roughly 90 percent of those employed in 1970 worked outside Smithton itself. Although this has changed slightly in recent years with the building of the mall in which Dot herself works, the city is still largely residential and dominated by single-family homes, which account for 90 to 95 percent of the housing stock.

Dot and her family live on the fringe of one of Smithton's new housing developments in a large, split-level home. When I last visited Smithton, Dot, her husband, Dan, her eldest daughter, Kit, and her mother were living in the house, which is decorated with Dot's needlework and crafts, projects she enjoyed when her children were young. Dot's other two children, Dawn, who is nineteen and married, and Joe, who is twenty-one, do not live with the family. Dot herself was forty-eight years old at the time of the study. Dan, a journeyman plumber, seems both bemused by Dot's complete absorption in romances and proud of her success at the bookstore. Although he occasionally reads thrillers and some nonfiction, he spends his leisure time with fellow union members or working about the house.

Although she is now a self-confident and capable woman, Dot believes she was once very different. She claims that she has changed substantially in recent years, a change she attributes to her reading and her work with people in the bookstore. When asked how she first began reading romances, she responded that it was really at her doctor's instigation. Although he did not suggest reading specifically, he advised her about fifteen years ago that she needed to find an enjoyable leisure activity to which she could devote at least an hour a day. He was concerned about her physical and mental exhaustion, apparently brought on by her conscientious and diligent efforts to care for her husband, three small children, and her home. When he asked her what she did for herself all day and she could list *only* the tasks she performed for others, he insisted that she learn to spend some time on herself if she did not want to land in a hospital. Remembering that she loved to read as a child, she decided to try again. Thus began her interest in romance fiction. Dot read many kinds of books at first, but she soon began to concentrate on romances for reasons she cannot now explain. Her reading became so chronic that when she discovered that she could not rely on a single shop to provide all of the latest releases by her favorite authors, she found it necessary to check four different bookstores to get all of the romances she wanted. Most of her customers commented that before they discovered Dot they did the same thing. Some still attend garage sales and flea markets religiously to find out-of-print books by authors whose more recent works they have enjoyed.

Dot would have continued as one of the legion of "silent" readers had not one of her daughters encouraged her to look for a job in a bookstore to make use of her developing expertise. Although hesitant about moving out into the public world, she eventually mustered the courage to try, soon finding employment at the chain outlet where she still works. She discovered that she thoroughly enjoyed the contact with other "readers," and, as she developed more confidence, she began to make suggestions and selections for uncertain buyers. In the first edition of her newsletter, she explained the subsequent events that led to the creation of her romance review:

> Soon it became apparent that the women who were regular customers were searching me out for my opinions on their selections. Also, the Area Supervisor of our store had noticed a sharply marked increase in sales of the general category of romances. . . . So the interviews and articles in . . . periodicals began and brought more attention to my socalled expertise.
>
> The idea for a newsletter and rating of new releases every month . . . belongs to my daughter, who felt we could make this available to a much larger group of women readers. As most of them know the prices of books are rising and the covers are not always a good indicator of the content of the book.[3]

With the help of her daughter, Kit, she planned, executed, and wrote the first edition of "Dorothy's Diary of Romance Reading," in April 1980. Despite reservations about taking up the role of critical mediator, she explained in her inaugural editorial that she was persuaded to such an authoritarian act by the intensity of her customers' needs and by the inability of the production system to meet them. "I know many women," she commented, "who need to read as an escape as I have over the years and I believe this is good therapy and much cheaper than tranquilizers, alcohol or addictive T.V. serials which most of my readers say bores them." She added that she intended to separate "the best or better books from the less well-written, so as to save the reader money and time." "However," she concluded, "I would never want to take from the ladies the right to choose their own reading materials, only to suggest from my own experience."[4]

Still conscious of the hierarchy implicit in the critic-consumer relationship, Dot continues to be careful about offering evaluative suggestions at the store. Her first question to a woman who solicits her advice is calculated to determine the kinds of romances the reader has enjoyed in the past. "If they are in my category," she explained in one of our interviews, "I start saying, 'OK, what was the last good book you read?' And then if they tell me that, I usually can go from there." Her services, like semi-programmed publication techniques, are designed to gauge already formulated but not fully expressed reader preferences, which she subsequently attempts to satisfy by selecting the proper material from a much larger corpus of published works. Dot can be more successful than distant publishing firms attempting the same service through market research because she personalizes selection at the moment of purchase in a way that the absent publishers cannot.

Dot's unusual success is a function of her participant's understanding of the different kinds of romances, acquired as the consequence of her voracious reading, and of her insistence on the individuality of her readers and their preferences. This is especially evident at the stage in her advising process when she finally displays a selection of books for her customers. "Sometimes," she laments, "I have people who say, 'Well, which one do *you* say is the best of these three?'" Her response indicates the depth of her respect for the singularity of readers and romances despite the fact that those readers are usually thought of as category readers and the romances considered formulaic performances:

> I will say, "They are not alike, they are not written by the same author, they are totally and completely different settings and I cannot say you will like this one better than this one because they are totally and completely different books." [But they always continue with] "Which one did you like best?" And I'll say, "Don't try to pin me down like that because its not right." I won't go any further. They have to choose from there because otherwise you're getting sheep. See, I like it when some of my women say, "Hey, I didn't care for that book." And I say, "Hey, how come?"[5]

Because Dot is ever mindful of her readers' dissatisfaction with some of the material flowing from the New York publishers and simultaneously aware of their desire to maintain and satisfy their own personal tastes, she has created a role for herself by facilitating a commercial exchange that benefits the reader as much as it does the producer. At the same time, Dot continues to perpetuate generic distinctions within a category that the publishers themselves are trying to rationalize and standardize. Hers is a strategy which, if not consciously calculated to empower readers with a selective ability, at least tends to operate in that way. By carefully identifying a book's particular historical setting, by relating the amount of sexually explicit description it contains, by describing its use of violence and cruelty, and by remarking about its portrayal of the heroine/hero relationship, she alerts the reader to the book's treatment of the essential features that nearly all of her customers focus on in determining the quality of a romance.

In addition to recognizing individual tastes and respecting personal preferences, Dot also performs another essential function for her regular customers. Although I suspect she was not always as effective at this as she is now, she capably defends her readers' preferences for romance fiction *to themselves.* One would think this unnecessary because so many of her customers come to her expressly seeking romances, but Dot finds that many of her women feel guilty about spending money on books that are regularly ridiculed by the media, their husbands, and their children. Dot encourages her customers to feel proud of their regular reading and provides them with a model of indignant response that they can draw upon when challenged by men who claim superior taste. By questioning them rhetorically about whether their romance reading is any different from their husbands' endless attention to televised sports, she demonstrates an effective rejoinder that can be used in the battle to defend the leisure pursuit they enjoy so much but which the larger culture condemns as frivolous and vaguely, if not explicitly, pornographic.

Dot's vociferous defense of her customers' right to please themselves in any way that does not harm others is an expression of her deeply held belief that women are too often the object of others' criticisms and the butt of unjustified ridicule. Although she is not a feminist as most would understand that term, she is perfectly aware that women have been dismissed by men for centuries, and she can and does converse eloquently on the subject. During my second stay in Smithton, she admitted to me that she understands very well why women have pushed for liberal abortion laws and remarked that even though her devoutly held religious convictions would prevent her from seeking one herself, she believes all women should have the right to *choose* motherhood and to control their own bodies. She also feels women should have the right to work and certainly should be paid equally with men. Many of our conversations were punctuated by her expressions of anger and resentment at the way women are constantly "put down" as childish, ignorant, and incapable of anything but housework or watching soap operas.

At first glance, Dots' incipient feminism seems deeply at odds with her interest in a literary form whose ultimate message, one astute observer has noted, is that "pleasure for women is men."[6] The traditionalism of romance fiction will not be denied here, but it is essential to point out that Dot and many of the writers and readers of romances interpret these stories as chronicles of female triumph. Although the particular way they do so will be explored later, suffice it to say here that Dot believes a good romance focuses on an intelligent and able heroine who finds a man who recognizes her special qualities and is capable of loving and caring for her as she wants to be loved. Thus Dot understands such an ending to say that female independence and marriage are compatible rather than mutually exclusive. The romances she most values and recommends for her readers are those with "strong," "fiery" heroines who are capable of "defying the hero," softening him, and showing him the value of loving and caring for another.

It is essential to introduce this here in order to take account adequately of Dot's personal influence on her customers and on their preferences in romance fiction. Because she is an exceptionally strong woman convinced of her sex's capabilities, when she expresses her opinions about a woman's right to pleasure, Dot not only supports her customers but confers legitimacy on the preoccupation they share with her. I suspect that in providing this much-needed reinforcement Dot also exerts an important influence on them that must be taken into account. She encourages her customers to think well of themselves not only by demonstrating her interest in them and in their desires but also by presenting them with books whose heroines seem out of the ordinary. Therefore, while the members of the Smithton group share attitudes about good and bad romances that are similar to Dot's, it is impossible to say whether these opinions were formed by Dot or whether she is simply their most articulate advocate. Nonetheless, it must be emphasized that this group finds it possible to select and construct romances in such a way that their stories are experienced as a reversal of the oppression and emotional abandonment suffered by women in real life. For Dot and her customers, romances provide a utopian vision in which female individuality and a sense of self are shown to be compatible with nurturance and care by another.

All of the Smithton readers who answered the questionnaire were female. Dot reported that although she suspects some of the men who buy romances "for their wives" are in fact buying them for themselves, all of the people she regularly advises are women. While the few houses that have conducted market-research surveys will not give out exact figures, officials at Harlequin, Silhouette, and Fawcett have all indicated separately that the majority of romance readers are married women between the ages of twenty-five and fifty. Fred Kerner, Harlequin's vice-president for publishing, for instance, recently reported to Barbara Brotman, of the *Chicago Tribune,* that "Harlequin readers are overwhelmingly women of whom 49 percent work at least part-time. They range in age from 24 to 49, have average family incomes of $15,000–20,000 and have high school diplomas but haven't completed college."[7] Harlequin will reveal little else about its audience, but a company executive did tell Margaret Jensen that the Harlequin reading population matches the profile of the "North American English-speaking female population" in age, family income, employment status, and geographical location.[8] For example, he said that 22 percent of the female population and Harlequin readers are between the ages of twenty-five and thirty-four. Carol Reo, publicity director for Silhouette Romances, has also revealed that the romance audience is almost entirely female, but indicates that 65 percent of Silhouette's potential market is under the age of forty and that 45 percent attended college.[9] If these sketchy details are accurate, the Smithton readers may be more representative of the Silhouette audience than they are of Harlequin's.[10] Unfortunately, the lack of detailed information about the total American audience for Harlequins as well as for other kinds of romances makes it exceedingly difficult to judge the representivity of the Smithton group. Still, it appears evident that the Smithton readers are somewhat younger than either Jensen's Harlequin readers or the Mills and Boon audience.

The age differential may account for the fact that neither Dot nor many of her customers are Harlequin fans. Although Dot reviews Harlequins and slightly more than half of her customers (twenty-four) reported reading them, a full eighteen indicated that they *never* read a Harlequin romance. Moreover, only ten of Dot's customers indicated that Harlequins are among the kinds of romances they *most* like to read. The overwhelming preference of the group was for historicals, cited by twenty (48 percent) as their favorite subgenre within the romance category.[11] Because historicals typically include more explicit sex than the Harlequins and also tend to portray more independent and defiant heroines, we might expect that this particular subgenre would draw younger readers who are less offended by changing standards of gender behavior. This would seem to be corroborated by the fact that only two of the women who listed Harlequins as a favorite also listed historicals.

In addition, the Smithton group also seemed to like contemporary mystery romances and contemporary romances, which were cited by another twelve as being among their favorites. Silhouettes are contemporary romances and, like the historicals, are less conventional than the Harlequins. Not only is their sexual description more explicit but it is not unusual for them to include heroines with careers who expect to keep their jobs after marriage. The similarity between Smithton's tastes and the content of the Silhouettes may thus explain why both audiences are younger than that for the relatively staid Harlequins.

Despite the discrepancies in the various reports, romance reading apparently correlates strongly with the years of young adulthood and early middle age. This is further borne out in the present study by the Smithton women's responses to a question about when they first began to read romances. Although fifteen (36 percent) of the women reported that they began in adolescence between the ages of ten and nineteen, sixteen (38 percent) indicated that they picked up the habit between the ages of twenty and twenty-nine. Another ten (24 percent) adopted romance reading after age thirty.[12]

Thirty-two women (76 percent) in the Smithton group were married at the time of the survey, a proportion that compares almost exactly with the 75 percent of married women included in Jensen's group.[13] An additional three (7 percent) of the Smithton women were single, while five (12 percent) were either widowed, separated, or divorced and not remarried.

Moreover, most of the women in the Smithton group were mothers with children *under* age eighteen (70 percent). Indeed, within the group, only five (12 percent) reported having no children at all. Nine (21 percent) of the Smithton women reported only one child, twelve (29 percent) claimed two children, eleven (27 percent) had three children, and three (7 percent) had four children. Interestingly enough, only five (12 percent) reported children under the age of five, while twenty-four of the women indicated that they had at least one child under age eighteen. Eleven (27 percent), however, reported that all of their children were over age eighteen. Fifteen (36 percent) reported children between ten and eighteen, and another fifteen (36 percent) had at least one child over age eighteen. The relatively advanced age of the Smithton readers' children is not surprising if one takes into account the age distribution of the women themselves and the fact that the mean age at first marriage within the group was 19.9 years.

Once again, the limited size of the sample and the lack of corroborating data from other sources suggest caution in the formation of hypotheses. Nonetheless, it appears that within the Smithton group romance reading correlates with motherhood and the care of children *other* than infants and toddlers.[14] This seems logical because the fact of the older children's attendance at school would allow the women greater time to read even as the children themselves continued to make heavy emotional demands on them for nurturance, advice, and attentive care. It will be seen later that it is precisely this emotional drain caused by a woman's duty to nurture and care for her children and husband that is addressed directly by romance reading at least within the minds of the women themselves.

Given the fact that fifteen (36 percent) of the Smithton readers reported children age ten and under, it should not be surprising to note that sixteen of the women (38 percent) reported that in the preceding week they were keeping house and/or caring for children on a full-time basis. Another nine (21 percent) were working part-time, while still another nine (21 percent) were holding down full-time jobs. In addition, two women failed to respond, two stated that they were retired, one listed herself as a student, and three indicated that they were currently unemployed and looking for work. These statistics seem to parallel those of the Mills and Boon study which found that 33 percent of the sample was represented by full-time housewives, while another 30 percent included housewives with full- or part-time jobs. Both studies suggest that romance reading is very often squeezed into busy daily schedules.

Although Fred Kerner's comment about the average $15,000–$20,000 income of the Harlequin audience is not very illuminating, neither is it at odds with the details reported by Dot's customers. Although four (10 percent) did not answer the question, eighteen (43 percent) in the group indicated a family income of somewhere between $15,000 and $24,999. Another fourteen (33 percent) claimed a joint income of $25,000 to $49,999, while four (10 percent) listed family earnings of over $50,000. The greater affluence of the Smithton group is probably accounted for by the fact that Dot's bookstore is located in one of the twelve most affluent counties in a state with 115. The median family income in Smithton, as reported by the 1970 United States census, was almost $11,000, which compares with the state median income of just slightly less than $9,000.

Before turning to the group's reading history and patterns, it should be noted that exactly half of the Smithton readers indicated that they had earned a high school diploma. Ten (24 percent) of the women reported completing less than three years of college; eight (19 percent) claimed at least a college degree or better. Only one person in the group indicated that she had not finished high school, while two failed to answer the question. Once again, as the Smithton readers appear to be more affluent than Harlequin readers, so also do they seem better educated; the Harlequin corporation claims that its readers are educated below even the statistical norm for the North American female population.

One final detail about the personal history of the Smithton women ought to be mentioned here: attendance at religious services was relatively high among Dot's customers. Although eight (19 percent) of the women indicated that they had not been to a service in the last two years, fifteen (36 percent) reported attendance "once a week or more," while another eight (19 percent) indicated attendance "once or a few times a month." Another nine (21 percent) admitted going to services a few times a year, while two (5 percent) did not answer the question. The women reported membership in a wide variety of denominations. Eight (19 percent) of the women indicated that they were Methodists and eight (19 percent) checked "Christian but non-denominational." The next two groups most heavily represented in the sample were Catholics and Baptists, each with five (12 percent) of the Smithton women.

When the reading *histories* of these women are examined, it becomes clear that, for many of them, romance reading is simply a variation in a pattern of leisure activity they began early in life. Indeed, twenty-two of Dot's customers reported that they first began to read for pleasure before age ten. Another twelve (27 percent) adopted the habit between the ages of eleven and twenty. Only seven (17 percent) of the Smithton women indicated that they began pleasure reading after their teen years. These results parallel earlier findings about the adoption of the book habit. Phillip Ennis found in 1965, for instance, that of the 49 percent of the

American population who were "current readers," 34 percent consisted of those who started reading early in life and 15 percent consisted of those who began reading at an advanced age.[15]

When *current* reading habits are examined, however, it becomes clear that the women think that it is the romances that are especially necessary to their daily routine. Their intense reliance on these books suggests strongly that they help to fulfill deeply felt psychological needs. Indeed, one of the most striking findings to come out of the Smithton study was that thirty-seven (88 percent) of Dot's readers indicated that they read religiously every day. Only five of her regular customers claimed to read more sporadically. Twenty-two of the women, in fact, reported reading more than sixteen hours per week, and another ten (24 percent) claimed to read between eleven and fifteen hours weekly.[16] When asked to describe their typical reading pattern once they have begun a new romance, eleven (26 percent) selected the statement, "I won't put it down until I've finished it unless it's absolutely necessary." Thirty more indicated reading "as much of it as I can until I'm interrupted or have something else to do." None of Dot's customers reported a systematic reading pattern of "a few pages a day until done," and only one admitted that she reads solely when she is in the mood. These figures suggest that the Smithton women become intensely involved in the stories they are reading and that once immersed in the romantic fantasy, Dot's customers do not like to return to reality without experiencing the resolution of the narrative.

This need to see the story and the emotions aroused by it resolved is so intense that many of the Smithton women have worked out an ingenious strategy to insure a regular and predictable arrival at the anticipated narrative conclusion. Although they categorize romances in several ways, one of the most basic distinctions they make is that between "quick reads" and "fat books." Quick reads contain less than 200 pages and require no more than two hours of reading time. Harlequins, Silhouettes, and most Regencies are considered quick reads for occasions when they know they will not be able to "make it through" a big book. If, for example, a woman has just finished one romance but still "is not ready to quit," as one of my informants put it, she will "grab a thin one" she knows she can finish before going to sleep. Fat books, on the other hand, tend to be saved for weekends or long evenings that promise to be uninterrupted, once again because the women dislike having to leave a story before it is concluded. This kind of uninterrupted reading is very highly valued within the Smithton group because it is associated with the pleasure of spending time alone.[17] . . . [T]he Smithton readers' strategies for avoiding disruption or discontinuity in the story betoken a profound need to arrive at the *ending* of the tale and thus to achieve or acquire the emotional gratification they already can anticipate.

The remarkable extent of their familiarity with the genre is attested to by the number of romances these women read each week. Despite the fact that twenty-six (62 percent) of Dot's customers claimed to read somewhere between one and four books *other* than romances every week, more than a third (fifteen) reported reading from five to nine romances weekly. An additional twenty-two (55 percent) completed between one and four romances every week, while four women indicated that they consume anywhere from fifteen to twenty-five romances during that same period of time. This latter figure strikes me as somewhat implausible because it implies a reading rate of one hundred romances a month. I think this is unlikely given the fact that far fewer romances were issued monthly by publishers at the time of the study. Of course, the women could be reading old romances, but the figure still seems exaggerated. Nonetheless, it is evident that Dot's customers read extraordinary amounts of romance fiction.

Although their chronic reading of these books might sound unusual or idiosyncratic, the Yankelovich findings about romance reading, as noted before, indicate that romance readers are generally heavy consumers. Most, however, are probably not as obsessed as the Smithton readers seem to be. Unfortunately, the Yankelovich discovery that the average romance reader had read nine romances in the last six months does not tell us what proportion of the group read an even larger number of novels. Although 40 percent of the heavy readers (those who had read more than twenty-five books in the last six months) reported having read a romance, thus suggesting the possibility of a correlation between high levels of consumption and romance reading, the study gives no indication of how many of the romance readers actually read anywhere near the number the Smithton women report, which ranges from twenty-four to more than six hundred romances every six months.[18] I think it safe to say that the Smithton group's reliance on romances is not strictly comparable to that of the occasional reader. Rather, Dot's customers are women who spend a significant portion of every day participating vicariously in a fantasy world that they willingly admit bears little resemblance to the one they actually inhabit. Clearly, the experience must provide some form of required pleasure and reconstitution because it seems unlikely that so much time and money would be spent on an activity that functioned merely to fill otherwise unoccupied time.

The women confirmed this in their answers to a directed-response question about their reasons for reading romance fiction. When asked to rank order the three most important motives for romance reading out of a list of eight, nineteen (45 percent) of the women listed "simple relaxation" as the first choice. Another eight (19 percent) of the readers reported that they read romances "because reading is just for me; it is my time." Still another six (14 percent) said they read "to learn about faraway places and times"; while five (12 percent) insisted that their primary reason is "to escape my daily problems." When these first choices are added to the second and third most important reasons for reading, the totals are distributed as in Table 2.1:

TABLE 2.1

Question: Which of the Following Best Describes Why You Read Romances?

a. To escape my daily problems	13
b. To learn about faraway places and times	19
c. For simple relaxation	33
d. Because I wish I had a romance like the heroine's	5
e. Because reading is just for me; it is my time	28
f. Because I like to read about the strong, virile heroes	4
g. Because reading is at least better than other forms of escape	5
h. Because romantic stories are never sad or depressing	10

On the basis of these schematic answers alone I think it logical to conclude that romance reading is valued by the Smithton women because the experience itself is *different* from ordinary existence. Not only is it a relaxing release from the tension produced by daily problems and responsibilities, but it creates a time or space within which a woman can be entirely on her own, preoccupied with her personal needs, desires, and pleasure. It is also a means of transportation or escape to the exotic or, again, to that which is different.

It is important to point out here that the responses to the second questionnaire are different in important ways from the answers I received from the women in the face-to-face interviews and in the first survey. At the time of my initial visit in June 1980, our conversations about their reasons for romance reading were dominated by the words "escape" and "education." Similarly, when asked by the first question-naire to describe briefly what romances do "better" than other books available today, of the thirty-one answering the undirected question, fourteen of the first respondents *volunteered* that they like romance fiction because it allows them to "escape." It should be noted that "relaxation" was given only once as an answer, while no woman mentioned the idea of personal space.

Both answers *c* and *e* on the second form were given initially in the course of the interviews by two unusually articulate readers who elaborated more fully than most of the women on the meaning of the word "escape." They considered these two answers synonymous with it, but they also seemed to prefer the alternate responses because they did not so clearly imply a desire to avoid duties and responsibilities in the "real" world. Although most of the other women settled for the word "escape" on the first questionnaire, they also liked their sister readers' terms better. Once these were introduced in the group interviews, the other women agreed that romance reading functions best as relaxation and as a time for self-indulgence. Because the switch seemed to hint at feelings of guilt, I decided to add the more acceptable choices to the second survey. Although both answers *c* and *e* also imply movement away from something distasteful in the real present to a somehow more satisfying universe, a feature that appears to testify to romance reading's principal function as a therapeutic release and as a provider of vicarious pleasure, the fact of the women's preference for these two terms over their first spontaneous response suggests again that the women harbor complex feelings about the worth and pro-priety of romance reading.

The women provided additional proof of their reliance on romance reading as a kind of tranquilizer or restorative agent in their responses to questions about pre-ferred reading times and the habit of rereading favorite romances. When asked to choose from among seven statements the one that best described their reading pat-tern, twenty-four (57 percent) eschewed specification of a particular time of day in order to select the more general assertion, "It's hard to say when I do most of my reading, since I read every chance I get." Another fourteen claimed to read mostly in the evenings, usually because days were occupied by employment outside the home. In the case of either pattern, however, romances are not picked up idly as an old magazine might be merely to fill otherwise unoccupied time. Rather, romance reading is considered so enjoyable and beneficial by the women that they deliber-ately work it into busy schedules as often and as consistently as they can.

Rereading is not only a widely practiced habit among the Smithton women but tends to occur most frequently during times of stress or depression. Three-fourths of Dot's customers reported that they reread favorite books either "sometimes" (twenty-one) or "often" (eleven). They do so, they explained in the interviews, when they feel sad or unhappy because they know exactly how the chosen book will affect their state of mind. Peter Mann similarly discovered that 46 percent of his Mills and Boon readers claimed to reread "very often," while another 38 percent reported repeat reading "now and then."[19] Unfortunately, he has provided no further information about why or when the women do so. Although it is possible that they may reread in order to savor the details of particular plots, it is clear that for the most part the Smithton women do not. For them, rereading is an activity engaged in expressly to lift the spirits. The following comment from one of the first questionnaires illustrates nicely the kind of correlation the Smithton women see between their daily needs and the effects of romance reading: "Romances are not depressing and very seldom leave you feeling sad inside. When I read for enjoyment I want to be entertained and feel lifted out of my daily routine. And romances are the best type of reading for this effect. Romances also revive my usually optimistic outlook which often is very strained in day-to-day living." Although all of Dot's customers know well that most romances end happily, when their own needs seem unusually pressing they often refuse even the relatively safe gamble of beginning a new romance. Instead, they turn to a romance they have completed previously because they already know how its final resolution will affect them. Romance reading, it would seem, can be valued as much for the sameness of the response it evokes as for the variety of the adventures it promises.

Interestingly enough, the Smithton readers hold contradictory opinions about the repetitious or formulaic quality of the fiction they read. On the one hand, they are reluctant to admit that the characters appearing in romances are similar. As Dot's daughter, Kit, explained when asked to describe a typical heroine in the historical romance, "there isn't a typical one, they all have to be different or you'd be reading the same thing over and over." Her sentiments were echoed frequently by her mother's customers, all of whom claim to value the variety and diversity of romance fiction.

On the other hand, these same women exhibit fairly rigid expectations about what is permissible in a romantic tale and express disappointment and outrage when those conventions are violated. In my first interview with Dot, she discussed a particular author who had submitted a historical novel to her publisher. Although the author explained repeatedly that the book was not a romance, the publisher insisted on packaging it with a standard romance cover in the hope of attracting the huge romance market. The author knew this would anger that audience and, as Dot remarked, "she was not surprised when she got irate letters." Clearly, romances may not deviate too significantly if regular readers are to be pleased. They expect and, indeed, rely upon certain events, characters, and progressions to provide the desired experience.

Dot herself often finds it necessary but difficult to overcome her customers' fixed expectations when she discovers a romance she thinks they will enjoy even though it fails to follow the usual pattern. In the case of *The Fulfillment,* for example, which Dot loved and wanted to share with her women, she worked out an entire speech to get them to buy the book and to read it through. The following is a verbatim transcription of her recreation of that speech: "Now this is a good book —but please don't think that it is the run of the mill. It isn't. At one point in this book, you're gonna want to put it down—and you're gonna say, 'Dot didn't tell me this'—and I said, 'Don't put it down. You keep reading.' Every one of them came back and said, 'You were right. I thought why did she give me this book?' They said, 'I kept reading like you said and it was great.'" The problem with this particular book was the fact that the hero died three-quarters of the way through the tale. However, because the author had worked out an unusually complex plot involving the heroine simultaneously with another equally attractive man in an acceptable way, the women did not find her sudden remarriage distasteful. Without Dot's skillful encouragement, however, most of the women would never have read the book past the hero's death.

Dot also tries to circumvent set expectations in her newsletter. She occasionally tells booksellers and readers about books classified by their publishers as something other than a romance. Erroneous categorization occurs, she believes, because the publishers really do not understand what a romance is and thus pay too much attention to meaningless, superficial details that lead to mistaken identifications. Because Jacqueline Marten's *Visions of the Damned* suffered this fate, Dot attempted to alert her readers to the problem classification. Her way of doing so provides an essential clue to the proper identification of a romance, which the women rely on despite their claim that all romantic novels are different. Of Marten's story, she wrote, "This book, because of cover and title, was classed as an occult. What a mistake! *Visions* is one of the best love stories I've read of late. Get it and read it. I loved it."[20] Although *Visions of the Damned* concerns itself with extrasensory perception and reincarnation, Dot believes that the book's proper plot structure is what makes it a romance. It is not the mere use of the romantic subject matter that qualifies Marten's book as a romance, she explained, but rather its manner of developing the loving relationship. As Dot remarked in a later interview, "Not all love stories are romances." Some are simply novels about love.

If the Smithton readers' stipulations are taken seriously, a romance is, first and foremost, a story about a woman. That woman, however, may not figure in a larger plot simply as the hero's prize, as Jenny Cavileri does, for instance in Erich Segal's *Love Story,* which the Smithton readers claim is not a romance. To qualify as a romance, the story must chronicle not merely the events of a courtship but *what it feels like* to be the *object* of one. Dot's customers insist that this need not be accomplished by telling the story solely from the heroine's point of view, although it is usually managed in this way. Although five of the women refuse to read first-person narratives because they want to be privy to the hero's thoughts and another ten indicate that they prefer to see both points of view, twenty-three of Dot's regular customers indicate that they have no preference about the identity of the narrator. However, all of the women I spoke to, regardless of their taste in narratives, admitted that they want to identify with the heroine as she attempts to comprehend, anticipate, and deal with the ambiguous attentions of a man who inevitably cannot understand her feelings at all. The point of the experience is the sense of exquisite tension, anticipation, and excitement created within the reader as she imagines the possible resolutions and consequences for a woman of an encounter with a member of the opposite sex and then observes that once again the heroine in question has avoided the ever-present potential for disaster because the hero has fallen helplessly in love with her.

In all of their comments about the nature of the romance, the Smithton women placed heavy emphasis on the importance of *development* in the romance's portrayal of love. The following two definitions were echoed again and again in other remarks:

> Generally there are two people who come together for one reason or another, *grow to love each other* and *work together solving problems* along the way—united for a

purpose. They are light easy reading and always have a happy ending which makes one feel more light-hearted.

I think [a romance] is a man and woman meeting, the growing awareness, the culmination of the love—*whether it's going to jell or if it's going to fall apart*—but they [the heroine and the hero] have recognized that they have fallen in love [emphasis added].

The women usually articulated this insistence on process and development during discussions about the genre's characteristic preoccupation with what is typically termed "a love-hate relationship." Because the middle of every romantic narrative must create some form of conflict to keep the romantic pair apart until the proper moment, many authors settle for misunderstanding or distrust as the cause of the intermediary delay of the couple's happy union. Hero and heroine are shown to despise each other, overtly, even though they are "in love," primarily because each is jealous or suspicious of the other's motives and consequently fails to trust the other. Despite the frequency with which this pattern of conflict is suddenly explained away by the couple's mutual recognition that only misunderstanding is thwarting their relationship, the Smithton women are not convinced when a hero decides within two pages of the novel's conclusion that he has been mistaken about the heroine and that his apparent hatred is actually affection. Dot's customers dislike such "about faces"; they prefer to see a hero and heroine gradually overcome distrust and suspicion and grow to love each other.

Although this depiction of love as a gradual process cannot be considered the defining feature of the genre for all of the Smithton women, slightly more than half (twenty-three) believe it one of the "three most important ingredients" in the narrative. As might have been predicted, when responding to a request to rank order narrative features with respect to their importance to the genre, Dot's customers generally agreed that a happy ending is indispensable. Twenty-two of the women selected this as the essential ingredient in romance fiction out of a list of eleven choices, while a total of thirty-two listed it in first, second, or third place. The runner-up in the "most important" category, however, was "a slowly but consistently developing love between hero and heroine," placed by twenty-three of the women in first, second, or third place. Considered almost equally important by Dot's customers was the romance's inclusion of "some detail about the heroine and the hero after they have finally gotten together."[21] Twenty-two of the women thought this one of the three most important ingredients in the genre. Table 2.2 summarizes the ranking responses of the Smithton women.

The obvious importance of the happy ending lends credence to the suggestion that romances are valued most for their ability to raise the spirits of the reader. They manage to do so, the rankings imply, by involving that reader vicariously in the gradual evolution of a loving relationship whose culmination she is later permitted to enjoy in the best romances through a description of the heroine's and hero's life together after their necessary union. When combined with the relative unimportance of detailed reports about sexual encounters, it seems clear that the Smithton readers are interested in the verbal working out of a romance, that is, in the reinterpretation of misunderstood actions and in declarations of mutual love rather than in the portrayal of sexual contact through visual imagery.

Beatrice Faust has recently argued in *Women, Sex, and Pornography* that female sexuality is "tactile, verbal, intimate, nurturant, process-oriented and somewhat

TABLE 2.2

Question: What Are the Three Most Important Ingredients in a Romance?

Response	First Most Important Feature	Second Most Important Feature	Third Most Important Feature	Total Who Checked Response In One of Top Three Positions
a. A happy ending	22	4	6	32
b. Lots of scenes with explicit sexual description	0	0	0	0
c. Lots of details about faraway places and times	0	1	2	3
d. A long conflict between hero and heroine	2	1	1	4
e. Punishment of the villain	0	2	3	5
f. A slowly but consistently developing love between hero and heroine	8	9	6	23
g. A setting in a particular historical period	3	4	3	10
h. Lots of love scenes with some explicit sexual description	3	7	3	13
i. Lots of love scenes without explicit sexual description	0	3	1	4
j. Some detail about heroine and hero after they've gotten together	1	7	14	22
k. A very particular kind of hero and heroine	3	4	3	10

inclined to monogamy," traits she attributes to biological predisposition and social reinforcement through culture.[22] Although there are important problems with Faust's reliance on biology to account for female preferences in sexual encounters as well as with her assertion that such tastes characterize all women, her parallel claim that women are not excited by the kinds of visual displays and explicit description of physical contact that characterize male pornography is at least true of the Smithton readers. Dot and her customers are more interested in the affective responses of hero and heroine to each other than in a detailed account of their physical contact. Interestingly enough, the Smithton women also explained that they do not like explicit description because they prefer to imagine the scene in detail by themselves. Their wish to participate in the gradual growth of love and trust and to witness the way in which the heroine is eventually cared for by a man who also confesses that he "needs" her suggests that the Smithton women do indeed want to see a woman attended to sexually in a tender, nurturant, and emotionally open way. It should be added that these preferences also hint at the existence of an equally powerful wish to see a man dependent upon a woman.

Although Dot's customers will not discuss in any detail whether they themselves are sexually excited by the escalation of sexual tension in a romance, they willingly acknowledge that what they enjoy most about romance reading is the opportunity to project themselves into the story, to become the heroine, and thus to share her surprise and slowly awakening pleasure at being so closely watched by someone who finds her valuable and worthy of love. They have elaborated this preference into a carefully articulated distinction between good and bad romances, which differ principally in the way they portray the hero's treatment of the heroine.

A substantial amount of popular and even scholarly writing about mass-produced entertainment makes the often correct assumption that such fare is cynically engineered to appeal to the tastes of the largest possible audience in the interest of maximum profit.[23] However, a certain portion of it is still written by sincere, well-meaning people who are themselves consumers of the form they work in and indeed proponents of the values it embodies. Despite publishers' efforts at rationalization of romance production through the use of carefully calculated "tip sheets to writers," the genre is not yet entirely written by men and women who do it only to make money. Although many of the most successful authors in the field are professional writers, a significant number of them are "amateurs" drawn to the genre by a desire to write the kind of material they love to read. More often than not, it is the work of *these* women that the Smithton readers like best.

In a letter to the readers of Dot's newsletter, for instance, LaVyrle Spencer has explained that her first book "was written because of one very special lady, Kathleen Woodiwiss," whose book, *The Flame and the Flower*, "possessed me to the point where I found I, too, wanted to write a book that would make ladies' hearts throb with anticipation." She continued, "I even got to the point where I told myself I wanted to do it for her, Kathleen, to give her a joyful reading experience like she'd given me."[24] *The Fulfillment* resulted from this inspiration.

Jude Deveraux, another successful author, also commented in Dot's newsletter on Woodiwiss's role in her decision to become a writer. She so enjoyed *The Flame and the Flower* that she dashed out to buy two more romances to re-create the pleasure Woodiwiss's book had provided. "I planned to stay up all night and read them," she explained to Dot's subscribers, but "by ten o'clock I was so disgusted I threw the books across the room. They were nothing but rape sagas." She gave up, turned off the light and thought, "If I read the perfect romance, what would the plot be?" Deveraux spent the night creating dialogue in her head and when she arose the next morning, she began writing. The book that resulted, *The Enchanted Land,* with its independent heroine and thoughtful hero, was mentioned often by Dot's customers as one of their favorites.[25]

Even the incredibly prolific and very professional Janet Dailey confesses that she too began the career that has made her a millionaire, by some observers' reckoning, because she wanted to write the kinds of books she most enjoyed reading.[26] Convinced by her husband to go ahead and try, she set out to write a romance.

Since that day in 1968, millions of readers have informally acknowledged through their repeat purchases of her books that she understands very well what her readers want.

Given the fact that many romance writers were romance readers before they set pen to paper, it seems logical to expect that their views of the romance might parallel those held by their readers. Of course, this is not universally the case because many romances are considered failures by readers. Some otherwise popular books do not please the entire audience, thus bearing witness to the possibility of a discrepancy between writers' and readers' definitions and conceptions. Rosemary Rogers, for example, is universally detested by the Smithton readers who consider her books "trashy," "filthy," and "perverted." Her views of the romance are at least not representative of this group of regular readers.

Despite exceptions like these, it is striking to note that there is a distinct similarity between the Smithton conception of the romance and that implied in comments about the form by writers who are themselves enthusiastic readers. In an article on "Writing the Gothic Novel," for instance, Phyllis Whitney has cautioned aspiring writers, "no feeling, no story—and that's a rule!"[27] She explains that even though explicit sexual description must never appear in a gothic, this prohibition does not mean sexual feeling should not figure in the stories. In fact, she goes on to say, anticipation and excitement *must* "smolder" beneath the surface in scenes that are "underplayed, suggested rather than stated." That way, Whitney elaborates, "the reader's imagination will work for you."[28] She understands that women like the Smithton readers project themselves into the story by identifying with the heroine as she responds to the hero with all of her "strongly passionate nature." Whitney also knows that those women wish to be shown repeatedly that men can attend to a woman in the manner she most desires. To clarify her point she explains finally that "in the true love scenes, there is always an underlying tenderness that, for a woman, can be an exciting factor in sex—James Bond to the contrary."[29] Like Beatrice Faust and the Smithton women, Phyllis Whitney seems to believe that "women want to love and be made love to as they love babies—that is, in a nurturant fashion."[30] Whitney closes with perhaps her most central piece of advice: "I doubt that you can write Gothic novels unless you like reading them. . . . While I am in the process of writing, I am submerged in my heroine and her problems—and having a wonderful time. Me and all those dark-browed heroes! I'm sure this is the first necessary ingredient, though I'm mentioning it last."[31]

Her attitude has been echoed by Jeanne Glass, an editor at Pyramid Publications, a house that attempts to specialize in the kinds of romances the Smithton readers like. She has written that the sex in romances must be "sensual, romantic, breathy—enough to make the pulse race, but not rough-guy, explicit, constantly brutal." She adds that the predominant flavor must be an "understanding of female *emotions:* hesitancy, doubt, anger, confusion, loss of control, exhilaration, etc."[32]

These comments suggest that some romance writers agree with the Smithton group that a romance is a love story whose gradually evolving course must be experienced from the heroine's point of view. These writers understand that the goal and raison d'être of the genre is its actual, though perhaps temporary, effect on readers like the Smithton women. While explicit description of sexual encounters may be included in some of the genre's variations, the writers agree with their readers that the emphasis in the encounters must be on the love that is being conveyed through sexual contact and not on its physical details.

If readers' and writers' interpretations of their own experiences are taken into account, then, the romance cannot be dismissed as a mere pretense for masturbatory titillation. The reading experience is valued for the way it makes the reader feel, but the feeling it creates is interpreted by the women themselves as a general sense of emotional well-being and visceral contentment. Such a feeling is brought on by the opportunity to participate vicariously in a relationship characterized by *mutual* love and by the hero's quite unusual ability to express his devotion gently and with concern for his heroine's pleasure. The question that needs to be asked, therefore, is *why* the readers find it essential and beneficial to seek out this particular kind of vicarious experience. That can perhaps best be answered by comparing good and bad romances. In explaining what they do when they have determined a particular text's quality, the Smithton women provide clues to both the *deprivation* that prompts their activity and the *fears* that are assuaged and managed in the reading experience.

The reactions of the Smithton women to books they are not enjoying are indicative of the intensity of their need to avoid offensive material and the feelings it typically evokes. Indeed, twenty-three (55 percent) reported that when they find themselves in the middle of a bad book, they put it down immediately and refuse to finish it. Some even make the symbolic gesture of discarding the book in the garbage, particularly if it has offended them seriously. This was the universal fate suffered by Lolah Burford's *Alyx* (1977), a book cited repeatedly as a perfect example of the pornographic trash distributed by publishers under the guise of the romance.

Another nine (21 percent) of the women indicated that although they do not read the rest of the book, they at least skip to the ending "to see how it came out." In responding to the question about why she must read the ending of a book even in the face of evidence that the book is insulting, Maureen explained that to cease following a story in the middle is to remain suspended in the heroine's nightmare while she *is* the heroine. Her comments were corroborated by every other woman I spoke to who engaged in this kind of behavior. In elaborating upon the problem, Maureen also mentioned the kind of books that most upset her:

Maureen: A lot of your thicker books—it's rape—sometimes gang rape. I could not handle that in my own life. And since I'm living as the heroine, I cannot handle it in a book. And I hate myself for reading them. But if I start it, I have to get myself out of there, so I have to read my way out.

Interviewer: So you must finish a book?

Maureen: Yes, I have to finish it. Even if it's only skimming, one word per page —or sometimes I just read the ending. I have to finish it. But it leaves a bad taste in my mouth forever.

Because nearly all romances end in the union of the two principal characters, regardless of the level of violence inflicted on the heroine during the course of the story, by reading that "happy" conclusion Maureen at least formally assures herself that all works out for the heroine as it should. She cannot simply dismiss the story as a badly managed fiction precisely because she becomes so involved in the tale that she lives it emotionally as her own. She and other readers like her feel it necessary to continue the imaginative pretense just long enough to share the heroine's achievement of mutual love that is the goal of all romance-reading experiences.

This need to read one's way out of a bad situation and to resolve or contain all of the unpleasant feelings aroused by it is so strong in some of the Smithton readers that they read the whole book even when they hate it. In fact, ten (24 percent) of Dot's customers indicated that they *always* finish a book no matter what its quality. Nevertheless, this habit does not testify to a wish or even a need to see women abused. Rather, it is the mark of the intensity with which they desire to be told that an ideal love is possible *even in the worst of circumstances* and that a woman can be nurtured and cared for even by a man who appears gruff and indifferent.

It is necessary to raise this issue of the romance readers' attitude toward the violence that undeniably exists in some romances because several commentators, including Ann Douglas, have recently suggested that women enjoy the experience of reading about others of their sex who are mistreated by men. In "Soft-Porn Culture," Douglas asserts that "the women who couldn't thrill to male nudity in *Playgirl* are *enjoying* the titillation of seeing themselves, not necessarily as they are, but as some men would like to see them: illogical, innocent, *magnetized by male sexuality and brutality.*"[33] Although it is hard to disagree with her point about traditional male sexuality, which is still treated as compelling, especially in the Harlequins about which Douglas writes, there is good reason to believe that male brutality is a concern in recent romances, not because women are magnetized or drawn to it, but because they find it increasingly prevalent and horribly frightening.

Clifford Geertz maintains that all art forms, like the Balinese cockfight, render "ordinary everyday experience comprehensible by presenting it in terms of acts and objects which have had their practical consequences removed and been reduced . . . to a level of sheer appearance, where the meaning can be more powerfully articulated and more exactly perceived."[34] If Geertz is correct, then it seems likely that the romance's preoccupation with male brutality is an attempt to understand the meaning of an event that has become almost unavoidable in the real world. The romance may express misogynistic attitudes not because women share them but because they increasingly need to know how to deal with them.

The romance also seems to be exploring the consequences of attempts to counter the increased threat of violence with some sort of defiance. While the final effect of such a display may be, as Douglas claims, the formulation of the message, "don't travel alone"; "men can't stand it," "men won't let you get away with it,"[35] the motive behind the message is less one of total assent than one of resignation born of fear about what might happen if the message was ignored. Romantic violence may also be the product of a continuing inability to imagine any situation in which a woman might acquire and use resources that would enable her to withstand male opposition and coercion.

When the Smithton readers' specific dislikes are examined in conjunction with their preferences in romance fiction, an especially clear view of the genre's function as an artistic "display" of contemporary cultural habits develops. In particular, when the events and features that the readers *most* detest are taken as indicators of their fears, it becomes possible to isolate the crucial characteristics and consequences of gender relations that prove most troubling to the Smithton women. . . . [T]he same awful possibilities of violence that dominate bad romances are always evoked as potential threats to female integrity even in good romances, simply because women are trying to *explain* this situation to themselves. Because the explanation finally advanced in the good romance remains a highly conservative one of traditional categories and definitions, when events that occur in reality are displayed in the text, they are always reinterpreted as mere threats. However, in those romances where the potential consequences of male-female relations are too convincingly imagined or permitted to control the tenor of the book by obscuring the developing love story, the art form's role as *safe* display is violated. In that case, the story treads too closely to the terrible real in ordinary existence that it is trying to explain. Then, the romance's role as conservator of the social structure and its legitimizing ideology is unmasked because the contradictions the form usually papers over and minimizes so skillfully render the romantic resolution untenable even for the women who are usually most convinced by it.

Dot first acquainted me with the features of such a "bad" romance during our initial interview when she informed me that her customers can tell the difference between romances written by women and those written by men. She agrees with their dismissal of male-authored romances, she explained, because very few men are "perceptive" or "sensitive" and because most cannot imagine the kind of "gentleness" that is essential to the good romance. When asked to elaborate on the distinction between a good romance and a bad one, she replied that the latter was "kinky, you know, filled with sado-masochism, cruelty, and all sorts of things." She concluded decisively, "I detest that!"

Her readers apparently do too for in response to a question requesting them to select the three things that "should never appear in a romance" from a list of eleven choices, rape was listed by eleven of the women as the most objectionable feature, while a sad ending was selected by an additional ten. The rest of the group divided almost evenly over explicit sex, physical torture of the heroine or hero, and bed-hopping. Despite the apparent range of dislikes, when their rankings are summarized, clear objections emerge. The women generally agree that bed-hopping or promiscuous sex, a sad ending, rape, physical torture, and weak heroes have no place in the romance. Their choices here are entirely consistent with their belief in the therapeutic value of romance reading. The sad ending logically ranks high on their list of objections because its presence would negate the romance's difference and distance from day-to-day existence, dominated as it so often is by small failures, minor catastrophes, and ongoing disappointments. In addition, without its happy ending, the romance could not hold out the utopian promise that male-female relations can be managed successfully.

I suspect bed-hopping is so objectionable in a romance because the genre is exploring the possibilities and consequences for women of the American middle class of adopting what has been dubbed "the new morality." Most students of the romance have observed that after the 1972 appearance of Woodiwiss's unusually explicit *The Flame and the Flower*, romance authors were free to treat their heroines as sexual creatures capable of arousal and carnal desire. Indeed, the extraordinary popularity of Woodiwiss's novel and its rapid imitation by others seem to suggest that large numbers of American women had been affected by feminism and the sexual revolution of the 1960s. The strong reader distaste for bed-hopping or promiscuous sex suggests, however, that this change in sexual mores was and still is tolerable only within very strict limits. Hence, the "good" romance continues to maintain that a woman acknowledge and realize her feelings *only* within traditional, monogamous marriage. When another text portrays a heroine who is neither harmed nor disturbed by her ability to have sex with several men, I suspect it is classified as "bad" because it makes explicit the threatening implications of an unleashed feminine sexuality capable of satisfying itself outside the structures of patriarchal domination that are still perpetuated most effectively through marriage.[36] Such a portrayal also strays too close to the suggestion that men do not care for women as individuals but, as the saying goes, are interested only in one thing.

TABLE 2.3

Question: Which of the Following Do You Feel Should Never Be Included in a Romance?

Response	First Most Objectionable	Second Most Objectionable	Third Most Objectionable	Total
a. Rape	11	6	2	19
b. Explicit sex	6	2	1	9
c. Sad ending	10	4	6	20
d. Physical torture	5	6	7	18
e. An ordinary heroine	1	1	1	3
f. Bed-hopping	4	12	6	22
g. Premarital sex	0	0	1	1
h. A cruel hero	1	5	6	12
i. A weak hero	4	5	7	16
j. A hero stronger than the heroine	0	0	0	0
k. A heroine stronger than the hero	0	1	3	4

In fact, the Smithton women revealed that they suspected as much when they voiced their anger about male promiscuity and repeatedly complained about romances that advance the double standard. "We do not want to be told," one of Dot's customers explained, "that if you love a man you'll forgive him." Neither do they wish to adopt male standards; Dot and her customers would prefer that men learn to adhere to theirs. The Smithton women overwhelmingly believe that sex is a wonderful form of intimate communication that should be explored only by two people who care for each other deeply and intend to formalize their relationship through the contract of marriage. For them, the romance is neither a recommendation for female revolt nor a strictly conservative refusal to acknowledge any change. It is, rather, a cognitive exploration of the possibility of adopting and managing some attitude changes about feminine sexuality by making room for them within traditional institutions and structures that they understand to be protective of a woman's interests.

Rape and physical torture of the heroine and the hero are obviously objectionable because the readers are seeking an opportunity to be shown a happier, more trouble-free version of existence. Such features are probably also distasteful, however, because the romance, which is never simply a love story, is also an exploration of the meaning of patriarchy for women. As a result, it is concerned with the fact that men possess and regularly exercise power over them in all sorts of circumstances. By picturing the heroine in relative positions of weakness, romances are not necessarily endorsing her situation, but examining an all-too-common state of affairs in order to display possible strategies for coping with it. When a romance presents the story of a woman who is misunderstood by the hero, mistreated and manhandled as a consequence of his misreading, and then suddenly loved, protected, and cared for by him because he recognizes that he mistook the meaning of her behavior, the novel is informing its readers that the minor acts of violence they must contend with in their own lives can be similarly reinterpreted as the result of misunderstandings or of jealousy born of "true love." The readers are therefore assured that those acts do not warrant substantial changes or traumatic upheaval in a familiar way of life.[37]

Woodiwiss's handling of what one reader called "a little forceful persuasion" is acceptable to the Smithton women because they are fully convinced by her attempt to show that the hero's sexual sway over the heroine is always the product of his passion and her irresistibility. Indeed, one publishing house understands this quite well, for in its directions to potential writers it states that rape is not recommended but that one will be allowed under specific conditions if the author feels it is necessary to make a point.[38] Should that rape occur "between the heroine and the hero," the directions specify, it must "never be initiated with the violent motivation that exists in reality" because "a woman's fantasy is to lose control" with someone who really cares for her. "A true rape" can be included only if "it moves the story forward" and if it happens to someone other than the heroine.

Vicious or "true" rape upsets the tenuous balance for most of the Smithton readers because they feel they would not be able to forgive or explain away an overtly malicious act. They cannot understand how a heroine finds it within herself to ignore such an event, forgive the man who violated her, and then grow to love him. As Ann, one of Dot's most outspoken customers, put it, "I get tired of it if they [the heroes] keep grabbing and using sex as a weapon for domination because they want to win a struggle of the wills. I'm tending to get quite a few of these in Harlequins and I think they're terrible." Her comment prompted excited discussion among those in the interview group who had read the recent Harlequins. All of the women agreed that they found Harlequin's new, more explicit preoccupation with male violence nauseating, and several even admitted that they stopped buying them to avoid being subjected to this form of male power. The following explanation of several Harlequin plots was given by another of Dot's customers:

> Four of the eight in the last shipment—they're married and separated four to eight years and all of a sudden *he* decides that they should have stayed together and *he* punishes her. They're gonna get together and live happily ever after, after *he* punishes her! Right!
> That sounds terrible.
> Well, they were. He tricks her into coming back or meeting with him or whatever and he has some sort of powerhold over her either emotionally or physically—either he'll take her child away or ruin her father. He's determined to win her back. She's good enough to have him now.[39]

This reader's scorn for a typical pattern of explanation in romance fiction makes it clear that there are limits to what can be justified by evoking the irrationality of passionate love. Although opinions about acceptability probably vary tremendously within the entire romance audience, Dots' readers at least seem to agree about the conditions that must be met. Violence is acceptable to them only if it is described sparingly, if it is controlled carefully, or if it is *clearly* traceable to the passion or jealousy of the hero. On the other hand, if it is represented as brutal and vicious, if it is extensively detailed and carried out by many men, or if it is depicted as the product of an obvious desire for power, these same women find that violence offensive and objectionable. This curious and artificial distinction that they draw between "forceful persuasion" and "true rape" is a function of the very pressing need to know how to deal with the realities of male power and force in day-to-day existence.

I suspect their willingness to see male force interpreted as passion is also the product of a wish to be seen as so desirable to the "right" man that he will not take "no" for an answer. Because he finds her irresistible, the heroine need not take any responsibility for her own sexual feelings. She avoids the difficulty of choosing whether to act on them or not. Although female sexuality is thus approvingly incorporated into the romantic fantasy, the individual ultimately held responsible for it is not the woman herself but, once again, a man.

If the qualities of a bad romance reveal the fears and concerns that are troubling to the women who read them, the characteristics they identify with good romances point to the existence of important needs and desires that are met and fulfilled by the perfect romantic fantasy. According to Dot and her customers, the relative excellence of a romance is a function of its treatment of three different aspects of the story. These include the personality of the heroine, the character of the hero, and the particular manner in which the hero pursues and wins the affections of the heroine. If these individuals and relationships are not presented properly, not even ingenious plotting will rescue the novel from "the garbage dump."

On first discussing romances with the Smithton readers, I was struck by the fact that individual books were inevitably registered in their memories as the stories of particular *women*. When specific titles were volunteered to illustrate a point, they were always linked with a capsule plot summary beginning with a statement about the heroine and continuing with the principal events of what was, to the speaker, her tale. Because of her perceived centrality in the romance and because of their admitted tendency to project themselves into the heroine's being, the Smithton readers hold particularly exacting expectations about the qualities the heroine should have and the kinds of behavior she should exhibit.

So consistent are their feelings about heroines, in fact, that no discrepancy appears between their orally reported preferences and those acknowledged on the anonymous questionnaires. Dot's customers inevitably responded to my query about the characteristics of a good heroine with the statement that she must have three traits: intelligence, a sense of humor, and independence. On the questionnaire, nineteen (45 percent) of the women selected intelligence from a list of nine other possibilities as the characteristic they *most* liked to see in a heroine, while nine (21 percent) picked a sense of humor. The only other traits to score significantly were femininity and independence. When the group's rankings are totaled, intelligence joins independence and a sense of humor as the three traits that score significantly higher than all of the others. It seems especially important to note that three-fourths of the group selected intelligence (79 percent) and a sense of humor (74 percent) at least once, whereas independence was chosen by almost half (48 percent) of the Smithton women. Femininity, with its connotation of demure deference was, however, still a choice of fourteen of the Smithton readers.

It may seem curious to insist here on the importance of the heroine's intelligence and independence to the Smithton women when so many "objective" students of the genre have commented on her typical passivity and quivering helplessness.[40] This harsh analytical judgment, however, is often founded on an assessment of the heroine's ultimate success in solving a mystery, making her desires known, or in refusing to be cowed by the hero. The *results* of her actions, in short, are always measured on a scale whose highest value is accorded the autonomous woman capable of accomplishing productive work in a nondomestic sphere. While the romantic heroine understandably compares badly with this ideal woman, it is important to note that neither Dot nor her readers find such an ideal attractive nor do they scrutinize and evaluate the heroine's success in effecting change or in getting others to do what she wants in order to assess her character. The heroine's personality is, instead, inevitably and securely established for them at the beginning of the tale through a series of simple observations about her abilities, talents, and career choice. Because the Smithton women accept those assertions at face value, they search no further for incidents that might comment on or revise her early portrayal. Not only do they believe in the heroine's honest desire to take care of herself, but they also believe in the mimetic accuracy of the extenuating circumstances that always intervene to thwart her intended actions. The Smithton women are, in sum, significantly more inclined than their feminist critics to recognize the inevitability and reality of male power and the force of social convention to circumscribe a woman's ability to act in her own interests. It must also be said that they are comfortable with the belief that a woman should be willing to sacrifice extreme self-interest for a long-term relationship where mutually agreed-upon goals take precedence over selfish desire.

The point I want to make here is that when analysis proceeds from within the belief system actually brought to bear upon a text by its readers, the analytical interpretation of the meaning of a character's behavior is more likely to coincide with that meaning as it is constructed and understood by the readers themselves. Thus the account offered to explain the desire to experience this particular fantasy is also more likely to approximate the motives that actually initiate the readers' decisions to pick up a romance. While the romantic heroine may appear foolish, dependent, and even pathetic to a woman who has already accepted as given the equality of male and female abilities, she appears courageous, and even valiant, to another still unsure that such equality is a fact or that she herself might want to assent to it.

The Smithton women seem to be struggling simultaneously with the promise and threat of the women's movement as well as with their culture's now doubled capacity to belittle the intelligence and activities of "the ordinary housewife." Therefore, while they are still very conservative and likely to admit the rightness of traditional relations between men and women, at the same time they are angered by men who continue to make light of "woman's work" as well as by "women's libbers" whom they accuse of dismissing mothers and housewives as ignorant, inactive, and unimportant. Their desire to believe that the romantic heroine is as intelligent and independent as she is asserted to be even though she is also shown to be vulnerable and most interested in being loved is born of their apparently unconscious desire to realize some of the benefits of feminism within traditional institutions and relationships—hence, the high value attached to the simple *assertion* of the heroine's special abilities. With a few simple statements rather than with truly threatening action on the part of the heroine, the romance author demonstrates for the typical reader the compatibility of a changed sense of the female self and an unchanged social arrangement. In the utopia of romance fiction, "independence" and a secure individual "identity" are never compromised by the paternalistic care and protection of the male.

. . . I would like to quote here from a lengthy and exuberant discussion carried on in one of the interviews when I asked Dot, her daughter, Kit, and Ann to describe the "ideal" romantic heroine. Rather than list a series of abstract traits as others generally did, these women launched into a fifteen-minute, communally produced plot summary of Elsie Lee's *The Diplomatic Lover* (1971). The delight with which they described the heroine and what they perceived to be her constant control of her situation is as good an example as any of the desire they share with feminists to believe in the female sex's strength and capabilities and in themselves as well. When I asked them why they liked the book so much after they told me they had xeroxed the text for their own use (the book is now out of print), the extended reply began in the following way:

Dot: It's just classic.

Ann: She *decides* that she wants to lose her virginity and picks *him*.

Kit: Well, he's really nice looking; he's a movie star and he's . . .

Dot: Well, the thing is, actually, because she is in a modern workaday world. She's in Washington, D.C., in the diplomatic corps.

Kit: And *she* makes the decision, you know.

Dot: And she's the only one [in the diplomatic community] who's a virgin and her name is Nanny.

Ann: Yes.

Dot: And they call her Nanny-No-No because she's always saying no, no, no!

Ann: She knows, she's read all the textbooks; but she's just never found anyone that set her blood to boiling.

Dot: And she's known him for years.

Ann: But he walks into the room at this one party and all of a sudden . . .

Kit: *She* makes the decision! It's her birthday.

Ann: She mentally licks her chops.

Kit: She's twenty-three. She decides, "Well, this is it!"

Ann: Yes.

Dot: But you know it's not distasteful. There's nothing . . . it was unusual.

Kit: It was very intimate.

Dot: It's not bold.[41]

In the midst of recounting the rest of the tale, they proudly exclaimed that Nanny "spoke six languages," was "a really good artist," and "did not want to marry him even though she was pregnant" because she believed he was an "elegant tomcat" and would not be faithful to her. These untraditional skills and unconventional attitudes are obviously not seen as fulfilling or quite proper by Lee herself because they are legitimated and rendered acceptable at the novel's conclusion when the hero convinces Nanny of his love, refuses to live without her, and promises to take care of her in the future. Here is the group's recitation of this moment:

Dot: He starts stalking her and this is visually . . .

Kit: It's hysterical.

Dot: You can see it.

Kit: She's backin' off.

Dot: She's trying to get to the stairway to get to her room.

Kit: And make a mad dash.

Ann: She's what they call a "petite pocket Venus type."

Dot: Yes, and he's stalking her and she's backing away and saying, "No, I won't marry you!"

Ann: "I ain't going!"

Kit: "No, just forget that!"

Dot: "No, I don't need you!"

Ann: "And he says I'll camp on your doorstep; I'll picket; unfair to, you know . . ."

As in all romances, female defiance is finally rendered ineffectual and childlike as well as unnecessary by Lee's conclusion. Nonetheless, if we are to understand the full meaning of the story for these women, it is essential to recognize that their temporary reveling in her intelligence, independence, self-sufficiency, and initiative is as important to their experiencing of the book as the fact of her final capture by a man who admits that he needs her. Indeed, after recounting the resolution of this tale, Dot, Kit, and Ann relived again her "seduction of him" by marveling over the moment "when she asks him, and he's drinking and he about chokes to death!"

In novels like *The Diplomatic Lover,* which the Smithton women like best, the happy ending restores the status quo in gender relations when the hero enfolds the heroine protectively in his arms. That ending, however, can also be interpreted as an occasion for the vicarious enjoyment of a woman's ultimate triumph. Dot's readers so interpret it because the heroine, they claim, maintains her integrity on her own terms by exacting a formal commitment from the hero and simultaneously provides for her own future in the only way acceptable to her culture.

The Smithton readers' interest in a strong but still traditional heroine is complemented by their desire to see that woman loved by a very special kind of hero. As noted earlier, these women will read many romances they do not especially like, even when the hero mistreats the heroine, because the experience of the happy ending is more important to them than anything else and because it successfully explains away many individual incidents they do not condone. Nevertheless, they prefer to see the heroine desired, needed, and loved by a man who is strong and masculine, but equally capable of unusual tenderness, gentleness, and concern for her pleasure. In fact, when asked to rank ten male personality traits as to desirability, not one of the Smithton readers listed independence in first, second, or third place. Although this might be explained by suggesting that the women felt no need to single this characteristic out because they assumed that men are, by nature, independent, their interview comments suggest otherwise. Throughout their discussions of particular books, they repeatedly insisted that what they remembered and liked most about favorite novels was the skill with which the author described the hero's recognition of his own deep feelings for the heroine and his realization that he could not live without her. While the women want to feel that the heroine will be protected by the hero, they also seem to want to see her dependency balanced by its opposite, that is, by the hero's dependence on her. In this context, the Smithton women's constant emphasis on the importance of mutuality in love makes enormous sense.

I do not want to suggest here that male protectiveness and strength are not important elements in the romantic fantasy; they are. Remember, sixteen (38 percent) of the women indicated that they think a weak hero is one of the three most objectionable features in a romance. In addition, almost 25 percent of Dot's customers agreed that out of nine traits strength is the third most important in a hero. Still, neither strength nor protectiveness is considered as important as intelligence, gentleness, and an ability to laugh at life, all of which were placed significantly more often by the readers in one of the three top positions on the questionnaire.

TABLE 2.4

Question: *What Qualities Do You Like to See in a Hero?*

Response	Most Important	Second Most Important	Third Most Important	Total
a. Intelligence	14	11	5	30
b. Tenderness	11	8	7	26
c. Protectiveness	3	4	7	14
d. Strength	3	3	9	15
e. Bravery	1	4	2	7
f. Sense of humor	8	5	6	19
g. Independence	0	0	0	0
h. Attractiveness	2	5	3	10
i. A good body	0	2	2	4
j. Other	0	0	0	0
Blank			1	1

However, because Dot and her customers rarely initiated discussion of the romantic hero and just as seldom volunteered opinions about specific male characters, it has been difficult to develop a complex picture of their ideal or of the motivation prompting its formation. Even when their responses are displayed in a graph, certain mysteries persist.

The principal difficulty involves the marked preference for an "intelligent" hero. Although it is hard to say why intelligence was ranked so high by the Smithton women, it is possible that the choice is both consistent with the high value they place on books, learning, and education and their own upward mobility as well as a way of reaffirming male excellence and agentivity without also automatically implying female inferiority. The word did appear in discussions of the ideal hero, but the women offered little that would explain its prominence in their question- naire responses. A few oral comments seemed to hint at the existence of an expec- tation that an "intelligent" man would be more likely to appreciate and encourage the extraordinary abilities of the ideal heroine, but this link was not volunteered consistently enough to warrant its formulation as the motive behind the fantasy. Equally hard to explain is the emphasis on a sense of humor, although I suspect the interest in this trait masks a desire to see a hero who is up to a "verbal duel" with the heroine. Not only does this create the air of "lightness" so important to the Smithton women, but it also helps to show off the heroine's tart-tongued facil- ity to advantage.

This vagueness about the actual content of the hero's personality persisted throughout many commentaries that tended to center instead on his ability to establish the proper relationship with the heroine. The Smithton women are less interested in the particularities of their heroes as individuals than in the roles the most desirable among them perform. Gentleness and tenderness figure often in their accounts of favorite novels not so much as character traits exhibited by par- ticular men but as the distinguishing feature of the attention accorded the heroine by all good heroes in the outstanding novels. The focus never shifts for these read- ers away from the woman at the center of the romance. Moreover, men are rarely valued for their intrinsic characteristics but become remarkable by virtue of the special position they occupy vis-à-vis the heroine. The romantic fantasy is there- fore not a fantasy about discovering a uniquely interesting life partner, but a ritual wish to be cared for, loved, and validated in a particular way.

In distinguishing the ideal romance from Rosemary Rogers's "perversions," one of the five customers I interviewed at length wondered whether her editor had been male because, she reasoned, "it's a man's type book." When pressed to elabo- rate, she retorted, "because a man likes the sex in it, you know, Matt Helm and all that type." The distinction she sees here between sex and romance was continually employed by the Smithton women to differentiate pornography, which they associ- ate with men, from their own interest in "insightful love," which they wish men could manage. As Joy said of the recent Harlequins, "all they worry about is sex— that's the first thing on their minds. They don't worry about anything else." She continued, "they don't need that; they need humor and love and caring." Similarly, in one of our final discussions, Dot also elaborated on the differences between pornography and romance and between men and women and, in doing so, identi- fied in a wistful tone the particular characteristic she and her customers believe all men should possess:

> I've always thought that women are more insightful into men's psyches than men are into women's. Well, men just don't take the time. They just don't. And it's always been interesting to me that psychiatrists are probably . . . 85 to 90 percent of the psychiatrists in this country are men and I'm sure they know the book. I'm sure they know the textbook. But as far as insightful, I think that is one of the most

rare commodities that there is . . . is an insightful man. . . . I don't think men look deep. I think they take even a man at face value. Whatever they see—that's what the man is.

What the Smithton women are looking for in their search for the perfect romantic fantasy is a man who is capable of the same attentive observation and intuitive "understanding" that they believe women regularly accord to men. . . . [T]he fantasy generating the ideal romantic story thus fulfills two deeply felt needs that have been activated in women by early object-relations and cultural conditioning in patriarchal society. On the one hand, the story permits the reader to identify with the heroine at the moment of her greatest success, that is, when she secures the attention and recognition of her culture's most powerful and essential representative, a man. The happy ending is, at this level, a sign of a woman's attainment of legitimacy and personhood in a culture that locates both for her in the roles of lover, wife, and mother.

On the other hand, by emphasizing the intensity of the hero's uninterrupted gaze and the tenderness of his caress at the moment he encompasses his beloved in his still always "masculine" arms, the fantasy also evokes the memory of a period in the reader's life when she was the center of a profoundly nurturant individual's attention. Because this imaginative emotional regression is often denied women in ordinary existence because men have been prompted by the culture's asymmetrical conditioning to deny their own capacities for gentle nurturance, it becomes necessary to fulfill this never-ending need in other areas. Nancy Chodorow has suggested, in *The Reproduction of Mothering,* that one way for women to provide this essential sustenance for themselves is through the mothering of others. By taking care of a child in this intense emotional way and by identifying with her child, Chodorow reasons, a woman is able to nurture herself, albeit vicariously. However, Chodorow does not comment at any length about whether this vicarious care and attention prove a perfectly adequate substitute. The ideal romance, at least as it is conceived by the Smithton women, argues effectively that it is not. Its stress on the emotional bonding between hero and heroine suggests that women still desire to be loved, cared for, and understood by an adult who is singularly capable of self-abnegating preoccupation with a loved one's needs. . . .

NOTES

1. In the course of completing this study of the Smithton readers, I have learned of at least five other such groups functioning throughout the country. Most seem to be informal networks of neighbors or co-workers who exchange romances and information about these books on a regular basis. I have also been told of a group similar to Dot's clustered about a Texas bookseller and have received information about the California-based "Friends of the English Regency," which also publishes a review newsletter and holds an annual Regency "Assemblee" at which it confers the "Georgette" award on favorite Regency romances. There is no way to tell how common this "reading club" phenomenon is, but it is worth investigation. If these clubs are widely relied upon to mediate the mass-production publishing process by individualizing selection, then a good deal of speculation about the meaning of mass-produced literature based on the "mass man" [sic] hypothesis will have to be reviewed and possibly rewritten.

2. These and all other figures about Smithton were taken from the *Census of the Population, 1970.* I have rounded off the numbers slightly to disguise the identity of Smithton.

3. Dorothy Evans, "Dorothy's Diary of Romance Reading" (mimeographed newsletter), April 1980, pp. 1–2.

4. Ibid., p. 2.
5. All spoken quotations have been taken directly from taped interviews. Nearly all of the comments were transcribed verbatim, although in a few cases repeated false starts were excised and marked with ellipses. Pauses in a speaker's commentary have been marked with dashes. I have paragraphed lengthy speeches only when the informant clearly seemed to conclude one topic or train of thought in order to open another deliberately. Lack of paragraphing, then, indicates that the speaker's comments continued apace without significant rest or pause.
6. Ann Bar Snitow, "Mass Market Romance: Pornography for Women Is Different," *Radical History Review* 20 (1979): 150.
7. Barbara Brotman, "Ah Romance! Harlequin Has an Affair for Its Readers," *Chicago Tribune* 2 June 1980, p. B1.
8. Margaret Jensen, "Women and Romantic Fiction: A Case Study of Harlequin Enterprises, Romances, and Readers," Ph. D. dissertation, McMaster University, 1980, p. 289.
9. Quoted in Brotman, "Ah, Romance!," p. B1.
10. See also Peter H. Mann, *A New Survey: The Facts about Romantic Fiction* (London: Mills and Boon, 1974), passim.
11. Readers were instructed to identify the particular kind of romance they liked to "read the most" from a list of ten subgenres. The titles had been given to me by Dot during a lengthy discussion about the different kinds of romances. Although I expected the women to check only one subgenre, almost all of them checked several as their favorites. The categories and totals follow: gothics, 6; contemporary mystery romances, 5; historicals, 20; contemporary romances, 7; Harlequins, 10; Regencies, 4; family sagas, 1; plantation series, 3; spy thrillers, 0; transcendental romances, 0; other, 2.
12. It should be pointed out, however, that these findings could also indicate that romances were not heavily advertised or distributed when the majority of women in this sample were teenagers. Thus, the fact that so many have picked up the romance habit may be as much a function of the recent growth of the industry as of any particular need or predisposition on the part of women at a particular stage in their life cycle. Still, . . . romances do address needs associated with the role of mothering for *this* particular group of readers.
13. Jensen, "Women and Romantic Fiction," pp. 290–91.
14. Jensen also reports that all of the married women in her sample have children and that three-quarters have children still living at home (ibid., p. 291).
15. Cited in Yankelovich, Skelly and White, *The 1978 Consumer Research Study on Reading and Book Purchasing,* prepared for the Book Industry Study Group (Darien, Conn.: The Group, 1978), p. 325.
16. This compares with the eight-hour weekly average claimed by book readers who read fiction for leisure as reported in Yankelovich, Skelly and White, ibid., p. 126.
17. Although the Smithton women also commented, as did Jensen's informants, on the ease with which "light reading" like Harlequins and Silhouettes can be picked up and put down when other demands intervene, all of Dot's customers with whom I spoke expressed a preference for finishing a romance in one sitting. Jensen does not say whether her readers would have preferred to read in this way, although she does comment rather extensively on the fact that it is the material circumstances of their jobs as housewives and mothers that most often necessitate what she calls "snatch" reading. She refers to an alternate pattern of reading several books, one after the other, as the "binge." This is not exactly equivalent to the Smithton readers' practice with fat books, but some of them did mention engaging in such behavior as a special treat to themselves. See Jensen, "Women and Romantic Fiction," pp. 300–301 and 312–14.
18. Yankelovich, Skelly and White, *The 1978 Consumer Research Study on Reading,* pp. 141, 144.
19. Mann, *A New Survey,* p. 17.
20. Evans, "Dorothy's Diary," April 1980, p. 1.
21. I included this choice on the final questionnaire because in many of the interviews the

women had expressed a distaste for romances that end abruptly with the declaration of love between the principal characters.

22. Beatrice Faust, *Women, Sex, and Pornography: A Controversial and Unique Study* (New York: Macmillan, 1980), p. 67.

23. Richard Hoggart is one of the few who disagrees with this argument. See his comments in *The Uses of Literacy: Changing Patterns in English Mass Culture* (Fair Lawn, N.J.: Essential Books, 1957), pp. 171–75. Jensen has also acknowledged that many Harlequin authors "apparently share the backgrounds, attitudes, and fantasies of their women readers" ("Women and Romantic Fiction," pp. 118–19).

24. Quoted in Evans, "Dorothy's Diary," May 1980, p. 2.

25. Quoted in Evans, "Dorothy's Diary," Newsletter #4, 1980, p. 2. (This issue is not dated by month.)

26. Phyllis Berman, "They Call Us Illegitimate," *Forbes* 6 (March 1978): 38.

27. Phyllis Whitney, "Writing the Gothic Novel," *Writer* 80 (February 1967): 10.

28. Ibid.

29. Ibid., p. 11.

30. Faust, *Women, Sex, and Pornography,* p. 63.

31. Whitney, "Writing the Gothic Novel," p. 43.

32. Quoted in Jeanne Glass, "Editor's Report," *Writer* 90 (April 1977): 33.

33. Ann Douglas, "Soft-Porn Culture," *New Republic* 30 August 1980, p. 28 (italics added).

34. Clifford Geertz, "Deep Play: Notes on the Balinese Cockfight," in *The Interpretation of Cultures,* p. 443 (New York: Basic Books, 1973).

35. Douglas, "Soft-Porn Culture," p. 25.

36. On the connection between patriarchy and marriage, see Heidi I. Hartmann, "The Family as Locus of Class, Gender, and Political Struggle: The Example of Housework," *Signs* 6 (1981): 366–76.

37. None of the Smithton women commented on whether they had ever been hit, pushed around, or forced to have sexual relations against their will, although several did tell me that they know this goes on because it happens to their friends. In summarizing current studies on wife abuse, Joanna Bunker Rohrbaugh has commented in *Women: Psychology's Puzzle* (New York: Basic Books, 1979) that "many researchers in this field agree with Judge Stewart Oneglia's estimate that '50 percent of all marriages involve some degree of physical abuse of the woman'" (p. 350). Rohrbaugh also points out that "studies that define wife abuse as anything from an occasional hard slap to repeated, severe beatings suggest that there are 26 million to 30 million abused wives in the United States today" (p. 350). If these figures are accurate, it seems clear that a good many romance readers may very well need to be given a model "explanation" for this sort of behavior.

38. I would like to thank Star Helmer for giving me a copy of Gallen Books' "tipsheet" for contemporary romances.

39. The italics have been added here to indicate where Ann placed special emphasis and changed her intonation during her remarks. In each case, the emphasis conveyed both sarcasm and utter disbelief. Two of the most difficult tasks in using ethnographic material are those of interpreting meanings clearly implied by a speaker but not actually said and adequately conveying them in written prose.

40. See, especially, Tania Modleski, "The Disappearing Act: A Study of Harlequin Romances," *Signs* 5 (1980): 444–48.

41. Again, the italics have been added here to indicate where special emphasis was conveyed through intonation. In each case, the emphasis was meant to underscore the distance between this heroine's behavior and that usually expected of women.

J O H N   F I S K E

MADONNA

Madonna, who has been a major phenomenon of popular culture throughout the
late 1980s, is a rich terrain to explore. Her success has been due at least as much
to her videos and her personality as to her music—about which most critics are
disparaging. It is also significant that her fans and her publicity materials, along
with journalistic reports and critiques, pay far more attention to what she looks
like, who she is, and what she stands for than to what she sounds like.

In this chapter, then, I concentrate on Madonna's appearance, her personality,
and the words and images of her songs, for these are the main carriers of her most
accessible meanings. This is not to say that her music is unimportant, for it is the
music that underpins everything else and that provides the emotional intensity or
affect without which none of the rest would *matter* to her fans. But it does point to
the fact that the pleasures of music are remarkably resistant to analysis, and are
equally difficult to express in the words and images that are so important in the circulation of culture.

Before her image became known, Madonna was not a success: at the start, at
least, her music was not enough on its own to turn her into a major resource of
popular culture. In the autumn of 1984 she was signed to Sire Records, which is
"where Warner Brothers put people they don't think will sell" (*Countdown
Magazine Special Annual* 1985: 2). She got some dance club play for "Borderline"
and "Holiday," but the *Madonna* LP was selling only slowly. *Like a Virgin,* her second LP, had been made but not released. Warner Brothers then gave Arthur
Pierson a tiny budget to make a rock video of "Lucky Star." He shot it in an after-
noon against a white studio backdrop, and the resulting video pushed the song into
the top ten. The *Madonna* album's sales followed suit, and *Like a Virgin* was
released for the Christmas market. Both LPs held the number one position for a
number of weeks. The film *Desperately Seeking Susan* was released in March 1985,
which added an adult audience to the teenage (largely female) one for the songs
and videos. The film worked to support the videos in establishing the "Madonna
look," a phrase that the media repeated endlessly in 1985 and one that Madonna
capitalized on by establishing her Boy Toy label to sell crucifix earrings, fingerless
lace gloves, short, navel-exposing blouses, black lacey garments, and all the visual
symbols she had made her own.

A concert tour started in April (in the foyers, of course, items of the Madonna look were for sale) and an old film, A *Certain Sacrifice,* that never made cinema release was dug up for the home video market. Also dug up and published in *Playboy* and *Penthouse* were old art school nude photos, and at the end of 1985, her wedding to Sean Penn became a world wide multimedia event, despite its "secret" location. In other words, she was a fine example of the capitalist pop industry at work, creating a (possibly short-lived) fashion, exploiting it to the full, and making a lot of money from one of the most powerless and exploitable sections of the community, young girls.

But such an account is inadequate (though not necessarily inaccurate as far as it goes) because it assumes that the Madonna fans are merely "cultural dopes," able to be manipulated at will and against their own interests by the moguls of the culture industry. Such a manipulation would be not only economic, but also ideological, because the economic system requires the ideology of patriarchal capitalism to underpin and naturalize it. Economics and ideology can never be separated.

And there is no shortage of evidence to support this view. Madonna's videos exploit the sexuality of her face and body and frequently show her in postures of submission (e.g., "Burning Up") or subordination to men. Her physical similarity to Marilyn Monroe is stressed (particularly in the video of "Material Girl"), an intertextual reference to another star commonly thought to owe her success to her ability to embody masculine fantasy. In the *Countdown* 1985 poll of the top 20 "Sex/Lust Objects" Madonna took third place and was the only female among 19 males (*Countdown,* December 1985: 35). All this would suggest that she is teaching her young female fans to see themselves as men would see them; that is, she is hailing them as feminine subjects within patriarchy, and as such is an agent of patriarchal hegemony.

But, if her fans are not "cultural dopes," but actively choose to watch, listen to, and imitate her rather than anyone else, there must be some gaps or spaces in her image that escape ideological control and allow her audiences to make meanings that connect with *their* social experience. For many of her audiences, this social experience is one of powerlessness and subordination, and if Madonna as a site of meaning is not to naturalize this, she must offer opportunities for resisting it. Her image becomes, then, not a model meaning for young girls in patriarchy, but a site of semiotic struggle between the forces of patriarchal control and feminine resistance, of capitalism and the subordinate, of the adult and the young.

The field of cultural studies, in its current state of development, offers two overlapping methodological strategies that need to be combined and the differences between them submerged if we are to understand this cultural struggle. One derives from ethnography, and requires us to study the meanings that the fans of Madonna actually *do* (or appear to) make of her. This involves listening to them, reading the letters they write to fanzines, or observing their behavior at home or in public. The fans' words or behavior are not, of course, empirical facts that speak for themselves; rather, they are texts that need "reading" theoretically in just the same way as the "texts of Madonna" do.

This brings us to the other strategy, which derives from semiotic and structuralist textual analysis. This involves a close reading of the signifiers of the text—that is, its physical presence—but recognizes that the signifieds exist not in the text itself, but extratextually, in the myths, countermyths, and ideology of their culture. It recognizes that the distribution of power in society is paralleled by the distribution of meanings in texts, and that struggles for social power are paralleled by semiotic struggles for meanings. Every text and every reading has a social and therefore political dimension, which is to be found partly in the structure of the text itself and partly in the social relations of the reader and the way they are brought to bear upon the text.

It follows that the theory that informs any analysis also has a social dimension that is a necessary part of the "meanings" the analysis reveals. Meanings, therefore, are relative and varied: what is constant is the *ways* in which texts relate to the social system. A cultural analysis, then, will reveal both the way the dominant ideology is structured into the text and into the reading subject, and those textual features that enable negotiated, resisting, or oppositional readings to be made. Cultural analysis reaches a satisfactory conclusion when the ethnographic studies of the historically and socially located meanings that *are* made are related to the semiotic analysis of the text. Semiotics relates the structure of the text to the social system to explore *how* such meanings are made and the part they play within the cultural process that relates meanings both to social experience and to the social system in general.

So Lucy, a 14-year-old fan, says of a Madonna poster:

> She's tarty and seductive . . . but it looks alright when she does it, you know, what I mean, if anyone else did it it would look right tarty, a right tart you know, but with her its OK, it's acceptable. . . . with anyone else it would be absolutely outrageous, it sounds silly, but it's OK with her, you know what I mean. (November 1985)

We can note a number of points here. Lucy can only find patriarchal words to describe Madonna's sexuality—"tarty" and "seductive"—but she struggles against the patriarchy inscribed in them. At the same time, she struggles against the patriarchy inscribed in her own subjectivity. The opposition between "acceptable" and "absolutely outrageous" not only refers to representations of female sexuality, but is an externalization of the tension felt by adolescent girls when trying to come to terms with the contradictions between a positive feminine view of their sexuality and the alien patriarchal one that appears to be the only one offered by the available linguistic and symbolic systems. Madonna's "tarty" sexuality is "acceptable"—but to whom? Certainly to Lucy, and to girls like her who are experiencing the problems of establishing a satisfactory sexual identity within an oppressing ideology, but we need further evidence to support this tentative conclusion. Matthew, aged 15, not a particular fan of Madonna, commented on her marriage in the same discussion. He thought it would last only one or two years, and he wouldn't like to be married to her "because she'd give any guy a hard time." Lucy agreed that Madonna's marriage would not last long, but found it difficult to say why, except that "marriage didn't seem to suit her," even though Lucy quoted approvingly Madonna's desire to make it an "open marriage." Lucy's problems probably stem from her recognition that marriage is a patriarchial institution and as such is threatened by Madonna's sexuality; the threat of course is not the traditional and easily contained one of woman as whore, but the more radical one of woman as independent of masculinity. As we shall see later, Madonna denies or mocks a masculine reading of patriarchy's conventions for representing women. This may well be why, according to *Time* (May 27, 1985), many boys find her sexiness difficult to handle and "suspect that they are being kidded" (p. 47). Lucy and Matthew both recognize, in different ways and from different social positions, that Madonna's sexuality *can* offer a challenge or a threat to dominant definitions of femininity and masculinity.

"Madonna's Best Friend," writing to *Countdown Magazine,* also recognizes Madonna's resistance to patriarchy:

> I'm writing to complain about all the people who write in and say what a tart and a slut Madonna is because she talks openly about sex and she shows her belly button and she's not ashamed to say she thinks she's pretty. Well I admire her and I think she has a lot of courage just to be herself. All you girls out there! Do you think you have nice eyes or pretty hair or a nice figure? Do you ever talk about boys or sex with friends? Do you wear a bikini? Well according to you, you're a slut and a tart!! So have you judged Madonna fairly?
> Madonna's Best Friend, Wahroonga, NSW. (*Countdown* December 1985: 70)

Praising Madonna's "courage just to be herself" is further evidence of the felt difficulty of girls in finding a sexual identity that appears to be formed in their interests rather than in the interests of the dominant male. Madonna's sexualization of her navel is a case in point:

> The most erogenous part of my body is my belly button. I have the most perfect belly button—an inny, and there's no fluff in it. When I stick a finger in my belly button I feel a nerve in the centre of my body shoot up my spine. If 100 belly buttons were lined up against a wall I would definitely pick out which one was mine.
> (*Madonna: Close up and Personal,* London: Rock Photo Publications, 1985)

What is noticeable here is both her pleasure in her own physicality and the fun she finds in admitting and expressing this pleasure: it is a sexual-physical pleasure that has nothing to do with men, and in choosing the navel upon which to center it, she is choosing a part of the female body that patriarchy has not conventionally sexualized for the benefit of the male. She also usurps the masculine pleasure and power of the voyeur in her claim to be able to recognize her navel, in all its proudly proclaimed perfection, among a hundred others. Madonna offers some young girls the opportunity to find meanings of their own feminine sexuality that suit them, meanings that are "independent." Here are some other Madonna fans talking:

> She's sexy but she doesn't need men . . . she's kind of there all by herself. (*Time* May 27, 1985: 47)
> She gives us ideas. It's really women's lib, not being afraid of what guys think. (*Time* May 27, 1985: 47)

The sense of empowerment that underlies these comments is characteristic of her teenage fans. A group of "wanna-bes," fans dressed in their own variants of Madonna's look, were interviewed on MTV in November 1987 during Madonna's "Make My Video" competition. When asked why they dressed like that, they replied, "It makes people look at us" or "When I walk down the street, people notice." Teenage girls, in public, are, in our culture, one of the most insignificant and self-effacing categories of people; the self-assertiveness evidenced here is more than mere posturing, it is, potentially at least, a source of real self-esteem. The common belief that Madonna's "wanna-bes" lack the imagination to devise their own styles of dress and merely follow her like sheep ignores the point that in adopting her style they are aligning themselves with a source of power.

The "Make My Video" competition showed how frequently the pleasures offered by Madonna to her fans were associated with moments of empowerment. In the competition fans were invited to make a video for the song "True Blue," and MTV devoted 24 hours to playing a selection of the entries. Many of the videos played with the theme of power, often at an unachievable, but not unimaginable, level of fantasy, such as one in which schoolgirls overpowered and tied up a teacher who denigrated Madonna; only by admitting her brilliance was he able to earn his freedom. Another took power fantasy to its extreme: it began with home-movie-type shots of two toddlers playing on a beach; the girl is suddenly wrapped up in a towel in the form of the U.S. flag, while the boy is wrapped in one in the form of the hammer and sickle. The video shows the American girl and Russian boy growing up in their respective countries, all the while telephoning and writing constantly to each other. Eventually she becomes president of the United States and he of the USSR, and they prevent an imminent nuclear war by their love for each other.

Another, less extreme, video made much closer connections between the empowered fan and her everyday life. The heroine sees her boyfriend off at a train station, then turns and joyfully hugs her female friend waiting outside. They dance-walk down the street and shop for clothes in a street market. At home, the friend dresses up in various Madonna-influenced outfits while the heroine looks on and applauds. Each outfit calls up a different type of boy to the door—all of whom are rejected, to the delight of the two girls. The heroine's boyfriend returns, and the final shot is of the three of them, arms interlinked, dancing down the street—then the camera pulls back to reveal one of the rejected boys on the friend's other arm, then continues pulling back to reveal in sequence each of the rejected boys hanging on her arm in a long line. The video shows girls using their "look" to control their relationships, and validating girl-girl relationships as powerfully, if not more so, as girl-boy ones.

In this video, as with the live "wanna-bes" interviewed in the same program, control over the look is not just a superficial playing with appearances, it is a means of constructing and controlling social relations and thus social identity. The sense of empowerment that Madonna offers is inextricably connected with the pleasure of exerting some control over the meanings of self, of sexuality, and of one's social relations.

But, like all pop stars, she has her "haters" as well as her fans:

> When I sit down on a Saturday and Sunday night I always hear the word Madonna and it makes me sick, all she's worried about is her bloody looks. She must spend hours putting on that stuff and why does she always show her belly button? We all know she's got one. My whole family thinks she's pathetic and that she loves herself. Paul Young's sexy sneakers. (*Countdown Annual* 1985: 109)

Here again, the "hate" centers on Madonna's sexuality, expressed as her presenting herself in whorelike terms, painting and displaying herself to arouse the baser side of man. But the sting comes in the last sentence, when the writer recognizes Madonna's apparent enjoyment of her own sexuality, which he (the letter is clearly from a masculine subject, if not a biological male) ascribes to egocentricity, and thus condemns.

Madonna's love of herself, however, is not seen as selfish and egocentric by girls; rather, it is the root of her appeal, the significance of which becomes clear when set in the context of much of the rest of the media addressed to them. McRobbie (1982) has shown how the "teenage press" typically constructs the girl's body and therefore her sexuality as a series of problems—breasts the wrong size or shape, spotty skin, lifeless hair, fatty thighs, problem periods—the list is endless. The advertisers, of course, who are the ones who benefit economically from these magazines, always have a product that can, at a price, solve the problem.

This polarization of Madonna's audience can be seen in the 1986 *Countdown* polls. She was top female vocalist by a mile (polling four times as many votes as the second-place singer) and was the only female in the top 20 "Sex/Lust Objects," in which she came third. But she was also voted into second place for the Turkey of the Year award. She's much loved or much hated, a not untypical position for a woman to occupy in patriarchy, whose inability to understand women in feminine terms is evidenced by the way it polarizes femininity into the opposing concepts of virgin-angel and whore-devil.

Madonna consciously and parodically exploits these contradictions:

> "When I was tiny," she recalls, "my grandmother used to beg me not to go with men, to love Jesus and be a good girl. I grew up with two images of women: the virgin and the whore. It was a little scary." (*National Times* August 23/29, 1985: 9)

She consistently refers to these contradictory meanings of woman in patriarchy: her video of "Like a Virgin" alternates the white dress of Madonna the bride with the black, slinky garb of Madonna the singer; the name Madonna (the virgin mother) is borne by a sexually active female; the crucifixes adopted from nuns' habits are worn on a barely concealed bosom or in a sexually gyrating navel. "Growing up I thought nuns were very beautiful. . . . They never wore any makeup and they just had these really serene faces. Nuns are sexy" (Madonna, quoted in the *National Times* August 23/29, 1985: 9).

But the effect of working these opposite meanings into her texts is not just to call attention to their role in male hegemony—a woman may either be worshipped and adored by a man or used and despised by him, but she has meaning only from a masculine-subject position. Rather, Madonna calls into question the validity of these binary oppositions as a way of conceptualizing woman. Her use of religious iconography is neither religious nor sacrilegious. She intends to free it from this ideological opposition and to enjoy it, use it, for the meanings and pleasure that it has for *her*, not for those of the dominant ideology and its simplistic binary thinking:

> I have always carried around a few rosaries with me. One day I decided to wear (one) as a necklace. Everything I do is sort of tongue in cheek. It's a strange blend —a beautiful sort of symbolism, the idea of someone suffering, which is what Jesus Christ on a crucifix stands for, and then not taking it seriously. Seeing it as an icon with no religiousness attached. It isn't sacrilegious for me. (*National Times* August 23/29, 1985: 10)

The crucifix is neither religious, nor sacrilegious, but beautiful: "When I went to Catholic schools I thought the huge crucifixes nuns wore were really beautiful."

In the same way, her adolescent girl fans find in Madonna meanings of femininity that have broken free from the ideological binary opposition of virgin: whore. They find in her image positive feminine-centered representations of sexuality that are expressed in their constant references to her independence, her being herself. This apparently independent, self-defining sexuality is as significant as it is only because it is working within and against a patriarchal ideology. And the patriarchal meanings must be there for the resisting meanings to work against. *Playboy* (September 1985), on behalf of its readers, picks up only her patriarchal and not her resistant sexuality:

> Best of all her onstage contortions and Boy Toy voice have put sopping sex where it belongs—front and center in the limelight (p. 122)

But even as it recognizes Madonna's patriarchal sexuality, *Playboy* has to recognize her parodic undermining of it, the control she exerts over the way she uses the dominant ideology but is not subjected to it:

> The voice and the body are her bona fides, but Madonna's secret may be her satirical bite. She knows a lot of this image stuff is bullshit: she knows that *you* know. So long as we're all in on the act together, let's enjoy it. (p. 127)

Some of the parody is subtle and hard to tie down for textual analysis, but some, such as the references to Marilyn Monroe and the musicals she often starred in, is more obvious. The subtler parody lies in the knowing way in which Madonna uses the camera, mocking the conventional representations of female sexuality while at the same time conforming to them. Even one of her ex-lovers supports this: "Her image is that of a tart, but I believe it's all contrived. She only pretends to be a gold digger. Remember, I have seen the other side of Madonna" (Prof. Chris Flynn, quoted in *New Idea*, January 11, 1986: 4).

Madonna knows she is putting on a performance, and the fact that this knowingness is part of the performance enables the viewer to answer a different interpellation from that proposed by the dominant ideology, and thus occupy a resisting subject position. The sensitive man watching her "Material Girl" performance knows, as she does, as we might, that this is only a performance. Those who take the performance at face value, who miss its self-parody, either are hailed as ideological subjects in patriarchy or else they reject the hailing, deny the pleasure, and refuse the communication:

> *The National Enquirer,* a weekly magazine devoted to prurient gossip, quotes two academic psychiatrists denouncing her for advocating teenage promiscuity, promoting a lust for money and materialism, and contributing to the deterioration of the family. Feminists accuse her of revisionism, of resurrecting the manipulative female who survives by coquetry and artifice. "Tell Gloria (Steinem) and the gang," she retorts, "to lighten up, get a sense of humour. And look at my video that goes with Material Girl. The guy who gets me in the end is the sensitive one with no money." (*National Times* August 23/29, 1985: 10)

Madonna consistently parodies conventional representations of women, and parody can be an effective device for interrogating the dominant ideology. It takes the defining features of its object, exaggerates and mocks them, and thus mocks those who "fall" for its ideological effect. But Madonna's parody goes further than this: she parodies not just the stereotypes, but the way in which they are made. She represents herself as one who is in control of her own image and of the process of making it. This, at the reading end of the semiotic process, allows the reader similar control over her own meanings.

Madonna's excesses of jewelry, of makeup, of trash in her style offer similar scope to the reader. Excessiveness invites the reader to question ideology: too much lipstick interrogates the tastefully made-up mouth, too much jewelry questions the role of female decorations in patriarchy. Excess overspills ideological control and offers scope for resistance. Thus Madonna's excessively sexual pouting and lipstick can be read to mean that she looks like that not because patriarchy determines that she should, but because she knowingly chooses to. She wears religious icons (and uses a religious name) not to support or attack Christianity's role in patriarchy (and capitalism) but because she chooses to see them as beautiful, sexy ornaments. She makes her own meanings out of the symbolic systems available to her, and in using their signifiers and rejecting or mocking their signifieds, she is demonstrating her ability to make her own meanings.

The video of "In the Groove" demonstrates this clearly. The song is the theme song of the film *Desperately Seeking Susan,* and the video is a montage of shots from the film. The film is primarily about women's struggle to create and control their own identity in contemporary society, and in so doing to shape the sort of relationships they have with men. The viewers of the video who have seen the film will find plenty of references that can activate these meanings, but the video can also be read as promoting the Madonna look, her style. She takes items of urban living, prises them free from their original social and therefore signifying context, and combines them in new ways and in a new context that denies their original meaning. Thus the crucifix is torn from its religious context and lacy gloves from their context of bourgeois respectability, or, conversely, of the brothel; the bleached blonde hair with the dark roots deliberately displayed is no longer the sign of the tarty slut, and the garter belt and stockings no longer signify soft porn or male kinkiness.

This wrenching of the products of capitalism from their original context and recycling them into a new style is, as Chambers (1986) has pointed out, a practice typical of urban popular culture:

> Caught up in the communication membrane of the metropolis, with your head in front of a cinema, TV, video or computer screen, between the headphones, by the radio, among the record releases and magazines, the realization of your "self" slips into the construction of an image, a style, a series of theatrical gestures.
>
> Between what is available in the shops, in the market, and the imprint of our desires, it is possible to produce the distinctive and the personalized. Sometimes the result will stand out, disturb and shock the more predictable logic of the everyday. . . .
>
> The individual *constructs* her or himself as the object of street art, as a public icon: the body becomes the canvas of changing urban signs. (p. 11)

In this street-produced bricolage of style, the commodities of the capitalist industries are purified into signifiers: their ideological signifieds are dumped and left behind in their original context. These freed signifiers do not necessarily mean *something,* they do not acquire new signifieds; rather, the act of freeing them from their ideological context signifies their users' freedom from that context. It signifies the power (however hard the struggle to attain it) of the subordinate to exert some control in the cultural process of making meanings.

The women in *Desperately Seeking Susan* who are struggling to control their social identity and relationships are participating in the same process as subcultures are when they recycle the products of the bourgeoisie to create a style that is theirs, a style that rejects meaning and in this rejection asserts the power of the subordinate to free themselves from the ideology that the meaning bears.

Madonna's videos constantly refer to the production of the image; they make her control over its production part of the image itself. This emphasis on the making of the image allows, or even invites, an equivalent control by the reader over its reception. It enables girls to see that the meanings of feminine sexuality *can be* in their control, *can* be made in their interests, and that their subjectivities are not necessarily totally determined by the dominant partriarchy.

The constant puns in Madonna's lyrics also invite this creative, producerly relation to the text. Puns arise when one word occurs in two or more discourses, and while the immediate context may give one priority, traces of the other(s) are always present. The pun never makes a final, completed sense of the relationship between these various discourses—it leaves them at the stage of collision and invites the reader first to recognize the pun and second to produce her or his sense out of this meeting of discourse. Within a pun, the play of contradictions and similarities is remarkably free and open. "Like a Virgin" opens with the following lyrics:

> I made it through the wilderness
> Somehow I made it through
> Didn't know how lost I was
> Until I found you
> I was beat
> Incomplete
> I'd been had, I was sad and blue
> But you made me feel
> Yeah you made me feel
> Shiny and new
> Like a virgin
>
> Touched for the very first time
> Like a virgin
> When your heart beats next to mine
> Gonna give you all my love boy
> My fear is fading fast
> Been saving it all for you
> 'Cause only love can last.

In *Understanding Popular Culture*, Chapter 5, I note how the semiotic excess of puns makes them particularly common in popular culture. Madonna's lyrics are no exception. Woven through these lines are puns playing with at least four discourses —religion, particularly religious love, sexuality or physical love, romantic love, and a discourse of street-wisdom, of urban survival. Thus, *made it* has the street-wise meaning of survived or came out on top, but also the sexual meaning of sexual conquest and, in its association with *wilderness,* echoes of Christ's survival and resistance of temptation. It is absent from the discourse of romantic love. *Wilderness,* too, is, in the religious discourse, the wilderness of the New Testament, but it is also the wilderness of contemporary urban life without true romantic love, the secular equivalent of religious love. So we could continue. *Lost* is sexually "lost," a loose woman whose experience is only of sex, not of romance; it is also lost in the streets, and has echoes of Christ or the Israelites lost in the wilderness. *I've been had* similarly has a street-wise and a sexual meaning. So by the time we get to *virgin,* the word has become a semiotic supermarket—the religious virgin, the sexual virgin (which the singer clearly is *not*), the emotional romantic virgin, (which, like the religious virgin, she *is*), and the naive virgin who has "been had" and "lost" in the streets. *Touched* also has religious meanings of "laying on of hands" or "blessing," physical ones of sexuality, emotional ones of true love, and street-wise ones of near madness or loss of control.

The relationship between these discourses is open, unresolved and requires active, productive readers. The similarities and differences among religious love, romantic love, sexual experience, and street-wisdom are left reverberating and active, not closed off. There is no final meaning that says, for instance, that religious love contradicts sexuality but supports romantic love and invalidates street-wisdom. One cannot simply conclude that street wisdom and physical sexuality are rejected, and romantic and religious love affirmed. Romantic love may be placed in a negative relationship to sexuality and urban survival, or it may be a development out of them, a growth for which they provide the soil. Puns do not preach: they raise issues, questions, and contradictions, and invite the imaginative participation (and therefore pleasure) of the reader in their resolution.

The form of the pun always resists final ideological closure: the potential meanings provoked by the collision of different discourses is always greater than that proposed by the dominant ideology. Thus, "Boy Toy," the name Madonna has given to her range of products and the media apply to her, can be read as *Playboy* (September 1985) does when it calls her the "world's number one Boy Toy" (p. 122) or "The compleat Boy Toy" (p. 127). In this reading Madonna is a toy for boys, but the pun can also mean the opposite, that the boy is the toy for her, as she toys with the men in "Material Girl." This is the reading that Madonna herself prefers when she says:

> I like young boys—15 or 16 year olds are the best. I like them smooth and thin. I want to caress a nice smooth body not a hulk. [()*Madonna: Close up and Personal,* London: Rock Photo Publications, 1985)

The video of "Burning Up" is built around puns, parodic excess, and contradictions. The narrative shows Madonna in a white dress lying writhing on a road, as she sings of her helpless passion for her uncaring lover who is driving toward her in a car, presumably to run over her. Her love for the boy makes her as (apparently) helpless a victim as the stereotyped female tied to the railroad track in many a silent movie. But the last shot of the video shows her in the driver's seat of the car, a knowing, defiant half smile on her lips, with the boy nowhere to be seen. This narrative denial of female helplessness runs throughout the performance as a countertext to the words of the lyric.

So when she sings, "Do you want to see me down on my knees? I'm bending over backward, now would you be pleased," she kneels on the road in front of the advancing car, then turns to throw her head back, exposing her throat in the ultimate posture of submission. But her tone of voice and her look at the camera as she sings have a hardness and a defiance about them that contradict the submissiveness of her body posture and turn the question into a challenge, if not a threat, to the male.

The puns in "Burning Up" are more subdued and less balanced than those in "Like a Virgin," though they also play with the two discourses of the sexual and the religious. The sexual may be given a greater emphasis in the text, but the discourse of religion is not far below the surface as Madonna sings of kneeling and burning, of her lack of shame and the something in her heart that just won't die. This yoking of sexuality and religion appears to be performing the traditional ideological work of using the subordination and powerlessness of women in Christianity to naturalize their equally submissive position in patriarchy, but, as in "Material Girl," the text provides the reader with ample opportunities to undermine the dominant ideology while wryly recognizing its presence in the representation, for again the representation of women's sexuality includes the means of that representation and therefore questions its ideological effectivity. The introductory sequence exhibits this clearly. In the 33 seconds before Madonna is shown singing, there are 21 shots:

(1)   female eye, opening
(2)   white flowers, one lights up
(3)   female mouth, made up (probably Madonna's)
(4)   blue car, lights go on
(5)   Madonna in white, lying on road
(6)   male Grecian statue with blank eyes
(7)   goldfish in bowl
(8)   close-up of male statue, eyes light up
(9)   midshot of statue, eyes still lit up
(10) extreme close-up of eye of statue, still lit up
(11) chain around female neck, tightened so that it pinches the flesh
(12) blurred close-up of Madonna, with the chain swinging loose
(13) laser beam, which strikes heavy bangles, manaclelike on female wrist
(14) laser beam on goldfish in bowl
(15) Madonna removing dark glasses, looking straight at camera
(16) Madonna sitting on road
(17) Madonna removing dark glasses
(18) Madonna lying on her back on the road
(19) the dark glasses on the road, an eye appears in one lens, greenish electronic effects merge to realistic image of eye
(20) Madonna sitting on road, facing camera
(21) close-up of Madonna on road, tilting her head back

This sequence has two main types of image, ones of looking and ones of subordination or bondage. Traditionally, as the eyes of the Greek statue tell us, looking has been a major way by which men exercise power over women, and the resulting female subordination is shown by Madonna's submissive postures on the road. The goldfish caught in the bowl is an ironic metaphor for the woman held in the male gaze. But the laser beam is a modern "look," impersonal, not the traditional male eye beam, and this can cut the female free from her bonding manacles, free the goldfish from the bowl. Similarly, Madonna's singing frees the chain that has previously been tightened around her neck. Later in the video, as Madonna sings of wanting her lover, and wanting to know what she has to do to win him, she tightens and then loosens the same chain about her neck; the next shot is a collage of male eyes, into which Madonna's lips are inserted as she sings. The pattern is repeated; her performance shows how women can be free from the look and the power of the male. Removing the dark glasses as she looks at us is a sign of her control of the look: we see what she allows us to. The glasses replace her lying on the road, but instead of her apparent submissiveness, they gain an active, electronic, all-seeing eye. Similarly, the video of "Lucky Star" opens and closes with Madonna lowering and raising dark glasses as she looks at the camera, again controlling what we see. In "Borderline," the male photographer is a recurring image, as Madonna parodies the photographic model she once was while singing of her desire for freedom. The resulting photograph is shown on the cover of a glossy magazine (called *Gloss!*) being admired by men.

Madonna knows well the importance of the look. This is a complex concept, for it includes how she looks (what she looks like), how she looks (how she gazes at others, the camera in particular), and how others look at her. Traditionally, looking has been in the control of men; Freud even suggests it is an essentially masculine way of exerting control through an extension of voyeurism, but Madonna wrests this control from the male and shows that women's control of the look (in all three senses) is crucial to their gaining control over their meanings within patriarchy.

The ideological effectivity of this is evidenced in a student essay:

> There is also a sense of pleasure, at least for me and perhaps a large number of other women, in Madonna's defiant look or gaze. In *Lucky Star* at one point in the dance sequence Madonna dances side on to the camera, looking provocative. For an instant we glimpse her tongue: the expectation is that she is about to lick her lips in a sexual invitation. The expectation is denied and Madonna appears to tuck her tongue back into her cheek. This, it seems, is how most of her dancing and grovelling in front of the camera is meant to be taken. She is setting up the sexual idolization of women. For a woman who has experienced this victimization, this setup is most enjoyable and pleasurable, while the male position of voyeur is displaced into uncertainty. (Robyn Blair, 19-year-old fan)

The look (in all senses of the word), meanings of self and of social relations, and power or powerlessness are interdetermined concepts—each one requires the other two to complete it. Madonna offers her fans access to semiotic and social power; at the basic level this works through fantasy, which, in turn, may empower the fan's sense of self and thus affect her behavior in social situations. This sort of empowering fantasy is pleasurable to the extent that it reverses social norms, and, when the fantasy can be connected to the conditions of everyday life—when, that is, it is a relevant fantasy—it can make the ideal into the achievable. The first two fan videos described above may be wish-fulfillment fantasies, but the third brings the fantasized ideal within reach of the everyday. The first two evidence the desire for empowerment; the third explores ways of achieving it. Fantasy is not adequately described by writing it off as mere escapism; it can, under certain conditions, constitute the imagined possibilities of small-scale social change, it may provide the motive and energy for localized tactical resistances. . . .

REFERENCES

Chambers, I. (1986). *Popular Culture: The Metropolitan Experience.* London: Methuen.

Fiske, J. (1989). *Understanding Popular Culture.* Boston: Unwin Hyman.

McRobbie, A. (1982). "*Jackie:* An Ideology of Adolescent Femininity," in B. Waites, T. Bennett, and G. Martin (eds.) *Popular Cultures: Past and Present* (pp. 263–283). London: Croom Helm/ Open University Press.

A N D R E A   P R E S S   A N D
E L I Z A B E T H   C O L E

WOMEN LIKE US:

WORKING-CLASS WOMEN RESPOND TO

TELEVISION REPRESENTATIONS

OF ABORTION

In this study, our goal is to articulate discourses of gender and class used by groups of working-class women in the contemporary United States. First, in studying discourses of gender and class characterizing dominant media representations of the abortion issue, we attempt to establish the cultural background against which women's ideas about this issue in particular and gender and class more generally are conceived and expressed. Second, by examining variations and nuances within the discourse of particular groups of women and differences among groups, we seek to illustrate the complexity and fluidity of women's discourses and to emphasize both their resonance with and resistance to mass media discourse. The ultimate goal of the work is to use the example of abortion to promote a rethinking of the notion of media hegemony and, more specifically, of the relation of women to social class and gender identities and political discourse in the contemporary United States.

THEORETICAL CONTEXT

Recent studies of the mass media audience, influenced by postmodernist critiques of the concept of the subject and by developments in feminist theory and research, have exposed the communication field's traditional attempts to construct scientific studies of the popular cultural audience (Willis 1978; McRobbie 1978, 1981, 1984; Morley 1980; Hobson 1982; Radway 1984; Long 1986, 1987; Lull 1987; Seiter et al. 1989; Seiter 1990; Liebes and Katz 1990; Press 1991). Critiques have identified such studies as yet another academic and political effort to subject the populations studied to the hegemonic structuring already taking place in their very constitution as media audiences. In contrast, newer studies have emphasized "resistances" to power occurring at individual and small-group levels.

Widespread criticism of traditional audience studies has altered the research techniques and theoretical orientations that predominate in the field. For example, many recent studies tend to feature qualitative rather than quantitative methodological approaches. Some have embraced critical historical methods (May 1980; Rosenzweig 1983; Peiss 1986; Gabler 1988) to ask new questions about the ways historically specific audiences have created and used popular cultural forms to structure and restructure their own identities as critical subjects.

Others, interested in more current practices, have turned to ethnographic methodologies (Bacon-Smith 1992; Brown 1991a, 1991b; Press 1991; Radway 1984, 1988). Ethnographic researchers face the paradox of studying the subject in an age of postmodernist insights that challenge the existence of unified, reflective subjects in any traditional sense, substituting instead a more diffuse (but less easily researchable) notion of constructed subjectivity (Baudrillard 1988; Radway 1988; Scott 1988; Lyotard 1984).[1] Yet unlike the abstract theorizing that marks postmodernist texts, ethnography requires a level of faith in the possibility of creative activity at the level of the subject and in the potential of ethnographers to come to understand their subjects, which is often difficult to maintain in the face of theoretical challenges to our customary notions of the subject. This paradox has led to an unfortunate and growing split in the field between those most deeply affected by the postmodernist critique and those more interested in practicing the new research techniques spawned in its wake.

This seeming contradiction between theory and method has particularly affected scholars using ethnographic techniques to study the popular cultural audience. Most centrally, the question of the way mass media audiences constitute and reconstitute themselves as subjects who at times resist cultural hegemonies and at others accommodate them has preoccupied researchers in this field, continually posing challenges to traditional notions of the subject (Radway 1988; Grossberg 1988, 1989; Fiske 1989a, 1989b, 1990). Increasingly, in these studies, scholars eschew notions of a unified subject, thereby accommodating the postmodernist critique. As a result, newer studies contrast sharply in form and theoretical orientation with slightly older studies in the field (e.g., Morley 1980; Hobson 1982; Radway 1984). In fact, it has proved difficult to alter the actual working notion of subjectivity that informs most current work, particularly if one is to maintain the political thrust inspiring most cultural studies of the audience. Those in the vanguard have produced theoretical critiques of earlier works, theoretical tracts, and research proposals for ethnographic work based on these new ideas, but little actual audience research has itself been produced based on these critiques. Feminist scholars have been particularly affected by this paradox, as ethnographic methodologies have been attractive to feminist researchers looking specifically at the female audience (McRobbie 1978, 1981, 1984; Hobson 1982; Radway 1984; Press 1991).[2]

The new direction in feminist cultural studies is toward more historically and geographically specific studies of particular groups of women. The pitfalls of essentialism are effectively avoided as studies become increasingly specific in scope.[3] The theoretical disadvantage of such studies from the perspective of more traditional feminist aims is the perhaps unavoidable fact that it is impossible to generalize about "the female audience" or the popular cultural subject at all. Researchers now seek to examine different groups of women for their increasingly differentiated political dialogue; they construe the media as similarly political and multivocal. Although the terms of postmodernist theorizing have been useful in pointing out the fluid, shifting nature of group identities, this approach often seems to depoliticize such studies by emphasizing only the fluidity of boundaries rather than the actual positions they represent and the actors who constitute them. Most feminist research, inspired by political concerns and in search of political actors, stops short of totalizing deconstructions of the subject and retains an affinity for ethnography for these reasons. It is in this tradition that we locate the study discussed in the remainder of this chapter.

ABORTION, TELEVISION, AND SOCIAL CLASS

In this study, we try to incorporate some of the insights of the postmodernist critique of the subject in specifying the way the political perspective and identity of two groups of working-class women resonate with and resist the dominant political discourses and the construction of a particular political subject they confront in the mass media. To accomplish this, we focus on the moral, intellectual, personal, and political issue of abortion.

Current mass media organs often discuss the issue of abortion. In addition, most women have at least thought about the issue of abortion in relation to their own experience or to that of family and friends. One of the few political issues almost universally experienced at both the private (or personal) and the public (or political) level, abortion is especially useful for examining how specific groups of women constitute themselves as political and intellectual actors in the contemporary United States.

The relationship between our cultural thinking about abortion and social class issues has long been a theme in feminist defenses of the pro-choice position (Ginsburg 1989, Luker 1984)[4] but has never explicitly entered more popularly accessible discussions of abortion from either the pro-choice or pro-life sides of the abortion debate. Others have analyzed in great depth the conventions marking abortion rhetoric in our culture's literature and mass media (Condit 1990). Nevertheless, the social class issues that implicitly riddle the representations of abortion in mass media have been virtually ignored, as has the potential impact this feature may have on both pro-life and pro-choice constituencies. On prime-time television, for example, the medium we examine here, images of economically needy women seeking abortions predominate over images of middle-class women in similar circumstances, despite the fact that large numbers of middle-class women seek abortions as well (Condit 1990; Petchesky 1990; Luker 1984). The abortion-seeking subject on television is a working-class, female subject, articulated by a series of signifiers typical of television's portrayal of working-class women.

Television representations are produced at every level—writers, producers, actors, directors—by the middle class. In fact, television representations of the experience and identity of working-class women in our culture represent a middle-class cosmology or perspective on working-class experience. These representations may or may not correspond to the representations and interpretations working-class women themselves might create were they given the opportunities for expression they currently lack in our culture. On a more obvious level, representations of the working class on television falsely unify experiences differentiated in fact by ethnic, geographical, religious, and employment-related factors.

In this chapter, we examine working-class women's responses to the working-class subjects characterized in two abortion scenarios aired on prime-time television. The first is an episode of the police drama "Cagney and Lacey," the second a fictionalized account of the real-life Norma McCorvey (alias Jane Roe in real life,

Ellen Russell in the fictionalized version) broadcast in the made-for-television movie *Roe vs. Wade*. In particular, we compare responses to these programs made by several groups of pro-choice[5] working-class women. These groups, composed of nonactivist women, were chosen specifically to fill the gap in the feminist literature about abortion with information about "ordinary" women's views.

Our findings build on conclusions made in Press's recent book (1991). In research for that work, Press found that working-class women accept television's depiction of middle-class life as normal and as normative, in that many view achieving a middle-class lifestyle as a goal of their own lives. In contrast to middle-class women, working-class women value what they define to be "realism" in television. But often they define realism as images of middle-class life rather than middle-class constructions of their own lives and experience. When television does portray the working class, women become extremely critical of its images, which allegedly lack the realism they seek. In this chapter, we seek to extend Press's research by drawing more finely the distinctions and trends that occur within working-class women's discourse, including about television.

At one level, our study seeks to afford working-class women the opportunity to respond to and criticize middle-class representations of their own experience. At another, broader level, we seek to explicate pro-choice working-class women's implicit articulation of a more general critique of the pro-choice subject as essentially a middle-class subject, the outgrowth of a discourse rooted in middle-class representations of working-class experience in our culture. Normally the pro-choice position is defined simply as one of a bipolar set of opinions characterizing the abortion debate. In general, this view excludes mention of the different types of subject positions possible under the rubric of "pro-choice."

ABORTION ON PRIME TIME

Over the last two decades, television entertainment's representation of abortion decisions has coalesced around a norm of what one scholar terms "generally acceptable abortions" (Condit 1990). What this means, in effect, is that on television, middle-class or upper-class women can legitimately abort only in cases of rape or incest, to save the life of the mother, or if genetic testing reveals a severely deformed fetus. Aborting to further a woman's career or to maintain a middle-class level of comfort for the family is not morally condoned in these representations. Single middle-class women may seek abortions, but in general these are portrayed as the selfish solution to a problem having other possible resolutions. Although middle-class women may be seen to agonize over abortions contemplated for these reasons, in television treatments they are customarily spared the consequences of such decisions by acts of nature (sudden miscarriage or the realization of false pregnancy) relieving the necessity for choices the dominant media find unacceptable. Usually, it is poor or working-class women only who actually obtain abortions in the end.

These norms did not always characterize television representations of abortion. They evolved, in part, in response to public protest over earlier, more liberal representations. For example, in two episodes of "Maude" broadcast on CBS in 1972, the lead character opted for an abortion primarily because she felt too old to raise another child. The network was flooded with angry calls and letters from viewers objecting to this rationale for abortion (Montgomery 1989). Future network programming responded to this history by aiming toward explicitly balanced representations of the issue. Ultimately this approach meant that women's ability to choose abortion freely would no longer be morally sanctioned or could be sanctioned only under very specific circumstances, such as in the case of women who face mitigating economic circumstances. Only women who are too poor to care properly for a child or are for whatever reason economically unstable are permitted on prime-time television to have morally approvable abortions. Even for these women, evidence of the responsibility of their decisions must be made abundantly clear. Either they must acknowledge the irresponsibility of their actions, or they must demonstrate that obtaining an abortion will contribute to their efforts to raise themselves out of their economically unstable situation into the boundaries of the middle class.

Television depictions of the abortion issue articulate our society's general ambivalence toward the issue. By depicting abortions only in cases of apparently extreme hardship, television attempts to offer a balanced representation. In this way, the medium captures the issue as it is contested and resolves it in a way that a majority finds palatable or at least reasonably inoffensive.

We have chosen two separate abortion stories that fall under this prime-time umbrella of acceptable representations of the issue. One, an episode of "Cagney and Lacey" originally broadcast in 1985, offers an immigrant Hispanic heroine who seeks an abortion to allow her to finish school and better her family circumstances. The other, a made-for-television movie broadcast in 1990 entitled *Roe vs. Wade*, details the struggles of the real-life woman Norma McCorvey who unsuccessfully sought an abortion in Texas in 1970 and ultimately challenged the legality of prohibitive abortion laws in the landmark case decided by the U.S. Supreme Court in 1972.

The "Cagney and Lacey" episode used in this study embodies television's characteristic pro-choice slant (although pro-life elements are present for balance) and pictures a prototypically acceptable abortion scenario. The main plot involves police sergeant Christine Cagney and her partner police officer Mary Beth Lacey (who is five months pregnant in the episode) being called upon to protect a Latina (and by implication, Catholic) woman, Mrs. Herrera, who is intimidated by angry antiabortionists while attempting to enter an abortion clinic. Soon after, someone bombs the clinic, inadvertently killing a transient old man. Cagney and Lacey are assigned to uncover the bomber and ultimately discover that a somewhat crazed member of the picketing right-to-life group is responsible.

Mrs. Herrera is depicted as poor (her husband is on disability). While she is conflicted about the abortion, Mrs. Herrera is convinced that her dreams of becoming a well-paid court stenographer will be unattainable should she give birth to a child now. She mentions in particular her fear of going on welfare and her belief that she will be forced to drop out of school if she has the child. Mrs. Herrera's plight makes one of television's strongest arguments in favor of abortion: that the lives of poor women will be ruined beyond repair by the burden of an unwanted child. Another strong argument in favor of abortion is made when Lacey, talking to her husband in bed, tells of her frightening experience as a teenager seeking an illegal abortion, which led her to fly to Puerto Rico to obtain one legally, an expense that, as a self-supporting student at the time, she could ill afford. Lacey also mentions in an argument with Cagney the plight of rape and incest victims. The abortion clinic doctor bemoans the clinic's bombing by referring to twelve-year-olds who have sought abortions there because they had nowhere else to turn.[6]

But the logic that abortion is most legitimate and necessary in the case of poor women predominates on the show.

In their desire to avoid inflaming activists on either side as the "Maude" episodes had done years earlier (Montgomery 1989), producers of this "Cagney and Lacey" episode consciously sought to achieve a balanced presentation of the abortion issue. Several characters clearly articulate different sorts of pro-life as well as pro-choice arguments (Condit 1990). Balance is also attempted through the presence of an articulate pro-life spokesperson, Mrs. Crenshaw, a white middle-class woman who is head of the pro-life organization sponsoring the demonstration. We also hear Cagney's father, a retired Irish-Catholic police officer who believes abortion is murder.

Despite the overt attempts at balance, the show represents abortion as an acceptable choice but only after careful consideration and under specific conditions, which are present in the case of Mrs. Herrera. The show favors women's right to safe, legal abortions more so than it does arguments in support of the pro-life perspective. This view is supported by Condit (1990) and most of the groups, both pro-choice and pro-life, whose members viewed the tape in our study. Yet Mrs. Herrera's abortion is framed in a particular way. She is not an independent, well-employed, middle-class woman as is the Barnard-educated Cagney. Although arguments in favor of the latter's right to abortion are made on the show, the actual abortion subplot it contains concerns a working-class woman rather than the middle-class Cagney, and even her desire for an abortion is portrayed as morally ambiguous. While in the end it appears that Mrs. Herrera has chosen abortion, the act is left unseen; her ambivalence and fears are highlighted, perhaps to maintain viewer sympathy with her. Choice is legitimated but only just: In extreme or seemingly extreme circumstances, a woman may legitimately opt for abortion, provided it is a last resort for one who feels herself emotionally and—possibly most significant—*financially* backed against the wall.

The television movie *Roe vs. Wade* presents a working-class heroine who, unlike the respectable Mrs. Herrera, doesn't play by the rules. Ellen Russell lives a defiantly anti-middle-class lifestyle and takes no recognizable steps toward achieving middle-class status. Unstable, with little family support, no good options for employment, and no history or anticipation of a stable relationship with a man, Ellen is a relentlessly nonconformist figure with few if any prospects for attaining middle-class status. Hard-drinking and rough-talking, Ellen defies conventional family values in telling us "I'm a loner; I don't mess with nobody and I don't want nobody messing with me." Her lack of prospects for conventional family life are fully matched by the lack of promise in her employment history. Traveling with a carnival when we meet her, Ellen quits the job upon learning that she is pregnant for reasons that are not altogether clear to us. She unsuccessfully searches for another job all during her pregnancy; her failure to find anything at all mandates the necessity of giving away her child, although Ellen makes it clear throughout her pregnancy that she feels herself financially incapable of supporting a child in any case.

Ellen's earlier first pregnancy had led her to marry a man who beat her for alleged unfaithfulness when he learned she was pregnant. The marriage ended abruptly after the abuse. Ellen's extremely critical mother forced her to sign away daughter Cheryl's care in the best interests of the child. Ellen's mother became guardian of Cheryl, Ellen moved away, and now, living a transient life, Ellen rarely sees her daughter. Ellen found the experience of giving up her child extremely painful. She thought constantly of Cheryl and felt she could not live through the experience of giving away another child. Yet she could not see her way clear to keeping her second child either, in part because of her guilt at giving up Cheryl ("If I could afford it, wouldn't I be raising Cheryl?"). Ellen's mother makes it clear that she is unwilling to raise a second child for her, thus eliminating that option as an end to the pregnancy.

Ellen's only way out of her dilemma, as she sees it, is to have an abortion. Yet in 1970 abortion is illegal in Texas. She could obtain one legally in New York or California but lacks the money to travel to either state. She tries to obtain an illegal back-alley abortion but is frightened away by the conditions of the operating room. She asks a doctor to help her obtain an abortion but he refuses ("I'm not going to break the law"). He will only refer her to a lawyer to help arrange an adoption. This lawyer also refuses her request to refer her to a doctor willing to perform the abortion. Instead, he introduces her to two attorneys interested in challenging Texas laws prohibiting the performing of abortion. Ellen cooperates with the attorneys, telling them "You ladies are my last hope." She believes or at least hopes that their suit will be settled in time for her to obtain an abortion. Although they are ultimately successful—and in 1972 antiabortion statutes are overturned nationwide—the final decision comes too late for Ellen. In the end, she goes through with her pregnancy and gives the baby up for adoption. We see a heartbreaking scene in the delivery room, where the nurses will not allow her even once to hold or look at her child. Following the experience, Ellen becomes so depressed that she attempts suicide. She is unsuccessful, however, and the movie ends with her reading in the newspapers that her case has succeeded when brought to the Supreme Court. Despite her momentary anger toward the lawyers for not making her abortion possible, in the end Ellen is grateful to have participated in so momentous a lawsuit.

Unlike Mrs. Herrera, Ellen does not play by the rules of middle-class society. Even if Texas laws could have been changed in time for her to obtain it, her abortion would not have helped her enter into the middle class or even become a more stable member of the working class. It would merely have spared her the pain of giving up yet another child, a pain already felt very keenly every time Ellen's thoughts turned to her daughter Cheryl. We are told nothing of her plans to further her education or obtain job skills or even of her resolve to attain steady employment. Yet Ellen is portrayed in a heroic light, a pioneer of the feminist fight against restrictive abortion laws. Her story is meant to be uplifting. Sympathetically drawn, Ellen remains spunky despite the many obstacles she faces in her life, restrictive abortion laws among them. She and other women like her, the movie implies, are victimized by these laws. Ellen's story is meant to offer some justification for the feminist struggle to change them and for the continuing fight to uphold the *Roe v. Wade* decision.[7]

METHODOLOGY

To date we have conducted focus-group interviews with twenty-nine groups of two to five women, usually in the home of one of the respondents; the total number of respondents to date is eighty-eight.[8] Of these, four working-class pro-choice groups, four working-class pro-life groups, and two middle-class groups from each perspective viewed *Roe vs. Wade;* four working-class pro-choice groups, two working-class pro-life groups, four middle-class pro-choice groups, and two middle-class pro-life groups viewed "Cagney and Lacey."[9] Interviews began with a series of questions about the respondents' activities as a group, their typical pattern of discussion about moral issues, and their television viewing habits. Later we asked them to describe and discuss their experiences with either their own decisions about unwanted pregnancies or those of friends or relatives. They were encouraged to talk about the considerations that women they know made in order to reach their reproductive decisions and to give us their thoughts as well on the topic. The respondents then viewed either a thirty-minute version of the "Cagney and Lacey" abortion episode from which subplots and commercials had been edited or the first thirty-five minutes of the *Roe vs. Wade* television movie (using identical wording, we told each group how the story ended following this segment). After viewing the tape, the women were asked specific questions about their reactions to the positions expressed by the characters in the show. Prior to each interview, respondents completed a questionnaire concerning basic demographic information, media-use habits, and general opinions about abortion. The sessions generally lasted from two and a half to three and a half hours. All group interviews were taped and later transcribed and coded.

PRO-CHOICE WORKING-CLASS RESPONSES

Generally, working-class women reject television images of women making abortion decisions, permeated as they are with television's particular focus on the experiences and problems of working-class women seeking abortions. Although responses from each of the groups we explore in the study excerpted here vary, all resist the terms prime-time television uses to define the abortion issue. Pro-life women, for example, are distanced from television in a very general way. Their vision of the world includes utopian hopes for the ability of families and communities to come together and support women, particularly women in need. Because the terms of this vision are essentially absent from television, these women by definition feel excluded by its images, as they are in so many ways excluded from mainstream society in the United States.

Working-class pro-choice women are also alienated from television representations of abortion but in a more complicated way given that the pro-choice perspective does predominate on the medium. Both the middle-class-identified and the working-class-identified pro-choice working-class groups object to the victimization of working-class women in television portrayals; neither group accepts that these women are powerless or even very disadvantaged. But middle-class-identified women feel the relatively powerless ought to pay for their faults, that they should not be free to depend on others or on the state to solve problems they themselves have created. Their support for the pro-choice perspective is qualified by this fear of granting irresponsible women too much freedom and support. In contrast, working-class-identified women focus their criticisms on the authorities and corrupt professionals whom they partially blame for their own difficulties. Their pro-choice position is based in part on objections to any policies that might further the authority of the state.

Working-class pro-choice groups are unified in their almost universal affection for and support of Mrs. Herrera, the lead character in the "Cagney and Lacey" episode. Mrs. Herrera, it seems, is a relatively uncontroversial heroine of a television abortion story. Pregnant within marriage, working hard in school, worried about her husband, and troubled over the morality of abortion, Mrs. Herrera faces her abortion decision in a way that makes her as acceptable to these women as she is to middle-class pro-choice women and even to some pro-life women. Working-class pro-choice women particularly find it easy to identify with Mrs. Herrera's struggle to be upwardly mobile. Yes, they agree, it is difficult to finish school while caring for a child and receiving welfare. One woman even recalls her social worker's advice to delay schooling until her children are of school age:

> **Respondent 1:** Well, in her situation I could see why she'd want to do it. She'd be better off doing it than to have the baby and have to give up everything and then, you know, not be able to take care of her kids in the future. It's really, really hard to go to school when you have kids and people try to make it look like there's a chance and there isn't. There's almost this much chance. . . . One in a million people make it. I'm trying right now to go to beauty school and get help from the state, and the lady's just telling me, "Don't even try it." The lady from the welfare office, she's saying, "You won't be able to afford to pay the babysitter, you won't be able to do this." I don't want to give you such a negative aspect, but they told me not to do it.

Other working-class pro-choice women mention the fact that the disabled Mr. Herrera might need care as well, worrying that Mrs. Herrera will be unable to meet the needs of her husband as well as her child. They see her desire for an abortion as understandable in this light. In all, reactions to Mrs. Herrera are relatively untroubled and supportive. Women in these groups find that her situation presents a strong argument justifying legalized abortion.

In contrast, Ellen Russell's situation provokes a more troubled reaction. Ellen is received by pro-choice working-class women on a continuum ranging from lukewarm approval to extreme disapproval. While women do not tend to condemn Ellen's right to abortion, they disapprove more generally of her lifestyle and the circumstances that led to this unwanted pregnancy in particular, as in these comments:

> **Respondent 3:** She was not the type to raise a child, definitely. No, her lifestyle was not that. . . . I don't think it would be conducive to raising a child. Of course there are a lot of children who live with carnivals and things of that nature who are truly remarkable people. Her own personal lifestyle, however, leaves something to be desired there. She's rather loose there.

> **Respondent 4:** She needs to get a little more responsible with where she's sleeping around or what she's doing while she's there though. A little more responsible sex.

Some women object explicitly to the fact that Ellen's case was used to illustrate abortion. Why not invoke the image of middle-class women in abortion clinics?

> **Respondent 4:** But that's not true [that it's only women like Ellen who have abortions]. Doctors' wives can have one. Attorneys' wives, you know. You can be a well-to-do woman and still want an abortion. You don't have to be a street person, and they made it look like only the bad people. . . . Well, this kind of made me feel like that because she was from a rough part of town or she acted rough and tough and

she liked to hang out in bars and all this. . . . That's not reality. In reality any woman could need an abortion whether she's on the streets, in a fifty-thousand- or four-hundred-thousand-dollar home.

We suspected that women as audiences would receive and construct television images according to the way they construe their identities and their relationship to dominant groups. Thus we expected women's responses to these two quite distinctive heroines to vary according to women's sense of their own identity in relationship to other groups in the broader society. In fact, these expectations were largely confirmed in our results. In contrast to the less controversial Mrs. Herrera, who aspires to middle-class status, Ellen Russell is depicted as a working-class woman who appears to have no real prospects of leaving her class, nor does she actively seek them. Among pro-choice working-class groups, there are two different sets of responses to her character that emphasize the multivocality of working-class discourse and identity in our culture. These two discourses mark deep divisions within working-class women's experience and in their attitudes toward middle-class life and societal authority. The first group we term "middle-class-identified"; these women embrace middle-class values and sharply criticize working-class women they see on television. The other group we term "working-class-identified"; these women identify themselves as outsiders vis-à-vis more mainstream society and are more apt to sympathize with the problems attributed to working-class women and their lives on television.[10] Women's evaluations of Ellen vary in relation to how working-class-identified versus middle-class-identified women are themselves. Initial pretelevision interviews indicate that women vary widely along this dimension. We will consider the responses to the character of Ellen in particular and to *Roe vs. Wade* in general made by members of one prototypical group chosen to represent each category.

WORKING-CLASS-IDENTIFIED WOMEN

While some working-class women see themselves as no different from and/or aspiring toward the middle class, others construct a very different self-identity, one more working-class-identified. The latter is well encapsulated by the words of one woman who asked us what groups we were interviewing. Wanting to respond honestly but unwilling to use explicitly the terminology of social class, we rather euphemistically responded that we were sampling different occupational groups. Our subject responded "Oh, you mean high class, middle class, and no class, like us!" Another woman, from another working-class-identified pro-choice group, explained that we could feel free to use her first name (though as a matter of policy we do not), since "No one who was a professor would know who I was." This lack of concern for anonymity contrasts sharply with middle-class-identified women's attitudes; they were so concerned with anonymity that they took false names from the very beginning of the interview tape, a position uncommon among the women interviewed. The former quotation acknowledges that women of the working-class-identified group neither identify with nor necessarily aspire to membership in the middle class. The speaker emphasizes the assured sense of anonymity and invisibility women in this group experience based on the feeling of discontinuity from other social groups. In the discussion that follows, we choose the group from which the former quote originated as our prototype representing the working-class-identified category.

Working-class-identified women tend to be suspicious of middle-class authority in ways middle-class-identified women are not. Their speech is littered with references to their distrust of middle-class (and, by extension, societal) authority. For example, this group strongly criticizes Ellen's attorneys for "using" her to further their careers. On the show, the attorneys tell us they have not been entirely honest with Ellen, in that they never told her this was their first case. Indeed, after the first verdict, Ellen accuses them of misleading her into thinking the case would be decided in time for her to have an abortion (the show leaves the facts surrounding this issue somewhat ambiguous). However, in the show a balancing attempt is made to depict attorney Sarah Weddington's concern for Ellen in their conversations.

The group responds to this situation as follows:

AP: What did you think of how the women lawyers handled their contacts with her? The way they treated her?

Respondent 4: I don't think they were very fair and honest with her right up front. I think they misled her. I don't think she realized in the beginning how long it really would take.

Respondent 3: Well, they didn't tell her either [that it would take] two months.

Respondent 4: And then here you see her all of a sudden and she's got this big old belly. And I think they took this case on . . . they believed in it and they believed in woman's choice, but I think they did it to set their career off. I think it was done selfishly on their part, because like they both said, "We're not telling her the truth—neither one of us has ever litigated."

AP: So you thought the women lawyers were sort of misleading her?

Respondent 3: I think so, I think they were just trying to further themselves. I don't think they really came down to the bottom line with her, and I don't think she was really smart enough to question them thoroughly enough on the situation.

Respondent 1: It was just any light of hope.

Respondent 2: They told her in May and it was March, she was just like . . .

Respondent 4: She was in limbo, she didn't know what to do. She was just believing what they told her.

Respondent 3: Since there was nothing available at that point in time in Texas, that they would give her some alternatives. But they didn't even suggest anything. I think they did it to further their own careers, and they're probably rich wealthy lawyers now.

The group goes on to agree that the lawyers should have helped Ellen obtain a legal abortion in New York and mentions several other ways the attorneys might also have helped Ellen once they realized their case would not be resolved in time for her to obtain an abortion:

AP: Do you think they should have given her the money to go to New York to get the abortion?

Respondent 2: You know, that crossed my mind, that if they would have really cared, you know, they could have probably done that. They looked like they . . .

Respondent 4: Had they have done that, wouldn't that have just thrown the case right out the window and they—wouldn't that have thrown the case right out the window? Wouldn't that have stopped all court procedures had they done something like that?

Respondent 1: How would they know?

Respondent 3: She was using a fictitious name anyway.

Respondent 4: Well, that's true, that's true.

Respondent 3: Why couldn't she have gone to some abortion clinic or Planned Parenthood or however they did it at that point in time in New York and used another fictitious name? Who's to say where the money came from? How would anybody know where the money came from? Unless one of the three said something.

Women in this group are much more effusive in detailing the possible ways her attorneys might have helped Ellen than are women in other pro-life and pro-choice groups, even though most agree that the attorneys used Ellen to further their own goals and careers. This is consistent with the group's generally critical attitude toward professionals and authorities of any kind.

In contrast to their critical attitude toward authority, working-class-identified women are less critical of Ellen herself than are any other working-class women interviewed. One woman, for example, praises Ellen's unwillingness to go on welfare, attributing it to her pride and independence. These women find Ellen's pride and stubbornness admirable.

Working-class-identified women are also more inclined than others to identify with Ellen, finding that her character and situation have parallels for them or others in their families or friend groups. One woman in the group, after viewing the show, retells the story of her niece she had mentioned in the pretelevision discussion, noting at several points her similarity to Ellen. Like Ellen, her niece as a teen had one child whom relatives had (almost entirely) raised; the niece became pregnant again soon after the birth. Our respondent had paid for her niece's abortion of the second pregnancy. The experiences of women in this group and their family connections lead them to accept the way *Roe vs. Wade* portrays Ellen's lack of resources. In contrast to pro-life women in particular, who as explained elsewhere (Press 1992) insist that Ellen has not fully tapped all family resources available to her, these women feel that at times such resources do not exist.

In sum, what marks the distinctive perspective of working-class-identified women is not necessarily their experiences but their interpretations of these experiences. They view themselves as not altogether unlike Ellen. Thus they reject what they perceive to be Ellen's powerlessness in favor of a more empowered embrace of her identity. They identify with Ellen and see many of her positive qualities.

MIDDLE-CLASS-IDENTIFIED WOMEN

In contrast, working-class women who are middle-class-identified see themselves as essentially members of the middle class already. Unlike working-class-identified women, they take great pains to construct a picture of themselves as completely separate from the members of their class, who don't work responsibly, don't have drive and ambition, take drugs or drink heavily, are "drifters," and have sex irresponsibly. One woman characteristically differentiates herself from those "others" who would accept public assistance as follows:

> **Respondent 2:** Many of us may have been in a situation at one time or another where we've struggled, and we've made real hard attempts to avoid using those sources or may have been denied those sources for various reasons.

In the following discussion, we rely on the remarks of a group we've chosen to represent the prototype of the middle-class-identified pro-choice perspective.

In contrast with their working-class-identified counterparts, middle-class-identified women are relentlessly critical of Ellen's character. Many of Ellen's unconventional traits directly offend women in this group. For example, unlike women in the working-class-identified group, these women interpret Ellen's unwillingness to go on welfare as evidence of ignorant "Texican" attitudes about who is trash and who isn't.

Women in the middle-class-identified group fill in the narrative's unsaid elements, completing Ellen's character sketch with details that ultimately make her an even more striking object of disapproval. One often criticized but only sketchily drawn aspect of Ellen's situation, for example, is the circumstances under which she became pregnant. We are not told anything about the baby's father or her relationship with him. All Ellen tells us is that he is "not interested," presumably in helping her either to raise the child or to obtain an abortion.

One member of the middle-class-identified group, however, articulates in some detail her belief that Ellen probably sleeps around: "I don't sleep with a man three days after I meet him," she ventures, implying that Ellen does precisely this (although there is no evidence to this effect on the show except a similar unsupported accusation made by Ellen's mother). This woman and others in the group are quite willing to fill in the details of Ellen's character with a series of negative qualities not necessarily intended in the television portrayal:

> **Respondent 4:** She obviously did not want to be pregnant. Obviously. She didn't seem to be in a long–term relationship. It sounded like it was just some guy passing through town or one of the other carnies. . . . OK, I've known him for a month or two months or however long. Personally, I don't go to bed with somebody three days after I meet them, but that's just me [laughs]. It just seemed it wasn't that she was in this long-term involved, stable relationship. [It was] not even necessarily long term—it seemed like it was just like a one-night stand basically. Oops, I got pregnant. You've got to be a little more careful, you know.

Respondent 3: She even said to her father and mother he was just a guy. That's too bad.

Respondent 2: I think it seemed like she was constantly in an environment where drinking might be available. She might have been drunk at the time of the pregnancy, you don't know.

The women in the group jump off from their discussion by using their construction of Ellen's character to rationalize their plan to sterilize women who have had too many abortions, thus draining either government money or bleeding insurance companies dry. Such irresponsible behavior, they reason, should be stopped, particularly when their taxes or health care costs are affected by it or when it wastes doctors' valuable time:

Respondent 4: Those are the people who line up frequently, using abortion as birth control. There's a whole lot easier, cheaper, less painful ways to have birth control than to keep getting abortions. We have people at work that [say things like] "I think I'm pregnant again, I don't think I can go through my fourth abortion." "You're twenty-two, what do you mean your fourth abortion?" "Well, I didn't want to go to the drug store." "Well, then cross your legs and go home!" [Several jokes are made by group members here.]

AP: Do you think that people like that should also have access to abortions?

Respondent 4: I think they should have access to voluntary sterilization.

Respondent 3: Precisely.

Respondent 4: Have sex three times and you're out of here. . . . No, I . . . [laughter].

Respondent 3: There has to be some kind of control. We need a national computerized system here. Get an abortion in Boone, Kentucky, . . . and then if they move to Ypsilanti, Michigan, to get another abortion—that's it, chick. Twice and you're out! I'm serious, OK? *We are the government* [emphasis added], we have a responsibility to stop all this endless waste. It's a waste of money, it's a waste of good professional time. Why should some doctor spend all the time aborting some woman? I know one who has had seven abortions! I'm ahead of you. Why should some doctor spend good medical time and taxpayers' money or anybody's money to keep aborting the same person over and over again?

These women recoil from a situation in which abortions are too free and easy to obtain, constructing a vision that would rely on centralized authorities to promote responsible behavior by limiting women's access to them. Members of this group show no hesitation in invoking societal authorities to discipline women they feel are too free and easy. In fact, they identify with these authorities explicitly in their speech, insisting that "We are the government."

Most strongly criticized by these women generally is Ellen's lack of self-reliance. Ellen is a woman "looking for a handout," the very type of person most likely to end up with a free ride from the welfare system—and probably the least deserving of it. They find Ellen's job search and her continual complaint that she cannot find work unconvincing: "She kept saying she kept trying to find a job, that there wasn't any work. Yet she could go out and have fun with her friends." Ellen gets no credit, as she did from the working-class-identified women, for her reluctance to go on public assistance (although somehow, given the group's attitude, it seems that she should). For this group, her other irresponsible qualities completely override this virtue.

Most telling of the group's particularly accepting attitude toward authority, and in sharp contrast to their working-class-identified counterparts, is the way middle-class-identified women characterize Ellen's relationship with the middle-class attorneys who take her case to the Supreme Court in an attempt to legalize abortion. Whereas working-class-identified women criticize the attorneys for using Ellen to get ahead, this group simply acknowledges this situation matter-of-factly. When asked if they thought her attorneys ought to have flown Ellen to New York to obtain a legal abortion, they chant an indignant "no" in a unison that rarely occurs in group interviews of this nature. They argue that Ellen did not "contract" in advance with her lawyers for this kind of help. Perhaps had she been shrewd enough to demand it in the beginning, she might deserve it. Rather than garnering their sympathy through her naïveté, Ellen in their view ought to pay for her lack of sophistication and strategy. Her attorneys owed her no help, nor did she deserve any. In fact, the group reacts with some disbelief that anyone would take this position; it seems to offend their most basic convictions in the importance of individual self-reliance. In contrast, working-class-identified women express compassion for Ellen's inability to look out for her own interests more successfully.

Overall, the middle-class-identified group's criticisms of Ellen help the members construct their own identities in opposition to hers. The women's tendency to separate themselves from Ellen's character and social group is emphasized by their reconstruction of the experiences of a child of one of their members, in marked contrast to the working-class-identified woman's tale of her niece described in the preceding section. In this case, a group member's daughter, Arlene, had become pregnant while still in high school, causing her to drop out of school and have an abortion. (All names attributed in the context of respondents in this study are pseudonyms.) Shortly thereafter, she became pregnant again and decided to keep the baby, although she remained unmarried. She later married the father briefly and was now divorced. She was currently working, caring for her daughter, and planning to attend school part-time in the future.

Members of the group collectively assume an unusual, almost reverent tone when discussing this girl's experience. The attitude is particularly remarkable when compared to the tone they later assume to discuss and evaluate Ellen's character, as in these passages:

Respondent 3: Arlene is a very mature young lady, always has been. Her actions at that time may not have been considered mature, but her decisions were correct for her at that time.

Respondent 2: She has an unusual confidence and responsibility. I think a lot of that comes from the support that she's received. It's an unusual circumstance in that she has a real friendship I think with her mom and with Pete [her stepfather].

Group members repeat several times "Arlene is an exceptionally mature individual" and variations thereof. No one criticizes Arlene's character, despite her actions. Ellen, on the other hand, disliked strongly by all group members, is criticized as morally loose and irresponsible for actions strikingly similar to those of Arlene.

While the group's regard for her mother's feelings certainly accounts in part for their reluctance to criticize Arlene, what comes across in their discussion is the feeling that the women strongly believe what they are saying. Our interpretation could of course be mistaken, but the women really seem to like Arlene and to admire her strength in surviving and making the best of difficult circumstances. We conclude that the divergence in these women's feelings toward Arlene and Ellen may be accounted for by their desire to separate themselves from media images of "those immoral" working-class people like Ellen.

This interpretation is strengthened by the group's view of welfare abusers. The women strongly disapprove of the "lazy, irresponsible" people who receive government assistance—who use food stamps to buy "lobster dinners" for all their friends. The system is flawed, people have no incentive to work, and ultimately the women would like to see it wiped out altogether. These abstractly expressed opinions on the subject, however, contrast sharply with the women's descriptions of the actual people on welfare that they meet at work. One woman, for example, takes job applications at her place of employment (a large discount supermarket-hardware establishment). She sympathetically describes applicants coming to her who "should have been paid yesterday," single fathers whose children haven't eaten in days, and others in extreme need of aid. She and the group strongly agree that these people are in need of assistance. When discussing them, the women criticize the welfare system for not being generous enough, for not meeting the needs of such people quickly enough. The woman in charge of hiring such applicants goes on to describe the decisions she must make regarding their work abilities. Often such people "need a chance" as she puts it; they could be efficient workers despite their lack of experience, high school degrees, or other paper qualifications. These attitudes toward the actual people she encounters in the course of her job, many of whom end up as her co-workers, contradict the way she and her friends characterize the scheming masses on welfare—and also the way they seem to place Ellen in this category despite her insistence on remaining off welfare. Again, such contrasts might be explained by the women's desire to separate themselves and those they work with from the bulk of working-class and poor people "out there," thereby strengthening their construction of and identification with a middle-class-identified subject position. Alternately, the women may actually be interested in separating themselves from media representations of the working class that are imposed from above and manufactured by the middle class. In sum, in this instance working-class women in our middle-class-identified group put aside their personal experience in favor of expressing more abstract commitments to principles often untouched by their own specific experience. Mass media are often evaluated similarly, with reference to their commitment to principle rather than their own experience with reality. When experience and principle conflict, the conflict is often decided in favor of the latter rather than the former.

CONCLUSION

Working-class pro-choice women's responses to the television characters of Mrs. Herrera and Ellen Russell may be divided into two main prototypes. In contrast to their essentially sympathetic response to Mrs. Herrera, working-class women's responses to Ellen question rather than assume the perspective of Ellen's middle-class creators who sympathize with her while creating a narrative that disempowers her almost entirely. What unifies both sets of pro-choice working-class women's responses is that each group resists this disempowering presentation of Ellen's self, objecting to its fundamental terms and logic. To working-class pro-choice women in both groups, Ellen can take charge—or at least can assume more control—of her life more so than she is pictured as capable of doing. One of the reasons Mrs. Herrera fares so well in comparison with Ellen is precisely because she is inter-preted as in control of her destiny, while Ellen is not. Neither group of women is willing to relinquish this vision of control. Perhaps in the end, they identify too strongly with television's working-class women and refuse to concede a lack of control in their own lives, as they do in Ellen's.

Class and group differences in these responses correspond to the different lan-guages invoked in defense of the pro-choice position by members of these two groups. Preliminary data indicate that middle-class pro-choice women embrace a uniformly liberal language to justify their support of an individual's right to make her own private decisions (Press 1992). This language is qualified, however, in the case of pro-choice working-class women, as their responses to its mass media incarnations illustrate. Media afford them the opportunity to respond to middle-class perspectives on working-class life and to resist them by putting forth their own interpretations and evaluations of such experiences. In this way an alternative working-class identity is constructed—their own.

Middle-class-identified working-class women resist the sympathetic middle-class constructions of their own identity that pepper the mass media. Rather than acknowledge the limitations of class, these women steadfastly deny the existence of any limits at all. They resist the liberal, therapeutic[11] worldview that acknowledges with sympathy the personal problems and handicaps faced by many and that Ellen's portrayal automatically calls up in our study's middle-class respondents. Instead, they embrace more conservative threads in our culture. They oppose the welfare state, insisting that we are all equal and that government ought to be limited, allow-ing us to obtain what we deserve by dint of our own hard efforts and perseverance. This belief in a low profile for government also leads this group to embrace generally pro-choice tenets concerning abortion. Yet the group's adherence to the pro-choice perspective is a qualified one. The right to abortion ought not to justify an irresponsible freedom for women. Women giving evidence of exercising their free-dom irresponsibly ought to have that freedom curtailed. In addition to the rhetoric of rights, then, the group members invoke notions of the good as well in their moralis-tic interpretation of Ellen and in their prescriptions concerning the ways in which immoral behavior ought to be curtailed. This is the "communitarian" strain in their thought (Sandel 1984). Communitarianism contrasts community-based notions of what is "good" to the Kantian liberal rhetoric of "rights" most often used to support the pro-choice position in our public political discourse. A qualified, communitarian pro-choice perspective better describes the group's position than does our more customary, undifferentiated use of the pro-choice label to construct a pro-choice political subject. The women envision a hierarchical community in which the smarter and more able must care, however unwillingly, for those less intelligent and responsible. In this view, the latter ought to pay for their burdensome qualities: The danger of abortion, welfare, and unemployment benefits is that things may become too easy for them, threatening the triumph of the sensible—themselves and the authorities with whom they feel interchangeable.

For working-class-identified women, in contrast, the dangers are reversed: More restrictive abortion laws may mean that central control of women might become too easy for the authorities who reign, persons whose interests are inevitably at odds with their own. Working-class-identified pro-choice respondents also resist media portrayals of their condition. Like their middle-class-identified counterparts, women in this group dislike Ellen; they find her irresponsible and irritatingly —but unconvincingly—helpless. Yet rather than blame Ellen for her plight, they are suspicious of both the professional and familial authorities—the doctor, her lawyers, and her mother. Television's benevolent professionals do not impress them in the least. Ellen's salvation lies not in obeying authority and conforming to society's rules but in learning to navigate these rules to the best of her ability, as do these women in the course of their lives. For this group, criticisms of television focus on articulating and exposing its sanctioning of authorities and the rights of authorities to interfere in women's lives.

Whether or not these women personally condone abortion (and often by their own admission they do not), women in this group are reluctant to invoke societal authority to outlaw it. They remain unconvinced that they should support the authorities who rule their society and communities. In their experience, such authorities are more likely to persecute them than to work to secure their rights. The group's propensity, then, is to support policies designed to limit the authorities' reach, as is the case with the pro–choice stance on abortion. Unlike the middle-class-identified group, working-class-identified women do not put their faith in notions of the good that then must be supported by societal and community authorities. Consequently, their liberal support for the right to free choice is more unqualified, as they are reluctant to allow authorities any more personal power over their lives than the considerable and sufficient amount that, in their view, is already exercised.

Television readily captures both a moralistic attitude toward abortion as well as a rights-oriented defense of the pro-choice position in its portrayal of "generally acceptable abortions." Both characters, Mrs. Herrera and Ellen Russell, are painted sympathetically as poor women who find they must make the extremely difficult decision to abort unplanned children. Middle-class-identified women accept these portraits at face value, whereas working-class-identified women do not.[12] Instead, working-class women make distinctions and judgments within these television images of their own group.

Some judgments result from aspirations of these women toward middle-class identity and consequent rejection of a fixed working-class identity for themselves or any other members of their class. If easy access to abortion for all women must be somewhat sacrificed in the construction of this alternative identity, the middle-class-identified women are willing to pay this price, in part because they believe it won't affect "sensible" people like themselves. The responses of middle-class-identified women to television images in these instances can be seen as evidence that they resist hegemonic interpretations of abortion dilemmas and hegemonic constructions of their own identities as subjects. But the basis for this resistance is an ultimate conformity to hegemonic notions of what upward mobility, middle-class identity, and middle-class membership really mean. In this sense, then, working-class women in this subgroup are ultimately thwarted in their attempt to truly resist dominant meanings and definitions of their identities and actions and the parameters of their world.

Pro-choice working-class-identified women offer a different order of critique. They reject not only images of themselves created by the middle class but those created to portray the middle class as well. Their overall skepticism of television maintains a distance from it that is absent for their middle-class-identified counterparts. These women more successfully maintain their guard in the face of mass media's efforts to define their self-identities. Their constructions do not match the public incarnations of the pro-choice subject to which the media have helped inure us. As Glendon notes, public "political rhetoric has grown increasingly out of touch with the more complex ways of speaking that Americans employ around the kitchen table, in their schools, workplaces, and in their various communities of memory and mutual aid" (1991, xii). Our study illustrates some of the differences between the way the pro-choice political subject is constructed in our public political rhetoric, as incarnated in the mass media, and the ways in which pro-choice subjectivity is constructed by members of two groups of pro-choice working-class women. Glendon's observation is well illustrated by our findings. We hope through this study to achieve a more sophisticated view of the ways in which concrete political subjectivities are constituted in our society in response to their more undifferentiated incarnation in dominant media forms.

This study offers an example of the new tradition of feminist research studying the popular cultural audience. Unlike more traditional audience research, the methodologies employed here allow women to speak for themselves and with each other in the context of television viewing, questionnaire answering, and in-depth interviewing. The focus-group methodology allows women to engage in semipublic discourse during the interview, which enables us to observe and interpret differences between this type of discourse as it occurs in the presence and absence of television. Our focus on social class differences among women (and racial differences in the larger study) adds a dimension to feminist audience research that has too often either overgeneralized from white middle-class samples or ignored class and racial differences among women altogether. It challenges the customary pro-life/pro-choice dichotomy that excludes explicit reference to the ways members of different social classes articulate their positions on abortion differently. Our research indicates that "pro-choice" as we commonly define it indeed derives from middle-class conceptions of the world, of individuals, of the experience of haves and have-nots, and of pregnancy and childbearing and women's related dilemmas.[13] The information presented here may shed light on some of the difficulties the pro-choice movement has experienced in presenting a unified political front during recent and ongoing abortion struggles.

Information about the ways in which different groups of women form and express their identities as subjects against the background of hegemonic cultural and media discourses will, we hope, help us to develop more fully notions about the forms of subjectivity that characterize postmodern society. Perhaps further awareness of these forms will lead increasingly to more effective ways of coming to know and understand the varieties of subjectivity we continually encounter in our work and in our lives.

NOTES

1. This approach has been written about extensively in the anthropological literature; see, for example, Rabinow (1977); Geertz (1983, 1988); Clifford and Marcus (1986); Marcus and Fischer (1986).

2. See Long (1989) for a detailed overview of the work currently being done in feminist cultural studies.

3. Essentialism is defined by some as the abstract and ahistorical construction of "the female subject." Feminist cultural studies that emphasize concrete historical or current studies of a specific and situated female popular cultural audience have generally led away from essentialism on one level, stressing as they do the study of concrete, historically situated cultural subjects. Yet on another level, the temptation of constructing an equally essentialized, resisting female subject that can be effectively contrasted to the male subject more customary in cultural theory has been a continuing problem, if only because such language often seems central to feminist problematics. Missing in this work is a sense of the socially and historically situated nature of the subjects studied; somehow the terms of feminist theory have made these details seem, at times, superfluous luxuries, not really essential to the political thrust of these works. See Harding (1991) and Long (1989) for a good discussion and critique of essentialism. Also, see Scott's (1988) review of several then-current works in feminist theory whose authors she criticizes for this tendency.

4. Both Ginsburg (1989) and Luker (1984) have noted that the social class constituencies of pro-life and pro-choice activist groups differ, pro-life groups appearing more working class in character.

5. The categories of "pro-life" and "pro-choice," as we argue elsewhere (Press and Cole 1992), falsely dichotomize working-class women's actual positions on abortion. Interviews reveal that women often disagree with the basic presumptions behind the existence of these two opinion categories. We retain use of these two categories, however, for descriptive purposes.

6. Our analysis of this episode is indebted to Condit's (1990) discussion.

7. *Roe vs. Wade* was broadcast at an extremely critical time in the politics of abortion in the United States. It coincided with an increase nationwide in state-level struggles to pass laws prohibiting the use of public funding for poor women's abortions. Ellen's story certainly serves as an example to those campaigning for restrictions against state-funded abortions of the difficulties poor women seeking abortions might face in the absence of available state funds.

8. See Krueger (1988), Glick et al. (1987-88), Basch (1987), and Watts and Ebbutt (1987) on the methodology of focus-group interviews. Most women interviewed to date have been white, although some groups include black women as well.

9. Women's class membership is not always easy to assess; see Rubin (1979) for a discussion of the difficulties involved. She discusses her difficulties in determining the class status of women as opposed to that of men or families. She found that "In some instances, a husband's status still clearly determines the wife's; in others, it clearly does not. Those are the easy ones. But that leaves the cases where there is no clarity" (1979, 216). Like Rubin, we found it necessary to make some judgments, using background questionnaire data on each participant. In general, working-class women were employed in a blue- or pink-collar position (Howe 1978), and/or had two years of college or less, and/or were married to a man fitting these characteristics.

10. These labels are coined primarily from tendencies exhibited in women's pretelevision discussions. In these rather far-ranging discussions, women answered several general questions concerning their patterns of media use and their attitudes about politics, morality, and abortion. Working-class women's answers to these questions can be grouped into two main categories based on their relationship to authority. The first are women who seem comfortable identifying with reigning authorities in our social and political system, themselves primarily middle or upper class ("middle-class-identified" women). These women identify themselves as the same as middle-class women, although by our measures they would be considered in the working class. In the second group are antiauthoritarian women who do not identify with

middle-class authorities ("nonmiddle-class- or working-class-identified"). These women hold views that are not generally supportive of social authorities in the United States. Posttelevision discussions reveal that they do not identify themselves in the same category with the middle-class characters on the television shows we showed them.

Women in the two groups we discuss here happen to occupy different positions within the working class. The middle-class-identified group is composed of low-level managers. Members of the working-class-identified group work in positions likely to be classified as "below" those occupied by the other group; their connection to the more stable working-class group is more tenuous, with some women supporting themselves with relatively transient work. Of course, one must be careful of generalizing this link between ideology and position based on the small sample the study includes.

11. See Bellah et al. (1984) for a fuller description of middle-class worldviews in our culture. In particular, Bellah and colleagues describe the therapeutic perspective and the origins of liberalism in middle-class outlooks generally.

12. See Press (1992) for fuller explication of data on middle-class women's responses to these characters.

13. See also Press and Cole (1992) on dissonance within the pro-choice discourse and on the inability of this category to articulate adequately a particular political discourse and subject position.

REFERENCES

Agar, Michael H. 1980. *The Professional Stranger: An Information Introduction to Ethnography.* New York: Academic Press.

Bacon-Smith, Camille. 1992. *Enterprising Women.* Philadelphia: University of Pennsylvania Press.

Basch, Charles E. 1987. "Focus Group Interview: An Underutilized Research Technique for Improving Theory and Practice in Health Education." *Health Education Quarterly* 14 (4): 411–448.

Baudrillard, Jean. 1988. *Selected Writings.* Stanford, Calif.: Stanford University Press.

Bellah, Robert N., Richard Madsen, William M. Sullivan, Ann Swidler, and Steven M. Tipton. 1984. *Habits of the Heart: Individualism and Commitment in American Life.* Berkeley: University of California Press.

Brown, Mary Ellen, 1991a. "Knowledge and Power: An Ethnography of Soap-Opera Viewers." Pp. 178–197 in *Television Criticism,* ed. Leah Vande Berge and Lawrence Wenner. New York: Longman.

———. 1991b. "Soap Opera as a Site of Struggle: The Politics of Interpretation." *Media Development* 2: 23–26.

Clifford, James, and George E. Marcus. 1986. *Writing Culture.* Berkeley and Los Angeles: University of California Press.

Condit, Celeste Michelle. 1990. *Decoding Abortion Rhetoric: Communicating Social Choice.* Urbana and Chicago: University of Illinois Press.

D'Acci, Julie. 1987. "The Case of *Cagney and Lacey.*" Pp. 203–225 in *Boxed in: Women and Television,* ed. Helen Baehr and Gillian Dyer. New York: Pandora Press.

Fiske, John. 1987. *Television Culture.* London and New York: Methuen.

———. 1989a. *Reading the Popular.* Boston: Unwin Hyman.

———. 1989b. *Understanding Popular Culture.* Boston: Unwin Hyman.

———. 1990. "Ethnosemiotics: Some Personal and Theoretical Reflections." *Cultural Studies* 4(1): 85–97.

Flax, Jane. 1987. "Postmodernism and Gender Relations in Feminist Theory." *Signs* 12(4): 621–641.

Fonow, Mary Margaret, and Judith A. Cook, eds. 1991. *Beyond Methodology: Feminist Scholarship as Lived Research.* Bloomington: Indiana University Press.

Gabler, Neal. 1988. *An Empire of Their Own: How the Jews Invented Hollywood.* New York: Crown.

Geertz, Clifford. 1973. *The Interpretation of Cultures.* New York: Basic Books.

———. 1983. *Local Knowledge: Further Essays in Interpretive Anthropology.* New York: Basic Books.

———. 1988. *Works and Lives: The Anthropologist as Author.* Stanford, Calif.: Stanford University Press.

Ginsburg, Faye D. 1989. *Contested Lives: The Abortion Debate in an American Community.* Berkeley: University of California Press.

Glendon, Mary Ann. 1991. *Rights Talk: The Impoverishment of Political Rhetoric.* New York: Free Press.

Glick, Deborah C., Andrew Gordon, William Ward, et al. 1987–88. "Focus Group Methods for Formative Research in Child Survival: An Ivoirian Example." *International Quarterly of Community Health Education* 8(4): 298–316.

Grossberg, Lawrence. 1987. "The In-Difference of Television." *Screen* 28(2): 28–45.

———. 1988. "Wandering Audiences, Nomadic Critics." *Cultural Studies* 2(3): 377–391.

———. 1989. "On the Road with Three Ethnographers." *Journal of Communication Inquiry* 13(2): 23–26.

Harding, Sandra. 1991. *Whose Science? Whose Knowledge? Thinking from Women's Lives.* Ithaca, N.Y.: Cornell University Press.

Hobson, Dorothy. 1982. *Crossroads: The Drama of a Soap Opera.* London: Methuen.

Howe, Louise Kapp. 1978. *Pink Collar Workers: Inside the World of Women's Work.* New York: Avon.

Krueger, Richard A. 1988. *Focus Groups: A Practical Guide for Applied Research.* Beverly Hills, Calif.: Sage.

Liebes, Tamar, and Elihu Katz. 1990. *The Export of Meaning: Cross-Cultural Readings of "Dallas."* Oxford and New York: Oxford University Press.

Long, Elizabeth. 1986. "Women, Reading, and Cultural Authority: Some Implications of the Audience Perspective in Cultural Studies." *American Quarterly* 38: 591–612.

———. 1987. "Reading Groups and the Crisis of Cultural Authority." *Cultural Studies* 1(2): 306–327.

———. 1989. "Feminism and Cultural Studies: Britain and America." *Critical Studies in Mass Communication* 6(4): 427–435.

Luker, Kristin. 1984. *Abortion and the Politics of Motherhood.* Berkeley: University of California Press.

Lull, James, ed. 1987. *Popular Music and Communication.* Newbury Park, Calif.: Sage.

Luttrell, Wendy. 1989. "Working-Class Women's Ways of Knowing: Effects of Gender, Race, and Class." *Sociology of Education* 62 (January): 33–46.

Lyotard, Jean Francois. 1984. *The Postmodern Condition: A Report on Knowledge,* trans. Geoff Bennington and Brian Massumi. Minneapolis: University of Minnesota Press.

Maguire, Patricia. 1987. *Doing Participatory Research: A Feminist Approach.* Amherst, Mass.: Center for International Education.

Marcus, George E., and Michael M. J. Fischer. 1986. *Anthropology as Cultural Critique.* Chicago and London: University of Chicago Press.

May, Larry. 1980. *Screening Out the Past: The Birth of Mass Culture and the Motion Picture Industry.* New York: Oxford University Press.

McDonnell, Kathleen. 1984. *Not an Easy Choice: A Feminist Re-examines Abortion.* Boston: South End Press.

McRobbie, Angela. 1978. "Working-Class Girls and the Culture of Femininity." Pp. 96–108 in *Women Take Issue,* ed. Women's Studies Group. London: Hutchinson.

———. 1981. "Just Like a *Jackie* Story." Pp. 113–128 in *Feminism for Girls,* ed. Angela McRobbie and Trisha McCabe. London: Routledge.

———. 1984. "Dance and Social Fantasy." Pp. 130–162 in *Gender and Generation,* ed. Angela McRobbie and Mica Nava. New York and London: Macmillan.

Montgomery, Kathryn C. 1989. *Target: Prime Time.* New York: Oxford University Press.

Morley, David. 1980. *The Nationwide Audience: Structure and Decoding.* London: British Film Institute.

————. 1986. *Family Television*. London: Comedia.

Nicholson, Linda. 1986. *Gender and History: The Limits of Social Theory in the Age of the Family*. New York: Columbia University Press.

Peiss, Kathy. 1986. *Cheap Amusements: Working Women and Leisure in Turn-of-the-Century New York*. Philadelphia: Temple University Press.

Petchesky, Rosalind Pollack. 1990. *Abortion and Woman's Choice: The State, Sexuality, and Reproductive Freedom*. Boston: Northeastern University Press.

Press, Andrea. 1991. *Women Watching Television: Gender, Class, and Generation in the American Television Experience*. Philadelphia: University of Pennsylvania Press.

————. 1992. "Mass Media and Moral Discourse: The Impact of Television on Modes of Reasoning About Abortion." *Critical Studies in Mass Communication* 8: 421–441.

Press, Andrea, and Elizabeth R. Cole. 1992. "Pro-Choice Voices: Discourses of Abortion Among Pro-Choice Women." *Perspectives on Social Problems* 4: 73–92.

Rabinow, Paul. 1977. *Reflections on Fieldwork in Morocco*. Berkeley and Los Angeles: University of California Press.

Radway, Janice. 1984. *Reading the Romance: Women, Patriarchy, and Popular Literature*. Chapel Hill: University of North Carolina Press.

————. 1986. "Identifying Ideological Seams: Mass Culture, Analytical Method, and Political Practice." *Communication* 9: 93–123.

————. 1988. "Reception Study: Ethnography and the Problems of Dispersed Subjects." *Cultural Studies* 2(3): 359–376.

Reeves, Jimmie L., and Richard Campbell. 1991. "The Politics and Poetics of Drug Transgression: Crusading Journalists on Crack Street." Paper presented at the November meetings of the Speech Communication Association, Atlanta, Georgia.

Roberts, Helen, ed. 1981. *Doing Feminist Research*. London: Routledge and Kegan Paul.

Rosenzweig, Roy. 1983. *Eight Hours for What We Will: Workers and Leisure in an Industrial City, 1870–1920*. Cambridge: Cambridge University Press.

Rubin, Lillian. 1979. *Women of a Certain Age: The Midlife Search for Self*. New York: Harper and Row.

Sandel, Michael J., ed. 1984. *Liberalism and Its Critics*. Oxford: Basil Blackwell.

Sanjek, Roger, ed. 1990. *Fieldnotes: The Makings of Anthropology*. Ithaca, N.Y., and London: Cornell University Press.

Scott, Joan Wallach. 1988. *Gender and the Politics of History*. New York: Columbia University Press.

Seiter, Ellen. 1990. "Making Distinctions in TV Audience Research: Case Study of a Troubling Interview." *Cultural Studies* 4(1): 61-84.

Seiter, Ellen, Hans Borchers, Gabriele Kreutzner, and Eva-Maria Warth, eds. 1989. *Remote Control: Television, Audience, and Cultural Power*. London and New York: Routledge.

Watts, Mike, and Dave Ebbutt. 1987. "More than the Sum of the Parts: Research Methods in Group Interviewing." *British Educational Research Journal* 13(1): 25–34.

Willis, Paul. 1978. *Profane Culture*. London: Routledge and Kegan Paul.

JANET STAIGER

TABOOS AND TOTEMS:

CULTURAL MEANINGS OF

THE SILENCE OF THE LAMBS

By the fifth week of the release of *Silence of the Lambs* (1991), the debates over the film had solidified into a set of propositions: 1) that whether or not Jonathan Demme had intended to create a homophobic film, the character of the serial murderer had attributes associated with stereotypes of gay men; 2) that in a time of paranoia over AIDS and increased violence directed toward gays in the United States, even suggesting connections between homosexuals and serial murderers was irresponsible; but 3) that the character of Clarice Starling played by Jodie Foster was a positive image of a woman working in a patriarchal society and, thus, empowering for women viewers. The diversion in views produced a consequent division: two non-dominant groups, some gay men and some feminists (both straight and lesbian), found themselves at odds over evaluating the film.

The controversy further escalated when several activists "outed" Jodie Foster. "Outing" is the recent practice by some people to declare publically that certain individuals are homosexual or bisexual[1] even though those people have not chosen to make their sexual preferences known. The argument for doing this is that it is hypocritical for famous people to remain private about such preferences if they participate in public activities which perpetuate homophobia. Rather they should help promote gay rights.

Foster's outing produced in the most vitriolic counter-analysis the claim that Foster was being outed because she was a strong woman and that she was being "offer[ed] up [by gay activists] as a sacrifice in the furtherance of gay visibility."[2] "You don't have to look far," the woman argued, "to find a reason why a culture with screen idols such as Marilyn Monroe and Judy Garland would object so vociferously to an actress like Jodie Foster. Like their straight brothers, the gay men who condemn Jodie Foster and *Lambs* are out to destroy a woman who doesn't put male interests first and doesn't conform to their idea of what a woman should be. Under the guise of promoting gay consciousness, they're falling back on the same reliable weapon that men have used for centuries against women who claim a little too much for themselves—they're calling her a dyke."

Although other women were not so strong in their condemnation of Foster's outing, all thirteen of those women whose views of the movie, *Silence of the Lambs,* I had available to me expressed praise for the film. These included at least two lesbians, one of whom criticized Larry Kramer of ACT UP for his "patronizing" attitude toward Foster, trying to treat her as a "disobedient daughter."[3]

Whether Foster is or is not a lesbian or bisexual "in real life" is not the point of this essay. Whether the character she plays in *Silence of the Lambs* is or is not a lesbian is also not at issue here. What I shall be pursuing instead is the ultimate *stitching* together of gay and woman that became the "climax" of the discussion. I shall argue that this possibility, while not inevitable, is grounded in its reception context and process. What I shall be doing here is what I call historical reception studies. This research attempts to illuminate the cultural meanings of texts in specific times and social circumstances to specific viewers, and it attempts to contribute to discussions about the spectorial effects of films by moving beyond text-centered analyses.

Because I wish to give you an application of this rather than an extended theoretical argument, I will simply lay out several hypotheses informing my research:

1) Immanent meaning in a text is denied.

2) "Free readers" do not exist either.

3) Instead, contexts of social formations and constructed identities of the self in relation to historical conditions explain the interpretation strategies and affective responses of readers. Thus, receptions need to be related to specific historical conditions as *events*.

4) Furthermore, because the historical context's discursive formation is contradictory and heterogeneous, *no* reading is unified.

5) The best means currently available for analyzing cultural meanings exist in poststructuralist and ideological textual analyses. These methods, of necessity, draw upon multiple theoretical frameworks and perspectives such as deconstructionism, psychoanalysis, cognitive psychology, linguistics, anthropology, cultural studies Marxism, and feminist, ethnic and minority, lesbian and gay studies. They do so with a clear understanding that the connections and differences among the frameworks and perspectives must be theorized.

Consequently, historical reception studies work combines contemporary critical and cultural studies to understand why distinct interpretive and affective experiences circulate historically in specific social formations. In a case study, the following steps might occur:

1) An object of analysis is determined. This object is an *event*, not a text: that is, it is a set of interpretations or affective experiences produced by individuals from an encounter with a text or set of texts within a social situation. It is not an analysis of the text except in so far as to consider what textually might be facilitating the reading.

2) Traces of that event are located. Here I shall be using primarily traces in the form of printed prose and images, but when available, oral accounts would be very good sites of additional evidence. The print and images include

about twenty reviews, news articles, letters to papers, advertisements, illustrations, and publicity which circulated in the major mass media.

3) The traces are analyzed textually and culturally. That is, as new historians elucidate causal processes to explain conjunctions called "events" and then characterize the social significance of these events in relation to specific groups of people, so too does this research. Furthermore, the analyses avoid categorizing receptions into preferred, negotiated, or resistant readings. Rather the processes of interpretation are described since more richness in explanation can be achieved than by reducing readings to three specific generalizations.

4) Finally, the range of readings is considered not only by what seems possible at that moment but also by what the readings did not consider. That is, structuring absences are as important as well.

My project will be to work toward explicating the event of the "sacrificial" outing of Jodie Foster. I shall argue that, although this event might be explained simply through contemporary U.S. stereotypes of lesbians—i.e., a strong woman must be a lesbian—or even because of informal oral communication circulated by gays and lesbians about Foster's sexual preferences, the possibility of making such an inference was facilitated by the critical response *Silence of the Lambs* received. Furthermore, Foster's outing is symptomatic of current cultural taboos and totems. Thus, calling Foster a lesbian is more overdetermined linguistically, psychoanalytically, and culturally than it might appear.

In this initial study of the event, three specific reading strategies occur.[4] These are: 1) the construction of binary oppositions with deployments of high and low, good and bad attributions; 2) the use of metaphor and analogy; and 3), most pertinent to the event, the hybridization or grafting of incompatible terms together. This practice is activated from the prior two strategies and even finds its motivation from one of the dominant metaphors in the discourse.

TABOOS

Perhaps because many writers have gone to film school or because thinking in oppositions so colors our everyday lives, reviewers of *Silence of the Lambs* often structured their plot analyses around a central binary opposition. The most obvious opposition was one between Hannibal "The Cannibal" Lecter and Jame "Buffalo Bill" Gumb. One reviewer notices that Lecter is upper class and witty while Gumb is a "working-class lout."[5] The reviewer even emphasizes how this sets up an audience to sympathize with the "good" Lecter and to find disgusting the "bad" Gumb. He critically summarizes, "Lecter: rich, wise, clever, helpful, and funny. Gumb: working-class, stupid, dense, and dull. Lecter: straight. Gumb: gay. Lecter: abstract evil; Gumb: evil incarnate." David Denby characterizes the Lecter/Gumb opposition as between "an unimaginable vicious genius; the other merely rabid and weird."[6] Another reviewer writes that the film has "two villains who represent quite different incarnations of evil. Buffalo Bill a grotesque enigma, has absolutely no redeeming virtues. But Lecter is strangely sympathetic, a symbol of muzzled rage."[7]

Important to this evaluation is that Lecter's victims are bureaucrats and authority figures, such as the census taker whose liver he ate with a nice Chianti.

Meanwhile, Gumb goes after young, overweight women. Additionally, of course, Gumb is played as effeminate—something remarked upon by several reviewers who also acknowledged the gay community's concern about the film.

Binary oppositions are commonly deployed in ways such that the two terms in the opposition are not equal. Peter Stallybrass and Allon White in *The Politics and Poetics of Transgression* argue that cultural oppositions often duplicate themselves in various discursive realms.[8] That is, hierarchies reproduce themselves across various symbolic systems such as psychic forms, the human body, geographical spaces, and social orders. To justify these figurations, one symbolic system will refer to the other to warrant its ordering. An obvious example would be the equation commonly made between the head as exalted and the lower anatomy as base; the physical body is written over by a metaphysical discourse.[9]

This hierarchization of binary oppositions functions analogically to legitimate Lecter's cannibalism. Thus, the class attributions, choice of victims, and socialized behavior patterns are read not merely as oppositions but ones with values attached which reinforced each other. Viewers routinely enjoyed Lecter, particularly as played by Anthony Hopkins. *Variety's* reviewer symptomatically jokes: the "juiciest part is Hopkins."[10] Lecter, of course, offers an interesting problem since he breaks a taboo which would so normally be described as the horror for a film.

Can we explain the spectators' acceptance of this transgression beyond the functioning of the textual array of values attached to the binary oppositions? Freud writes in *Totem and Taboo* that taboos are occasionally breached only to reassert the boundaries authenticating them. One instance of such a breach is the ritual eating of something considered taboo. Such a thing might even be the plant or animal which the tribe considers to be its totem. Totems stand as symbols for the group.

But according to Freud, they are also causal explanations. The totem is the tribe's origin, the "father" of the tribe. Thus, Freud links the ritual eating of totems to the Oedipal story and argues that what has been established as out-of-bounds (e.g., killing one's father) is in the ritual the symbolic consumption of the totem's character. A current example of such a ritual act, Freud writes, is the Christian communion. Drinking wine and eating bread is devouring one's own kind. Lecter, of course, foregoes the more oblique symbolism: he actually eats members of the tribe but for the same purpose.[11] Lecter's ingestation of his own kind, authorized as the incorporation of the bodies of authority figures and legitimated through socially originated hierarchies of binary oppositions, provides both textual and contextual determinations for spectators to accept, and even find pleasure in, his destruction of boundaries.

Consequently, and as part of the weirdly disconcerting pleasure of the event, the reviewers make all sorts of jokes about accepting the broken taboo as if they too wish to participate in the ritual. These jokes occur in the form of puns, doubly validating as they are by puns being a lawful disruption of traditional meanings. For example, Denby writes: "The horrors of the scene are brought off with, well, taste."[12] Another reviewer notes, "Buffalo Bill is famous for killing women, skinning them and leaving the cocoon of an exotic moth in their mouths. Lecter made his name by eating the flesh of his victims raw. All of that may sound a little hard to swallow."[13] One columnist gives Demme a "C- in Mise-en-Scène 101 for the way he fleshes out (so to speak) the villainous Jame Gumb on screen."[14] Notice that all of these wisecracks are made apologically, because they do, indeed, open fissures in social categorizing. Headlines are particularly susceptible to word play, and the discursive motif continues there. Examples include: "Overcooked Lambs," "Skin Deep: Jonathan Demme's Chatter of the Hams," and "Gluttons for Punishment."[15]

Thus, a very powerful and significant binary opposition between Lecter and Gumb is constructed and circulated by viewers of the film. A second structuring binary opposition is proposed by Denby and J. Hoberman who point out that Clarice Starling has several fathers with which to contend.[16] Hoberman expands the comparison: Crawford, the FBI agent, is her daytime dad who is rational; Lecter, her nighttime father, is a "charismatic suitor."[17] This reading of the film as an incest story is transformed in other reviews. As one writer suggests, *Silence of the Lambs* can be seen as about Starling who is "changing, trying to formulate an identity."[18] Interpreting the film as an Oedipal passage for Starling is reinforced *visually* by iconographic materials published with the reviews. Most illustrations were supplied by Orion in its publicity kit. These feature Lecter standing behind Starling with Crawford behind both of them. Some illustrations cut out Crawford; others left him in. All three people face forward so that Crawford and Lecter seem to be peering over Starling's shoulder.

Reading *Silence of the Lambs* as an initiation/Oedipal story fits in an eerie way a discussion of the slasher genre by Carol Clover. She argues that in this genre women are victimized by psychopathic killers. However, she continues that it would be an error to assume that slasher pictures are simply cases of misogyny. For one thing, we ought not imagine that gender characteristics determine viewer identification.[19] This is particularly important with cinematic representation in which the physical body is often so powerful as an immediate signifier of gender. Furthermore, viewer identification does not necessarily remain stably located to a single character throughout a film. For instance, Clover believes that in slasher movies identification seems to alter during the course of the picture from sympathizing with the killer to identifying with the woman-hero. Clover also argues that the (apparently male) monster is usually characterized as bisexual while the woman-hero is not so simply a "woman." She is often "unfeminine," even tracking the killer into "his underground labyrinth."[20]

The ultimate confrontation in the slasher film, Clover believes, is between a "shared femininity" and a "shared masculinity" in which the monster is castrated. Thus, the woman-hero is able to appropriate, referring to Linda Williams's work, "all those phallic symbols'" of the killer's. Moreover, and important here, the woman-hero is "a congenial double for the adolescent male" who is now negotiating sexual identity. The woman-hero is a safe identificatory substitute for a male, with the repressed plot about male-to-male relations. The woman-hero is thus a "homoerotic stand-in."

Psychoanalytical discourse is widespread, and Hoberman, among others, is familiar with it. Thus, the historical discourse of psychoanalysis may be abetting his reading the film as an Oedipal crisis for Starling, one that ends "happily." Starling is permitted to join the FBI; Lecter rewards her with unfettered independence from threats by him. Furthermore, and most significantly, Starling kills Gumb, symbol of aberrant sexual behavior, thus overtly denying homoeroticism while permitting it to exist in the apparently heterosexual Crawford-Starling pair.

Thus, one way some reviewers seem to have read the film is Starling-as-Masquerading-Woman who accedes into patriarchy. However, another way exists to understand parts of the interpretive reception of *Silence of the Lambs*. To explore that I need to draw out further the second interpretive strategy: the functions of metaphor and analogy.

TOTEMS

We can assume that some reviewers of the movie read the original novel which is thus part of the potential context for interpreting the film. The novel employs a rather hackneyed device: the various characters are linked to animals, with a theme of natural preying.[21] At the first meeting between Crawford and Starling, Crawford describes Lecter's behavior: "It's the kind of curiosity that makes a snake look in a bird's nest" (6). Starling, of course, is thus forewarned. Later, added to Lecter's attributes is the classic connection of the snake being the devil: "Dr. Lecter's eyes are maroon and they reflect the light in pinpoints of red" (16); his tongue flickers in and out of his face (144). Thus, the metaphor builds a set of parallelisms: body attributes equal snake equals devil; therefore, evil.

The animal motif as metaphor and category for social cognition, perhaps set up by having read the novel, perhaps from Starling's name itself—or from the title of the film—perhaps from habit, permeates reception discourse about *Silence of the Lambs.* Lecter is a "cobra"[22] who lives in a "snake pit of an asylum."[23] He makes "hissing, vile, intimate remarks to women."[24]

The initiation theme crisscrosses with this motif. Starling is described as "mole-like" for her penetration of the killers' habitats. She descends into the "dungeon-like bowels" of the prison;[25] she raids the "basement of death."[26] Stuart Klawans points out that Starling must overcome all sorts of obstacles: the initial course in the opening shots, a "labyrinth of offices," "a mazelike dungeon."[27]

But Starling is not always, or usually, the one doing the preying. "Lecter plays cat and mouse with Clarice."[28] For viewers, Starling can become the totem animal with whom she identifies: *she* is the "lamb in wolves' territory."[29] Also crossing is the devil association. Starling "must defend herself at all times, lest [Lecter] eat her soul."[30]

Social discourses are never uniform nor logical even as they try to map hierarchies across semantic categories. In the reception of *Silence of the Lambs,* Lecter's meaning is mobile; some times on the top, other times on the bottom. This inversion is most obvious when he is positioned not to counsel but to threaten Starling. The photographs of the series of father figures with Starling could be read another way. Some men reviewers took Starling to be a woman-victim. Could readers perceive Starling as a woman in danger?

In a discussion of the representation of the naked female body, Margaret R. Miles points out that by the 15th century, a common visual motif is the positioning of a woman in a frontal pose with the figure of Adam, her lover, standing behind her.[31] Or, Adam is transformed into the Figure of Death and the woman dances with him. Or in even more threatening and troubling images, Death copulates with the woman in sadomasochistic brutalism. These images are reminiscent of representations of vampirism, a later connection of animals, eating, sexuality, and death. Miles argues that their significance is the patriarchal connection of woman with sin, sex, and death. But she also notes that "Julia Kristeva has stated that [while] 'significance is inherent in the human body,' . . . little more can be said about *what* is signified until one examines the meanings of bodies in their particular religious and social contexts."[32]

Hauntingly, then, another theme in the critical reception of the film is the ambiguous threat of Lecter to Starling as woman-victim. When they discussed it, many reviewers did take the threat to be sexual in some way. Added to this was the suggestion of pandering by Crawford who sends Starling to Lecter hoping, as Vincent Canby puts it, "to arouse his interest."[33] This reading, however, does not mean that Starling is necessarily being read psychically as female, with the sexuality as heterosexual—in fact it would be repressed polymorphous sexuality—but it does open the space for such a reception. This opens for discussion another feature in the array of interpretations.

MINOTAURS AND MOTHS

Women who discussed the film in the public discourse that I surveyed liked *Silence of the Lambs* and seemed especially to sympathize with Starling. Julie Salamon describes Starling as "an attractive woman of unexceptional size doing what used to be thought of as a man's job. . . . She is a rare heroine, a woman who goes about her work the way men do in movies, without seeming less a woman."[34] Amy Taubin praises the movie as a "feminist film" which "suggests that [sexuality and sexual role] fantasies can be exumed and examined, and that their meanings can be shifted." Taubin goes on to invert traditional mythology: after describing Starling's discussions with Lecter as "the meeting of Oedipus and the Sphinx," she claims that the pleasure of the film is "the two-hour spectacle of a woman solving the perverse riddles of patriarchy—all by herself."[35]

Again, Starling is being placed in the narrative position traditionally given to a male. However, in Taubin's scenario, Lecter is not the patriarchal father. Rather, Lecter must fit in the slot of the Sphinx, the monstrous hybrid with the upper torso of a woman and the lower torso an amalgamation of animal body parts. Although symptomatically its gender is unknown, the Sphinx has traditionally been associated with the "maternal." Interestingly, however, no other reviewer surveyed suggested that Lecter had any feminine traits, perhaps because by contrast he seemed masculine compared with Gumb.[36]

Another monstrous hybrid is also mentioned in the reviews. Hoberman retitles the movie "Nancy Drew Meets the Minotaur." The Minotaur is a double inversion of the Sphinx, for its lower body is that of a human male while its head is that of a bull.[37] Thus, the human body halves that define the two beasts are reversed as well as the genders. Furthermore, the Minotaur is absolutely knowable as male since the lower portion of its body is entirely visible—the area legitimated by medical discourse as that which defines and describes sexual difference.[38] This Minotaur association is reinforced through the labyrinth metaphors mentioned earlier.

The third reading strategy is hybridization, the grafting together of irreconcilables. The associations with these particular mythical beasts are some evidence of this. Note, in particular, that what is grotesque is not the blurring of boundaries or even their transgression, which is the case for Lecter's cannibalism in which he ingests another and takes on its attributes. Rather what is disturbing is the all-too-apparent, the *see-able*, combination of disparate semantical categories: human/animal. Again, Hoberman's discourse is particularly insightful. About Gumb, he writes, "[Buffalo Bill] is a jarring billboard of discordant signs—a figure stitched together like the Frankenstein monster."[39]

Hoberman's vocabulary, then, gives us the thread to another pattern of interpretation motivated by the text and mobilized by the historical context. Gumb received his nickname because he skins his victims and sews those skins together to make himself an outfit. Literally stripping the women of their outer raiment, Gumb tries to fashion himself into the woman he desires to be. All of the reviewers decide he is the ultimate monster.

Working from Kristeva's thoughts about the abject, Barbara Creed has recently argued that the horror to be confronted in some films is not just the phallic mother but, finally, the archaic mother of the imaginary, pre-Oedipal experience.[40] The monstrous horror is not the castrated female but the maternal authority which threatens the "obliteration of the self."

Many of the reviewers observe that Gumb's behavior is readable as effeminate, leading to the inference, despite lines of dialogue, that he is homosexual. As the reviewer for the Los Angeles *Reader* puts it, Gumb has a "swishy stage-homosexual posturing."[41] This association seems to be emphasized and commented upon by a sketch accompanying a *Village Voice* article in which Gumb holds a needle and thread while Starling has a pencil and paper. Again, Starling is face forward in the foreground with the threat behind her, looking toward her. No matter her gender, Gumbo's is by cultural categories feminized.

Also reinforcing this threat of the engulfing maternal monster is Gumb's totem: the death's-head moth, so named because the markings on its back resemble those of a skull. It is this animal which he wishes to imitate in its transformation into beauty; it is this totem which he shoves down his victims' throats. Klawans observes that Jack the Ripper is considered to be the first serial killer, whom Klawans notes arrives when women start living on their own in the city.[42] Furthermore, to make his self apparent, to construct his own identity, the serial killer will repeat his signature at each crime scene. By "pattern, [the killer] writes in code with his victims' bodies."[43] The film, then, meticulously follows common lore about such behavior. The death's-head moth functions symbolically to write "Gumb" on the bodies of women. According to the movie plot, Gumb did this as well to forecast his forthcoming transformation and new link to the identity "woman." Holding the moth in their mouths, the women's interiors are now exteriorized—their skins gone but their bodies the cocoon for a new beauty.

This association of moth, maternity, and monster is strongly prepared for extratextually, so the fact that viewers responded to it is not surprising. For *Silence of the Lambs*, the moth was a major motif in the advertising campaign through the posters of it covering Starling's mouth.[44] But the ad's image does not have the moth *in* Starling's throat. It would not be visible. It covers her mouth, hiding an orifice. In this film, and in symptomatic displacement, inversions have existed all over the interpretational landscape. Outsides become insides both in Lecter's cannibalism and Gumb's scripting his forthcoming transformation.

Furthermore, the moth is *stitched* across her mouth. Starling is figured and readable as a hybrid monster as well. If she is easily thought of as an individual in search of her identity, she, like Gumb, can be associated with the moth. She is interpretable as part of his clan. But this stitching is across the mouth, leaving Starling, like that of so many victims, silenced.

Recall that readers have also equated Starling with the lambs she tried to save from slaughter. After death, lambs have two functions: they can be eaten; their hides can be worn. In both cases, the sacrifice is incorporated by the killer—internally via swallowing and externally via masquerading as an other. In both cases, difference and identity are threatened. Klawans writes, why is the audience being worked over in *Silence of the Lambs*? "The best answer . . . and it's a good one—is that the protagonist is a woman. She might even be a lesbian." Other *male* writers also publicly regarded this a distinct possibility prior to the outing of Foster.[45] Thus, although Starling *is* a woman, she may not be a *"normal"* woman. We thus have a complete quadrant of gender and sexual preferences available in the film: Lecter: heterosexual male; female victims; (heterosexual) females; Gumb: homosexual male; Starling: homosexual female. Reading Starling as a lesbian, however, is not a direct result of textual evidence but an inference from the interpretive strategies and the discursive context of the film.

Mary Douglas writes in *Purity and Danger* that social pollution comes from threats to the political and cultural unity of a group.[46] Social pollution anxieties can be rewritten over the human body in a concern for its orifices since body openings "are connected symbolically to social preoccupations about exits and entrances."[47] In my analysis of this public discourse, the most apparent danger was from incorporating or transgressing traditional oppositions. Douglas believes that one way to cancel such a social pollution is a confessional rite.

As the release date for *Silence of the Lambs* neared, Orion and the producers used the Hollywood strategy of attracting attention to it by giving several benefit shows. One party was for the AIDS Project in Los Angeles. In the United States in 1991, this gesture of concern cannot be disassociated with the public assumption that AIDS is primarily a disease of gay men and lower-class drug-users. Gay activists immediately read the event as a pollution rite: "They [are attempting] to launder the film by using . . . an organization whose clients are mostly gay to offset criticism."[48] To gay activists, the act of trying to imply concern for homosexuals was thus an inverted confession of the homophobia of the film.

This event occurred extratextually and prior to the film's opening. Thus, its existence determined the reception of the film for many viewers. When the film went on to do good box office, the intensity of the threat increased. For gay activists, an external threat—wide reinforcement of the notion that effeminate men are psychopathic serial killers—was not only being ignored by massive numbers of audience members but likely being, again, incorporated into public mythologies. Thus, some gay activists chose to blur the line which is so often crossed: the difference between fiction and real social life.

Notice that gay activists did not try to argue that *Starling* was a lesbian. Like Orion, they made the argument that the movie had some (obscure) value to social life. Like Orion, they made the argument extratextually: *Jodie Foster* was a lesbian. In a time in which homo- or bisexuality is threatened as a personal identity—threatened not just by social stereotyping but by real physical threats from homophobic violence—"sacrificing" Foster seems logical. That is, pointing out the hypocrisy of the filmmakers by arguing that Foster had not yet come to terms with her own identity and sexual preferences was necessary if society was ever to come to terms with its notions of "monsters."

As I have indicated, Foster might well have come under attack simply because of stereotypes of the strong woman as a lesbian as well as informal oral communication about her, but motifs in the advertising and film, combined with reading strategies by its viewers, reinforced the credibility of the accusation by those who chose to out her. Starling's gender is ambiguous. She is easily read as a "son" in a patriarchal identity crisis; she is easily read as "unfeminine," tracking archaic mothers in their lairs; she is easily read as a hybrid—a moth-person. And within a structural square of oppositions and inversions, her position is the most "other":

not heterosexual, not male. She could be the lamb sacrificed in punishment for the film's expressed homophobia and repressed polymorphous sexuality.

Of course, other people pointed out that those choosing to out her were in an odd way accepting the notion that being called a lesbian would be humiliating. And that, in any case, Foster was being denegrated or patronized just as women so often are in our culture. As I mentioned earlier, women—both straight and lesbian—uniformly defended her and the movie as a positive, powerful representation of a female.

In closing I wish to underline what I have been doing theoretically. This study is an attempt to indicate how contemporary theoretical frameworks can be useful in determining the cultural meanings (with the plural emphasized) of a specific text. What I have not done is to try to unify the text or the readings by asserting that one reading or set of oppositions or displacements is more viable than another. I have tried to provide the *range* of readings and to give an initial account of what might explain that range.

Additionally, my *primary* evidence for the cultural meanings of the events was not derived from a textual reading of the film. It came from public discourse. From that discourse, mediated though it is, I determined what textual, extratextual, and social determinants might account for the readings in my sample. I did not, although I might have, discuss significant absences in the discourse, a critical one being "blood," which is obviously significant considering how AIDS is transmitted.

Determining the cultural meaning of a text is full of assumptions and pitfalls. Interpreting interpretations is viciously circular. Additionally, the discourse I used i[s] public and therefore already suspect. It is by no means representative of its culture—although I would be willing to argue that it has some relation to it as well as an effect on it. Given these (and other) problems, however, I still believe that research of this sort is helpful in a project of trying to under[stand] how individuals interpret the world and how they use discourse to shape, or reshape, that world. While I have made no decision about the political gesture of outing, I do believe I need to work toward understanding what acts of resistance such as that one mean in my social formation.

What this investigation has reaffirmed for me, then, is that at this time homosexuality, bisexuality, or ambiguous sexual preference is threatening to a wide range of readers. Gumb's death as an "unnatural" person is met with a sigh of relief. "Sick" though the movie's ending may be, Lecter's continued career as a cannibal of authority figures is met with a shaky laugh of pleasure. Maybe this is because Lecter's act of murder is one that dominant culture takes to be a normal ritual of incorporation: father to son, not the hybriding of monsters such as men who sew rather than model themselves after appropriately masculine authority figures.

NOTES

I would like to thank Eithne Johnson for preparing such an interesting Ph.D. reading list, Beth Wichterich for helping me understand parts of the events, and audiences at the 1991 Nordiskt Filmsymposium (Lund, Sweden), the Women's Research Seminars at the University of Texas at Austin, and the University of Wisconsin-Madison for giving me very valuable responses to drafts of this essay.

1. In this paper I will usually not refer to bisexuality as a sexual preference. However, bisexuality should be considered an implied option throughout.

2. Leslie Larson, "Foster Freeze," [Letter to] *Village Voice* (April 2, 1991) [n.p.—from *Silence of the Lambs* clipping file, Academy of Motion Picture Arts and Sciences Margaret Herrick Library—hereafter SLfile]. Background, descriptions, and debates preceding this can be

found in David J. Fox, "Gays Decry Benefit Screening of 'Lambs,'" *Los Angeles Times* (February 4, 1991) [n.p. SLfile]; Michael Musto, "La Dolce Musto," *Village Voice* (February 12, 1991) [n.p. SLfile]; Amy Taubin, "Demme's Monde," *Village Voice* (February 19, 1991), pp. 64, 76–77; Lisa Kennedy, ed., "Writers on the *Lamb*," *Village Voice* (March 5, 1991), pp. 49, 56; Michelangelo Signorile, "*Lamb* Chops," [Letter to] *Village Voice*, (March 12, 1991) [n.p. SLfile]; [Letters to] *Village Voice* (March 19, 1991) [n.p. SLfile]; Elaine Dutka, "'Silence' Fuels a Loud and Angry Debate," *Los Angeles Times* (March 20, 1991) [n.p. SLfile]; and Michael Bronski, "Reel Politic," *Z Magazine* 4: 5 (May, 1991), pp. 80–84.

3. Julie Salamon, "Weirdo Killer Shrink Meets the G-Girl," *Wall Street Journal* (February 14, 1991); Amy Taubin, "Demme's Monde"; Lisa Kennedy, "Writers"; Martha Gever (in Kennedy, ed., "Writers"); C. Carr (in Kennedy, ed. "Writers"); Sheila Benson, "Why Do Critics Love These Repellent Movies?," *Los Angeles Times Calendar* (March 17, 1991); Andrea Kusten, Letters, *Village Voice* (March 19, 1991); Anna Hamilton Phelan, Tammy Bruce, and Phyllis Frank quoted in Elaine Dutka, "' Silence' Fuels a Loud and Angry Debate"; Leslie Larson, "Foster Freeze"; B. Ruby Rich, quoted in Bronski, "Reel Politic"; Maria Magenit, quoted in Bronski, "Reel Politic."

4. If I were explaining something else about the reception of *Silence of the Lambs*, other features and practices in the discourse might be pertinent.

5. Henry Sheehan, "Overcooked Lambs," *Los Angeles Reader* (February 15, 1991), pp. 29–30. These footnotes contain only the sources which I quote from; other reviews were part of my sample.

6. David Denby, "Something Wilder," *New York* 24: 7 (February 18, 1991), pp. 60–61.

7. Brian D. Johnson, "The Evil That Men Do," *Maclean's* (February 18, 1991), pp. 51–52.

8. Peter Stallybrass and Allon White, *The Politics and Poetics of Transgression* (London: Methuen, 1986).

9. "A recurrent pattern emerges: the 'top' attempts to reject and eliminate the 'bottom' for reasons of prestige and status, only to discover, not only that it is in some way frequently dependent upon that low-Other . . . but also that the top *includes* the low symbolically, as a primary eroticized constituent of its own fantasy life. The result is a mobile, conflictual fusion of power, fear and desire in the construction of subjectivity: a psychological dependence upon precisely those Others which are being rigorously opposed and excluded at the social level. It is for this reason that what is *socially* peripheral is so frequently *symbolically* central (like long hair in the 1960s)" (Stallybrass and White, *Politics and Poetics*, p. 5).

10. "Cart," "The Silence of the Lambs," *Variety* (February 11, 1991), p. 109.

11. Sigmund Freud, *Totem and Taboo: Resemblances Between the Psychic Lives of Savages and Neurotics* [1918], trans. A. A. Brill (New York: Vintage Books, 1946). "The cannibalism of primitive races derives its more sublime motivation in a similar manner. By absorbing parts of the body of a person through the act of eating we also come to possess the properties which belonged to that person" (p. 107).

12. Denby, "Something Wilder."

13. Johnson, "The Evil."

14. Stephen Harvey, in Kennedy, ed., "Writers." p. 49.

15. Henry Sheehan, "Overcooked Lambs," p. 29; John Powers, "Skin Deep: Jonathan Demme's Chatter of the Hams," *L.A. Weekly* (February 15–21, 1991), p. 27: Stanley Kauffmann, "Gluttons for Punishment," *New Republic* (February 18, 1991), p. 48.

16. J. Hoberman, "Skin Flick," *Village Voice* (February 19, 1991), p. 61.

17. As Hoberman notices, in the original novel, Starling's relation with her mother is a dominant theme. In the film, her mother's death and its meaning to Starling are repressed, with the film concentrating on Starling's need to deal with her father's death.

18. Terrence Rafferty, "Moth and Flame," *New Yorker* (February 25, 1991), pp. 87–88.

19. Carol J. Clover, "Her Body, Himself: Gender in the Slasher Film," *Representations* 20 (Fall, 1987), pp. 187–228.

20. Starling was widely perceived by the viewers to be unfeminine. She was variously referred to in her role as an FBI recruit. Although Orion's publicity materials described her as "gutsy,"

repeating verbatim studio handout sheets is taboo among reviewers; equally unsettling might have been the unconscious connection between that adjective and Lecter's idiosyncratic diet. Here, however, Starling is variously relabeled to be "tenacious," "sturdy," "tough," "resourceful," "persistent," "ambitious," "driven." The *Silence of the Lambs* publicity materials, Orion Pictures [SLfile].

21. Thomas Harris, *The Silence of the Lambs* (New York: St. Martin's, 1988).
22. Rafferty, "Moth and Flame."
23. Peter Travers, "Snapshots from Hell: The Silence of the Lambs," *Rolling Stone* (March 7, 1991), pp. 87–88.
24. Denby, "Something Wilder."
25. Chuck Smith, "Hollywood Horror," *Vanguard* (April 19, 1991) [n.p. SLfile].
26. Hoberman, "Skin Flick."
27. Stuart Klawans, "Films," *The Nation* (February 25, 1991), pp. 246–47.
28. Powers, "Skin Deep."
29. Smith, "Hollywood Horror."
30. Richard A. Blake, "Visions of Evil," *America* 64: 10 (March 16, 1991), p. 292. *Commonweal's* reviewer implies the film is about Faust and Mephisto. The *Rolling Stone* headline says the film has "snapshots from hell."
31. Margaret R. Miles, *Carnal Knowing: Female Nakedness and Religious Meaning in the Christian West* (New York: Vintage Books, 1989).
32. Miles, *Carnal Knowing,* pp. 12 and xi.
33. Vincent Canby, "Methods of Madness in 'Silence of the Lambs,'" *New York Times* (February 14, 1991), p. C17.
34. Salamon, "Wierdo Killer."
35. Amy Taubin, in Kennedy, ed., "Writers."
36. Reviewers did at times discuss him not only as monstrous but as alien or an extraterrestrial.
37. In *Alice Doesn't: Feminism, Semiotics, Cinema* (Bloomington: Indiana University Press, 1984), Teresa de Lauretis's analysis of narrativity and gender uses the Oedipal myth with its stories of meeting the Sphinx and the Minotaur tale as part of her argument about patriarchy's construction of desire. This odd coincidence is not particularly troublesome to explain since the equation is widely known through feminist discourse, and Taubin and Hoberman both are familiar with that discourse. We do not need to assume anything more than common social and discursive networks provoked this conjunction of terms.
38. Arnold I. Davidson, "Sex and the Emergence of Sexuality," *Critical Inquiry* 14: 1 (Autumn, 1987), pp. 16–48, writes that it was through psychiatry that a split was made between anatomical sex and psychological sex. Medicalization takes over, investigating for visual evidence of gender both externally and internally.
39. Hoberman, "Skin Flick."
40. Barbara Creed, "Horror and the Monstrous-Feminine: An Imaginary Abjection," *Screen* 27: 1 (January–February, 1986), pp. 44–70.
41. Sheehan, "Overcooked Lambs."
42. And as psychoanalysis as a discourse begins its dissemination.
43. Klawans, "Films."
44. It was derived from the novel but appears even during publicity generated while the film was in production. Its potency is obvious from the fact that the ad campaign recently won an award for the best movie poster of the year. Eithne Johnson informs me that the posters used Dali's "punning" picture of women to create the skull. Furthermore, moths and butterflies have a long-standing association with the vagina. No reviewer, however, made note of either.
45. Klawans, "Films"; Smith, "Hollywood Horror."
46. Mary Douglas, *Purity and Danger: An Analysis of the Concepts of Pollution and Taboo* (New York: Praeger, 1966), p. 122.
47. Douglas, *Purity,* p. 126.
48. Richard Jennings quoted in Fox, "Gays Decry Benefit Screening of 'Lambs.'"

JOHN   FROW

ECONOMIES OF VALUE

*The privileging of the self through the pathologizing of the Other remains
the key move and defining objective of axiology.*[1]

From this point onwards I address you, my silent reader, explicitly as a cultural intellectual: an address which may go astray, but which enables me to abandon that pretence of universality—the pretence of the absence of position—which lends such a
false glow of transparency to academic writing. I assume, for the sake of argument,
that when I say "we" from now on I am speaking to and partly for men and women
belonging to a local fraction of the class that I have tried to describe in the
previous chapter; I assume that "we" have certain—but by no means all—
class-specific interests in common; and that these have to do above all with the
investments we have made in knowledge and its social relations. I assume you share
my uncertainties about the value of our knowledge and about—the topic of this final
chapter—the positions that we are able to occupy within the field of cultural value.

   I argued earlier that it is no longer either possible or useful to understand cultural production in terms of a general economy of value, and thus that we can no
longer imagine ourselves into a vantage point from which conflicting judgements
of value could be reconciled. What may in some sense always have been the case
has become self-evidently so now: that different social groups employ criteria of
value which may well be incompatible and irreconcilable. Lotman's distinction
between the aesthetic of opposition that organizes post-Romantic high culture,
and the aesthetic of repetition that organizes much of folk and popular culture is
perhaps the simplest way of exemplifying this incompatibility; but in general the
disjunctions between the organizing aesthetics of European and non-European
cultures, between "men's" and "women's" genres (in so far as this opposition can be
sustained), between religious and "aesthetic" functionalizations of a text, between
literate and oral cultures, between the cultural norms of different age-classes or
different sexual subcultures or different national regions, and so on, can be taken
as indications of a vastly more complex network of differentiations which is not, or
is no longer, reducible to a single scale.

Yet it is precisely this assumption of a set of uniform criteria, or of a uniform hierarchy of criteria, that has played the major organizing role in the most authoritative and entrenched practices of reading—with the inevitable effect of repressing the difference and the specificity of other practices, casting them as naïve or exotic or perverse. Within a "modernist" regime of value, commensuration between regimes (the application to diverse texts and reading practices of a single standard) can occur only by way of an absolute disvaluation of those practices that fail to measure up. When Umberto Eco, for example, constructs the concept of an "average reader" of the James Bond texts who functions as a figure of literalness, he does so by ignoring the systems of cultural reference that structure popular readings. He simply misses many of the intertextual references (like the parody by the Bond films of other popular films, including earlier films in the Bond series) around which forms of popular "knowingness" are constructed.[2] Eco

> construes sophisticated reading as being subject to a distinctive form of social and cultural organization because he is familiar with the determinations which organize it. Lacking such familiarity with the determinations which mould and configure popular reading, such reading is conceived as being socially and culturally unorganized. . . . [P]opular reading is conceived as a mere lack, characterized by the absence of the determinations which mould sophisticated reading.[3]

Alternatively, certain theorists who are in principle willing to grant the sheer difference between frameworks of value, their irreducibility to a single perspective, nevertheless seek to reserve some ultimate criterion which, "in the last instance," allows for an absolute discrimination between more and less valuable texts. A favourite amongst semioticians is the criterion of informational complexity, understood as a purely formal and abstract criterion, by virtue of which some texts are more likely than others to be put to a multiplicity of uses and engage a multiplicity of quite divergent interests. But Barbara Herrnstein Smith is right, I think, to argue that among the competencies given by the acquisition of cultural capital is the ability to move between diverse cultural codes and to cope with, and indeed enjoy, structural complexity; thus the texts most highly valued by semioticians (and other intellectuals) "will tend to be those that gratify the exercise of such competencies and engage interests of that kind."[4] However desirable they might seem, such criteria are therefore by no means universal, and cannot form the basis of an aesthetic that could reconcile diverse criteria of value at a high level of abstraction.

As soon as it is conceded that there no longer exists a general economy of value, however, a series of difficult consequences comes into play.

For the category of value does not disappear with the collapse of a general economy;[5] it continues to organize every local domain of the aesthetic and every aspect of daily life, from the ritualized discussions of movies or books or TV programmes through which relations of sociability are maintained, to the fine discriminations of taste in clothing or food or idiom that are made by every social class and every status subculture, to the organization of school and university curricula, museum and gallery exhibitions, and the allocation of commercial and public financing to the culture industries. There is no escape from the discourse of value, and no escape from the pressure and indeed the obligation to treat the world as though it were fully relational, fully interconnected. But what becomes entirely problematical is just the possibility of relation: that is, of critical movement across the spaces between *incommensurate* evaluative regimes. If the use of cultural objects is something more than a matter of individual preference (and the whole vocabulary of "preference" as it is elaborated by the rationalist individualism of neoclassical economics simply begs the question of why different choices are made and of whether some choices are better than others; "preference" has the great theoretical advantage of being ineffable),[6] then it becomes a problem to account for the systemic formation of value without assuming criteria that hold good right across the cultural field.

One possible strategy for dealing with this transformed economy would be through a move that seems, in fact, to get neatly beyond the whole problem of valuation. The move involves deciding that, rather than engaging *in* a discourse of value, calculating the relative worth of this text against that text according to some impossibly universal criterion of value, the job of the critic is rather to analyse the social relations of value themselves: to analyse the discourses of value, the socially situated frameworks of valuation from which value judgements are generated by readers. More broadly, this would be an analysis not only of norms and procedures but of the institutional structures through which value is formed, transmitted, and regulated; of the social distribution of literacy; of the mechanisms for the training and certification of valuing subjects; of the multiplicity of formations of value, differentiated by age, by class, by gender, by race, and so on.

Such a practice of dispassionate analysis, where normativity is passed from the subject to the object of study, has the virtue of generosity towards the very different, often contradictory discourses of value held by different groups; rather than privileging the values of an intellectual élite, proclaiming as universal a set of norms that can be demonstrated to be historically and culturally variable—norms of "good taste" that are invariably class- and gender-specific—it concedes in advance the validity of the discrepant norms of other social groups: a validity that is now always relative to those groups and grounded in them, as are the norms of a socially situated high culture.

Certainly this seems to me an indispensable first step in dealing with questions of value. It has the major flaw, however, of being unable to comprehend its own position, in ways that matter, within the ambit of its analysis. It is as though the understanding of value took place within some space that was free of social conflict, free of the play of interests, free of prejudice and misunderstanding; and as though (in a counter-movement to that passage of normativity from subject to object) the principle of totalization had been displaced from the object, the cultural field, to the self-effacing space of analysis itself. Methodological objectivism works as a denial of the principle that "'culture' is always relational, an inscription of communicative processes that exist, historically, *between* subjects in relations of power."[7]

Cultural studies has occasionally made the analogy between some of its own claims to disinterest and the procedures of ethnomethodology, in particular ethnomethodology's refusal of any position that would be external to the values and codes of the group, the *ethnos,* it is studying: its refusal, that is, of any metadiscourse. Indeed, because of ethnomethodology's bias in favour of practical, everyday sociological reasoning, professional sociology is given no privileged status whatsoever, and its procedures and its theoretical problems are of interest only as one more example of the use of reflexivity to construct and maintain a reality.

Given this absence of a privileged meta-level (since neither the sociologist nor the philosopher has any special claim to expertise denied to ordinary people, who are just as expert in the rules that govern social reality), there can be no *critique* of everyday processes: as Harold Garfinkel puts it, "there can be nothing to quarrel with or to correct about practical sociological reasoning," and "ethnomethodological studies are not directed to formulating or arguing correctives. They are useless when they are done as ironies."[8]

Such a position seems to me to have clearly conservative political implications —at best it can give rise to a kind of political quietism. Nor does it seem to me even possible to avoid the practice of "irony": to avoid, that is, the disaffected criticality of intellectual knowledge, since, as Bob Hodge and Alec McHoul argue in their analysis of the strategy of "ethnomethodological indifference," although "the text is supposed to speak for itself, untouched by sociological hands, it is nevertheless the case that the commentary—coming after the moment of action and data-collection—*gives* the character of truth to its text."[9] Indeed, the very desire to avoid normative or prescriptive forms of reasoning inevitably leads to a repression of the privileged status of sociological enquiry, as well as its links to social power.

A further strategy closely related to this strategy of dispassionate analysis of value systems is the espousal or at least the acceptance of a kind of happy relativism: a model (which we might call "postmodern") of the world as being irreducibly plural and informed by no principle of totalization.

Zygmunt Bauman, for example, sets up an opposition between two distinct modes of intellectual practice. On the one hand he posits a framework characteristic of modernity, according to which the orderly totality of the world is patterned by the uneven distribution of probabilities, and order is exerted by their manipulation. The stochastic nature of this universe thus implies no final chaos and no separation of knowledge from practice; on the contrary, "effectivity of control and correctness [of knowledge] are tightly related (the second explains the first, the first corroborates the second), whether in laboratory experiment or societal practice." On the other hand, there is what he calls the postmodern worldview of "an unlimited number of models of order, each one guaranteed by a relatively autonomous set of practices. Order does not precede practices and hence cannot serve as an outside measure of their validity. Each of the many models of order makes sense solely in terms of the practices which validate it," and is upheld by the beliefs of a "community of meanings." These local forms of knowledge are not subject to any higher-level principle of explanation: "there are no criteria for evaluating local practices which are situated outside traditions, outside 'localities.' Systems of knowledge may only be evaluated from 'inside' their respective traditions." Thus, "if, from the modern point of view, relativism of knowledge was a problem to be struggled against and eventually overcome in theory and in practice, from the postmodern point of view relativity of knowledge (that is, its 'embeddedness' in its own communally supported tradition) is a lasting feature of the world."[10]

This "postmodern" model continues to have the merit of openness towards the discrepant and often disdained structures of value of different social groups; in asserting the validity and the local specificity of a plurality of practices and codes of valuation it refuses to maintain the privilege of any one culture over any other. But this openness can easily become a kind of contempt in its own right, since it entails a certain indifference towards the otherness of other domains; no domain of value has anything to say to or about any other, and indeed there is an active prohibition on intercommunication; each domain is hermetically sealed from each of the others.

A more complex and more restless formulation of the problem of commensuration between heterogeneous value systems can be found in the work of Jean-François Lyotard. Following his turn, after the major texts of the early 1970s, from an energetics to a "generalized rhetoric,"[11] it is possible to isolate two main phases in this formulation.

The first is built around the concept of language games and the problematic of incommensurability between games that Lyotard derives from it. The form that Lyotard gives to this idea of an absence of measure is the postulate that the diversity of languages (including the diversity of ends informing them) cannot be reconciled at a higher logical level. Three different reasons are given to support this thesis. The least interesting, and the most dogmatically offered, is the argument that prescriptives cannot be derived from descriptives. The second has to do with the impossibility of transcending what he calls "story" or "opinion"[12] in order to attain a mode of understanding that could not itself be objectified as story.[13] The third reason is ethico-political rather than logical: it is an argument that the postulate of an integrating metadiscourse represents an attempt to impose discursive homogeneity where there not only is but ought to be heterogeneity. Far from constituting a problem, the diversity of language games is a prerequisite for the openness of the social system; conversely, the achievement of a "consensus"—and therefore of an end to discussion—would represent a form of violence (or "terror") done to the dynamic of social argument.

The mode of relativism that Lyotard describes in this phase of his work could perhaps be called an absolute relativism, and it generates precisely the contradictions implied by the oxymoron. As Samuel Weber observes of the argument of *Just Gaming*, where a universally binding prescriptive is formulated in order to maintain and underpin the value of singularity, "the concept of absolute, intact singularity" remains "tributary to the same logic of identity that sustains any and all ideas of totality"; and "the concern with 'preserving the purity' and singularity 'of each game' by reinforcing its isolation from the others gives rise to exactly what was intended to be avoided: 'the domination of one game by another', namely, the domination of the prescriptive."[14]

The second "phase" of Lyotard's later work (one that in part overlaps chronologically with the "first") can be read as an attempt to overcome the insoluble problems that attach to any notion of *pure* heterogeneity, of *absolute* difference. Here, with the introduction of the concepts of the *différend* and of the genre of discourse, the question of the linkage (or "slippage") between sentences displaces that of incommensurability—although the latter still remains the starting point for Lyotard's thinking. Whilst at one level translation between sentences belonging to different regimes continues not to be possible,[15] what is, however, not only possible but absolutely unavoidable is the linkage (*enchaînement*) of one sentence to another. The function of the genre of discourse is to bring sentences that may belong to quite distinct regimes within the ambit of a single end, a single teleology. It does not follow from this, however, that the incommensurability between sentences is eliminated or reconciled, since "another genre of discourse can inscribe it into another finality. Genres of discourse do nothing more than shift the differend from the level of regimens to that of ends."[16] And this process of reinscription, of shifting "ends," is in principle endless.

One way of describing the movement in Lyotard's thought that is sketched here would be to say that there is a passage from an ontology of the sentence to a pragmatics of the sentence—to a concern with the uses to which sentences are put. Rather than formulating a general rule about the necessary separation of language games, Lyotard describes a process which encompasses both the practical commensuration of sentences as they are tied together by a discursive telos, and the endless dissociation of sentences as they are put to conflicting uses (or as there is conflict over the uses to which they may be put). This is to say that commensuration is possible (and is a practical necessity) not at the level of a metadiscourse that would somehow reconcile the semantic and pragmatic tensions between sentences, but at the more limited, "local," and always contested level of the genre. It is not that there is no metadiscourse, but that there are many of them. If this conclusion ends by restating the problem of the lack of measure between distinct orders of knowledge and value (and if, as Connor notes, it continues to beg the question of the ground against which radical difference can be perceived),[17] it does so, nevertheless, no longer on the basis of an assertion of the self-contained purity of these orders, but in the recognition of the constant passage and the complex and conflictual transactions between them.

For Lyotard as for Wittgenstein, the entrenched separateness of language games is grounded in the specificity of the forms of life in which they are embedded.[18] What is at stake politically—at least for Lyotard—in this correlation is the irreducible diversity of human interests, and in particular a deep suspicion of any claim to represent a universally valid structure of interest—a claim typically made by the *particular* class of intellectuals.[19] But much hangs on the way these two orders of being are bound together (and, indeed, on the conceptual separation made between them in the first place).

The problem is that of the forms of unity and identity ascribed to social groups; it is a problem that has been particularly acute for cultural studies, with its habitual reliance on a sociological relativism. At the limit, if aesthetic texts and practices of knowledge are closely tied to shared forms of life, and if their force is purely relative to these forms, then they are deprived of all except the most limited cognitive power—since they have no hold over any other domain. There is no scope for challenging the givenness of a cultural order: if every social group, every valuing community or subculture produces only those texts that express and validate its way of life, there is no *strong* ground from which to argue for alternative forms of textuality or indeed alternative ways of life.

A more general objection to the relativization of texts and codes of reading to communities, however, might be the organicism inherent in the notion of community itself: a concept that evokes the pre-industrial village rather than the abstract and highly mediated cultural spaces of the late twentieth century. The model of a plurality of valuing communities or subcultures is a model of a dispersed set of social clusters which are at once separate and self-contained; as John Guillory argues, the concept posits social identity as the basis for the solidarity of evaluation (and disagreement is therefore always a priori evidence of belonging to a different community: the argument is in this sense circular). Thus the concept of value cannot adequately account for differences of judgement *within* a valuing community, since it is used above all to "exalt the difference of the community from other communities."[20]

It is probably not, I think, any longer problematic to say that value is always *value-for*, always tied to some valuing group; what does raise a problem is the fact that in our world the boundaries of communities are always porous, since most people belong to many valuing communities simultaneously; since communities overlap; and since they're heterogeneous. Moreover, to tie texts to forms of life in this way assumes that texts enter exhaustively into their context, without residue, and without the possibility of further, unpredicted, and perhaps unpredictable uses being made of them. The concept of community in cultural studies works as an *archè*, an organic and unifying origin.

Janice Radway speaks of the naturalization of presence inherent in the comparable concept of an empirical "audience," and hence of the difficulty of theorizing "the dispersed, anonymous, unpredictable nature of the use of mass-produced, mass-mediated cultural forms," where the receivers of such forms "are never assembled fixedly on a site or even in an easily identifiable space" and "are frequently not uniformly or even attentively disposed to systems of cultural production, or to the messages they issue."[21]

But rather than adopting her tactic of attempting an even more exhaustive empirical analysis, a total ethnography, of "the ever-shifting kaleidoscope of cultural circulation and consumption,"[22] it seems to me more useful (and more economical) to posit a mediating institutional mechanism to account both for the diversity of value and for the absence of any simple or necessary coincidence between social groups and the structure of valuation.

The concept I want to propose is that of the *regime of value*, a semiotic institution generating evaluative regularities under certain conditions of use, and in which particular empirical audiences or communities may be more or less fully imbricated. Arjun Appadurai uses the concept in this sense to define the cultural framework within which very variable investments are made in the exchange of commodities. Adopting from Simmel the notion that economic value has no general existence but is always the particular result of "the commensuration of two intensities of demand," and that this commensuration takes the form of "the exchange of sacrifice and gain," he argues that it is thus exchange that underlies the formation of value, and exchange occurs within specific regimes where "desire and demand, reciprocal sacrifice and power interact to create economic value in specific social situations."[23] Regimes of value are mechanisms that permit the construction and regulation of value-equivalence, and indeed permit cross-cultural mediation. Thus the concept

> does *not* imply that every act of commodity exchange presupposes a complete cultural sharing of assumptions, but rather that the degree of value coherence may be highly variable from situation to situation, and from commodity to commodity. A regime of value, in this sense, is consistent with both very high and very low sharing of standards by the parties to a particular commodity exchange. Such regimes of value account for the constant transcendence of cultural boundaries by the flow of commodities, where culture is understood as a bounded and localized system of meanings. (p. 15)

The regime of value constitutes "a broad set of agreements concerning what is desirable, what a reasonable 'exchange of sacrifices' comprises, and who is permitted to exercise what kind of effective demand in what circumstances" (p. 57); this regulation is always political in its mediation of discrepant interests.

The concept is roughly similar to Tony Bennett's concept of the *reading forma-*

tion, which is likewise used to bypass a sociological realism that would tie modes of reading directly to social groups. The reading formation is a semiotic apparatus, a "set of discursive and intertextual determinations that organize and animate the practice of reading, connecting texts and readers in specific relations to one another by constituting readers as reading subjects of particular types and texts as objects-to-be-read in particular ways."[24] What this means is that neither texts nor readers have an existence independent of these relations; that every act of reading, and hence every act of ascribing value, is specific to the particular regime that organizes it. Texts and readers are not separable elements with fixed properties but "variable functions within a discursively ordered set of relations,"[25] and apparently identical texts and readers will function quite differently within different regimes.

Regimes of value are thus relatively autonomous of and have no directly expressive relation to social groups. In the case of "high"-cultural regimes, this relative autonomy is an effect of historical survivals and of the relative autonomy of the modern educational apparatus, both of which then give rise to interpretative and evaluative traditions that do not directly reflect class interests; in the case of "popular" regimes, their relative autonomy has less to do with the historical persistence of codes of value (although this is still a factor) than with the way the mass media work to form audiences that cross the borders of classes, ethnic groups, genders, and indeed nations. The concept of regime expresses one of the fundamental theses of work in cultural studies: that no object, no text, no cultural practice has an intrinsic or necessary meaning or value or function; and that meaning, value, and function are always the effect of specific (and changing, changeable) social relations and mechanisms of signification.

Thus the regimes that make up the domain of "high" culture consist of sets of interlocking institutions framing particular kinds of practice and producing certain axiological regularities: school curricula; classroom trainings in appropriate responses and evaluations; the certification of academic expertise and the structure of professional careers in cultural production and cultural criticism; the institutions of the theatre, the concert hall, the museum, and the art gallery; the art market; the publishing industry (and the "quality" niches within it); specialist and non-specialist journals and magazines; criticism and reviews in the *feuilleton* sections of newspapers and of radio and television programming; peer-group cultures, and the conversational rituals that sustain evaluative codes; particular patterns of work and leisure, and particular codes of status-discrimination; and so on. As the composition of this network, together with the protocols and criteria by which value is articulated, vary historically, so too do the particular functions performed by "high" culture (*one* of these, but not the only one, may be to reinforce the discrepancy between aesthetic and economic discourses of value, as a way of designating aesthetic—that is, non-economic—value as a marker of status).

Like the regimes of high culture, although often in less self-assertive ways, the regimes of "popular" culture too tend to take on the task of reinforcing the disjunction between the two discourses of value—the task of converting commodities into non-economic values (aesthetic values, which may however take an ethical and experiential form). And they too are organized around complex apparatuses of codification, of formal or informal trainings, and of status marking. There may well, of course, be regimes of value whose central principle is the inappropriateness of "evaluation"; Eric Michaels makes this case for the Australian Aboriginal art of the Western desert, which is based on a principle of reproduction and on inherited authorship rights,[26] and similar arguments have been made for some forms of post-modernist art. The point, though, is that even such an ethos of non-evaluation must be organized and regulated by a definite and historically particular regime.

An essay on graffiti by Susan Stewart neatly crystallizes the different framings and consequences that arise when a cultural form is positioned by different evaluative regimes.[27] As an "indigenous or folk form carried out by a community of writers relatively homogeneous in age (9–16)" (p. 165) the practice of graffiti-writing in New York and Philadelphia situates itself in one sense firmly outside "the aesthetic" and within a politics of the (re-)appropriation of space; in another sense, however, it is practised in accordance with quite specifically aesthetic codes. It possesses a comprehensive vocabulary of evaluation (an anti-language which often inverts the standard terms of approval, and which, giving special weight to the criteria of difficulty and frequency, values "elegance, speed, grace, and the sensuality of the body") (p. 171); and a distinctive technical vocabulary to describe its tools and its activities. A well-defined hierarchy of practitioners structures a semi-formal apprenticeship system:

> beginners (called "toys") work with master writers as apprentices. The toy generally progresses from writing simple "tags" (signatures made with markers or spray paints) on any surface to writing "throw-ups" (larger tags thrown onto inaccessible surfaces or the outsides of subway cars) to writing "pieces" (short for masterpieces: symbolic and/or figurative works such as landscapes, objects, letters, or characters drawn on a variety of surfaces). (p. 165)

The dominant code is one of stylistic individuation, expressed in the triumphant formalization of handwriting and repeated insistently across public space in such a way as to "serve purely as a mark of presence, the concrete evidence of an individual existence and the reclamation of the environment through the label of the personal" (p. 165). The investment in frequency of production is borrowed from advertising and publicity, and the act of writing is "a tautological process of self-promotion miming the reflexive signifiers of advertising and 'packaging'"; the borrowing should however be read, Stewart argues, as "a matter of adaptation, manipulation, and localization" (p. 166). For this aesthetics of the signature works both within and against commodity culture, figuring the writer at once as brand name and as the repetition of resistance to the repetitions of commodity culture.

Whereas, for the writers, graffiti works[28] as an appropriation of privatized public space, a reduction of the public-monumental to the scale of the handwritten name, which "contrast[s] to the monument's abstraction and stasis the signature's personality, mobility, and vernacular, localized audience" (p. 169), within a quite different regime of value—that which organizes the readings of city officials—gaffiti relates to public space as dirt and crime. A key term here is "defacement": as with the defacement of coinage, graffiti "is considered a threat to the entire system of meanings by which [public] surfaces acquire value, integrity, and significance" (p. 168). Specifically, it is a threat to the system of property values, and a mark of the failure of state policing of the common domain.

It thus ties into a wider semiotic network in which it is read as an ethico-political, not as an aesthetic, practice. Explicitly placed outside the realm of the cultural, it is linked to "the dirty, the animal, the uncivilized, and the profane" (p. 168). Its producers are (incorrectly) assumed all to be of Afro-American or Latin descent, and are characterized as deviant (members of criminal gangs, or even insane). Despite the absence of a sexual thematics in graffiti, which focuses entirely on the representation of the proper name, it is organized within this regime as an *obscene* form: writing in the wrong place. And, in order that the vast resources expended on "graffiti maintenance" can be legitimated, it is characterized, despite its physical durability, as a reversible or erasable form: like dirt, and unlike the artwork, it contains within it the necessity of its own removal.

The conflict between these two axiological regimes is fought out at the level of the streets and the subways. A third regime, however, moves the scene of value off the streets and into the coffee-table books and the galleries. Stewart describes two wings, the "liberal" and the "avant-garde," of the aesthetic appropriation of graffiti (the difference between them is a matter of a family quarrel within the knowledge class). The liberal solution to the "graffiti problem" involves one of two demands: either that writers paint over their work, or that they become art students, redeploying their talents in the traditional studio genres. Stewart calls these approaches "insidious": the "'encouragement' of the writer's creativity is in effect a matter of disciplinary punishment, a punishment that takes as its thematic a generalized representation and simultaneous suppression of the signature which had been at the centre of the graffiti artist's work" (p. 170). To "reform" the writers of graffiti—to channel their skills into the codes of a discrepant aesthetic formation through a process of retraining—is at once an aesthetic and a political project, one that involves a repression of the social conditions of necessity and possibility of graffiti writing and a determined attempt to keep up appearances.

The avant-garde aesthetic, by contrast, seeks to retain the signature of the writer, but to retain it in the fetishized and saleable mode of "a self-conscious intentionality which places the artist intertextually within the tradition as it is defined by critics and the art establishment in general" (p. 172). This tradition (that of "a progression of individual artefacts worked by individual masters") (ibid.) displaces the local and recent culture of autograph graffiti into a place where it figures as "the spontaneous, the primitive, the real of this tradition—a real located in nature and the body. Here the invention of a tradition for graffiti, particularly as a form of 'folk art,' is the invention of both nostalgia and currency. Graffiti is valued as a dying art form, the romantic heir to abstract expressionism and pop art" (p. 173). The movement to a regime of *taste* substitutes a new object —graffiti produced on canvas as an object of appreciation—for the mobile and difficult autograph on the subway car, or the logo rapidly inscribed on the side of a bank. Within this regime, "the valuation of graffiti is an effort to accommodate through adaptation a novel threat to the status of the art object in general. To the extent that graffiti writers move off the street and into the gallery, the threat will be met" (p. 174).

A final regime of value—one that brackets the status of graffiti as art in order to refuse a "liberal pluralism of aesthetic judgements" (p. 163) according to which each regime confronts the "same" object from different perspectives—is that somewhat less visible regime from within which Stewart herself writes, and which makes it possible for her to play off the "street" regime against the others. Like the aesthetic regime, its conditions of existence are the possession of extensive cultural capital; it differs, perhaps, in its greater ability to elaborate a distance from immediate class interests (or, to put this differently, in its prosecution of an alternative set of interests).

The concept of regimes of value makes two things possible. First, by specifying the *mechanism* by means of which "extratextual" determinations like social position are translated into reading practices (mechanisms of training in the recognition and use of distinct codes of value) and the formal or informal institutions within which they operate, it demonstrates the irreducibility of semiotic codes to class or race or age or gender—and, conversely, it stresses the point that, because of this very non-equivalence, class and race and age and gender are always to an important degree imagined (but not imaginary) structures. Second, it makes it possible to rethink the relation between canonical (or "high") and non-canonical (or "popular") culture, as *practices* of value rather than as collections of texts with a necessary coherence: the text of graffiti can figure just as well within a "high"-cultural regime as within a "popular" regime. This is not to revert to a use of these categories as *substantive* or internally coherent categories; it is merely to accept the fact that the concepts of a "high" and a "popular" regime continue to organize the cultural field and to produce ideological effects of cultural distinction. (At the same time, this shift from texts to practices underlines the spuriousness of those defences of "the canon" which assume that texts have intrinsic worth.)

Judgements of value are always choices made within a particular regime. This is not to say that the regime determines which judgement will be made, but that it specifies a particular range of possible judgements, and a particular set of appropriate criteria; in setting an agenda, it also excludes certain criteria and certain judgements as inappropriate or unthinkable. Regimes therefore allow for disagreement, specifying the terms within which it can be enacted. Disagreement may also take place in the space of overlap between regimes, or between discrepant and non-intersecting regimes; but in a sense disagreement is only ever really possible where *some* agreement on the rules of engagement can be held in common.

If commensurability of criteria within a regime enables both concurrent and divergent judgements to be made, the incommensurability of criteria *between* regimes thus tends to preclude the possibility of productive exchange. Disagreement of this kind can be settled by an agreement to disagree, or by the attempt to impose one set of criteria over another. The latter has traditionally been the way of high culture and its institutions, if only because those institutions have had the power to do so; and the universalization of high-cultural values may take the shape either of a discrediting of other criteria of value, or of an appropriation of those criteria.

The difficulties that arise from any attempt to avoid the politics of totalizing judgement are often cast in terms of the philosophical dilemma of axiological (and, by implication, epistemological) relativism. At their core lies, I think, the anxiety generated by the fiction that is strategically posited by any politically informed relativism: the fiction that, in order to neutralize my own inevitable partiality, I should consider all domains of value to be *formally* equivalent. (This, it should be noted, is also the fiction put into place by any democratic electoral system: that, however passionately I may believe in the rightness of one party, I must suspend this belief in order to recognize the formal right of any other political party to win power, and, conversely, to accept as politically legitimate the possibility that my party will lose. This suspension of belief, for all its apparent ordinariness in the established democracies, depends upon a sophisticated politics of knowledge.)[29] What causes anxiety is a belief that recognition of the equal right of other values to *formal* (but not necessarily substantive) respect implies that all values or arguments must therefore be considered equally "valid"; and that this means that all arguments, by being held equal, are thus in some sense trivialized. Arguments, on this reading, cannot be defended or adjudicated because there is no possibility of winning an argument.

One response to this would be to elaborate a theory of what it means for an argument or a value to be *locally* valid: that is, for it to be judged correct or incorrect within a specific and limited framework, where such a judgement is entirely appropriate, but beyond which it ceases to hold any force. But Barbara Herrnstein Smith is on stronger ground in refusing the terms of the dilemma altogether. If the concepts of validity and objectivity, which continue to be presupposed by the arguments against relativism, are rejected as vacuous, this by no means entails that judgements of value cannot be evaluated and said to be better or worse (just as Foucault's argument that judgements of truth and falsity are always generated within a particular regime of truth does not mean that he himself will not make such judgements within a particular regime). What is entailed is that judgements of value and truth are relative to a social position of enunciation and to a set of conditions of enunciation (which are not necessarily the same for each instance of an utterance). "Better" and "worse" will be meaningful terms to the extent that a framework of valuation is agreed, and that the authority of speakers is accepted, at least provisionally, within it.

Nevertheless, neither of these responses confronts the question of how it is possible to make judgements across the boundaries of regimes. The analogy between the strategic fictions deployed by axiological relativism and by political democracy can perhaps serve to clarify the limits of the former, since these fictions belong to a larger historical framework. Both the rational valuing subject and the citizen endowed with rights and with formal equality before the law are aspects of the bourgeois subject of legal contract, a figure that integrates the dimensions of rational economic calculation, ethical integrity, consistency of will over time, and positional equality within and for the duration of the contractual framework.[30] The figure of the bourgeois subject (I use the concept in a historically specific sense) is neither a pure illusion nor a straightforward social gain, since the formal equalities on which it is predicated are always systematically interwoven with, and work to conceal, structural inequalities in the economic sphere and the actual control of the legal and political spheres by the dominant class. Relativism of value and of knowledge is closely connected with—and is perhaps even a logical extrapolation from—this structure of formal equality; and this connection, which is *formally* "progressive," indicates both its political usefulness (it is not a position from which we can ever afford to retreat, out of nostalgia for a social order, past or future, free of these fictions), and its limitations. In so far as cognitive relativism posits a plurality of equivalent spheres, it necessarily fails to conceive of inequalities and asymmetries between these spheres (and therefore leaves the existing distribution of power untouched); and it is likely to conceptualize valuing communities in terms of self-contained positional identities, such that difference is posited between rather than within spheres of value.

In order to move beyond the limitations of relativism (which does not mean the reinstatement of some non-positional perspective), it becomes necessary to redefine the notion of positionality itself, together with the notion of representation on which it depends. The crucial argument here, it seems to me, is the one that follows when regimes of value are detached from a directly expressive relation to a social community. To speak is then never quite the same thing as "to express the interests of" or "to stand for" a particular group. At the same time, the dissociation of regime from group means that it is likely that members of any group will belong to more than one regime of value. This is particularly the case with "cultural" intellectuals, who are specifically trained in the ability to switch codes, to move readily between different practices of reading and of valuation.

Two sets of questions branch out from these difficult and intricate problems of positionality. The first is a set of practical difficulties within the cultural institutions. Given the fact (if this is conceded) of incommensurability between different regimes of value, and given the intense social interests that play around these fractures and asymmetries, how is it possible for judgements of value to be applied in the routine and everyday manner required by school and university curricula, by editorial decision-making, by decisions about arts funding and research funding, and about the exhibition of artefacts? What gets floor-space and wall-space in the museum and the gallery? What gets discussed in the arts pages of the newspapers and magazines? What do we teach our students: the canonical texts (whose authority they cannot otherwise fight against because they do not know them)? non-canonical texts (and don't these then become precisely an alternative *canon*)?[31] some mix of the two—and if so, then according to which criteria do we choose?[32] Is it possible to bypass the uncanny symbiosis of "high" culture and "popular" culture, their mutually reinforcing sacralization, in order to make possible a continual estrangement of the frames within which texts are normally and normatively read? Is it *practically* possible, as Steven Connor proposes, to live with "the paradoxical structure of value as immanent transcendence,"[33] a system of contingent universals—and indeed, is it "practically" possible not to?[34] These are questions not just about criteria, but about whose stories get told, and, crucially, about who gets to make these decisions, who doesn't, and on what grounds.

In the first instance, of course, these are questions not about individual decisions but about institutional structures. Training in the protocols of reading and in the formulation of value is received in part in the institutions of mass education and mass culture, which are detached from local cultures and local communities; and which are, in that sense, and in that sense only, "universal." These are the institutions controlled by the knowledge class—the class of intellectuals in the broadest sense of the term.[35]

At this point, then, I return to the question of the "interests" of intellectuals: that is, above all, their institutional interest in cultural capital and its distribution. I shall use what I take to be an unresolved problem in a passage of Andrew Ross's *No Respect*[36] as a way of getting at the articulation of this interest with the institutional distinction between high and low culture.

Ross begins the passage, towards the end of the book, with a concise argument about the effects of distinction brought about by the disdain felt by high-cultural intellectuals for popular culture: "the exercise of cultural taste, wherever it is applied today, remains one of the most efficient guarantors of anti-democratic power relations, and, when augmented by the newly stratified privileges of a knowledge society, gives rise to new kinds of subordination" (p. 227). No longer just the lackeys of the ruling class, intellectuals are themselves the holders of significant social power which is manifested precisely in the exercise of judgement. To intellectual "disdain" Ross counterposes popular "disrespect":

Intellectuals today are unlikely to recognize . . . what is fully at stake in the new *politics of knowledge* if they fail to understand why so many cultural forms, devoted to horror and porn, and steeped in chauvinism and other bad attitudes, draw their popular appeal from expressions of disrespect for the lessons of educated taste. The sexism, racism, and militarism that pervades these genres is never expressed in a pure form (whatever that might be); it is articulated through and alongside social resentments born of subordination and exclusion. A politics that only preaches about the sexism, racism, and militarism while neglecting to rearticulate the popular, resistant appeal of the disrespect will not be a popular politics and will lose ground in any contest with the authoritarian populist languages that we have experienced under Reaganism and Thatcherism.

And Ross goes on to warn that

for many intellectuals, such a politics has always been and still is difficult to imagine, let alone accept, because of its necessary engagement with aggressively indifferent attitudes toward the life of the mind and the protocols of knowledge; because it appeals to the body in ways which cannot always be trusted; and because it trades on pleasures which a training in political rationality encourages us to devalue. But the challenge of such a politics is greater than ever because in an age of expert rule, the popular is perhaps the one field in which intellectuals are least likely to be experts. (pp. 231–2)

This argument is the culmination of a book that meticulously documents the ways in which the notion of "the popular" has served as an emblem by means of which North American intellectuals, and indeed intellectuals elsewhere in the world, have figured their relation to an imaginary Other. To take one case, for 1950s left intellectuals like Sydney Finkelstein and Eric Hobsbawm, American jazz "had become the ideal embodiment of an authentic music by the people, for the people"; and

similar claims for the authenticity of an organic communitarian culture would also be made in the subsequent course of rock music by musicians, youth leaders, and pop critics at the height of the equally short-lived rock counterculture in the late sixties. But the period of jazz's authentic "moment" as a legitimate populist art, from the late forties of Finkelstein to the late fifties of Hobsbawm, no longer belonged to the large, popular audience it had once enjoyed. Instead, it belonged to traditional intellectuals in possession, finally, of their Holy Grail, and, increasingly, to the organic black intellectual voices of musicians. (p. 93)

In developing this argument through a series of case studies—the cultural politics of the Popular Front, the Cold War critique of mass culture, Pop Art and camp, the feminist anti-pornography movement—Ross is scrupulous not to counterpose intellectual constructions of the popular to some more authentic mode of popular consumption. Contrasting the North American with the European appropriation of American popular culture, he says:

While the American experience of commercial popular culture was, of course, much more *lived* and direct, we should not fall into the trap of assuming that it was less mediated or fantasmatic. The uses made of comic strips, science fiction, "Detroit" styling, Westerns, rock'n'roll, advertising, etc., by different social groups cannot be read as if they were spontaneous responses to real social conditions. On the contrary, they represent an imaginary relation to these conditions, and one which is refracted through the powerful lens of the so-called American Dream—a pathologically seductive infusion of affluence, sublimated ordinariness and achieved utopian pleasure. The American as a dream American. (p. 149)

The very cogency of Ross's analysis, however, makes it difficult to understand just how to take his urging that intellectuals must learn to "engage" with the anti-intellectualism of popular culture. On the one hand, this appeal assumes (although Ross qualifies this assumption elsewhere) that the power of the knowedge class is in some sense the dominant social power, and it thereby both underplays the dominant role of capital (intellectuals may run the schools and the mass media, but they do not own them), and accepts what may be a kind of scape-goating of intellectuals. At the same time, Ross offers no indications of how, or from what political position, such an "engagement" might be possible without a repetition of that imaginary identification in which intellectuals have constructed "the popular" as a fantasy of otherness. There are clear limits to the extent to which it is possible for intellectuals to associate themselves with anti-intellectual-ism; and there are limits to how far they can or should suspend their critique of, for example, racism, sexism, and militarism. By the same token, Ross begs the question of the bad faith that might be involved in intellectuals identifying with a position that directly attacks their own status and activity, including that very act of identification. There are, after all, already strong traditions of intellectual anti-intellectualism in the United States (and elsewhere), exemplified currently by those New Right intellectuals who identify a "politically correct" liberal intelli-gentsia as the holders of real social power.

Let me put in the deliberately exaggerated form of a double-bind the central aporia that I see for cultural studies in confronting these questions of value: the impossibility either of espousing, in any simple way, the norms of high culture, in so far as this represents that exercise of distinction which works to exclude those not possessed of cultural capital; or, on the other hand, of espousing, in any simple way, the norms of "popular" culture to the extent that this involves, for the posses-sors of cultural capital, a fantasy of otherness and a politically dubious will to speak on behalf of this imaginary Other.

Despite its exaggerated form, this dilemma is, I think, a real one, and one that we should not seek to resolve too quickly; it speaks to the heart of the political dif-ficulty of being a cultural intellectual in a world where culture is defined by its relation to one or another market in distinction. It is a dilemma that may not nec-essarily take the form of personal anxiety—indeed, a postmodern floating between cultural regimes may be deeply pleasurable—but it poses difficult questions about pedagogic strategy, about political effectivity, and about the organization of cultural institutions.

My intention in posing the dilemma in this way is not to argue that intellectuals should keep their distance from popular culture, but to argue that they should not idealize it as their mystical Other, precisely because they themselves are not sepa-rate from this Other. As Larry Grossberg argues:

We are always and already one (if not many) of the masses. Consequently, we cannot start by dividing up the terrain according to our own maps of tastes and distastes (although our travelogues are always contaminated by them), or our own sense of some imaginary boundary which divides a mythic (and always dominant) mainstream from a magical (and always resisting or reflexive) marginality, or our own notion of an assumed gulf between our intellectual self and our popular-media self.[37]

The overlap between regimes of value is the condition that makes it possible to move between incommensurate regimes, at the same time as it both produces and frustrates the will to totalizing judgement. One possible model for such a process of crossover between regimes organized by incompatible criteria perhaps already exists, in the rather routine form of the study of literary texts from different historical periods: in the form, that is, not just of an analysis of historically differentiated norms of production and reception, but of a refusal either completely to privilege the present (making its categories the standard of familiarity from which the strangeness of other historical categories deviates) or completely to forget it (so that history becomes unhistorical in its pure estrangement from present interests). This is the model of a hermeneutics, understood not as a method of depth interpretation but as the mediation of interpretative frameworks. I invoke this model not in order to suggest that a ready-made and properly functioning paradigm for cultural studies exists elsewhere,[38] nor to announce a new set of scholarly tasks, but simply to indicate one of the ways in which an openness to cultural difference might be compatible with an established and regularized methodology, rather than being a matter of unreproducible spontaneity.

One other key locus for the experience, or rather the construction, of otherness as a central disciplinary moment is of course ethnography. This is a model which has had an increasing influence on cultural studies, though often in ways that reflect little knowledge of ethnographic procedures[39] or the complexity of ethnography's own methodological reflection (in recent years, for example, its problematization of the forms of writing through which the object of ethnography is formed as at once exotic and familiar).[40] The exemplary aspect of ethnography in this context, however, must surely be no more than the brute fact of its complicity with colonial (and neo-colonial, and post-colonial) domination.[41]

The second set of questions is separate from but directly connected to the first set. They are ethical and political questions: who speaks? who speaks for whom? whose voice is listened to, whose voice is spoken over, who has no voice? whose claim to be powerless works as a ruse of power? under what circumstances is it right or wrong, effective or ineffective, to speak for others? And how can relations of enunciative power—which by definition are shifting and situational—adequately be described?

A recent essay by Linda Alcoff may serve as a point of entry to these questions of representation (in both senses of the word).[42] Alcoff casts the question of representation in terms of enunciative modality, the relation between social position and the semantics of utterance. Beginning with the "growing recognition that where one speaks from alters the truth of what one says, and thus that one cannot assume an ability to transcend one's location," she then extends this on the one hand to the argument that "the practice of privileged persons speaking for or on behalf of less privileged persons has actually resulted (in many cases) in increasing or reinforcing the oppression of the group spoken for" (pp. 6–7), and on the other hand (shifting from persons to discursive positions) to the thesis that "certain contexts and locations are allied with structures of oppression, and certain others are allied with resistance to oppression. Therefore all are not politically equal, and, given that politics is connected to truth, all are not epistemically equal" (p. 15).

Alcoff's aim is to produce something like an ethics, or an ethico-politics, of speaking. Her argument is complicated, however, by the collapse, during the course of the essay, of the solidity of the concept of position (or "context" or "social location"). Thus she concedes that the notion of social location cannot be used as an index of determinant origin, since speakers can never be said to be fully in control of the meanings of utterances, and certainly have little control over the uses that are made of them. To be an "author" is not to be the source of an utterance, but rather to be *credited* as its source; and the import of an utterance cannot be deduced simply from its propositional content or from the enunciative position or credentials of its speaker, since the utterance will also generate an open-ended chain of effects which is not reducible to either of those two moments.

In order to retrieve from this concession some of the force of the concept of enunciative modality—but also to guard against the converse danger of the *reduction* of meaning to social position—Alcoff introduces a more qualified model of the semantics of context: location "bears on" meaning and truth rather than determining them, and it is multiple and mobile. The act of speaking from within a group is consequently "immensely complex. To the extent that location is not a fixed essence, and to the extent that there is an uneasy, underdetermined, and contested relationship between location on the one hand and meaning and truth on the other, we cannot reduce evaluation of meaning and truth to a simple identification of the speaker's location" (pp. 16–17).

Moreover, even so far as the thesis linking a privileged right and competence to speak with symbolic oppression holds good, the appropriate response to this link is not necessarily to abdicate from speaking for others. For two reasons: first, because such a response "assumes that one *can* retreat into one's own discrete location and make claims entirely and singularly based on that location that do not range over others"; and second, because "even a complete retreat from speech is of course not neutral since it allows the continued dominance of current discourses and acts by omission to reinforce their dominance" (p. 18). Whereas the act of speaking for others denies those others the right to be the subjects of their own speech, the refusal to speak on behalf of the oppressed, conversely, assumes that they are in a position to act as such fully empowered subjects.

Alcoff's argument here follows closely that of Gayatri Spivak in "Can the Subaltern Speak?"[43] where, taking issue with Foucault and Deleuze's influential remarks on the "fundamental . . . indignity of speaking for others,"[44] she argues that any invocation of the oppressed as self-representing and "fully in control of the knowledge of their own oppression" (p. 274) serves to effect a double concealment: on the one hand, of the fact that these self-representing oppressed are still (since they are *invoked* to play a role) a fact of discourse, a representation; and, on the other, of the role of intellectuals in constructing this self-negating representation, their representation of themselves as transparent. There can be no simple refusal of the role of judge or of universal witness, since to do so is to denegate the institutional conditions, consequences, and responsibilities of intellectual work.[45]

The particular circumstances under which it is appropriate or inappropriate to represent the interests of others, and to attempt to bracket off one's own interests in the process, are of course always complex and contingent; precisely because of the complexity of the category of position. What Alcoff's argument usefully does, however, is move away from a naïve realism of social positionality towards a more differentiated politics of enunciation.

The problem with tying an utterance to social position or social "identity" is that the latter tends to act as (or to be taken as) something fully external to discourse, the place of the Real *as against* the discursive. But position and identity are discursively realized and imagined; and they are shifting and multiple. Speaking positions, and the authority (or lack of it) that accompanies them, are, however, powerful and very real performative *effects*. By this I mean that they are the effects of discursive institutions of authorization which selectively credit the speaker with membership of one or more speech communities and with a place on one or more hierarchies of authority and credibility. They are not effects, that is to say, of "objective" social position, but of an imputed position; they are moments of a semiotic politics, not reflections of a political reality that takes place elsewhere.[46]

There is no point of leverage *outside* the politics of representation, only an endless and unequal negotiation of relations of power within it (and within its institutions, which are largely controlled but not owned by the knowledge class). The determinations operating on the rights of "cultural" intellectuals to speak for others are twofold, and pull in contradictory directions. The first (an enabling condition) is the "uneasiness" of the relation between group and speaker, the slight but significant detachment of speaking position from *representation* of a speech community (in the sense of standing for it, sharing its characteristics).[47] I have used the concept of regime of value to theorize this partial detachment. Like the infinitesimal swerve of Lucretius's atoms, it is this gap that allows the universe of discourse to be at once rule-governed and open-ended. The second determination is their membership of a social class with real, though ambivalent, class interests in the implementation of modernity. The privileged possession of cultural capital translates into an exercise of power that can well take the form of an apparent self-negation or self-abasement.

"Culture is our specific capital," says Bourdieu, "and, even in the most radical probing, we tend to forget the true foundation of our specific power, of the particular form of domination we exercise."[48] In seeking to place the work of cultural intellectuals in the framework of a class formation and a set of more or less definite class interests, I have sought to make this work less transparent, and so to take seriously the ways in which it might further the knowledge class's own interests rather than those of the groups for whom intellectuals claim to speak, or any more universal interest.

One response to this shift towards the interests of intellectual work might be simply to condemn those interests, to find them irrelevant to the real stakes in social struggle; but if it is true that intellectual work is indeed structured by a specific (if ambivalent) social interest, then such a response can only miss the point (and indeed can only be made from within the structure of interest that it denounces). A different kind of response might be to give serious attention—as Gouldner, for example, does—to the progressive political potential of the knowledge class. In Gouldner's analysis, the political interests of the New Class are defined by its revolutionizing relation to the mode of production (the modernizing imperative to "make it new") and its ambivalent relation to the classes above and beneath it. In the advanced industrial economies it serves as "a technical intelligentsia whose work is subordinate to the old moneyed class. The New Class is useful to the old for the technical services it performs and, also, to legitimate the society as modern and scientific."[49] As its effective control over production grows, however, so does its political power *vis-à-vis* the bourgeoisie. In the political sphere proper, it is only through the New Class that the old dominant class can exercise an influence on state policy, and "as the organizational units of the economy and state become larger and more bureaucratic, the survival and control of the old class becomes more attenuated, more indirect, ever more dependent on the intelligentsia of the New Class" (p. 50). In terms both of its relation to the mode of production and its relation to the bourgeoisie, then, the New Class is an inherently progressive political force, and indeed is "a centre of whatever human emancipation is possible in the foreseeable future" (p. 83). It neither restricts the forces of production nor develops them only in so far as they are profitable; in its commitment to an ideal of freedom of knowledge it embodies a rationality which is broader than the merely instrumental; it is internationalist and cosmopolitan; and by extension—this is perhaps the most dated aspect of Gouldner's argument—its politics are logically left-wing.

A strong form of this thesis can be found in a recent essay of Pierre Bourdieu's which uncharacteristically abandons the sceptical detachment of the sociologist in order to argue directly for the necessity of a corporatist politics of intellectuals.[50] At its most basic, this is an argument that intellectuals should recognize their right to "accord themselves what every other group accords itself, i.e., the right to publicly defend their vision of the world, as particular and self-interested as it might be" (p. 110). In particular, they should accord themselves the right to defend the autonomy of intellectual work against the various powerful threats to it: threats to funding, to working conditions, to the right to autonomy both from commercial pressures and from political direction of the goals of research, threats to the right to disseminate knowledge in the public domain, and indeed to the concept of a public domain itself. Despite compelling reasons, intellectuals have not usually been adept at such self-defence: they

> have often emphasized the defence of major universal causes and rejected the defence of their own interests as merely corporatist, forgetting that the defence of the universal presupposes the defence of the defenders of the universal. . . . They can do this without remorse or moral hesitation since, by defending themselves as a whole, they defend the universal. (p. 103)

What this universal might be is never spelled out precisely, but, as with Gouldner's conception of the culture of critical discourse that characterizes the New Class of intellectuals, it seems to be grounded in the first instance in the norms and protocols of scientific work; in the free dissemination of scientific knowledge; and in the fact that intellectual work is formed in the rejection of particularisms. It is contrasted to commercially oriented research, to the bureaucratic regulation of knowledge, and to journalism.

The claim that Bourdieu makes is not precisely that intellectuals represent a universal class, since they "have not escaped the universal temptation to universalize their particular interests" (p. 109). There are, however, two reasons why they are

capable of a certain kind of class generosity. The first is "their situation as dominated dominators or, more precisely, as dominated parties within the field of power
—a situation which leads them to feel solidarity with any and all the dominated,
despite the fact that, being in possession of one of the major means of domination,
cultural capital, they partake of the dominant order" (ibid.). The other is the capacity for self-reflexivity given by intellectual work (for example, sociology), and thus
their awareness of "the *privileges* underlying their claims to the universal" (p. 110).
The politics of intellectuals will be a "corporatism of the universal" to the extent
that it seeks to universalize the privileged conditions of their own existence.

What this argument promises is a way out of that politics of the alibi whereby
intellectuals claim the right to speak from a position of relative power on behalf of
the powerless and the dispossessed. It is, however, a wrong argument. It relies for
all its force on a distinction between "real" intellectuals and "pseudo-" intellectuals
(the treacherous clerks within the disciplines, the bureaucrats and journalists
without); but this distinction is impossible to maintain without at the same time
destroying any notion of the possible unity of the class fraction of intellectuals.
Like so many other accounts of the intelligentsia, it massively overestimates the
social value of intellectual work. And it discards all of that elementary suspicion
that causes Gouldner to describe the New Class of intellectuals as a *"flawed* universal class"—flawed in the sense that its interests do not coincide with those of
other social classes.[51] The alternative to the claim to the disinterestedness of the
knowledge classs[52] is not simply that it should commit itself to the defence of its
own class interests. As Bourdieu himself has made abundantly clear, cultural capital is always at best a partial good: at once an instrument of knowing (and in that
sense *potentially* universal), and an instrument of class distinction.

To say that we must be as suspicious of the interests of intellectuals as we are of
any other social interests is not to imply that we should or somehow could reject
them. To the contrary: we can act in good faith only as long as we recognize that
there is no escape from the consequences of possession of cultural capital, just as
there is no way of getting outside the game of value judgement and the game of
cultural distinction. At the same time, this structure of interest means that it is
politically crucial for intellectuals not to universalize the competences they possess
as norms which can be used to totalize the cultural field.

The question of our relation to regimes of value is not a personal but an institutional question. A key condition of any institutional politics, however, is that intellectuals do not denegate their own status as possessors of cultural capital; that they
accept and struggle with the contradictions that this entails; and that their cultural
politics, right across the spectrum of cultural texts, should be openly and without
embarrassment presented as their politics, not someone else's.

NOTES

1. Barbara Herrnstein Smith, *Contingencies of Value: Alternative Perspectives for Critical Theory*
   (Cambridge, Mass.: Harvard University Press, 1988), 38.
2. Noel King reminds me, however, that Eco's book on Bond was written in the 1960s within a
   particular theoretical paradigm. His "oversights" are not so much a matter of failure of
   insight as of the critical institution that draws a particular line between what should and
   what need not be known.
3. Tony Bennett and Janet Woollacott, *Bond and Beyond: The Political Career of a Popular Hero*
   (London and New York: Methuen, 1987), 79.
4. *Contingencies of Value*, 51.

5. The concept of value of course has a long genealogy in the disciplines of aesthetics and economics. Just as the category of labour, according to Marx, could achieve philosophical abstraction and generality only on the historical basis of "a very developed totality of real kinds of labour," so the category of value became a recognizable philosophical *problem* only under particular historical circumstances. John Guillory and Mary Poovey have each documented the emergence of the category of value in its modern aesthetic sense in the break-up of the discipline of moral philosophy (the key figure here is Adam Smith, and the disintegration of moral philosophy can be traced in the distance between the *Theory of Moral Sentiments* and *The Wealth of Nations*). What emerges, more precisely, is what Barbara Herrnstein Smith calls a "double discourse of value": a relation of mutual exclusion between the autonomy of the aesthetic and the instrumentality of the commodity. This split is undermined almost from the beginning, however, by the reluctant or repressed recognition not only of the commodity status of artworks but also of the aesthetic dimension of commodities (Poovey takes *fashion* as the paradigm case of the constructedness of desire; its logic exposes "both the persistence of aesthetic concerns within economic exchanges, and the persistence of a market logic in the domain of beauty or art"). Thus, Guillory argues, "the 'double discourse of value' is historically determined by the fact that while it is not possible for any object *not* to have a relation to the market, to the objective condition of universal commensuration, this relation cannot be defined by the simple reduction of the object (not even the commodity) to the quantum of exchange value." This might suggest that that whole powerful tradition—including the work of Bataille and of Baudrillard—that opposes an economy of exchange to an economy of the gift, and the calculations of exchange value to the spontaneity of use value, is ultimately unworkable, because of the interpenetration of these two economies. Karl Marx, *Grundrisse: Foundations of the Critique of Political Economy (Rough Draft)*, trans and forward by Martin Nicholaus (Harmondsworth: Penguin, 1973), 104; John Guillory, *Cultural Capital: The Problem of Literary Canon Formation* (Chicago: University of Chicago Press, 1993), 325; Mary Poovey, "Aesthetics and Political Economy in the Eighteenth Century," in George Levine and Carolyn Williams (eds.), *Aesthetics and Ideology* (New Brunswick, N.J.: Rutgers University Press, forthcoming); Smith, *Contingencies of Value*, 127.
6. Cf. John Fekete, "Introductory Notes for a Postmodern Value Agenda," in John Fekete (ed.), *Life After Postmodernism: Essays on Value and Culture* (New York: St Martin's Press, 1987), p. viii.
7. James Clifford, "Introduction: Partial Truths," in James Clifford and George E. Marcus (eds.), *Writing Culture: The Poetics and Politics of Ethnography* (Berkeley: University of California Press, 1986), 15.
8. Harold Garfinkel, *Studies in Ethnomethodology* (New Jersey: Prentice-Hall, 1967), p. viii.
9. Bob Hodge and Alec McHoul, "The Politics of Text and Commentary," *Textual Practice*, 6: 2 (1992), 193–4.
10. Zygmut Bauman, *Legislators and Interpreters: On Modernity, Postmodernity and Intellectuals* (Cambridge: Policy Press, (1987), 3–4.
11. Geoff Bennington, *Lyotard: Writing the Event* (Manchester: Manchester University Press, 1988), 117: "Once the libidinal language is recognized as essentially that (a language), and can in principle become one more *dispositif* rather than a general ground of explanation for all *dispositifs*, then a general field of 'façons de parler' is opened up, which might be described in terms of a generalized rhetoric."
12. Cf. Jean-François Lyotard and Jean-Loup Thébaud, *Just Gaming*, trans. Wlad Godzich, Theory and History of Literature, Vol. 20 (Minneapolis: University of Minnesota Press, 1985), 43: "We are always within opinion, and there is no possible discourse of truth on the situation. And there is no such discourse because one is caught up in a story, and one cannot get out of this story to take up a metalinguistic position from which the whole could be dominated. We are always immanent to stories in the making, even when we are the ones telling the story to the other."
13. Jean-François Lyotard, *The Differend: Phrases in Dispute*, trans. Georges Van Den Abbeele,

Theory and History of Literature, Vol. 46 (Minneapolis: University of Minnesota Press, 1988), 138.

14. Samuel Weber, "Afterword: Literature—Just Making It," in *Just Gaming*, 103, 104.

15. In *Just Gaming* (pp. 53–4) Lyotard makes the distinction that "languages are translatable, otherwise they are not languages; but language games are not translatable, because if they were, they would not be language games. It is as if one wanted to translate the rules and strategies of chess into checkers." This makes it clear, of course, that non-translatability is part of the *definition* of language games.

16. *The Differend*, 29.

17. Steven Connor, *Theory and Cultural Value* (Oxford: Basil Blackwell, 1992), 112.

18. There is a useful genealogy of the term *Lebensformen* as Wittgenstein found it "in the air" in Vienna (most immediately among the neo-Kantian characterologists) in Allan Janik and Stephen Toulmin, *Wittgenstein's Vienna* (New York: Simon and Schuster, 1973), 230 ff.

19. In a discussion of racism, Immanuel Wallerstein has made an explicit claim that the value of universality is specific to the small class of "cadres," whereas "by assuming a particularist stance—whether of class, of nation or of race—the working strata are expressing an instinct of self-protection against the ravages of a universalism that must be hypocritical within a system founded both on the permanence of inequality and on the process of material and social polarization." Étienne Balibar and Immanuel Wallerstein, *Race, Nation, Class: Ambiguous Identities* (London: Verso, 1991), 230. I think it is possible to accept that this argument is correct without thereby being driven to abandon all aspiration to the achievement of "universal" values.

20. Guillory, *Cultural Capital*, 278.

21. Janice Radway, "Reception Study: Ethnography and the Problems of Dispersed Audiences and Nomadic Subjects," *Cultural Studies*, 2: 3 (1988), 361.

22. Ibid.

23. Arjun Appadurai, "Introduction: Commodities and the Politics of Value," in Arjun Appadurai (ed.), *The Social Life of Things: Commodities in Cultural Perspective* (Cambridge: Cambridge University Press, 1986), 4.

24. Tony Bennett, "Texts in History: The Determinations of Readings and Their Texts," *Journal of the Midwest Modern Language Association*, 18: 1(1985), 7.

25. Ibid. 10.

26. Eric Michaels, "Bad Aboriginal Art," *Art and Text*, 28 (1988), 59–73.

27. Susan Stewart, "Ceci Tuera Cela: Graffiti as Crime and Art," in John Fekete (ed.), *Life After Postmodernism: Essays on Value and Culture* (New York: St Martin's Press, 1987), 161–80; references will be given in the text.

28. I have followed Stewart, and common usage, in treating "graffiti" as a singular collective noun.

29. Cf. Adam Przeworski, *Democracy and the Market: Political and Economic Reforms in Eastern Europe and Latin America* (Cambridge: Cambridge University Press, 1991), 93. In making this analogy I do not want to downplay the extent to which political choice in most of the established democracies has become virtually meaningless.

30. Cf. Betty Mensch, "Freedom of Contract as Ideology," *Stanford Law Review*, 33 (Apr. 1981), 753–92; Roberto Mangabeira Unger, *The Critical Legal Studies Movement* (Cambridge, Mass.: Harvard University Press, 1986), 63 ff.

31. "What should have been clear before now is that the canonizing effect does not in the least require a stable corpus of works in which to be embodied. Since canonization depends not on what one says about texts, so much as where one says it from, there is no real reason why a postmodernist world of shifting or open canons need do anything to the canonizing effect of discourses within institutions, except perhaps to make them ideologically more subtle and inconspicuous." Steven Connor, "The Modern and the Postmodern as History," *Essays in Criticism*, XXXVII: 3 (1987), 188; cf. Guillory, *Cultural Capital*, 81: "The movement to open or expand the canon might be regarded, among other things, as a belated attempt to save the bourgeois sociolect by expanding its base of textual representation."

32. For an extended analysis of the problems that arise from such basic pedagogic questions, cf. Charlotte Brunsdon, "Problems with Quality," *Screen*, 31: 1 (1990), 67–90.

33. Connor, *Theory and Cultural Value*, 33.

34. Cf. ibid. 2: "It is both the desire for an absolute grounding of political practice, and the attempt to imagine a political practice without grounding, which are hopelessly impractical and unresponsive to the practical complexity attaching to questions of value."

35. Bruce Robbins has useful things to say about the profession of literary studies, *qua* profession, in *Secular Vocations: Intellectuals, Professionalism, Culture* (London: Verso, 1993).

36. Andrew Ross, *No Respect: Intellectuals and Popular Culture* (London and New York: Routledge, 1989). Page references are given in the text.

37. Lawrence Grossberg, "Wandering Audiences, Nomadic Critics," *Cultural Studies*, 2: 3 (1988), 385.

38. I have made detailed criticisms of Gadamerian hermeneutics in *Marxism and Literary History* (Cambridge, Mass. and Oxford: Harvard University Press and Basil Blackwell, 1986), 224–7.

39. Cf. Virginia Nightingale, "What's 'Ethnographic' about Ethnographic Audience Research?," *Australian Journal of Communication* 16 (1989), 50–63.

40. James Clifford and George E. Marcus (eds.), *Writing Culture: The Poetics and Politics of Ethnography* (Berkeley: University of California Press, 1986); James Clifford, *The Predicament of Culture: Twentieth-Century Ethnography, Literature, and Art* (Cambridge, Mass.: Harvard University Press, 1988); George E. Marcus and Michael M. J. Fischer (eds.), *Anthropology as Cultural Critique: An Experimental Moment in the Human Sciences* (Chicago: University of Chicago Press, 1986); Clifford Geertz, *Works and Lives: The Anthropologist as Author* (Stanford, Calif.: Stanford University Press, 1988); Edward Said, "Representing the Colonized: Anthropology's Interlocutors," *Critical Inquiry*, 15 (1989), 205–25; Johannes Fabian, *Time and the Other: How Anthropology Makes Its Object* (New York: Columbia University Press, 1983).

41. Is it necessary to add that this is in no way meant to impugn the integrity of practising anthropologists, or to overlook the sensitivity that the discipline has developed to the relations of power that hold between it and the peoples it studies? The criticism is structural and historical, and it draws to a large extent upon a political critique developed within the profession itself.

42. Linda Alcoff, "The Problem of Speaking for Others," *Cultural Critique*, 20 (1991–2), 5–32; further references will be given in the text.

43. Gayatri Chakravorty Spivak, "Can the Subaltern Speak?" in Cary Nelson and Lawrence Grossberg (eds.), *Marxism and the Interpretation of Culture* (Urbana: University of Illinois Press, 1988), 271–313.

44. "Intellectuals and Power: A Conversation Between Michel Foucault and Gilles Deleuze," in Michel Foucault, *Language, Counter-Memory, Practice,* trans. Donald F. Bouchard and Sherry Simon (Ithaca, NY: Cornell University Press, 1977), 209.

45. Elsewhere Spivak writes: "The position that only the subaltern can know the subaltern, only women can know women, and so on, cannot be held as a theoretical presupposition . . . for it predicates the possibility of knowledge on identity." Gayatri Chakravorty Spivak, "A Literary Representation of the Subaltern: A Woman's Text from the Third World," *In Other Worlds: Essays in Cultural Politics* (New York and London: Methuen, 1987), 253–4.

46. I elaborate some of the political aspects of the distinction between knowing and being supposed to know in "Discipline and Discipleship," *Textual Practice*, 2: 3 (1988), 307–23.

47. Cf. the discussion by Boltanski and Thévenot of the procedures by which structures of typicality (generality) are constructed: Luc Boltanski and Laurent Thévenot, *De la justification: Les Économies de la grandeur* (Paris: Gallimard, 1991). Cf. also John Guillory's argument in *Cultural Capital* (pp. 6–7) that the politics of canon critique has operated as a kind of displacement of the liberal-pluralist politics of representation. The assumption it makes is that of a "homology between the process of *exclusion,* by which socially defined minorities are excluded from the exercise of power or from political representation, and the process of *selection,* by which certain works are designated canonical, others noncanonical. . . . Canonical and noncanonical authors are supposed to *stand for* particular social groups, dom-

inant or subordinate." This is, in all senses of the word, an *imaginary* politics; it relies on an essentialist conception of social "identity" and it misrecognizes the specific location of the canon (and its critique) in the institution of the school.

48. Pierre Bourdieu, *In Other Words: Essays Toward a Reflective Sociology*, trans. Matthew Adamson (Stanford, Calif.: Stanford University Press, 1990), 107.

49. Alvin Gouldner. *The Future of Intellectuals and the Rise of the New Class* (New York: Oxford University Press, 1979), 11–12.

50. Pierre Bourdieu, "The Corporatism of the Universal: The Role of Intellectuals in the Modern World," trans. Carolyn Betensky, *Telos,* 81 (Fall 1989), 99–110; further references are given in the text.

51. Gouldner, *The Future of Intellectuals,* 83.

52. The *locus classicus* for this claim is Mannheim's description of the *freischwebende Intelligenz* (Max Weber's term) as "a relatively classless stratum." Karl Mannheim, *Ideology and Utopia: An Introduction to the Sociology of Knowledge,* trans. Louis Wirth and Edward Shils (New York: Harvest, 1936), 155 ff.

V

LIMITATIONS AND DIFFICULTIES
OF RECEPTION STUDY

This anthology has suggested that in the last ten years many new developments have transformed reception study, which now includes not only phenomenological, neopragmatist, and post-Marxist approaches but also "practical" literary studies, cultural studies, and historical accounts of books and reading. In light of these new developments, several criticisms of and objections to reception study deserve reevaluation. For the most part, these criticisms identify three faults of reception study: its implicit conservatism, its dubious relativism, and, in its poststructuralist versions, its ahistorical character.

The first criticism, reception study's implicit conservatism, can take a political as well as a subtle Derridean form. An example of the political form comes from Christopher Norris, who says that, by rejecting Derridean ideological critique, Stanley Fish's reception study imposes on critics the narrow rules of the professional "game" (109). Similarly, Daniel O'Hara warns us that "a Stanley Fish can all too readily be taken, even by [oppositional] critics who should know better, as a plausible representative of the academic left" (7).[1] To an extent, this objection rightly asserts that reception study encourages critics to engage in ordinary literary criticism, instead of challenging conventions or undermining established ideologies. Certainly Fish divorces criticism from politics because he considers criticism professional, not engaged or oppositional. This anthology indicates, however, that the liberal neopragmatism of Mailloux, the post-Marxism of Bennett, and the reception studies of Jane Austen, *The Silence of the Lambs,* women romance readers, and Madonna's music do not by any means ignore politics or reaffirm the professional "game."

The more subtle, Derridean version of this first objection asserts that, irreducible and, hence, subversive, the figural language or rhetorical forms of a text sustain many different interpretations. Since radical Derrideans maintain that, as a result, the rhetorical forms undermine the ideologies of a text or a reader, they argue that to grant the reader control of the text is to accept established interpretive practices and their ideological justification. In keeping with this view, Norris argues that Fish accepts conventional practices or established interpretations of the reader because Fish denies the subversive import of figural language (109; see also O'Hara, 133–43).

Although Paul de Man does not undertake a radical critique of ideology, he too complains that, despite many virtues, Jauss's theory of reading preserves conventional interpretive practices. In "History and Reading," de Man claims that, on the one hand, Jauss's account of the "horizon of expectation" successfully articulates the relationship of poetics and hermeneutics, textual structure and interpretive activity, and semiotics and literary history. That is, because of this notion, Jauss treats interpretation as the individual concretization of a "polysemic" textual structure that remains inexhaustible. On the other hand, de Man argues that the irreducible "play" of the signifier undermines this relationship of textual structure and reader's interpretation. A mimetic practice, the "horizon of expectations" has psychological import incompatible with the signifier's formal properties. Because of this mimetic practice, Jauss does not rigorously pursue the logic of the signifier; rather, his reading of Baudelaire's "Spleen II," especially his "decorous" analysis of "Boucher" or his "sublimated" interpretation of "sphinx," suggests that he quickly reaestheticizes the signifier's effects so that nothing "unpleasant can occur."

In response to de Man's criticisms, Jauss has denied that his aesthetics imitates empirical reality in a neoclassical fashion or ignores the unpleasant effects of the signifier (204–5). He argues that, on the contrary, deconstruction and reception study both oppose logocentrism, traditional philology, and classical aesthetics on the grounds that, always partial, understanding shows insights as well as blindnesses; however, he still defends the cognitive import of aesthetics, and he remains curious why de Man "opposed to the aesthetic the destructive power of the poetic equated with rhetoric" (205).

Actually, all reception theorists are vulnerable to this Derridean objection because all reception theory assumes that the conventions of interpretive practice limit the play of the signifier. What justifies them is, in part, the pedagogical practices whereby readers learn to read. As Jonathan Culler points out, someone has to teach readers that the aporias, gaps, and figural play subverting interpretive norms or aesthetic ideals require what de Man terms rigorous reading (114). The Derridean objection ignores the institutional contexts of interpretive practices, which the text's polysemic figural language may resist but from which it cannot altogether escape. To acknowledge these academic contexts is not, moreover, to adopt a conservative politics or to choose "the professional game"; indeed, there is no way to escape the game. As Fish says, the opposition to criticism's professional contexts is itself a professional gambit (1985). In addition, given the humanities' depressed state, one has to question the political value of this antiprofessional opposition, which fosters public distrust of the humanities.

Since this acknowledgment of criticism's institutional limitations implicitly denies that texts express universal values, critics have raised the second objection: reception study's relativism. They argue that, because reception study allows incompatible interpretive communities, rhetorical practices, or reading formations, rather than transcendental entities or universal ideals, reception study lapses into solipsism or fails to establish agreement or reform the profession.[2] To an extent, this objection too suggests that reception study blandly accommodates its academic contexts. To a greater extent, this objection implies that, because reception study repudiates objective truth or universal values, it cannot defend the humanities against conservative jeremiads or establish a consensus of professional scholars or political officials. As Reed Way Dasenbrock says, "We've Done It to Ourselves."

John Guillory pursues a version of this argument in "Discourses of Value." Although Guillory does not claim that the relativism of reception study has caused the humanities' socioeconomic difficulties, he does suggest that, because it critiques criticism's aesthetic "foundations," its concept of reading formations or interpretive communities break down. His argument is that, to acknowledge "the essential plurality of values," reception study allows distinct valuing communities, rather than autonomous aesthetic norms. Should the members of the community disagree, the community would readily break down into smaller and smaller units. Unable to preserve the requisite unity or solidarity of its members, the community would lapse into anarchy.

This criticism of reception study's "relativism" rightly indicates that without normative ideals the notion of "interpretive community" or "reading formation" reveals serious limitations; nonetheless, even though reception theorists critique foundational aesthetics, they do not assume that an interpretive community lacks normative ideals. Jauss explains the methods, practices, assumptions, and beliefs that constitute the "horizon of expectations" of the reader and his or her society. This "community" of readers does not lack public import or fail to bind its members, as Guillory claims, because the text, as a normative force, can transcend its readers and articulate new beliefs and values. Fish grants that incommensurate interpretive communities cannot engage in "rational" communication or transform each other, but he argues that, since the members of an interpretive community evaluate each others' readings, reception study has social norms, not "relativist" individual nor universal aesthetic grounds. Moreover, he construes the reader's interpretive community as a formal construct explaining interpretive differences, not a substantial entity requiring solidarity and/or imposing conformity.

Steven Mailloux admits that Fish's theory has relativist import but argues that his rhetorical hermeneutics need not imply incommensurable or "relativist" interpretive practices or preclude a rational consensus. Richard Rorty believes that the neopragmatist critique of philosophy's epistemological foundations cannot be relativist because it moves beyond traditional philosophy; similarly, Mailloux, who accepts Rorty's view, denies that his critique of literature's aesthetic foundations can be relativist. While Mailloux grants that divergent views can destroy a "liberal society," he argues that it will overcome its incommensurable views and preserve its solidarity but only by virtue of its growing enlightenment, not its transcendent aesthetic norms.

Guillory's critique of Tony Bennett's reception theory takes a slightly different turn. Guillory objects that Bennett considers aesthetic discourse "the narrative of a dominant social group's ideological universalization of its particular interests and historical situation"—a position that produces anarchy. Such an objection, however, misconstrues Bennett's argument. Although Bennett maintains that the established "reading formations" governing the reader's activity construct their own social relations (21), he limits their authority to the disciplinary force exercised by schools and universities, not by dominant social groups or classes. Guillory also considers Bennett's "conspiratorial" relativism central to "left-liberal" reception theory; however, Fish and Mailloux's liberal or professional ideals are based on consensus or individual choice, whereas Bennett's reading formations impose conformity on their members but do not lapse into anarchy because the reading formations enable schools and universities to discipline readers, ensuring that they constitute proper political/ethical subjects.

In still another charge, Guillory denies that reception study can adequately explain how the changing institutional contexts of criticism influence it. Similarly, Paul Bové rejects reception study not only because it accepts the conservative scholars' hostility to "oppositional" theory and multicultural studies (5) but also because it lacks what he terms "[c]ritical intelligence" which "involves a demystification of intellectuals' sense of their independence, a constant genealogical self-criticism, and research into specific discourses and institutions as part of the struggle against oppressive power" (47; see also Dasenbrock, 1995, 182; and Sprinker, 155). In this way the objections that reception study plays the professional "game" and lapses into relativism bring us to the third objection, that, as Guillory says, reception study fails to engage in "historical self-reflection" (324).

In "Confrontations with Radicalness," Robert Holub forcefully defends the historical profundity of reception study. He argues, however, that American criticism has repeatedly failed to recognize this historical depth. He blames this failure on poststructuralist critics such as de Man and Fish, who share what he calls a corrosively negative "radicalness." In his terms, their radical criticism creates a "deeply seated malaise" that "undercuts" reception theory "without offering much in the way of an alternative."

It is true that much American criticism does not appreciate the profound historical insight of Jauss or European reception study. It is also true, however, that Fish's, Mailloux's, and Bennett's critiques of foundational aesthetic theory need not lead to ahistoricism and a terrible "malaise." Indeed, while de Man's critique of theory demands "technically correct readings" (119), Fish's critique of theory justifies reception study. His approach lacks Jauss's historical depth, but his account of reception study has historical insight because, as his interpretation of Milton's *Lycidas* indicates, he assumes that readers learn the generic features and interpretive cruxes of Milton's poetry within historically specific contexts that mark the readers' membership in a particular interpretive community.

Mailloux also critiques "foundational" theory, but his reception study displays greater historical depth than Fish's. Like Jauss, who claims that the historical study of the reader's "horizon of expectations" resolves the longstanding opposition between objective, historical criticism and subjective, formal criticism, Mailloux maintains that historical reception study overcomes the pernicious warfare of textual or authorial "realists," who expect the structure of a text or the intention of an author to govern the reader's activity, and reader-oriented "idealists," who, like Fish, expect the reader's conventions and beliefs to explain his or her interpretive activity. Instead of promoting a hermeneutics of self and other, Mailloux urges critics to stop doing theory. More importantly, unlike de Man and Fish, Mailloux claims that to reject theory is to focus "on the rhetorical dynamics among interpreters within specific cultural settings. . . . [T]heory soon turns into rhetorical history" (144–45). Mailloux critiques theory in a poststructuralist fashion, but his critique still turns to "rhetorical history." He shows, for example, that twentieth-century readers debated the racial issues posed by *The Adventures of Huckleberry Finn* because these readers disputed the politics of the newly established formal criticism. By contrast, nineteenth-century readers ignored these issues because these readers meant to stop a spreading juvenile delinquency, which they termed the "bad boy syndrome" (104–29, 86–99).

As we already noted, Bennett rejects the traditional Marxist "dualism" whereby an objective history grounds an indeterminate text or culture but still examines the historical development of the "reading formations" regulating the reader's activity. In *Outside Literature,* Bennett maintains, for instance, that during the nineteenth century, when the schools turned literature into a "moral technology," the ideal teacher and, subsequently, the many-layered text made the reader's interpretive activity the basis of his or her unending ethical improvement (177–80). In other words, like de Man and Fish, Mailloux and Bennett critique literary theory on poststructuralist grounds, but their new kinds of reception study still have significant historical import. More importantly, the poststructuralist critique of theory opens reception study to literature's broad new areas, including women's, African-American, and multicultural literatures, popular culture, the ordinary reader, and the history of the book. As this anthology has shown, reception studies of these new areas do not limit criticism to the "professional game," deny it significant public influence, or deprive it of sociohistorical substance. On the contrary, the study of these new areas enables criticism to address the pressing sociohistorical issues raised not only by the humanities' political divisions but also by the media's growing influence and by reading's emerging history.

NOTES

1. O'Hara says that Fish's empiricist view of local, practical interpretation precludes radical, structural change and affirms the status quo (133–41). In "The Discipline of the Syllabus," Greg Jay complains that Mailloux's "critique of literariness through rhetorical hermeneutics . . . threatens to underestimate or misrepresent the liberating power that comes with categories of the literary or the aesthetic as they challenge or subvert dominant ideological or social frames of interpretation" (113). Similarly, Terry Eagleton complains that postmodern theory disables radical opponents of the capitalist system just when that system has gotten more powerful than ever (381).

2. See, for example, Dasenbrock, 1993, 18–32. Dasenbrock formulates this objection to relativism in other ways too. For instance, he says that, since significant disagreement requires some notion of truth, proponents of reception theory can form only a supportive circle of mutually congratulatory persons (1995, 558–60). He also objects that "as long as we insist on the community-specific nature of truth . . . we have no coherent response to any hostile description of our community" (1995, 182). Suresh Raval maintains that Fish is relativist because he gives up objectivity as well as convincing and unconvincing reasons (80–81). Giles Gunn attributes to Mailloux a "relativist world" that, "while acknowledging the historicity of all interpretive acts, including its own, in effect denies the possibility of critically comparing and evaluating them. We are thus left hermeneutically with the spectacle of history as a conflict . . . of interpretations among which it is impossible, from what I can tell, to adjudicate" (62). Etienne Balibar and other Marxists address the theory of Althusser and the post-Marxists, not reception study, but they maintain that "genuine" Marxist theory "takes its distance from any form of 'constructivism' or relativism, even in the sophisticated form given it by Foucault" (Balibar, 163; see also Sprinker, 829–31).

WORKS CITED

Balibar, Etienne. "Althusser's Object." *Social Text* 39 (summer 1994): 157–88.

Bennett, Tony. *Outside Literature*. New York: Routledge, 1990.

Bové, Paul. *In the Wake of Theory*. Hanover, N.H.: Wesleyan University Press, 1992.

Culler, Jonathan. *Structuralist Poetics: Structuralism, Linguistics and the Study of Literature*. Ithaca, N.Y.: Cornell University Press, 1975.

Dasenbrock, Reed Way. "Do We Write the Text We Read?" In *Literary Theory After Davidson*, edited by Reed Way Dasenbrock, 18–36. University Park: Pennsylvania State University Press, 1993.

———. "Truth and Methods." *College English* 57 (1995): 546–61.

———. "We've Done It to Ourselves: The Critique of Truth and the Attack on Theory." In *PC Wars: Politics and Theory in the Academy*, edited by Jeffrey Williams, 172–83. London: Routledge, 1995.

de Man, Paul. *The Resistance to Theory*. Minneapolis: University of Minnesota Press, 1986.

Eagleton, Terry. *The Ideology of the Asesthetic*. Cambridge, Mass.: Blackwell, 1990.

Fish, Stanley. "Anti-Professionalism." *New Literary History* 17 (1985): 89–108.

Guillory, John. *Cultural Capital: The Problem of Literary Canon Formation*. Chicago: University of Chicago Press, 1993.

Gunn, Giles. "Approaching the Historical." In *Reconceptualizing American Literary/Cultural Studies: Rhetoric, History, and Politics in the Humanities*, edited by William E. Cain, 59–72. New York: Garland, 1996.

Jauss, Robert. "Response to Paul de Man." In *Reading de Man Reading*, edited by Lindsay Waters and Wlad Godzich, 202–8. Minneapolis: University of Minnesota Press, 1989.

Jay, Gregory S. "The Discipline of the Syllabus." In *Reconceptualizing American Literary/Cultural Studies: Rhetoric, History, and Politics in the Humanities*, edited by William E. Cain, 101–16. New York: Garland, 1996.

Mailluoux, Steven. *Rhetorical Power*. Ithaca, N.Y.: Cornell University Press, 1989.

Norris, Christopher. *What's Wrong with Postmodernism: Critical Theory and the Ends of Philosophy*. Baltimore: Johns Hopkins University Press, 1990.

O'Hara, Daniel. *Radical Parody: American Culture and Critical Agency After Foucault*. New York: Columbia University Press, 1992.

Raval, Suresh. *Grounds of Literary Criticism*. Urbana: University of Illinois Press, 1998.

Sprinker, Michael. "The Current Conjuncture in Theory." *College English* 51 (1989): 825–34.

READING AND HISTORY

Some writers, not very remote from Jauss in time and place, have denied the effi-
cacy of a theory of interpretation based on the public reception of a work of literature and have discarded it as a mere side-effect devoid of hermeneutic interest.
Walter Benjamin's dogmatic pronouncement at the onset of his essay entitled "The
Task of the Translator" is a relevant case in point: "Nowhere does a concern for the
reception of a work of art or of an artform aver itself fruitful for its understanding. . . . No poem is addressed to a reader, no painting to its beholder, no sym-
phony to its listeners."[1] The passage is quoted by Rainer Warning, together with a
passage from Adorno, as a prime example of author or production oriented essentialism.[2] But is this really the case? When Jauss identifies the power of canonical
essences in the writings of Curtius, Lukács, and Gadamer, he is on safe ground,
but when the same is being said about Benjamin, Adorno, and Heidegger—three
names that, for all that separates them, belong together in this context—things are
not so simple. Benjamin, for instance, in the very essay from which the just-quoted
passage is taken, could not be more explicit in his critique of Platonic essences as
a model for history when he rejects the validity of the notion of copy or representation (Abbild) as an approach to literary texts. Nor could one be more eloquently
explicit than he is, in the same essay, about the historicity of literary understanding
—although the notion of history that Benjamin here invokes certainly differs considerably from Jauss's. By invoking the "translation" rather than the reception or
even the reading of a work as the proper analogon for its understanding, the negativity inherent in the process is being recognized: we all know that translations can
never succeed and that the task (Aufgabe) of the translator also means, as in the
parlance of competitive sports, his having to give up, his defeat "by default." But
"translation" also directs, by implication, the attention to language, rather than
perception, as the possible locus for this negative moment. For translation is, by
definition, intralinguistic, not a relationship between a subject and an object, or
a foreground and a background, but between one linguistic function and another.
Throughout the essay, Benjamin's point is that translation, as well as the insuper-
able difficulty that inhabits its project, exposes certain tensions that pertain
specifically to language: a possible incompatibility between proposition (Satz)
and denomination (Wort) or between the literal and what he calls the symbolic
meaning of a text or, within the symbolic dimension itself, between what is being

symbolized and the symbolizing function. The conflict is stated, in most general terms, as existing between what language means (*das Gemeinte*) and the manner in which it produces meaning (*die Art des Meinens*). It is certainly true that, in Benjamin's essay and elsewhere in his writings, these tensions are, to some degree, suspended in what he refers to as pure language: *die reine Sprache*. But it is equally clear that this apparent transcendence does not occur in the realm of art but in that of the sacred. Between Benjamin's *reine Sprache* and Valéry's *poésie pure* there is very little in common. Far from being nostalgia or a prophecy of the sacred, poetic language, of which the inherent inadequacy is made explicit in its translation, is what has to be forgotten to find access to the sacred: in the poetic translations that Hölderlin made of Sophocles "meaning collapses from abyss to abyss, until it threatens to lose itself in the bottomless depths of language." In such a sentence, "abyss" should perhaps be read as technically and neutrally as in any trivial "mise en abîme." The existential pathos is counterbalanced by the fact that these "bottomless depths" of language are also its most manifest and ordinary grammatical dimensions, the specific linguistic categories that Benjamin can list with some precision. What this does to Benjamin's subsequent claims of transcendence (or to their perhaps falacious understanding *as* transcendence) is not our present concern. It establishes however that, as far as poetry and its history are concerned, there can be no question of essences. The rejection of a conception of poetry as message or reception is not the result of an essentialist conception of literature but of the critique of such a conception. With numerous qualifications, something similar could be said of Heidegger's essay "On the Origin of the Work of Art," which Jauss summarizes (and dismisses) as an assertion of a "timeless present" or a "self sufficient presence" of the work of art, a simplification that does scant justice to Heidegger's dialectical concept of historical preservation (*Bewahrung*) on which Jauss himself, possibly by way of Gadamer, is dependent.[3]

The point is not to oppose to each other philosophical traditions some of which Jauss could easily enlist on his side of the question. Rather, the reference to Benjamin's essay draws attention to the possibility that a concept such as "horizon of expectation" is not necessarily applicable, without further elaboration, to the arts of language. For all the obstacles to understanding mentioned by Benjamin belong specifically to language rather than to the phenomenal world; consequently, the expectation that they could be mastered by analogy with processes that stem from the psychology of perception is by no means certain. Husserl himself, among others, could be invoked to caution against the possibility of such a mistranslation.[4] The hermeneutics of experience and the hermeneutics of reading are not necessarily compatible. This does not imply that the solutions proposed by Jauss are inadequate or that the recourse to perception can or should be avoided altogether; the opposite is the case. It does mean, however, that the horizon of Jauss's methodology, like all methodologies, has limitations that are not accessible to its own analytical tools. The limitation, in this case, has to do with linguistic factors that threaten to interfere with the synthesizing power of the historical model. And it also means that these same factors will then exercise a more or less occult power over Jauss's own discourse, especially over the details of his textual interpretations.

At first sight, this hardly seems to be the case. Jauss is by no means adverse to taking the linguistic aspects of texts into consideration, nor is he in any way on the defensive in dealing with the work of linguists. His preference, however, goes to linguists who attempt to mediate between the communicative and the aesthetic function of language, to what one could call the stylists of communication theory. Jauss has argued from the start that the recognition of the formal and aesthetic aspects of a text are not to be separated from historical investigations having to do with its reception; a good formalist, by the strength of his own performance, has to become a historian. The Czech linguist Felix V. Vodička, whose work is often cited with approval by Jauss and other Konstanz theoreticians, has made this explicit in his conception of reception as the historical "concretization" of a linguistic structure. The element of negativity that, in Jauss's horizon of expectation is located in the nonawareness of the background, resides, in Vodička and in the Prague linguists generally, in the characterization of literary language as a language of *signs*. Just as an element of not-knowing is built within the model of the horizon, the concept of literary sign implies an element of indeterminacy and of arbitrariness. In the words of Jan Mukařovský, a leading figure of the Prague Linguistic Circle, as quoted by Vodička: "Although the work of literature is closely dependent in its effect on communication by signs, it depends on it in such a manner that it is the dialectical negation of an actual communication."[5] The ensuing polysemy is mastered by inscribing it within the historical and social continuum of particular receptions or "concretizations." Structural aesthetics as practiced by the Prague circle are therefore far from being a threat to Jauss. His historical concepts seem to dovetail perfectly with their linguistic terminology. This theoretical alliance achieves a genuine synthesis between hermeneutics and poetics. Is this to say that Benjamin's anxieties about the semantics of poetic language are convincingly laid to rest by the concerted investigations of both linguists and historians?

The answer will depend on a term that until now we were able to keep in abeyance. When Vodička speaks of concretizations, he strongly insists that these are *aesthetic* concretizations, just as Jauss's reception is an *aesthetic* reception, an *aesthetic* process. How "aesthetic" is to be understood here is not self-evident. For Mukařovský, the aesthetic quality of the work of literature, like its historical quality, is a function of its sign-structure. In the analysis of poetic diction "the structure of the linguistic sign holds the center of attention, whereas the (nonpoetic) functions are oriented toward extralinguistic instances and goals exceeding the linguistic sign."[6] The focus, in poetic texts, on the process of signification rather than on significance is what is said to be specifically aesthetic. The arbitrary and conventional aspects of the sign thus acquire value as aesthetic features and it is by this same conventionality that the collective, social, and historical dimensions of the work can be reintegrated. This is the very point at which the procedures of a historian such as Jauss and poeticians such as Vodička or Mukařovský converge. It is Jauss's considerable merit to have perceived and demonstrated the linkage between reception and semiotics. The condensation of literary history and structural analysis occurs by ways of the category of the aesthetic and depends for its possibility on the stability of this category.

This stability, however, remains problematic for many philosophers. A concatenation of the aesthetic with the meaning-producing powers of language is a strong temptation to the mind but, precisely for that reason, it also opens up a Pandora's box. The aesthetic is, by definition, a seductive notion that appeals to the pleasure principle, a eudaemonic judgment that can displace and conceal values of truth and falsehood likely to be more resilient to desire than values of pleasure and pain. Nietzsche, who is acutely aware of aesthetic powers as tools of the will, warns that judgments based on pleasure or on pain "are the silliest *expressions* of judgments imaginable—by which, of course, I (Nietzsche) do not mean to say that the judgments which become audible in this manner have to be silly."[7] Aesthetic reactions can never be considered as central causes (*Ursachen*) but only as trivial side-effects (*Nebensachen*): "they are value judgments *of the second order* which are derived from a centrally dominant value; they consider the useful and the harmful in a purely affective mode and are therefore absolutely volatile and dependent."[8] The considerable interest they hold for the historian or for the critical philosopher is symptomatological rather than systematic: they are philosophically significant to the extent that their power to mislead points to other causes. Hegel's massively misunderstood treatment of the aesthetic as a provisional (*vorläufig*, a word that also occurs in Benjamin[9]) form of cognition is entirely in the spirit of his continuators Kierkegaard and Nietzsche. This means, among other things, that whenever the aesthetic is invoked as an appeal to clarity and control, whenever, in other words, a symptom is made into a remedy for the disorder that it signals, a great deal of caution is in order. Jauss's straightforward equation of the aesthetic with the pleasure principle, as in the essay on Valéry and Goethe, or as is implicit in his subsequent book on *Aesthetic Experience and Literary Hermeneutics*,[10] is in itself symptomatic. And when this same principle is then made to link up with the more objective properties of language revealed by linguistic analysis, the suspicion arises that aesthetic judgment has trespassed beyond its legitimate epistemological reach. As is to be expected in such a case, the traces of this transgression become noticeable by the omission, rather than by the misrepresentation, of certain features of language.

Characteristic of such omissions is Jauss's lack of interest, bordering on outright dismissal, in any considerations derived from what has, somewhat misleadingly, come to be known as the "play" of the signifier, semantic effects produced on the level of the letter rather than of the word or the sentence and which therefore escape from the network of hermeneutic questions and answers. Such a concern with "the instances of the letter" is particularly in evidence, as is well known, among certain French writers not generally included within Jauss's own critical canon of relevant *Fachliteratur*. He has always treated such Parisian extravagances with a measure of suspicion and even when, under the pressure of their persistence as well as of genuine affinities between their enterprise and his own, he acknowledged some of their findings, it has always been a guarded and partial recognition. There are good pedagogical and ideological reasons, of local rather than general interest, for this reserve. The tactics of exclusion, on the other hand, are so familiar as to constitute, within the community of literary scholarship, a mass reaction: in a long tradition, more familiar even in the world of *haute couture* than of literary theory, what is made in Paris is often thought of as more fashionable than sound. What is in fashion in Paris is tolerable only as window display, not for everyday wear. Yet, as we know from Baudelaire, fashion, *la mode,* is itself a highly significant and, precisely, aesthetic and historical category that historians should not underestimate. When it becomes fashionable to dismiss fashion, clearly something interesting is going on, and what is being discarded as *mere* fashion must also be more insistent, and more threatening, than its frivolity and transcience would seem to indicate. What is being dismissed, in the context of our question, is the play of the signifier, the very same topic (if it can thus be called) which Friedrich Schlegel singled out when the displeasure of his readers, the accusation of frivolity, forced him, in 1800, to suspend publication of the *Athenäum*.[11]

In the practice of his own textual interpretation, Jauss pays little attention to the semantic play of the signifier and when, on rare occasions, he does so, the effect is quickly reaestheticized before anything unpleasant might occur—just as any word-play is so easily disarmed by assimilating it to the harmlessness of a mere pun or *calembour*. Thus, in a recent article that makes use of one of Baudelaire's Spleen poems as a textual example,[12] Jauss comments judiciously on the lines in which the name of the eighteenth-century painter Boucher is made to pseudo-rhyme with the word "débouché" (uncorked)

> . . . un vieux boudoir
> Où les pastels plaintifs et les pâles Boucher,
> Seuls, respirent l'odeur d'un flacon débouché.

In a rare Lacanian moment, Jauss suggests that what he calls a "grotesque" effect of verbal play—the rhyme-pair Boucher/débouché—is also something more uncanny: "The still harmonius representation of the last perfume escaping from the uncorked bottle overturns (*kippt um*) into the dissonant connotation of a 'decapitated' rococo painter Boucher" (p. 157). After having gone this far, it becomes very hard to stop. Should one not also notice that this bloody scene is made gorier still by the presence of a proper name (Boucher) which, as a common name, means butcher, thus making the "pâle Boucher" the agent of his own execution? This pale and white text of recollection (the first line of the poem is "J'ai plus de souvenirs que si j'avais mille ans") turns red with a brutality that takes us out of the inwardness of memory, the ostensible *theme* of the poem, into a very threatening literality to which an innocent art-term such as "dissonance" hardly does justice. Much more apt is Jauss's very concrete and undecorous, almost colloquial, word "umkippen" (to overturn), which "overturns" the beheaded Boucher as if he were himself an uncorked "flacon" spilling his blood. That this would happen to the proper name of a painter, and by means of a merely "grotesque" and frivolous play on words tells us a great deal about the difficult-to-control borderline (or lack of it) between the aesthetics of *homo ludens* and the literal incisiveness of *Wortwitz*. For reasons of decorum, the gap that Jauss has opened, by his own observation, in the aesthetic texture of the language is at once reclosed, as if the commentator felt that he might betray the integrity of the text with which he is dealing.

This hesitation, this restraint before giving in to the coarseness and the potential violence of the signifier is by no means to be condemned as a lack of boldness. After all, Baudelaire himself does not threaten us, or himself, directly, and by keeping the menace wrapped up, as it were, within a play of language, he does not actually draw blood. He seems to stop in time, to fence with a foil[13]—for how could anyone be hurt by a mere rhyme? Yet, the poetic restraint exercised by Baudelaire differs entirely from the aesthetic restraint exercised by Jauss. For the play on words, as we all know from obscene jokes, far from preserving decorum dispenses with it quite easily, as Baudelaire dispensed with it to the point of attracting the attention of the *police des moeurs*. What it does not dispense with, unlike decorum (a classical and aesthetic concept), is the ambiguity of a statement that because it is a verbal thrust and not an actual blow, allows itself to be taken figurally but, in so doing, opens up the way to the performance of what it only seems to feign or prefigure. The false rhyme on Boucher/débouché is a figure, a paranomasis. But only after we have, with the assistance of H. R. Jauss, noticed and recognized it as such does the actual threat inherent in the fiction produced by the actual hands of the painter (who is also a butcher) become manifest. This no longer describes an aesthetic but a poetic structure, a structure that has to do with what Benjamin identified as a nonconvergence of "meaning" with "the devices that produce meaning," or what Nietzsche has in mind when he insists that eudaemonic judgments are inadequate "means of expression" of a cognition. Since this poetic (as distinguished from aesthetic) structure has to do with the necessity of deciding whether a statement in a text is to be taken as a figure or à la lettre, it pertains to rhetoric. In this particular instance, Jauss has come upon the rhetorical dimension of language; it is significant that he has to draw back in the face of his own discovery.

But how can it be said that Jauss swerves from the consideration of rhetoric where he has so many perceptive and relevant things to say about it, and does so without any trace of the restraint for which I am both praising and blaming him in his gloss on Baudelaire's poem? An extended study of his writings, going well beyond the decorous limits of an introduction, would show that something similar to what happens in the essay on Spleen occurs whenever rhetorical categories are at stake. One hint may suffice. In a polemical exchange with Gadamer about the rhetoric of classicism (p. 30), classical art is assimilated to a rhetoric of mimesis (the Aristotelian rhetorical category par excellence), and opposed to medieval and modern art, which are said to be nonmimetic and nonrepresentational. A rhetorical trope serves as the ground of a historical system of periodization that allows for the correct understanding of meaning; once again, a poetic and a hermeneutic category have been seamlessly articulated. But if this assertion seems so reasonable, is it not because it corresponds to a received idea of literary history rather than being the result of a rigorous linguistic analysis? The alternative to *mimesis* would be, one assumes, allegory, which all of us associate with medieval and, at least since Benjamin, with modern art. If we then ask whether Jauss's own model for reading, the horizon of expectation, is classical or modern, one would have to say that it is the former. For it is certainly, like all hermeneutic systems, overwhelmingly mimetic: if literary understanding involves a horizon of expectation it resembles a sense of perception, and it will be correct to the precise extent that it "imitates" such a perception. The negativity inherent in the Husserlian model is a negativity within the sensory itself and not its negation, let alone its "other." It is impossible to conceive of a phenomenal experience that would not be mimetic, as it is impossible to conceive of an aesthetic judgment that would not be dependent on imitation as a constitutive category, also and especially when the judgment, as is the case in Kant, is interiorized as the consciousness of a subject. The concept of nonrepresentational art stems from painting and from a pictorial aesthetic that is firmly committed to the phenomenalism of art. The allegory, or allegoresis, which Jauss opposes to mimesis, remains firmly rooted in the classical phenomenalism of an aesthetics of representation.

"Allegory," however, is a loaded term that can have different implications. A reference to Walter Benjamin can again be helpful, all the more so since Jauss alludes to him in the same essay on Baudelaire from which I have been quoting. In his treatment of allegory Benjamin plays, by anticipation, the part of Hamann in a debate in which Jauss would be playing the part of Herder. For him, allegory is best compared to a commodity; it has, as he puts it in a term taken from Marx, *Warencharakter,* "matter that is death in a double sense and that is anorganic." The "anorganic" quality of allegory is, however, not equivalent, as Jauss's commentary seems to suggest (p. 179), to the negation of the natural world; the opposition between organic and anorganic, in Benjamin, is not like the opposition between *organisch* and *aorganisch*, familiar from the terminology of idealist philosophy in Schelling and also in Hölderlin. The commodity is anorganic because it exists as a mere piece of paper, as an inscription or a notation on a certificate. The opposition is not between nature and consciousness (or subject) but between what exists as language and what does not. Allegory is material or materialistic, in Benjamin's sense, because its dependence on the letter, on the literalism of the letter, cuts it off sharply from symbolic and aesthetic syntheses. "The subject of allegory can only be called a grammatical subject"; the quotation is not from Benjamin but from one of the least valued sections of Hegel's *Lectures on Aesthetics*,[14] the canonical bible, still for Heidegger, of the phenomenalism of art. Allegory names the rhetorical process by which the literary text moves from a phenomenal, world-oriented to a grammatical, language-oriented direction. It thus also names the moment when aesthetic and poetic values part company. Everyone has always known that allegory, like the commodity and unlike aesthetic delight, is, as Hegel puts it, "icy and barren."[15] If this is so, can one then still share Jauss's confidence that "the allegorical intention, pursued to the utmost of *rigor mortis*, can still reverse (*umschlagen*) this extreme alienation into an appearance of the beautiful" (205)?[16] If the return to the aesthetic is a turning away from the language of allegory and of rhetoric, then it is also a turning away from literature, a breaking of the link between poetics and history.

The debate between Jauss and Benjamin on allegory is a debate between the classical position, here represented by Jauss, and a tradition[17] that undoes it, and that includes, in the wake of Kant, among others Hamann, Friedrich Schlegel, Kierkegaard, and Nietzsche. The debate occurs in the course of interpreting Baudelaire's poem "Spleen II." The poem deals with history as recollection, *souvenir*, Hegel's *Erinnerung*. Jauss's precise and suggestive reading carefully traces the manner in which an inner state of mind (spleen) is first compared to an outside object (ll. 2 and 5), then asserted to *be* such an object (l. 6), then becomes the voice of a speaking subject that declares itself to be an object (l. 8), and finally culminates in the dialogical relationship of an apostrophe by this subject to a material object that has itself acquired consciousness:

> —Désomais tu n'es plus, ô matière vivante!
> Qu'un granit entouré d'une vague épouvante, . . .
> [ll. 19–20]

At the conclusion of the poem, the enigmatic figure of "Un vieux sphinx" appears and is said, however restrictively and negatively, to be singing:

> Un vieux sphinx . . .
> Ne chante qu'aux rayons du soleil qui se couche.
> [ll. 22–24]

Jauss convincingly identifies this sphinx as the figure of the poetic voice and his song as the production of the text of "Spleen II" (pp. 169, 170). We rediscover the not unfamiliar, specular (that is to say solar and phenomenal) conception of a "poetry of poetry,"[18] the self-referential text that thematizes its own invention, prefigures its own reception, and achieves, as aesthetic cognition and pleasure, the recovery from the most extreme of alienations, from the terror of encrypted death. "The dissonance of the statement is aesthetically harmonized by the assonance and the balance between the various textual layers" (p. 182). "In a successfully elaborated form, the literary representation of terror and anxiety is always already, thanks to aesthetic sublimation, overcome" (p. 167). The promise of aesthetic sublimation is powerfully argued, in a manner that leaves little room for further questioning.

The assurance that further questioning nevertheless should take place has little to do with one's own spleen, with pessimism, nihilism or the historical necessity to overcome alienation. It depends on powers of poetic analysis, which it is in no one's power to evade. One of the thematic textual "layers" of "Spleen II" that remain constant throughout the text is that of the mind as a hollow container, box, or grave and the transformation of this container, or of the corpse contained in it, into a voice:

> mon triste cerveau.
> C'est une pyramide, un immense caveau,
> Qui contient plus de morts que la fosse commune.
> —Je suis un cimetière abhorré de la lune,
>
> . . . .
>
> —Désormais tu n'es plus, ô matière vivante!
> Qu'un granit entouré d'une vague épouvante,
> Assoupi dans le fond d'un Saharah brumeux;
> Un vieux sphinx ignoré du monde insoucieux,
> Oublié sur la carte, et dont l'humeur farouche
> Ne chante qu'aux rayons du soleil qui se couche.

The transformation occurs as one moves from mind (as recollection) to pyramid and to sphinx. It occurs, in other words, by an itinerary that travels by way of Egypt. Egypt, in Hegel's *Aesthetics,* is the birthplace of truly symbolic art, which is monumental and architectural, not literary. It is the art of memory that remembers death, the art of history as *Erinnerung.* The emblem for interiorized memory, in Hegel, is that of the buried treasure or mine (*Schacht*), or perhaps, a well.[19] Baudelaire, however, fond though he is of well-metaphors, uses "pyramid," which connotes, of course, Egypt, monument and crypt, but which also connotes, to a reader of Hegel, the emblem of the sign as opposed to the symbol.[20] The sign, which pertains specifically to language and to rhetoric, marks, in Hegel, the passage from sheer inward recollection and imagination to thought (*Denken*), which occurs by way of the deliberate forgetting of substantial, aesthetic, and pictorial symbols.[21] Baudelaire, who in all likelihood never heard of Hegel, happens to hit on the same emblematic sequence[22] to say something very similar. The decapitated painter lies, as a corpse, in the crypt of recollection and is replaced by the sphinx who, since he has a head and a face, can be apostrophized in the poetic speech of rhetorical figuration. But the sphinx is not an emblem of recollection but, like Hegel's sign, an emblem of forgetting. In Baudelaire's poem he is not just "oublié" but "oublié sur la carte," inaccessible to memory because he is imprinted on paper, because he is himself the inscription of a sign. Contrary to Jauss's assertion—"for who could say with more right than the sphinx: j'ai plus de souvenirs que si j'avais mille ans"—the sphinx is the one least able to say anything of the sort. He is the grammatical subject cut off from its consciousness, the poetic analysis cut off from its hermeneutic function, the dismantling of the aesthetic and pictorial world of "le soleil qui se couche" by the advent of poetry as allegory. What he "sings" can never be the poem entitled "Spleen"; his song is not the sublimation but the forgetting, by inscription, of terror, the dismemberment of the aesthetic whole into the unpredictable play of the literary letter. We could not have reached this understanding without the assistance of Jauss's reading. His work confronts us with the enigma of the relationship between the aesthetic and the poetic and, by so doing, it demonstrates the rigor of its theoretical questioning.

NOTES

1. Walter Benjamin, "Die Aufgabe des Übersetzers" in *Illuminationen* (Frankfurt, 1961), p. 56. English translation in *Illuminations*, trans. Harry Zohn (New York, 1968).
2. Rainer Warning, *Rezeptionsästhetik: Theorie und Praxis* (Munich, 1975), p. 9.
3. Jauss, *Toward an Aesthetic of Reception*, trans. Timothy Bahti (Minneapolis, Min, 1980), p. 63. Subsequent citations are given parenthetically [note added by editors].
4. See Husserl, *Logical Investigations*, trans. J. N. Findlay (London, 1970), Vol. II; also J. P. Schobinger, *Variationen zu Walter Benjamins Sprachmeditationen*, (Basel/Stuttgart, 1979), p. 102, and Jacques Derrida, *La Voix et le phénomène* (Paris, 1967), especially chapter VII, "Le supplément d'origine," pp. 98–117.
5. Warning, *Rezeptionsästhetik*, p. 89.
6. Jan Mukařovský, *The Word and Verbal Art*, trans. John Burbank and Peter Steiner, with a foreword by René Wellek (Yale University Press, 1977), p. 68.
7. Friedrich Nietzsche, "Nachlass," in *Werke in drei Bänden*, ed. Karl Schlechta (Munich, 1956), III, p. 683.
8. Ibid., III, p. 685.
9. Benjamin, *Illuminationen*, p. 62: "Damit ist allerdings zugestanden, dass alle Übersetzung nur eine irgendwie *vorläufige* Art ist, sich mir der Fremdheit der Sprachen auseinanderzusetzen."
10. H. R. Jauss, *Ästhetische Erfahrung und literarische Hermeneutik I* (Munich, 1977).
11. Friedrich Schlegel, "Über die Univerständlichkeit" in *Kritische Schriften*, ed. Wolfdietrich Rasch (Munich, 1970), pp. 530–42.
12. H. R. Jauss, "The Poetic Text Within the Change of Horizons of Reading: The Example of Baudelaire's 'Spleen II'" in *Toward an Aesthetic of Reception*, pp. 139–85.
13. In "Über einige Motive bei Baudelaire," *Illuminationen*, p. 210, Benjamin quotes the lines from another of the *Fleurs du Mal* poems:
   Je vais m'éxercer seul à ma fantasque escrime,
   Flairant dans tous les coins les hasardes de la rime, . . .
   (Le Soleil)
14. *Vorlesungen über die Ästhetik* (Werkausgabe), I, p. 512.
15. *Ibid.*, I, p. 512.
16. "*Erscheinung des Schönen*" is, of course, the traditional Hegelian vocabulary for the aesthetic experience. The "umkippen" of Jauss's earlier, corrosive observation on Baudelaire's play on *Boucher/débouché* (157), which suggests the demolition of the aesthetic idol as if it were the *colonne Vendôme* or any monument honoring a tyrant, is now replaced by the more dignified "umschlagen." Taken literally, however, *schlagen* (to beat) in the cliché *umschlagen* is rather more threatening than *kippen* (to tilt).
17. The use of "tradition" in this context is one of the numerous occasions in which one can share Rousseau's naive regret that we have no diacritical mark at our disposal by which to

indicate irony. It also indicates that, try as I may, when I seem to be reproaching Jauss for not freeing himself from classical constraints, I am not more liberated from them than he is.

18. "Poesie der Poesie" is a concept frequently developed in connection with Paul Valéry, whose authority as a poetician is, for various and complex reasons, overrated in Germany. The "Valérization" of Mallarmé and of Baudelaire is a case in which Harold Bloom's notion of belatedness would have a salutary effect.

19. *Enzyklopädie der philosophischen Wissenschaften* (Werkausgabe), III, § 453, p. 260.

20. *Ibid.*, III, § 458, p. 270.

21. *Ibid.*, III, § 464, p. 282.

22. That the coincidence may be due to common occult sources in Hegel and Baudelaire obscures rather than explains the passage. It distracts the reader from wondering why the use of this particular emblematic code can be "right" in a lyric poem as well as in a philosophical treatise.

JOHN GUILLORY

THE DISCOURSE OF VALUE

It must be emphasized that literary theory's new discourse of value, whether or not it happens to be linked explicitly to a relativist or neopragmatist theoretical agenda, is usually "progressive," in whatever political senses that word can bear. This was true even of rhetorical reading in its later phase, and even though the de Manian critique of "aesthetic ideology" engaged the political at one remove, as an "episte-mological" critique of aesthetic pleasure rather than aesthetic value. The effect of an openly progressive critique of aesthetics is to position the "aesthetic" and the "political" as the discursive antithesis of current critical thought, and thus to enjoin a choice between them. It would be embarrassing at this date to claim for aesthetics any privilege in relation to the political, as embarrassing as an argument for "absolute" or "transcendent" values—the dismal chorus of most reactionary thought. In the context of critical theory, however, it may be surprising to some that the concept of the aesthetic was never rejected within the Marxist tradition, the very body of theory which cultural conservatives are likely to blame for the cur-rent critique of aesthetics. It is only necessary to invoke Marx's famous comments on the transhistorical appeal of Greek art, from the introduction to the *Grundrisse*, to confirm that Marx himself scarcely reduced the work of art to "ideology"; and it would be easy to demonstrate that the theory of ideology in the Marxist tradition has nearly without exception attributed to the domain of the aesthetic the capacity to produce a critique of the capitalist social order analogous to, and not at all superseded by, the critique produced in such a text as *Capital*.[1] A rehearsal of this tradition, up to and beyond Althusser's theory of the work of art's "internal distan-ciation" from the operation of the ideological[2] would confirm this fact; but in lieu of such a history it will be useful to set before us Adorno's valedictory comment in *Aesthetic Theory* on the refusal of the aesthetic, a comment characteristically both tart and dialectical:

> Take a look at the widespread inclination (which to this day has not been mitigated by education) to perceive art in terms of extra-aesthetic or pre-aesthetic criteria. This tendency is, on the one hand, a mark of atrocious backwardness or of the regressive consciousness of many people. On the other hand, there is no denying that the tendency is promoted by something in art itself. If art is perceived strictly in aesthetic terms, then it cannot be properly perceived in aesthetic terms.[3]

I would suggest that his statement is quite representative of the Marxist tradition, even of the most recent work of Terry Eagleton, Frederic Jameson, or Frank Lentricchia.[4] If this tradition can now be tacitly assimilated to the dismissal of aesthetic discourse, the arguments for dismissing the aesthetic do not derive from Marxist theory. One may conjecture that the very ease with which that tradition is misremembered, or spuriously rewritten, argues for the origin of the critique in an academic consensus much larger than the sphere of Marxist theory, and possessing the force of "axiology" for current critical practice.

The historical circumstance of Marxism's long-standing alliance with aesthetics has recently been drawn to our attention in an essay by a Marxist critic, Tony Bennett, entitled "Really Useless 'Knowledge': A Political Critique of Aesthetics," which argues that this alliance has indeed been an embarrassment to Marxist theory, and that "The time is long past . . . when the project of a Marxist aesthetic ought finally to have been laid to rest."[5] I shall briefly take note of Bennett's argument . . . in order to establish a basis for the point just proposed, that the refusal of the aesthetic is an epistemic feature of current critical practice, constituting a consensus powerful enough to enlist in an alliance of "left" critiques even the form of left critique—Marxist theory—historically sympathetic to aesthetics. What one would like to understand here is the nature of the consensus which produces, at the same historical moment, a thorough refusal of the aesthetic in left-liberal criticism, and a certain embarrassment within Marxist theory at the legacy of Marxism's long-standing alliance with aesthetic discourse.

Bennett acknowledges as a premise of his argument the importance of a distinction between aesthetic discourse, which "construes the aesthetic as a distinctive mode of the subject's mental relation to reality," and "discourses of value," the "much more numerous and heterogeneous array of discourses which regulate the social practice of valuing within different valuing communities" (35). More to the point, we should emphasize (Bennett does not) that there is a discourse of aesthetics long before there is any conception of "aesthetic value." This can be confirmed on philological grounds by the fact that the word "value" scarcely ever appears in *The Critique of Judgment,* or in the other texts cited as the ur-texts of aesthetics. The concept of value does appear quite prominently, however, in the central texts of political economy (Smith, Ricardo, Marx), but the current critique of value is not especially interested in these texts, and makes no reference to them. How, then, has the concept of the aesthetic come to be so indissolubly linked to a concept of value whose basic meaning can be taken for granted (however contested particular values may be), and without reference to the discourse of political economy? Bennett's argument traces the *problem* of aesthetic value (but not the concept, the *word*) to the central problem of Kantian aesthetics: an attempt to give the grounds or conditions for judgments of taste in the constitution of a perceiving subject—in the faculty of judgment—rather than in the properties of an aesthetic object. Kant argues typically in the first paragraph of *The Critique of Judgment* (the passage cited by Bennett):

> In order to distinguish whether anything is beautiful or not, we refer the representation, not by the understanding to the object for cognition, but by the imagination (perhaps in conjunction with understanding) to the subject and its feeling of pleasure or pain. The judgement of taste, therefore, is not a judgement of cognition,

and is consequently not logical but aesthetical—which means that it is one whose determining ground can be *no other than subjective.* (37)

In quoting even this much of Kant, Bennett already recovers more of the history of aesthetics than is usually invoked in the current critique, since within the present consensus the fundamental thesis of aesthetic discourse is always abbreviated as the thesis of the transhistorical or transcendental value of the *object,* the work of art. Kant defines the problem of the aesthetic as the problem of demonstrating the conditions for the hypothetical universality and therefore "disinterestedness" of aesthetic judgment, adduced usually as the simple determination of a perception of the "beautiful" or the "sublime" (and for Kant the examples are usually adduced from nature, not from works of art). The problem of value, on the other hand, could not possibly enter into this problematic until two such objects of aesthetic perception are *compared.* It is only at this point, when judgments differ, that the universality of aesthetic perception is revealed to be restricted to certain individuals or social groups; and a little further analysis would reveal that the work of art rather than the object in nature will ordinarily provide the occasion for such a contradiction between the actual and the hypothetical universality of aesthetic judgment. It is relatively easy to read out of this contradiction another version of the narrative of a dominant social group's ideological universalization of its particular interests and historical situation, an ideology which we can be sure will be asserted along a variety of fronts, especially in the context of "values." (Herrnstein Smith similarly remarks on the "move to assign dominant status to the *particular* conditions and perspectives that happen to be relevant to or favored by that person, group, or class.") Bennett argues—and this point is worthy of emphasis—that aesthetic discourse is the peculiarly *exemplary* form of such ideological assertion. By contrast with most discourses of value, which "have effect solely within the limits of particular valuing communities," aesthetic discourse "is the form taken by discourses of value which are hegemonic in ambition and, correspondingly, universalist in their prescriptive ambit, and which have, as their zone of application, those practices nominated as aesthetic" (36). It would seem that it is primarily by means of aesthetics that a concept of a "general" or "universal" subject can be formulated for ideology. And thus one can see why it should have become important for recent critiques to call the claims of aesthetics into question; for aesthetics appears on this account somehow to be the ideology of ideologies, the *source* of the ideological effect of subject-formation.

What Bennett discovers in casting a disillusioned glance at the obscure origins of aesthetic discourse is the concealing of this universal subject in claims about the value of the object: "Once this determining ground has been universalized . . . aesthetic discourse tilts on its axis, as the properties of the subject which guarantee the universality of aesthetic judgement are transferred to the object. Value, transfixed in the singular gaze of the universal subject, solidifies and takes form as the property of the object" (38). It should be pointed out, however, that the transference of aesthetic properties to the object was precisely what aesthetic discourse in its Kantian form considered to be problematic, and what it therefore designated as a kind of necessary error: Kant remarks that in the judgment of beauty, one "will therefore speak of the beautiful as if beauty were a characteristic of the object and the judgment logical (constituting a cognition of the object by means of concepts of it), although it is only aesthetical and involves merely a reference of the representation of the object to the subject" (46). In spite of such qualifications in the text of Kant, Herrnstein Smith too can dispatch, with no more ado than Bennett, Kant's fiction of "subjective universality" by referring casually to "objective—in the sense of universal subjective—validity."[6] In other words Kant's "subjective universality" is not the name of a theoretical *problem* but an overt-covert claim to objective validity, an assertion of the objective value of the aesthetic object. As a fraudulent discourse of the subject, then, aesthetics as such can be discarded and replaced with an overt discourse of "subjects"—the true constituents of "valuing communities."

This is in fact what Bennett proposes as the inescapable conclusion of a critique of aesthetics, and on behalf of a more "politically useful" discourse which inaugurates its project as the choice between aesthetics and politics:

> The political utility of discourses of value, operating via the construction of an ideal of personality to which broadly based social aspirations can be articulated, is unquestionable.
>
> There is, however, no reason to suppose that such discourses must be hitched up to the sphere of universality in order to secure their effectivity. To the contrary, given the configuration of today's political struggles, it is highly unlikely that an ideal of personality might be forged that would be of equal service in the multiple, intersecting but, equally, non-coincident foci of struggle constituted by black, gay, feminist, socialist and, in some contexts, national liberation politics. In particular conjunctures, to be sure, an ideal of personality may be forged which serves to integrate—but always temporarily—such forces into a provisional unity. But this is not the basis for a generalizable and universalisable cultural politics. Nor is this the time for such a politics. (49)

The critique of aesthetics always assumes a concept of value grounded in the notion of a "valuing community" or "communities." Yet insofar as Bennett represents such communities as constitutively "black, gay, feminist, socialist," etc., he opens the concept of the "valuing community" to the same logical objection cogently advanced by Mary Louise Pratt against similar notions of "subcommunities" proposed by linguists: "What the 'subcommunity' approach does not do, however, is see the dominated and dominant *in their relations with each other*—this is the limitation imposed by the imaginings of a community."[7] Such "imaginings" reinstate a kind of local "subjective universality," functioning with vigorous exclusivity in the various valuing communities to construct black values, or gay values, or feminist values; but also, for other communities, "American" values, and "fundamentalist Christian" values, and "white male" values, and "heterosexual" values. Any of these communities might also construct objects of value (let us say, "canons") which can only be properly valued within the respective community of the object's production. I have already suggested [elsewhere], in considering Fish's notion of an "interpretive community," that such a logical contradiction fatally afflicts the critique of canon formation, and that in practice there is very little to arrest the disintegrative force breaking communities down into progressively smaller groups precisely in order to confirm a distinct, ideal, and homogeneous social identity as the basis of the solidarity, and thus the *values* of the community.

NOTES

1. We have recently been reminded of this fact by Patrick Brantlinger in his *Crusoe's Footprints: Cultural Studies in Britain and America* (New York: Routledge, 1990), 73.
2. See Althusser's "Letter on Art in Reply to André Aspre," in *Lenin and Philosophy*, trans. Ben Brewster (New York: Monthly Review Press, 1971).
3. T. W. Adorno, *Aesthetic Theory*, trans. C. Lenhardt (London: Routledge, 1970), 9.
4. Eagleton's views of the work of art in this context are fairly represented by his chapter on "Marxism and Aesthetic Value," in *Criticism and Ideology* (London: Verso, 1976). Lentricchia has recently repudiated those literary materialists who "speak as if the real enemy were the aesthetic" in an inteview with Imre Salusinszky, *Criticism in Society* (New York: Methuen, 1987), 200. More recently Perry Anderson has observed in his *English Questions* (London: Verso, 1992): "For aesthetic value is not to be dispatched so easily—the wish to finish with it recalling Dobrolyubov, or Bazarov, more than Marx or Morris. Railing at canons is not the same as replacing them, which they have resisted. Evacuation of the terrain of literary evaluation in the traditional sense necessarily leaves its conventional practitioners in place" (243).
5. Tony Bennett, "Really Useless 'Knowledge': A Political Critique of Aesthetics," in *Thesis Eleven* 12 (1985), 33.
6. Barbara Herrnstein Smith, *Contingencies of Value: Alternative Perspectives for Critical Theory* (Cambridge: Harvard University Press, 1988), 66.
7. Mary Louise Pratt, "Linguistic Utopias," in *The Linguistics of Writing: Arguments between Language and Literature,* ed. Nigel Fabb et al. (New York: Methuen, 1987), 56.

R O B E R T   H O L U B

CONFRONTATIONS WITH RADICALNESS

The responses of [Stanley] Fish, [Paul] de Man, and [Samuel] Weber to Iser and Jauss are certainly very different. Fish, from a position of neopragmatic skepticism, attacks the notions of determinacy and indeterminacy, the very cornerstones of Iser's theory; de Man, in a more deconstructive fashion, criticizes *Rezeptionsästhetik* for its inattentiveness to language; and Weber, from a similar although slightly more Lacanian perspective, assails an obsolete manner of critical endeavor couched in the terminology of reader response. Yet I would maintain that all three share a common ground, one that can perhaps be described best by the word "radicalness." The dominant objection to reception theory in the eighties is captured by these three critics insofar as they represent alternatives that appear to undo, in a fundamental way, the projects proposed by Iser and Jauss. The question that presents itself, then, is what constitutes this radicalness. In order to investigate this we may leave aside for the moment an evaluation of the validity of each critique, since the force of the respective criticisms derives as much from the style as from the content. Let us then return briefly to the objections and formulations of Fish, de Man, and Iser in order to look more closely at the kind of radical gestures employed to confront reception theory; for in examining this radical gesturing we will also encounter major paradigms from the dominant discourse of literary theory as it has been practiced in the United States for the past two decades.

The first feature we can discern in all three confrontations might be called the metacritical maneuver. This consists in portraying the theory to be criticized as a local and confined response. The metacritic implicitly claims the ability to oversee literary theory, and from this higher, broader, and quasi-transcendental perspective the theorist under consideration appears naive and limited. We have already seen that Fish prominently employs this strategy to discredit Iser's work. A theory of response that depends on a distinction between indeterminate and determinate elements will be an efficient machine for generating readings, Fish maintains, but these readings are in no way more valid, more accurate, or more faithful than any others since they are perforce the products of an arbitrary interpretive convention. But de Man and Weber assume a similar superior position with regard to their subjects. For the former this is most obvious in his discussion of the classical trappings of Jauss's horizon of expectations. We have already seen above that de Man likens Jauss's project of interpretation to correct perception. For this reason Jauss can

CONFRONTATIONS WITH RADICALNESS • 341

never fathom the radical otherness of the truly allegorical. "The negativity inherent in the Husserlian model is a negativity within the sensory itself and not its negation, let alone its 'other.'"[1] The message here, as in Fish's review, is that the aesthetics of reception operates within the strictures of a narrow framework, and that de Man is able to stand outside this framework and observe options unseen or unseeable by Jauss. The same is true of Weber's remarks. He correctly notes Iser's dependence on the construction of visual images for his theory of response, but from his privileged perspective he can envision this process of visualization as well as the nonimagistic alternatives. The point here is that American radicalness entails a certain way of disqualifying the validity of an adversarial theory. A "nonradical" approach is not so much wrong or incorrect or invalid as it is naive, limited, and limiting. Reception theory is not criticized on its own terms, for what it does, or how it performs, but placed in a perspective in which this sort of criticism is superfluous.

A second strategy employed by this brand of radicalness is to attribute to the criticized theory an unwitting retention of superannuated philosophical or theoretical tenets. Since anything old is immediately suspect, reception theorists who openly rely on tradition will appear unacceptable. This disqualification of the heritage is found most clearly in the observations of de Man and Weber. Both criticize reception theory for adhering to phenomenological models and for not paying more attention to recent developments in the theory of language, particularly in France. De Man . . . is especially candid about this topic. After noting the absence of "play" in Jauss's work, he writes:

> Such a concern with "the instances of the letter" is particularly in evidence, as is well known, among certain French writers not generally included within Jauss's own critical canon of relevant *Fachliteratur*. He has always treated such Parisian extravagances with a measure of suspicion and even when, under the pressure of their persistence as well as of genuine affinities between their enterprise and his own, he acknowledged some of their findings, it has always been a guarded and partial recognition.[2]

Weber makes a similar point when he contends that Iser never manages to break through to a new notion of criticism, and actually falls back into an all too familiar pattern. "It is remarkable, then," he writes, "that *The Act of Reading*, which begins precisely by questioning the traditional conception of literature as a repository of univocal meaning, nevertheless gravitates toward the very position it sets out to criticize."[3] The rhetoric of the radical avant-garde clearly valorizes novelty, rupture, and discontinuity, while it scorns progress, tradition, and dialectical process. The surest means of gaining the upper hand on an adversary, in fact, is to reveal his or her dependence on a heritage that predates the insights of Lacan or Derrida.

A final element of the American radicalness I have been describing is its negativity. If we consider that reception theory offers a positive model of how to deal with literary texts, then the result of these various confrontations has been to undercut this positivity without offering much in the way of an alternative. Fish's objections to the problem of the given and the supplied call into question not only Iser's theory of response, but any endeavor to come to terms with the reading process, including, one might add, his own. By setting the stakes at the level of the linguistic code, he undermines the coherence of any more limited approach to literary reception and effect. De Man's procedure in dealing with Jauss is similar in that he suggests the impossibility of every hermeneutic project—insofar, of course, as this project makes claims to truth. In opening up texts to an unavoidable linguistic instability, he necessarily forfeits any certainty in interpretation. All critical endeavor, including de Man's, are always already undone before they have been conceived. Finally Weber's alternative to Iser's critical model remains hazy because his assumptions allow only negation. Indeed, his final sentence speaks of a reading that "is forever caught in an act it can never quite get together."[4] But once again this avowal of futility ultimately boomerangs; with equal justification we could turn around and attack his own interpretation of "The Figure in the Carpet," or, for that matter, of *The Act of Reading* itself. In denying a transcendental position and the authority of the author, Weber would appear to cancel his own authority as well. Iser, it turns out, is not the only one "caught in the act of reading"; for according to the premises outlined by Weber this is a universal fate. It would be absurd to deny that these three critics of reception theory negate critical activity. In a paradoxical fashion the criticisms that they offer open up texts to an abundance of interpretive possibilities. But these possibilities are ultimately and fundamentally repetitions of a task whose outcome is already known. The lesson we learn is that criticism is doomed to perform an action that has been always already undone and negated before it begins.

The radicalness of American theory thus remains entangled in a self-canceling mechanism of ironic one-upmanship and a spiral of infinitely negative speculation. What is perhaps more disturbing than this Sisyphean state of affairs, however, is the rather dubious political valence of this radicalness. All three critiques make gestures in the direction of progressive politics, but it is difficult to determine whether this gesture is the sign of a greeting or a hasty departure. Fish upbraids Iser for his popularity with American academics. His theory, we are told, is "particularly well suited to the pluralism of most American literary criticism."[5] Iser embraces a safe and comfortable liberalism; no one warns against reading him (except perhaps Fish); he is not on anyone's hit list. This may very well be true, but why Fish is more dangerous and why the writers on his list pose more of a threat—and to whom?—is not clear at all. De Man's faint gesture to the political comes with his citation of Benjamin, who is called upon to play the foil to the traditional, classical Jauss. Benjamin is placed in a succession of radical subversion from Hamann to Nietzsche, but de Man conveniently ignores what precisely he was trying to subvert. No mention is made of his marxist affiliations, his ties with Brecht, or his anticapitalist views. Weber, who is most aware of the problem, nevertheless fares no better than his would-be radical colleagues. His claim to revolutionary politics exhausts itself in remarks directed against Iser's audience. He maintains, for example, that the addressees of Iser's work consist of similarly minded, transcendence-oriented professionals. Later he takes a swipe at Iser's reception "in the land that has traditionally fancied itself the home of rugged individualism." And he chastises his work for its "semblance of secular pluralism" and its "atmosphere of liberalism."[6] But his putatively more radical critique, as we have seen, offers no alternative in terms of either a positive theory or a possible politics.

American confrontations with reception theory thus disclose a deeply seated malaise in critical circles. . . . Forever employing a self-defeating metacriticism that attacks the very transcendental position from which it apparently makes its own categorical pronouncements, the currently fashionable radicalness heralds a permanent and self-consuming revolution of novelty and negativity. While it pretends to have political implications, when questioned about its politics, it has nothing comprehensible to say. For its element is exclusively that of the logos that it so often debunks, but is condemned to employ. Its most important objective is not to further knowledge, a proposition in which it no longer believes, but to render its own arguments impervious to attack. Perhaps this is the reason that the sophistry of the radically skeptical antitheoretical position could gain such widespread attention during the eighties as well.[7] All this does not mean that the preceding criticisms of reception theory are unjustified; nor does it let reception theorists off the hook for their abysmal ignorance of what has been going on in these avant-garde circles in the United States and France. But it does suggest that a deeper understanding of the traditions and the ramifications of the work of the best reception theorists might still play a fruitful role in American criticism. Although the border crossing of reception theory may never benefit from such an understanding, it could have the function of promoting a genuine debate concerning the possibilities and limits of radicalness.

NOTES

1. Paul de Man, Introduction, *Toward an Aesthetic of Reception,* by Hans Robert Jauss (Minneapolis: University of Minnesota Press, 1982), p. xxii.
2. De Man, Introduction, pp xix–xx.
3. Samuel Weber, "Caught in the Act of Reading," *Demarcating the Disciplines: Philosophy Literature Art,* Glyph Textual Studies 1 (Minneapolis: University of Minnesota Press, 1986), p. 199.
4. Weber, "Caught in the Act of Reading," p. 212.
5. Stanley Fish, "Why No One's Afraid of Wolfgang Iser," *Diacritics* 11, no. 1 (1981): 3.
6. Weber, "Caught in the Act of Reading," p. 200.
7. See W. J. T. Mitchell, *Against Theory: Literary Studies and the New Pragmatism* (Chicago: University of Chicago Press, 1985).

BIBLIOGRAPHY: RECEPTION STUDIES

The following bibliography of reception studies in English is divided into four major categories: general theories, texts and authors, the history of the book, and mass and popular culture. Owing to the volume of work done in these areas, particularly in reception theory and literary criticism, and to the bibliographies available in older anthologies, this bibliography is not designed to be comprehensive. The bibliographies for the first two categories emphasize work done since 1990, although important earlier studies are also included. The bibliography for texts and authors is limited to reception studies of British, American, and continental European literatures, which form the three subdivisions for that section. In the bibliography as a whole, several works could have appeared in more than one of the four major divisions, but to avoid repetition we have listed each item only in the category that best reflects its emphasis.

I. GENERAL THEORIES

Ahrens, Rudiger, and Heinz Antor, eds. *Text, Culture, Reception: Cross Cultural Aspects of English Studies.* Heidelberg: Carl Winter Universitatsverlag, 1992.

Allor, Martin. "The Politics of Producing Audiences." In *The Audience and Its Landscape,* edited by James Hay, Lawrence Grossberg, and Ellen Wartella, 209–19. Boulder, Colo.: Westview, 1996.

Ang, Ien. "Culture and Communication: Towards an Ethnographic Critique of Media Consumption in the Transnational Media System." *European Journal of Communication* 5 (1990): 239–60.

———. "Ethnography and Radical Contextualization in Audience Studies." *In The Audience and Its Landscape,* edited by James Hay, Lawrence Grossberg, and Ellen Wartella, 247–62. Boulder, Colo.: Westview, 1996.

Babrow, A. S. "Theory and Method in Research on Audience Motives." *Journal of Broadcasting and Electronic Media* 32 (1988): 471–87.

Bennett, Tony. *Culture: A Reformer's Science.* St. Leonards, Australia: Allyn & Unwin, 1998.

———. "Figuring Audiences and Readers." *In The Audience and Its Landscape,* edited by James Hay, Lawrence Grossberg, and Ellen Wartella, 145–59. Boulder, Colo.: Westview, 1996.

――――. *Formalism and Marxism.* London: Methuen, 1979.

――――. "Marxism and Popular Fiction." *Literature and History* 7 (1981): 138–65.

――――. *Outside Literature.* New York: Routledge, 1990.

――――. "Texts in History: The Determinations of Readings and Their Texts." *Journal of the Midwest Modern Language Association* 18, no. 1 (spring 1985): 1–16.

Berg, Henk de. "Reception Theory or Perception Theory?" Rpt. in *The Systemic and Empirical Approach to Literature and Culture as Theory and Application,* edited by Steven Totosy de Zepetnek and Irene Sywenky, 23–30. Siegen, Germany: Institute for Empirical Literature and Media Research, Siegen University, 1997.

Bérubé, Michael. *Public Access: Literary Theory and American Cultural Politics.* London: Verso, 1994.

Biocca, F. A. "Opposing Conceptions of the Audience: The Active and the Passive Hemispheres of Mass Communication Theory." *In Communication Yearbook,* vol. 11, edited by J. A. Anderson, 51–80. Newbury Park, Calif.: Sage, 1988.

Bird, Elizabeth. "Travels in Nowhere Land: Ethnography and the 'Impossible' Audience." *Critical Studies in Mass Communication* 9 (1992): 250–60.

Blumler, Jay G. "The Role of Theory in Uses and Gratifications Studies." *Communication Research* 6 (1979): 9–36.

Brunt, Rosiland, and Martin Jordan. "Constituting the Television Audience: A Problem of Method." In *Television and Its Audience,* edited by Phillip Drummond and Richard Paterson, 231–49. London: British Film Institute, 1988.

Budd, Mike, Robert M. Entman, and Clay Steinman. "The Affirmative Character of U.S. Cultural Studies." *Critical Studies in Mass Communication* 7 (1990): 169–84.

Bump, Jerome, "The Family Dynamics of the Reception of Art." *Style* 31 (1997): 328–50.

Cain, William. E., ed. *Reconceptualizing American Literary/Cultural Studies: Rhetoric, History, and Politics in the Humanities.* New York: Garland, 1996.

Carragee, K. M. "Interpretive Media Study and Interpretive Social Science." *Critical Studies in Mass Communication* 7 (1990): 81–96.

Chartier, Roger. "Labourers and Voyagers: From the Text to the Reader." Rpt. in *Readers and Reading,* edited by Andrew Bennett, 132–49. New York: Longman, 1995.

Cobley, Paul. "Throwing Out the Baby: Populism and Active Audience Theory." *Media, Culture and Society* 16 (1994): 677–87.

Corner, John. "Meaning, Genre, and Context: The Problematics of 'Public Knowledge' in the New Audience Studies." In *Mass Media and Society,* edited by James Curran and Michael Gurevitch, 267–84. London: Arnold, 1991.

Cupchik, Gerald C. "Identification as a Basic Problem for Aesthetic Reception." In *The Systemic and Empirical Approach to Literature and Culture as Theory and Application,* edited by Steven Totosy de Zepetnek and Irene Sywenky, 11–22. Siegen, Germany: Institute for Empirical Literature and Media Research, Siegen University, 1997.

Curran, James. "The New Revisionism in Mass Communication Research: A Reappraisal." *European Journal of Communication* 5 (1990): 135–64.

Dasenbrock, Reed Way. "Do We Write the Text We Read?" In *Literary Theory After Davidson*, edited by Reed Way Dasenbrock, 18–36. University Park: Pennsylvania State University Press, 1993.

———. "Truth and Methods." *College English* 57 (1995): 546–61.

———. "We've Done It to Ourselves: The Critique of Truth and the Attack on Theory." In *PC Wars: Politics and Theory in the Academy*, edited by Jeffrey Williams, 172–83. London: Routledge, 1995.

de Man, Paul. Introduction to *Toward an Aesthetic of Reception*, by Hans Robert Jauss. Translated by Timothy Bahti. Minneapolis: University of Minnesota Press, 1982.

Dev, Amiya. "Globalization and Literary Value." In *The Search for a New Alphabet: Literary Studies in a Changing World*, edited by Harald Hendrix, Joost Klock, Sophie Levie, and Will van Peer, 62–66. Amsterdam: Benjamins, 1996.

Erickson, Peter. "On the Origins of American Feminist Shakespeare Criticism." *Women's Studies: An Interdisciplinary Journal* 26 (1997): 1–26.

Fioretos, Aris. "To Read Paul de Man." Rpt. in *Responses on Paul de Man's Wartime Journalism*, edited by Werner Hamacher, Neil Hertz, and Thomas Keenan, 165–72. Lincoln: University of Nebraska Press, 1989.

Fish, Stanley. "Anti-Professionalism." *New Literary History* 17 (1985): 89–127.

———. "Being Interdisciplinary Is So Very Hard To Do." *Profession* 89: 15–22.

———. "Consequences." *Critical Inquiry* 11 (1985): 433–58.

———. *Is There a Text in This Class? The Authority of Interpretive Communities.* Cambridge, Masso.: Harvard University Press, 1980.

———. *Professional Correctness: Literary Studies and Political Change.* Oxford: Clarendon Press of Oxford University Press, 1995.

Fiske, John. "The Cultural Economy of Fandom." In *The Adoring Audience: Fan Culture and Popular Media*, edited by Lisa Lewis, 30–49. London: Routledge, 1992.

Fokkema, Douwe, and Elrud Ibsch. *Theories of Literature in the Twentieth Century: Structuralism, Marxism, Aesthetics of Reception, Semiotics.* London: Hurst, 1995.

Fouquier, E. "Figures of Reception: Concepts and Rules for a Semiotic Analysis of Mass Media Reception." *Research in Marketing* 4 (1988): 331–47.

Frow, John. "Economies of Value." In *Cultural Studies and Cultural Value*, 131–69. Oxford: Clarendon Press of Oxford University Press, 1995.

Greenblatt, Stephen. "What Is the History of Literature?" *Critical Inquiry* 23 (1997): 460–81.

Grossberg, Lawrence. "The Contexts of Audiences and the Politics of Difference." *Australian Journal of Communication* 16 (1989): 13–35.

———. "Is There a Fan in the House? The Affective Sensibility of Fandom." In *The*

Adoring Audience: Fan Culture and Popular Media, edited by Lisa Lewis, 50–65. London: Routledge, 1992.

———. "Wandering Audiences, Nomadic Critics." *Cultural Studies* 2 (1988): 377–91.

Grossman, Jeffrey. "The Reception of Walter Benjamin in the Anglo-American Literary Institution." *German Quarterly* 65 (1992): 414–28.

Guillory, John. "Bourdieu's Refusal." *Modern Language Quarterly* 58 (1997): 367–98.

Hall, Stuart. "Encoding/Decoding." In *Culture, Media, Language,* edited by Stuart Hall, Dorothy Hobson, Andrew Lowe, and Paul Willis, 128–38. London: Hutchinson, 1980.

Harding, James M. "Given Movement: Determinant Response, Textual Givens, and Hegelian Moments in Wolfgang Iser's Reception Theory." *Diacritics* 23, no. 1 (spring 1993): 40–52.

Headley, John M. "Tommaso Campanella and Jean de Launoy: The Controversy over Aristotle and His Reception in the West." *Renaissance Quarterly* 43 (1990): 529–550.

Höijer, Birgitta. "Studying Viewers' Reception of Television Programmes: Theoretical and Methodological Considerations." *European Journal of Communication* 5 (1990): 29–56.

Holland, Peter, and Hanna Scolnicov, eds. *Reading Plays: Interpretation and Reception.* Cambridge: Cambridge University Press, 1991.

Holub, Robert C. *Crossing Borders: Reception Theory, Poststructuralism, Deconstruction.* Madison: University of Wisconsin Press, 1992.

———. "Reception Theory: School of Constance." Rpt. in *The Cambridge History of Literary Criticism, VIII: From Formalism to Poststructuralism,* edited by Raman Selden, 319–46. Cambridge: Cambridge University Press, 1995.

Ingram, Susan. "The Trouble with Harry, Or: Producing Walter Benjamin's Anglo-American Reception." *Carleton Germanic Papers* 25 (1997): 78–90.

Janssen, Susanne. "Literary Reputation and Authors' Intervention in Critical Reception." Rpt. in *The Systemic and Empirical Approach to Literature and Culture as Theory and Application,* edited by Steven Totosy de Zepetnek, and Irene Sywenky, 278–97. Siegen, Germany: Institute for Empirical Literature and Media Research, Siegen University, 1997.

Jauss, Hans Robert. *Toward an Aesthetic of Reception.* Translated by Timothy Bahti. Minneapolis: University of Minnesota Press, 1982.

———. "The Theory of Reception: A Retrospective of Its Unrecognized Prehistory." In *Literary Theory Today,* edited by Peter Collier and Helga Geyer-Ryan, 53–73. Cambridge, England: Polity, 1990.

———. "The Identity of the Poetic Text in the Changing Horizon of Understanding." In *The Identity of the Literary Text,* edited by Mario J. Valdis and Owen Miller, 146–74. Toronto: University of Toronto Press, 1985.

———. "Response to Paul de Man." In *Reading de Man Reading,* edited by Lindsay

Waters and Wlad Godzich, 202–08. Minneapolis: University of Minnesota Press, 1989.

———. *Question and Answer: Forms of Dialogic Understanding.* Edited and translated by Michael Hays. Minneapolis: University of Minnesota Press, 1989.

Jensen, Klaus Bruhn. "After Convergence: Constituents of a Social Semiotics of Mass Media Reception." In *The Audience and Its Landscape,* edited by James Hay, Lawrence Grossberg, and Ellen Wartella, 63–73. Boulder, Colo.: Westview, 1996.

———. "The Past in the Future: Problems and Potentials of Historical Reception Studies." *Journal of Communication* 43, no. 4 (autumn 1993): 20–28.

———. "Qualitative Audience Research: Toward an Integrative Approach to Reception." *Critical Studies in Mass Communication* 4 (1987): 21–36.

Kalman, G. C. "Signs/Signals of Literariness: Sign Theory vs Reception Theory." In *Signs of Humanity,* vol. 1, edited by Michel Balat, Janice Deledalle-Rhodes, and Gérard Deledalle, 513–19. Berlin: Mouton de Gruyter, 1992.

Katz, Elihu. "Viewers Work." In *The Audience and Its Landscape,* edited by James Hay, Lawrence Grossberg, and Ellen Wartella, 9–21. Boulder, Colo.: Westview, 1996.

Kubey, Robert. "On Not Finding Media Effects: Conceptual Problems in the Notion of an 'Active' Audience." In *The Audience and Its Landscape,* edited by James Hay, Lawrence Grossberg, and Ellen Wartella, 187–205. Boulder, Colo.: Westview, 1996.

Landauer, Carl. "Auerbach's Performance and the American Academy: Or, How New Haven Stole the Idea of Mimesis." In *Literary History and the Challenge of Philology: The Legacy of Erich Auerbach,* edited by Seth Lerer, 179–94. Stanford, Calif.: Stanford University Press, 1996.

Lembo, Ronald, and Kenneth H. Tucker. "Culture, Television, and Opposition: Rethinking Cultural Studies." *Critical Studies in Mass Communication* 7 (1990): 97–116.

Lindenberger, Herbert. "On the Reception of Mimesis." Rpt. in *Literary History and the Challenge of Philology: The Legacy of Erich Auerbach,* edited by Seth Lerer, 195–213. Stanford, Calif.: Stanford University Press, 1996.

Loveridge, Mark. "If Everything Else Fails, Read the Instructions: Further Echoes of the Reception Theory Debate." *Connotations: A Journal for Critical Debate* 4 (1994-1995): 151–64.

Mailloux, Steven. *Rhetorical Power.* Ithaca, N.Y.: Cornell University Press, 1989.

———. *Interpretive Conventions: The Reader in the Study of American Fiction.* Ithaca, N.Y.: Cornell University Press, 1982.

———. "Articulation and Understanding: The Pragmatic Intimacy between Rhetoric and Hermeneutics." Rpt. in *Hermeneutics and Rhetoric In Our Time,* edited by Walter Jost and Michael Hyce, 1–33. New Haven, Conn.: Yale University Press, 1995.

———. *Reception Histories: Rhetoric, Pragmatism, and American Cultural Politics.* Ithaca, N.Y.: Cornell University Press, 1998.

———. "Rhetorical Hermeneutics Revisited." *Text and Performance Quarterly* 11 (1991): 233–48.

McCormick, Kathleen. "Teaching, Studying, and Theorizing the Production and Reception of Literary Texts." *College Literature* 19, no. 2 (June 1992): 4–18.

———. *The Culture of Reading and the Teaching of English.* New York: Manchester University Press, 1994.

McGregor, Graham, and R. S. White, eds. *Reception and Response: Hearer Creativity and the Analysis of Spoken and Written Texts.* London: Routledge, 1990.

Merquior, Jose Guilherme. "Notes on the American Reception of Foucault." *Stanford French Review* 15 (1991): 25–35.

Morley, David. "Active Audience Theory: Pendulums and Pitfalls." *Journal of Communication* 43, no. 4 (autumn 1993): 13–19.

———. "Changing Paradigms in Audience Studies." In *Remote Control: Television, Audiences, and Cultural Power,* edited by Ellen Seiter, Hans Borchers, Gabriele Kreuttzner, and Eva-Maria Warth, 16–43. London: Routledge, 1989.

———. "Texts, Readers, Subjects." In *Culture, Media, Language,* edited by Stuart Hall, Dorothy Hobson, Andrew Lowe, and Paul Willis, 163–73. London: Hutchinson, 1980.

Murphy, Richard J. "Russian Formalism and German Reception Theory: A Reconsideration: Continuities in the Methodologies of Victor Shklovsky and Wolfgang Iser." *Germano-Slavica: A Canadian Journal of Germanic and Slavic Comparative Studies* 6 (1990): 339–49.

Newcomb, H. "On the Dialogic Aspects of Mass Communication." *Critical Studies in Mass Communication* 1 (1984): 34–50.

Nicholsen, Shierry Weber. "Toward a More Adequate Reception of Adorno's Aesthetic Theory: Configurational Form in Adorno's Aesthetic Writings." *Cultural Critique* no. 18 (spring 1991): 33–64.

Perin, Constance. "The Reception of New, Unusual, and Difficult Art." Rpt. in *The Artist Outsider: Creativity and the Boundaries of Culture,* edited by Michael D. Hall and Eugene W. Metcalf, 172–97. Washington, D.C.: Smithsonian, 1994.

Press, Andrea. "Toward a Qualitative Methodology of Audience Study: Using Ethnography to Study the Popular Culture Audience." In *The Audience and Its Landscape,* edited by James Hay, Lawrence Grossberg, and Ellen Wartella, 113–30. Boulder, Colo.: Westview, 1996.

Radway, Janice. "The Hegemony of 'Specificity' and the Impasse in Audience Research: Cultural Studies and the Problem of Ethnography." In *The Audience and Its Landscape,* edited by James Hay, Lawrence Grossberg, and Ellen Wartella, 235–45. Boulder, Colo.: Westview, 1996.

———. "Reception Study: Ethnography and the Problems of Dispersed Audiences and Nomadic Subjects." *Cultural Studies* 2 (1988): 359–76.

Ragland-Sullivan, Ellie. "The Eternal Return of Jacques Lacan." In *Literary Theory's Future(s),* edited by Joseph Natoli, 33–81. Urbana: University of Illinois Press, 1989.

Rayburn, J. D., II, and Philip Palmgreen. "Merging Uses and Gratifications Expectancy-Value Theory." *Communication Research* 11 (1984): 537–62.

Redfield, Marc. "De Man, Schiller, and the Politics of Reception." *Diacritics* 20, no. 3 (fall 1990): 50–70.

Reid, Roddey. "Foucault in America: Biography, 'Culture War,' and the New Consensus." *Cultural Critique* no. 35 (winter 1996): 179–211.

Richter, David. "The Unguarded Prison: Reception Theory, Structural Marxism, and the History of the Gothic Novel." *Eighteenth Century* 30, no. 3 (autumn 1989): 3–17.

Saenz, M. "Television Viewing as a Cultural Practice." *Journal of Communication Inquiry* 16, no. 2 (summer 1992): 37–51.

Schroder, Kim Christian. "Convergence or Antagonist Traditions? The Case of Audience Research." *European Journal of Communication* 2 (1987): 7–31.

Seaman, William R. "Active Audience Theory: Pointless Populism." *Media, Culture and Society* 14 (1992): 301–11.

Segers, Rien T. "Dynamics and Progress in Literary Studies? Some Notes on a Neglected Topic in Literary Scholarship with Special Reference to Reception." Rpt. in *Celebrating Comparativism*, edited by Katalin Kurtosi and Jozsef Pal, 169–205. Szeged, Hungary: Gold, 1994.

Smith, Louise Z. "In Search of Our Sisters' Rhetoric: Teaching Through Reception Theory." Rpt. in *Practicing Theory in Introductory College Literature Courses*, edited by James M. Cahalan and David B. Downing, 72–84. Urbana, Ill.: National Council of Teachers of English, 1991.

Stierle, Karlheinz. "Studium: Perspectives on Institutionalized Modes of Reading." *New Literary History* 22 (1991): 115–27.

Swanson, David L. "Audience Research: Antimonies, Intersections, and the Prospect of a Comprehensive Theory." In *The Audience and Its Landscape*, edited by James Hay, Lawrence Grossberg, and Ellen Wartella, 53–62. Boulder, Colo.: Westview, 1996.

Taylor, Gary. "The Rhetorics of Reception." In *Crisis in Editing: Texts of the English Renaissance*, edited by Randall McLeod, 19–59. New York: AMS, 1994.

Woodmansee, Martha, and Peter Jaszi, eds. *The Construction of Authorship: Textual Appropriation in Law and Literature*. Durham, N.C.: Duke University Press, 1994.

Wren-Lewis, Justin. "The Encoding-Decoding Model: Criticisms and Redevelopments for Research on Decoding." *Media, Culture and Society* 5 (1983): 179–97.

Wunsch, Marianne. "The Status and Significance of Reception Studies in Literary History." Rpt. in *Proceedings of the XIIth Congress of the International Comparative Literature Association V: Space and Boundaries in Literary Theory and Criticism*, edited by Roger Bauer, Douwe Wessel Fokkema, and Michael de Graat, 324–30. Munich: Iudicium, 1990.

Ziarek, Krzysztof. "The Reception of Heidegger's Thought in American Literary Criticism." *Diacritics* 19, no. 3/4 (fall/winter 1989): 114–26.

Zutshi, Margot. "Hans Robert Jauss's Rezeptionsasthetik—Theory and Application." Rpt. in *New Ways in Germanistik*, edited by Richard Sheppard, 95–111. New York: Berg, 1990.

2. TEXTS AND AUTHORS

ENGLISH LITERATURE

Allison, Jonathan. "The Attack on Yeats." *South Atlantic Review* 55, no. 4 (November 1990): 61–73.

Allott, Miriam. "Attitudes to Shelley: The Vagaries of a Critical Reputation." In *Essays on Shelley*, edited by Miriam Allott, 1–38. Totowa, N.J.: Barnes & Noble, 1982.

Altman, Joel B. "'Prophetic Fury': Othello and the Economy of Shakespearean Reception." *Studies in the Literary Imagination* 26, no. 1 (spring 1993): 85–113.

Aske, Martin. "Keats, the Critics, and the Politics of Envy." In *Keats and History*, edited by Nicholas Roe, 46–64. Cambridge: Cambridge University Press, 1995.

Barnett, Louise K. "Betty's Freckled Neck: Swift, Women, and Women Readers." In *1650–1850: Ideas, Aesthetics, and Inquiries in the Early Modern Era*, vol. 4, edited by Kevin L. Cope, Laura Morrow, and Anna Battigeli, 233–45. New York: AMS, 1998.

Basker, James G. "Samuel Johnson and the American Common Reader." *The Age of Johnson* 6 (1993): 3–30

Birrell, T. A. "A Reception of T. S. Eliot: Texts and Contexts." *English Studies* 69 (1988): 518–533.

Boheemen Saaf, Christine van. "Purloined Joyce." In *Re: Joyce: Text, Culture, Politics*, edited by John Brannigan, Geoff Ward, and Julian Wolfreys, 246–57. New York: St. Martin's, 1998.

Brodie, Laura Fairchild. "Jane Austen and the Common Reader: 'Opinions of *Mansfield Park*,' 'Opinions of *Emma*,' and the Janeite Phenomenon." *Texas Studies in Literature and Language* 37 (1995): 54–71

Brown, Homer. "The Institution of the English Novel: Defoe's Contribution." *Novel: A Forum on Fiction* 29 (1996): 299–318.

Brownlee, Kevin, and Sylvia Huot, eds. *Rethinking the Romance of the Rose: Text, Image, Reception*. Philadelphia: University of Pennsylvania Press, 1992.

Champion, Margret G. "Reception Theory and Medieval Narrative: Reading *Pearl* as a Novel." *Neophilologus* 76 (1992): 629–37.

Cohen, Philip. "Stamped on His Works: The Decline of Samuel Butler's Literary Reputation." *The Journal of the Midwest Modern Language Association* 18, no. 1 (spring 1985): 64–81.

Court, Franklin E. "The Critical Reception of Pater's *Marius*." *English Literature in Transition (1880–1920)* 27 (1984): 124–39.

Crick, Bernard. "The Reception of *Nineteen Eighty-Four*." In *George Orwell and Nineteen Eighty-Four: The Man and the Book*, 97–103. Washington, D.C.: Library of Congress, 1985.

Dane, Joseph A. *Who Is Buried in Chaucer's Tomb?: Studies in the Reception of Chaucer's Book*. East Lansing: Michigan State University Press, 1998.

Davies, Alistair. "Contexts of Reading: The Reception of D. H. Lawrence's *The Rainbow* and *Women in Love*." In *The Theory of Reading*, edited by Frank Gloversmith, 199–222. Totowa, N.J.: Barnes & Noble, 1984.

Donaldson, Ian. "'Not of an Age': Jonson, Shakespeare, and the Verdicts of Posterity." In *New Perspectives on Ben Jonson*, edited by James Hirsh, 197–214. Madison, N.J.: Fairleigh Dickinson University Press, 1997.

Donaldson, Sandra. "'For Nothing Was Simply One Thing': The Reception of Elizabeth Barrett Browning's 'A Curse for a Nation.'" *Studies in Browning and His Circle* 20 (1993): 137–44.

Dubruck, Edelgard E. "Inviting Tacit Agreement: 'The Pardoner's Tale' and Its Modern Reception." In *The Living Middle Ages: Studies in Mediaeval English Literature and Its Tradition*, 103–113. Stuttgart: Belser Wissenschaftlicher Dienst, 1989.

Engel, Elliot D., and Margaret F. King. "Pickwick's Progress: The Critical Reception of *The Pickwick Papers* from 1836–1986." *Dickens Quarterly* 3 (1986): 56–66.

Felperin, Howard. "Bardolatry Then and Now." In *The Appropriation of Shakespeare: Post-Renaissance Reconstructions of the Works and the Myth*, edited by Jean I. Marsden, 129–44. New York: St. Martin's, 1991.

Ferguson, Margaret W. "Renaissance Concepts of the 'Woman Writer.'" In *Women and Literature in Britain*, 1500–1700, edited by Helen Wilcox, 143–68. Cambridge: Cambridge University Press, 1996.

Fitzgerald, Mary E. F. "The Unveiling of Power: 19th Century Gothic Fiction in Ireland, England and America." In *Literary Interrelations: Ireland, England and the World*, vol. 2, edited by Wolfgang Zach and Heinz Kosok, 15–25. Tubingen, Germany: Narr, 1987.

Foakes, R. A. *Hamlet versus Lear: Cultural Politics and Shakespeare's Art*. Cambridge: Cambridge University Press, 1993.

Fredeman, William E. "Scholarly Resources: The Pre-Raphaelites in Canada." *Journal of Pre-Raphaelite Studies* 6/7 (fall/spring 1997–1998): 191–216.

Froula, Christine. "Corpse, Monument, Hypocrite Lecteur: Text and Transference in the Reception of 'The Waste Land.'" *Text: An Interdisciplinary Journal of Textual Studies* 9 (1996): 297–314.

Gaillet, Lynee Lewis. "Reception of Elizabeth Barrett Browning's *Aurora Leigh*: An Insight into the Age's Turmoil over the Representation of Gender and Theories of Art." *Studies in Browning and His Circle* 20 (1993): 115–22.

Goldstein, Philip. "Criticism and Institutions: The Conflicted Reception of Jane Austen's Fiction." *Studies in the Humanities* 18 (1991): 35–55.

Greaves, Richard L. "Bunyan through the Centuries: Some Reflections." *English Studies* 64 (1983): 113–21.

Greene, Donald. "An Anatomy of Pope Bashing." In *The Enduring Legacy: Alexander Pope Tercentenary Essays*, edited by G. S. Rousseau and Pat Rogers, 241–81. Cambridge: Cambridge University Press, 1988.

Gumbrecht, Hans Ulrich. "Strangeness as a Requirement for Topicality: Medieval Literature and Reception Theory." *L'Esprit Createur* 21, no. 2 (summer 1981): 5–12.

Hammond, Brean. "'Our Toils Obscure, and A' That': Burns and the Burns Myth." In *Anglistentag*, edited by Han Ulrich Seeber and Walter Gobel, 9–19. Tubingen, Germany: Niemeyer, 1993.

Handley, Graham. *Jane Austen*. New York: St. Martin's, 1992.

Healy, Thomas. "Past and Present Shakespeares: Shakespearian Appropriations in Europe." In *Shakespeare and National Culture*, edited by John J. Joughin and John Drakakis, 206–32. New York: Manchester University Press, 1997.

Hung, Eva. "The Introduction of Dickens into China (1906–1960): A Case Study in Target Culture Reception." *Perspectives: Studies in Translatology* 1 (1996): 29–41.

Ikegami, Tadahiro. "A Short History of Langland Studies in Japan." *Yearbook of Langland Studies* 11 (1997): 157–62.

Jackman, Christine. "Few Women Care for *Beowulf*." *Tessera* 10 (1991): 55–64.

Jackson, Dennis. "'At Last, the Real D. H. Lawrence'? The Author and the Editors: A Reception History, 1975–93." In *Editing D. H. Lawrence: New Versions of a Modern Author*, edited by Charles L. Ross and Dennis Jackson, 211–38. Ann Arbor: University of Michigan Press, 1995.

Johnson, Claudia L. "The Divine Miss Jane: Jane Austen, Janeites, and the Discipline of Novel Studies." *boundary* 2 23, no. 3 (fall 1996): 143–63.

Kelley, Theresa M. "Poetics and the Politics of Reception: Keats's 'La Belle Dame sans Merci.'" *ELH* 54 (1987): 333–62.

Klein, Holger. "Preface: Receiving *Hamlet* Reception." *New Comparison* no. 2 (autumn 1986): 5–13.

Kolbrener, William. *Milton's Warring Angels: A Study of Critical Engagements*. Cambridge: Cambridge University Press, 1997.

Korshin, Paul J. "Johnson's *Rambler* and Its Audiences." In *Essays on the Essay: Redefining the Genre*, edited by Alexander J. Butrym, 92–105. Athens: University of Georgia Press, 1989.

Krier, Theresa M., ed. *Refiguring Chaucer in the Renaissance*. Gainesville: University Press of Florida, 1998.

Lynn, Steven. "Johnson's Critical Reception." In *The Cambridge Companion to Samuel Johnson*, edited by Greg Clingham, 240–53. Cambridge: Cambridge University Press, 1997.

Malone, Catherine. "'We Have Learnt to Love Her More than Her Books': The Critical Reception of Bronte's *Professor*." *Review of English Studies* 47 (1996): 175–87.

Mayer, Robert. "The Reception of *A Journal of the Plague Year* and the Nexus of Fiction and History in the Novel." *ELH* 57 (1990): 529–55.

McCormack, Kathleen. "Reproducing Molly Bloom: A Revision History of the Reception of 'Penelope,' 1922–1970." In *Molly Blooms: A Polylogue on 'Penelope' and Cultural Studies,* edited by Richard Pearce, 17–39. Madison: University of Wisconsin Press, 1994.

———. "Reading *Ulysses* within the History of Its Production and Reception." In *Approaches to Teaching Joyce's Ulysses,* edited by Kathleen McCormick and Erwin R. Steinberg, 87–96. New York: Modern Language Association of America, 1993.

Muir, Kenneth. "Changing Interpretations of Shakespeare." In *The New Pelican Guide to English Literature, Vol. 2: The Age of Shakespeare,* edited by Boris Ford and Brian Vickers, 384–403. Harmondsworth, England: Penguin, 1982.

Newey, Vincent. "Keats, History, and the Poets." In *Keats and History,* edited by Nicholas Roe, 165–93. Cambridge: Cambridge University Press, 1995.

Novy, Marianne L. *Engaging with Shakespeare: Responses of George Eliot and Other Women Novelists.* Iowa City: University of Iowa Press, 1998.

Pearsall, Derek. "The Gower Tradition." In *Gower's* Confessio Amantis: *Responses and Reassessments,* edited by Alastair J. Minnis, 179–97. Woodbridge, England: Brewer, 1983.

Pedley, Colin. "'Terrific and Unprincipled Compositions': The Reception of *Lovers' Vows* and *Mansfield Park.*" *Philological Quarterly* 74 (1995): 297–316.

Pointner, Frank Erik. "Bardolatry and Biography: Romantic Readings of Shakespeare's Sonnets." In *British Romantics as Readers: Intertextualities, Maps of Misreading, Reinterpretations,* edited by Michael Gassenmeier, Petra Bridzun, Jens Martin Gurr, and Frank Erik Pointner, 117–36. Heidelberg: Carl Winter Universitatsverlag, 1998.

Radcliffe, David Hill. *Edmund Spenser: A Reception History.* Columbia, S.C.: Camden, 1996.

Rain, D. C. "Richardson's Character: A Case Study in an Author's Reputation." *English: The Journal of the English Association* 43 (1994): 193–208.

Ridley, Florence H. "The Friar and the Critics." In *The Idea of Medieval Literature: New Essays on Chaucer and Medieval Culture in Honor of Donald R. Howard,* edited by James M. Dean and Christian Zacher, 160–72. Newark: University of Delaware Press, 1992.

Robinson, Fred C. "Beowulf in the Twentieth Century." In *1996 Lectures and Memoirs,* edited by Majorie Chibnall, 45–62. Oxford: Oxford University Press, 1997.

Rodden, John. "My Orwell, Right or Left." *Canadian Journal of History* 24 (1989): 1–15.

Rooksby, Rikky. "A Century of Swinburne." In *The Whole Music of Passion: New Essays on Swinburne,* edited by Rikky Rooksby and Nicholas Shrimpton, 1–21. Brookfield, Vt.: Ashgate, 1993.

Rose, Ellen Cronan. "From Supermarket to Schoolroom: Doris Lessing in the United States." In *In Pursuit of Doris Lessing: Nine Nations Reading,* edited by Claire Sprague, 74–88. New York: St. Martin's, 1990.

Rozmovits, Linda. *Shakespeare and the Politics of Culture in Late Victorian England.* Baltimore: Johns Hopkins University Press, 1998.

Rude, Donald W., and Kenneth W. Davis. "The Critical Reception of the First American Edition of *The Nigger of the 'Narcissus.'*" *Conradian* 16, no. 2 (May 1992): 46–56.

Sabor, Peter. "The Rediscovery of Frances Burney's Plays." In *Lumen, XIII,* edited by Donald W. Nichol and Margarete Smith, 145–56. Edmonton, Alberta: Academic, 1994.

Segall, Jeffrey. "Culture, Politics, and Ideology in the Reception of *Ulysses.*" In *Approaches to Teaching Joyce's* Ulysses, edited by Kathleen McCormick and Erwin R. Steinberg, 42–48. New York: Modern Language Association of America, 1993.

———. *Joyce in America: Cultural Politics and the Trials of* Ulysses. Berkeley and Los Angeles: University of California Press, 1993.

Shawcross, John T. "Allegory, Typology, and Didacticism: *Paradise Lost* in the Eighteenth Century." In *Enlightening Allegory: Theory, Practice, and Contexts of Allegory in the Late Seventeenth and Eighteenth Centuries,* edited by Kevin L. Cope, 41–74. New York: AMS, 1993.

Smith, Diane M. "Confronting Socialism: The Naturalist Novel and Its Reception in Europe." *Works and Days* 7, no. 2 (fall 1989): 81–90.

Szonyi, Gyorgy E. "Self-Representation and Canon-Formation in the Late Renaissance: The Reception of Philip Sidney and Balint Balassi." In *Celebrating Comparativism,* edited by Katalin Kurtosi and Jozsef Pal, 447–59. Szeged, Hungary: Gold, 1994.

Taylor, Gary. *Reinventing Shakespeare: A Cultural History from the Restoration to the Present.* London: Weidenfeld & Nicholson, 1989.

Taylor, Richard C. "'Future Retrospection': Rereading Sheridan's Reviewers." In *Sheridan Studies,* edited by James Morwood and David Crane, 47–57. Cambridge: Cambridge University Press, 1995.

Thompson, Nicola Diane. *Reviewing Sex: Gender and the Reception of Victorian Novels.* New York: New York University Press, 1996.

———. "'Something Both More and Less Than Manliness': Gender and the Literary Reception of Anthony Trollope." *Victorian Literature and Culture* 22 (1994): 151–71.

Turner, James Grantham. "Novel Panic: Picture and Performance in the Reception of Richardson's *Pamela.*" *Representations* no. 48 (1994): 70–96.

Von Maltzahn, Nicholas. "Laureate, Republican, Calvinist: An Early Response to Milton and *Paradise Lost.*" *Milton Studies* 29 (1993): 181–98.

Wall, Stephen. "Ranking *Lord of the Flies* as Literature." In *Readings on* Lord of the Flies, edited by Clarice Swisher, 134–89. San Diego: Greenhaven, 1997.

Watts, Cedric. "*Heart of Darkness.*" In *The Cambridge Companion to Joseph Conrad,* edited by J. H. Stape, 45–62. Cambridge: Cambridge University Press, 1996.

Weimann, Robert. "A Divided Heritage: Conflicting Appropriations of Shakespeare in (East) Germany." In *Shakespeare and National Culture,* edited by John Drakakis and John J. Joughin, 173–205. New York: Manchester University Press, 1997.

Widdowson, Peter. *Hardy in History: A Study in Literary Sociology.* London: Routledge, 1989.

Wittreich, Joseph. "Milton's Transgressive Maneuvers: Receptions (Then and Now) and the Sexual Politics of *Paradise Lost.*" In *Milton and Heresy,* edited by Stephen Dobranski and John P. Rumrich, 244–66. Cambridge: Cambridge University Press, 1998.

Wixson, Douglas. "Reception Theory and the Survival of Orwell's *Nineteen Eighty-Four.*" *North Dakota Quarterly* 55, no. 2 (spring 1987): 72–86.

Woodcock, George. "Orwell's Changing Repute." *Queen's Quarterly* 88 (1981): 250–55.

Zimmermann, Heiner O. "Is Hamlet Germany? On the Political Reception of *Hamlet.*" In *New Essays on* Hamlet, edited by John Manning and Mark Thornton Burnett, 293–318. New York: AMS, 1994.

AMERICAN LITERATURE

Allen, Gay Wilson, and Ed Folsom, eds. *Walt Whitman and the World.* Iowa City: University of Iowa Press, 1995.

Arac, Jonathan. Huckleberry Finn *as Idol and Target: The Functions of Criticism in Our Time.* Madison: University of Wisconsin Press, 1997.

Axton, Marie. "Hemingway's Literary Reputation in England." *Hemingway Review* 11, special issue (summer 1992): 4–13.

Banks, Marva. "*Uncle Tom's Cabin* and Antebellum Black Response." In *Readers in History: Nineteenth-Century American Literature and the Contexts of Response,* edited by James L. Machor, 209–27. Baltimore: Johns Hopkins University Press, 1993.

Bassett, John E. "The Critical Reception of Thomas Wolfe's Posthumous Novels." *Resources for American Literary Study* 22 (1996): 79–102.

Baym, Nina. *Novels, Readers, and Reviewers: Responses to Fiction in Antebellum America.* Ithaca, N.Y.: Cornell University Press, 1984.

Bérubé, Michael. *Marginal Forces/Cultural Centers: Tolson, Pynchon, and the Politics of the Canon.* Ithaca, N.Y.: Cornell University Press, 1992.

Blair, John G. "Asian-American Writing-as-Culture-Studies: The Difference That Distance Makes." *Hitting Critical Mass: A Journal of Asian-American Cultural Criticism* 4 (1996): 27–37.

Bobia, Rosa. *The Critical Reception of James Baldwin in France.* New York: Peter Lang, 1997.

Bodziock, Joseph. "The Weight of Sambo's Woes." Rpt. in *Perspectives of Black Popular Culture,* edited by Harry B. Shaw, 166–79. Bowling Green, Oh.: Popular, 1990.

Bredella, Lothar. "Understanding a Foreign Culture through Assimilation and Arthur Miller's *The Crucible* and Its Dual Historical Context." Rpt. in *Text, Culture, Reception: Cross Cultural Aspects of English Studies,* edited by Rudiger Ahrens and Heinz Antor, 475–521. Heidelberg: Carl Winter Universitatsverlag, 1992.

Buckingham, Willis. "Poetry Readers and Reading in the 1890s: Emily Dickinson's First Reception." In *Readers in History: Nineteenth-Century American Literature and the Contexts of Response*, edited by James L. Machor, 164–79. Baltimore: Johns Hopkins University Press, 1993.

Burkholder, Robert E. "The Contemporary Reception of *English Traits*." In *Emerson Centenary Essays*, edited by Joel Myerson, 156–72. Carbondale: Southern Illinois University Press, 1982.

Ceniza, Sherry. "'Being a Woman . . . I Wish to Give My Own View': Some Nineteenth-Century Women's Responses to the 1860 *Leaves of Grass*." In *The Cambridge Companion to Walt Whitman*, edited by Ezra Greenspan, 110–34. Cambridge: Cambridge University Press, 1995.

Cohn, Deborah. "'He Was One of Us': The Reception of William Faulkner and the U.S. South by Latin American Authors." *Comparative Literature Studies* 34 (1997): 149–69.

Corkin, Stanley. "*Sister Carrie* and the Industrial Life: Objects and the New American Self." *MFS: Modern Fiction Studies* 33 (1987): 605–19.

Davis, Sara deSaussure, and Philip D. Beidler, eds. *The Mythologizing of Mark Twain*. Tuscaloosa: University of Alabama Press, 1984.

Ennis, Stephen. "The Literary Initiation of John Dos Passos." *Papers of the Bibliographical Society of America* 88 (1994): 87–92.

Fabre, Michel. "Richard Wright's Critical Reception in France—Censors Right and Left, Negritude Intellectuals, the Literary Set, and the General Public." *Mississippi Quarterly* 50 (1997): 307–25.

Fisch, Audrey A. "'Exhibiting Uncle Tom in Some Shape or Other': The Commodification and Reception of *Uncle Tom's Cabin* in England." *Nineteenth-Century Contexts* 17 (1993): 145–58.

———. "'Repetitious Accounts So Piteous and So Harrowing': The Ideological Work of American Slave Narratives in England." *Journal of Victorian Culture* 1 (1996): 16–34.

Fischer, Victor. "Huck Finn Reviewed: The Reception of *Huckleberry Finn* in the United States, 1885–1897." *American Literary Realism* 16, no. 1 (spring 1983): 1–57.

Gates, Henry Louis, Jr. "Literary Theory and the Black Tradition." In *Figures in Black: Words, Signs, and the "Racial" Self*, 3–58. New York: Oxford University Press, 1987.

Goldstein, Philip. "Critical Realism or Black Modernism?: The Reception of *Their Eyes Were Watching God*." *Reader: Essays in Reader-Oriented Theory, Criticism, and Pedagogy* no. 41 (spring 1999): 54–73.

Grant, Jennifer. "Reinterpreting Dickinson: Recognizing the Disruptive Imaginary." *Dickinson Studies* 79 (1991): 18–29 and 39–44.

Grimstead, David. "Anglo-American Racism and Philis Wheatley's 'Sable Veil,' 'Length'ned Chain,' and 'Knitted Heart.'" In *Women in the Age of the American Revolution*, edited by Ronald Hoffman, Peter J. Albert, and Linda K. Kerber, 338–444. Charlottesville: University Press of Virginia, 1989.

Gutman, Huck, ed. *As Others Read Us: International Perspectives on American Literature.* Amherst: University of Massachusetts Press, 1991.

Hamand, Wendy F. "'No Voice from England': Mrs. Stowe, Mr. Lincoln, and the British in the Civil War." *New England Quarterly* 61 (1988): 3–24.

Harris, Susan K. "Responding to the Text(s): Women Readers and the Quest for Higher Education." In *Readers in History: Nineteenth-Century American Literature and the Contexts of Response,* edited by James L. Machor, 259–82. Baltimore: Johns Hopkins University Press, 1993.

Headrick, Paul. "'Brilliant Obscurity': The Reception of *The Enormous Room.*" *Spring: The Journal of the E. E. Cummings Society* 1 (1992): 46–76.

Hewitt, Rosalie. "Henry James's *The American Scene:* Its Genesis and Its Reception, 1905–1977." *Henry James Review* 1 (1980): 179–96.

Holly, Carol. "The British Reception of Henry James's Autobiographies." *American Literature* 57 (1985): 570–87.

Jiji, Vera. "Reviewers' Responses to the Early Plays of Eugene O'Neill: A Study in Influence." *Theatre Survey* 29 (1988): 69–80.

Johnston, Carol. "The Critical Reception of *Of Time and the River.*" *Thomas Wolfe Review* 11, no. 1 (spring 1987): 45–54.

Jones, Buford. "'Decies Repitita Placebit': The Critical Reception of *Twice-Told Tales,* 1837–1842." *Nathaniel Hawthorne Review* 14, no. 1 (spring 1988): 1–6.

Keesey, Douglas. "*Vineland* in the Mainstream Press: A Reception Study." *Pynchon Notes* nos. 26/27 (spring/fall 1990): 107–13.

Leff, Leonard J. "A Thunderous Reception: Broadway, Hollywood, and *A Farewell to Arms.*" *The Hemingway Review* 15, no. 2 (spring 1996): 33–51.

Levine, Robert S. "*Uncle Tom's Cabin* in *Frederick Douglass' Paper*: An Analysis of Reception." *American Literature* 64 (1992): 71–93.

Lewis, Robert W. "The Inception and Reception of Hemingway's *A Farewell to Arms.*" *Hemingway Review* 9, no. 1 (fall 1989): 90–95.

Liberman, M. M. "The Responsibility of the Novelist: The Critical Reception of *Ship of Fools.*" *Criticism* 8 (1966): 377–88.

McElrath, Joseph R., Jr. "Stephen Crane in San Francisco: His Reception in *The Wave.*" *Stephen Crane Studies* 2, no. 1 (spring 1993): 2–18.

Machor, James L. "Historical Hermeneutics and Antebellum Fiction: Gender, Response Theory, and Interpretive Contexts." In *Readers in History: Nineteenth-Century American Literature and the Contexts of Response,* edited by James L. Machor, 54–84. Baltimore: Johns Hopkins University Press, 1993.

———. "Informed Reading and Early Nineteenth-Century American Fiction." *Nineteenth-Century Literature* 47 (1992): 320–48.

———. "Poetics as Ideological Hermeneutics: American Fiction and the Historical Reader of the Early Nineteenth Century." *Reader* no. 25 (spring 1991): 49–64.

Mailloux, Steven. "Reading as a Historical Act: Cultural Rhetoric, Bible Politics, and Fuller's 1845 Review of Douglass's *Narrative.*" In *Readers in History: Nineteenth-Century American Literature and the Contexts of Response,* edited by James L. Machor, 3–31. Baltimore: Johns Hopkins University Press, 1993.

———. "Rhetorical Hermeneutics as Reception Study: *Huckleberry Finn* and 'The Bad Boy Boom.'" In *Reconceptualizing American Literary/Cultural Studies: Rhetoric, History, and Politics in the Humanities,* edited by William Cain, 35–56. New York: Garland, 1996.

Messmer, Marietta. "Dickinson's Critical Reception." In *The Emily Dickinson Handbook,* edited by Gudren Grabber, Roland Hagenbuchle, Christine Miller, and Richard Sewall, 299–322. Amherst: University of Massachusetts Press, 1998.

Morey, Frederick L. "Great, Deep or Interesting? E.D. and Her Importance." *Dickinson Studies* 46 (1983): 29–38.

Morris, Timothy. *Becoming Canonical in American Poetry.* Urbana: University of Illinois Press, 1995.

Neilson, Jim. *Warring Fictions: Cultural Politics and the Vietnam War Narrative.* Jackson: University Press of Mississippi, 1998.

Nelson, Emmanuel. "Critical Deviance: Homophobia and the Reception of James Baldwin's Fiction." *Journal of American Culture* 14, no. 3 (fall 1991): 91–96.

Pells, Richard. *Not Like Us: How Europeans Have Loved, Hated, and Transformed American Culture since World War II.* New York: HarperCollins, 1997.

Person, Leland, Jr. "Melville and the Reviewers: The Irony of (Mis)reading." *Melville Society Extracts* no. 72 (February 1988): 3–5.

Phillipson, John S. "The Reception of *Look Homeward, Angel* in England: 1930 and 1958." *Thomas Wolfe Review* 17, no. 2 (fall 1993): 55–60.

Price-Stephens, Gordon. "The British Reception of William Faulkner 1929–1962." *Mississippi Quarterly* 18 (1965): 119–200.

Procopiow, Norma. "The Early Critical Reception of William Carlos Williams." *William Carlos Williams Newsletter* 5, no. 1 (spring 1979): 12–16.

Reardon, William R. "O'Neill Since World War II: Critical Reception in New York." *Modern Drama* 10 (1967): 289–99.

Richmond, Marion, "The Early Critical Reception of *The Portrait of a Lady.*" *Henry James Review* 7 (1986): 158–63.

Roy, Jackie. "Black Women Writing and Reading." Rpt. in *Black Women's Writing,* edited by Gina Wisker, 43–54. New York: St. Martin's, 1993.

Savoy, Eric. "Reading Gay America: Walt Whitman, Henry James, and the Politics of Reception." In *The Continuing Presence of Walt Whitman: The Life after the Life,* edited by Robert K. Martin, 3–15. Iowa City: University of Iowa Press, 1992.

Scharnhorst, Gary. "Hawthorne's Reception in England 1845–1849." *Nathaniel Hawthorne Review* 16, no. 2 (fall 1990): 13–15.

Scholonick, Robert J. "Politics and Poetics: The Reception of Melville's *Battle Pieces and Aspects of the War.*" *American Literature* 49 (1977): 422–30.

Simmonds, Roy S. "The British Critical Reception of Hemingway's *The Garden of Eden.*" *Hemingway Review* 8, no. 2 (spring 1989): 14–21.

Skerl, Jennie, and Robin Lydenberg, eds. *William S. Burroughs at the Front: Critical Reception, 1959–1989.* Carbondale: Southern Illinois University Press, 1991.

Skilton, David. "Some Victorian Readings of American Fiction." In *The Origins and Originality of American Culture,* edited by Tibor Frank, 113–20. Budapest: Akademiai Kiado, 1984.

Smith, David L. "Representative Emersons: Versions of American Identity." *Religion and American Culture* 2 (1992): 159–80.

Smith, F. Lannom. "The American Reception of *Leaves of Grass*: 1855–1882." *Walt Whitman Review* 22 (1976): 137–56.

Stephens, Robert O. "Hemingway's British and American Reception: A Study in Values." In *Hemingway: A Revaluation,* edited by Donald R. Noble, 83–97. New York: Whitson, 1983.

Templin, Charlotte. "Mass Culture, Gender, and Cultural Authority: The Reception of Erica Jong's *How to Save Your Own Life.*" The *Centennial Review* 38, no. 1 (winter 1994): 95–110.

Thomas, M. Wynn. "'A New World of Thought': Whitman's Early Reception in England." *Walt Whitman Review* 27 (1981): 74–78.

Tompkins, Jane. "Masterpiece Theater: The Politics of Hawthorne's Literary Reputation." *American Quarterly* 36 (1984): 617–42.

Upton, Lee. "The Remaking of a Poet: Louise Bogan." *The Centennial Review* 36 (1992): 557–72.

Verhoeven, W. M., ed. *James Fenimore Cooper: New Historical and Literary Contexts.* Amsterdam: Rodopi, 1993.

Wallace, James D. *Early Cooper and His Audience.* New York: Columbia University Press, 1986.

Walser, Richard. "Boston's Reception of the First American Novel." *Early American Literature* 17 (1982): 65–74.

Wasserman, Reneta R. Mautner. "The Reception of Cooper's Work and the Image of America." *ESQ: A Journal of the American Renaissance* 32 (1986): 183–200.

Weinstein, Cindy. "Melville, Labor, and the Discourses of Reception." Rpt. in *The Cambridge Companion to Herman Melville,* edited by Robert S. Levine, 202–23. Cambridge: Cambridge University Press, 1998.

Whitfield, Stephen J. "Cherished and Cursed: Toward a Social History of *The Catcher in the Rye.*" *New England Quarterly* 70 (1997): 567–600.

Wilcoxon, Hardy C. "Chinese American Literature beyond the Horizon." *New Literary History* 27 (1996): 313–28.

Williams, John. *Fiction as False Document: The Reception of E. L. Doctorow in the Postmodern Age.* Columbia, S.C.: Camden House, 1996.

Woodress, James. "The Making and Reception of *My Antonia.*" In *Approaches to Teaching My Antonia,* edited by Susan J. Rosowski, 37–42. New York: Modern Language Association, 1989.

Zehr, Janet S. "The Response of Nineteenth-Century Audiences to Louisa May Alcott's Fiction." *American Transcendental Quarterly* 1 (1987): 323–42.

CONTINENTAL EUROPEAN LITERATURE

Aldridge, A. Owen. "Voltaire Then and Now: Paradoxes and Contrasts in His Reputation." In *Enlightenment Studies in Honour of Lester G. Crocker,* edited by Alfred Bingham and Virgil W. Topazio, 1–17. Oxford: Voltaire Foundation, 1979.

Alsip, Barbara W. "*L'Avare*: History of Scholarship." *Oeuvres et Critiques: Revue Internationale d'Etude de la Reception Critique d'Etude des Oeuvres Littéraires de Langue* 6, no. 1 (1981): 99–110.

Altman, Janet Gurkin. "A Woman's Place in the Enlightenment Sun: The Case of F. de Graffigny." *Romance Quarterly* 38 (1991): 261–72.

Bahr, Ehrhard. *The Novel as Archive: The Genesis, Reception, and Criticism of Goethe's Wilhelm Meisters. Wanderjahre.* Columbia, S.C.: Camden House, 1998.

Bathrick, David. "Productive Mis-Reading: GDR Literature in the USA." *GDR Bulletin* 16, no. 2 (fall 1990): 1–6.

Berman, Russell A. "Producing the Reader: Kafka and the Modernist Organization of Reception." *Newsletter of the Kafka Society of America* 6, no. 1/2 (June/December 1982): 14–18.

Carr, Robert. "Crossing the First World/Third World Divides: Testimonial, Transnational Feminisms, and the Postmodern Condition." In *Scattered Hegemonies: Postmodernity and Transnational Feminist Practices,* edited by Inderpal Grewal and Caren Kaplan, 153–72. Minneapolis: University of Minnesota Press, 1994.

Chen, Xiaomei. "Occidentalist Theater in Post-Mao China: Shakespeare, Ibsen, and Brecht As Counter Others." In *Streams of Cultural Capital: Transnational Cultural Studies,* edited by David Liu Palumbo and Hans Ulrich Gumbrecht, 155–77. Stanford, Calif.: Stanford University Press, 1997.

Clayton, J. Douglas, ed. *Chekhov Then and Now: The Reception of Chekhov in World Culture.* New York: Peter Lang, 1997.

Fallaize, Elizabeth. "Reception Problems for Women Writers: The Case of Simone de Beauvoir." In *Women and Representation,* edited by Diana Knight and Judith Still, 43–56. London: WIF, 1995.

Farrelly, Daniel J. *Goethe in East Germany, 1949–1989: Toward a History of Goethe Reception in the GDR.* Columbia, S.C.: Camden House, 1998.

Fernandez-Morera, Dario. "Cervantes and the Aesthetics of Reception." *Comparative Literature Studies* 28 (1981): 405–19.

Gelber, Mark H., ed. *The Jewish Reception of Heinrich Heine*. Tubingen, Germany: Niemeyer, 1992.

Giametti, A. Bartlett, ed. *Dante in America: The First Two Centuries*. Binghamton, N.Y.: Medieval & Renaissance Texts & Studies, 1983.

Greene, Ellen, ed. *Re-Reading Sappho: Reception and Transmission*. Berkeley and Los Angeles: University of California Press, 1996.

Haase, Donald, ed. *The Reception of Grimm's Fairy Tales: Responses, Reactions, Revisions*. Detroit: Wayne State University Press, 1993.

Hoffmann, Werner. "The Reception of the *Nibelungenlied* in the Twentieth Century." In *A Companion to the* Nibelungenlied, edited by Winder McConnell, 127–52. Columbia, S.C.: Camden House, 1998.

Hohendahl, Peter Uwe, and Sander L. Gilman, eds. *Heinrich Heine and the Occident: Multiple Identities, Multiple Receptions*. Lincoln: University of Nebraska Press, 1991.

Jackson, Robert Louis. "Dostoevsky in the Twentieth Century." *Dostoevsky Studies: Journal of the International Dostoevsky Society* 1 (1980): 3–10.

Johnson, Dane. "The Rise of Gabriel Garcia Marquez and Toni Morrison." In *Cultural Institutions of the Novel*, edited by Deidre Lynch and William B. Warner, 129–56. Durham, N.C.: Duke University Press, 1996.

Kennedy, William J. *Authorizing Petrarch*. Ithaca, N.Y.: Cornell University Press, 1994.

King, Adele, ed. *Camus's* L'Etranger: *Fifty Years On*. New York: St. Martin's, 1992.

Kolin, Philip C. "Venus and/or Adonis among the Critics." In *Venus and Adonis: Critical Essays*, edited by Philip C. Kolin, 3–65. New York: Garland, 1997.

Larsen, Neil. "Cortazar and Postmodernity: New Interpetive Liabilities." In *Julio Cortazar: New Readings*, edited by Carlos J. Alonso, 57–75. Cambridge: Cambridge University Press, 1998.

McLeod, Glenda K., ed. *The Reception of Christine de Pizan from the Fifteenth Through the Nineteenth Centuries: Visitors to the City*. Lewiston, N.Y.: Mellen, 1991.

Mistacco, Vicki. "Plus ca change . . . : The Critical Reception of *Emily L.*" *The French Review: Journal of the American Association of Teachers of French* 66 (1992): 77–88.

Mufti, Aamir. "Reading the Rushdie Affair: An Essay on Islam and Politics." *Social Text* no. 29 (winter 1991): 95–116.

Nash, Jerry C. "'The Poet of One Poem': Du Bellay, Walter Pater, and Modern Aesthetic Criticism." *Oeuvres et Critiques: Revue Internationale d'Etude de la Reception Critique d'Etude des Oeuvres Litteraires de Langue* 20, no. 1 (1995): 113–19.

Parker, Stephen Jan. "Critical Reception." In *The Garland Companion to Vladimir Nabokov*, edited by Vladimir E. Alexandrov, 67–75. New York: Garland, 1995.

———. "Nabokov Studies: The State of the Art." In *The Achievements of Vladimir Nabokov: Essays, Studies, Reminiscences, and Stories from the Cornell Nabokov Festival*, edited by George Gibian and Stephen Jan Parker, 81–97. Ithaca, N.Y.: Center for International Studies, Committee on Soviet Studies, Cornell University, 1984.

Patterson, Michael. "Brecht's Legacy." In *The Cambridge Companion to Brecht,* edited by Peter Thomson and Glendyr Sacks, 273–87. Cambridge: Cambridge University Press, 1994.

Paulson, Ronald. *Don Quixote in England: The Aesthetics of Laughter.* Baltimore, Johns Hopkins University Press, 1998.

Picchi, Mario. "The Centenary of Guy de Maupassant." *Italian Books and Periodicals: Cultural and Bibliographic Review* 36, no. 1/2 (January/December 1993): 23–25.

Raizis, Marius Byron. "Romantic Readings of Homer." In *British Romantics as Readers: Intertextualities, Maps of Misreading, Reinterpretations,* edited by Michael Gassenmeier, Petra Bridzun, Jens Martin Gurr, and Frank Erik Pointner, 55–69. Heidelberg: Carl Winter Universitatsverlag, 1998.

Rincon, Carlos. "Streams out of Control: The Latin American Plot." In *Streams of Cultural Capital: Transnational Cultural Studies,* edited by Liu David Palumbo and Hans Ulrich Gumbrecht, 179–98. Stanford, Calif.: Stanford University Press, 1997.

Sammons, Jeffrey L. "Problems of Heine Reception: Some Considerations." *Monatshefte fur Deutschen Unterricht, Deutsche Sprache und Literatur* 73 (1981): 383–391.

Schmidt, Peter Lebrecht. "Reception Theory and Classical Scholarship: A Plea for Convergence." In *Hypatia: Essays in Classics, Comparative Literature, and Philosophy Presented to Hazel E. Barnes on Her Seventieth Birthday,* edited by William M. Calder, Ulrich K. Goldsmith, and Phyllis B. Kevevan, 67–77. Boulder: Colorado Associated University Press, 1985.

Schulz, H. J. "American German Literary Reception." In *Proceedings of the Tenth Congress of the International Comparative Literature Association,* vol. 1, edited by Anna Balakian, James J. Wilhelm, Douwe W. Fokkema, Edward C. Smith, III, Claudio Guillen, Peggy Escher, and M. J. Valdes, 244–50. New York: Garland, 1985.

Schutjer, Karin. "The Semiotics of Individuality and the Problem of Reception in Holderlin's *Empedokles.*" *Colloquia Germanica: Internationale Zeitschrift fur Germanistik* 30 (1997): 227–50.

Sinnigen, John H. "The Contexts of Canon Formation." *Anales Galdosianos* 25 (1990): 129–32.

Slater, Maya. "Moliere and His Readers." In *Reading Plays: Interpretation and Reception,* edited by Hanna Scolnicov and Peter Holland, 161–74. Cambridge: Cambridge University Press, 1991.

Smith, Dawn L. "Cervantes and His Audience: Aspects of Reception Theory in *El retablo de las maravillas.*" In *The Golden Age Comedia: Text, Theory, and Performance,* edited by Charles Ganelin and Howard Mancing, 249–61. West Lafayette, Ind.: Purdue University Press, 1994.

Ugrinsky, Alexej, ed. *Goethe in the Twentieth Century.* New York: Greenwood, 1987.

Van Zuylen, Marina. "From Horror Vacui to the Reader's Boredom: *Bouvard et Pecuchet* and the Art of Difficulty." *Nineteenth-Century French Studies* 22 (1993/1994): 112–22.

Waddington, Patrick. "Some Salient Phases of Turgenev's Critical Reception, I: 1853–1870; II: 1870–1883." In *Ivan Turgenev and Britain*, edited by Patrick Waddington, 1–56. Oxford: Berg, 1995.

3. HISTORY OF THE BOOK

Allen, James Smith. "Critics in Search of a Text: Reviewers as an Interpretive Community in Modern France." *Proceedings of the Annual Meeting of the Western Society for French History* 18 (1991): 439–46.

———. "A Distant Echo: Reading Jules Michelet's *L'Amour* and *La Femme* in 1859–1860." *Nineteenth-Century French Studies* 16, no. 1/2 (fall/winter 1987/88): 30–46.

———. *In the Public Eye: A History of Reading in Modern France, 1800–1940.* Princeton, N.J.: Princeton University Press, 1991.

———. *Popular French Romanticism: Authors, Readers, and Books in the Nineteenth Century.* Syracuse, N.Y.: Syracuse University Press, 1981.

Brewer, John. "Reconstructing the Reader: Prescriptions, Texts and Strategies in Anna Larpent's Reading." In *The Practice and Representation of Reading in England*, edited by James Raven, Helen Small, and Naomi Tadmor, 226–45. Cambridge: Cambridge University Press, 1996.

Brieger, Peter H. "Pictorial Commentaries to the *Commedia*." In *Illuminated Manuscripts* of The Divine Comedy, edited by Peter H. Brieger, Millard Meiss, and Charles Southward Singleton, 81–113. Princeton, N.J.: Princeton University Press, 1969. Vol. 1.

Brooks, Jeffrey. "The Educated Response: Literature for the People." In *When Russia Learned to Read: Literacy and Popular Literature, 1861–1917*, 295–352. Princeton, N.J.: Princeton University Press, 1985.

Chartier, Roger. *The Cultural Uses of Print in Early Modern France.* Translated by Lydia G. Cochrane. Princeton, N.J.: Princeton Univeristy Press, 1987.

———. *The Order of Books: Readers, Authors, and Libraries in Europe between the Fourteenth and Eighteenth Centuries.* Translated by Lydia G. Cochrane. Cambridge, England: Polity, 1994.

Coleman, Janet. *Medieval Readers and Writers, 1350–1400.* New York: Columbia University Press, 1981.

Coleman, Joyce. *Public Reading and the Reading Public in Late Medieval England and France.* Cambridge: Cambridge University Press, 1996.

Cooper, Allene. "Science and the Reception of Poetry in Postbellum American Journals." *American Periodicals* 4 (1994): 24–46.

Cruse, Amy. *The Englishman and His Books in the Early Nineteenth Century.* New York: Crowell, 1930.

———. The Victorians and Their Books. London: Allen, 1935

Darnton, Robert. "First Steps Toward a History of Reading." *Australian Journal of French Studies* 23 (1986): 5–30.

———. "Readers Respond to Rousseau: The Fabrication of Romantic Sensitivity." *The Great Cat Massacre and Other Episodes of French Cultural History.* New York: Basic Books, 1984. 215–56.

———. "Toward a History of Reading." *Wilson Quarterly* 13, no. 4 (fall 1989): 86–102.

Davidson, Cathy N. *Revolution and the Word: The Rise of the Novel in America.* New York: Oxford University Press, 1986.

Eberly, Rosa A. *Citizen Critics: Literary Public Spheres.* Urbana: University of Illinois Press, 2000.

Fabian, Bernhard. "English Books and Their Eighteenth-Century German Readers." In *The Widening Circle: Essays on the Circulation of Literature in Eighteenth-Century Europe,* edited by P. J. Korshin, 117–96. Philadelphia: University of Pennsylvania Press, 1976.

Fergus, Jan. "Provincial Servants' Reading in the Late Eighteenth Century." In *The Practice and Representation of Reading in England,* edited by James Raven, Helen Small, and Naomi Tadmor, 202–25. Cambridge: Cambridge University Press, 1996.

Flesch, Juliet. "Bring Love to Book: The Compilation and Reception of a Bibliography." *Publishing History* 40 (1996): 99–107.

Flint, Kate. *The Woman Reader: 1837–1914.* New York: Oxford University Press, 1993.

Forster, Antonio. "'The Self–Impanelled Jury': The Reception of Review Journals, 1749–1760." In *Studies in Newspaper and Periodical History, 1993 Annual,* edited by Michael Harris, 27–51. Westport, Conn.: Greenwood, 1993.

Gaisser, Julia Haig. *Catullus and His Renaissance Readers.* Oxford: Clarendon Press of Oxford University Press, 1993.

Gallaway, W. F., Jr. "The Conservative Attitude Toward Fiction, 1780–1830." *PMLA* 55 (1940): 1041–59.

Gerrard, Teresa. "New Methods in the History of Reading: 'Answers to the Correspondents' in the *Family Herald,* 1860–1900." *Publishing History* 43 (1998): 53–69.

Gilmore, William. *Reading Becomes a Necessity of Life: Material and Cultural Life in Rural New England, 1780–1835.* Knoxville: University of Tennessee Press, 1989.

Ginzburg, Carlo. *The Cheese and the Worm: The Cosmos of a Seventeenth-Century Miller.* London: Routledge and Kegan Paul, 1980.

Hall, David D. *Cultures of Print: Essays in the History of the Book.* Amherst: University of Massachusetts Press, 1996.

———. "The History of the Book: New Questions? New Answers?" *Journal of Library History* 21 (1986): 27–36.

Hancock, Maxine. "Bunyan as Reader: The Record of *Grace Abounding.*" *Bunyan Studies* 5 (1994): 68–84.

Harris, Kate. "John Gower's 'Confessio Amantis': The Virtue of Bad Texts." In *Manuscripts and Readers in Fifteenth-Century England,* edited by Derek Pearsall, 27–40. Cambridge, England: Brewer; Totowa, N.J.: Biblio Distribution, 1983.

Hayward, Jennifer Poole. *Consuming Pleasures: Active Audiences and Serial Fiction from Dickens to Soap Operas.* Lexington: University of Kentucky Press, 1997.

Henkin, David. *City Reading: Written Words and Public Spaces in Antebellum New York.* New York: Columbia University Press, 1998.

Huot, Sylvia. The Romance of the Rose *and Its Medieval Readers: Interpretation, Reception, Manuscript Transmission.* Cambridge: Cambridge University Press, 1993.

Johnson, Barbara. *Reading* Piers Plowman *and* The Pilgrim's Progress. Carbondale: Southern Illinois University Press, 1992.

Kallendorf, Craig. *Virgil and the Myth of Venice: Books and Readers in the Italian Renaissance.* Oxford: Clarendon Press of Oxford University Press, 1999.

Kaufman, Paul. "Readers and Their Reading in Eighteenth-Century Lichfield." *The Library* 28 (1973): 108–15.

———. "The Reading of Plays in the Eighteenth Century." *Bulletin of the New York Public Library* 73 (1969): 562–80.

Lerer, Seth. *Chaucer and His Readers: Imagining the Author in Late-Medieval England.* Princeton, N.J.: Princeton University Press, 1993.

Lewis, Suzanne. *Reading Images: Narrative Discourse and Reception in the Thirteenth Century Illuminated Apocalypse.* New York: Cambridge University Press, 1995.

McCarthy, John A. "The Art of Reading and the Goals of the German Enlightenment." *Lessing Yearbook* 16 (1984): 79–94.

McHenry, Elizabeth. "Forgotten Readers: African-American Literary Societies and the American Scene." In *Print Culture in a Diverse America,* edited by James P. Danky and Wayne A. Wiegard, 149–72. Urbana: University of Illinois Press, 1998.

Magnuson. Paul. *Reading Public Romanticism.* Princeton, N.J.: Princeton University Press, 1998.

Myerson, Joel. "The Contemporary Reception of the Boston *Dial.*" *Resources for American Literary Study* 3 (1973): 203–20.

Nord, David Paul. "Reading the Newspaper: Strategies and Politics of Reader Response, Chicago, 1912–17." *Journal of Communication* 45, no. 3 (summer 1995): 66–93.

———. "Religious Reading and Readers in Antebellum America." *Journal of the Early Republic* 15 (1995): 241–72.

———. "A Republican Literature: Magazine Reading and Readers in Late-Eighteenth-Century New York." In *Reading in America: Literature and Social Change,* edited by Cathy N. Davidson, 114–39. Baltimore: Johns Hopkins University Press, 1989.

———. "Working-Class Readers: Family, Community, and Reading in Late Nineteenth-Century America." *Communication Research* 13 (1986): 156–81.

Orians, G. Harrison. "Censure of Fiction in American Romances and Magazines, 1789–1810." *PMLA* 52 (1937): 195–214.

Pawley, Christine. "Better than Billiards: Reading and the Public Library in Osage,

Iowa, 1890–95." In *Print Culture in a Diverse America,* edited by James P. Danky and Wayne A. Wiegard, 173–99. Urbana: University of Illinois Press, 1998.

Pearson, Jacqueline. *Women's Reading in Britain, 1750–1835: A Dangerous Recreation.* Cambridge: Cambridge University Press, 1999.

Richardson, Brian. *Printing, Writers, and Readers in Renaissance Italy.* Cambridge: Cambridge University Press, 1999.

Rose, Jonathan. "Rereading the English Common Reader: A Preface to the History of Audiences." *Journal of the History of Ideas* 53 (1992): 47–70.

Rowland, William G. *Literature and the Marketplace: Romantic Writers and Their Audiences in Great Britain and the United States.* Lincoln: University of Nebraska Press, 1996.

Saenger, Paul. "Silent Reading: Its Impact on Late Medieval Script and Society." *Viator: Medieval and Renaissance Studies* 13 (1982); 367–414.

Sicherman, Barbara. "Reading *Little Women*: The Many Lives of a Text." In *U.S. History as Women's History: New Feminist Essays,* edited by Linda Kerber, Alice Kesslar Harris, and Kathryn Kish Sklar, 245–66. Chapel Hill: University of North Carolina Press, 1995.

———. "Sense and Sensibility: A Case Study of Women's Reading in Late-Victorian America." In *Reading in America: Literature and Social Change,* edited by Cathy N. Davidson, 201–25. Baltimore: Johns Hopkins University Press, 1989.

Somerset, Fiona. *Clerical Discourse and Lay Audience in Late Medieval England.* Cambridge: Cambridge University Press, 1998.

Stevenson, Robert L. "Prescription and Reality: Reading Advisors and Reading Practice, 1860–1880." *Book Research Quarterly* 6 (1990/91): 43–61.

Stock, Brian. *The Implications of Literacy: Written Language and Models of Interpretation in the Eleventh and Twelfth Centuries.* Princeton, N.J.: Princeton University Press, 1983.

Sutherland, J. A. *Victorian Fiction: Writers, Publishers, Readers.* Basingstoke, England: Macmillan, 1995.

Tadmor, Naomi. "'In the Even My Wife Read to Me': Women, Reading and Household Life in the Eighteenth Century." In *The Practice and Representation of Reading in England,* edited by James Raven, Helen Small, and Naomi Tadmor, 162–74. Cambridge: Cambridge University Press, 1996.

Taylor, John Tinnon. *Early Opposition to the English Novel: The Popular Reaction from 1780 to 1830.* New York: King's Crown, 1943.

Thomas, Amy M. "Literature in Newsprint: Antebellum Family Newspapers and the Uses of Reading." In *Reading Books: Essays on the Material Text and Literature in America,* edited by Michele Moylan and Lane Styles, 101–16. Amherst: University of Massachusetts Press, 1996.

Ward, Albert. *Book Production[,] Fiction and the German Reading Public 1740–1800.* Oxford: Clarendon Press of Oxford University Press, 1974.

Warner, William Beatty. *Licensing Entertainment: The Elevation of Novel Reading in Britain, 1684–1750.* Berkeley and Los Angeles: University of California Press, 1998.

Woodmansee, Martha. "Toward a Genealogy of the Aesthetic: The German Reading Debate of the 1790s." *Cultural Critique* 11 (winter 1988/89): 203–21.

Zboray, Ronald J. *A Fictive People: Antebellum Economic Activity and the American Reading Public.* New York: Oxford University Press, 1993.

———. "The Letter and the Fiction Reading Public in Antebellum America." *Journal of American Culture* 10, no. 1 (spring 1987): 27–34.

Zboray, Ronald J., and Mary Saracino Zboray. "Books, Reading, and the World of Goods in Antebellum New England." *American Quarterly* 48 (1996): 587–622.

———. "'Have You Read . . . ?' Real Readers and Their Responses in Antebellum Boston and Its Region." *Nineteenth-Century Literature* 52 (1997): 139–70.

———. "Political News and Female Readership in Antebellum Boston and Its Region." *Journalism History* 22, no. 1 (spring 1996): 2–14.

———. "Reading and Everyday Life in Boston: The Diary of David F. and Mary D. Child." *Libraries and Culture: A Journal of Library History* 32 (1997): 285–323.

———. "Transcendentalism in Print: Production, Dissemination, and Common Reception." In *The Transcendent and the Permanent: The Transcendental Movement and Its Contexts,* edited by Charles Capper and Conrad Edick Wright, 310–81. Boston: Massachusetts Historical Society, 1999.

4. TEXTS, GENRES, AND AUDIENCES IN MASS AND POPULAR CULTURE

Ableman, R. "Motivations for Viewing 'The 700 Club.'" *Journalism Quarterly* 65 (1988): 112–18.

———. "'PTL Club' Viewer Uses and Gratifications." *Communication Quarterly* 37 (1989): 54–66.

———. "Religious Television Uses and Gratifications." *Journal of Broadcasting and Electronic Media* 31 (1987): 293–307.

Abrahamsson, V. B. "When Women Watch Television . . . ." *Nordicom Review* 2 (1993): 37–52.

Adams, R. C., and G. M. Webber. "The Audience for, and Male vs. Female Reactions to, *The Day After.*" *Journalism Quarterly* 61 (1984): 812–16.

Allen, Richard L., and William T. Bielby. "Black Attitudes and Behaviors Toward Television." *Communication Research* 6 (1979): 437–62.

Allen, Robert C. "Reader-Oriented Criticism and Television." In *Channels of Discourse: Television and Contemporary Criticism,* edited by Robert C. Allen, 74–112. Chapel Hill: University of North Carolina Press, 1987.

———. "Relocating the Site of the Audience." *Critical Studies in Mass Communication* 5 (1988): 217–33.

Alperstein, N. M. "Imaginary Social Relationships with Celebrities Appearing on

Television Commercials." *Journal of Broadcasting and Electronic Media* 35 (1991): 43–58.

Ang, Ien. "Feminist Desire and Female Pleasure: On Janice Radway's *Reading the Romance.*" *Camera Obscura* 16 (1998): 179–92.

———. "Melodramatic Identification: Television Fiction and Women's Fantasy." In *Television and Women's Culture: The Politics of the Popular,* edited by Mary Ellen Brown, 75–88. Newbury Park, Calif.: Sage, 1990.

———. "Wanted: Audiences. On the Politics of Empirical Audience Studies." In *Remote Control: Television, Audiences, and Cultural Power,* edited by Ellen Seiter, Hans Borchers, Gabriele Kreuttzner, and Eva-Maria Warth, 96–115. London: Routledge, 1989.

———. *Watching "Dallas": Soap Opera and the Melodramatic Imagination.* New York: Methuen, 1985. Ansley, Cassandra. "How to Watch *Star Trek.*" *Cultural Studies* 3 (1989): 323–39.

Ang, Ien, and Joke Hermes. "Gender and/in Media Consumption." In *Mass Media and Society,* edited by James Curran and Michael Gurevitch, 307–28. London: Arnold, 1991.

Austin, Bruce A., and John W. Myers. "Hearing-Impaired Viewers and Prime-Time Television." *Journal of Communication* 34, no. 4 (autumn 1984): 60–71.

Bacon-Smith, Camille. *Enterprising Women: Television Fandom and the Creation of Popular Myth.* Philadelphia: University of Pennsylvania Press, 1992.

Baker, Martin. "Seeing How Far You Can See: On Being a 'Fan' of 2000 A.D." In *Reading Audiences: Young People and the Media,* edited by David Buckingham, 159–83. Manchester: Manchester University Press, 1993.

Bantz, Charles R. "Exploring Uses and Gratifications: A Comparison of Repeated Uses of Television and Reported Uses of Favorite Program Types." *Communication Research* 8 (1982): 352–79.

Barker, Martin. "Taking the Extreme Case: Understanding a Fascist Fan of Judge Dred." In *Trash Aesthetics: Popular Culture and Its Audience,* edited by Deborah Cartmell, I. Q. Hunter, Heidi Kaye, and Imelda Whelan, 14–30. London: Pluto, 1997.

Barrow, Austin S. "Audience Motivation, Viewing Contexts, Media Content, and Form: The Interactional Emergence of Soap Opera Entertainment." *Communication Studies* 41 (1990): 343–61.

Becker, Lee B. "Measurement of Gratifications." *Communication Research* 6 (1979): 54–73.

———. "Two Tests of Media Gratifications: Watergate and the 1974 Election." *Journalism Quarterly* 53 (1976): 29–33.

Bennett, Tony, and Janet Woollacott. *Bond and Beyond: The Political Career of a Popular Hero.* New York: Methuen, 1987.

Bielby, Denise and C. Lee Harrington. "Reach Out and Touch Someone: Viewers,

Agency, and Audiences in the Television Experience." In *Viewing, Reading, Listening: Audiences and Cultural Reception,* edited by Jon Cruz and Justin Lewis, 81–100. Boulder, Colo.: Westview, 1994.

Biltereyst, Daniel. "Qualitative Audience Research and Transnational Media Effects: A New Paradigm?" *European Journal of Communication* 10 (1995): 245–70.

———. "Resisting American Hegemony: A Comparative Analysis of the Reception of Domestic US Fiction." *European Journal of Communication* 5 (1990): 469–97.

Blumler, Jay G., and Elihu Katz, eds. *The Uses of Mass Communications: Current Perspectives in Gratifications Research.* Beverly Hills, Calif.: Sage, 1974.

Bobo, Jacqueline. *Black Women as Cultural Readers.* New York: Columbia University Press, 1995.

Bodroghkozy, Aniko. "'Is This What You Mean by Color TV?' Race, Gender, and Contested Meanings in NBC's *Julia*." In *Private Screenings: Television and the Female Consumer,* edited by Lynn Spiegel and Denise Mann, 143–67. Minneapolis: University of Minnesota Press, 1992.

Bottomore, Stephen. "The Panicking Audience?: Early Cinema and the 'Train Effect.'" *Historical Journal of Film, Radio and Television* 19 (1989): 177–216.

Bourgalt, Louise M. "The 'PTL Club' and Protestant Viewers: An Ethnographic Study." *Journal of Communication* 35, no. 1 (winter 1985): 132–48.

Bovill, M., R. M. McGregor, and Mallory Wober. "Audience Reactions to Parliamentary Television." In *Televising Democracies,* edited by Bob Franklin, 149–69. New York: Routledge, 1992.

Boyarin, Jonathan. "Voices Around the Text: The Ethnography of Reading at Mesivta Tifereth Jerusalem." In *The Ethnography of Reading,* edited by Jonathan Boyarin, 212–37. Berkeley and Los Angeles: University of California Press, 1991.

Brown, Jane D., and Laurie Schulze. "The Effects of Race, Gender, and Fandom on Audience Interpretations of Madonna's Music Videos." *Journal of Communication* 40, no. 1 (winter 1990): 88–102.

Brown, Mary Ellen. "Knowledge and Power: An Ethnography of Soap-Opera Viewers." In *Television Criticism,* edited by Leah Vande Berge and Lawrence Wenner, 178–97. New York: Longman, 1991.

———. *Soap Opera and Women's Talk: The Pleasure of Resistance.* Thousand Oaks, Calif.: Sage, 1994.

Brundson, Charlotte, and David Morley. *Everyday Television: Nationwide.* London: British Film Institute, 1978.

Brunt, Rosiland. "Engaging with the Popular: Audiences for Mass Culture and What to Say about Them." In *Cultural Studies,* edited by Lawrence Grossberg, Cary Nelson, and Paula A. Treichler, 69–76. New York: Routledge, 1992.

———. "The Politics of 'Bias': How Television Audiences View Current Affairs." In *Propaganda, Persuasion, and Polemic,* edited by J. Hawthorn, 141–56. London: Arnold, 1987.

t, J., and S. C. Rockwell. "Evolving Cognitive Models in Mass Communication Reception Processes." In *Responding to the Screen: Reception and Reaction Processes*, edited by J. Bryant and D. Zillmann, 217–60. Hillsdale, N.J.: Erlbaum, 1991.

Buckingham, David. "Boys' Talk: Television and the Policing of Masculinity." In *Reading Audiences: Young People and the Media*, edited by David Buckingham, 89–115. Manchester: Manchester University Press, 1993.

————. *Children Talking Television: The Making of Television Literacy*. Washington, D.C.: Taylor and Francis, 1993.

————. "Doing Them Harm? Children's Conceptions of the Negative Effects of Television." In *Social Learning from Broadcast Television*, edited by Karen Swan, Carla Meskill, and Steven DeMaio, 25–44. Creskill, N.J.: Hampton, 1998.

————. *Moving Images: Children's Emotional Responses to Television*. Manchester: Manchester University Press, 1996.

————. *Public Secrets: "EastEnders" and Its Audience*. London: British Film Institute, 1987.

————. "What Are Words Worth? Interpreting Children's Talk about Television." *Cultural Studies* 5 (1991): 228–45.

————. ed. *Reading Audiences: Young People and the Media*. Manchester: Manchester University Press, 1993.

Caldarola, V. J. "Reading the Television Text in Outer Indonesia." *Howard Journal of Communication* 4, no. 1/2 (summer/fall 1992): 28–49.

Canary, Daniel L., and Brian H. Spitzberg. "Loneliness and Media Gratifications." *Communication Research* 20 (1992): 800–21.

Cantor, Joanne, and Amy I. Nathanson. "Children's Fright Reactions to Television News." *Journal of Communication* 46, no. 4 (autumn 1996): 139–52.

Cantor, Joanne, and Sandra Reilly. "Adolescents' Fright Reactions to Television Films." *Journal of Communication* 32, no. 1 (winter 1982): 87–99.

Cantor, Joanne, Barbara J. Wilson, and Cynthia Hoffner. "Emotional Responses to a Televised Nuclear Holocaust Film." *Communication Research* 13 (1986): 257–77.

Christenson, P. "Preadolescent Perceptions and Interpretations of Music Videos." *Popular Music and Society* 16, no. 3 (fall 1992): 63–74.

Cohen, Jodi R. "Critical Viewing and Participatory Democracy." *Journal of Communication* 44, no. 4 (autumn 1994): 98–113.

————. "The 'Relevance' of Cultural Identity in Audiences' Interpretations of Mass Media. "*Critical Studies in Mass Communication* 8 (1991): 442–54.

Collins, Ava. "Intellectuals, Power and Quality Television." *Cultural Studies* 7 (1993): 28–45.

Collins, James. "Watching Ourselves Watch Television, Or Who's Your Agent?" *Cultural Studies* 3 (1989): 261–81.

Cooks, L. M., and M. P. Orbe. "Beyond Satire: Selective Exposure and Selective Perception in 'In Living Color.'" *Howard Journal of Communication* 4 (1993): 217–33.

Cooper, Brenda. "The Relevancy of Gender Identity of Spectators' Interpretations of *Thelma and Louise.*" *Critical Studies in Mass Communication* 16 (1999): 20–41.

Corner, John, Kay Richardson, and Natalie Fenton. *Nuclear Reactions: Form and Response in Public Issue Television.* London: Libbey, 1990.

Crook, S. "Television and Audience Activity: The Problem of the Television/Viewer Nexus in Audience Research." *Australian and New Zealand Journal of Sociology* 25 (1989): 356–80.

Cruz, Jon. "Testimonies and Artifacts: Elite Appropriations of African-American Music in the Nineteenth Century." In *Viewing, Reading, Listening: Audiences and Cultural Reception,* edited by Jon Cruz and Justin Lewis, 125–51. Boulder, Colo.: Westview, 1994.

Cruz, Jon, and Justin Lewis, eds. *Viewing, Reading, Listening: Audiences and Cultural Reception.* Boulder, Colo.: Westview, 1994.

Cunningham, Stuart, and Elizabeth Jacka. "Neighborly Relations: Cross-Cultural Reception Analysis and Australian Soaps in Britain." *Cultural Studies* 8 (1994): 509–26.

D'Acci, Julie. *Defining Women: Television and the Case of Cagney and Lacey.* Chapel Hill: University of North Carolina Press, 1994.

Dahlgren, Peter. "The Modes of Reception: For a Hermeneutics of TV News." In *Television in Transition,* edited by Phillip Drummond and Richard Paterson, 235–49. London: British Film Institute, 1985.

———. "What's the Meaning of This?: Viewers Plural Sense-Making of T.V. News." *Media, Culture and Society* 10 (1988): 285–301.

Dávidházi, Péter. *The Romantic Cult of Shakespeare: Literary Reception in Anthropological Perspective.* New York: St. Martin's, 1998.

Dickinson, Roger, Ramaswami Harindranath, and Olga Linné, eds. *Approaches to Audiences.* Boulder, Colo.: Westview, 1998.

Dohnalik, Jacek. "Uses and Gratifications of 'Return to Eden' for Polish Viewers." *European Journal of Communication* 4 (1989): 307–28.

Dorr, Amiée. *Television and Children: A Special Medium for a Special Audience.* Beverly Hills, Calif.: Sage, 1986.

Drotner, Kirsten. "Media Ethnography: An Other Story?" *Nordicom Review* 2 (1993): 1–13.

Durkin, Kevin. "Children's Accounts of Sex-Role Stereotypes in Television." *Communication Research* 11 (1984): 341–62.

Eastman, S. T., and K. E. Riggs. "Television Sports and Ritual: Fan Experiences." *Sociology of Sport Journal* 11 (1994): 249–74.

Ehrenreich, Barbara, Elizabeth Hess, and Gloria Jacobs. "Beatlemania: Girls Just Want to Have Fun." In *The Adoring Audience: Fan Culture and Popular Media,* edited by Lisa Lewis, 84–106. London: Routledge, 1992.

Facorro, L. B., and M. DeFleur. "A Cross-Cultural Experiment on How Well Audiences Remember News Stories from Newspaper, Computer, Television, and Radio Sources." *Journalism Quarterly* 70 (1993): 585–601.

Fever, J. "Reading *Dynasty*: Television and Reception Theory." *South Atlantic Quarterly* 88 (1989): 443–60.

Fiske, John. "Audiencing: Cultural Practices and Cultural Studies." In *Handbook of Qualitative Research*, edited by N. K. Denzin and Y. S. Lincoln, 189–98. Thousand Oaks, Calif.: Sage, 1994.

———. "British Cultural Studies and Television." In *Channels of Discourse: Television and Contemporary Criticism*, edited by Robert C. Allen, 254–89. Chapel Hill: University of North Carolina Press, 1987.

———. "Ethnosemiotics: Some Personal and Theoretical Reflections." *Cultural Studies* 4 (1990): 85–99.

———. "Madonna." In *Reading the Popular*, 95–113. Boston: Unwin Hyman, 1989.

———. "Moments of Television: Neither the Text Nor the Audience." In *Remote Control: Television, Audiences, and Cultural Power*, edited by Ellen Seiter, Hans Borchers, Gabriele Kreuttzner, and Eva-Maria Warth, 56–78. London: Routledge, 1989.

———. "Popular Television and Commercial Culture: Beyond Political Economy." In *Television Studies: Textual Analysis*, edited by Gary Burns and Robert J. Thompson, 21–40. New York: Praeger, 1989.

———. *Television Culture*. London: Methuen, 1987.

Frank, Ronald E., and Marshall G. Greenberg. *Audiences for Television*. Beverly Hills, Calif.: Sage, 1982.

———. *The Public's Use of Television*. Beverly Hills, Calif.: Sage, 1980.

Frazer, Elizabeth. "Teenage Girls Reading *Jackie*." *Media, Culture and Society* 9 (1987): 407–25.

Frost, Richard, and John Stauffer. "The Effects of Social Class, Gender, and Personality on Psychological Responses to Film Violence." *Journal of Communication* 37, no. 1 (winter 1987): 29–45.

Fuller, Linda K. The Cosby Show: *Audiences, Impact, and Implications*. Westport, Conn.: Greenwood, 1992.

Furno-Lamunde, D., and J. Anderson. "The Uses and Gratifications of Rerun Viewing." *Journalism Quarterly* 69 (1992): 362–72.

Galloway, John J., and F. Louise Meek. "Audience Uses and Gratifications: An Expectancy Model." *Communication Research* 8 (1981): 435–49.

Geraghty, Christine. "Audiences and 'Ethnography': Questions of Practice." In *The Television Studies Book*, edited by Christine Geraghty and David Lusted, 141–57. London: Arnold, 1998.

Gillespie, Marie. "*The Mahabharate*: From Sanskrit to Sacred Soap. A Case Study of the Reception of Two Contemporary Television Versions." In *Reading Audiences:*

Young People and the Media, edited by David Buckingham, 48–73. Manchester: Manchester University Press, 1993.

———. *Television, Ethnicity and Cultural Change.* London: Routledge, 1995.

Graber, Doris A. *Processing the News: How People Tame the Information Tide.* New York: Longman, 1984.

Gray, Ann. "Reading the Audience." *Screen* 28, no. 3 (summer 1987): 24–35.

Greenberg, Bradley S., R. Linsangan, and A. Soderman. "Adolescents' Reactions to Television Sex." In *Media, Sex, and the Adolescent,* edited by Bradley S. Greenberg, Jane D. Brown, and Nancy L. Buerrel-Rothfuss, 196–226. Cresskill, N.J.: Hampton, 1993.

Gripsrud, Josten. "Toward a Flexible Methodology in Studying Media Meaning." *Critical Studies in Mass Communication* 7 (1990): 129–46.

Groden, Debra. "The Interpreting Audience: The Therapeutics of Self-Help Book Reading." *Critical Studies in Mass Communication* 8 (1991): 404–20.

Gunter, Barrie. "The Perceptive Audience." In *Communication Yearbook,* vol. 11, edited by J. A. Anderson, 22–50. Newbury Park, Calif.: Sage, 1988.

———. *Poor Reception: Misunderstanding and Forgetting Broadcast News.* Hillsdale, N.J.: Erlbaum, 1987.

Gunter, Barrie, Jill McLear, and Brian Clifford. *Children's Views about Television.* Aldershot, England: Avebury. Brookfield, Vt.: Gower, 1991.

Gunter, Barrie, and Rachel Viney. *Seeing Is Believing: Religion and Television in the 1990s.* London: Libbey, 1994.

Gunter, Barrie, and Mallory Wober. "The Gulf Crisis and Television: The People's Response in Britain." In *Desert Storm and the Mass Media,* edited by Bradley S. Greenberg and Walter Ganzt, 281–98. Creskill, N.J.: Hampton, 1993.

———. *The Reactive Viewer: A Review of Research on Audience Reaction Measurement.* London: Libbey, 1992.

———. *Violence on Television: What the Viewers Think.* London: Libbey and Independent Broadcasting Authority, 1988.

Hacker, Kenneth L., Tara G. Coste, and Daniel F. Kamm. "Oppositional Readings of Network Television News: Viewer Deconstruction." *Discourse and Society* 2 (1991): 183–202.

Hagen, Ingunn. "The Ambivalences of TV News Viewing: Between Ideals and Everyday Practices." *European Journal of Communication* 9 (1994): 193–220.

———. "Expectations and Consumption Patterns in TV News Viewing." *Media, Culture and Society* 16 (1994): 415–28.

Hall, J. L., C. Miller, and J. Hanson. "Music Television: A Perceptions Study of Two Age Groups." *Popular Music and Society* 10, no. 4 (1986): 17–28.

Hallam, J., and M. Marshment. "Framing Experience: Case Studies in the Reception of *Oranges Are Not the Only Fruit.*" *Screen* 36 (1995): 1–15.

Hamilton, N. F., and Alan M. Rubin. "The Influence of Religiosity on Television Viewing." *Journalism Quarterly* 69 (1992): 667–78.

Hardy, Simon. *The Reader, The Author, His Woman and Her Lover: Soft-Core Pornography and Heterosexual Men.* London: Cassell, 1998.

Harindranath, Ramaswami. "Documentary Meanings and Interpretive Contexts: Observations on Indian 'Repertoires.'" In *Approaches to Audiences,* edited by Roger Dickinson, Ramaswami Harindranath, and Olga Linné, 283–97. Boulder, Colo.: Westview, 1998.

Harper, Sue, and Vincent Porter. "Moved to Tears: Weeping in the Cinema in Postwar Britain." *Screen* 37 (1996): 152–73.

Harrington, C. Lee. "'Is Anyone Out There Sick of the News?!' TV Viewer's Responses to Non-Routine News Coverage." *Media, Culture and Society* 20 (1998): 471–94.

Harrington, C. Lee, and Denise Bielby. *Soap Fans: Pursuing Pleasure and Making Meaning in Everyday Life.* Phildelphia: Temple University Press, 1995.

Hart, A. "Understanding Television Audiences." *Journal of Educational Television* 18 (1992): 5–21.

Hawkins, Robert Parker. "The Dimensional Structure of Children's Perceptions of Television Reality." *Communication Research* 4 (1977): 299–320.

Hay, James, Lawrence Grossberg, and Ellen Wartella, eds. *The Audience and Its Landscape.* Boulder, Colo.: Westview, 1996.

Hermes, Joke. "Media, Meaning and Everyday Life." *Cultural Studies* 7 (1993): 493–506.

Hermes, Joke, and Veronique Schutgens. "A Case of the Emperor's New Clothes? Reception and Text Analysis of the Dutch Feminist Magazine *Opzis.*" *European Journal of Communication* 7 (1992): 307–34.

Hitchen, Jacqueline C., and Chingching Chang. "Effects of Gender Schematic Processing and the Reception of Political Commercials for Men and Women Candidates." *Communication Research* 22 (1995): 430–58.

Hobson, Dorothy. *"Crossroads": The Drama of a Soap Opera.* London: Methuen, 1982.

———. "Housewives and the Mass Media." In *Culture, Media, Language,* edited by Stuart Hall, Dorothy Hobson, Andrew Lowe, and Paul Willis, 105–14. London: Hutchinson, 1980.

———. "Soap Operas at Work." In *Remote Control: Television, Audiences, and Cultural Power,* edited by Ellen Seiter, Hans Borchers, Gabriele Kreuttzner, and Eva-Maria Warth, 150–67. London: Routledge, 1989.

Hofstetter, C. Richard, William A. Schultz, and Sean M. Mahoney. "The Elderly's Perception of Television Ageist Stereotyping: Television or Contextual Aging?" *Communication Reports* 6 (1993): 92–100.

Höijer, Birgitta. "Social Psychological Perspectives in Reception Analysis." In *Approaches to Audiences,* edited by Roger Dickinson, Ramaswami Harindranath, and Olga Linné, 166–83. Boulder, Colo.: Westview, 1998.

————. "Socio-Cognitive Structures and Television Reception." *Media, Culture and Society* 14 (1992): 583–603.

Höijer, Birgitta, K. Nowak, and S. Ross. "Reception of Television as a Cognitive and Cultural Process." *Nordicom Review* 1 (1992): 1–14.

Hoover, S. M. "The Meaning of Religious Television: The '700 Club' in the Lives of Its Viewers." In *American Evangelicals and the Mass Media,* edited by Q. J. Shultze, 231–52. Grand Rapids, Mich.: Academic Books/Zondervan, 1990.

Howard, J., G. Rothbart, and L. Sloan. "The Response to 'Roots': A National Survey." *Journal of Broadcasting* 22 (1978): 279–88.

Hunt, D. M. *Screening the Los Angeles "Riots": Race, Seeing and Resistance.* New York: Cambridge University Press, 1997.

Jarvie, I. C. "Fanning the Flames: Anti-American Reaction to *Operation Burma* (1945)." *Historical Journal of Film, Radio and Television* 1 (1981): 117–37.

Jenkins, Henry. "*Star Trek* Rerun, Reread, Rewritten: Fan Writing as Textual Poaching." *Critical Studies in Mass Communication* 5 (1988): 85–107.

————. "'Strangers No More, We Sing': Filking and the Social Construction of the Science Fiction Fan Community." In *The Adoring Audience: Fan Culture and Popular Media,* edited by Lisa Lewis, 208–36. London: Routledge, 1992.

————. *Textual Poachers: Television Fans and Participatory Culture.* New York: Routledge, 1992.

Jensen, Klaus Bruhn. *Making Sense of the News: Towards a Theory and an Experimental Model of Reception for the Study of Mass Communication.* Aarhus, Denmark: Aarhus University Press, 1986.

————. "News as Social Resource: A Qualitative Empirical Study of the Reception of Danish Television News." *European Journal of Communication* 3 (1988): 275–301.

————. "Reception as Flow: The 'New Television Viewer' Revisited." *Cultural Studies* 8 (1994): 293–305.

————. "Television Futures: A Social Action Methodology for Studying Interpretive Communities." *Critical Studies in Mass Communication* 7 (1990): 129–46.

————. "When Is Meaning? Communication Theory, Pragmatism, and Mass Media Reception." In *Communication Yearbook,* vol. 14, edited by J. A. Anderson, 3–32. Newbury Park, Calif.: Sage, 1991.

————. ed. *News of the World: World Cultures Look at Television News.* London: Routledge, 1998.

Jensen, Klaus Bruhn, and Karl Erik Rosengren. "Five Traditions in Search of the Audience." *European Journal of Communication* 5 (1990): 207–39.

Jhally, Sut. "MTV, Cultural Politics and the Sex Wars: The Strange and Illuminating Case of *Dreamworlds.*" *Media Information Australia* no. 64 (May 1992): 48–59.

Jhally, Sut, and Justin Lewis. *Enlightened Racism: The Cosby Show, Audiences, and the Myth of the American Dream.* Boulder, Colo.: Westview, 1992.

Johnson, E. "Credibility of Black and White Newscasters to a Black Audience." *Journal of Broadcasting* 28 (1984): 365–68.

Jones, F. G. "The Black Audience and the BET Channel." *Journal of Broadcasting and Electronic Media* 34 (1990): 477–86.

Kaiser, S. B., and J. L. Chandler. "Audience Responses to Appearance Codes: Old-Age Imagery in the Media." *The Gerontologist* 28 (1988): 692–99.

Katz, Elihu, Jay G. Blumler, and Michael Gurevitch. "Uses and Gratifications Research." *Public Opinion Quarterly* 37 (1974): 509–23.

Katz, Elihu, and Tamar Liebes. "Decoding *Dallas*: Notes from a Cross-Cultural Study." In *Inter/Media: Interpersonal Communication in a Media World*, 3rd ed., edited by Gary Gumpert and Robert Cathcart, 97–109. Oxford: Oxford University Press, 1986.

———. "Interacting with *Dallas*: Cross Cultural Readings of American TV." *Canadian Journal of Communication* 15 (1990): 45–66.

———. "Mutual Aid in the Decoding of *Dallas*": Preliminary Notes from a Cross-Cultural Case Study." In *Television in Transition,* edited by Phillip Drummond and Richard Paterson, 187–98. London: British Film Institute, 1985.

Katz, Elihu, Tamar Liebes, and Sumiko Iwao. "Neither Here Nor There: Why 'Dallas' Failed in Japan." *Communication* 12 (1991): 99–110.

Kepplinger, Hans Mathias. "Content Analysis and Reception Analysis." *American Behavioral Scientist* 33 (1989): 175–82.

Kielwasser, A. P., and M. A. Wolf. "The Appeal of Soap Opera: An Analysis of Process and Quality in Dramatic Serial Gratifications." *Journal of Popular Culture* 23 (1989): 111–24.

Kim, JungKee, and Alan M. Rubin. "The Variable Influence of Audience Activity on Media Effects." *Communication Research* 24 (1997): 107–35.

Kippax, Susan, and John P. Murray. "Using the Mass Media: Need Gratification and Perceived Utility." *Communication Research* 7 (1980): 335–60.

———. "Using Television: Programme Content and Need Gratification." *Politics* 12 (1977): 56–69.

Klingler, Barbara. "Film History Terminable and Interminable: Recovering the Past in Reception Studies." *Screen* 38 (1997): 107–28.

Krugman, D. M., S. A. Shamp, and K. F. Johnson. "Video Movies at Home: Are They Viewed Like Film or Like Television?" *Journalism Quarterly* 68 (1991): 120–30.

Lanzetta, John T., Denis B. Sullivan, Roger D. Masters, and Gregory J. McHugo. "Emotional and Cognitive Responses to Televised Images of Political Leaders." In *Mass Media and Political Thought: An Information-Processing Approach,* edited by Sidney Kraus and Richard M. Perloff, 85–116. Beverly Hills, Calif.: Sage, 1985.

Larsson, L. "Another (Hi)Story: On Women's Reading and Swedish Weeklies." *Nordicom Review* 2 (1993): 15–24.

Lawrence, P. A. and Philip Palmgreen. "A Uses and Gratifications Analysis of Horror Films Preference." In *Horror Films: Current Research on Audience Preferences and Reactions*, edited by James B. Weaver and Ronald C. Tamborini, 161–78. Mahwah, N.J.: Erlbaum, 1996.

Leal, Ondina, and Rubin George Oliver. "Class Interpretations of a Soap Opera Narrative: The Case of the Brazilian *Novela* 'Summer Sun.'" *Theory, Culture and Society* 5 (1988): 81–89.

Lee, M. L. and C. H. Cho. "Women Watching Television: An Ethnographic Study of Korean Soap Opera Fans in the U.S." *Cultural Studies* 4 (1990): 30–44.

Lembo, Ronald. "Is There Culture After Cultural Studies?" In *Viewing, Reading, Listening: Audiences and Cultural Reception*, edited by Jon Cruz and Justin Lewis, 33–54. Boulder, Colo.: Westview, 1994.

Levy, Mark R. "VCR Use and the Concept of Audience Activity." *Communication Quarterly* 35, no. 3 (summer 1987): 267–75.

Levy, Mark R., and Susan Windahl. "Audience Activity and Gratifications: A Conceptual Clarification and Exploration." *Communication Research* 11 (1984): 51–78.

Levy, Mark R., and Sven Windahl. "The Concept of Audience Activity." In *Media Gratifications Research: Current Perspectives*, edited by Karl Erik Rosengren, Lawrence A. Wenner, and Philip Palmgreen, 109–22. Beverly Hills, Calif.: Sage, 1985.

Lewis, Justin. "Decoding Television News." In *Television in Transition*, edited by Phillip Drummond and Richard Paterson, 205–34. London: British Film Institute, 1985.

———. *The Ideological Octopus: An Exploration of Television and Its Audience*. London: Routledge, 1991.

Lewis, Lisa, ed. *The Adoring Audience: Fan Culture and Popular Media*. London: Routledge, 1992.

Lichtenstein, Allen, and Lawrence B. Rosenfeld. "Uses and Misuses of Gratifications Research: An Explication of Media Functions." *Communication Research* 10 (1983): 97–109.

Lichterman, P. "Self-Help Reading as a Thin Culture." *Media, Culture and Society* 14 (1992): 421–47.

Liebes, Tamar. "Cultural Differences in the Retelling of Television Fiction." *Critical Studies in Mass Communication* 5 (1988): 277–92.

———. "Decoding Television News: The Political Discourse of Israeli Hawks and Doves." *Theory and Society* 21 (1992): 357–81.

Liebes, Tamar and Elihu Katz. *The Export of Meaning: Cross-Cultural Readings of Dallas*. Oxford: Oxford University Press, 1990.

———. "On the Critical Abilities of Television Viewers." In *Remote Control: Television, Audiences, and Cultural Power*, edited by Ellen Seiter, Hans Borchers, Gabriele Kreuttzner, and Eva-Maria Warth, 204–21. London: Routledge, 1989.

————. "Patterns of Involvement in Television Fiction: A Comparative Analysis." *European Journal of Communication* 1 (1986): 151–72.

Liebes, Tamar, and Rivka Ribak. "In Defense of Negotiated Readings: How Moderates on Each Side of the Conflict Interpret Intifada News." *Journal of Communication* 44, no. 2 (spring 1994): 108–24.

————. "A Mother's Battle Against Television News: A Case Study of Political Socialization." *Discourse and Society* 2 (1991): 203–22.

Lind, Rebecca Ann. "Ethical Sensitivity in Viewer Evaluations of a T.V. News Investigative Report." *Human Communication Research* 23 (1997): 535–61.

————. *Viewer Response to Ethical Issues in Television News.* Columbia, S.C.: Association for Education in Journalism and Mass Communication, 1993.

Lind, Rebecca Ann, and D. L. Rarick. "Public Attitudes Toward Ethical Issues in TV Programming: Multiple Viewer Orientations." *Journal of Mass Media Ethics* 7 (1992): 133–50.

Lindlof, Thomas R. "Media Audiences as Interpretive Communities." In *Communication Yearbook,* vol. 11, edited by J. A. Anderson, 81–107. Newbury Park, Calif.: Sage, 1988.

————. "The Qualitative Study of Media Audiences." *Journal of Broadcasting and Electronic Media* 35 (1991): 23–42.

Lindlof, Thomas R., and Debra Grodin. "When Media Use Can't Be Observed: Some Problems and Tactics of Collaborative Audience Research." *Journal of Communication* 40, no. 4 (autumn 1990): 8–28.

Livingstone, Sonia M. "Audience Reception: The Role of the Viewer in Retelling Romantic Drama." In *Mass Media and Society,* edited by James Curran and Michael Gurevitch, 285–306. London: Arnold, 1991.

————. "Audience Research at the Crossroads: The 'Implied Audience' in Media and Cultural Theory." *European Journal of Cultural Studies* 1 (1998): 193–217.

————. "Interpreting a Television Narrative: How Different Viewers See a Story." *Journal of Communication* 40, no. 1 (winter 1990): 72–85.

————. "Interpretive Viewers and Structured Programs." *Communication Research* 16 (1989): 25–57.

————. *Making Sense of Television: The Psychology of Audience Interpretation.* London: Pergamon, 1990.

————. "The Resourceful Reader: Interpreting Television Characters and Narratives." In *Communication Yearbook,* vol. 15, edited by S. A. Deetz, 58–90. Newbury Park, Calif.: Sage, 1992.

————. "The Rise and Fall of Audience Research: An Old Story with a New Ending." *Journal of Communication* 43, no. 4 (autumn 1993): 5–12.

————. "Viewers' Interpretations of Soap Opera: The Role of Gender, Power, and Morality." In *Television and Its Audience,* edited by Phillip Drummond and Richard Paterson, 83–107. London: British Film Institute, 1988.

————. "Watching Talk: Gender and Engagement in the Viewing of Audience Discussion Programmes." *Media, Culture and Society* 16 (1994): 429–47.

————. "Why People Watch Soap Operas: An Analysis of the Explanations of British Viewers." *European Journal of Communication* 3 (1988): 55–80.

Livingstone, Sonia M., and Peter Lunt. *Talk on Television: Audience Participation and Public Debate*. London: Routledge, 1994.

Livingstone, Sonia M., Mallory Wober, and Peter Lunt. "Studio Audience Discussion Programmes: An Analysis of Viewers' Preferences and Involvement." *European Journal of Communication* 9 (1994): 355–80.

Lometti, Guy E., Byron Reeves, and Carl R. Bybee. "Investigating the Assumptions of Uses and Gratifications Research." *Communication Research* 4 (1977): 321–38.

Long, Elizabeth. "Textual Interpretation as Collective Action." In *The Ethnography of Reading*, edited by Jonathan Boyarin, 180–211. Berkeley and Los Angeles: University of California Press, 1992.

————. "Women, Reading, and Cultural Authority: Some Implications of the Audience Perspective in Cultural Studies." *American Quarterly* 38 (1986): 591–612.

Lull, James. *Inside Family Television: Ethnographic Research on Television Audiences*. London: Routledge, 1990.

————. "The Social Uses of Television." *Human Communication Research* 6 (1980): 197–209.

McDonald, D. G., and S. D. Reese. "Television News and Audience Selectivity." *Journalism Quarterly* 64 (1987): 763–68.

MacGregor, Brent, and David E. Morrison. "From Focus Groups to Editing Groups: A New Method of Reception Analysis." *Media, Culture and Society* 17 (1995): 141–50.

McIlwraith, Robert D., and John R. Schallow. "Adult Fantasy Life and Patterns of Media Use." *Journal of Communication* 33, no. 1 (winter 1983): 78–91.

McLeod, Jack M., and Lee B. Becker. "The Uses and Gratifications Approach." In *Handbook of Political Communication*, edited by Dan D. Nimmo and Keith R. Sanders, 67–100. Beverly Hills, Calif.: Sage, 1981.

McQuail, Denis. "Gratifications Research and Media Theory: Many Models or One?" In *Media Gratifications Research: Current Perspectives*, edited by Karl Erik Rosengren, Lawrence A. Wenner, and Philip Palmgreen, 149–67. Beverly Hills, Calif.: Sage, 1985.

————. "With the Benefit of Hindsight: Reflections on Uses and Gratifications Research." In *Approaches to Audiences*, edited by Roger Dickinson, Ramaswami Harindranath, and Olga Linné, 151–65. Boulder, Colo.: Westview, 1998.

McQuail, Denis, Jay G. Blumler, and F. R. Brown. "The Television Audience: A Revised Perspective." In *Sociology of Mass Communication*, compiled by Denis McQuail. New York: Penguin, 1972.

Mankekar, P. "National Texts and Gendered Lives: An Ethnography of Television Viewers in a North Indian City." *American Ethnologist* 20 (1993): 543–63.

Mares, Marie-Louise, and Joanne Cantor. "Elderly Viewers' Responses to Televised Portrayals of Old Age." *Communication Research* 19 (1992): 459–78.

Means Coleman, Robin R. *African American Viewers and the Black Situation Comedy.* New York: Garland, 1998.

Merrick, Helen. "The Readers Feminism Doesn't See: Feminist Fans, Critics and Science Fiction." In *Trash Aesthetics: Popular Culture and Its Audience,* edited by Deborah Cartmell, I. Q. Hunter, Heidi Kaye, and Imelda Whelan, 48–65. London: Pluto, 1997.

Messaris, Paul, and Jisuk Woo. "Image vs. Reality in Korean-Americans' Responses to Mass-Media Depictions of the United States." *Critical Studies in Mass Communication* 8 (1991): 74–90.

Miller, Toby. "Following." In *The Avengers,* 145–59. London: British Film Institute, 1997.

Miyazaki, Toshiko. "Housewives and Daytime Serials in Japan: A Uses and Gratifications Perspective." *Communication Research* 8 (1981): 323–41.

Moffitt, M. A. "Articulating Meaning: Reconceptions of the Meaning Process, Fantasy/Reality, and Identity Leisure Activities." *Communication Theory* 3 (1993): 231–51.

———. "Leisure Fiction and the Audience: Meanings and Communication Strategies." *Women's Studies in Communication* 16, no. 2 (fall 1993): 27–61.

Moores, Shaun. *Interpreting Audiences: The Ethnography of Media Consumption.* London: Sage, 1993.

———. "Texts, Readers, and the Contexts of Reading: Developments in the Study of Media Audiences." *Media, Culture and Society* 12 (1990): 9–29.

Morley, David. *Family Television: Cultural Power and Domestic Leisure.* London: Comedia, 1986.

———. *The "Nationwide" Audience: Structure and Decoding.* London: British Film Institute, 1980.

———. *The Nationwide Television Studies.* London: Routledge, 1999.

———. "Populism, Revisionism, and the 'New' Audience Research." In *Cultural Studies and Communication,* edited by Jim Curran, David Morley, and V. Walkerdine, 279–93. New York: St. Martin's, 1996.

———. *Television, Audiences, and Cultural Studies.* London: Routledge, 1992.

Morley, David, and Roger Silverstone. "Domestic Communication—Technologies and Meanings." *Media, Culture and Society* 12 (1990): 31–55.

Morris, Meaghan. "Banality in Cultural Studies." In *Logics of Television: Essays in Cultural Criticism,* edited by Patricia Mellencamp, 14–43. Bloomington: Indiana University Press, 1990.

Moss, Gemma. "Girls Tell the Teen Romance: Four Reading Histories." In *Reading Audiences: Young People and the Media,* edited by David Buckingham, 116–34. Manchester: Manchester University Press, 1993.

Mullen, Bob. *Consuming Television: Television and Its Audience*. Oxford: Blackwell, 1997.

———. *Not a Pretty Picture: Ethnic Minority Views on Television*. Aldershot, England: Avebury, 1996.

Nakayama, Thomas K., and Lisa N. Peñaloza. "Madonna T/Races: Music Videos Through the Prism of Color." In *The Madonna Connection: Representational Politics, Subcultural Identities, and Cultural Theory*, edited by Cathy Schwichtenberg, 39–55. Boulder, Colo.: Westview, 1993.

Neuman, W. R. "Television and American Culture: The Mass Medium and the Pluralist Audience." *Public Opinion Quarterly* 46 (1982): 471–87.

Nightengale, Virginia. *Studying Audiences: The Shock of the Real*. London: Routledge, 1996.

———. "What's Ethnographic about Ethnographic Audience Research?" *Australian Journal of Communication* 16 (1989): 50–63.

Norden, Martin F., and Kim Wolfson. "Cultural Influences on Film Interpretation Among Chinese and American Students." In *Current Research in Film: Audience, Economics, and Law*, vol. 2, edited by Bruce A. Austin, 21–34. Norwood, N.J.: Ablex, 1986.

Oliver, Mary Beth. "Adolescents' Enjoyment of Graphic Horror: Effects of Viewers' Attitudes and Portrayals of Victims." *Communication Research* 20 (1993): 30–50.

Osborn, D. K., and R. C. Endsley. "Emotional Reactions of Young Children to TV Violence." *Child Development* 42 (1971): 321–31.

Palmgreen, Philip, and P. A. Lawrence. "Audiences, Gratifications, and Consumption of Theatrical Films: The Rest of the Story." In *Current Research in Film: Audiences, Economics, Law*, vol. 5, edited by Bruce A. Austin, 39–55. Norwood, N.J.: Ablex, 1991.

Palmgreen, Philip, and J. D. Rayburn, II. "Uses and Gratifications and Exposure to Public Television: A Discrepancy Approach." *Communication Research* 6 (1979): 155–79.

Palmgreen, Philip, Lawrence A. Wenner, and J. D. Rayburn, II. "Gratifications Discrepancies and News Program Choice." *Communication Research* 8 (1981): 451–78.

———. "Relations Between Gratifications Sought and Obtained: A Study of Television News." *Communication Research* 7 (1980): 161–92.

Press, Andrea. "Class and Gender in the Hegemonic Process: Class Differences in Women's Perceptions of Television Realism and Identification with Television Characters." *Media, Culture and Society* 11 (1989): 229–51.

———. "Class, Gender, and the Female Viewer: Women's Responses to *Dynasty*." In *Television and Women's Culture*, edited by Mary Ellen Brown, 158–82. Newbury Park, Calif.: Sage, 1990.

———. *Women Watching Television: Gender, Class, and Generation in the American Television Experience*. Philadelphia: University of Pennsylvania Press, 1991.

Press, Andrea, and Elizabeth Cole. "Women Like Us: Working-Class Women Respond to Television Representations of Abortion." In *Viewing, Reading, Listening: Audiences and Cultural Reception*, edited by Jon Cruz and Justin Lewis, 55–80. Boulder, Colo.: Westview, 1994.

Radway, Janice. *Reading the Romance: Women, Patriarchy, and Popular Literature.* Chapel Hill: University of North Carolina Press, 1984.

Reep, Diana C., and Faye H. Dambrot. "In the Eye of the Beholder: Viewer Perceptions of TV's Male/Female Working Partners." *Communication Research* 15 (1988): 51–69.

Reeves, Nicholas. "Cinema, Spectatorship and Propaganda: *Battle of the Somme* (1916) and Its Contemporary Audience." *Historical Journal of Film, Radio and Television* 17 (1997): 5–28.

Reid, Evelyn Cauleta. "Television Viewing Habits of Young Black Women in London." *Screen* 30, no. 1/2 (winter/spring 1989): 114–21.

Richards, Chris. "Taking Sides? What Young Girls Do with Television." In *Reading Audiences: Young People and the Media*, edited by David Buckingham, 24–47. Manchester: Manchester University Press, 1993.

Richards, Jeffrey. "Wartime British Cinema Audiences and the Class System: The Case of 'Ships with Wings.'" *Historical Journal of Film, Radio and Television* 7 (1987): 129–41.

Richardson, Kay, and John Corner. "Reading Reception: Mediation and Transparency in Viewers' Accounts of a TV Programme." *Media, Culture and Society* 8 (1986): 485–508.

Riggs, Karen E. *Mature Audiences: Television and the Elderly.* New Brunswick, N.J.: Rutgers University Press, 1998.

Roscoe, Jane, Harriette Marshall, and Kate Gleeson. "The Television Audience: A Reconsideration of the Taken-for-Granted Terms 'Active,' 'Social' and 'Critical.'" *European Journal of Communication* 10 (1995): 87–108.

Rosengren, Karl Erik, Lawrence A. Wenner, and Philip Palmgreen, eds. *Media Gratifications Research: Current Perspectives.* Beverly Hills, Calif.: Sage, 1985.

Ross, K. "But Where's the Me in It? Disability, Broadcasting and the Audience." *Media, Culture and Society* 19 (1997): 669–77.

Rubin, Alan M. "Audience Activity and Media Use." *Communication Monographs* 60 (1993): 98–105.

———. "Ritualized and Instrumental Television Viewing," *Journal of Communication* 34, no. 3 (summer 1984): 67–77.

———. "Television Uses and Gratifications: The Interactions of Viewing Patterns and Motivations." *Journal of Broadcasting* 27 (1983): 37–51.

———. "Uses of Daytime Television Soap Operas by College Students." *Journal of Broadcasting and Electronic Media* 29, no. 3 (summer 1985): 241–58.

Rubin, Alan M., and Elizabeth M. Perse. "Audience Activity and Satisfaction with Favorite Television Soap Opera." *Journalism Quarterly* 65 (1988): 368–75.

———. "Audience Activity and Soap Opera Involvement: A Uses and Effects Investigation." *Human Communication Research* 14 (1987): 246–68.

———. "Audience Activity and Television News Gratifications." *Communication Research* 14 (1987): 58–84.

Rubin, Alan M., and Sven Windahl. "The Uses and Dependency Model in Mass Communication." *Critical Studies in Mass Communication* 3 (1986): 184–99.

Ruddock, A. "Scientific Criticism? A Critical Approach to the Resistive Audience." *New Jersey Journal of Communication* 6, no. 1 (spring 1998): 59–80.

Sampedro, Víctor. "Grounding the Displaced: Local Media Reception in a Transnational Context." *Journal of Communication* 48, no. 2 (spring 1988): 125–43.

Schaefer, R. J., and R. K. Avery. "Audience Conceptualizations of 'Late Night with David Letterman.'" *Journal of Broadcasting and Electronic Media* 37 (1993): 253–75.

Schlesinger, P., R. E. Dobash, R. P. Dobash, and C. Weaver. *Women Viewing Violence.* London: British Film Institute, 1992.

Schrag, R. L., and L. B. Rosenfeld. "Assessing the Soap Opera Frame: Audience Perceptions of Value Structures in Soap Operas and Prime-Time Serial Dramas." *Southern Speech Communication Journal* 52 (1987): 362–76.

Schreiber, Elliot S., and Douglas A. Boyd. "How the Elderly Perceive Television Commercials." *Journal of Communication* 30, no. 1 (winter 1980): 61–70.

Schroder, Kim Christian. "Audience Semiotics, Interpretive Communities and the 'Ethnographic Turn' in Media Research." *Media, Culture and Society* 16 (1994): 337–47.

———. "Cultural Quality: Search for a Phantom? A Reception Perspective of Judgments of Cultural Value." In *Media Cultures*, edited by Michael Skovmand and Kim Christian Schoder, 199–219. London: Sage, 1992.

———. "*Dynasty* in Denmark: Towards a Social Semiotics of the Media Audience." *Nordicom Review* 1 (1988): 6–13.

———. "The Pleasure of *Dynasty*: The Weekly Reconstruction of Self-Confidence." In *Television and Its Audience,* edited by Phillip Drummond and Richard Paterson, 61–82. London: British Film Institute, 1988.

Schulze, Laurie, Anne Barton White, and Jane D. Brown. "'A Sacred Monster in Her Prime': Audience Construction of Madonna as Low-Other." In *The Madonna Connection: Representational Politics, Subcultural Identities, and Cultural Theory,* edited by Cathy Schwichtenberg, 15–37. Boulder, Colo.: Westview, 1993.

Seiter, Ellen. "Making Distinctions in TV Audience Research: A Case Study of a Troubling Interview." *Cultural Studies* 4 (1990): 61–84.

———. *Television and New Media Audiences.* Oxford: Clarendon Press of Oxford University Press, 1999.

Seiter, Ellen, Hans Borchers, Gabrielle Kreuttzner, and Eva-Maria Warth. "'Don't Treat Us Like We're So Stupid and Naive': Toward an Ethnography of Soap Opera Viewers." In *Remote Control: Television, Audiences, and Cultural Power,* edited by Ellen Seiter, Hans Borchers, Gabriele Kreuttzner, and Eva-Maria Warth, 223–47. London: Routledge, 1989.

————. eds. *Remote Control: Television, Audiences, and Cultural Power.* London: Routledge, 1989.

Sender, Katherine. "Selling Sexual Subjectivities: Audiences Respond to Gay Window Advertising." *Critical Studies in Mass Communication* 16 (1999): 172–96.

Shapiro, M. E., and T. Biggers. "Emotion-Eliciting Qualities in the Motion Picture Viewing Situation and Audience Evaluations." In *Current Research in Film: Audiences, Economics, and Law,* vol. 3, edited by Bruce A. Austin, 1–11. Norwood, N.J.: Ablex, 1987.

Shattuc, Jane. "Conclusion: The Inconclusive Audience." In *The Talking Cure: TV Talk Shows and Women,* 171–98. New York: Routledge, 1997.

Shaw, Irene, and David S. Newell. *Violence on Television: Programme Content and Viewer Perception.* London: British Broadcasting Corporation, 1972.

Sigman, Stuart J., and Donald L. Fry. "Differential Ideology and Language Use: Readers' Reconstructions and Descriptions of News Events." *Critical Studies in Mass Communication* 2 (1985): 307–22.

Silj, Alessandro, and Manuel Alvarado. *East of Dallas: The European Challenge to American Television.* London: British Film Institute, 1988.

Smoodin, Eric. "'This Business of America': Fan Mail, Film Reception, and *Meet John Doe.*" *Screen* 37 (1996): 111–28.

Snead, Peter. "Hollywood's Message to the World: The British Response in the Nineteen Thirties." *Historical Journal of Film, Radio and Television* 1 (1981): 19–32.

Spiegel, Lynn. "Television and the Family Circle: The Popular Reception of a New Medium." In *Logics of Television: Essays in Cultural Criticism,* edited by Patricia Mellancamp, 73–97. Bloomington: Indiana University Press/London: British Film Institute, 1990.

Spurlin, William J. "Rhetorical Hermeneutics and Gay Identity Politics: Rethinking American Cultural Studies." In *Reconceptualizing American Literary/Cultural Studies: Rhetoric, History, and Politics in the Humanities,* edited by William E. Cain, 169–93. New York: Garland, 1996.

Stacey, Jackie. *Star Gazing: Hollywood and Female Spectatorship.* London: Routledge, 1994.

————. "Textual Obsessions: Methodology, History, and Researching Female Spectatorship." *Screen* 34 (1993): 260–74.

Staiger, Janet. *Interpreting Films: Studies in the Historical Reception of American Cinema.* Princeton, N.J.: Princeton University Press, 1992.

————. "Taboos and Totems: Cultural Meanings of *The Silence of the Lambs.*" In *Film*

Theory Goes to the Movies, edited by Jim Collins, Harry Radner, and Ava Preacher Collins, 142–54. New York: Routledge, 1993.

Steiner, Gary. *The People Look at Television: A Study of Audience Attitudes.* New York: Knopf, 1963.

Steiner, Linda. "Oppositional Decoding as an Act of Resistance." *Critical Studies in Mass Communication* 5 (1988): 1–15.

Sun, Se-Wen, and James Lull. "The Adolescent Audience for Music Videos and Why They Watch." *Journal of Communication* 36, no. 1 (winter 1986): 115–25.

Swanson, David L. "The Continuing Evaluation of the Uses and Gratifications Approach." *Communication Research* 6 (1979): 3–7.

———. "Gratifications Seeking, Media Exposure, and Audience Interpretations: Some Directions for Research." *Journal of Broadcasting and Electronic Media* 31 (1987): 237–54.

———. "Political Communication Research and the Uses and Gratifications Model: A Critique." *Communication Research* 6 (1979): 37–53.

———. "The Uses and Misuses of Uses and Gratifications." *Human Communication Research* 3 (1977): 214–21.

Swanson, David L., and A. S. Babrow. "Uses and Gratifications: The Influence of Gratification-Seeking and Expectancy-Value Judgments on the Viewing of Television News." In *Rethinking Communication,* vol. 2, edited by Brenda Dervin and the International Communication Association, 361–75. Newbury Park, Calif.: Sage, 1989.

Taylor, Helen. *Scarlett's Women: Gone with the Wind and Its Female Fans.* London: Virago, 1989.

Thumin, Janet. "'A Live Commercial for Icing Sugar.' Researching the Historical Audience: Gender and Broadcasting Television in the 1950s." *Screen* 36 (1995): 48–55.

Tsivian, Yuri. *Early Cinema in Russia and Its Cultural Reception.* Chicago: University of Chicago Press, 1994.

Tulloch, John, and Henry Jenkins. *Science Fiction Audiences.* London: Routledge, 1995.

Tulloch, Marian, and John Tulloch. "Representing and Reading Strikes: Television, Industrial Relations, and Audiences." *Media Information Australia* no. 70 (November 1993): 34–42.

Valkenburg, Patti M., and Sabine C. Janssen. "What Do Children Value in Entertainment Programs? A Cross-Cultural Investigation." *Journal of Communication* 49, no. 2 (spring 1999): 3–21.

Wells, A. "Images of Popular Music Artists: Do Male and Female Audiences Have Different Views?" *Popular Music and Society* 12, no. 3 (fall 1988): 1–17.

Wenner, Lawrence A. "Gratifications Sought and Obtained in Program Dependency: A Study of Network Evening News Programs and *60 Minutes.*" *Communication Research* 9 (1982): 539–60.

————. "Political News on Television: A Reconsideration of Audience Orientation." *Western Journal of Speech Communication* 47 (1983): 380–95.

White, R. A. "Media Reception Theory: Emerging Perspectives." *INTERCOM: Revista Brasiliera de Comunicação.* 16, no. 1 (January–June 1993): 8–21.

Wilson, Tony. *Watching Television: Hermeneutics, Reception, and Popular Culture.* Cambridge,: Polity, 1993.

Wober, Mallory, and S. Fazal. "Neighbors at Home and Away: British Viewers' Perceptions of Australian Soap Operas." *Media Information Australia* no. 71 (February 1994): 78–87.

Wolf, Michelle A. "How Children Negotiate Television." In *Natural Audiences: Qualitative Research of Media Uses and Effects,* edited by Thomas P. Lindlof, 58–94. Norwood, N.J.: Ablex, 1978.

Wood, Julian. "Repeatable Pleasures: Notes on Young People's Use of Video." In *Reading Audiences: Young People and the Media,* edited by David Buckingham, 184–201. Manchester: Manchester University Press, 1993.

Wright, John C., Dale Kunkel, Marites Pinon, and Aletha C. Huston. "How Children Reacted to Televised Coverage of the Space Shuttle Disaster." *Journal of Communication* 39, no. 2 (spring 1989): 27–45.

PERMISSIONS

"The Identity of the Poetic Text in the Changing Horizon of Understanding," by Hans Robert Jauss is reprinted with permission from *The Identity of the Literary Text*, edited by Mario Valdes and Owen Miller (Toronto: University of Toronto Press, 1985)

"Yet Once More," by Stanley Fish is reprinted by permission from *Professional Correctness* (Oxford: Clarendon Press, 1995)

"Interpretation and Rhetorical Hermeneutics," by Steven Mailloux is reprinted from Steven Mailloux, *Reception Histories: Rhetoric, Pragmatism, and American Cultural Politics*. Copyright ©1998 Cornell University. Used by permission of the publisher, Cornell University Press. An earlier version of this essay appeared as "Rhetorical Hermeneutics Revisited," *Text and Performance Quarterly* 11 (1991), pp. 223–44. Used by permission of the National Communication Association. Another version of this essay has appeared in Critrical Terms for Literary Study, University of Chicago Press.

"Texts in History: The Determinations of Readings and Their Texts," by Tony Bennett is reprinted with permission from *The Journal of the Midwest Modern Language Association* 18:1 (Spring 1985): 1–16

"1790," by Gary Taylor is reprinted with permission from *Reinventing Shakespeare: A Cultural History from the Renaissance to the Present* (New York: Oxford University Press, 1987), pp. 102–116, 120–133, and 14–151.

"Literary Theory and the Black Tradition," by Henry Louis Gates, Jr., is reprinted from *Figures in Black: Words, Signs, and the "Racial" Self*, by Henry Louis Gates Jr.. Copyright © 1989 by Henry Louis Gates, Jr. Used by Permission of Oxford University Press, Inc.

Claudia L. Johnson, "The Divine Miss Jane: Jane Austen, Janeites, and the Discipline of Novel Studies," *boundary* 2 23:2 (Fall 1996): 143–63. ©1996, Duke University Press. All Rights Reserved. Reprinted with permission.

Jane Tompkins, "Masterpiece Theater: The Politics of Hawthorne's Reputation," *American Quarterly* 36 (1984): 617–642. ©1984. The American Studies Association. Reprinted by Permission of the Johns Hopkins University Press.

"First Steps Toward a History of Reading," by Robert Darnton is reprinted with permission from *Australian Journal of French Studies* 23.1 (January-April 1986): 5–30

James Smith Allen, "Reading the Novel," *In the Public Eye: A History of Reading in Modern France, 1800-1940* (Princeton: Princeton University Press, 1991), pp. 275–302. ©1991 Reprinted by permission of Princeton University Press.

Janice Radway, "Readers and Their Romances," *Reading the Romance: Women, Patriarchy, and Popular Literature* by Janice A. Radway. Copyright © 1984 by the University of North Carolina Press. Used by permission of the publisher.

"Madonna," by John Fiske is reprinted with permission from *Reading the Popular* (Boston: Unwin Hyman, 1989), pp. 95–113.

Andrea Press and Elizabeth Cole, "Women Like Us: Working-Class Women Respond to Television Representations of Abortion," *Viewing, Reading, Listening: Audiences and Cultural Reception*, edited by John Cruz and Justin Lewis. Copyright © 1994 by Westview Press. Reprinted by permission of Westview Press, a member of Perseus Books, L.L.C.

Janet Staiger, "Taboos and Totems: Cultural Meanings of *The Silence of the Lambs*," in *Film Theory Goes to the Movies*, edited by Jim Collins, Harry Radner, and Ava Preacher Collins. Reproduced by permission of Taylor & Francis/Routledge, Inc., http://www.routledge-ny.com.

"Economies of Value" © John Frow 1995, is reprinted from *Cultural Studies and Cultural Value* (1995) by permission of Oxford University Press.

"Reading and History," by Paul de Man is reprinted with permission from pp. xv-xxv from his Introduction to *Toward an Aesthetic of Reception* by Hans Robert Jauss, translated by Timothy Bahti (Minneapolis: University of Minnesota Press, 1982)

"The Discourse of Value" by John Guillory is reprinted with permission from his *Cultural Capital* (Chicago: University of Chicago Press, 1993)

Robert Holub, "Confrontations with Radicalness" from *Crossing Borders*. ©1992. Reprinted by permission of The University of Wisconsin Press.

INDEX

Abortion, and social class, 261; television depictions of, 261–64.

Adams, Richard, on "The Gentle Boy," 139.

Adorno, Theodor, influence on reception study, 22, 24.

Alcoff, Linda, on the politics of speaking, 309–11.

Allen, James Smith, 180–202.

Amo, Wilhelm, the education and writing of, 111.

antibellum criticism, 140–41; of Hawthorne and Melville, 141–42,

Austen, Jane, and gay men, 119; and H. W. Garrod's "Depreciation," 122; and Janeites, 122; and Rudyard Kipling's "The Janeites," 122–24; and sister-love, 119–20.

Bakhtin, Mikhail, 14–15.

Baudelaire, Charles, "Spleen II," 328, 330–31; Hans Robert Jauss on, 328–29, 330–31.

Bauman, Zygmunt, 297.

Benjamin, Walter, and the critique of essentialism, 324–25.

Black art, and black humanity, 113–14; the documentary status of, 106–8; twentieth-century confusions of art and propaganda in, 115–16.

book publications, German versus French, 163.

Booth, Wayne, 127–28.

Bourdieu, Pierre, 312–13.

Burke, Edmund, 84–6.

"Burning Up," control of the gaze in, 257–58; parodic sexuality of, 256–57.

Byron, Lord George Gordon, on *Hamlet*, 82–3

Cagney and Lacey, pro-choice episode of, 263–64; working-class, pro-choice women's responses to, 266–67.

Chartier, Roger, 174–75.

classics, 133–34, 149–51; decanonizing of, 24–5.

Cobbett, William, 88.

Coleridge, Samuel Taylor, 80–1.

cultural studies, methodologies of, 247–48; new theories of reception of, 205; versus cultural rhetoric studies, 45–7.

Daniel, Book of, 40–1.

Darnton, Robert, 160–79.

De Man, Paul, 324–33; Jauss' response to, 319.

Desperately Seeking Susan, 253–54.

dialog, definition of, 9; types of, 9–11.

Dickinson, Emily, a poem of, 40–1, 43–4.

discourses of value, 295–96.

Douglass, Fredric, *the Narrative of the Life of Fredric Douglass*, 110.

Eco, Umberto, 295.

ethnographic studies, paradox of, 260.

ethnomethodology, 296–97; 309.

Fiske, John, 246–58.

Frow, John, 67; 294–317.

Gadamer, Hans-Georg, 13–14.

Gates, Henry Louis, Jr., 105–17.

Gouldner, Alvin, 311–12.

Grossberg, Lawrence, 308–09.

Guillory, John, 299.

Harding, D. W., 125.

Hawthorne, Nathaniel, and the New England Clerisy, 145–47; neglect of the genius of, 135.

Hazlitt, William, 82, 87.

history of the book, definitions of, 155–56.

Holub, Robert, 339–42.

Huckleberry Finn, dreams and racism in, 42–3.

Jauss, Hans Robert, 7–28; allegory versus mimesis in, 329–30; and the aesthetic, 326–27; and linguists, 325–26; and the play of the signifier, 322–28; as practical critic, 75–6.

Jefferson, Thomas, 106–07.

Johnson, Claudia, 118–32.

Kean, Edmund, 83.

Keats, John, on Shakespeare, 81.

La Nouvelle Héloïse, 161.

Laclau, Ernesto, 64–5.

Lamb, Charles, 81–2.

L'Assommoir, 190–92.

Le Lys rouge, 193–96.

Leavis, F. R., 125–126, 128.